Lecture Notes in Computer Science 13141

More information about this series at https://link.springer.com/bookseries/558

Björn Þór Jónsson · Cathal Gurrin ·
Minh-Triet Tran · Duc-Tien Dang-Nguyen ·
Anita Min-Chun Hu · Binh Huynh Thi Thanh ·
Benoit Huet (Eds.)

MultiMedia Modeling

28th International Conference, MMM 2022
Phu Quoc, Vietnam, June 6–10, 2022
Proceedings, Part I

 Springer

Editors
Björn Þór Jónsson ⓘ
IT University of Copenhagen
Copenhagen, Denmark

Cathal Gurrin ⓘ
Dublin City University
Dublin, Ireland

Minh-Triet Tran ⓘ
University of Science, VNU-HCM
Ho Chi Minh City, Vietnam

Duc-Tien Dang-Nguyen ⓘ
University of Bergen
Bergen, Norway

Anita Min-Chun Hu ⓘ
National Tsing Hua University
Hsinchu, Taiwan

Binh Huynh Thi Thanh ⓘ
Hanoi University of Science and Technology
Hanoi, Vietnam

Benoit Huet ⓘ
Median Technologies
Valbonne, France

ISSN 0302-9743   ISSN 1611-3349 (electronic)
Lecture Notes in Computer Science
ISBN 978-3-030-98357-4   ISBN 978-3-030-98358-1 (eBook)
https://doi.org/10.1007/978-3-030-98358-1

This Springer imprint is published by the registered company Springer Nature Switzerland AG
The registered company address is: Gewerbestrasse 11, 6330 Cham, Switzerland

Preface

These two-volume proceedings contain the papers accepted at MMM 2022, the 28th International Conference on MultiMedia Modeling.

Organized for more than 25 years, MMM has become a respected and well-established international conference bringing together excellent researchers from academic and industrial areas. MMM is considered a core-B conference. During the conference, novel research works from MMM-related areas (especially multimedia content analysis; multimedia signal processing and communications; and multimedia applications and services) are shared along with practical experiences, results, and exciting demonstrations. The 28th edition of the conference was organized in Vietnam during June 6–10, 2022. Due to the COVID-19 pandemic, the conference date had been shifted back by a number of months from the original scheduled dates. Despite the pandemic, MMM 2022 received a large number of submissions organized in different tracks.

Specifically, 212 papers were submitted to MMM 2022 tracks. Each paper was reviewed by at least three reviewers from the Program Committee, while the TPC chairs and special event organizers acted as meta-reviewers and assisted in the decision-making process. Out of 163 regular papers, 71 were accepted for the proceedings. In particular, 35 papers were accepted for oral presentation (acceptance rate of 21%) and 36 papers for poster presentation (acceptance rate of 22%). Regarding the remaining tracks, 23 special session papers were submitted with 13 accepted for oral presentation. Additionally, one paper was accepted (from three submitted) for a new Brave New Ideas track and six demonstration papers were accepted. Finally, there were 16 papers accepted for participation at the Video Browser Showdown 2022.

The special sessions are traditionally organized to extend the program with novel challenging problems and directions. The MMM 2022 program included four special sessions:

- MAPTA - Multimedia Analytics Perspectives, Tools and Applications
- MULTIMED - Multimedia and Multimodal Analytics in the Medical Domain and Pervasive Environments
- MACHU - Multimedia Analytics for Contextual Human Understanding
- MDRE - Multimedia Datasets for Repeatable Experimentation

Besides the four special sessions, the 11th Video Browser Showdown represented an important highlight of MMM 2022 with 16 participating systems in this exciting (and challenging) competition. In addition, three highly respected speakers were invited to MMM 2022 to present their impressive talks and results in multimedia-related topics.

Last but not least, we would like to thank all members of the MMM community who contributed to the MMM 2022 event. We also thank all authors of submitted papers, all reviewers, and all members of the MMM 2022 organization team for their great work and support. They all helped MMM 2022 to be an exciting and inspiring international event for all participants!

June 2022

Björn Þór Jónsson
Cathal Gurrin
Minh-Triet Tran
Duc-Tien Dang-Nguyen
Anita Min-Chun Hu
Binh Huynh Thi Thanh
Benoit Huet

Organization

General Chairs

Björn Þór Jónsson   IT University of Copenhagen, Denmark
Cathal Gurrin   Dublin City University, Ireland
Minh-Triet Tran   University of Science, VNU-HCM, Vietnam

Community Direction Chairs

Tat-Seng Chua   National University of Singapore, Singapore
Jan Zahálka   Czech Technical University in Prague,
                              Czech Republic
Maria Eskevich   CLARIN, The Netherlands

Technical Program Chairs

Duc-Tien Dang-Nguyen   University of Bergen, Norway
Anita Min-Chun Hu   National Tsing Hua University, Taiwan
Huynh Thi Thanh Binh   Hanoi University of Science and Technology,
                              Vietnam

Technical Program Coordinator

Benoit Huet   EURECOM, France

Demo Chairs

Aaron Duane   IT University of Copenhagen, Denmark
Binh Nguyen   University of Science, VNU-HCM, Vietnam

Local Arrangement Chairs

Tien Dinh   University of Science, VNU-HCM, Vietnam
Vu Nguyen   University of Science, VNU-HCM, Vietnam
Vu Lam   University of Science, VNU-HCM, Vietnam

Video Browser Showdown Chairs

Klaus Schoeffmann   University of Klagenfurt, Austria
Werner Bailer   JOANNEUM RESEARCH, Austria
Jakub Lokoč   Charles University, Czech Republic
Cathal Gurrin   Dublin City University, Ireland

Publication Chair

Vinh-Tiep Nguyen   University of Information Technology,
                                 VNU-HCM, Vietnam

Steering Committee

Phoebe Chen   La Trobe University, Australia
Tat-Seng Chua   National University of Singapore, Singapore
Kiyoharu Aizawa   University of Tokyo, Japan
Cathal Gurrin   Dublin City University, Ireland
Benoit Huet   EURECOM, France
Klaus Schoeffmann   University of Klagenfurt, Austria
Richang Hong   Hefei University of Technology, China
Björn Þór Jónsson   IT University of Copenhagen, Denmark
Guo-Jun Qi   University of Central Florida, USA
Wen-Huang Cheng   National Chiao Tung University, Taiwan
Peng Cui   Tsinghua University, China

Web Chairs

Omar Shahbaz Khan   IT University of Copenhagen, Denmark
Mai-Khiem Tran   University of Science, VNU-HCM, Vietnam
Viet-Tham Huynh   University of Science, VNU-HCM, Vietnam

Organizing Agency

Minh-Hung Nguyen-Tong   CITE, Vietnam

Special Session Organizers

Multimedia Datasets for Repeatable Experimentation (MDRE)

Cathal Gurrin   Dublin City University, Ireland
Duc-Tien Dang Nguyen   University of Bergen, Norway
Björn Þór Jónsson   IT University of Copenhagen, Denmark
Klaus Schoeffmann   University of Klagenfurt, Austria

Multimedia Analytics: Perspectives, Tools and Applications (MAPTA)

Björn Þór Jónsson	IT University of Copenhagen, Denmark
Stevan Rudinac	University of Amsterdam, The Netherlands
Xirong Li	Renmin University of China, China
Cathal Gurrin	Dublin City University, Ireland
Laurent Amsaleg	CNRS-IRISA, France

Multimedia Analytics for Contextual Human Understanding (MACHU)

Duc-Tien Dang-Nguyen	University of Bergen, Norway
Minh-Son Dao	NICT, Japan
Cathal Gurrin	Dublin City University, Ireland
Ye Zheng	South Central University for Nationalities, China
Thittaporn Ganokratanaa	KMUTT, Thailand
Hung Tran-The	Deakin University, Australia
Zhihan Lv	Qingdao University, China

MULTIMED: Multimedia and Multimodal Analytics in the Medical Domain and Pervasive Environments

Georgios Meditskos	Centre for Research and Technology Hellas, Information Technologies Institute, Greece
Klaus Schoeffmann	University of Klagenfurt, Austria
Leo Wanner	ICREA – Universitat Pompeu Fabra, Spain
Stefanos Vrochidis	Centre for Research and Technology Hellas, Information Technologies Institute, Greece
Athanasios Tzioufas	National and Kapodistrian University of Athens, Greece

Program Committee and Reviewers (Regular and Special Session Papers)

Esra Açar Çelik	Fortiss Research Institute, Germany
Naushad Alam	Dublin City University, Ireland
Ahmed Alateeq	Dublin City University, Ireland
Laurent Amsaleg	IRISA, France
Evlampios Apostolidis	Centre for Research and Technology Hellas, Information Technologies Institute, Greece
Ognjen Arandjelovic	University of St Andrews, UK
Werner Bailer	JOANNEUM RESEARCH, Austria
Kai Uwe Barthel	HTW Berlin, Germany
Ilaria Bartolini	University of Bologna, Italy
Christian Beecks	University of Münster, Germany

Zhenzhen Hu	Hefei University of Technology, China
Jen-Wei Huang	National Cheng Kung University, Taiwan
Lei Huang	Ocean University of China, China
Benoit Huet	EURECOM, France
Tran-The Hung	Deakin University, Australia
Ichiro Ide	Nagoya University, Japan
Konstantinos Ioannidis	Centre for Research and Technology Hellas, Information Technologies Institute, Greece
Bogdan Ionescu	Politehnica University of Bucharest, Romania
Adam Jatowt	UIBK, Austria
Peiguang Jing	Tianjin University, China
Hyun Woo Jo	Korea University, South Korea
Björn Þór Jónsson	IT University of Copenhagen, Denmark
Yong Ju Jung	Gachon University, South Korea
Anastasios Karakostas	Centre for Research and Technology Hellas, Greece
Ari Karppinen	Finnish Meteorological Institute, Finland
Omar Shahbaz Khan	IT University of Copenhagen, Denmark
Tran Thuong Khanh	University of Oulu, Finland
Koichi Kise	Osaka Prefecture University, Japan
Markus Koskela	CSC - IT Center for Science Ltd., Finland
Calvin Ku	National Tsing Hua University, Taiwan
Yu-Kun Lai	Cardiff University, UK
Minh-Quan Le	University of Science, VNU-HCM, Vietnam
Tu-Khiem Le	Dublin City University, Ireland
Andreas Leibetseder	Alpen-Adria-Universität Klagenfurt, Austria
Jiatai Lin	Guangdong University of Technology, China
Yu-Hsun Lin	National Tsing Hua University, Taiwan
Xueting Liu	Caritas Institute of Higher Education, Hong Kong
Jakub Lokoc	Charles University, Czech Republic
Stephane Marchand-Maillet	Viper Group - University of Geneva, Switzerland
Lux Mathias	University of Klagenfurt, Austria
Mitsunori Matsushita	Kansai University, Japan
Thanassis Mavropoulos	Centre for Research and Technology Hellas, Greece
Georgios Meditskos	Aristotle University of Thessaloniki, Greece
Frank Mejzlik	Charles University, Czech Republic
Robert Mertens	BHH University of Applied Sciences, Germany
Vasileios Mezaris	Centre for Research and Technology Hellas, Greece
Weiqing Min	ICT, China
Phivos Mylonas	Ionian University, Greece

Binh Nguyen	University of Science, VNU-HCM, Vietnam
Hien Nguyen	University of Information Technology, VNU-HCM, Vietnam
Manh-Duy Nguyen	Dublin City University, Ireland
Thao-Nhu Nguyen	Dublin City University, Ireland
Thi Oanh Nguyen	Hanoi University of Science and Technology, Vietnam
Thu Nguyen	SimulaMet, Norway
Nguyen Nhung	University of Manchester, UK
Tu Van Ninh	Dublin City University, Ireland
Naoko Nitta	Osaka University, Japan
Noel E. O'Connor	Dublin City University, Ireland
Vincent Oria	NJIT, USA
Tse-Yu Pan	National Tsing Hua University, Taiwan
Jian-Wei Peng	National Cheng Kung University, Taiwan
Ladislav Peska	Charles University, Czech Republic
Yannick Prié	LS2N - University of Nantes, France
Athanasios Psaltis	Centre for Research and Technology Hellas, Greece
Georges Quénot	Laboratoire d'Informatique de Grenoble, France
Fazle Rabbi	University of Bergen, Norway
Miloš Radovanović	University of Novi Sad, Serbia
Amon Rapp	University of Turin, Italy
Benjamin Renoust	Osaka University, Japan
Luca Rossetto	University of Zurich, Switzerland
Stevan Rudinac	University of Amsterdam, The Netherlands
Mukesh Saini	Indian Institute of Technology Ropar, India
Shin'ichi Satoh	National Institute of Informatics, Japan
Klaus Schoeffmann	University of Klagenfurt, Austria
Heiko Schuldt	University of Basel, Switzerland
Jie Shao	University of Electronic Science and Technology of China, China
Xi Shao	Nanjing University of Posts and Telecommunications, China
Ujjwal Sharma	University of Amsterdam, The Netherlands
Koichi Shinoda	Tokyo Institute of Technology, Japan
Hong-Han Shuai	National Chiao Tung University, Taiwan
Mei-Ling Shyu	University of Miami, USA
Vassilis Sitokonstantinou	National Observatory of Athens, Greece
Tomas Skopal	Charles University, Czech Republic
Alan F. Smeaton	Dublin City University, Ireland
Natalia Sokolova	University of Klagenfurt, Austria

Thanos Stavropoulos	Centre for Research and Technology Hellas, Information Technologies Institute, Greece
Li Su	University of Chinese Academy of Sciences, China
Lifeng Sun	Tsinghua University, China
Shih-Wei Sun	Taipei National University of the Arts, Taiwan
Mario Taschwer	University of Klagenfurt, Austria
Georg Thallinger	JOANNEUM RESEARCH, Austria
Diego Thomas	Kyushu University, Japan
Christian Timmerer	University of Klagenfurt, Austria
Ly-Duyen Tran	Dublin City University, Ireland
Minh-Triet Tran	University of Science, VNU-HCM, Vietnam
Thanh-Hai Tran	TU Wien, Austria
Thy Thy Tran	Technische Universität Darmstadt, Germany
Ngo Thanh Trung	Osaka University, Japan
Wan-Lun Tsai	National Cheng Kung University, Taiwan
Athina Tsanousa	Centre for Research and Technology Hellas, Information Technologies Institute, Greece
Shingo Uchihashi	FUJIFILM Business Innovation Corp., Japan
Habib Ullah	Norwegian University of Life Sciences, Norway
Tiberio Uricchio	University of Florence, Italy
Lucia Vadicamo	ISTI-CNR, Italy
Guido Vingione	Serco, Italy
Muriel Visani	University of La Rochelle, France
Stefanos Vrochidis	Centre for Research and Technology Hellas, Information Technologies Institute, Greece
Qiao Wang	Southeast University, China
Xiang Wang	National University of Singapore, Singapore
Xu Wang	Shenzhen University, China
Zheng Wang	University of Tokyo, Japan
Wolfgang Weiss	JOANNEUM RESEARCH, Austria
Tien-Tsin Wong	Chinese University of Hong Kong, Hong Kong
Marcel Worring	University of Amsterdam, The Netherlands
Xiao Wu	Southwest Jiaotong University, China
Sen Xiang	Wuhan University of Science and Technology, China
Yingqing Xu	Tsinghua University, China
Ryosuke Yamanishi	Kansai University, Japan
Toshihiko Yamasaki	University of Tokyo, Japan
Keiji Yanai	University of Electro-Communications, Japan
Gang Yang	Renmin University of China, China
Yang Yang	University of Electronic Science and Technology of China, China

Contents – Part I

Learning

Multimedia for Medical Applications (Special Session)

Applications 2

Multimedia Analytics for Contextual Human Understanding (Special Session)

Applications 3

Image Analytics

Speech and Music

Multimodal Analytics

Contents – Part II

Demonstration Papers

Video Browser Showdown 2022

Best Paper Session

Real-time Detection of Tiny Objects Based on a Weighted Bi-directional FPN

Yaxuan Hu[1], Yuehong Dai[1(✉)], and Zhongxiang Wang[2]

[1] University of Electronic Science and Technology of China, Chengdu, China
daiyh@uestc.edu.cn
[2] ShenZhen East-Win Technology Co., LTD., Shenzhen, China

Abstract. Tiny object detection is an important and challenging object detection subfield. However, many of its numerous applications (e.g., human tracking and marine rescue) have tight detection time constraints. Namely, two-stage object detectors are too slow to fulfill the real-time detection needs, whereas one-stage object detectors have an insufficient detection accuracy. Consequently, enhancing the detection accuracy of one-stage object detectors has become an essential aspect of real-time tiny objects detection. This work presents a novel model for real-time tiny objects detection based on a one-stage object detector YOLOv5. The proposed YOLO-P4 model contains a module for detecting tiny objects and a new output prediction branch. Next, a weighted bi-directional feature pyramid network (BiFPN) is introduced in YOLO-P4, yielding an improved model named YOLO-BiP4 that enhances the YOLO-P4 feature input branches. The proposed models were tested on the Tiny-Person dataset, demonstrating that the YOLO-BiP4 model outperforms the original model in detecting tiny objects. The model satisfies the real-time detection needs while obtaining the highest accuracy compared to existing one-stage object detectors.

Keywords: Tiny object detection · Bi-directional feature pyramid network · Real-time detection · YOLOv5

1 Introduction

Object detection is a critical component of computer vision research that focuses on the recognition and localization of objects in images. Detecting tiny objects is an essential but challenging object detection area with many applications, including surveillance, tracking [17], aided driving [18], remote sensing image analysis [10], and marine rescue [16]. Tiny object detection deals with very small objects in images of extremely low resolution. An increase in resolution yields blurred images, making it difficult to extract enough features for learning. These characteristics pose a significant challenge for tiny object detection.

Current object detection algorithms can be broadly classified into one-stage and two-stage object detection algorithms. One-stage object detection algorithms are fast and enable very rapid detection while ensuring a specific degree of

© Springer Nature Switzerland AG 2022
B. Þór Jónsson et al. (Eds.): MMM 2022, LNCS 13141, pp. 3–14, 2022.
https://doi.org/10.1007/978-3-030-98358-1_1

detection accuracy. These algorithms include SSD [2], RetinaNet [1], and YOLO series (YOLOv3 [3], YOLOv4 [4], YOLOv5 [5]). In contrast, two-stage object detection algorithms are extremely accurate. Thus, algorithms such as Faster-RCNN [6] and Mask R-CNN [7] have higher detection accuracy than one-stage detection algorithms, but their detection speed is typically worse. Many application scenarios, such as personnel tracking and sea rescue, pose strict requirements on the model's detection time. The two-stage object detection algorithm cannot meet the real-time detection requirements, and the one-stage object detection algorithm's detection accuracy is insufficient. Therefore, the one-stage object detection algorithms' detection accuracy improvement has become a significant concern in the tiny object detection domain.

This paper studies the accuracy problems in detecting tiny objects and, as a result, proposes an improved approach and advances the parameter settings in the training process. The proposed algorithm, named YOLO-P4, enhances the tiny object detection accuracy. YOLO-P4 is based on the YOLOv5 one-stage object detection algorithm but includes both a new prediction branch and a module specialized for detecting tiny objects, thus substantially improving the model's effectiveness.

However, it is important to note that YOLO-P4 improves the accuracy at the expense of detection speed. Thus, YOLO-BiP4 is also proposed to improve detection speed. The algorithm builds on a new feature fusion structure called weighted bi-directional feature pyramid network (BiFPN) [2], but the structure was modified for the YOLO-P4 feature layer. As a result, the YOLO-BiP4 algorithm reduces the number of model parameters while maintaining detection accuracy and improving the detection speed to satisfy the real-time detection requirements.

2   Related Work

The proposed algorithm for tiny object detection is based on BiFPN, a multiscale feature fusion approach. This section briefly introduces the two parts of tiny object detection and multiscale feature fusion.

2.1   Tiny Object Detection

Many research efforts were directed at handling the lack of information and large size differences between the object and the background to improve the accuracy and speed of tiny object detection. For example, Kis et al. [8] used data enhancement to increase the number of tiny objects via oversampling images containing the tiny objects and copy-pasting them. Gong et al. [9] focused on the fact that image feature fusion is affected by the dataset scale distribution, introducing a fusion factor α to enhance the fusion effect between feature pyramid network's (FPN) layers. Liu et al. [10] proposed UAV-YOLO, which modified the ResNet structure by changing the number of layers and the connection of modules. As a result, the network's receptive field was enlarged, and its semantic feature extraction capability improved. Jiang et al. [11] proposed a simple and effective scale matching method to achieve a favorable tiny object representation by aligning the tiny objects' scales in datasets for pre-training and learning. The listed methods approach the tiny object detection from different angles striving to improve its performance.

2.2   Multiscale Feature Fusion

Feature fusion combines features from different image scales. The vast majority of the current target detection algorithms use a high feature layer after repeated downsampling for target classification and regression, significantly affecting the tiny object detection. Note that since the tiny object size is very small, the available features are limited. As the network deepens, it is difficult to preserve enough features at high sampling rates, and their detailed information may be completely lost. This problem is tackled by fusing shallow and deep image features to enhance the tiny object feature extraction. Shallow features have higher resolution and contain more detailed location information. However, these features undergo fewer convolutions, making them noisier and less semantic. In contrast, deeper features contain more robust semantic information but have lower resolution and poorer perception of details. Thus, an efficient fusion of shallow and deep features is vital to ensure tiny object detection accuracy.

FPN [12] is a classical image feature fusion network. It has a top-down network structure with lateral connections and constructs feature maps of various sizes and high-level semantic information. FPN extracts features for images of each scale and produces multi-scale feature representations with strong semantic information for every level's feature map. Nevertheless, it significantly increases the network inference time and occupies considerable memory, seriously affecting the model's operational efficiency.

To overcome the discussed FPN's drawbacks, scholars have proposed various FPN structures. Liu et al. [13] developed a Path Aggregation Network (PANet), which adds a bottom-up path aggregation network to FPN to fully integrate the features from different feature layers and greatly improve the detection. The YOLOv5 model's neck utilizes FPN and PANet. Kim et al. [14] considered the features' contextual information and proposed a parallel FPN. A multi-scale context aggregation module serves to resize the parallel feature mappings to the same size while aggregating their contextual information to obtain each level of the final feature pyramid. As a result, this action reduces the performance differences between features at each level. BiFPN is another FPN improvement. In contrast to treating features of different scales equally, BiFPN introduces a weighting mechanism to balance the feature information. While considering the distinct contributions of features at different scales, weights are assigned to each branch involved in feature fusion to perform adaptive learning. BiFPN deletes nodes with only one input or output edge and adds an extra edge between the output and output nodes at the same level. Thus, more features can be fused without increasing consumption (see Fig. 1).

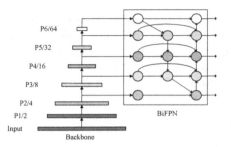

Fig. 1. The structure of BiFPN and backbone

3   The Proposed Model

3.1   YOLO-P4

According to the COCO dataset [15] definition, a small object is an object of fewer than 32 × 32 pixels. Several practical applications require performing remote acquisition of images, which typically have a large resolution, but the object to be detected is small. For example, in the Tiny-Person [16] dataset, the training contains a total of 21599 labels, among which 6872 labels are less than 3 pixels in length or width.

Within this work, the object smaller than 20 pixels is considered a tiny target, and they directly lead to the model's low detection efficiency. The detection results of using the YOLOv5s model to detect an image in Tiny-Person are shown in Fig. 2(a). One can note from the figure that there are several undetected targets. The reasons stem from the YOLOv5s structure (see Fig. 3). In the model's backbone part, four downsampling operations are performed first, and then the P3, P4, and P5 feature layers are fused in the neck part for target prediction. The input image is sized 640 × 640, the detection layer size of P5 is 20 × 20, which serves to detect targets of size 32 × 32 or larger. The P4 feature layer corresponds to a detection layer of size 40 × 40 and is used to detect targets of size 16 × 16 or larger. Finally, the P3 feature layer has 80 × 80 size and can detect targets of size 8 × 8 or larger.

(a) YOLOv5s detection results   (b) YOLOs-P4 detection results

Fig. 2. Comparison of detection results

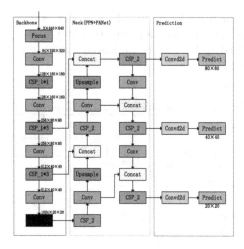

Fig. 3. The structure of YOLOv5s

The current three detection layers typically serve for detecting objects with a size above 8 × 8. When the object size is smaller than 8 × 8, the detection accuracy drops dramatically. Nevertheless, the size of tiny objects is generally smaller than 8 × 8. Further, as noted previously, downsampling drastically reduces the feature information, preventing one from extracting sufficient information. An analysis revealed that the input image size could be upgraded to 960 × 960 so that the detection layer size of the P3 feature layer is 120 × 120. Then, the tiny object size is expanded 2.25 times, and more valuable features can be extracted. The images of P2, P3, P4, and P5 feature layers with input sizes of 640 and 960 are visualized in Fig. 4. One can note that the P3 feature layer of the 960 × 960 image contains more effective information than the 640 × 640 image.

However, although the number of effective features contained in the P3 feature layer is boosted by increasing the input image size, the small scale of a tiny object renders effective features retained after two downsamplings too few to extract sufficient information. Figure 3 shows that the features in P3 provide insufficient information for tiny object feature extraction. Thus, using the information in the P2 feature layer is necessary, ensuring it participates in the feature fusion process.

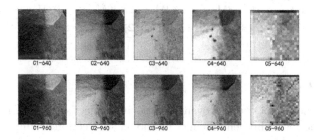

Fig. 4. Feature layer display for different input sizes

Therefore, to involve P2 in feature fusion, the original model's structure was extended by adding a module for detecting tiny objects and a new output detection branch (Predict-Tiny). The improved model is called YOLO-P4, and its structure is depicted in Fig. 5.

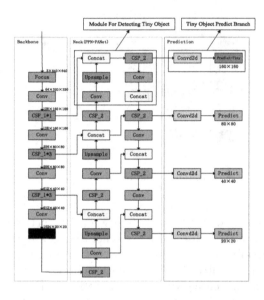

Fig. 5. The structure of YOLOv5s-P4

Compared with the original model in Fig. 3, one can note that YOLO-P4 adds another upsampling before the tiny object detection layers and after the original model is upsampled twice to fuse P2 with tiny objects' rich features. Further, it adds a new output detection branch, which greatly improves the model's detection of tiny objects.

Table 1. Number of models' parameters

Model	YOLOv5x	YOLOv5l	YOLOv5m	YOLOv5s
Original	88.40M	47.37M	21.47M	7.25M
P4	96.48M	51.72M	23.46M	7.93M
BiP4	**78.26M**	**44.16M**	**21.51M**	8.10M

3.2   YOLO-BiP4

Recall that the YOLOv5 improvement for tiny object detection increases the inference time loss while enhancing the model's detection. Namely, adding an upsampling and a new detection layer introduces many parameters, leading to the model inference time loss. In FPN-PANet, the number of parameters passing through the upsampling layer doubles with each additional upsampling layer. Table 1 compares the number of parameters in the original and the improved YOLO-P4 models. The table shows that there are more parameters in YOLO-P4 than in the original model. The parameters increase the corresponding inference time, which is unsuitable for the task at hand. Therefore, the YOLO-BiP4 algorithm is proposed to ensure sufficient detection accuracy without significantly increasing the inference time.

The analysis reveals that controlling the number of parameters reduces the inference time loss. YOLO-P4's neck part has a structure of FPN+PANet. Not to increase the inference time significantly, BiFPN is introduced.

In contrast to other feature fusion methods, BiFPN introduces a weighting mechanism that enables different features treatment. Each branch involved in feature fusion is assigned a weight based on their contributions at different scales during feature fusion. Then, adaptive learning is employed during model training to ensure the model's detection accuracy. Figure 1 presents the BiFPN structure, which fuses five feature layers in turn. When performing fusion, the weights are set in the following ways. Let P_i denote the feature at layer i, and w_i is that feature's fusion weight.

1) Unbounded fusion: Addition is performed directly on the fusion branches. It is equivalent to the one where each fusion branch's weight is equal to one (i.e., $w_i = 1, \forall i$).

2) Softmax-based fusion: the output follows the formula

$$Output = \sum_{i=1}^{4} \frac{exp(w_i))}{\sum_{j=1}^{4} exp(w_j))} \cdot P_i \tag{1}$$

3) Fast normalized fusion: The ReLU function is introduced before the calculation to ensure that weight is greater than zero. $\epsilon = 0.0001$ is a small value to avoid numerical instability. The output equation is

$$Output = \sum_{i=1}^{4} \frac{w_i}{\epsilon + \sum_{j=1}^{4} w_j} \cdot P_i \tag{2}$$

The improved BiFPN is introduced into the YOLO-P4 model, yielding the YOLO-BiP4 architecture. Specifically, one of the BiFPN's input feature layers is removed, changing the number of feature layers at the input side from five to four (namely, P2, P3, P4, and P5). The BiP4 structure is built using both top-down and bottom-up rules, and the fast-normalized fusion is used to set the weights. Figure 6 depicts the YOLO-BiP4 structure.

Figure 6 demonstrates that YOLO-BiP4 removes the vertices with only one input or output edge, thus reducing the number of parameters by a certain amount. Such a design can effectively improve the model's detection speed.

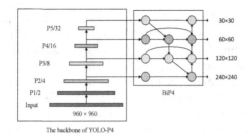

The backbone of YOLO-P4

Fig. 6. The structure of YOLO-BiP4

4   Experiments

4.1   Evaluation Methods and Datasets

In the object detection field, the model's detection effectiveness is commonly measured using the *mean average precision* (mAP). Furthermore, in models requiring real-time detection, the number of parameters and the model's detection speed are also crucial. Typically, a model is said to satisfy the real-time detection requirement when its detection speed is greater than 30 *frames per second* (FPS). Therefore, this work studies these three aspects in a multidimensional analysis of the model performance.

Tiny-Person is a dataset for tiny object detection collected from high-quality video and web images. It contains 72,651 annotations of human targets with low resolution in visual effects. In total, there are 1610 images, including 794 images in the training set and 816 images in the test set. The average absolute scale of all objects in the Tiny-Person dataset is 18 pixels, while the average size is less than 5 × 5. More than 30% of the objects span less than 3 pixels in height or width, all of which can be called tiny objects.

4.2   Experimental Environment and Parameter Description

The hardware environment used in the experiments reported herein consisted of a CoreTM i7-7700HQCPU@2.80 GHz, GeForce GTX1070 graphics card for training, and RTX3090 graphics card for testing. The main software used was Pycharm 2020.2. The configured virtual environment was based on Python 3.9, and the utilized deep learning framework was Pytorch 1.8.0.

A series of YOLOv5 models were studied, including the original models (i.e., YOLOv5s, YOLOv5m, YOLOv5l, and YOLOv5x), the model with improved input parameters (i.e., YOLOv5-960), and the models with improved network structure (i.e., YOLOv5-P4 and YOLOv5-BiP4). The trained models result from 200 training epochs on the Tiny-Person dataset using the Adam optimizer with a learning rate set to 0.001.

Table 2. Detection accuracy for different test sizes when the training size is 640. The results reported as mAP (%)

TIS	YOLOv5x	YOLOv5l	YOLOv5m	YOLOv5s
640	27.70	27.63	27.47	26.97
960	35.94	35.26	34.08	33.15
1408	38.77	38.18	36.71	**36.64**
1536	**38.86**	**38.68**	**36.82**	36.49

Table 3. Detection speed for different test sizes when the training size is 640. The results reported as FPS

TIS	YOLOv5x	YOLOv5l	YOLOv5m	YOLOv5s
640	110.51	198.89	328.08	490.83
960	45.43	89.09	143.55	333.72
1408	23.26	45.32	77.58	181.18
1536	15.43	37.52	61.16	126.38

4.3 Comparison of Improved Detection Results

The experiments aimed at improving the input parameters were performed first. The input size ranged from 640 to 960, and the mAP and detection speed were compared for each YOLOv5 model over 200 epochs. The experiments show that increasing the input images' size during testing can effectively improve the models' detection. The experiments comparing the detection speed and accuracy for both the training and test input image sizes are shown in Tables 2, 3, 4 and 5. Here, TIS stands for Test Image Size.

As shown in the table, increasing the input image size enhances the detection accuracy for both training and testing but hampers the detection speed. The model whose training input was of size 960 improves its detection over the course of the training, but its detection speed decreases. The results demonstrate that the detection accuracy and speed are optimal when the input size equals 1408 for the model test. As a result, the following experiments' input parameters were based on a training input sized 960 and a testing input sized 1408.

YOLO-P4 adds a module that fuses the P2 feature layer in the original model to improve the extraction of effective tiny object features. Further, a new output prediction branch called Predict-Tiny that is dedicated to tiny object detection is introduced. Tables 6 and 7 show the YOLO-P4's detection accuracy and speed when the training size equals 960, and the testing size is 1408.

Experiments show that adding the fusion module and the output prediction branch significantly improves the YOLO-P4's detection accuracy but decreases the detection speed in turn. Nevertheless, except for the YOLOx-P4 model, the proposed models can all meet the real-time detection requirement. Compared to the model before the improvement (i.e., YOLOv5), the detection accuracy has

Table 4. Detection accuracy for different test sizes when the training size is 960. The results reported as mAP (%)

TIS	YOLOv5x	YOLOv5l	YOLOv5m	YOLOv5s
640	29.58	29.52	29.30	26.64
960	37.88	37.75	37.37	35.34
1408	**42.59**	**41.95**	41.75	40.89
1536	42.32	41.93	**42.27**	**41.08**

Table 5. Detection speed for different test sizes when the training size is 960. The results reported as FPS

TIS	YOLOv5x	YOLOv5l	YOLOv5m	YOLOv5s
640	108.28	207.18	335.43	497.41
960	54.31	90.32	143.76	323.87
1408	24.34	46.75	84.96	179.62
1536	15.23	37.83	68.38	155.91

Table 6. Model's detection accuracy comparison. The results reported as mAP (%)

Model	YOLOv5x	YOLOv5l	YOLOv5m	YOLOv5s
Original	42.59	41.95	41.75	40.89
P4	**45.90**	**45.69**	**44.79**	42.77
BiP4	45.66	44.61	44.29	**43.26**

Table 7. Model's detection speed comparison. The results reported as FPS

Model	YOLOv5x	YOLOv5l	YOLOv5m	YOLOv5s
Original	24.34	46.75	84.96	179.62
P4	18.36	36.92	45.91	91.51
BiP4	21.08	40.45	62.23	109.78

improved by 7.8%, 8.9%, 7.3%, and 4.6%, respectively. Figure 2(a) and 2(b) show the detection results before and after the improvement, where the differences are highlighted using the black boxes.

Table 1 compares the number of parameters in YOLO-P4 to those in the original YOLOv5 model. Note that detection speed decreases as the number of parameters increases.

Next, the YOLO-P4 model structure was improved by introducing the BiFPN structure to reduce the number of parameters and enhance the detection speed. The BiFPN structure is improved by removing one input, thus reducing the number of model parameters and significantly increasing the model's detection

Table 8. Comparison of different models detection results in Tiny-Person dataset

Model	mAP (%)	FPS
YOLOx-BiP4 (Ours)	45.66	21.08
YOLOl-BiP4 (Ours)	**44.61**	**40.45**
YOLOm-BiP4 (Ours)	44.29	62.23
YOLOv5l	41.95	46.75
YOLOv4	32.83	44.87
NAS-FPN	37.75	18.06
RetinaNet-101	33.53	5.20
SSD-513	31.2	8.10
Faster R-CNN	47.35	5.80

speed. The improved model's accuracy and speed are shown in Tables 6 and 7, respectively, whereas the corresponding number of parameters is given in Table 1.

Tables 6 and 7 show that, compared to YOLO-P4, the improved YOLO-BiP4 model reduced the number of parameters while increasing the detection speed by 14.8%, 9.6%, 35.5%, and 20.1%, respectively. Furthermore, the improved model maintained the YOLO-P4's detection accuracy. Compared to YOLOv5-960, the YOLO-BiP4's detection accuracy is 7.2%, 6.3%, 6.1%, and 5.8% higher, respectively.

Finally, Table 8 shows the YOLO-BiP4's detection results and contrasts them to other one-stage and two-stage models' performances on the Tiny-Person dataset. Table 8 demonstrates that the proposed YOLO-BiP4 model achieves the highest accuracy of a one-stage model for detecting tiny objects while satisfying the real-time detection requirements.

5   Conclusions and Future Works

Building on the YOLOv5 algorithm, this paper first proposed YOLO-P4, an improved algorithm for tiny object detection. A module dedicated to tiny object detection was added to fuse the P2 feature layer with sufficient object features, and an output prediction branch was added to predict tiny objects. Experiments demonstrate that such modifications improve the YOLO-P4's average accuracy in detecting tiny objects by 7.2%. Then, YOLO-BiP4 is proposed to reduce the number of model parameters and improve the detection speed. YOLO-BiP4 is based on YOLO-P4 but introduces the BiFPN structure to improve the YOLO-P4's feature layer. This modification results in the average reduction of the number of parameters by 10.9%, while the detection speed increased by 19.9% on average. The proposed model achieves the highest accuracy of the one-stage tiny object detectors while considering the real-time detection requirement. However, the detection speed is still insufficient despite the tiny object detection accuracy improvement. Thus, simultaneous improvement of the detection accuracy and speed remains a critical direction for future research.

References

1. Lin, T.Y., Goyal, P., Girshick, R., et al.: Focal loss for dense object detection. In: Proceedings of the IEEE International Conference on Computer Vision, pp. 2980–2988 (2017)
2. Tan, M., Pang, R,. Le, Q.V.: Efficientdet: scalable and efficient object detection. In: Proceedings of the IEEE/CVF Conference on Computer Vision and Pattern Recognition, pp. 10781–10790 (2020)
3. Redmon, J., Farhadi, A.: Yolov3: an incremental improvement. arXiv preprint arXiv:1804.02767 (2018)
4. Bochkovskiy, A., Wang, C.Y., Liao, H.Y.M.: Yolov4: optimal speed and accuracy of object detection. arXiv preprint arXiv:2004.10934 (2020)
5. Glenn, J.: ultralytics/yolov5: v3.1 - Bug Fixes and Performance Improvements. https://github.com/ultralytics/yolov5 (2020)
6. Ren, S., He, K., Girshick, R., et al.: Faster r-cnn: towards real-time object detection with region proposal networks. Adv. Neural Inf. Process. Syst. **28**, 91–99 (2015)
7. He, K., Gkioxari, G., Dollár, P., et al.: Mask r-cnn. In: Proceedings of the IEEE International Conference on Computer Vision, pp. 2961–2969 (2017)
8. Kisantal, M., Wojna, Z., Murawski, J., et al.: Augmentation for small object detection. arXiv preprint arXiv:1902.07296 (2019)
9. Gong, Y., Yu, X., Ding, Y., et al.: Effective fusion factor in FPN for tiny object detection. In: Proceedings of the IEEE/CVF Winter Conference on Applications of Computer Vision, pp. 1160–1168 (2021)
10. Liu, M., Wang, X., Zhou, A., et al.: UAV-YOLO: small object detection on unmanned aerial vehicle perspective. Sensors **20**(8), 2238 (2020)
11. Jiang, N., Yu, X., Peng, X., et al.: SM+: refined scale match for tiny person detection. In: ICASSP 2021–2021 IEEE International Conference on Acoustics, Speech and Signal Processing (ICASSP), pp. 1815–1819. IEEE (2021)
12. Lin, T.Y., Dollár, P., Girshick, R., et al.: Feature pyramid networks for object detection. In: Proceedings of the IEEE Conference on Computer Vision and Pattern Recognition, pp. 2117–2125 (2017)
13. Liu, S., Qi, L., Qin, H., et al.: Path aggregation network for instance segmentation. In: Proceedings of the IEEE Conference on Computer Vision and Pattern Recognition, pp. 8759–8768 (2018)
14. Kim, S.W., Kook, H.K., Sun, J.Y., et al.: Parallel feature pyramid network for object detection. In: Proceedings of the European Conference on Computer Vision (ECCV), pp. 234–250 (2018)
15. Lin, T.-Y., Maire, M., Belongie, S., Hays, J., Perona, P., Ramanan, D., Dollár, P., Zitnick, C.L.: Microsoft COCO: common objects in context. In: Fleet, D., Pajdla, T., Schiele, B., Tuytelaars, T. (eds.) ECCV 2014. LNCS, vol. 8693, pp. 740–755. Springer, Cham (2014). https://doi.org/10.1007/978-3-319-10602-1_48
16. Yu, X., Gong, Y., Jiang, N., et al.: Scale match for tiny person detection. In: Proceedings of the IEEE/CVF Winter Conference on Applications of Computer Vision, pp. 1257–1265 (2020)
17. Chen, L., Ai, H., Zhuang, Z., et al.: Real-time multiple people tracking with deeply learned candidate selection and person re-identification. In: 2018 IEEE International Conference on Multimedia and Expo (ICME), pp. 1–6. IEEE (2018)
18. Chen, J., Bai, T.: SAANet: spatial adaptive alignment network for object detection in automatic driving. Image Vision Comput. **94**, 103873 (2020)

Multi-modal Fusion Network for Rumor Detection with Texts and Images

Boqun Li, Zhong Qian, Peifeng Li$^{(\boxtimes)}$, and Qiaoming Zhu

School of Computer Science and Technology, Soochow University, Suzhou, China
20205227046@stu.suda.edu.cn, {qianzhong,pfli,qmzhu}@suda.edu.cn

Abstract. Currently, more and more individuals tend to publish texts and images on social media to express their views. Inevitably, social media platform has become a media for a large number of rumors. There are a few studies on multi-modal rumor detection. However, most of them simplified the fusion strategy of texts and images and ignored the rich knowledge behind images. To address the above issues, this paper proposes a Multi-Modal Model with Texts and Images (M^{3}TI) for rumor detection. Specifically, its Granularity-fusion Module (GM) learns the multi-modal representation of the tweet according to the relevance of images and texts instead of the simple concatenation fusion strategy, while its Knowledge-aware Module (KM) retrieves image knowledge through the advanced recognition method to complement the semantic representation of image. Experimental results on two datasets (English PHEME and Chinese WeiBo) show that our model M^{3}TI is more effective than several state-of-the-art baselines.

Keywords: Rumor detection · Coarse-grained and fine-grained · Image knowledge

1 Introduction

Rumors, a variety of false information which is widely spread on the social media, can publicize false information, spread panic, mislead the public, and cause terrible effects. For example in Iran, with the rise of COVID-19 cases and deaths, the use of so-called "traditional" and "Islamic" anti-coronavirus drugs has been sought after by some people. However, these drugs without safety certification are very dangerous to the human body. Hence, considering the potential panic and threat caused by rumors, rumor detection on social media efficiently and as early as possible is a way to control rumor propagation.

Twitter and Microblog have become the focus of rumor detection research because of their huge number of users and wide propagation. To reduce manpower and implement automatic rumor detection, a large number of methods based on neural network have been proposed [2,8,11,17] and almost all typically only considered single modality, i.e., text, and largely ignored the visual data and knowledge behind images. Only a few studies focused on both texts

© Springer Nature Switzerland AG 2022
B. Þór Jónsson et al. (Eds.): MMM 2022, LNCS 13141, pp. 15–27, 2022.
https://doi.org/10.1007/978-3-030-98358-1_2

These folks sure hope so. Lineup surprisingly short.

Fig. 1. Example of multi-modal tweet.

and images [5,16,18]. However, most of them simplified the fusion strategy of texts and images and ignored the richer knowledge behind images. For example, Wang et al. [16] simply concatenated textual features and visual features to get multi-modal features. Jin et al. [5] proposed to use attention mechanism to fuse text and image features. Zhang et al. [18] proposed a multi-channel CNN for combining text, text knowledge, image features. However, all of them only used the high-dimensional representation learnt by images, and did not pay attention to the rich semantic knowledge behind images.

Nevertheless, take Fig. 1 as an example, the methods above have following issues: 1) These strategies adopted similar fusion method for different samples which are unable to pinpoint the key region of text (*"Lineup surprisingly short"*), let alone the simple concatenating strategy; 2) All of them used the high-dimensional representation learnt by images which only captured underlying features of the visual layer (such as *"person"*), for better understanding the image, we prefer to acquire semantic knowledge of the concept layer (such as *"crowd"* or *"mass"*) to prove *"Lineup surprisingly short"* belongs to rumor.

To address the above issues, we propose a M̲ulti-M̲odal M̲odel with T̲exts and I̲mages (M³TI) to detect rumors, which mainly considers three features, i.e., texts, images, and image knowledge. Firstly, our Granularity-fusion Module (GM) using a coarse-grained and fine-grained fusion mechanism is introduced to learn the latent connection from images and source texts. Then, our knowledge-aware Module (KM) integrates the image knowledge[1] and the source texts to capture the full semantic meaning of images. Finally, the multi-modal representation and knowledge representation extracted by GM and KM, respectively, are fed into a classification module with reply representation for rumor detection. Experimental results on two publicly available datasets (English PHEME and Chinese WeiBo) show that our model M³TI is more effective than several state-of-the-art baselines. To sum up, our main contributions can be summarized as the following three aspects:

(1) We applied a novel fusion strategy on multi-modal rumor detection to generalize better under different cases in reality, in which Granularity-fusion

---

[1] The image knowledge consists of the entities with brief introduction and is extracted by an object recognition tool(https://ai.baidu.com/tech/imagerecognition/general).

Module uses a coarse-grained and fine-grained fusion mechanism to consider the relevance between images and texts.

(2) We exploited image knowledge consisting of entities with introduction to complement semantic meaning of images. As far as we know, it is the first time to use image knowledge for rumor detection and Knowledge-aware Module helps the model intuitively understand image and context together.

(3) We experimentally demonstrated that our model is more robust and effective on two public datasets from the real world.

2 Related Work

The neural network models have been proved effective in rumor detection. Compared with traditional machine learning, neural network can save a lot of manpower and learn the representation of various information more effectively.

Rumor Detection on Texts. Various methods using text modality have been proposed in rumor detection. Among them, Ma et al. [9] proposed the hierarchical attention to notice the specific sentences conducive to rumor detection. Li et al. [7] used user information, attention mechanism and multi-task learning to detect rumors. They added the user credibility information to the rumor detection layer, and applied the attention mechanism in the hidden layer of the rumor detection layer and stance detection layer. Khoo et al. [6] proposed a rumor detection model named PLAN based on attention, in which only texts were considered, and user interaction was achieved by self-attention.

Multi-modal Rumor Detection. There are only a few work on multi-modal rumor detection. EANN proposed by Wang et al. [16] included three components: feature extractor, fake news detector and event discriminator. It only simply concatenated the visual features and text features to obtain multi-modal features. We believe that the concatenation strategy breaks up the connection among words and visual data. Jin et al. [5] proposed a multi-modal detection model att-RNN and emphasized the importance of social context features. The attention mechanism was used to capture the association between the visual features and the text/social joint features. Zhang et al. [18] proposed a model MKEMN to learn the multi-modal representation of the tweet and retrieve the knowledge about the entities from texts. Different from Zhang et al. we further use the image information to obtain the entities in the image, which can make use of images more intuitively and effectively.

Other Multi-modal Tasks. Emotion analysis and sarcasm detection are related to rumor detection, and there are a few relative methods based on multi-modal content in these aspects. Although the inputs are different, their fusion mechanism can inspire our tasks. Poria et al. [12] used multi-core learning to fuse different modalities. Gu et al. [4] aligned text and audio at the word level and applied attention mechanism to fuse them. Cai et al. [1] proposed to use the attribute features in the image, then applied early fusion and late fusion between these attributes and texts to detect whether a sentence is ironic.

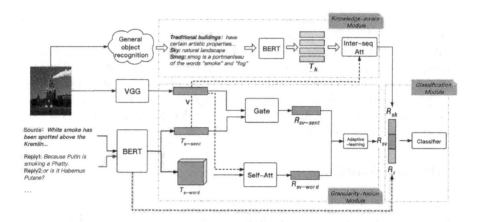

Fig. 2. Multi-modal model with texts and images (M³TI) for rumor detection

3   Approach

3.1   Overview

We define a thread, i.e., $thread = \{S_0, I_0, R_1, R_2, ..., R_n\}$, where S_0 means source tweet, I_0 is the image attached to S_0 and it may be null which depends on whether the user published the image, R_i is the i-th tweet in chronological order, n means that the thread has n relevant replies. The goal of our model is to classify the thread as *"Rumor"* or *"Non-Rumor"*.

Figure 2 shows the architecture of our proposed Multi-Modal Model with Texts and Images (M³TI) for rumor detection. Our model mainly includes the following three parts: Granularity-fusion Module (corresponding to Sect. 3.2), Knowledge-aware Module (corresponding to Sect. 3.3), and Classification Module (corresponding to Sect. 3.4).

We briefly introduce the process of three modules above. Firstly, source tweet and image are fused through Coarse-grained and Fine-grained Mechanism to obtain two fused vectors. Adaptive Learning Mechanism is used to balance them. Secondly, we combine the source text and image knowledge through Inter-Sequence Attention. At last, we make use of two vectors obtained by two modules mentioned above and information of replies to detect rumors.

3.2   Granularity-Fusion Module

Text Encoder. Text encoder module aims to produce the text representation for a given source text S_0. Firstly, we feed source text into a Bert-Base-Uncased [3] model to capture the contextual information, "$[CLS]$" is used to represent its sentence-level vector $T_{s-sent} = [s_1, s_2, ..., s_{768}]$ and the embedding corresponding to each token in the source text is used to represent the word-level vector matrix $T_{s-word} = [s_{w1}, s_{w2}, ..., s_{wn}]$, where n is the number after word segmentation of each source text, $s_{wi} \in \mathbb{R}^{768}$ is used as the embedding of each token after word segmentation. We also get sentence-level vector of replies $R_r \in \mathbb{R}^{768}$.

Visual Encoder. Given an image (I_0) , we firstly resize the image to 224×224 pixels, then feed it into the vision sub-network to generate $v \in \mathbb{R}^{512}$. The structure of its front layers is the same as VGG-16 [14] network. We modify the last two full connection layers of VGG-16. Only the parameters of the last two full connection layers will be updated when training.

Coarse-grained Fusion. When fusing different modalities, one representation may overwhelm another, resulting in biased representation. Sangwan et al. [13] have proved that the Gating Mechanism is very effective for balancing two different modalities. We concatenate T_{s-sent} and v to obtain the weight w' which represents the weight of the text modality w.r.t. image modality, and then obtain the transformed representation $R_{sv-sent} \in \mathbb{R}^{768}$ as follows.

$$w = T_{s-sent} \oplus v \tag{1}$$

$$w' = softmax(w) \tag{2}$$

$$R_{sv-sent} = w' T_{s-sent} \tag{3}$$

Fine-grained Fusion. In order to accurately pinpoint the specific region of source text highly relevant to the image. We apply an image-guided text attention method. Given an image vector v, we firstly map v into text space through fully connected layer to obtain v', and use Q to imply the relationship between image and words. M represents the new embedding matrix calculated from the weight matrix W and T_{s-word}. Finally we obtain the attention distribution over each region of text, where $R_{sv-word} = [r_1, r_2, ..., r_{768}]$, the r_i denotes the weight of attention from the i-th region of text features towards the image representation. The Self-Att Mechanism equations are as follows.

$$v' = fully\_connected(v) \tag{4}$$

$$Q = v' T_{s-word} \tag{5}$$

$$W = softmax([\sum_{i=1}^{768} Q_{1_i}, ..., \sum_{i=1}^{768} Q_{n_i}]) \tag{6}$$

$$M = W^T T_{s-word} = [m_1, ..., m_n] \tag{7}$$

$$R_{sv-word} = [\sum_{t=1}^{n} m_{t_1}, ..., \sum_{t=1}^{n} m_{t_{768}}] \tag{8}$$

Adaptive Learning. We utilize an adaptive gate $e \in \mathbb{R}^{768}$ to combine relevance from the coarse-grained representation and the fine-grained representation. The final representation $R_{sv} \in \mathbb{R}^{768}$ is computed as follows.

$$e = softmax(W_e(R_{sv-sent} \oplus R_{sv-word}) + b_e) \tag{9}$$

$$R_{sv} = (1 - e) \odot R_{sv-sent} + e \odot R_{sv-word} \tag{10}$$

where W_e, b_e are the trainable parameters of adaptive learning mechanism. $\oplus$ is concatenation and $\odot$ is the element-wise multiplication.

3.3 Knowledge-Aware Module

Knowledge Encoder. In previous work, Cai et al. [1] have proved that using image recognition method to identify image entities is beneficial for model to understand context. The image entities with brief introduction are extracted as image knowledge through object recognition method, where only image entities higher than the recognition threshold (i.e., 0.6) will be recognized. We concatenate the entities with their introduction, and then feed them into the shared Bert to obtain several image knowledge vectors $T_k \in \mathbb{R}^{m*768}$, where m is the number of entities recognized in the image.

Inter-sequence Attention. Then, the Inter-sequence Attention is used to obtain the fusion representation. M_{sk} including $\{T_{s-sent}, T_{k1}, T_{k2}, ..., T_{km}\}$ represents a sequence set. We need to initialize a training parameter $v \in \mathbb{R}^{768}$ to obtain the knowledge fusion representation $R_{sk} \in \mathbb{R}^{768}$ as follows.

$$M_{sk} = [T_{s-sent}, T_k] \tag{11}$$

$$M = tanh(M_{sk}) \tag{12}$$

$$\alpha = softmax(v^T M) \tag{13}$$

$$R_{sk} = tanh(M_{sk}\alpha^T) \tag{14}$$

3.4 Classification Module

We get the fusion vector of image knowledge and source text (R_{sk}), fusion vector of source text and attached image (R_{sv}), and vector of replies (R_r). We use two full connection layers as our classifier, the activation function of the output layer is tanh, and the loss function is the cross entropy function.

$$R_I = R_{sk} \oplus R_{sv} \oplus R_r \tag{15}$$

$$R = tanh[W_b(W_a(R_I) + b_a) + b_b] \tag{16}$$

where W_a, b_a, W_b, b_b are the trainable parameters of classifier.

4 Experimentation

4.1 Experimental Settings

In this paper, two public datasets are used to evaluate our model, i.e., English PHEME and Chinese WeiBo, in which the source tweets containing images and we crawl them. The data distribution of PHEME and WeiBo is shown in Table 1.

Table 1. Distribution of datasets

	PHEME	WeiBo
Events	6425	4664
Users	50,593	2,746,818
Tweets	105,354	3,805,656
Average length of tweets	13.6	99.9
Rumors	2403	2313
Non-rumors	4022	2351
Images in rumors	739	1982
Images in non-rumors	1667	1861
Percentage of rumors with images	30.75%	85.69%
Percentage of non-rumors with images	41.45%	79.16%
Percentage of all the threads with images	37.45%	82.40%

For PHEME and WeiBo, we randomly divided the data, and used the same processing method as Sujana et al. [15], 80% of the data was used as the training set, 10% as the validation set, and the remaining 10% as the test set. Similar to Ma et al. [10], we calculated the accuracy, precision, recall and F1 score to measure the performance of rumor detection.

We firstly preprocess our data such as deleting tags, emotions and removing retweets. In order to better fit the situation that may occur in reality, the source tweets in our datasets contain images randomly, it just depends on whether the user published the image. If the source tweet does not contain image, we uniformly give them a blank image without any information. For the images contained in the source tweets, we adjust the size to 224 × 224 pixels and normalize them. We use Adam optimizer to update the parameters, dropout is 0.2 and the learning rate is 10^{-5}.

4.2 Experimental Results

The corresponding baselines will be briefly described below.

SVM. A SVM classifier using bag-of-words and N-gram (e.g., 1-gram, bigram and trigram) features.

CNN. A convolutional neural network model (CNN) for obtaining the representation of each tweet followed by a softmax layer.

BiLSTM. A bidirectional RNN-based tweet model that considers the context of the target and tweet.

PLAN [6]. A model uses the maximum pooling layer at the word-level to obtain the tweet representation and the transformer encoder to encode at tweet-level, and finally obtains a high-level representation.

Table 2. Results of comparison with different baselines

Dataset	Method	Acc	Pre	Rec	F1
PHEME	SVM	0.688	0.518	0.512	0.515
	CNN	0.795	0.731	0.673	0.701
	BiLSTM	0.794	0.727	0.677	0.701
	PLAN	0.871	0.859	0.863	0.861
	att-RNN	0.880	0.868	0.869	0.869
	MKEMN	0.891	0.884	0.879	0.881
	Our Model	**0.901**	**0.893**	**0.890**	**0.892**
WeiBo	SVM	0.818	0.819	0.818	0.818
	CNN	0.897	0.897	0.897	0.897
	BiLSTM	0.929	0.931	0.929	0.929
	PLAN	0.939	0.939	0.938	0.938
	att-RNN	0.932	0.932	0.932	0.931
	MKEMN	0.942	0.942	0.942	0.942
	Our Model	**0.957**	**0.958**	**0.957**	**0.957**

att-RNN [5]. A multi-modal detection model based on LSTM, using attention mechanism to capture the association between the visual features and the text/social joint features.

MKEMN [18]. A model combining multi-modal content with external knowledge for rumor detection, and using memory network to measure the differences between different events.

Comparing the experimental results in Table 2, it can be seen that the proposed method achieves the best results both on Acc and F1. From Table 2, we can draw the following observations:

(1) The SVM model performs worst among all methods. This is for the reason that it is built with the hand-crafted features which have limitation for the task of rumor detection.

(2) CNN and BiLSTM have comparable performance in both datasets. In addition, BiLSTM outperforms CNN in WeiBo. We can see that the average length of tweets in WeiBo is much longer than PHEME from Table 1. This suggests that BiLSTM can better capture the forward and backward semantic dependence which is more suitable for long sentences.

(3) In PHEME, multi-modal att-RNN performs better than single-modal PLAN, but in WeiBo, att-RNN performs worse than PLAN. The phenomenon we can see from Table 1 that fewer users in PHEME publish more events, which indicates that users in PHEME are more social intensive. In this case, users are more inclined to publish images strongly related to texts in order to prove narration. att-RNN adopts the similar fusion strategy regardless of the relevance between image and text. So it will only perform better when images are highly relevant to texts.

Table 3. Ablation experiment results (**Text**: Text modality;　**Image**: Image modality; **Coarse**: Coarse Grained Fusion;　**Fine**: Fine Grained Fusion;　**Knowledge**:Image Knowledge)

	Text	Image	Coarse	Fine	Knowledge	Acc	Pre	Rec	F1
PHEME	✓					0.866	0.853	0.861	0.856
		✓				0.639	0.320	0.500	0.390
	✓	✓				0.869	0.870	0.843	0.854
	✓	✓	✓			0.854	0.845	0.835	0.840
	✓	✓		✓		0.883	0.874	0.873	0.873
	✓	✓	✓	✓		0.891	0.883	0.880	0.882
	✓	✓			✓	0.888	0.885	0.869	0.876
	✓	✓	✓	✓	✓	**0.901**	**0.893**	**0.890**	**0.892**
WeiBo	✓					0.931	0.932	0.931	0.931
		✓				0.523	0.526	0.525	0.515
	✓	✓				0.933	0.934	0.934	0.934
	✓	✓	✓			0.936	0.936	0.936	0.936
	✓	✓		✓		0.872	0.875	0.872	0.872
	✓	✓	✓	✓		0.947	0.947	0.947	0.947
	✓	✓			✓	0.944	0.945	0.944	0.944
	✓	✓	✓	✓	✓	**0.959**	**0.959**	**0.960**	**0.959**

(4) MKEMN performs well on both datasets due to its effective fusion strategy, which integrates text, image and textual knowledge on different channels for better capturing semantic information.

(5) Compared with all baselines, our model outperforms other methods in most cases. We attribute the superiority to two properties: a)The GM module took the relevance between image and text into account and learned a multi-modal representation according to the correlation size that can accurately express the user's view. b)The KM module extracted the semantic knowledge from visual data to provide evidence for the judgment.

4.3 Ablation

In this section, we compare among the variants of M^{3}TI with respect to the following two aspects to demonstrate the effectiveness of our model: the usage of fusion strategy, and the usage of image knowledge. We conducted the ablation experiments as shown in Table 3 and we can conclude that:

(1) The model based on text modality is superior to model based on image modality, which is obvious because the text features contain more rich semantic information.

(2) When we simply concatenate image features and text features, the improvement of result is not obvious compared with text features alone, which shows that concatenation can not be effectively used as multi-modal representation.

(3) In PHEME, the effect of fine-grained fusion vector is better, but in WeiBo, the effect of coarse-grained fusion vector is better. As described in Sect. 4.2, the sample collection of PHEME and WeiBo is different, in PHEME, the relevance between texts and images is higher than WeiBo dataset. We can prove that fine-grained is fit for the dataset where image has strong relevance with text and coarse-grained is fit for the other case.

(4) However, when GM module uses Adaptive-learning ("√" on both "Coarse" and "Fine") to balance coarse-grained vector and fine-grained vector, the result is significantly improved, which shows that the GM module can mine the relevance between images and texts and learn an optimal representation according to the relevance.

(5) When we use image knowledge, the results are also improved. This is obvious because it provides more understandable semantic information for the model.

Based on the analysis above, the following conclusions can be drawn, i.e., 1) The coarse-grained and fine-grained fusion mechanism combined by adaptive-learning plays an important role in fusing text and image; 2) Image knowledge is useful for our model to better understand context.

4.4 Case Study

To illustrate the importance of text, image and image knowledge for rumor detection, we present several intuitive cases into Table 4 and compare the predicted results of our model with the single-modal model. These cases explain our fusion strategy and how image knowledge and reply information work.

For Case 1, the rumor case was successfully detected by our proposed model, but ignored by the single-modal model based on text. Because the text content alone is not enough to give sufficient evidence while the image attached to it provides clues for detection. When the image and text are highly correlated, our model may increase the proportion of fine-grained vector to pinpoint important region of text "*Lineup surprisingly short*"; In the image knowledge, from the word "*demonstration*", we can more intuitively find that this thread belongs to rumor; With the help of the wordcloud of replies (we preprocess some unnecessary tags), the frequent words like "*much*" and "*long*" are contrary to the "*surprisingly short*". Therefore, such a thread that seems difficult to judge from the text alone can be accurately recognized by our model.

While in Case 2, the non-rumor case was successfully detected by our proposed model, but ignored by the single-modal model based on image. From the image alone, we can only get the information of four men in the photo, which can't judge the correctness of the statement that "*four cartoonists were killed*", but the view of replies (i.e., "*RIP*","*kill*") is more firm. When the relevance between source text and attached image is not strong, and the image can not provide effective evidence, our model may try to enhance the proportion of

Table 4. Cases

Number	Image	Source/Image knowledge	Reply-wordcloud
1		**Source:** *These folks sure hope so. Lineup surprisingly short.* **Image knowledge:** **street:** *Street is one of administrative division...* **demonstration:** *public activities and events: a way of modern society public opinion*	
2		**Source:** *Paris media attack kills 4 cartoonists including chief editor. #AFP* **Image knowledge:** **group photo:** *a close-up, a photograph of several people together* **man:** *male human being*	
3		**Source:** *The internet has now pronounced @PutinRF dead #putindead* **Image knowledge:** **Putin:** *Public figure and President of Russia, Vladimir Putin has been nominated for the Nobel Peace Prize*	

coarse-grained vector, so as to reduce the noise of irrelevant images. Combined with the views of commentators, we can successfully determine it as a non-rumor.

As shown in Case 3, the image and text are highly related. The image seems to learn "strong" evidence to prove that the text content is correct, and the replies are inadequate, our model may make mistakes. Although we all know that this is a rumor now, under the circumstances at that time, it will be difficult for our model to judge the authenticity of this tweet.

5   Conclusion

In this paper, we propose a Multi-Modal Model with Texts and Images (M³TI), which explores a novel fusion strategy according to the relevance of texts and images, and semantic knowledge behind images. Our Granularity-fusion Module utilizes the adaptive gate to balance coarse-grained features and fine-grained features which can generalize well for different cases. Moreover, Knowledge-aware Module offers more intuitive image knowledge. In the comparative experiments of PHEME and WeiBo datasets, compared with other methods, our method uses three modalities, i.e., text, image, image knowledge, and achieves the best effect. In the future work, we will continue to study the fusion method to integrate images and texts effectively under misleading circumstances.

Acknowledgments. The authors would like to thank the three anonymous reviewers for their comments on this paper. This research was supported by the National Natural Science Foundation of China (Nos. 61836007 and 62006167.), and the Priority Academic Program Development of Jiangsu Higher Education Institutions (PAPD).

References

1. Cai, Y., Cai, H., Wan, X.: Multi-modal sarcasm detection in twitter with hierarchical fusion model. In: Proceedings of the 57th Annual Meeting of the Association for Computational Linguistics, pp. 2506–2515 (2019)
2. Chen, W., Zhang, Y., Yeo, C.K., Lau, C.T., Lee, B.S.: Unsupervised rumor detection based on users' behaviors using neural networks. Pattern Recogn. Lett. **105**, 226–233 (2018)
3. Devlin, J., Chang, M.W., Lee, K., Toutanova, K.: Bert: pre-training of deep bidirectional transformers for language understanding. arXiv preprint arXiv:1810.04805 (2018)
4. Gu, Y., Yang, K., Fu, S., Chen, S., Li, X., Marsic, I.: Multimodal affective analysis using hierarchical attention strategy with word-level alignment. In: Proceedings of the Conference. Association for Computational Linguistics. Meeting, vol. 2018, p. 2225. NIH Public Access (2018)
5. Jin, Z., Cao, J., Guo, H., Zhang, Y., Luo, J.: Multimodal fusion with recurrent neural networks for rumor detection on microblogs. In: Proceedings of the 25th ACM International Conference on Multimedia, pp. 795–816 (2017)
6. Khoo, L.M.S., Chieu, H.L., Qian, Z., Jiang, J.: Interpretable rumor detection in microblogs by attending to user interactions. In: Proceedings of the AAAI Conference on Artificial Intelligence, vol. 34, pp. 8783–8790 (2020)
7. Li, Q., Zhang, Q., Si, L.: Rumor detection by exploiting user credibility information, attention and multi-task learning. In: Proceedings of the 57th Annual Meeting of the Association for Computational Linguistics, pp. 1173–1179 (2019)
8. Lu, Y.J., Li, C.T.: GCAN: graph-aware co-attention networks for explainable fake news detection on social media. arXiv preprint arXiv:2004.11648 (2020)
9. Ma, J., Gao, W., Joty, S., Wong, K.F.: Sentence-level evidence embedding for claim verification with hierarchical attention networks. Association for Computational Linguistics (2019)
10. Ma, J., et al.: Detecting rumors from microblogs with recurrent neural networks (2016)
11. Ma, J., Gao, W., Wong, K.F.: Detect rumor and stance jointly by neural multi-task learning. In: Companion Proceedings of the Web Conference 2018, pp. 585–593 (2018)
12. Poria, S., Cambria, E., Gelbukh, A.: Deep convolutional neural network textual features and multiple kernel learning for utterance-level multimodal sentiment analysis. In: Proceedings of the 2015 Conference on Empirical Methods in Natural Language Processing, pp. 2539–2544 (2015)
13. Sangwan, S., Akhtar, M.S., Behera, P., Ekbal, A.: I didn't mean what i wrote! exploring multimodality for sarcasm detection. In: 2020 International Joint Conference on Neural Networks (IJCNN), pp. 1–8. IEEE (2020)

14. Simonyan, K., Zisserman, A.: Very deep convolutional networks for large-scale image recognition. arXiv preprint arXiv:1409.1556 (2014)
15. Sujana, Y., Li, J., Kao, H.Y.: Rumor detection on twitter using multiloss hierarchical bilstm with an attenuation factor. arXiv preprint arXiv:2011.00259 (2020)
16. Wang, Y., et al.: Eann: event adversarial neural networks for multi-modal fake news detection. In: Proceedings of the 24th ACM Sigkdd International Conference on Knowledge Discovery & Data Mining, pp. 849–857 (2018)
17. Wu, L., Rao, Y., Zhao, Y., Liang, H., Nazir, A.: DTCA: decision tree-based co-attention networks for explainable claim verification. arXiv preprint arXiv:2004.13455 (2020)
18. Zhang, H., Fang, Q., Qian, S., Xu, C.: Multi-modal knowledge-aware event memory network for social media rumor detection. In: Proceedings of the 27th ACM International Conference on Multimedia, pp. 1942–1951 (2019)

PF-VTON: Toward High-Quality Parser-Free Virtual Try-On Network

Yuan Chang, Tao Peng$^{(\boxtimes)}$, Ruhan He, Xinrong Hu, Junping Liu, Zili Zhang, and Minghua Jiang

Engineering Research Center of Hubei Province for Clothing Information,
Wuhan Textile University, Wuhan 430200, China
pt@wtu.edu.cn

Abstract. Image-based virtual try-on aims to transfer a target clothes onto a person has attracted increased attention. However, the existing methods are heavily based on accurate parsing results. It remains a big challenge to generate highly-realistic try-on images without human parser. To address this issue, we propose a new Parser-Free Virtual Try-On Network (PF-VTON), which is able to synthesize high-quality try-on images without relying on human parser. Compared to prior arts, we introduce two key innovations. One is that we introduce a new twice geometric matching module, which warps the pixels of the target clothes and the features of the preliminary warped clothes to obtain the final warped clothes with realistic texture and robust alignment. The other is that we design a new U-Transformer, which is highly effective for generating highly-realistic images in try-on synthesis. Extensive experiments show that our system outperforms the state-of-the-art methods both qualitatively and quantitatively.

Keywords: Virtual Try-On · Parser-free · Geometric matching · U-Transformer

1 Introduction

Virtual try-on enables consumers to experience themselves wearing different clothes without physically wearing them, which attracts extensive attention from the computer graphics and computer vision communities. To realize virtual try-on, a number of methods have been proposed. These methods can be classified as 3D model based approaches and 2D image based ones. The 3D methods [3,6,10,22] require additional 3D measurements and more computing power. In contrast, 2D methods without leveraging any 3D information are more broadly applicable. However, since available datasets [13] for 2D image try-on are composed of pairs of pictures (clothes and a person wearing the clothes),

This work is supported by Science Foundation of Hubei under Grant No. 2014CFB764 and Department of Education of the Hubei Province of China under Grant No. Q20131608.

we cannot access to the ground-truth after clothing transfer. Thus, it is still challenging to cast virtual try-on into a supervised task.

State-of-the-art method [13] solve this by masking the clothing region on the reference person with both a pose estimator [4] and a human parser [9]. Then, try-on module is trained to reconstruct the person image from the masked person image and the clothes image. The early methods [13,18,29] adopt a two-stage strategy. First, the target clothes is warped to align with the reference person by using a Thin-Plate Spline (TPS) [1] based warping method, and then the texture is mapped to the refined result with a composition mask. These methods continuously improve the warping effect, but try-on results are blurry. Thus, a number of methods [5,31,32] with an additional semantic prediction module are proposed. These methods use a predicted semantics to generate each semantic part of the human body and improve the try-on performance. However, it is worth noting that human parser is prone to errors. When the parsing results are slightly wrong, these methods will generate highly-unrealistic try-on images. To be independent on human parser, Issenhuth et al. [17] adopts a teacher-student paradigm where the parser-based teacher network is trained in the standard way (reconstruction) before guiding the parser-free student network to pay attention to the initial task (try-on). Recently, based on teacher-student paradigm, Ge et al. [8] proposes a new teacher-tutor-student strategy where the generated images by the parser-based teacher network as tutor knowledge and uses it as input of the parser-free student network, which is supervised by the real person image (teacher knowledge). Meanwhile, different from the previous warping module with TPS transformation, inspired by the Han et al. [11], their method designs a new warping module with five flow networks. However, in all cases of the person strikes a complex posture (i.e. self-occlusions and cross-arms), the alignment is not accurate and the texture of clothes is confused.

Based on our research and experiment, there are some key problems in the existing methods. In terms of clothing warping, the warping strategy with TPS transformation can obtain warped clothes with rich details, but cannot fully align with the reference person. The warping strategy with flow network can be aligned with the reference person in most cases. However, when the person strikes a complex posture, this warping strategy would lead to terrible results. In terms of try-on synthesis, no matter whether the teacher-student paradigm is used or not, the existing methods are affected by the parsering results and generate highly-unrealistic try-on images. Meanwhile, most of the existing methods adopt a simple ResNet [14] or U-Net [23] for generating try-on images. However, due to the limitation of kernel size and receptive field, the regular convolution cannot capture sufficient contextual information when the person strikes a complex posture, making the image synthesis fail. Some experimental results of recent state-of-the-art methods are shown in the Fig. 1. As shown in the first row, the previous methods have the problems of strange sleeve length and texture distortion. As shown in the second row, when person strikes a complex posture, the details of arms and clothes cannot be accurately generated. Recent method (PF-AFN) hopes to be independent of accurate parsing results, but the results of the third row show that it is still affected. As a result, existing methods are still insufficient to synthesize highly-realistic try-on images without human parser.

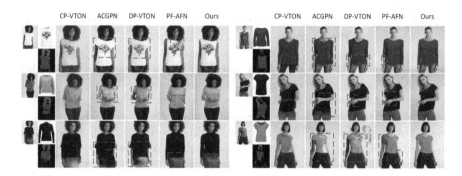

Fig. 1. Comparing our method with recent state-of-the-art virtual try-on methods.

To address these issues, we proposed a new Parser-Free Virtual Try-On Network (PF-VTON) for synthesizing high-quality try-on images without relying on parsing results. Specifically, we first use a parser-based teacher network to generate a try-on image (fake person image), and then take it as input to train a parser-free student network, which is supervised by the real person image. In the teacher network, we use a three-stage pipeline (including semantic prediction module, clothing warping module, and try-on synthesis module), which is widely used in image-based virtual try-on tasks. There are two key challenges to solve the problems of clothing warping and try-on synthesis mentioned in the above article. In terms of clothing warping, we introduce a new clothing warping strategy with twice geometric matching to warp the pixels of the target clothes and the features of the preliminary warped clothes. The clothing warping strategy is used in the parser-based teacher network, which not only preserves the texture details of target clothes but also makes the warped clothes completely aligned with the reference person. In terms of try-on synthesis, considering that the core idea of the Transformer [28], i.e., multi-head self-attention, has been demonstrated successfully in computer vision, we add the attention mechanism into the U-Net structure to form a new U-Transformer structure. The U-Transformer is used in try-on synthesis module to solve the problem that long-distance dependence cannot be captured due to the limitation of kernel size and receptive field, and synthesize high-quality try-on images when the person strikes a complex posture. These two strategies can make our teacher network generate higher quality images and better train the student network. To remove human parser and pose estimator at inference time, we distill the teacher network and use the output of teacher network as input to train the student network. Unlike the teacher networks, semantic prediction module and feature transformation of clothing warping module are not included in the student networks. Moreover, pixel transformation of clothing warping module and try-on synthesis module have the same architecture as the teacher network, but different inputs and ground-truth.

The main contributions can be summarized as follows: First, we introduce a new twice geometric matching module to warp the pixels and features of clothes. The strategy can get warped clothes with realistic texture and robust alignment.

Second, we design a new U-Transformer to solve the problem of long-distance dependence in complex situations and improve the performance of try-on. Finally, we propose a new Parser-Free Virtual Try-On Network (PF-VTON), which greatly improves the performance of try-on and generates high-quality try-on images without relying on parsing results. Experiments show that our system outperforms the state-of-the-art methods both qualitatively and quantitatively.

2   Related Works

2.1   Fashion Analysis and Image Synthesis

More and more people have conducted extensive research on fashion related tasks due to their closely related to the real-world has huge profit potentials. Most of the existing works focus on fashion image analysis [20,25], fashion recommendation [12], and fashion editing [16]. Compared with recent work on interactive search, virtual try-on is the more challenging, since it requires preserving the characteristics of target clothes while generating highly-realistic try-on images.

2.2   Transformer

Transformers [28] has achieved much success in the past few years. Recently, the application field of transformer has expanded from natural language processing [2,26] to computer vision [7,33]. The core idea of the Transformer, i.e., attention, has been demonstrated successfully on various tasks. In the image-based virtual try-on, the existing methods use ResNet or U-Net for try-on synthesis. However, due to limited receptive fields of the convolution kernels, these methods are hard to build global dependencies, which are crucial for highly-realistic try-on synthesis in challenging contexts. Our proposed U-Transformer utilizes the strong abilities of attention mechanism, especially the multi-head attention mechanism in the transformer [28], to model long-range interactions and spatial relationships between each semantic part of the human body.

2.3   Virtual Try-On

Virtual try-on can be classified as 3D model based approaches and 2D image based ones. Due to the 3D methods [3,6,10,22] require additional 3D measurements and more computing power, the 2D methods [5,8,13,17,18,29,31,32] are more broadly applicable. The previous methods [13,18,29] used a two-stage strategy and continuously improved the performance of clothing warping, but try-on results are blurry. Afterwards, some methods [5,31,32] proposed semantic prediction module to improve the overall performance, which require accurate human parsing. When the parsing results are slightly wrong, these methods generate highly-unrealistic try-on images. The recent state-of-the-art methods [8,17] adopted knowledge distillation strategy to realize virtual try-on without human parser. These mehods hope to be independent of accurate parsing results, but the try-on images are still affected.

3   PF-VTON

The proposed PF-VTON is shown in the Fig. 2. The teacher-student strategy is adopted, and the images generated by teacher network are used as input to train student network.

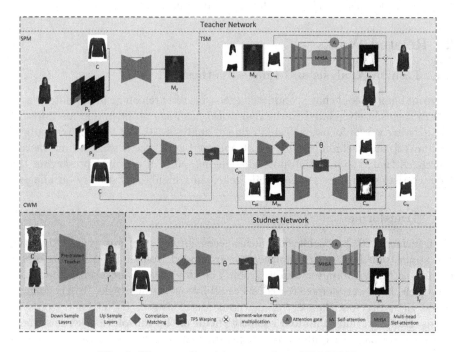

Fig. 2. The overall architecture of our PF-VTON.

3.1   Teacher Network

We train the teacher network with data (C, I) following the existing image-based methods [29], where C and I indicate the target clothes and the image of the person wearing this clothes. We first use a pose estimator [4] and a human parser [9] to obtain the 18-channel pose heat map P and semantic map M of the reference person respectively. Next, we fuse the clothing and arm regions of M into the background to obtain a cloth-agnostic semantic map and use it to get a non-target region image I_n of the reference person. Meanwhile, we use the mask of the face and hair regions in M to get a head image. We also resize M to get a coarse body shape. Then, we transform P into a binary pose map with 18 points and connect the 18 points to obtain a 3-channel pose connection map.

Our semantic prediction module (SPM) is used to predict semantic layout after try-on, which uses a standard U-Net [23] structure similar to previous methods. Specifically, we concatenate cloth-agnostic semantic map, binary pose map, and pose connection map as person representation P_1, and combine it with C to predict a semantic map M_p with the ground-truth supervision M. Because P_1 does not contain any clothing information, the predicted semantic results are not limited by the clothes of the reference person. Moreover, the standard weighted cross-entropy loss with increased weights for arm and background classes is used to train this module to better handle complex cases.

Our clothing warping module (CWM) is used to warp target clothes to warped clothes that aligns with the pose of the reference person. Inspired by [5], we also adopt feature transformation. The difference is that we introduce a clothing warping strategy with twice geometric matching to warp the pixels and features of clothes. The strategy can get warped clothes with realistic texture and robust alignmen. In the pixel transformation, we concatenate coarse body shape, binary pose map, and head image as person representation P_2, and combine it with C as input to warp C to a warped clothes C_{pt} with the ground-truth supervision I_c, where I_c is the clothes worn on the reference person. We use $L1$ loss, perceptual loss and grid constraint loss [18] to train this module. The loss function includes three components shown in Eq. (4). $L_1(C_{pt}, I_c)$ is an $L1$ loss between C_{pt} and I_c. $L_p(C_{pt}, I_c)$ is a perceptual loss [27]. We use the pre-trained VGG_{19} as ϕ and weighted sum the $L1$ norms of last five layer feature maps in ϕ to represent perceptual losses between inputs. Inspired by [18], we also introduce a grid constraint loss $L_c(G_x, G_y)$, where $G_x(x, y)$, $G_y(x, y)$, H_G and W_G are the coordinates of the grid to be mapped and height and width of the grid, respectively. The loss is introduced to serve as a constraint on TPS by minimizing the absolute difference distance of two neighboring grid intervals, which retains the characteristic of clothes after pixel transformation. The loss of pixel transformation L_{pt} is a weighted sum of the four losses described above:

$$L_l(C_{pt}, I_c) = \|C_{pt} - I_c\|_1 \tag{1}$$

$$L_p(C_{pt}, I_c) = \sum_{i=1}^{5} \lambda_i \|\phi_i(C_{pt}) - \phi_i(I_c)\|_1 \tag{2}$$

$$L_c(G_x, G_y) = \sum_{x}^{H_G} \sum_{y}^{W_G} (\|G_x(x, y - 1) - G_x(x, y)\|$$
$$- |G_x(x, y + 1) - G_x(x, y)\|| + \|G_y(x - 1, y)$$
$$- G_y(x, y)| - |G_y(x + 1, y) - G_y(x, y)\||) \tag{3}$$

$$L_{pt} = \lambda_l L_1(C_{pt}, I_c) + \lambda_p L_p(C_{pt}, I_c) + \lambda_c L_c \tag{4}$$

In the feature transformation, we first concatenate P_2 and C_{pt} as input to obtain a TPS parameters, and then use an encoder to extract features from the concatenation of C_{pt} and predicted clothing mask M_{pc} of M_p. Finally, these extracted features are warped and fed to the corresponding layer of the decoder. The decoder outputs a warped clothes C_{ft} and a clothing composition mask C_m. The C_{pt} and C_{ft} are then fused together using C_m to synthesize final warped clothes C_w:

$$C_w = (1 - C_m) \odot C_{ft} + C_m \odot C_{pt} \tag{5}$$

where $\odot$ represents element-wise matrix multiplication. We use $L1$ loss, perceptual loss to train this module. The loss function L_{ft} includes five components shown in Eq. (6), where M_c is the mask of clothing region in reference person.

$$L_{ft} = \lambda_l L_l(C_m, M_c) + \lambda_l L_l(C_{fw}, I_c) + \lambda_l L_l(C_w, I_c)$$
$$+ \lambda_p L_p(C_{fw}, I_c) + \lambda_p L_p(C_w, I_c) \tag{6}$$

Our try-on synthesis module (TSM) is used to synthesize try-on images. To achieve highly-realistic virtual try-on, the U-Transformer is adopted to overcome the lack of global context information in U-Net to deal with virtual try-on tasks in complex situations. The inductive bias with transitional invariance and local sensitivity determines that convolutional neural network (CNN) only focuses on local information and lacks the overall grasp of the data itself. In contrast, transformer can model long-distance dependencies, but using full transformer would lead to inability to fit in small tasks. Due to the available virtual try-on dataset is a toy level, using transformer structure alone can not get better results than using CNN structure alone. Thus, we propose a U-Transformer with the advantages of CNN and transformer. The U-Transformer takes the U-Net as the backbone and adds attention mechanism at three levels. First, inspired by [21], we add attention gate in the skip connection to highlight salient features of the local region while suppressing irrelevant regions in an input image useful for achieving accurate spatial recovery in the decoder. Second, we add self-attention to encoder-decoder for capturing the relationship between distant pixels and understanding the global structure of the feature graph. The self-attention formulation is given in Eq. (7):

$$\text{Attention}(Q, K, V) = \text{softmax}(\frac{QK^T}{\sqrt{d_k}})V \tag{7}$$

where a self-attention module takes three inputs, a matrix of queries $Q \in \mathbb{R}^{n \times d_k}$, a matrix of keys $K \in \mathbb{R}^{n \times d_k}$ and a matrix of values $V \in \mathbb{R}^{n \times d_k}$. Finally, we add multi-head self-attention between the bottom of encoder-decoder to connect each element in the highest feature maps and explicitly model the complete context information. The multi-head self-attention is shown below.

$$\text{MultiHead}(Q, K, V) = \text{Concat}(\text{head}_1, ..., \text{head}_h)W^O$$
$$\text{where head}_i = \text{Attention}(QW_i^Q, KW_i^K, VW_i^V)$$

where the projections are parameter matrices $W_i^Q \in \mathbb{R}^{d_{model} \times d_k}$, $W_i^K \in \mathbb{R}^{d_{model} \times d_k}$, $W_i^V \in \mathbb{R}^{d_{model} \times d_v}$ and $W^O \in \mathbb{R}^{hd_v \times d_{model}}$. The U-Transformer is used to explore the relationship between people and clothes in the field of virtual try-on, so as to generate highly-realistic try-on images. Specifically, we first concatenate I_n, M_p, and C_w as input to generate a preliminary synthesis image I_s and predict an image composition mask I_m. Then, I_s and C_w are fused together using I_m to synthesize final try-on image I_f:

$$I_f = (1 - I_m) \odot I_s + I_m \odot C_w \tag{8}$$

where $\odot$ represents element-wise matrix multiplication. We use $L1$ loss, perceptual loss to train this module. The loss function L_{tsm} includes three components shown in Eq. (9).

$$L_{tsm} = \lambda_l L_l(I_m, M_c) + \lambda_l L_l(I_f, I) + \lambda_p L_p(I_f, I) \tag{9}$$

3.2 Student Network

In the teacher network, data (C, I) is used as input to generate the final try-on image I_f. After training the teacher network, we randomly select a different clothes C' and generate a try-on image I', that is the image of person in I wearing C'. The student network uses a pixel transformation and a U-Transformer for end-to-end learning. Specifically, we first use C and I' as input to get a warped clothes C_{pt}, and then take C_{pt} and I' to generate a try-on image I'_f with the ground-truth supervision real image I, where I'_m is predicted image composition mask and I'_f is synthesized in the same way as the teacher network. We use $L1$ loss, perceptual loss to train this network. The loss function L_s includes four components shown in Eq. (12), where λ_w and λ_s are hyperparameters of clothing warping and try-on synthesis respectively.

$$L_{warp} = L_l(C_{pt}, I_c) \tag{10}$$

$$L_{synthesis} = L_l(I'_m, M_c) + L_l(I'_f, I) + L_p(I'_f, I) \tag{11}$$

$$L_s = \lambda_w L_{warp} + \lambda_s L_{synthesis} \tag{12}$$

4 Experiments

We first describe the dataset and implementation details, and then compare our approach with CP-VTON [29], ACGPN [31], and PF-AFN [8]. Our PF-VTON is improved on the basis of CP-VTON. The ACGPN is the latest method for the virtual try-on method without teacher-student strategy, and the PF-AFN is the state-of-the-art for the virtual try-on. We present visual and quantitative results proving that our PF-VTON achieves state-of-the-art results.

4.1 Dataset

We conducted experiments on VITON [13] dataset, which is widely used in most image-based virtual try-on methods (CP-VTON [29], ACGPN [31], DP-VTON [5], and PF-AFN [8]). The entire dataset contains about 19,000 image pairs, each of which includes a front-view female image and a corresponding top-clothing image. Then, there are 16,253 cleaned pairs, which are split into a training set of 14,221 pairs and a validation set of 2,032 pairs. Finally, the images in the validation set were rearranged into unpaired pairs as the testing set. All input images are resized to 256×192 and the output images have the same resolution.

4.2   Implementation Details

Each modules of the teacher and student network was trained for 200K steps by setting the weights of losses $\lambda_l = \lambda_p = 1$, and batch-size 4. During the training of student networks, we set the $\lambda_w = 0.25$ and $\lambda_s = 1$. The learning rate is initialized as 0.0001 and the network is optimized by Adam optimizer [19] with the hyper-parameter $\beta_1 = 0.5$, and $\beta_2 = 0.999$. The encoder-decoder structure of each module is similar to U-Net [23]. Specifically, we use a 10-layer U-Net with five 2-strided down-sampling convolutional layers and five up-sampling layers.

4.3   Qualitative Results

We mainly perform visual comparison of our method with state-of-the-art methods in Fig. 3 and Fig. 4, including CP-VTON [29], ACGPN [31], DP-VTON [5], and PF-AFN [8]. To validate the performance of the proposed PF-VTON for virtual try-on, the comparison results are composed of two main aspects: warped clothes and try-on images.

Comparison of warped clothes is shown in Fig. 3. The baseline methods either fail to preserve complete details or fail to align accurately. CP-VTON directly warps the target clothes and preserve complete attributes of clothes, but the alignment effect is poor. The results of ACGPN are sometimes better and sometimes strange. DP-VTON allows better alignment without losing too

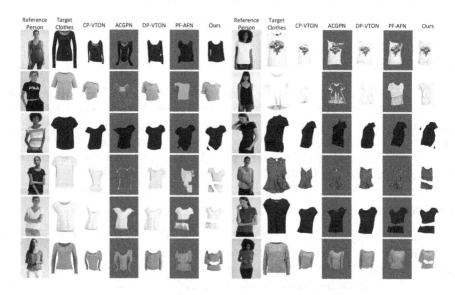

Fig. 3. Qualitative comparisons of warped clothes.

Fig. 4. Qualitative comparisons of try-on images.

much detail, but fully aligned clothes cannot be obtained in the case of occlusion. PF-AFN wants to be perfectly aligned with the reference person, but it produces worse results when occlusion occurs. Our PF-VTON preserves the characteristics of the target clothes and achieves complete alignment with the reference person. No other work has achieved this.

Comparison of try-on images is shown in Fig. 4. In the first two rows, when an error occurs in the parsing result, baseline models generate highly-unrealistic try-on images with visual artifacts. In the next row, when the pattern and pose of target clothes are complex, clothes with texture confusion are shown in the results of competition methods. In the fourth row, the baseline methods fail to transfer long-sleeved clothes to the corresponding region of the reference person. In the last two rows, when the person strikes a complex posture (i.e. self-occlusions and cross-arms), large misalignment occurs between the target clothes and the reference person. In such case, the baseline methods are insufficient to generate high-quality try-on images while preserving the attributes of clothes and people. In contrast, our PF-VTON can generate highly-realistic try-on images without relying on accurate parsing results while preserving both person's and cloth's attributes.

Table 1. The comparison of different methods under IS, SSIM and FID metrics.

Method	IS↑	FID↓	SSIM↑
CP-VTON	2.792	24.424	0.785
ACGPN	2.663	16.697	0.841
DP-VTON	2.886	13.980	0.871
PF-AFN	2.872	10.114	0.887
PF-VTON	**3.003**	**9.628**	**0.889**

4.4 Quantitative Results

We adopt inception score (IS) [24] to measure the perceptual quality of synthesized images. For IS, higher scores indicate better results. Due to the calculation formula of IS does not consider the ground truth and cannot reflect whether the generated image is close to the real image, Frechet Inception Distance (FID) [15] is used to overcome the above problems in IS. For FID, lower scores indicate better results. In addition, we also use Structural SIMilarity (SSIM) [30] to measure the similarity score, because most of the existing work uses it to evaluate the reconstruction performance. For SSIM, higher scores indicate better results. As shown in Table 1, compared with the previous parser-based methods, the overall performance of our PF-VTON is significantly improved. Meanwhile, compared with the recent parser-free method, our PF-VTON outperforms them in image quality, showing its great advantage in generating high-quality try-on images.

5 Conclusion

We propose a parser-free virtual try-on network (PF-VTON) to generates high-quality try-on images. In terms of clothing warping, our warping strategy can obtain warped clothes with realistic details and robust alignment. In terms of try-on synthesis, our U-Transformer can deal with long-distance dependence and generate highly-realistic try-on images in complex situations.

References

1. Belongie, S., Malik, J., Puzicha, J.: Shape matching and object recognition using shape contexts. IEEE Trans. Pattern Anal. Mach. Intell. **24**(4), 509–522 (2002)
2. Bhardwaj, R., Majumder, N., Poria, S., Hovy, E.: More identifiable yet equally performant transformers for text classification. arXiv preprint arXiv:2106.01269 (2021)
3. Brouet, R., Sheffer, A., Boissieux, L., Cani, M.P.: Design preserving garment transfer (2012)
4. Cao, Z., Simon, T., Wei, S.E., Sheikh, Y.: Realtime multi-person 2D pose estimation using part affinity fields. In: Proceedings of the IEEE Conference on Computer Vision and Pattern Recognition, pp. 7291–7299 (2017)

5. Chang, Y., et al.: Dp-vton: toward detail-preserving image-based virtual try-on network. In: ICASSP 2021–2021 IEEE International Conference on Acoustics, Speech and Signal Processing (ICASSP), pp. 2295–2299. IEEE (2021)
6. Chen, W., et al.: Synthesizing training images for boosting human 3D pose estimation. In: 2016 Fourth International Conference on 3D Vision (3DV), pp. 479–488. IEEE (2016)
7. Dosovitskiy, A., et al.: An image is worth 16×16 words: transformers for image recognition at scale. arXiv preprint arXiv:2010.11929 (2020)
8. Ge, Y., Song, Y., Zhang, R., Ge, C., Liu, W., Luo, P.: Parser-free virtual try-on via distilling appearance flows. In: Proceedings of the IEEE/CVF Conference on Computer Vision and Pattern Recognition, pp. 8485–8493 (2021)
9. Gong, K., Liang, X., Zhang, D., Shen, X., Lin, L.: Look into person: self-supervised structure-sensitive learning and a new benchmark for human parsing. In: Proceedings of the IEEE Conference on Computer Vision and Pattern Recognition, pp. 932–940 (2017)
10. Guan, P., Reiss, L., Hirshberg, D.A., Weiss, A., Black, M.J.: Drape: dressing any person. ACM Trans. Graph. (TOG) **31**(4), 1–10 (2012)
11. Han, X., Hu, X., Huang, W., Scott, M.R.: Clothflow: a flow-based model for clothed person generation. In: Proceedings of the IEEE/CVF International Conference on Computer Vision, pp. 10471–10480 (2019)
12. Han, X., Wu, Z., Jiang, Y.G., Davis, L.S.: Learning fashion compatibility with bidirectional LSTMs. In: Proceedings of the 25th ACM International Conference on Multimedia, pp. 1078–1086 (2017)
13. Han, X., Wu, Z., Wu, Z., Yu, R., Davis, L.S.: Viton: an image-based virtual try-on network. In: Proceedings of the IEEE Conference on Computer Vision and Pattern Recognition, pp. 7543–7552 (2018)
14. He, K., Zhang, X., Ren, S., Sun, J.: Deep residual learning for image recognition. In: Proceedings of the IEEE Conference on Computer Vision and Pattern Recognition, pp. 770–778 (2016)
15. Heusel, M., Ramsauer, H., Unterthiner, T., Nessler, B., Hochreiter, S.: Gans trained by a two time-scale update rule converge to a local nash equilibrium. In: Advances in Neural Information Processing Systems. pp. 6626–6637 (2017)
16. Hsiao, W.L., Katsman, I., Wu, C.Y., Parikh, D., Grauman, K.: Fashion++: minimal edits for outfit improvement. In: Proceedings of the IEEE/CVF International Conference on Computer Vision, pp. 5047–5056 (2019)
17. Issenhuth, T., Mary, J., Calauzènes, C.: Do not mask what you do not need to mask: a parser-free virtual try-on. In: Vedaldi, A., Bischof, H., Brox, T., Frahm, J.-M. (eds.) ECCV 2020. LNCS, vol. 12365, pp. 619–635. Springer, Cham (2020). https://doi.org/10.1007/978-3-030-58565-5_37
18. Jae Lee, H., Lee, R., Kang, M., Cho, M., Park, G.: La-viton: a network for looking-attractive virtual try-on. In: Proceedings of the IEEE/CVF International Conference on Computer Vision Workshops (2019)
19. Kingma, D.P., Ba, J.: Adam: a method for stochastic optimization. arXiv preprint arXiv:1412.6980 (2014)
20. Liu, J., Lu, H.: Deep fashion analysis with feature map upsampling and landmark-driven attention. In: Proceedings of the European Conference on Computer Vision (ECCV) Workshops (2018)
21. Oktay, O., et al.: Attention u-net: learning where to look for the pancreas. arXiv preprint arXiv:1804.03999 (2018)
22. Pons-Moll, G., Pujades, S., Hu, S., Black, M.J.: Clothcap: seamless 4D clothing capture and retargeting. ACM Trans. Graph. (TOG) **36**(4), 1–15 (2017)

23. Ronneberger, O., Fischer, P., Brox, T.: U-Net: convolutional networks for biomedical image segmentation. In: Navab, N., Hornegger, J., Wells, W.M., Frangi, A.F. (eds.) MICCAI 2015. LNCS, vol. 9351, pp. 234–241. Springer, Cham (2015). https://doi.org/10.1007/978-3-319-24574-4_28

24. Salimans, T., Goodfellow, I., Zaremba, W., Cheung, V., Radford, A., Chen, X.: Improved techniques for training GANs. In: Advances in Neural Information Processing Systems, pp. 2234–2242 (2016)

25. Shajini, M., Ramanan, A.: An improved landmark-driven and spatial-channel attentive convolutional neural network for fashion clothes classification. Visual Comput. **37**(6), 1517–1526 (2021)

26. Shao, B., Gong, Y., Qi, W., Cao, G., Ji, J., Lin, X.: Graph-based transformer with cross-candidate verification for semantic parsing. In: Proceedings of the AAAI Conference on Artificial Intelligence, vol. 34, pp. 8807–8814 (2020)

27. Simonyan, K., Zisserman, A.: Very deep convolutional networks for large-scale image recognition. arXiv preprint arXiv:1409.1556 (2014)

28. Vaswani, A., et al.: Attention is all you need. In: Advances in Neural Information Processing Systems, pp. 5998–6008 (2017)

29. Wang, B., Zheng, H., Liang, X., Chen, Y., Lin, L., Yang, M.: Toward characteristic-preserving image-based virtual try-on network. In: Proceedings of the European Conference on Computer Vision (ECCV), pp. 589–604 (2018)

30. Wang, Z., Bovik, A.C., Sheikh, H.R., Simoncelli, E.P.: Image quality assessment: from error visibility to structural similarity. IEEE Trans. Image Process. **13**(4), 600–612 (2004)

31. Yang, H., Zhang, R., Guo, X., Liu, W., Zuo, W., Luo, P.: Towards photo-realistic virtual try-on by adaptively generating-preserving image content. In: Proceedings of the IEEE/CVF Conference on Computer Vision and Pattern Recognition, pp. 7850–7859 (2020)

32. Yu, R., Wang, X., Xie, X.: VTNFP: an image-based virtual try-on network with body and clothing feature preservation. In: Proceedings of the IEEE/CVF International Conference on Computer Vision, pp. 10511–10520 (2019)

33. Zheng, S., et al.: Rethinking semantic segmentation from a sequence-to-sequence perspective with transformers. In: Proceedings of the IEEE/CVF Conference on Computer Vision and Pattern Recognition, pp. 6881–6890 (2021)

MF-GAN: Multi-conditional Fusion Generative Adversarial Network for Text-to-Image Synthesis

Yuyan Yang[1,2], Xin Ni[1,2], Yanbin Hao[1,2], Chenyu Liu[3], Wenshan Wang[3], Yifeng Liu[3], and Haiyong Xie[2,4(✉)]

[1] University of Science and Technology of China, Hefei 230026, Anhui, China
{sz987456,nx150012}@mail.ustc.edu.cn
[2] Key Laboratory of Cyberculture Content Cognition and Detection, Ministry of Culture and Tourism, Hefei 230026, Anhui, China
haiyong.xie@ieee.org
[3] National Engineering Laboratory for Risk Perception and Prevention (NEL-RPP), Beijing 100041, China
2011010090@bupt.cn, ww2468@columbia.edu, liuyifeng2@cetc.com.cn
[4] Advanced Innovation Center for Human Brain Protection, Capital Medical University, Beijing 100069, China

Abstract. The performance of text-to-image synthesis has been significantly boosted accompanied by the development of generative adversarial network (GAN) techniques. The current GAN-based methods for text-to-image generation mainly adopt multiple generator-discriminator pairs to explore the coarse/fine-grained textual content (*e.g.*, words and sentences); however, they only consider the semantic consistency between the text-image pair. One drawback of such a multi-stream structure is that it results in many heavyweight models. In comparison, the single-stream counterpart bears the weakness of insufficient use of texts. To alleviate the above problems, we propose a Multi-conditional Fusion GAN (MF-GAN) to reap the benefits of both the multi-stream and the single-stream methods. MF-GAN is a single-stream model but achieves the utilization of both coarse and fine-grained textual information with the use of conditional residual block and dual attention block. More specifically, the sentence and word features are repeatedly inputted into different model stages for textual information enhancement. Furthermore, we introduce a triple loss to close the visual gap between the synthesized image and its positive image and enlarge the gap to its negative image. To thoroughly verify our method, we conduct extensive experiments on two benchmarked CUB and COCO datasets. Experimental results show that the proposed MF-GAN outperforms the state-of-the-art methods.

Keywords: Text-to-Image · GAN · Triplet loss

1 Introduction

Text-to-image synthesis aims at generating high-resolution, photo-realistic and text-consistent images according to natural language descriptions, which is a

© Springer Nature Switzerland AG 2022
B. Þór Jónsson et al. (Eds.): MMM 2022, LNCS 13141, pp. 41–53, 2022.
https://doi.org/10.1007/978-3-030-98358-1_4

challenging task in computer vision and natural language processing. It drives research progress in multimodal learning and also has great potential applications, such as image editing, video games and computer-aided design.

Recently, many methods for text-to-image synthesis [6,13,17] are based on Attentional Generative Adversarial Network (AttnGAN) [16]. AttnGAN consists of two-stage generators, and generally encodes text descriptions into two kinds of vectors, namely, global sentence vector and local word vector. The first stage generator utilizes the sentence vector to generate low-resolution images, and the second stage generator generates high-resolution images based on the initial images and the spatial attention mechanism. More recently, many studies adopt a simple single-stream GAN for text-to-image generation (see, e.g., [14,19,20]). In particular, HDGAN [20] resembles a simple vanilla GAN, which has multiple side outputs and uses complicated hierarchical-nested adversarial objectives for training. DF-GAN [14] fuses image features and sentence features through several deep fusion blocks and adopts a one-way discriminator, instead of a two-way discriminator, to speed up the convergence of the generator. DTGAN [19] employs the visual loss to ensure that the generated images and real images have similar color distribution and shape.

These methods have proven to be useful. The single-stream structure is more efficient than the stacked structure, as the former contains only one generator and one discriminator, while the latter (e.g., AttnGAN) is more complex and consists of three generators, three generators, and a deep attentional multimodal similarity module. Thus the single-stream network is more preferable when it is necessary to decrease the run time and improve the stability of the generative model. However, it still has many shortcomings. Firstly, with the size of the feature map increasing, it becomes more and more difficult to fuse sentence vectors and image features through affine transformation only, and most fine-grained information at the word level may be lost during the generation process. Secondly, the one-way discriminator only pays attention to the matching information between texts and images, but ignores the fact that matching the generated images and real images can improve the quality of the generated images. Although visual loss can alleviate this problem, it neglects the information available from matching real and generated images.

To address these problems, we propose a novel Multi-conditional Fusion Generative Adversarial Network (MF-GAN), which has only one generator/discriminator pair without involving extra modules such as object detection. In the generator, we propose a Conditional Residual Block and a Dual Attention Block, respectively, to take advantage of sentence features and word features to model text-to-image mapping. In the discriminator, we first map the input image into the semantic space, then employ a triplet loss to pull the synthesized image towards its corresponding ground-truth image and push it away from another image that is associated with a different text description.

We summarize the contributions of our work as follows. Firstly, we propose a novel Multi-conditional Fusion Generative Adversarial Network (MF-GAN) for text-to-image generation, where sentence features and word features are applied for many times during image synthesis with only a single-stream GAN. Secondly, triplet loss is carried to improve the semantic consistency and image quality by making the generated image close to its related image and far away from the irrelevant image in the semantic space. To the best of our knowledge, it is the first time to introduce the triplet loss in text-to-image synthesis. Lastly, we conduct extensive experiments to quantify the advantages of MF-GAN. The experimental results show that MF-GAN outperforms the state-of-the-art methods on two standard benchmark datasets.

The remainder of this paper is structured as follows. Section 2 presents related works. Section 3 describes the overall framework of MF-GAN. three important components. Section 4 evaluates MF-GAN using two popular datasets. Section 5 concludes the paper with future works.

2   Related Work

The most popular and efficient text-to-image synthesis methods are GAN based methods. The application of GAN was first proposed by Reed *et al.* [10] in 2014. It contains a generator and a discriminator, where the former generates interrelated images from texts, and the latter tries to distinguish generated images from real images until it reaches the Nash equilibrium. However, the images generated by this method have low resolution. To address this problem, StackGAN [18] adopts a tree-like structure to improve the image quality. AttnGAN [16] adopts an attention-driven, multi-stage GAN for the fine-grained text-to-image generation, obtaining very promising results. Encouraged by the success of AttnGAN, researchers further improve its performance. For example, SEGAN [13] and SDGAN [17] apply siamese network [8] to fulfill low-level semantic diversity. MirrorGAN [9] regenerates the corresponding text description based on the generated images. CPGAN [6] designs a memory construction [1] to learn the meaningful visual features from each relevant image for a given word by using Bottom-Up and Top-Down Attention model and Yolo-V3.

Apart from the methods which take the stacked structure as the backbone as mentioned above, there are many ways to convert the generation process into multiple steps, which may lead to better performance on complex datasets such MSCOCO [7]. More specifically, IGSG [3] builds scene graphs from text descriptions first, which reason about the objects and their relationships. Then it uses a graph convolutional network to generate scene layouts from the scene graphs. Finally, a low-resolution image is generated by a Cascade Refinement Network. InferrGAN [2] decomposes the text-to-image generation into three steps: generating bounding boxes for each object in the text description, generating object shapes based on the bounding boxes, and generating the image conditioned on them. Moreover, ObjGAN [5] proposes an object-driven attention mechanism to provide fine-grained information for different components.

However, the training process of the generation process is slow and inefficient. To simplify the model, HDGAN [20] presents an extensible single-stream generator architecture. DF-GAN [14] also presents a novel simplified text-to-image backbone and Matching-Aware zero-centered Gradient Penalty to achieve the desired results without extra networks. DTGAN [19] adopts the attention modules and conditional normalization to fine-tune on each scale of feature maps.

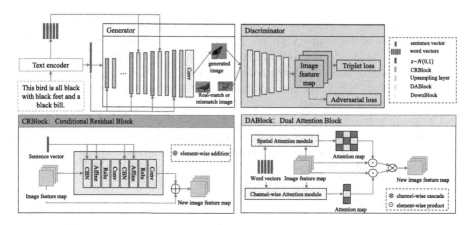

Fig. 1. The architecture of MF-GAN with only one generator/discriminator pair. The generator contains multiple CRBlocks (blue), DABlocks (yellow) and upsampling layers (orange). The discriminator contains multiple DownBlocks, which generate image features from the input images. Adversarial loss is calculated based on (text, generated image), (text, real-match image), and triplet loss is calculated based on (generated image, real-match image), (generated image, real-mismatch image). (Color figure online)

Different from the methods mentioned above, MF-GAN refines image features at the sentence level through conditional batch-normalization and affine transformation. Besides, the dual attention module is used only on the large scale of image features, which can focus on the word-level information. Additionally, inspired by [12], we also employ the triplet loss to generate more realistic and semantic consistent images.

3   Method

In this section, we present MF-GAN, a novel text-to-image adversarial generation network, aiming at refining image features at both sentence and word level and meanwhile improving semantic consistency by triplet loss.

3.1   Overall MF-GAN Architecture

MF-GAN is composed of three main components: a text encoder, a generator, and a discriminator, as illustrated in Fig. 1.

The text encoder aims at extracting the feature representations at both sentence level and word level from the natural language descriptions. We adopt a bi-directional Long Short-Term Memory (LSTM) pre-trained by [16] to learn the text representation. Specifically, it takes a sentence as input, and each word in the sentence corresponds to two hidden states in the bi-directional LSTM, one for each direction. These hidden states are utilized to represent the semantic meaning of each word, and the last hidden states are concatenated to form the global sentence vector. They are denoted by $\omega \in \mathbb{R}^{D \times N}$ and $s \in \mathbb{R}^D$, where D is the dimension of the word vector and sentence vector, N is the number of words. In other words, ω is a feature matrix of all words and its ith column ω_i is the feature vector of the ith word in the given sentence.

The generator has three inputs: the sentence feature vector s, the word feature matrix ω from the text encoder, and the noise vector z sampled from the standard normal distribution. To make full use of all these informations for generating high-quality images, we apply m upsampling layers $(U_1, U_2, ..., U_m)$ to enlarge image features, m Conditional Residual Blocks (CRBlock) $(R_0, R_1, ..., R_m)$ to fuse sentence information and image features, and two Dual Attention Blocks (DABlock) (A_1, A_2) to complement more fine-grained word-level information. Specifically, we have

$$
\begin{aligned}
&\hat{s} = F^{ca}(s); \quad h_0 = R_0(fc(z, \hat{s}), s); \\
&h_i = R_i(U_i(h_{i-1})) \ for \ i = 1, 2, 3, ..., m-2; \\
&h_j = R_j(U_j(A_j(h_{j-1}, \omega), h_{j-1})) \ for \ j = m-1, m; \ k = 1, 2; \\
&x = G(h_m).
\end{aligned}
\tag{1}
$$

where $(h_0, h_1, ..., h_m)$ are the hidden states generated by $(R_0, R_1, ..., R_m)$, which represents the image features with gradually growing resolutions and h_m is the final output with the highest resolution. F^{ca} is the Conditioning Augmentation [18] which converts the sentence vector s to the N_c-dimensional conditioning vector $\hat{s}$, which is concatenated to the N_z dimensional noise vector z sampled from the standard normal distribution. Then the result is fed into a fully connected layer and the first CRBlock R_0 to generate the 4×4 image feature h_0. CRBlock R_i and DABlock A_j are described in detail in Sect. 3.2 and 3.3, respectively.

The discriminator in our MF-GAN mainly contains several DownBlocks, each of which consists of several down-sampling layers and residual networks, converting input images into 4×4 image feature maps. Then the image features of the generated images, real-match images, and real-mismatch images are used to calculate the triplet loss (see Sect. 3.4) to improve semantic consistency. As a result, the discriminator needs to judge whether the corresponding image and text match according to the input image features and sentence features. In order to do so, we first compress the sentence vector s to N_d dimensions and spatially replicate it to form a $4 \times 4 \times N_d$ tensor. Then this tensor is concatenated with the image feature maps mentioned above, which is then fed into two convolutional layers to calculate the adversarial loss for the discriminator and generator:

$$
\begin{aligned}
L_{adv}^D = \ &\mathbb{E}_{x \sim P_{data}}[\max(0, 1 - D(x, s))] \\
&+ \frac{1}{2}\mathbb{E}_{G(z,x,\omega) \sim P_G}[\max(0, 1 + D(G(z, s, \omega), s))] \\
&+ \frac{1}{2}\mathbb{E}_{x \sim P_{misdata}}[\max(0, 1 + D(x, s))],
\end{aligned}
\tag{2}
$$

$$
L_{adv}^G = \mathbb{E}_{x \sim P_G}[D(G(z, s, \omega), s)],
\tag{3}
$$

where z is a noise sampled from the standard normal distribution, s is the sentence vector, ω is the word feature matrix, $P_{data}, P_G, P_{misdata}$ respectively denote the synthetic data distribution, real data distribution, and mismatching data distribution.

3.2 Conditional Residual Block

Our CRBlock aims at refining image features using text information as guidance. Specifically, we choose Conditional Batch Normalization (CBN) and Affine Transformation (Affine), which can take sentence vectors as conditions to predict the parameters of batch-normalization and linear transformation, respectively. As shown in Fig. 1, CRBlock receives two inputs: sentence vector and image feature map. Next we describe the CBN and Affine in detail.

CBN takes a batch of image features $x \in \mathbb{R}^{N \times C \times H \times W}$ and sentence vector s as input. It achieves the feature fusion as follows: First, it normalizes the mean and standard deviation for each feature channel; second, it learns the parameters γ_s and β_s from the conditions s; third, it learns a set of affine parameters $\gamma, \beta \in \mathbb{R}^C$ from data. The modified normalization function is formatted as

$$CBN(x|s) = (\gamma + \gamma_s) \times \frac{x - \mu(x)}{\sigma(x)} + (\beta + \beta_s), \tag{4}$$

where $\mu(x), \sigma(x) \in \mathbb{R}^C$ are the mean and standard deviation respectively. They are computed across the dimension of batch and spatial independently for each feature channel.

Affine is similar to CBN, which also receives two inputs: image features $x \in \mathbb{R}^{N \times C \times H \times W}$ and sentence vector s. It first predicts $\gamma_s, \beta_s \in \mathbb{R}^C$ from s via two one-hidden-layer MLPs. Then it fuses text information and image features, which can be formally expressed as follows:

$$AFF(x|s) = \gamma_s \times x + \beta_s. \tag{5}$$

3.3 Dual Attention Block

The purpose of our Dual Attention Block is to draw different sub-regions of the image condition on words that are most relevant to those sub-regions, and drawing the connection between words and channels. In implementation, we apply spatial attention and channel-wise attention to image features.

Spatial attention module takes the word feature $\omega \in \mathbb{R}^{D \times T}$ and the hidden image feature $h \in \mathbb{R}^{\hat{D} \times (H \times W)}$ as input. Note that ω_i is the D-dimensional feature vectors of the ith word (a total of T words), and h_i is the $\hat{D}$-dimensional feature vectors of ith sub-region of the image. We first map the word feature to the common semantic space of the image feature by a perception layer $U \in \mathbb{R}^{\hat{D} \times D}$, producing $\omega' = U\omega$. Then, we calculate the word-context vector for h_j, which represents the relevance between the word vectors and the jth sub-region:

$$c_j = \sum_{i=0}^{T-1} \beta_{j,i} \omega'_i, \ where \ \beta_{j,i} = \frac{\exp(s'_{j,i})}{\sum_{k=0}^{T-1} \exp(s'_{j,k})}, \tag{6}$$

where $s'_{j,i} = h_j^T \omega'_i$, and $\beta_{j,i}$ means the weight of the ith word when generating j^{th} sub-region of the image. Therefore, the output of spatial attention module is $(c_0, c_1, ..., c_{(H \times W)-1}) \in \mathbb{R}^{\hat{D} \times (H \times W)}$.

Channel-wise attention module has the same inputs as spatial attention module: the word features $\omega \in \mathbb{R}^{D \times T}$ and hidden image features $h \in \mathbb{R}^{\hat{D} \times (H \times W)}$. But it uses a different perception layer $V \in \mathbb{R}^{(H \times W) \times D}$ to convert the word feature into the common semantic space of the image features, producing $\omega'' = V\omega$. Then we apply similar method to calculate word-context vector c_j for the jth channel of the image feature, which is a dynamic representation of word vectors relevant to channels:

$$c_j = \sum_{i=0}^{T-1} \alpha_{j,i} \omega_i'', \; where \; \alpha_{j,i} = \frac{\exp(r'_{j,i})}{\sum_{k=0}^{T-1} \exp(r'_{j,k})}, \tag{7}$$

where $r'_{j,i} = h_j^T \omega''_i$, and $\alpha_{j,i}$ represents correlation values between channels and words across all spatial locations. Hence, the output of channel-wise attention module is $(c_0, c_1, ..., c_{\hat{D}-1}) \in \mathbb{R}^{(H \times W) \times \hat{D}}$.

Then we compute element-wise products of these two output attention maps from the above two modules and the original image features respectively. Finally, a new feature map is obtained after a channel-wise cascade processing.

3.4 Triplet Loss

To enhance the generation consistency, we apply triplet loss working on our discriminator and focus on the hardest negatives in a mini-batch. In practice, given a pair of generated image and corresponding real image (I_g, I_r), we choose its hardest negative image in this batch of real images by $I' = argmax_{I \neq I_r} d(D(I_g), D(I))$, where D means generating image features by a set of downsampling blocks in the discriminator and d means calculating the differences between two features. Then with the predefined margin α, we adopt the triplet loss as following:

$$L_{triplet} = \max(d(D(I_g), D(I_r)) - d(D(I_g), D(I')) + \alpha, \; 0). \tag{8}$$

The generator loss consists of triplet loss and adversarial loss:

$$L^G = L_{adv}^G + \lambda_T L_{triplet}, \tag{9}$$

where λ_T is a hyper-parameter for triplet loss.

The discriminator loss contains adversarial loss and Matching-aware zero-center gradient penalty (MA-GP) loss [14], which enables us to synthesize more realistic images through a zero-centered gradient penalty on real data:

$$L^D = L_{adv}^D + \lambda_M \mathbb{E}_{x \sim P_{data}}[(||\nabla_x D(x, s)|| + ||\nabla_s D(x, s)||)^p], \tag{10}$$

where p and λ_M are the hyper-parameters to balance two kinds of loss.

4 Experiment

4.1 Datasets and Training Details

We evaluate our MF-GAN for text-to-image generation on two widely used datasets. The first dataset is the CUB-200-2011 bird dataset [15], which contains 200 bird species with 11788 images. We split them into 8,855 training images and 2933 test images. Each image is annotated with 10 descriptions, 15 part locations, 312 binary attributes and 1 bounding box. We pre-process the CUB dataset to ensure that the bounding boxes of birds have greater-than-0.75 object-image size rations suggested by [18]. The second dataset is the COCO dataset [7], which contains 82783 images for training and 40504 images for validation, and each image has 5 descriptions. The greater number and types of images make the COCO dataset more challenging than the CUB dataset.

As for training details, we set $D = 256, N_c = 128, N_z = 100, N_d = 256$ and $W_0 = H_0 = 256$ by default. Then we train MF-GAN for 800 epochs on CUB and 120 epochs on COCO dataset by using Pytorch. Besides, we use Adam with $\beta_1 = 0.0$ and $\beta_2 = 0.9$ to optimize our training process. The learning rate is set to 0.0001 for generator and 0.0004 for discriminator according to Two Time-scale Update Rule (TTUR) [14]. The text encoder and its parameters are all same as the previous works [16].

4.2 Evaluation Metrics

Similar to previous works (*e.g.*, [14]), we adopt two metrics, Inception Score(IS) [11] and Frechet Inception Distance (FID) [14], to evaluate the performance.

Inception Score (IS). The Inception score aims to measure two indicators of GAN: the quality and diversity of the synthesized images. It is formulated as:

$$I = \exp(\mathbb{E}_x D_{KL}(p(y|x)||p(y))), \tag{11}$$

where x is a synthesized image and y is the label predicted by a pre-trained Inception v3 model. IS computes the KL-divergence between the distribution of $p(x|y)$ and $p(y)$. A higher IS score means that each generated image clearly belongs to a specific class and the labels are evenly distributed. But when the mode collapses, this result will have no reference value.

Frechet Inception Distance (FID). The FID has the same function as IS, but the difference is that it calculates the Frechet distance between the distribution of the real image r and the generated image x in the feature space of a pre-trained Inception v3 network. The FID is formulated as:

$$F(r, x) = ||\mu_r - \mu_x||_2^2 + Tr(\Sigma_r + \Sigma_x - 2\sqrt{\Sigma_r \Sigma_x}), \tag{12}$$

where $\mu_r, \mu_x, \Sigma_r, \Sigma_x$ are respective means and covariance of real data distribution and generated data distribution. Lower FID means that two distributions

Table 1. The IS and FID scores on CUB and COCO datasets.

Method	CUB		COCO	
	IS↑	FID ↓	IS↑	FID↓
AttnGAN [16]	4.36 ± 0.03	–	25.89 ± 0.47	35.49
ControlGAN [4]	4.58 ± 0.09	–	24.06 ± 0.60	–
SD-GAN [17]	4.67 ± 0.09	–	**35.69 ± 0.50**	–
SE-GAN [13]	4.67 ± 0.04	18.167	27.86 ± 0.31	32.28
DF-GAN [14]	4.86 ± 0.04	16.09	–	28.92
DTGAN [19]	4.88 ± 0.03	16.35	–	**23.61**
MF-GAN	**4.94 ± 0.07**	**15.52**	28.70 ± 0.22	27.95

are closer, the quality of synthesized images is higher and the diversity is better. Moreover, the FID is more sensitive to the model collapse, because only one category of images will cause really high FID score.

4.3 Quantitative Results

We compare MF-GANwith numerous text-to-image synthesis methods, including the classic method (*i.e.*, AttnGAN [16]), two AttnGAN based improved methods (*i.e.*, SD-GAN [17] and SE-GAN [13]), DF-GAN [14], controlGAN [4], and DTGAN [19]. Note that we do not choose CPGAN as it does not experiment on the CUB dataset and needs two extra pre-trained: Bottom-Up and Top-Down (BUTD) Attention model and Yolo-V3. The test results of all these approaches on CUB and COCO dataset are from their corresponding published results.

Table 1 shows the IS and FID scores on the CUB and COCO dataset. We make the following observations. First, MF-GAN outperforms SE-GAN which employs sliding loss to enrich image ID information in image synthesis by achieving inception scores of 4.94 and FID scores of 15.52. Second, MF-GAN improves the IS from 4.86 to 4.94 and reduce the FID from 16.09 to 15.52 compared to DF-GAN which also has a single-stream structure. These quantitative results on CUB dataset show that our MF-GAN generates images that have higher quality and diversity than other models. Third, Compared with AttnGAN, the FID value of our MF-GAN is greatly reduced. Moreover, our model decreases the FID from 28.92 to 27.95 compared with DF-GAN. It demonstrates that our DF-GAN outperforms the art-of-the-state methods on the COCO dataset.

4.4 Qualitative Results

We now compare the images generated by AttnGAN, DF-GAN, and MF-GAN. Figure 2 shows the qualitative results on the CUB dataset (the first four columns) and the COCO dataset (the last four columns). Note that the first row shows 8 texts extracted from the test set of CUB and COCO, and the following two rows show the sample images generated by AttnGAN, DF-GAN, and our MF-GAN, respectively, from the corresponding text.

Fig. 2. Sample images synthesized by AttnGAN, DF-GAN and MF-GAN conditioned on text descriptions from CUB (1–4 columns) and COCO (5–8 columns) datasets.

AttnGAN uses a stacked network structure to generate low-resolution images and add more details to it. In this way, once the initial generated images is completely distorted, it is difficult to further improve by the subsequent generators. In comparison, both DF-GAN and our MF-GAN adopt a single network structure, and the generated images are more realistic. For example, the images generated by AttnGAN in columns 1 to 3 lack the shape of the bird, and their color information does not match the corresponding text; however, the images generated by DF-GAN and our MF-GAN have the key characteristics of a bird.

In addition, when compared against DF-GAN, MF-GAN generates more details in both the background and the target object. As shown in columns 1 to 3, the birds in the last row are more complete than the previous row. Obviously, the COCO dataset is more challenging than the CUB bird dataset. It is difficult for all methods to generate complete and realistic images for all target objects in the text. However, the images generated by AttnGAN are distorted with greater probability (*e.g.*, images generated by AttnGAN in columns 5 to 8 can no longer find the approximate shapes of the person, sheep, pizza, and canoe). DF-GAN has made great progress on this basis, the generated images are more realistic and contain more objects, while our MF-GAN generates even more details than DF-GAN, and the overall details are richer (*e.g.*, in the 5th and 8th columns, the person and canoe generated by our model are more realistic).

4.5 Ablation Study

We next perform ablation experiments on the CUB dataset to verify the effectiveness of each component in our MF-GAN, which contains Conditional Residual Network (CRBlock), Dual Attention Block (DABlock) and triplet loss (Tloss) working on the discriminator. We first remove triplet loss from our MF-GAN, and then remove CRBlock by retaining affine transformation and removing

Table 2. Quantitative results of the models that remove the CRBlock, DABlock, Triplet loss (Tloss) from MF-GAN and replace with visual loss (Vloss) on CUB dataset.

Method	IS↑
MF-GAN without (DAB + CRB + Tloss)	4.31 ± 0.05
MF-GAN without (CRB + Tloss)	4.51 ± 0.03
MF-GAN without Tloss	4.70 ± 0.03
MF-GAN replace Tloss with Vloss	4.52 ± 0.04
MF-GAN	$\mathbf{4.94 \pm 0.04}$

conditional batch-normalization. Finally, we continue to remove DABlock. We test their performance on the CUB dataset, and the results are shown in Table 2.

After removing the triplet loss, the IS score decreases from 4.94 to 4.70, suggesting that the triplet loss is able to improve image quality and semantic consistency. Then we continue to remove our CRBlock, and the IS score further drops from 4.70 to 4.51, suggesting that the CRBlock is more effective than affine transformation only in the text-to-image generation task. Finally, we remove the DABlock, the IS score drops to 4.31, which shows that DABlock can indeed improve the quality of the generated images.

We also compare our triplet loss with visual loss. Note that we employ triplet loss to improve the quality of the generated images and the semantic consistency between texts and images by matching image ID information; however, visual loss proposed by [19] has the similar function, which computes the L1 loss based on the image features of real image and the generated image. In experiments, we keep the backbone of our model and hyper-parameters λ_T, but replace triplet loss with visual loss. The results are shown in Table 2, suggesting that the triplet loss is more efficient than the visual loss.

5   Conclusion

In this paper, we propose a novel and simple text-to-image synthesized method, Multi-conditional Fusion Generative Adversarial Network (MF-GAN), to model the image feature maps at both sentence and word level. In addition, we introduce the triplet loss to improve image quality and semantic consistency. Extensive experiments demonstrate that our MF-GAN outperforms the state-of-the-art methods on the CUB dataset and COCO dataset. Results of ablation study show the effectiveness of each module in MF-GAN on improving the image quality and semantic consistency. For future works, we plan to investigate object detection and semantic alignment for further improving semantic consistency.

Acknowledgments. We would like to thank the anonymous reviewers for their valuable suggestions. Haiyong Xie is the correspondence author. This work is supported in part by the National Key R&D Project (Grant No. SQ2021YFC3300088) and the Natural Science Foundation of China (Grant No. U19B2036).

References

1. Gulcehre, C., Chandar, S., Cho, K., Bengio, Y.: Dynamic neural turing machine with continuous and discrete addressing schemes. Neural Comput. **30**(4), 857–884 (2018)
2. Hong, S., Yang, D., Choi, J., Lee, H.: Inferring semantic layout for hierarchical text-to-image synthesis. In: Proceedings of the IEEE Conference on Computer Vision and Pattern Recognition, pp. 7986–7994 (2018)
3. Johnson, J., Gupta, A., Fei-Fei, L.: Image generation from scene graphs. In: Proceedings of the IEEE Conference on Computer Vision and Pattern Recognition, pp. 1219–1228 (2018)
4. Li, B., Qi, X., Lukasiewicz, T., Torr, P.H.: Controllable text-to-image generation. arXiv preprint arXiv:1909.07083 (2019)
5. Li, W., et al.: Object-driven text-to-image synthesis via adversarial training. In: Proceedings of the IEEE/CVF Conference on Computer Vision and Pattern Recognition, pp. 12174–12182 (2019)
6. Liang, J., Pei, W., Lu, F.: CPGAN: content-parsing generative adversarial networks for text-to-image synthesis. In: Vedaldi, A., Bischof, H., Brox, T., Frahm, J.-M. (eds.) ECCV 2020. LNCS, vol. 12349, pp. 491–508. Springer, Cham (2020). https://doi.org/10.1007/978-3-030-58548-8_29
7. Lin, T.-Y., et al.: Microsoft COCO: common objects in context. In: Fleet, D., Pajdla, T., Schiele, B., Tuytelaars, T. (eds.) ECCV 2014. LNCS, vol. 8693, pp. 740–755. Springer, Cham (2014). https://doi.org/10.1007/978-3-319-10602-1_48
8. Melekhov, I., Kannala, J., Rahtu, E.: Siamese network features for image matching. In: 2016 23rd International Conference on Pattern Recognition (ICPR), pp. 378–383. IEEE (2016)
9. Qiao, T., Zhang, J., Xu, D., Tao, D.: Mirrorgan: learning text-to-image generation by redescription. In: Proceedings of the IEEE/CVF Conference on Computer Vision and Pattern Recognition, pp. 1505–1514 (2019)
10. Reed, S., Akata, Z., Yan, X., Logeswaran, L., Schiele, B., Lee, H.: Generative adversarial text to image synthesis. In: International Conference on Machine Learning, pp. 1060–1069. PMLR (2016)
11. Salimans, T., Goodfellow, I., Zaremba, W., Cheung, V., Radford, A., Chen, X.: Improved techniques for training gans. arXiv preprint arXiv:1606.03498 (2016)
12. Schroff, F., Kalenichenko, D., Philbin, J.: Facenet: a unified embedding for face recognition and clustering. In: Proceedings of the IEEE Conference on Computer Vision and Pattern Recognition, pp. 815–823 (2015)
13. Tan, H., Liu, X., Li, X., Zhang, Y., Yin, B.: Semantics-enhanced adversarial nets for text-to-image synthesis. In: Proceedings of the IEEE/CVF International Conference on Computer Vision, pp. 10501–10510 (2019)
14. Tao, M., Tang, H., Wu, S., Sebe, N., Wu, F., Jing, X.Y.: DF-GAN: deep fusion generative adversarial networks for text-to-image synthesis. arXiv preprint arXiv:2008.05865 (2020)
15. Wah, C., Branson, S., Welinder, P., Perona, P., Belongie, S.: The Caltech-UCSD Birds-200-2011 Dataset. Technocal Report CNS-TR-2011-001, California Institute of Technology (2011)
16. Xu, T., et al.: Attngan: fine-grained text to image generation with attentional generative adversarial networks. In: Proceedings of the IEEE Conference on Computer Vision and Pattern Recognition, pp. 1316–1324 (2018)

17. Yin, G., Liu, B., Sheng, L., Yu, N., Wang, X., Shao, J.: Semantics disentangling for text-to-image generation. In: Proceedings of the IEEE/CVF Conference on Computer Vision and Pattern Recognition, pp. 2327–2336 (2019)
18. Zhang, H., et al.: Stackgan: text to photo-realistic image synthesis with stacked generative adversarial networks. In: Proceedings of the IEEE International Conference on Computer Vision, pp. 5907–5915 (2017)
19. Zhang, Z., Schomaker, L.: DTGAN: dual attention generative adversarial networks for text-to-image generation. arXiv preprint arXiv:2011.02709 (2020)
20. Zhang, Z., Xie, Y., Yang, L.: Photographic text-to-image synthesis with a hierarchically-nested adversarial network. In: Proceedings of the IEEE Conference on Computer Vision and Pattern Recognition, pp. 6199–6208 (2018)

Applications 1

Learning to Classify Weather Conditions from Single Images Without Labels

Kezhen Xie, Lei Huang$^{(\boxtimes)}$, Wenfeng Zhang, Qibing Qin, and Zhiqiang Wei

Faculty of Information Science and Engineering,
Ocean University of China, Qingdao, China
huangl@ouc.edu.cn

Abstract. Weather classification from single images plays an important role in many outdoor computer vision applications, while it has not been thoroughly studied. Despite existing methods have achieved great success under the supervision of weather labels, they are hardly applicable to real-world applications due to the reliance on extensive human-annotated data. In this paper, we make the first attempt to view weather classification as an unsupervised task, i.e., classifying weather conditions from single images without labels. Specifically, a two-step unsupervised approach, where weather feature learning and weather clustering are decoupled, is proposed to automatically group images into weather clusters. In weather feature learning, we employ a self-supervised task to learn the semantically meaningful weather features. To ensure weather features invariant to image transformations and extract discriminative weather features, we also introduce online triplet mining into the task. In weather clustering, a learnable clustering method is designed by mining the nearest neighbors as a prior and enforcing the consistent predictions of each image and it's nearest neighbors. Experimental results on two public benchmark datasets indicate that our approach achieves promising performance.

Keywords: Weather classification · Weather feature learning · Weather clustering

1 Introduction

Weather conditions influence our daily lives and industrial productions in many ways [1,2]. With the development of surveillance cameras and the convenience of outdoor images collection, weather recognition can be treated as a computer vision task. Weather recognition from outdoor images is the foundation of many computer vision applications, such as vehicle assistant driving system [3] and robotic vision [4]. Most existing methods in computer vision field are based on the hypothesis that the weather in outdoor images is clear, ignoring that some weather conditions, such as rain and haze, may cause complex visual effects. Such effects may degrade the performances significantly of outdoor vision systems [5]. Thus, weather recognition from single outdoor images is of great significance.

© Springer Nature Switzerland AG 2022
B. Þór Jónsson et al. (Eds.): MMM 2022, LNCS 13141, pp. 57–68, 2022.
https://doi.org/10.1007/978-3-030-98358-1_5

Despite the remarkable value, it has not been thoroughly studied to classify weather conditions from single outdoor images. Weather classification is the task of assigning a weather label from a predefined set of classes to an outdoor image. For example, the weather condition in an image is sunny, rainy or cloudy, etc. At present, the task is typically solved by training Convolutional Neural Networks (CNNs) [6–8] on the labeled weather datasets [2,5,9]. Under the supervised setup, the networks learn discriminative feature representations which are then classified to predetermined weather categories. However, the high annotation cost for weather images is a severe problem for the deep learning based approaches due to their intensive demand of data. When the ground-truth weather labels are not available during training, the loss cannot be calculated and the model cannot be trained using the existing weather classification methods. At present, there is no researches on how to classify weather conditions from single images without the supervision of weather labels during training. In the absence of supervision information, the desired goal is to group the images into different weather clusters, so that the images within the same cluster have the same or similar weather condition, while those in different clusters have different weather conditions.

Under this situation, we make the initial attempt by developing an unsupervised clustering method to assign outdoor images without labels to weather clusters. We propose a two-step learnable unsupervised approach, which is named Weather Clustering by Adopting Triplet mining and Nearest neighbors (WCATN), including weather feature learning and weather clustering. Firstly, we propose to learn weather feature representations through a pretext task in self-supervised manner, which does not require labeled data for learning. The weather representations are learned by optimizing the objective of the pretext task. To extract discriminative weather features which are invariant to image transformations, we also include a constraint to the cross entropy loss and introduce the triplet loss into the representation learning. Secondly, the previous representation learning approaches require K-means clustering for estimation, which is known to result in cluster degeneracy [10,11]. Instead, in this paper, we design a novel learnable clustering method for weather clustering. Specifically, the nearest neighbors of each sample, which are semantically meaningful, are minded through the pretext task as the prior for weather cluster learning. Each sample and its nearest neighbors are classified together in the clustering.

In summary, the main contributions of this paper are as follows:

(1) We propose a two-step learnable unsupervised approach for weather classification, which takes the first attempt to classify weather conditions from single outdoor images without labels.
(2) We propose to learn weather features through a pretext task in a self-supervised manner. We also introduce the online triplet mining into the learning to extact transformation-invariant and discriminative weather features.
(3) A learnable weather clustering method is designed by integrating the mined nearest neighbors. We classify each sample and its nearest neighbors together by imposing consistent and discriminative predictions for them.

2   Related Works

In this section, we present some classic and state-of-the-art methods of weather classification, and introduce a brief discussion on popular unsupervised learning approaches.

2.1   Weather Classification

Recently, deep CNNs have made great breakthroughs in computer vision tasks, such as image classification [6], image retrieval [12,13], etc. Excellent CNN architectures, e.g. AlexNet [6], VGG [7] and ResNet [8], have been designed and achieved superior performance than traditional approaches. Inspired by the great success of CNNs, some researchers introduced them into weather recognition tasks, which have shown their superiority than handcrafted features and traditional classifiers in conventional weather recognition methods.

In [14], Elhoseiny et al. employed AlexNet [6] to classify two-class weather conditions, and it achieved better results compared with the state-of-the-art handcrafted features based method [9]. In [15], Shi et al. applied VGG [7] to extract features from both the image and the foreground of the image for four-class weather recognition. Lin et al. [16] proposed the RSCM model based on CNN to discover regional properties and concurrency for multi-class weather classification. Additionally, Zhao [17] constructed a multi-task framework based on CNN to simultaneously deal with weather classification and weather-cue segmentation. In [18], The ResNet is extended with a channel-wise attention module to extract discriminative weather features, which are subsequently applied to inter-dependent weather classifiers for multi-label weather recognition. In [2], a CNN-RNN based approach is proposed for multi-label weather classification, where CNN extracts the visual features and then RNN further processes the features and mines the dependencies among weather classes.

2.2   Unsupervised Learning

For two-stage unsupervised approaches, representation learning is the first stage. Most popular representation learning methods [19,20] utilize self-supervised learning to extract feature representations from images without annotations. In self-supervised learning, a pretext task is adopted to learn the weights of a convolutional neural network. It learns the semantic features by minimizing the objective of the pretext task. Various pretext tasks have been studied, e.g., in-painting patches [20], predicting image rotations [19], performing instance discrimination [21], etc. Then the second stage evaluates the features by fine-tuning the network on a new task in a supervised manner. As for the cases without annotations, a clustering criterion (e.g. K-means) is needed and optimized independently, which may lead to imbalanced clusters [10] and they may not align with the semantic classes [11].

As an alternative, end-to-end unsupervised learning methods combine representation learning with image clustering. The first set of methods (e.g. DEC [22],

DAC [23]) utilizes the CNNs' architecture as the prior to cluster images. Another set (e.g. IMSAT [24], IIC [25]) proposes to learn clustering by the mutual information between the image and its augmentations. Generally, the methods rely on the initial features of the network are sensitive to initialization [11] and likely to absorb low-level features that useless for semantic clustering.

3   Method

In this section, we firstly illustrate the overview of the proposed approach. Then we present the two steps, i.e. weather feature learning and weather clustering, in details.

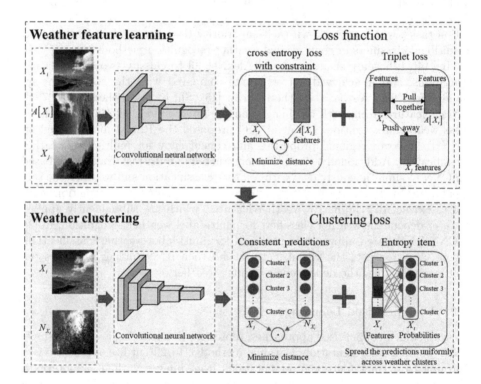

Fig. 1. Overall framework of our two-step learnable unsupervised approach for weather clustering. Step 1 learns to extract weather feature representations using a convolutional neural network in self-supervised manner. In the training stage, it combines the contrastive cross entropy loss, which is with constraint of minimizing the distance between image X_i and their augmentations $A[X_i]$, with triplet loss. Step 2 learns to cluster X_i and N_{X_i} (which is the nearest neighbors set of X_i, minded based on feature similarity) together. The clustering loss enforces the consistent predictions of X_i and N_{X_i} by minimizing the distance of their soft assignments over weather clusters C, and includes an entropy item to spread the predictions uniformly across C.

3.1 Overview

In order to classify weather conditions from single outdoor images without labels, we propose a two-step unsupervised approach, named WCATN (Weather Clustering by Adopting Triplet mining and Nearest neighbors), for weather clustering. The architecture of WCATN is demonstrated in Fig. 1, consisting of weather feature learning and weather clustering.

In weather feature learning, to extract high-level semantic features, we propose to learn weather feature representations via a pretext task in self-supervised manner, with a standard convolutional neural network as the backbone. The pretext task aims at minimizing the distance between each sample and its augmentation to learn weather features which are invariant to image transformations. Furthermore, an online triplet batch mining is also introduced to enforce the distance minimal than that between the sample and other samples. Besides, the nearest neighbors of each image are minded for weather clustering by the learned network.

In weather clustering, we integrate the semantically meaningful nearest neighbors into the learnable approach as a prior. As shown in Fig. 1, we classify each image and its nearest neighbors together. The designed clustering loss aims to impose the network to generate both consistent and discriminative predictions by maximizing their dot product after softmax. Moreover, an entropy term is included to spread the predictions of samples uniformly to the weather clusters.

3.2 Weather Feature Learning

In supervised learning for weather classification, each sample can be associated with the correct class through the use of ground-truth weather labels. Particularly, the mapping functions from images $D = \{X_1, \cdots, X_{|D|}\}$ to weather classes C are generally learned by optimizing the cross-entropy loss. However, when there are no ground-truth weather labels available in the datasets, we need to define a prior to get the estimate that which samples tend to belong the same cluster and which do not.

In end-to-end unsupervised clustering approaches, the architecture of CNNs is used as a prior [22,23] or the consistency between the images and the corresponding augmentations is enforced [24,25] to learn clusters. In both cases, the learning is sensitive to network initialization [11]. Besides, the network has not yet extracted high-level features from the image at the beginning of the training. This leads to that the clusters can easily absorb low-level information (e.g. edge, texture, contrast, color, etc.), which is far less semantically meaningful for weather clustering. To overcome these limitations and get a better prior for weather clustering, we propose to learn weather feature representations from the unlabeled images via a pretext task.

The pretext task τ learns an embedding function Φ_θ to map images to weather features in self-supervised manner in weather feature learning. Φ_θ is parameterized by a convolutional neural network with weights θ. There are several pretext tasks that can be used to learn the embedding function Φ_θ in literatures, e.g. in-painting [20], rotation prediction [19], instance discrimination [21], etc. However, in practice, certain pretext tasks are based on particular image transformations, leading to that the learned feature representations are covariant to the adopted transformation. It means that different transformations of the same image will result in different outputs for Φ_θ. This makes the learned feature representations inappropriate for weather clustering, where weather feature representations are needed to be invariant to image transformations. Thus, in order to learn more appropriate weather representations for clustering, we impose the pretext task τ to minimize the distance between the images X_i and the corresponding augmentations $A\,[X_i]$, as depicted below.

$$\min_\theta d\left(\Phi_\theta\left(X_i\right), \Phi_\theta\left(A\left[X_i\right]\right)\right) \tag{1}$$

Following [11,21], we employ the instance discrimination task, which meets the constraint in Eq. (1), as the pretext task to learn weather feature representations. Correspondingly, we introduce this constraint into the contrastive cross entropy loss of the task for training. However, it may be not optimal that Eq.(1) only considers the distance between image X_i and it's augmentation $A\,[X_i]$ pair, since it cannot guarantee the distance is minimal than that between X_i and other images. Thus, an online triplet batch mining is constructed as $\langle X_i, A\,[X_i], X_j \rangle$ in each training batch, and the triplet loss is applied to reducing the distance of positive pair $\langle X_i, A\,[X_i] \rangle$ and enlarging the negative pair $\langle X_i, X_j \rangle$. Note that $X_j\,(i \neq j)$ is randomly selected in each training batch. The triplet loss is formulated as:

$$L_{tri} = \sum |d_{a,p} - d_{a,n} + \alpha|_+ \tag{2}$$

where $d_{a,p} = \|\Phi_\theta\left(X_i\right) - \Phi_\theta\left(A\left[X_i\right]\right)\|_2^2$, $d_{a,n} = \|\Phi_\theta\left(X_i\right) - \Phi_\theta\left(X_j\right)\|_2^2$ and α is a margin threshold. By optimizing L_{tri}, the model can further learn transformation-invariant weather representations.

Images with similar weather conditions (i.e. similar high-level semantic features) are mapped more closely together by the embedding function Φ_θ. The reason is as follows. Firstly, the output of the pretext task is conditioned on the input images, forcing Φ_θ to extract specific weather information from the images. Secondly, Φ_θ has to discard the information from the input images which is not predictive for the high-level pretext task due to its limited capacity. It can be concluded that the pretext task can be utilized to extract semantically meaningful weather features in representation learning. Thus, we employ the weather feature representations extracted by the pretext task as the prior for weather clustering.

3.3   Weather Clustering

Though the weather features are extracted by pretext task in representation learning, naively applying the standard clustering algorithm K-means to the features can result in clustering degeneracy [10,11]. When a discriminative model learning the decision boundary, it can assign all its probability mass to the same weather cluster. This causes one cluster dominates the others. In this paper, we propose to design a learnable weather clustering method with mining the nearest neighbors of each sample as our prior.

Nearest Neighbors Mining. It is empirically found in [11] that the image X_i and it's K nearest neighbors (which are mined based on feature similarity) belong to the same semantic class in most cases for different values of K, rendering them appropriate for semantic clustering. Inspired by this, we propose to introduce the nearest neighbors mined through the pretext task as the prior for weather clustering.

In this paper, through weather feature learning, a model Φ_θ is trained on the unlabeled weather dataset D to solve the pretext task τ, i.e. instance discrimination task. For each sample $X_i \in D$, we mine its K nearest neighbors by calculating the feature similarity in the embedding space. The set N_{X_i} is defined as the neighbors of X_i.

Learnable Clustering. We integrate the semantically meaningful K nearest neighbors as the prior into a learnable weather clustering method. In this method, we aim to learn a weather clustering function Φ_η, which is parameterized by a convolutional neural network with weights η, to classify the image X_i and its nearest neighbors N_{X_i} together. Φ_η terminates in a softmax function to perform soft assignments over the weather clusters $C = \{1, \cdots, C\}$, with $\Phi_\eta(X_i) \in [0,1]^C$. The probability of image X_i being assigned to weather cluster c is represented by $\Phi_\eta^c(X_i)$. The weights of Φ_η are learned by minimizing the following objectives:

$$L = -\frac{1}{|D|} \sum_{X \in D} \sum_{k \in N_x} \log \langle \Phi_\eta(X), \Phi_\eta(k) \rangle + \lambda \sum_{c \in C} \Phi_\eta^{'c} \log \Phi_\eta^{'c} \tag{3}$$

$$\Phi_\eta^{'c} = \frac{1}{|D|} \sum_{X \in D} \Phi_\eta^c(X) \tag{4}$$

where $\langle \cdot \rangle$ represents the dot product operator. The first term in Eq. (3) enforces Φ_θ to make discriminative and consistent predictions for image X_i and its K nearest neighbor samples N_{X_i}. The dot production will reach maximum when the predictions of sample X_i and its neighbors are one-hot (discriminative) and they are assigned to the same weather cluster (consistent). In order to avoid Φ_η assigning all the samples to a single weather cluster, an entropy term (the second term in the Eq. (3)) is included, which spreads the predictions uniformly across the weather clusters C. The exact number of clusters is generally unknown in unsupervised learning. However, similar to previous achievements [22,23,25], we choose C equal to the number of ground-truth weather clusters for the purpose of evaluation.

4   Experiments

In this section, we firstly introduce the two experimental datasets and evaluation metrics, and then describe the implementation details. Finally, we present the results of the proposed approach.

4.1   Datasets and Evaluation Metrics

We perform the experimental evaluation on the MWI (Multi-class Weather Image) dataset [5, 26] and the MWD (Multi-class Weather Dataset) dataset [16]. Both of the datasets are publicly available and constructed specifically for weather understanding based on outdoor images. The MWI dataset contains 20,000 outdoor images and is annotated with 4 weather classes. The MWD dataset contains 65,000 images from 6 common weather categories, and is annotated with weather classes and attributes. In our work, the annotations of both datasets are omitted for training. We evaluate the results based on clustering accuracy (ACC), normalized mutual information (NMI) and adjusted rand index (ARI).

4.2   Implementation Details

We use a standard ResNet-50 backbone. For each sample, 10 nearest neighbors are minded through the pretext task. The instance discrimination task is adopted as the pretext task and implemented based on SimCLR [21]. The weights obtained from the weather feature learning is transferred to initiate the weather clustering. The weight on the entropy term is empirically set to $\lambda = 5$. The learning rate is initialized as 10^{-4} and the weight decay is set to 10^{-4}. All experiments are performed with the same backbone, pretext task, augmentations and hyper-parameters.

4.3   Experimental Results

To demonstrate the promising performance of the proposed approach, abundant experiments are conducted on the MWI and MWD dataset.

Table 1. Experimental results and comparisons with the state-of-the-art methods on the MWI dataset and MWD dataset.

Dataset metric	MWI			MWD		
	ACC	NMI	ARI	ACC	NMI	ARI
SWAV + Kmeans [27]	57.3	29.3	31.0	16.8	0.00098	0.3
simCLR + Kmeans [21]	42.0	6.3	6.6	21.4	3.4	5.1
DCCM [28]	32.4	16.3	30.2	35.6	22.6	16.3
GATCluster [29]	63.3	**32.0**	23.9	44.5	20.0	21.4
WCATN (Ours)	**65.1**	27.0	**33.8**	**46.9**	**26.7**	**21.9**

Table 1 compares the proposed approach with the state-of-the-art methods on two benchmarks. Our approach outperforms the prior unsupervised works by a large margin for weather clustering on both datasets. Firstly, we compare with the state-of-the-art unsupervised representation learning with K-means for clustering in the first two rows. As reported in Table 1, WCATN improves the performance by +7.8% in ACC, +2.8% in ARI on the NMI dataset than the SWAV+Kmeans method and obtains a close NMI. Furthermore, WCATN achieves best results on all the three metrics by a very large gap on the MWD dataset. This mainly because that we design a novel learnable clustering in WCATN instead of using Kmeans, which avoid the cluster degeneracy problem in Kmeans. Secondly, we compare with the state-of-the-art end-to-end unsupervised learning methods in the second two rows. It can be observed from Table 1 that the end-to-end learning methods outperform K-means clustering, and our approach perform better than these methods. WCATN achieves ACC = 65.1%, NMI = 27.0%, ARI = 33.8% on the MWI dataset and ACC = 46.9%, NMI = 26.7%, ARI = 21.9% on the MWD dataset, which is superior than the compared methods. The main reason may be that our learned clusters rely on more high-level semantic weather features, rather than on the initial weather features of the network. Overall, the proposed approach achieves promising results and is superior than the state-of-the-art unsupervised methods.

4.4   Ablation Study

To verify the effectiveness of important components of WCATN, we conduct ablation studies on both MWI and MWD datasets. Except for the specified changes in different comparisons, all employed experiments are under the same setting.

Effectiveness of Online Triplet Mining. To evaluate the influence of online triplet mining in weather feature learning, we conduct the experiments with WCATN-T, which removes the triplet mining from our approach. It can be observed from Table 2 that the WCATN outperforms WCATN-T on all the metrics on both datasets. Specifically, it improves the performance of ACC, NMI, ARI by +4.0%, +1.5%, +5.4% and +2.7%, +3.2%, +2.3% respectively on The MWI and MWD dataset. In brief, the results verified the effectiveness of online triplet mining for weather feature learning. This is because that triplet loss is applied to enforce the image and its augmentations to be mapped more closely than the negative pairs in the embedding space. Thus, the WCATN can further learn transformation-invariant and discriminative weather representations.

Effectiveness of the Nearest Neighbors. To evaluate the effectiveness of learning weather clustering using the nearest neighbors, we compare WCATN with WCATN-N, which replaces the nearest neighbors with image augmentations. As shown in Table 2, our proposed WCATN achieves 65.1% and 46.9% of ACC on the MWI and MWD dataset, which outperforms WCATN-N by +6.0%

Table 2. Ablation studies on both datasets for weather clustering. WCATN-T: compared with WCATN, this method removes the online triplet mining in the weather feature learning. WCATN-N: compared with WCATN, this method does not adopt the nearest neighbors. WCATN-N classifies the samples and their augmentations together in weather clustering.

Dataset metric	MWI			MWD		
	ACC	NMI	ARI	ACC	NMI	ARI
WCATN-T	61.1	25.5	28.4	44.2	23.5	19.6
WCATN-N	59.1	24.7	26.6	42.1	21.7	18.3
WCATN	**65.1**	**27.0**	**33.8**	**46.9**	**26.7**	**21.9**

and +4.8% respectively. It also achieves higher results of NMI and ARI on both datasets. Overall, the results demonstrate the effectiveness of the nearest neighbors in weather clustering. By classifying each sample and its nearest neighbors together, we impose discriminative and consistent predictions for them, which helps learn better weather representations for clustering learning.

4.5   Parameter Sensitivity

For each sample in the dataset, K nearest neighbors are mined in the embedding space for weather clustering. To study the influence of different number of K, we set $K = \{0, 5, 10, 15, 20, 25, 30\}$ in experiments during weather clustering step. We make comparison studies on the MWI dataset and the detailed experimental results are reported in Fig. 2. It achieves best at $K = 10$, with ACC = 65.1%, ARI = 33.8%, and NMI = 27%. Overall, the results are not very sensitive to variations of K, and remain stable even as increasing K to 30. We also include the case $K = 0$, i.e., enforcing consistent predictions for images and their augmentations instead of their nearest neighbors. It decreases the performance on the MWI dataset compared to $K = 5$, with –3.6% of ACC, –4.3% of NMI and –1.8% of ARI. This confirms that it can learn better weather representations by imposing coherent predictions between each sample and its nearest neighbors.

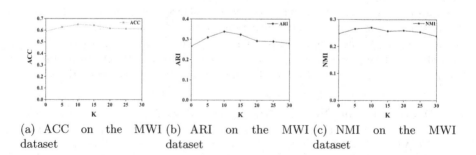

(a) ACC on the MWI dataset   (b) ARI on the MWI dataset   (c) NMI on the MWI dataset

Fig. 2. Comparisons of weather clustering performance on the MWI dataset using different number of the nearest neighbors K.

5   Conclusion

In this work, we propose to classify weather conditions from single images without labels. To achieve this goal, a two-step unsupervised approach is proposed to automatically group images into weather clusters. The first step is to obtain semantically meaningful weather features via employing a self-supervised task and introducing online triplet mining in weather feature learning. The second step is to learn weather clustering by classifying each sample and its nearest neighbors (which are mined based on feature similarity) together. In the future work, we plan to enhance clustering leaning for improving the performance of weather clustering.

Acknowledgements. This work is supported by the National Natural Science Foundation of China (No. 61872326, No. 62072418); Qingdao Independent Innovation Major Project (20-3-2-2-hy, 20-3-2-12-xx). This work got the data service from the Marine Environment Data Service System which supported by the National Key R&D Program of China (2019YFC1408405).

References

1. Lu, C., Lin, D., Jia, J., Tang, C.-K.: Two-class weather classification. IEEE Trans. Pattern Anal. Mach. Intell. **39**(12), 2510–2524 (2017)
2. Zhao, B., Li, X., Lu, X., Wang, Z.: A CNN-RNN architecture for multi-label weather recognition. Neurocomputing **322**, 47–57 (2018)
3. Ohn-Bar, E., Trivedi, M.M.: Are all objects equal? deep spatio-temporal importance prediction in driving videos. Pattern Recognit. **64**, 425–436 (2017)
4. Loncomilla, P., Ruiz-del-Solar, J., Martínez, L.: Object recognition using local invariant features for robotic applications: a survey. Pattern Recognit. **60**, 499–514 (2016)
5. Zhang, Z. Ma, H.: Multi-class weather classification on single images. In: 2015 IEEE International Conference on Image Processing (ICIP), pp. 4396–4400 (2015)
6. Krizhevsky, A., Sutskever, I., Hinton, G.E.: Imagenet classification with deep convolutional neural networks. In: Advances Neural Information Processing System, vol. 25, pp. 1097–1105 (2012)
7. Simonyan, K., Zisserman, A.: Very deep convolutional networks for large-scale image recognition. ArXiv Prepr. ArXiv14091556 (2014)
8. He, K., Zhang, X., Ren, S., Sun, J.: Deep residual learning for image recognition. In: Proceedings of the IEEE Conference on Computer Vision and Pattern Recognition, pp. 770–778 (2016)
9. Lu, C., Lin, D., Jia, J., Tang, C.-K.: Two-class weather classification. In: Proceedings of the IEEE Conference on Computer Vision and Pattern Recognition, pp. 3718–3725 (2014)
10. Caron, M., Bojanowski, P., Joulin, A., Douze, M.: Deep clustering for unsupervised learning of visual features. In Proceedings of the European Conference on Computer Vision, pp. 132–149 (2018)
11. Van Gansbeke, W., Vandenhende, S., Georgoulis, S., Proesmans, M., Van Gool, L.: Scan: learning to classify images without labels. In: European Conference on Computer Vision, pp. 268–285 (2020)

12. Qin, Q., Huang, L., Wei, Z., Xie, K., Zhang, W.: Unsupervised deep multi-similarity hashing with semantic structure for image retrieval. IEEE Trans. Circuits Syst. Video Technol. **31**, 2852–2865 (2020)

13. Zhang, W., Huang, L., Wei, Z., Nie, J.: Appearance feature enhancement for person re-identification. Expert Syst. Appl. 163, 113771 (2021)

14. Elhoseiny, M., Huang, S., Elgammal, A.: Weather classification with deep convolutional neural networks. In: 2015 IEEE International Conference on Image Processing (ICIP), pp. 3349–3353 (2015)

15. Shi, Y., Li, Y., Liu, J., Liu, X., Murphey, Y.L.: Weather recognition based on edge deterioration and convolutional neural networks. In: 2018 24th International Conference on Pattern Recognition (ICPR), pp. 2438–2443 (2018)

16. Lin, D., Lu, C., Huang, H., Jia, J.: RSCM: region selection and concurrency model for multi-class weather recognition. IEEE Trans. Image Process. **26**(9), 4154–4167 (2017)

17. Zhao, B., Hua, L., Li, X., Lu, X., Wang, Z.: Weather recognition via classification labels and weather-cue maps. Pattern Recognit. **95**, 272–284 (2019)

18. Xie, K., Wei, Z., Huang, L., Qin, Q., Zhang, W.: Graph convolutional networks with attention for multi-label weather recognition. Neural Comput. Appl. **33**(17), 11107–11123 (2021). https://doi.org/10.1007/s00521-020-05650-8

19. Gidaris, S., Singh, P., Komodakis, N.: Unsupervised representation learning by predicting image rotations. ArXiv Prepr. ArXiv180307728 (2018)

20. Pathak, D., Krahenbuhl, P., Donahue, J., Darrell, T., Efros, A.A.: Context encoders: feature learning by inpainting. In: Proceedings of the IEEE Conference on Computer Vision and Pattern Recognition, pp. 2536–2544 (2016)

21. Chen, T., Kornblith, S., Norouzi, M., Hinton, G.: A simple framework for contrastive learning of visual representations. In: International Conference on Machine Learning, pp. 1597–1607 (2020)

22. Xie, J., Girshick, R., Farhadi, A.: Unsupervised deep embedding for clustering analysis. In: International Conference on Machine Learning, pp. 478–487 (2016)

23. Chang, J., Wang, L., Meng, G., Xiang, S., Pan, C.: Deep adaptive image clustering. In: Proceedings of the IEEE International Conference on Computer Vision, pp. 5879–5887 (2017)

24. Hu, W., Miyato, T., Tokui, S., Matsumoto, E., Sugiyama, M.: Learning discrete representations via information maximizing self-augmented training. In: International Conference on Machine Learning, pp. 1558–1567 (2017)

25. Ji, X., Henriques, J.F., Vedaldi, A.: Invariant information clustering for unsupervised image classification and segmentation. In: Proceedings of the IEEE/CVF International Conference on Computer Vision, pp. 9865–9874 (2019)

26. Zhang, Z., Ma, H., Fu, H., Zhang, C.: Scene-free multi-class weather classification on single images. Neurocomputing **207**, 365–373 (2016)

27. Caron, M., Misra, I., Mairal, J., Goyal, P., Bojanowski, P., Joulin, A.: Unsupervised learning of visual features by contrasting cluster assignments. ArXiv Prepr. ArXiv200609882 (2020)

28. Wu, J., et al.: Deep comprehensive correlation mining for image clustering. In: Proceedings of the IEEE/CVF International Conference on Computer Vision, pp. 8150–8159 (2019)

29. Niu, C., Zhang, J., Wang, G., Liang, J.: Gatcluster: self-supervised gaussian-attention network for image clustering. In: European Conference on Computer Vision, pp. 735–751 (2020)

Learning Image Representation via Attribute-Aware Attention Networks for Fashion Classification

Yongquan Wan[1,3]([✉]), Cairong Yan[2], Bofeng Zhang[1], and Guobing Zou[1]

[1] School of Computer Engineering and Science, Shanghai University, Shanghai, China
[2] School of Computer Science and Technology, Donghua University, Shanghai, China
[3] School of Information Technology, Shanghai Jian Qiao University, Shanghai, China

Abstract. Attribute descriptions enrich the characteristics of fashion products, and they play an essential role in fashion image research. We propose a fashion classification model (M2Fashion) based on multi-modal data (text + image). It uses the intra-modal and inter-modal data correlation to locate relevant image regions under the guidance of attributes and the attention mechanism. Compared with traditional single-modal feature representation, learning embedding from multi-modal features can better reflect fine-grained image features. We adopt a multi-task learning framework that combines category classification and attribute prediction tasks. The extensive experimental result on the public dataset Deep-Fashion shows the superiority of our proposed M2Fashion compared with state-of-the-art methods. It achieves +1.3% top-3 accuracy rate improvement in the category classification task and +5.6%/+3.7% top-3 recall rate improvement in the attribute prediction of *part/shape*, respectively. A supplementary experiment on attribute-specific image retrieval on the DARN dataset also demonstrates the effectiveness of M2Fashion.

Keywordsss: Multi-modal · Classification · Prediction · Attention mechanism

1 Introduction

With the development of convolutional neural networks (CNN) and the publication of large-scale fashion datasets, significant progress has been made in fashion-related research, including fashion item recognition [1–3], fashion compatibility recommendation [4, 5], fashion attribute prediction [1, 6, 7] and fashion image retrieval [8–10]. Fashion category classification is a multi-class classification task, and fashion attribute prediction is a multi-label classification task. both of them generate helpful information for fashion items. Traditional classification methods usually only use the features learned from images as input and ignore the attribute information.

Figure 1 illustrates three fashion items in a fashion dataset. We can see that each image belongs to a category and has some attribute labels associated with it. The attribute labels of each fashion image reflect the category of the image. For example, an item with the '*strapless*' attribute is unlikely to be a pair of '*Jeans*', while an item with the '*mini*'

© Springer Nature Switzerland AG 2022
B. Þór Jónsson et al. (Eds.): MMM 2022, LNCS 13141, pp. 69–81, 2022.
https://doi.org/10.1007/978-3-030-98358-1_6

attribute is more likely to be a '*dress*'. In addition, there is a specific correlation between the attribute labels describing a fashion image, and they are not entirely independent. For example, '*denim*' and '*crochet*' will not be used to describe the same piece of clothing, while '*strapless*' and '*mini*' express the same piece of clothing because they are independent of each other. The use of labels and dependencies between labels helps to understand fashion items more accurately. Our goal is to use images and a group of known attribute labels to build a multi-modal classification model.

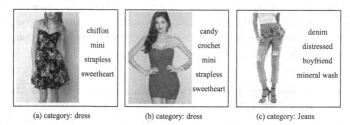

Fig. 1. Examples of fashion images and attributes. Image (a) and Image (b) share some attributes: *mini, strapless* and *sweetheart*, and they belong to the same category. Image (c) belongs to a separate category and has completely different attributes.

To support multi-modal interaction, we use two types of attention mechanisms to facilitate the interaction between visual and semantic information, i.e. an attribute-specific spatial attention module and an attribute-specific channel attention module. They enable the network to learn multi-modal features based on known attribute labels. In the model training phase, we represent the state of the labels as positive, negative or unknown to model them. Suppose we know the attribute state of image (a) and set it to true ('strapless') or false ('maxi'), the model can predict with a high degree of confidence that the image belongs to the 'upper body' category and has the 'mini' attribute. We compare our model with some competing methods on public datasets, which proves the model's superiority. The main contributions are as follows:

- We propose a fashion classification model (M2Fashion) based on multi-modal features. It is an attribute-guided attention-based model, which extracts more associated information between images and attributes to promote accurate fashion classification and attribute prediction. A channel attention module and a spatial attention module are integrated into the model for data fusion of two different modalities.
- We adopt a multi-task learning framework that combines category classification and attribute prediction tasks. Compared with other classification models, the attributes in our model are not independent, and their relationship is contained in the attribute hierarchy.
- Extensive experiments are carried out to compare the proposed model with several state-of-the-art models on public datasets. Experimental results show the superiority of the proposed model. In addition, M2Fashion is applied to an attribute-specific image retrieval tasks by removing the final classifier. This supplementary experiment also demonstrates the effectiveness of our model.

2 Related Work

Attribute Learning. The existing attribute learning methods can be categorized into two groups: 1) visual feature-based [9, 10]. They embed images in a common low-dimensional space and use the feature vectors in the low-dimensional space for attribute classification. 2) visual-semantic feature-based [11–13]. They learn joint representation by exploring the correlation between multi-modal content. Some of these methods use semantic information from attributes or annotated text to extract saliency or visual attention from the image. The above studies all learn visual/semantic features but ignore the relationship between attributes. Our work aims to mine the inner correlation of multiple attributes to learn fine-grained image representations.

Attention-Based Models. In recent years, the attention mechanism is widely used in computer vision and natural language processing. This technology has also been researched and applied in the field of fashion. Ji et al. [14] proposed a tag-based attention mechanism and a context-based attention mechanism to improve the performance of cross-domain retrieval of fashion images. Li et al. [15] proposed a joint attribute detection and visual attention framework for clothes image captioning. Ma et al. [16] proposed an attribute feature embedding network, which learns attribute-based embedding in an end-to-end manner to measure the attribute-specified fine-grained similarity of fashion items. Inspired by the success of the attention mechanism, we proposed to use two attribute-aware attention modules for fine-grained image classification tasks.

Multi-task Learning. Since it was proposed, multi-task learning (MTL) has achieved many successes in several domains, such as image classification with landmark detection [17], attribute-enhanced recipe retrieval [18], and visual question answering [19]. To explore the intrinsic correlation of attributes to obtain more reliable prediction results, we are motivated to build a multi-task framework to model the correlation and common representation of categories and multiple attributes of fashion images.

3 Methodology

3.1 Problem Formulation

Given a set of fashion items denoted by $D = \{(x_1, A_1), ..., (x_n, A_n)\}$, where $x_i (1 \leq i \leq n)$ is the i-th image, $x_i \in \mathbb{R}^{c \times h \times w}$ (c, h, and w are the number of channel, height, and weight respectively), $A_i = [a_{i1}, a_{i2}, ..., a_{iK}]$ is a multi-hot attribute vector which describes the image appearance with K semantic attributes, $a_{ij} \in \{-1, 0, 1\}$ ($1 \leq j \leq K$), and K is the number of all attributes. The attribute set is denoted as $\mathcal{A} = \{\mathcal{A}_1, \mathcal{A}_2, ..., \mathcal{A}_K\}$. The goal of our model is to map the unimodal representation from images and attributes to a joint semantic space, and learn a classifier $f(\bullet)$ in the joint space so that $y = f(x, A; \theta)$. In category classification tasks, y denotes the predicted image category, and in attribute prediction tasks, y denotes predicted attribute labels.

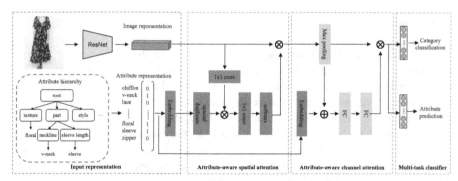

Fig. 2. The framework of our proposed model. It is made up of four key components, input representation module, attribute-aware spatial attention module, attribute-aware channel attention module, and multi-task classifier.

3.2 Network Structure

Figure 2 illustrates the framework of our model. It consists of four key components: input representation module, attribute-aware spatial attention (ASA) module, attribute-aware channel attention (ACA) module, and multi-task classifier. For an input image, the image embedding vector is extracted using ResNet pre-trained on ImageNet. Then, to learn the fine-grained features of the image, we use the image and multiple attributes to learn the feature representation. We adopt the architecture of [16] but add some changes to the method. In their work, spatial attention and channel attention of images guided by attributes are generated by embedding one attribute category such as 'sleeve_length'. In contrast, our model combines images and attribute values such as '3/4 sleeve' to generate attribute-guided attention. Our intuition is that images with the same attribute values will have more similar features. After that, these new attribute-aware features are fed into the attribute classifier.

Input Representation. To represent an image, we use ResNet, a CNN model pre-trained on ImageNet, as the backbone network. To maintain the spatial information of the image, we remove the last fully connected (FC) layer in CNN. Given an image $x_i \in \mathbb{R}^{h \times w \times 3}$, the feature extractor outputs a vector $\bar{x}_i \in \mathbb{R}^{h \times w \times d}$, where $h \times w$ is the size of the feature graph, and d is the number of channels. We represent the attribute label status as positive, negative, or unknown. They are represented by 1, −1 and 0, respectively. For an image x_i, we collect a set of labels embedded in A_i, the j-th element in A_i means the i-th image has the attribute a_{ij}. Attribute label embeddings $\bar{A}_i$ are learned from an embedding layer of size $d \times K$.

$$\bar{A}_i = f_1(A_i) = \delta(W_{a1}A_i), \tag{1}$$

where $W_{a1} \in \mathbb{R}^{d \times K}$ denotes transformation matrix, δ denotes the tanh activation function. Note that we broadcast $\bar{A}_i$ along the height and width dimension so that its shape is compatible to the image feature map $\bar{x}_i$.

Attribute-Aware Spatial Attention. An attribute is related to a specific visual region of the fashion image. For example, the attribute '*3/4 sleeve*' usually appears on either side of the middle area in the image, and to learn attribute-specific features such as '*sleeve length*', the regions around the sleeve will receive more attention. To calculate the attribute-specific image space attention, instead of using a single attribute category to guide attention, we use multiple attribute values to generate attribute embedding. These values are organized into a hierarchical structure, called attribute hierarchy.

Specifically, for an image x_i and its attribute labels A_i, we use I and T_1 to represent $\bar{x}_i$ and $\bar{A}_i$, respectively. First, we get the attribute guided spatial attention feature vector denoted as V_s, obtained by calculating the weighted average of the input image features according to the attribute label embedding. For image embedding I, we employ a convolution layer with d 1×1 convolutional kernels following a nonlinear tanh activation function to transform the dimension of the image to d. The mapped image feature vector is expressed as

$$f_2(I) = \delta(W_{v1}I), \tag{2}$$

where W_{v1} denotes a convolutional layer containing d 1×1 convolution kernels, and δ denotes the tanh activation function.

The attended image feature vector is fused with attribute feature using element-wise product followed with an activation function.

$$f_s(I, T_1) = \delta(W_{v2}(f_2(I) \odot T)), \tag{3}$$

where $\odot$ denotes element-wise product operation, W_{v2} is 1×1 convolutional layer, and δ denotes the tanh activation function. The attention weight is obtained through the softmax activation function.

$$\alpha_l^s = \frac{\exp(f_s(I_l, T_1))}{\sum_j^{h \times w} \exp(f_s(I_j, T_1))}. \tag{4}$$

Then, the spatial attention feature vector under the attention of attribute A_i can be obtained by the following calculation.

$$V_s = \sum_l^{h \times w} \alpha_l^s I_l, \tag{5}$$

where $\alpha_l^s \in R^{h \times w}$ is the attention weight, and I_l is the image feature at location l.

Attribute-Aware Channel Attention. We adopt the attention mechanism of Ma et al. [16] with one modification. In their work, they apply sum pooling on the output from ASEN module. In contrast, we adopt global max pooling on the feature map V_s to concentrate only on discriminative areas. For the attribute A_i, we employ a separate attribute embedding layer to generate an embedding vector with the same dimension as V_s,

$$\tilde{A}_i = f_3(A_i) = \delta(W_{a2}A_i), \tag{6}$$

where $w_{a2} \in \mathbb{R}^{c \times n}$ is the embedding parameter, and δ is the tanh activation function. For the convenience of understanding, we use T_2 to represent $\tilde{A}_i$. The spatial attended features and attribute embedding are fused by concatenation, then fed into two sequential FC layers to generate the attribute-aware channel attended feature. The attention weight $\alpha^c \in \mathbb{R}^c$ is calculated by

$$\alpha^c = \sigma(W_{c2}\sigma(W_{c1}[T_2, V_s])), \tag{7}$$

Where [,] represents the concatenation operation, σ represents the sigmoid activation function, and W_{c1} and W_{c2} are parameters of the FC layer. For simplicity of understanding, the bias in the formula is removed. The final output of ACA is obtained by the element-wise product of I_s and attention weight α_c.

$$V_c = \alpha^c \odot V_s. \tag{8}$$

Finally, we further employ an FC layer over V_c to generate the attribute-guided feature of the given image with known image labels.

$$Z = WV_c + b, \tag{9}$$

where $W \in \mathbb{R}^{c \times c}$ is the transformation matrix, and $b \in \mathbb{R}^c$ is the bias.

Multi-task Learning. In this paper, the MTL framework is used to predict the categories and attributes of images. We share feature vectors in two tasks, category classification and attribute prediction, which helps to share knowledge and distinguish subtle differences between different tasks. At the end of the network, we add two different branches, one for predicting categories of images and the other for predicting attributes of images. The shared attribute-guided image features output is fed to two branches, respectively. We use the cross-entropy loss for category classification, denoted as

$$L_{category} = -\frac{1}{N}\sum_{i=1}^{N}\{y_i^c \log(P(\hat{y}_i^c|Z_i)) + (1 - y_i)\log(1 - P(\hat{y}_i^c|Z_i))\}. \tag{10}$$

The output of the attribute prediction branch is passed into a sigmoid layer to squeeze the output between [0,1] and output $\hat{a}_j$. We use the binary cross-entropy loss for attribute prediction, denoted as

$$L_{attribute} = \sum_{j=1}^{K} a_j \log(p(\hat{a}_j|x_i)) + (1 - a_j)\log(1 - p(\hat{a}_j|x_i)), \tag{11}$$

where a_j is the j-th ground truth of the binary attribute label, $p(\hat{a}_j|x_i)$ is a component of $Y = [y_1, \cdots, y_k]$, and Y is the predicted attribute distribution.

3.3 Label Mask Training

We adopt the strategy of label masking training proposed in [20] to learn the correlation between labels and allow the model to perform multiple label classification with given partial labels. In the process of training, we mask a certain number of labels randomly and use the ground truth of other labels to predict masked labels. For K possible labels, we set certain labels Y_u as unknown labels for a particular sample, where $|Y_u|$ is a random number between 0.25K and K. Y_u are randomly sampled from all available labels Y, and their state is set as unknown. The remaining labels are known and denoted as Y_k. These labels in the known state will be used as input to the model along with the image, and our model predicts labels in the unknown state. In the training process, some labels are randomly masked as unknown, and the model learn the combination association of different known status labels. After the label mask training is incorporated, Eq. (11) is modified as

$$L_{attribute} = \sum_{j=1}^{K} E\{CE(Y_u, \hat{Y}_u | Y_k)\}. \tag{12}$$

3.4 Triplet Network Training

We use the triplet network shown in Fig. 3 to train our model, aiming to learn effective embedding and similarity measurements to minimize the distance between anchor and positive samples and maximize the distance between anchor and negative ones.

The construction process of the input data in the triplet network is as follows. Given an image triplet $\{x^a, x^p, x^n\}$, x^a is the anchor image, x^p is the positive image, and x^n is the negative image. The positive example image has at least one attribute that is the same as the anchor image, while the negative example does not have any attribute the same as the anchor image. Let $\{Z^a, Z^p, Z^n\}$ be the attribute attended feature embedding triplet. The similarity is defined as cosine similarity.

$$sim(Z^a, Z^p) = \frac{Z^a \cdot Z^p}{\|Z^a\| + \|Z^p\|}, sim(Z^a, Z^n) = \frac{Z^a \cdot Z^n}{\|Z^a\| + \|Z^n\|}. \tag{13}$$

We force the similarity between the anchor and the positive samples to be greater than the similarity between the anchor and the negative samples, i.e., $sim(Z^a, Z^p) > sim(Z^a, Z^n)$. Then we define a triplet ranking loss function based on hinge loss as

$$L_{tri} = max\{0, sim(Z^a, Z^p) - sim(Z^a, Z^n) + m\}, \tag{14}$$

where m represents the margin between two similarities. The total loss is defined as

$$L_{total} = L_{category} + \lambda L_{attribute} + \gamma L_{tri}, \tag{15}$$

where λ and γ are parameters that balance the contribution of all losses.

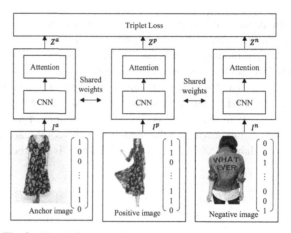

Fig. 3. The triplet network structure used to train our model.

4 Experiments

4.1 Experiments Settings

Datasets. We conduct our experiments on a public dataset Deepfashion [1], a large-scale clothes dataset. We choose its Category and Attribute Prediction benchmark (abbreviated as DeepFashion-C) that is more suitable for our tasks. DeepFashion-C contains 289,222 clothes images in 46 categories and five attribute categories with 1,000 attribute values. Each image is annotated with only one category and several attributes. We adopt the same train-valid-test division as [1].

Metrics. For image category classification, top-k accuracy is usually adopted as the evaluation metric. For image attribute prediction, the top-k recall rate used in [1] is traditionally used as the evaluation metric.

Implementation Details. The proposed model is implemented in the Pytorch framework with an NVIDIA GeForce GTX 1080Ti GPU. We use the ResNet 50 network pre-trained on ImageNet for feature extraction. The images are resized to 224×224. We use a 1×1 convolutional layer to reduce the dimension of the feature vector to 512. The multi-hot vector of the attributes is transformed to 512-dimensional vectors by an embedding layer followed by the tanh activation function. Then the image and attribute features are used to obtain spatial attention through the dot product operation. In the ACA module, we use a separated attribute embedding layer. We use SGD to train the triplet network, the total epoch is set to 20. The learning rate is 1e-5 and decays at the rate of 0.95 every epoch. We empirically set α to 1 and γ to 0.5 in Eq. (15).

Baselines. We conduct comparative tests with some baseline models. All models use the same triple sampling method for fine-tuning, but the training methods are different. WTBI [21] first trains a generalized similarity model, and then fine-tunes each type of clothing to obtain a class-independent model. DARN [8] constructs a tree structure for all attributes to form a semantic representation space of clothing images. FashionNet [1] extracts features and landmark location information from images, and combines them for training to predict image categories and attributes. Corbiere [9] uses weak label information and images crawled from the Internet to make dot products and predicts the probability of each word in the vocabulary. Attentive [3] uses a two-way convolutional recursive neural network to improve classification through landmark-aware attention and category-driven attention. Upsampling [22] increases the resolution of the feature map through up-sampling and uses the predicted landmark location as a reference to improve classification.

4.2 Experiment Results

We validate the performance of our model on the DeepFashion-C dataset, and Table 1 summarizes the performance of different methods in terms of top-k ($k = 3$, 5) recall rate for fashion classification and attribute prediction. Some clothing classification and attribute recognition results are show in Fig. 4. The following observations can be obtained.

Table 1. Performance comparison of different models on DeepFashion-C dataset

Models	Category		Texture		Fabric		Shape		Part		Style		All	
	Top-3	Top-5	Top-3	Top-5	Top-3	Top-5	Top-3	Top-5	Top-3	Top-5	Top-3	Top-5	Top-3	Top-5
WTBI	43.73	66.26	24.21	32.65	25.38	36.06	23.39	31.26	26.31	33.24	49.85	58.68	27.46	35.37
DARN	59.48	79.58	36.15	48.15	36.64	48.52	35.89	46.93	39.17	50.14	66.11	71.36	42.35	51.95
FashionNet	82.58	90.17	37.46	49.52	39.30	49.84	39.47	48.59	44.13	54.02	66.43	73.16	45.52	54.61
Corbiere	86.30	92.80	53.60	63.20	39.10	48.80	50.10	59.50	38.80	48.90	30.50	38.30	23.10	30.40
Attentive	90.99	95.78	50.31	65.48	40.31	48.23	53.32	61.05	40.65	56.32	68.70	**74.25**	51.53	60.95
Upsampling	91.16	96.12	56.17	65.83	**43.20**	53.52	58.28	67.80	46.97	57.43	**68.82**	74.13	54.69	63.74
Ours w/o ASA	91.89	96.13	55.61	65.17	40.12	54.73	59.70	68.98	49.17	59.19	64.48	71.82	52.64	62.37
Ours w/o ACA	90.12	95.15	54.73	64.82	39.45	53.27	58.21	66.72	47.87	57.53	60.54	68.61	50.47	60.07
Ours	**92.33**	**96.65**	**56.89**	**66.31**	40.42	**55.83**	**60.42**	**69.87**	**49.62**	**61.17**	65.38	72.79	**54.85**	**64.76**

- Our model outperforms all competitors in the category classification task and the attribute prediction task. For the former, our model improves the top-3 accuracy rate by 1.3%. For the latter, our model also improves the recall rate.
- We evaluate our model using only one attention module and get two variants: M2Fashion w/o ASA and M2Fashion w/o ACA. The former employs global max pooling instead of an attribute-aware spatial attention model to generate features. The latter utilizes vector V_s as the attribute-guide feature vector directly. We can see that removing the ASA or ACA module reduces the performance of the two subtasks, showing the effectiveness of both ASA and ACA modules.
- The classification task has a more significant impact on the *part*-related attribute prediction (+5.6% of top-3 recall rate) and the *shape*-related attribute prediction (+3.7%

Fig. 4. Results of clothing category classification and attribute prediction on DeepFashion-C dataset. The correct predictions are marked in green, and the wrong predictions are marked in red.

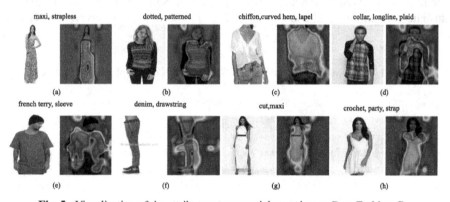

Fig. 5. Visualization of the attribute-aware spatial attention on DeepFashion-C.

top-3 recall rate) than the *texture*-related attribute prediction (+1.3% top-3 recall rate). It does not perform well on the *style*-related attribute prediction and the *fabric*-related attributes prediction because it is hard to focus the attention on these two attributes on the images. The classification of clothing is more dependent on the shape characteristics of clothing, and clothing classification can also promote the understanding of *shape*-related attributes.

4.3 Attention Visualization

Visualization of our attention mechanisms can be found in Fig. 5. We observe that the learned attention gives a higher response in the attribute-related areas, which shows that the attention helps find out which areas are relative to the given attribute. According to our observations, the attributes related to '*part*', such as '*maxi*' in Fig. 5(a) and '*sleeve*' in Fig. 5(e), are more likely to highlight local visual features. The attention map of attributes related to '*material*' or '*style*' focuses on the entire clothing.

4.4 Impact of Joint Learning and the Pooling Methods

The Impact of Joint Learning. We explore the correlation between category classification and attribute prediction. As shown in Table 2 (top), the results show that the joint learning of categories and attributes improves the accuracy of the two tasks. We found that after adopting the multi-task learning framework, in the classification task, the top-3 accuracy is increased by 4.1%, and the top-5 accuracy is increased by 3.0%; in the attribute prediction task, the top-3 recall rate is increased by 11.7%, and the top-5 recall rate is increased by 12.2%.

The Impact of Global Max Pooling. We use global max pooling instead of global average pooling to capture global context information. Global max pooling is sensitive to discriminative local features. The function of global maximum pooling is verified by ablation experiments. The results are shown in Table 2 (bottom). Global max pooling improves the recall rate of category classification and attribute prediction.

Table 2. Performance comparison of different learning methods and pooling methods.

Methods	Category		All	
	Top-3	Top-5	Top-3	Top-5
Category only	88.64	93.84	–	–
Attribute only	–	–	48.65	57.74
Category + attribute	**92.23**	**96.65**	**54.35**	**64.76**
GAP	91.72	95.84	53.63	62.84
GMP	**92.23**	**96.65**	**54.35**	**64.76**

Table 3. Performance comparison of attribute-specific fashion retrieval on DARN using MAP

Models	Category	Clothes button	Clothes color	Clothes length	Clothes pattern	Clothes shape	Collar shape	Sleeve length	Sleeve shape	All
Triplet	23.59	38.07	16.83	39.77	49.56	47.00	23.43	68.49	56.48	40.14
CSN	34.10	44.32	48.38	53.68	54.09	56.32	31.82	78.05	58.76	50.86
ASEN	36.69	46.96	**51.35**	56.47	54.49	60.02	34.18	80.11	60.04	53.31
Ours	**36.91**	**48.03**	51.14	**57.51**	**56.09**	**60.77**	**35.05**	**81.13**	**62.23**	**54.29**

4.5 A Case: Attribute-Specific Image Retrieval

The learned model can be applied to attribute-specific image retrieval tasks by removing the final classifier. For instance, given a query with an image and two labels *v-neckline* and *floral*, the model returns top-k similar images with these two labels.

We conduct the experiment on DARN [8] dataset, which contains about 253983 upper-clothing images and has a total of 9 attributes and 179 attribute values. We randomly divided the dataset into 8:1:1 for training, validation and test. Similar to [16], we use the metric of mean average precision (MAP) for evaluation. Following baselines are considered for comparison: Triplet Network, Conditional Similarity Network (CSN) [23], and Attribute specific embedding network (ASEN) [16].

Table 3 shows the results of attribute-specific image retrieval tasks on the DARN dataset. We can see that (1) the triplet network that learns the universal embedding space performs the worst; (2) our proposed M2Fashion outperforms other baselines. We attribute the better performance to the fact that M2Fashion uses multiple attribute labels and label masks to learn the association between labels and the attention of labels with images. In contrast, ASEN uses a single attribute category to guide attention.

5   Conclusions

In this paper, we explore fine-grained fashion image embedding to capture multi-modal content for fashion categorization. The proposed model adopts the visual-text attention mechanism to capture the association between different modal data and effectively uses any number of partial labels to perform multi-label and multi-class classification tasks. It also helps to discover how different attributes focus on specific areas of an image. In the future, we will study the impact of the hierarchical structure of attributes on the model and extend the model to hierarchical attribute prediction.

References

1. Liu, Z., Luo, P., Qiu, S., Wang, X., Tang, X.: DeepFashion: powering robust clothes recognition and retrieval with rich annotations. In: CVPR, pp. 1096–1104 (2016)
2. Dong, Q., Gong, S., Zhu, X.: Multi-task curriculum transfer deep learning of clothing attributes. In: WACV, pp. 520–529 (2017)
3. Wang, W., Xu, Y., Shen, J., Zhu, S.C.: Attentive fashion grammar network for fashion landmark detection and clothing category classification. In: CVPR, pp. 4271–4280 (2018)
4. Han, X., Wu, Z., Jiang, Y.G., Davis, L.S.: Learning fashion compatibility with bidirectional LSTMs. In: MM, pp. 1078–1086 (2017)
5. Hou, M., Wu, L., Chen, E., Li, Z., Zheng, V.W., Liu, Q.: Explainable fashion recommendation: a semantic attribute region guided approach. In: IJCAI, pp. 4681–4688 (2019)
6. Zhang, S., Song, Z., Cao, X., Zhang, H., Zhou, J.: Task-aware attention model for clothing attribute prediction. IEEE Trans. Circ. Syst. Video Technol. (TCSVT) **30**(4), 1051–1064 (2020)
7. Chen, M., Qin, Y., Qi, L., Sun, Y.: Improving fashion landmark detection by dual attention feature enhancement. In: ICCV Workshop, pp. 3101–3104 (2019)
8. Huang, J., Feris, R., Chen, Q., Yan, S.: Cross-domain image retrieval with a dual attribute-aware ranking network. In: ICCV, pp. 1062–1070 (2015)
9. Corbiere, C., Ben-Younes, H., Rame, A., Ollion, C.: Leveraging weakly annotated data for fashion image retrieval and label prediction. In: ICCV Workshop, pp. 2268–2274 (2017)
10. Chen, Q., Huang, J., Feris, R., Brown, L.M., Dong, J., Yan, S.: Deep domain adaptation for describing people based on fine-grained clothing attributes. In: CVPR, pp. 5315–5324 (2015)

11. Liao, L., He, X., Zhao, B., Ngo, C.W., Chua, T.S.: Interpretable multimodal retrieval for fashion products. In: MM, pp. 1571–1579 (2018)
12. Han, X., Wu, Z., Huang, P.X., Zhang, X., Zhu, M., Li, Y.: Automatic spatially-aware fashion concept discovery. In: ICCV, pp. 1463–1471 (2017)
13. Ferreira, B.Q., Costeira, J.P., Sousa, R.G., Gui, L.Y., Gomes, J.P.: Pose guided attention for multi-label fashion image classification. In: ICCV Workshop, pp. 3125–3128 (2019)
14. Ji, X., Wang, W., Zhang, M., Yang, Y.: Cross-domain image retrieval with attention modeling. In: MM, pp. 1654–1662 (2017)
15. Li, X., Ye, Z., Zhang, Z., Zhao, M.: Clothes image caption generation with attribute detection and visual attention model. Pattern Recogn. Lett. **141**, 68–74 (2021)
16. Ma, Z., Dong, J., Long, Z., Zhang, Y., He, Y., Xue, H.: Fine-grained fashion similarity learning by attribute-specific embedding network. In: AAAI, pp. 11741–11748 (2020)
17. Li, P., Li, Y., Jiang, X., Zhen, X.: Two-stream multi-task network for fashion recognition. In: ICIP, pp. 3038–3042 (2019)
18. Min, W., Jiang, S., Sang, J.: Being a supercook: joint food attributes and multimodal content modeling for recipe retrieval and exploration. IEEE Trans. Multimedia **19**(5), 1100–1113 (2017)
19. Lu, J., Goswami, V., Rohrbach, M., Parikh, D., Lee, S.: 12-in-1: Multi-task vision and language representation learning. In: CVPR, pp. 10437–10446 (2020)
20. Lanchantin, J., Wang, T., Ordonez, V., Qi, Y.: General multi-label image classification with transformers. In: CVPR, pp. 16478–16488 (2021)
21. Kiapour, M.H., Han, X., Lazebnik, S., Berg, A.C., Berg, T.L.: Where to buy it: matching street clothing photos in online shops. In: ICCV, pp. 3343–3351 (2015)
22. Liu, J., Lu, H.: Deep fashion analysis with feature map upsampling and landmark-driven attention. In: Leal-Taixé, L., Roth, S. (eds.) ECCV 2018. LNCS, vol. 11131, pp. 30–36. Springer, Cham (2019). https://doi.org/10.1007/978-3-030-11015-4_4
23. Veit, A., Belongie, S., Karaletsos, T.: Conditional similarity networks. In: CVPR (2017)

Toward Detail-Oriented Image-Based Virtual Try-On with Arbitrary Poses

Yuan Chang, Tao Peng$^{(\boxtimes)}$, Ruhan He, Xinrong Hu, Junping Liu, Zili Zhang, and Minghua Jiang

Engineering Research Center of Hubei Province for Clothing Information, Wuhan Textile University, Wuhan 430200, China
pt@wtu.edu.cn

Abstract. Image-based virtual try-on with arbitrary poses has attracted many attentions recently. The purpose of this study is to synthesize a reference person image wearing a target clothes with a target pose. However, it is still a challenge for the existing methods to preserve the clothing details and person identity while generating fine-grained try-on images. To resolve the issues, we present a new detail-oriented virtual try-on network with arbitrary poses (DO-VTON). Specifically, our DO-VTON consists of three major modules: First, a semantic prediction module adopts a two-stage strategy to gradually predict a semantic map of the reference person. Second, a spatial alignment module warps the target clothes and non-target details to align with the target pose. Third, a try-on synthesis module generates final try-on images. Moreover, to generate high-quality images, we introduce a new multi-scale dilated convolution U-Net to enlarge the receptive field and capture context information. Extensive experiments on two famous benchmark datasets demonstrate our system achieves the state-of-the-art virtual try-on performance both qualitatively and quantitatively.

Keywords: Virtual Try-On · Arbitrary poses · Spatial alignment · Dilated convolution

1 Introduction

Online apparel shopping has grown significantly and has become a regular part of our life. However, there exist significant differences between consumers and models that would lead to a poor user experience. Therefore, it is important for online apparel shopping to create an interactive shopping environment close to reality. The traditional pipeline [1,4,9,22] is to model humans and items as 3D objects and render them with computer graphics. However, the high computational costs and necessary annotated data for building 3D models make these methods expensive to build and maintain. In contrast, the image-based virtual try-on method without any 3D information to generate the try-on image. Thus, some fixed-pose visual try-on methods [3,6,10,17,28,34,35] were proposed and showed promising results. However, customers may want to try on new clothing with arbitrary poses for determining whether it looks good on them.

© Springer Nature Switzerland AG 2022
B. Þór Jónsson et al. (Eds.): MMM 2022, LNCS 13141, pp. 82–94, 2022.
https://doi.org/10.1007/978-3-030-98358-1_7

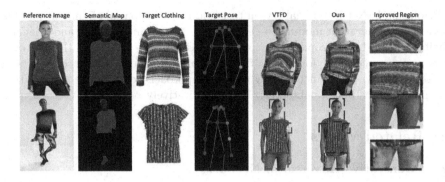

Fig. 1. Comparing our method with the state-of-the-art method [29].

Recently, to solve the problem of single view, some virtual try-on with arbitrary poses methods [5,13,14,29,36] were proposed. These methods have achieved promising results, but there are still some shortcomings in detail preservation and visual performance. The possible causes of these shortcomings are as follows: First, it is difficult to complete the semantic prediction of pose and clothes at one time. Second, overlooking warping non-target details and feeding non-target region image of the original reference person into the try-on generation stage, usually resulting in the loss of person identity. Finally, a simple U-Net [24] or ResNet [11] is not enough to synthesize fine-grained images. As shown in Fig. 1, the state-of-the-art method is insufficient to generate fine-grained images while preserving clothing details and person identity.

To address the above issues, we propose a detail-oriented virtual try-on network with arbitrary poses (DO-VTON). Specifically, the DO-VTON consists of three major modules. The first module is semantic prediction module (SPM), which is introduced to predict a semantic map by separating pose prediction and clothing prediction. The two-stage strategy makes the module more focused on a single task, so as to more accurately predict the semantic map after try-on. The second module is spatial alignment module (SAM), which is used to warp the target clothes and non-target details to align the target pose. As opposed to prior arts, we divide the module into two regions, and propose a unique non-target region alignment to preserve the non-target details and improve the overall visual performance. The third module is try-on synthesis module (TSM), which synthesizes final try-on images based on the outputs from the first two modules. In particular, the dilated convolution with different dilation rates is introduced to expand the receptive field and capture multi-scale features. We connect multiple dilated convolutions to form a multi-scale dilated convolution U-Net structure and use it in SAM and TSM to generate fine-grained images.

The main contributions can be summarized as follows. First, we adopt a two-stage semantic prediction strategy to gradually predict the semantic map of the reference person wearing the target clothes with the target pose, and divide spatial alignment into clothing alignment and non-target region alignment to preserve details in both regions. Second, we design a new multi-scale dilated convolution U-Net for virtual try-on task and use it in spatial alignment module and fusion generation module to generate the fine-grained details and alleviate artifacts. Third, we propose the complete DO-VTON, which greatly improves the performance of try-on image in detail preservation of target clothes and person identity. Experiments show that our approach achieves the state-of-the-art performance both qualitatively and quantitatively.

2 Related Works

2.1 Generative Adversarial Networks

One of the main architectures for deep image generation is Generative Adversarial Networks (GANs) [8], which can generate convincing images and show impressive results in various domains. Jetchev et al. [15] proposed a CAGAN based on CycleGAN [37] to solving image analogy problems, which is automatic swapping of clothes on fashion model photos. CAGAN is an early attempt to use the GAN method for virtual try-on, but it only uses the GAN method and overlooks warping the clothes according to the body shape lead to unsatisfactory try-on performance. Inspired by the success of GANs in various image generation tasks, we also use GAN loss [20,31] during the training phase.

2.2 Person Image Generation

Person image generation has recently attracted attention in media production and virtual reality. Ma et al. [19] proposed a pose-guided two-stage network that utilizes a coarse-to-fine strategy to first generate a coarse result that captures the global structure of a person and then refine the result in an adversarial way. Siarohin et al. [25] introduced deformable skip connections that can utilize a number of local affine transformations to decompose the overall deformation and alleviate pixel-to-pixel misalignment problem between different poses. Song et al. [27] proposed a decomposition strategy that first generates a semantic parsing transformation map and then synthesizes semantic-aware textures. Due to the above methods is insufficient to control the generation and preservation of clothes, they cannot directly be applied to the virtual try-on task.

2.3 Virtual Try-On

Virtual try-on methods can be classified as 3D model based approaches and 2D image based ones. Due to 3D methods [1,4,9,22] require additional annotated data and more computing power, 2D methods are more broadly applicable. The 2D methods can be further categorized based on whether to use paired datasets (clothes and a person wearing this clothes) or not. Unpaired methods [18,21,23] are suitable for solid color clothes, but they are difficult to generate exactly the same pattern or texture as clothes. Thus, we use paired datasets to complete virtual try-on. Early, some fixed-pose virtual try-on methods [3,6,10,28,34,35]

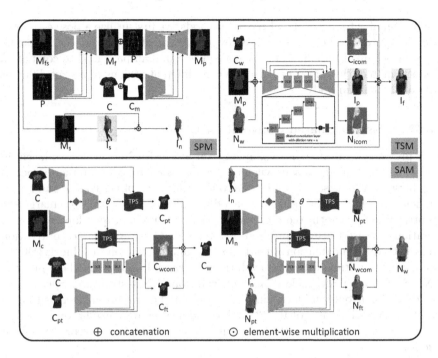

Fig. 2. The network architecture of the proposed DO-VTON.

were proposed and achieved some success, but they can only present a single try-on viewpoint. Recently, some new virtual try-on methods [5,13,14,29,36] that can simultaneously change the clothing item and person pose have been proposed. Dong et al. [5] proposed a Warp-GAN that warps target clothes into a synthesized human parsing map and alleviates blurry issues caused by the misalignment among different poses. Wang et al. [29] proposes a similar pipeline to fixed-pose methods, which first predicts semantics and warps target clothes, then synthesizes try-on images, and finally refines facial details. For the convenience of description, we call [29] VTFD for short. Due to the fact that VFTD completes semantic prediction of clothes and pose at one time, it can not obtain accurate semantic layout. Meanwhile, it directly uses the non-target details extracted from the original reference person as input, which only preserves the color of bottom clothes. In addition, the pipeline in which VTFD performs semantic prediction and spatial alignment at the same time also leads to many artifacts in try-on results, so there is still a gap between it and realistic virtual try-on.

3 DO-VTON

The network structure is shown in the Fig. 2. Our work aims at generating try-on images of a reference person wearing a target clothes with a target pose. The MG-VTON [5] and VTFD [29] are most relevant to the problem we are trying to solve. Similar to most virtual try-on methods, we first utilize a pose estimator [2] to compute the coordinates of 18 keypoints, and then convert the keypoints into an 18-channel pose heatmap. We also use a human parser [7] to compute a semantic map of the reference person, where different regions represent different parts of the human body.

3.1 Multi-scale Dilated Convolution U-Net

Many previous works only use a simple U-Net [24] or ResNet [11] is insufficient in generating fine-grained images when target pose is complex or interaction occlusions between the torso and limbs due to the limitation of kernel size and receptive field. To address this issue, we introduce dilated convolution to enlarge the receptive field and capture context information, and use multiple skip-connection operations to fuse features. Inspired by [30,33], we first use dilated convolution layers with different dilation rates to form a dilated convolution block (DCB), then connect multiple dilated convolution blocks and finally add them into the U-Net to form a multi-scale dilated convolution U-Net structure. Specifically, each dilated convolution block contains four dilated convolution layers with $3 * 3$ kernels and dilation rates of 1, 2, 3, and 4, and a standard convolution is used to adjust the number of channels. The four dilated convolution layers are defined as follows:

$$x_n = f_n(x_{n-1}), \qquad y_n = c(y_{n-1}(x), x_n) \tag{1}$$

where $x_0 = x$, x is the input of the dilated convolution block, x_n is the output of the dilated convolution layer with dilation rate $= $ n, f_n denotes operators implemented in step n, c represents the concatenation operator, and y_n is the result of concatenation with n steps. Finally, the three dilated convolution blocks are connected and positioned at the bottom of the U-Net. We use these connected dilated convolution blocks to fuse multi-scale features and deal with large spatial transformation problem in virtual try-on tasks.

3.2 Semantic Prediction Module

The semantic prediction module (SPM) is proposed to predict a semantic layout of reference person after changing pose and clothes. Many previous methods complete the semantic prediction of pose and clothes at one time, leading to cannot handle huge spatial misalignment between person and clothes. To address this issue, our SPM utilizes a two-stage strategy to predict the final semantic map by separating pose prediction and clothing prediction.

Specifically, the reference image is preprocessed to get a source semantic map M_s, and then the clothing and arm regions of M_s are fused into an indistinguishable region to get a fused source semantic map M_{fs}. In stage I, we take M_{fs} and target pose P as inputs to predict a preliminary fused semantic map M_f of the reference person with P. The M_f only changes the pose without wearing target clothes C. In stage II, we predict a final semantic map M_p of the reference person wearing C with P by using M_f, P, C and target clothing mask C_m.

At training phase, we adopt a standard cross-entropy loss in both stages. The ground-truth of each stage is obtained by semantic map of reference person with target pose. The model generalization ability is favorable since the final M_p is based on the fused M_{fs} without any information of original clothes. In addition, two masks are extracted from M_p as inputs of the spatial alignment module. One is the predicted clothing mask M_c, and the other is the predicted non-target mask M_n.

3.3 Spatial Alignment Module

The spatial alignment module (SAM) is proposed to warp target clothes and non-target details for fitting target pose. One of the challenges is huge spatial misalignment in virtual try-on with arbitrary poses. Most of the existing methods take non-target details extracted from original reference person as input to synthetize images, leading to only retain the color of bottom clothes. Thus, our SAM is divided into target clothing alignment and non-target region alignment. Inspired by [3], we use an improved warping strategy to take the place of traditional methods [28]. Meanwhile, we add the multi-scale dilated convolution U-Net into the feature transformation for better characteristic and alignment.

In the target clothing alignment, we first use a pixel transformation similar to geometric matching module in [28], including two feature extraction layers, a correlation layer, a regression network, and a thin-plate spline transformation module. Specifically, we take target clothes C and M_c extracted from M_p as inputs to obtain a spatial transformation parameter θ and a warped clothes based on pixel transformation C_{pt}. Then, the structure of feature transformation is divided into two branches. The upper branch uses a encoder to extract features from C, then uses θ obtained by pixel transformation to warp these features. The lower branch uses another encoder to extract features from C_{pt}, then connects these features with warped features from the upper branch, and feeds them to the corresponding layer of a decoder. The output of upper encoder is fed to the decoder through three connected dilated convolution blocks. The decoder outputs a warped clothes based on feature transformation C_{ft} and predicts a clothing composition mask C_{wcom}. The final warped clothes C_w is obtained by fusing C_{pt} and C_{ft}, guided by C_{wcom} as follows:

$$C_w = (1 - C_{wcom}) \odot C_{ft} + C_{wcom} \odot C_{pt} \qquad (2)$$

where $\odot$ represents element-wise multiplication.

At training phase of pixel transformation, we first adopt a strategy of combining $L1$ loss, VGG perceptual loss, and GAN loss. We use a discriminator structure given in pix2pixHD [31] with spectral normalization [20]. The $L1$ loss, VGG perceptual loss, and GAN loss are defined as follows:

$$L_{l1}(C_{pt}, C_t) = \|C_{pt} - C_t\|_1 \qquad (3)$$

$$L_{VGG}(C_{pt}, C_t) = \sum_{i=1}^{5} \lambda_i \|\phi_i(C_{pt}) - \phi_i(C_t)\|_1 \qquad (4)$$

$$L_{GAN} = E_{x,y}\left[log(D(x,y))\right] + E_{x,z}\left[log(1 - D(x,G(x,z)))\right] \tag{5}$$

where C_t is the clothes worn on the target person. We use the pre-trained $VGG19$ [26] as ϕ_i and weighted sum the $L1$ norms of last five layer feature maps in ϕ to represent perceptual losses between inputs. In GAN loss, x is input, y is the ground-truth C_t, and z is the noise which is an additional channel of input sampled from the standard normal distribution. Moreover, a transformation constraint loss L_{tc} [17] is also used to avoid shape distortion and texture confusion of clothes after pixel transformation. It is defined as follows:

$$
\begin{aligned}
L_{tc}(G_x, G_y) = \sum_x^{H_G} \sum_y^{W_G} (&\|G_x(x, y-1) - G_x(x,y)\| \\
&- |G_x(x, y+1) - G_x(x,y)\| + \|G_y(x-1, y) \\
&- G_y(x,y)| - |G_y(x+1,y) - G_y(x,y)\|)
\end{aligned}
\tag{6}
$$

where $G_x(x,y)$, $G_y(x,y)$, H_G, and W_G are the x and y coordinates of the grid to be mapped and height and width of the grid, respectively. The pixel transformation loss L_{pt} is a weighted sum of the four losses described above:

$$L_{pt} = \lambda_{l1} L_{l1} + \lambda_{VGG} L_{VGG} + \lambda_{GAN} L_{GAN} + \lambda_{tc} L_{tc} \tag{7}$$

The training of feature transformation is similar to the above process. We also use $L1$ loss, VGG perceptual loss, and GAN loss.

In the non-target region alignment, we take a non-target region image I_n and M_n as inputs, where I_n is the non-target region of source person. The non-target region alignment uses the same loss function to train the same network structure and generates a warped non-target region image based on pixel transformation N_{pt}, a warped non-target region image based on feature transformation N_{ft}, and a non-target composition mask N_{icom}. Finally, the final warped non-target region image N_w is obtained by fusing N_{pt} and N_{ft}, guided by N_{icom} as follows:

$$N_w = (1 - N_{wcom}) \odot N_{ft} + N_{wcom} \odot N_{pt} \tag{8}$$

where $\odot$ represents element-wise multiplication. The ground-truth is non-target region image of target person, which is extracted from the image of reference person wearing target clothes with target pose.

3.4   Try-On Synthesis Module

To synthesize fine-grained try-on images, we use the proposed multi-scale dilated convolution U-Net structure as generator to take the place of traditional U-Net [24] or ResNet [11] in the try-on synthesis module (TSM). Specifically, our TSM first takes M_p, C_w, and N_w as input to output a preliminary try-on image I_p, a clothing composition mask C_{icom}, and a non-target composition mask N_{icom}. Then, I_p, C_w, and N^w are fused together using C_{icom} and N_{icom} to synthesize a final try-on image I_f:

$$I_f = (1 - C_{icom}) \odot (1 - N_{icom}) \odot I_p + C_{icom} \odot C_w + N_{icom} \odot N_w \qquad (9)$$

where $\odot$ represents element-wise multiplication.

As training phase, we also apply $L1$ loss, VGG perceptual loss, and GAN loss to synthesize realistic try-on images.

4   Experiments

4.1   Datasets and Experimental Setup

We conduct experiments on MPV datasets [5] and VITON datasets [28], respectively. For a fair comparison, we use the same part of the MPV datasets as the state-of-the-art method VTFD [29], consisting of 14,754 three-tuples of the same person in the same clothes but with different poses. All images are resized to 256×192 resolution. The training set and testing set are 12,410 and 2,344 pairs respectively. Each network is trained for 200K steps by setting the weights of losses $\lambda_{l1} = \lambda_{GAN} = 1$, $\lambda_{VGG} = 10$, and batch-size 4. When transform constraint loss is used, we set the $\lambda_{tc} = 1$. The network is optimized by Adam optimizer [16] with $\beta_1 = 0.5$, $\beta_2 = 0.999$, a learning rate of 0.0002.

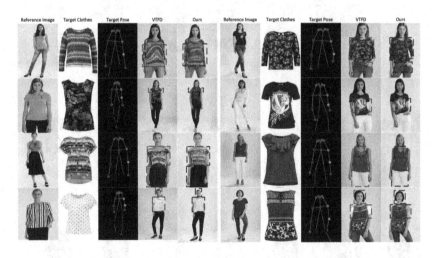

Fig. 3. Visual comparison on MPV datasets. Compared with the state-of-the-art virtual method (VTFD [29]), our method performs much better on warping target clothes, preserving non-target details, and generating fine-grained try-on images.

In addition, due to the lack of source code and dataset, many arbitrary-pose methods cannot be compared, such as MG-VTON [5]. In order to be more convincing, we conduct experiments on VITON dataset [28] and compare with the state-of-the-art methods (CP-VTON [28], ACGPN [34], DP-VTON [3], and PF-AFN [6]). The whole dataset contains 16,253 pairs, which are split into a training set of 14,221 and a testing set of 2,032 pairs. In the experiment, we remove the first stage of the two-stage semantic prediction module and the non-target region alignment of the spatial alignment module, and the other experimental details are the same as those constructed on MPV datasets.

4.2   Qualitative Results

Results of MPV are shown in Fig. 3. In the first row, the shape and texture are over-stretched in the results of the competing method. In the second row, the warped clothes are not aligned with the reference person. In the third row, the neckline of the clothes are not accurately generated and the bottom clothes are not well maintained. In the fouth row, the hair generated by the competing method is different from the reference person and many visual artifacts are generated. In contrast, our method obtains warped clothes with realistic texture and robust alignment, preserves non-target details such as bottom clothes and hair, and generates fine-grained try-on images.

Fig. 4. Visual comparison on VITON datasets. Compared with the recent fixed-pose methods (CP-VTON [28], ACGPN [34], DP-VTON [3], and PF-AFN [6]), our method generates fine-grained try-on images while preserving person's and cloth's attributes.

Results of VITON are shown in Fig. 4. In this visual comparison, we can see that our method generates fine-grained try-on images while preserving person's

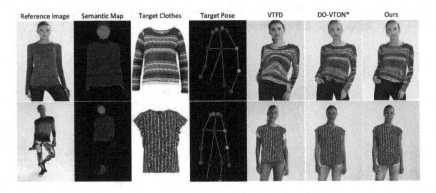

Fig. 5. Ablation study on the effect of multi-scale dilated convolution U-Net.

and cloth's attributes. It is worth noting that our method is not specifically for fixed-pose virtual try-on task, but it still achieves the state-of-the-art virtual try-on performance.

In addition, ablation study is conducted to evaluate the effectiveness of the prosposed multi-scale dilated convolution U-Net. DO-VTON* indicates DO-VTON use U-Net instead of the multi-scale dilated convolution U-Net. As shown in Fig. 5, benefited from the designed multi-scale dilated convolution U-Net, the full DO-VTON is able to alleviate artifacts and generate fine-grained try-on images. Moreover, these observations are corroborated by the quantitative results (Table 1).

4.3 Quantitative Results

The goal of virtual try-on with arbitrary poses is to generate high-quality images of a person wearing target clothes with target pose. Thus, we apply Structural SIMilarity (SSIM) [32] and (ii) Fréchet Inception Distance (FID) [12] to evaluate the performance of our method. SSIM is utilized to measure the similarity of the generated try-on image and ground-truth. A higher SSIM means more similarity. FID computes the Fréchet distance between the distribution of the real and generated dataset in the feature space. A lower FID means higher image quality and diversity. Table 1 lists SSIM and FID scores on MPV datasets by MG-VTON [5], VTFD [29], and our DO-VTON. The quantitative metrics demonstrate the superiority of our method over other methods.

Table 1. The SSIM and FID results of four methods on MPV datasets. DO-VTON* is DO-VTON variant for ablation study.

Method	SSIM↑	FID↓
MG-VTON	0.705	22.418
VTFD	0.723	16.006
DO-VTON*	0.732	14.938
DO-VTON	**0.739**	**14.699**

5 Conclusion

In this work, we propose a new DO-VTON which generates fine-grained try-on images while preserving person's and cloth's attributes. Specifically, we first utilize a two-stage strategy to predict semantic map, followed by warping target clothes and non-target details, and finally synthesize try-on images. Meanwhile, the multi-scale dilated convolution U-Net is used in our modules. Qualitative and quantitative results demonstrate that our method achieves the state-of-the-art performance.

Acknowledgement. This work is supported in part by the Science Foundation of Hubei under Grant No. 2014CFB764 and Department of Education of the Hubei Province of China under Grant No. Q20131608, and Engineering Research Center of Hubei Province for Clothing Information.

References

1. Brouet, R., Sheffer, A., Boissieux, L., Cani, M.P.: Design preserving garment transfer. ACM Trans. Graph. **31**(4), Article-No (2012)
2. Cao, Z., Simon, T., Wei, S.E., Sheikh, Y.: Realtime multi-person 2D pose estimation using part affinity fields. In: Proceedings of the IEEE Conference on Computer Vision and Pattern Recognition, pp. 7291–7299 (2017)
3. Chang, Y., et al.: Dp-vton: toward detail-preserving image-based virtual try-on network. In: ICASSP 2021–2021 IEEE International Conference on Acoustics, Speech and Signal Processing (ICASSP), pp. 2295–2299. IEEE (2021)
4. Chen, W., et al.: Synthesizing training images for boosting human 3D pose estimation. In: 2016 Fourth International Conference on 3D Vision (3DV), pp. 479–488. IEEE (2016)
5. Dong, H., et al.: Towards multi-pose guided virtual try-on network. In: Proceedings of the IEEE/CVF International Conference on Computer Vision, pp. 9026–9035 (2019)
6. Ge, Y., Song, Y., Zhang, R., Ge, C., Liu, W., Luo, P.: Parser-free virtual try-on via distilling appearance flows. In: Proceedings of the IEEE/CVF Conference on Computer Vision and Pattern Recognition, pp. 8485–8493 (2021)
7. Gong, K., Liang, X., Zhang, D., Shen, X., Lin, L.: Look into person: self-supervised structure-sensitive learning and a new benchmark for human parsing. In: Proceedings of the IEEE Conference on Computer Vision and Pattern Recognition, pp. 932–940 (2017)

8. Goodfellow, I., et al.: Generative adversarial nets. In: Advances in Neural Information Processing Systems, pp. 2672–2680 (2014)

9. Guan, P., Reiss, L., Hirshberg, D.A., Weiss, A., Black, M.J.: Drape: dressing any person. ACM Trans. Graph. (TOG) **31**(4), 1–10 (2012)

10. Han, X., Wu, Z., Wu, Z., Yu, R., Davis, L.S.: Viton: an image-based virtual try-on network. In: Proceedings of the IEEE Conference on Computer Vision and Pattern Recognition, pp. 7543–7552 (2018)

11. He, K., Zhang, X., Ren, S., Sun, J.: Deep residual learning for image recognition. In: Proceedings of the IEEE Conference on Computer Vision and Pattern Recognition, pp. 770–778 (2016)

12. Heusel, M., Ramsauer, H., Unterthiner, T., Nessler, B., Hochreiter, S.: Gans trained by a two time-scale update rule converge to a local nash equilibrium. In: Advances in Neural Information Processing Systems, pp. 6626–6637 (2017)

13. Hsieh, C.W., Chen, C.Y., Chou, C.L., Shuai, H.H., Cheng, W.H.: Fit-me: image-based virtual try-on with arbitrary poses. In: 2019 IEEE International Conference on Image Processing (ICIP), pp. 4694–4698. IEEE (2019)

14. Hsieh, C.W., Chen, C.Y., Chou, C.L., Shuai, H.H., Liu, J., Cheng, W.H.: Fashion-on: semantic-guided image-based virtual try-on with detailed human and clothing information. In: Proceedings of the 27th ACM International Conference on Multimedia, pp. 275–283 (2019)

15. Jetchev, N., Bergmann, U.: The conditional analogy gan: swapping fashion articles on people images. In: Proceedings of the IEEE International Conference on Computer Vision Workshops, pp. 2287–2292 (2017)

16. Kingma, D.P., Ba, J.: Adam: a method for stochastic optimization. arXiv preprint arXiv:1412.6980 (2014)

17. Lee, H.J., Lee, R., Kang, M., Cho, M., Park, G.: La-viton: a network for looking-attractive virtual try-on. In: 2019 IEEE/CVF International Conference on Computer Vision Workshop (ICCVW), pp. 3129–3132. IEEE (2019)

18. Lewis, K.M., Varadharajan, S., Kemelmacher-Shlizerman, I.: Vogue: try-on by stylegan interpolation optimization. arXiv preprint arXiv:2101.02285 (2021)

19. Ma, L., Jia, X., Sun, Q., Schiele, B., Tuytelaars, T., Van Gool, L.: Pose guided person image generation. arXiv preprint arXiv:1705.09368 (2017)

20. Miyato, T., Kataoka, T., Koyama, M., Yoshida, Y.: Spectral normalization for generative adversarial networks. arXiv preprint arXiv:1802.05957 (2018)

21. Neuberger, A., Borenstein, E., Hilleli, B., Oks, E., Alpert, S.: Image based virtual try-on network from unpaired data. In: Proceedings of the IEEE/CVF Conference on Computer Vision and Pattern Recognition, pp. 5184–5193 (2020)

22. Pons-Moll, G., Pujades, S., Hu, S., Black, M.J.: Clothcap: seamless 4D clothing capture and retargeting. ACM Trans. Graph. (TOG) **36**(4), 1–15 (2017)

23. Raj, A., Sangkloy, P., Chang, H., Hays, J., Ceylan, D., Lu, J.: SwapNet: image based garment transfer. In: Ferrari, V., Hebert, M., Sminchisescu, C., Weiss, Y. (eds.) ECCV 2018. LNCS, vol. 11216, pp. 679–695. Springer, Cham (2018). https://doi.org/10.1007/978-3-030-01258-8_41

24. Ronneberger, O., Fischer, P., Brox, T.: U-Net: convolutional networks for biomedical image segmentation. In: Navab, N., Hornegger, J., Wells, W.M., Frangi, A.F. (eds.) MICCAI 2015. LNCS, vol. 9351, pp. 234–241. Springer, Cham (2015). https://doi.org/10.1007/978-3-319-24574-4_28

25. Siarohin, A., Sangineto, E., Lathuiliere, S., Sebe, N.: Deformable gans for pose-based human image generation. In: Proceedings of the IEEE Conference on Computer Vision and Pattern Recognition, pp. 3408–3416 (2018)

26. Simonyan, K., Zisserman, A.: Very deep convolutional networks for large-scale image recognition. arXiv preprint arXiv:1409.1556 (2014)
27. Song, S., Zhang, W., Liu, J., Mei, T.: Unsupervised person image generation with semantic parsing transformation. In: Proceedings of the IEEE/CVF Conference on Computer Vision and Pattern Recognition, pp. 2357–2366 (2019)
28. Wang, B., Zheng, H., Liang, X., Chen, Y., Lin, L., Yang, M.: Toward characteristic-preserving image-based virtual try-on network. In: Proceedings of the European Conference on Computer Vision (ECCV), pp. 589–604 (2018)
29. Wang, J., Sha, T., Zhang, W., Li, Z., Mei, T.: Down to the last detail: virtual try-on with fine-grained details. In: Proceedings of the 28th ACM International Conference on Multimedia, pp. 466–474 (2020)
30. Wang, P., et al.: Understanding convolution for semantic segmentation. In: 2018 IEEE Winter Conference on Applications of Computer Vision (WACV), pp. 1451–1460. IEEE (2018)
31. Wang, T.C., Liu, M.Y., Zhu, J.Y., Tao, A., Kautz, J., Catanzaro, B.: High-resolution image synthesis and semantic manipulation with conditional gans. In: Proceedings of the IEEE Conference on Computer Vision and Pattern Recognition, pp. 8798–8807 (2018)
32. Wang, Z., Bovik, A.C., Sheikh, H.R., Simoncelli, E.P.: Image quality assessment: from error visibility to structural similarity. IEEE Trans. Image Process. **13**(4), 600–612 (2004)
33. Wu, T., Tang, S., Zhang, R., Cao, J., Li, J.: Tree-structured kronecker convolutional network for semantic segmentation. In: 2019 IEEE International Conference on Multimedia and Expo (ICME), pp. 940–945. IEEE (2019)
34. Yang, H., Zhang, R., Guo, X., Liu, W., Zuo, W., Luo, P.: Towards photo-realistic virtual try-on by adaptively generating-preserving image content. In: Proceedings of the IEEE/CVF Conference on Computer Vision and Pattern Recognition, pp. 7850–7859 (2020)
35. Yu, R., Wang, X., Xie, X.: VTNFP: an image-based virtual try-on network with body and clothing feature preservation. In: Proceedings of the IEEE/CVF International Conference on Computer Vision, pp. 10511–10520 (2019)
36. Zheng, N., Song, X., Chen, Z., Hu, L., Cao, D., Nie, L.: Virtually trying on new clothing with arbitrary poses. In: Proceedings of the 27th ACM International Conference on Multimedia, pp. 266–274 (2019)
37. Zhu, J.Y., Park, T., Isola, P., Efros, A.A.: Unpaired image-to-image translation using cycle-consistent adversarial networks. In: Proceedings of the IEEE International Conference on Computer Vision, pp. 2223–2232 (2017)

Parallel DBSCAN-Martingale Estimation of the Number of Concepts for Automatic Satellite Image Clustering

Ilias Gialampoukidis[1] ⓘ, Stelios Andreadis[1](✉) ⓘ, Nick Pantelidis[1], Sameed Hayat[2], Li Zhong[2], Marios Bakratsas[1], Dennis Hoppe[2], Stefanos Vrochidis[1] ⓘ, and Ioannis Kompatsiaris[1] ⓘ

[1] Information Technologies Institute, Centre for Research and Technology Hellas, Thessaloniki, Greece
{heliasgj,andreadisst,pantelidisnikos,mbakratsas,stefanos, ikom}@iti.gr

[2] University of Stuttgart - High Performance Computing Center Stuttgart, Stuttgart, Germany
{hpcshaya,li.zhong,hpcdhopp}@hlrs.de

Abstract. The necessity of organising big streams of Earth Observation (EO) data induces the efficient clustering of image patches, deriving from satellite imagery, into groups. Since the different concepts of the satellite image patches are not known a priori, DBSCAN-Martingale can be applied to estimate the number of the desired clusters. In this paper we provide a parallel version of the DBSCAN-Martingale algorithm and a framework for clustering EO data in an unsupervised way. The approach is evaluated on a benchmark dataset of Sentinel-2 images with ground-truth annotation and is also implemented on High Performance Computing (HPC) infrastructure to demonstrate its scalability. Finally, a cost-benefit analysis is conducted to find the optimal selection of reserved nodes for running the proposed algorithm, in relation to execution time and cost.

Keywords: Density-based clustering · Image clustering · High Performance Computing

1 Introduction

Recent years have witnessed an increasing availability of frequent and free-of-cost Earth Observation (EO) data, which promotes the involvement of satellite imagery analysis in several domains, from agriculture to disaster management, and from security and defence to blue economy. To support applications in this wide range of domains, various satellite-based solutions are proposed by the scientific community, with a particular focus on artificial intelligence methods and machine-learning approaches [22,30].

Nonetheless, the large streams of time series of remotely sensed images need to be organised in a contextual manner. The multimodal dimension of multispectral satellite images, i.e. Sentinel-2 images, as well as the different polarisation modes of satellite radar data, i.e. Sentinel-1 images, require effective and efficient management of the associated metadata, so as to group them into clusters. The lack of training data in

ⓒ Springer Nature Switzerland AG 2022
B. Þór Jónsson et al. (Eds.): MMM 2022, LNCS 13141, pp. 95–106, 2022.
https://doi.org/10.1007/978-3-030-98358-1_8

the EO domain results, though, to the inability of the EO downstream sector to apply supervised machine learning techniques for pattern recognition in satellite images. The problem has proven to be challenging when the number of clusters, that satellite image patches can be grouped in, is not known a priori and the labels are not known or not annotated. To that end, density-based algorithms are suitable [20], since they do not require the number of clusters as input, contrary to other clustering approaches, such as k-means. Density-based algorithms require as input two other parameters: the minimum number of points required to form a cluster, namely $minPts$, and the neighbourhood radius ϵ (density level). Nevertheless, their estimation is hard to be made and often requires several executions and combinations of outputs from multiple density levels.

Over twenty years ago, [8] introduced the now popular DBSCAN, a density-based algorithm for discovering clusters in large spatial databases with noise. DBSCAN is still used both in research and real-world applications, while it has inspired numerous extensions. In particular, DBSCAN-Martingale [11] estimates the number of clusters by optimizing a probabilistic process, which involves randomness in the selection of the density parameter. In this work we propose a novel, parallel version of the DBSCAN-Martingale, which is validated in clustering large datasets of satellite image patches from Sentinel-2 imagery. However, the parallelisation as well as the immense size of EO data bring on a new challenge, namely computational limitations. For this reason, this work also involves the transferring of the proposed algorithm to High Performance Computing (HPC) infrastructure, so as to show how these limitations can be overcome, to prove scalability and to achieve high efficiency.

The remainder of the paper is organised as follows. First, in Sect. 2 we discuss related publications that concern the optimisation of DBSCAN, either by optimising its parameters or its performance time. Section 3 presents the proposed algorithm, along with the necessary background, and describes the HPC infrastructure where the algorithm is transferred. Section 4 continues with the description of the dataset used for the evaluation of the algorithm, the results of the experiments, and a cost-benefit analysis to examine how time and cost range in relation to the number of used nodes. Finally, Sect. 5 concludes with a summary of the presented work and future steps.

2   Related Work

Due to its high popularity, the scientific community has focused on the improvement of DBSCAN, mainly in two directions: the optimisation of DBSCAN's parameters, i.e. $minPts$ and ϵ, and the performance time, proposing faster versions of the algorithm.

Regarding the parameters optimisation, the algorithm in [6] divides the dataset into multiple data regions, sets the appropriate parameters for each data region for local clustering, and finally merges the data regions. Kim et al. [19] focus on minimizing the additional computation required to determine the parameters by using the approximate adaptive ϵ-distance for each density while finding the clusters with varying densities that original DBSCAN cannot find. The author of [28] proposes a self-adaption grey DBSCAN algorithm that automatically selects its parameters, whereas Li et al. [25] calculate the parameters $minPts$ and ϵ based on the optimal k-value, selected after multiple iterations of k-clustering. Furthermore, in the works of [14] and [24], the problem of proper parameterisation is solved by applying the density peak algorithm and the natural neighbour algorithm respectively. In contrast to these works, the proposed algorithm aims to identify the most "stable" number of clusters by running DBSCAN for multiple ϵ and $minPts$ values, in a parallel manner.

As far as performance is concerned, several recent works present revisions of DBSCAN, aiming to reduce the computation time. Pandey et al. [31] target the time spent in the input/output (reading/writing data), while the work in [9] inspects the neighbourhoods of only a subset of the objects in the dataset, similarly to the modification of DBSCAN presented in [17] that requires computing only the densities for a chosen subset of points. Likewise, the approaches of [34] and [4] run on selected core points, the first based on locality sensitive hashing and the latter on k-nearest neighbours.

In addition, Ding & Yang [7] apply a novel randomized k-centre clustering idea to decrease the complexity of range query, which is a time-consuming step in DBSCAN. Cai et al. [2] improve the efficiency with Ada-DBSCAN, an extension that consists of a data block splitter and a data block merger, coordinated by local and global clustering, and Li et al. [23] with ADBSCAN, which identifies local high-density samples utilizing the inherent properties of the nearest neighbour graph. Other extensions that present good performance are 3W-DBSCAN [40] and the Bisecting Min Max DBSCAN [18].

The upsurge of distributed and HPC technology has motivated scientists to propose various parallel implementations of DBSCAN. The work in [39] presents a framework that divides data into partitions, calculates local DBSCAN results, and merges local results based on a merging graph. Deng et al. [5] enable parallel computing by a divide-and-conquer method that includes a simplified k-mean partitioning process and a reachable partition index, and Gong et al. [12] present a new approach that supports real-time clustering of data based on continuous cluster checkpointing. Additional parallelised versions of DBSCAN are found in the works of [21], [15] applying MapReduce, [41] with a parallel grid clustering algorithm, and [32], who developed a scalable distributed implementation of their own μDBSCAN.

The works in [38] and [16] manage to parallelise DBSCAN by using Quadtree data structure. In the latter, the solution distributes the dataset into smaller chunks and then utilizes the parallel programming frameworks such as Map-Reduce to provide an infrastructure to store and process these small chunks of data. The author of [26] utilizes Cover Tree to retrieve neighbours for each point in parallel and the triangle inequality to filter many unnecessary distance computations. Instead of performing range queries for all objects, AnyDBC by [29] iteratively learns the current cluster structure of the data and selects a few most promising objects for refining clusters at each iteration.

Finally, a further step to distributed implementations of DBSCAN is the optimisation of the involved stages. Chen et al. [3] propose improvements both in data partitioning and in merging. Han et al. [13] adopt a partitioning strategy based on kdtree, similar to [33], and a new merging technique by mapping the relationship between the local points and their bordering neighbours. Tyercha et al. [37] use a Hilbert curve to identify the centres for initial partitioning, Liyang et al. [27] optimise it with distance matrix and R-Tree based methods, and Song and Lee [35] suggest a cell-based data partitioning scheme, which randomly distributes small cells rather than the points themselves.

On the other hand, our work improves the performance by implementing the proposed algorithm in such a way that it can run on HPC, allocating the multiple realisations and iterations of DBSCAN in different nodes and cores.

3   Background and Methodology

3.1   Background and Notation

In this section we provide the notation that we deem necessary before presenting the proposed algorithm. As already mentioned, DBSCAN [8] has two parameters: ϵ and $minPts$. The parameter ϵ defines the radius of neighborhood around a point x (density level), while the parameter $minPts$ is the minimum number of neighbors within ϵ radius. $minPts$ is usually predefined based on the minimum size of the desired clusters. On the other hand, the density level ϵ is hard to be estimated and, even so, the algorithm is not able to output all clusters using one single density level. The cluster structure is visualised using the OPTICS [1] plot of reachability distances, where the dents represent clusters and it is also possible to observe the density level at which the desired clusters are extracted. For each density level ϵ, the output of DBSCAN is one clustering vector and is denoted by $C_{DBSCAN_{(\epsilon)}}$. In detail, given a dataset of n-instances, DBSCAN provides as output a clustering vector C with values the cluster IDs $C[j]$ for each instance $j = 1, 2, ..., n$, assigning each element j to a cluster. In case the j-th element is marked as noise, then the cluster ID is zero ($C[j] = 0$). For further definitions of the DBSCAN-Martingale process and its extension for providing the estimation of the number of clusters $\hat{k}$, the reader is referred to [10, 11].

3.2   The Proposed Parallel-DBSCAN-Martingale

The proposed parallel version of the DBSCAN-Martingale algorithm, which requires R realisations and T iterations of the DBSCAN algorithm, each one allocated in different nodes and cores, so that the algorithm can scale up using an HPC infrastructure, is presented step-by-step in Algorithm 1. Furthermore, the complete framework for its implementation is illustrated in Fig. 1. In brief, given a dataset of satellite images (e.g. Sentinel-1 or Sentinel-2), which are cropped into patches, any feature extraction technique can be applied and the resulted feature vectors can be used for clustering. As mentioned in Sect. 3.1, the OPTICS plot is used for selecting the maximum ϵ and then DBSCAN-Martingale is executed on different cores in parallel, for multiple values of $minPts$, in order to detect the most probable number of clusters, which is the final output of the framework.

3.3   HPC Infrastructure

In order to demonstrate the scalability of the proposed algorithm and achieve the best performance of clustering, Parallel-DBSCAN-Martingale is also run on HPC infrastructure. On these clusters, the environments are setup so that machine learning and deep learning algorithms can be processed effectively. In particular, the NEC Cluster platform (Vulcan) is provided by HLRS in order to accelerate the computation, shorten the running time and improve the performance. It is a heterogeneous cluster with currently 761 nodes of different types (Memory, CPU, Disk, Accelerators). For the experiments of Sect. 4, CascadeLake nodes (clx-25) have been used, which include Infiniband interconnect for high-speed transmission and high memory 384 GB. Especially, near real-time data analytics are enabled to be performed with the high amount of RAM. The

---

Algorithm 1. Parallel-DBSCAN-Martingale(N, T, R, w) return $\hat{k}$

1: Allocate N nodes and T cores
2: Set the number w of different values of $minPts$
3: Extract feature vectors per satellite image patch using any feature extraction method
4: Find ϵ_{max} using the maximum reachability distance from an OPTICS reachability plot
5: **for** $minPts \in \{minPts_1, minPts_2, ..., minPts_w\}$ **do**
6: $\quad$ $clusters = \emptyset, k = 0$
7: $\quad$ **for** $r = 1$ to R **do**
8: $\quad\quad$ Generate a random sample of T values in $[0, \epsilon_{max}]$
9: $\quad\quad$ Sort the generated sample $\epsilon_t, t = 1, 2, ..., T$
10: $\quad\quad$ **for** $t = 1$ to T **do**
11: $\quad\quad\quad$ compute $C_{DBSCAN(\epsilon_t)}$ distributed in each one of the T cores
12: $\quad\quad\quad$ compute $C^{(t)}$ distributed in each one of the T cores
13: $\quad\quad\quad$ update the cluster IDs
14: $\quad\quad\quad$ update the vector C
15: $\quad\quad\quad$ update $k = \max_j C[j]$
16: $\quad\quad$ **end for**
17: $\quad\quad$ $clusters =$ AppendTo($clusters, k$)
18: $\quad$ **end for**
19: $\quad$ $\hat{k} =$ mode($clusters$)
20: **end for**
21: compute $\delta_i = |\frac{\hat{k}_{i+1} - \hat{k}_i}{minPts_{i+1} - minPts_i}|, i = 1, 2, ..., w - 1$
22: compute $minPts$ such as: $minPts = \arg\min_i \delta_i$
23: find index i such that $minPts = minPts_i$
24: **return** $\hat{k}_i$

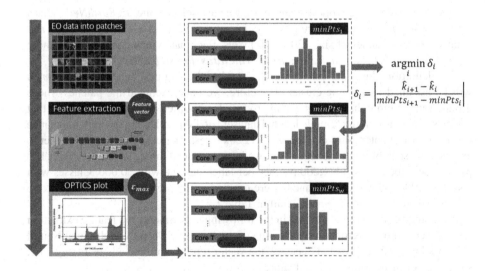

Fig. 1. The Parallel-DBSCAN-Martingale framework

high performance data analytics (HPDA) system naturally enables different kinds of machine learning and data analysis tasks, including the clustering task. The technical details of the NEC Cluster (Vulcan) are summarised in Table 1.

Table 1. Technical specification of the NEC Cluster (Vulcan) installed at HLRS.

	Vulcan CascadeLake nodes (clx-25)
Total number of nodes	84 nodes
Processors per node	2× Intel Xeon Gold 6248, 40 cores total @ 2.50 GHz
1 RAM per node	384 GB
Disk storage per node	No local storage
External parallel file system	∼500 TByte (shared), throughput of 6 GB/s
Operating system	CentOS 7
Available standard software	PBSPro, Apache Hadoop, Apache Spark, etc.
Main programming languages/Tools	C++, MPI, Python, etc.

4 Evaluation

The scope of this evaluation is not to compare the Parallel-DBSCAN-Martingale with other algorithms, but to prove that multiple iterations can result in the correct number of clusters and also to show the scalability of the solution on different HPC parameters.

4.1 Dataset Description

For the evaluation of the proposed algorithm, we have selected the *BigEarthNet*[1] dataset [36], which contains ground-truth annotation about Sentinel-2 satellite images and counts 590,326 patches of size 120×120 pixels. Each patch may contain one or more of the following labels: *water, rice, urban, vineyards, forest, bare rock,* and *snow.*

By definition clustering cannot handle a multi-labelling problem, since each patch will be assigned to a single cluster. Therefore, we have excluded the patches whose ground truth is more than one label and produced a modified version of the dataset that can be seen in the column "Single labeled dataset" of Table 2. Due to the high imbalance in the number of patches for each class (e.g. 220k forest, 1k rice, 52 rock) and in order to evaluate the scalability of the algorithm, we have produced three subsets: one with 100 patches per label, one with 1,000 patches per label and one with 30,000. Classes with less than 100/1,000/30,000 instances were omitted in the preparation of the respective subset. All subsets can be seen in detail in Table 2.

It should be also noted here that in the following experiments the feature extraction stage generated one vector per satellite image patch using a Deep Convolutional Neural Network layer, but as stated in Sect. 3.2, the vector representation could be of any type, such as color histograms or other feature vectors.

---

[1] http://bigearth.net/.

Table 2. Number of satellite image patches per label

Labels	Single labeled dataset	Subset 1	Subset 2	Subset 3
Water	71,549	100	1,000	30,000
Rice	1,122	100	1,000	–
Urban	33,411	100	1,000	30,000
Vineyards	2,749	100	1,000	–
Forest	220,406	100	1,000	30,000
Bare rock	52	–	–	–
Snow	61,707	100	1,000	30,000
Total	390,996	600	6,000	120,000

4.2 Results

For our experiments, T was set to 5, ϵ_{max} to 10, and w to 12, with $minPts$ varying from 5 to 16. For each $minPts$, Parallel-DBSCAN-Martingale estimated the probabilities of the number of clusters (for reasons of space, only the plot for $minPts = 11$ can be seen in Fig. 2a) and generated the final result in an unsupervised way, searching for the most "stable" number of clusters as an optimal solution (Fig. 2b), i.e. 6 for Subset 1.

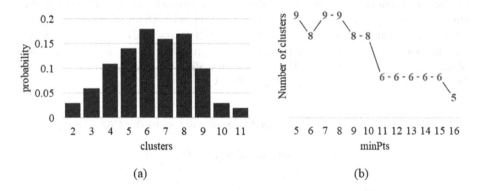

(a)   (b)

Fig. 2. (a) Probability of the number of clusters for $minPts = 11$ (b) Most probable number of clusters per $minPts$

Estimating the number of clusters with the highest probability for every $minPts$ requires significant computational effort. For Subset 1 (600 patches) and 100 realisations, it was possible to run Parallel-DBSCAN-Martingale in a personal computer with 4 cores and achieve an execution time of 12 s. However, it did not manage to run for Subset 2 (6,000 patches) or Subset 3 (120,000), indicating that it needs to be distributed in multiple processing nodes for scalability. Four runs were successful on the HPC infrastructure (presented in Sect. 3.3) with different parameters, i.e. the size of the dataset, the number of realisations and the available cores. All details for each run (parameters and execution time) can be found in Table 3. It should be highlighted here that on HPC, the proposed algorithm is able to cluster even within 40 min (2,400 s) satellite image patches that cover more than 172k m^2 (Run 3).

Table 3. Execution time of Parallel-DBSCAN-Martingale for different parameters

		PC	HPC			
		Run 1	Run 1	Run 2	Run 3	Run 4
Dataset	Number of patches	600	6,000	6,000	120,000	120,000
	Size of patches (MB)	50	501	501	10,020	10,020
	Square kilometers	864	8,640	8,640	172,800	172,800
T		5	5	5	5	5
R		100	10	1,000	10	1,000
Available cores		4	216	108	1,044	80
Time (seconds)		12	12	160	2,400	12,400

4.3 Cost-Benefit Analysis

After achieving the parallel execution of DBSCAN-Martingale on HPC, a further analysis has been conducted in order to investigate how time and cost range in relation to the number of reserved nodes. Regarding prices, we refer to HLRS fee schedule for 2020[2], where the computing cost for Cascade-lake 384 GB nodes is €1.31 per node * hour. The fluctuation of execution time (in hours) and execution cost (in euros) per number of nodes when running Parallel-DBSCAN-Martingale ($T = 5$, $R = 60$) is reported in Table 4 and also displayed as a line chart in Fig. 3.

Table 4. Time & cost analysis of multi-node execution of Parallel-DBSCAN-Martingale

Reserved nodes	Execution time (hours)	Execution cost (€)
1 (40 cores)	1.672	2.62
2 (80 cores)	0.822	2.62
3 (120 cores)	0.562	3.93
4 (160 cores)	0.533	5.24
5 (200 cores)	0.527	6.55
6 (240 cores)	0.273	7.86

---

[2] https://www.hlrs.de/solutions-services/academic-users/legal-requirements/.

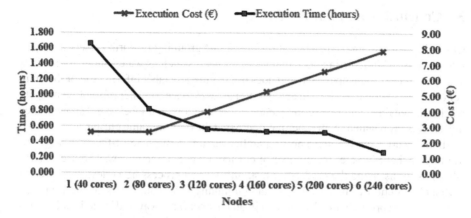

Fig. 3. Execution time (hours) and execution cost (€) vs nodes

Moreover, we define marginal cost m_i as:

$$m_i = \frac{v_{n_i} - v_{n_{i-1}}}{t_{n_i} - t_{n_{i-1}}}$$

where v_c is the price value, t_c is the processing time and n is the number of nodes. The fluctuation of marginal cost m_i is illustrated in Fig. 4 and shows that switching from 1 to 2 nodes is advantageous, since execution time is reduced by half with the exact same cost, while switching from 4 to 5 nodes is the least profitable option, considering that the cost increases, but the execution time remains almost the same.

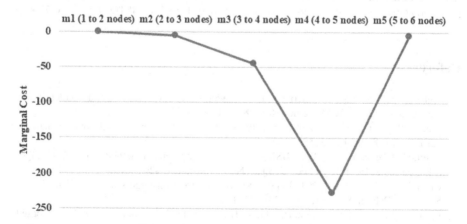

Fig. 4. Marginal cost while increasing number of nodes

5   Conclusion and Future Work

Clustering satellite image patches allows for a fast grouping of Earth Observation data into clusters of similar semantic content, i.e. concepts such as water, snow, forest, rice, etc. This process is unsupervised and does not require any label information or the number of clusters known a priori. In an operational level, once a cluster of satellite imagery patches is obtained and one of the patches is assigned with a label (e.g. "snow"), then this label is propagated to all other members (patches) of the same cluster.

In this work we presented a novel, parallel version of the state-of-the-art DBSCAN-Martingale that estimates the number of clusters in an automatic way. The use of HPC allows us to distribute the processing task into several processing nodes, thus offering a scalable solution to the EO Big Data community. The parameters of the proposed density-based approach are also learned in an unsupervised way and a stable solution is searched with many executions and realisations of the process, to get the optimal value for the number of clusters. Once the optimal number of clusters is obtained, then any traditional clustering algorithm (e.g. k-means) can be applied, having as input the estimated number of clusters and the vector representation of the satellite image patches. Parallel-DBSCAN-Martingale was evaluated in a subset of the BigEarthNet dataset and achieved to estimate the correct number of clusters, i.e. labels of the patches. It was also run successfully on HPC infrastructure, proving its scalability and increasing its efficiency. Finally, a cost-benefit analysis was conducted to detect the optimal selection of nodes for running this particular algorithm on this particular infrastructure.

Future work will focus on further experiments on HPC to discover the optimal usage of multiple cores, as well as on the parallelisation of other parts of DBSCAN-Martingale, such as the realisations.

Acknowledgement. This work has been supported by the EU's Horizon 2020 research and innovation programme under grant agreements H2020-101004152 CALLISTO and H2020-776019 EOPEN.

References

1. Ankerst, M., Breunig, M.M., Kriegel, H.P., Sander, J.: Optics: ordering points to identify the clustering structure. ACM Sigmod Rec. **28**(2), 49–60 (1999)
2. Cai, Z., Wang, J., He, K.: Adaptive density-based spatial clustering for massive data analysis. IEEE Access **8**, 23346–23358 (2020)
3. Chen, G., Cheng, Y., Jing, W.: DBSCAN-PSM: an improvement method of DBSCAN algorithm on spark. Int. J. High Perf. Comput. Netw. **13**(4), 417–426 (2019)
4. Chen, Y., et al.: KNN-BLOCK DBSCAN: fast clustering for large-scale data. IEEE Trans. Syst. Man Cybern. Syst. **51**, 3939–3953 (2019)
5. Deng, C., Song, J., Cai, S., Sun, R., Shi, Y., Hao, S.: K-DBSCAN: an efficient density-based clustering algorithm supports parallel computing. Int. J. Simul. Process Model. **13**(5), 496–505 (2018)
6. Diao, K., Liang, Y., Fan, J.: An improved DBSCAN algorithm using local parameters. In: Zhou, Z.-H., Yang, Q., Gao, Y., Zheng, Yu. (eds.) ICAI 2018. CCIS, vol. 888, pp. 3–12. Springer, Singapore (2018). https://doi.org/10.1007/978-981-13-2122-1_1

7. Ding, H., Yang, F.: On metric DBSCAN with low doubling dimension. arXiv preprint arXiv:2002.11933 (2020)
8. Ester, M., Kriegel, H.P., Sander, J., Xu, X., et al.: A density-based algorithm for discovering clusters in large spatial databases with noise. In: KDD, vol. 96, pp. 226–231 (1996)
9. Galán, S.F.: Comparative evaluation of region query strategies for DBSCAN clustering. Inf. Sci. **502**, 76–90 (2019)
10. Gialampoukidis, I., Vrochidis, S., Kompatsiaris, I.: A hybrid framework for news clustering based on the DBSCAN-martingale and LDA. In: MLDM 2016. LNCS (LNAI), vol. 9729, pp. 170–184. Springer, Cham (2016). https://doi.org/10.1007/978-3-319-41920-6_13
11. Gialampoukidis, I., Vrochidis, S., Kompatsiaris, I., Antoniou, I.: Probabilistic density-based estimation of the number of clusters using the DBSCAN-martingale process. Pattern Recogn. Lett. **123**, 23–30 (2019)
12. Gong, Y., Sinnott, R.O., Rimba, P.: RT-DBSCAN: real-time parallel clustering of spatio-temporal data using spark-streaming. In: Shi, Y., et al. (eds.) ICCS 2018. LNCS, vol. 10860, pp. 524–539. Springer, Cham (2018). https://doi.org/10.1007/978-3-319-93698-7_40
13. Han, D., Agrawal, A., Liao, W.k., Choudhary, A.: Parallel DBSCAN algorithm using a data partitioning strategy with spark implementation. In: 2018 IEEE International Conference on Big Data (Big Data), pp. 305–312. IEEE (2018)
14. Hou, J., Lv, C., Zhang, A., E, X.: Merging DBSCAN and density peak for robust clustering. In: Tetko, I.V., Kůrková, V., Karpov, P., Theis, F. (eds.) ICANN 2019. LNCS, vol. 11730, pp. 595–610. Springer, Cham (2019). https://doi.org/10.1007/978-3-030-30490-4_48
15. Hu, X., Liu, L., Qiu, N., Yang, D., Li, M.: A mapreduce-based improvement algorithm for DBSCAN. J. Algorithms Comput. Technol. **12**(1), 53–61 (2018)
16. Ibrahim, R., Shafiq, M.O.: Towards a new approach for empowering the mr-dbscan clustering for massive data using quadtree. In: 2018 IEEE 20th International Conference on High Performance Computing and Communications; IEEE 16th International Conference on Smart City; IEEE 4th International Conference on Data Science and Systems (HPCC/SmartCity/DSS), pp. 91–98. IEEE (2018)
17. Jang, J., Jiang, H.: DBSCAN++: towards fast and scalable density clustering. In: International Conference on Machine Learning, pp. 3019–3029. PMLR (2019)
18. Johnson, T., Prabhu, K., Parvatkar, S., Naik, A., Temkar, P.: The bisecting min max DBSCAN algorithm (2018)
19. Kim, J.H., Choi, J.H., Yoo, K.H., Nasridinov, A.: AA-DBSCAN: an approximate adaptive DBSCAN for finding clusters with varying densities. J. Supercomput. **75**(1), 142–169 (2019)
20. Kriegel, H.P., Kröger, P., Sander, J., Zimek, A.: Density-based clustering. Wiley Interdisc. Rev. Data Min. Knowl. Disc. **1**(3), 231–240 (2011)
21. Kumari, A., Shrivastava, V., Pandey, A.: Reduction of DBSCAN time complexity for data mining using parallel computing techniques (2019)
22. Lary, D.J., Alavi, A.H., Gandomi, A.H., Walker, A.L.: Machine learning in geosciences and remote sensing. Geosci. Front. **7**(1), 3–10 (2016)
23. Li, H., Liu, X., Li, T., Gan, R.: A novel density-based clustering algorithm using nearest neighbor graph. Pattern Recognit. **102**, 107206 (2020)
24. Li, J., Chen, Y.: Improved DBSCAN algorithm based on natural neighbors. Mod. Comput. **13** (2018)
25. Li, J., Han, X., Jiang, J., Hu, Y., Liu, L.: An efficient clustering method for DBSCAN geographic spatio-temporal large data with improved parameter optimization. Int. Arch. Photogram. Remote Sens. Spat. Inf. Sci. **42**, 581–584 (2020)
26. Li, S.S.: An improved DBSCAN algorithm based on the neighbor similarity and fast nearest neighbor query. IEEE Access **8**, 47468–47476 (2020)
27. Liyang, L., Hongzhen, S., Shen, W., Jinyu, L.: Parallel implementation of DBSCAN algorithm based on spark (2016)

28. Lu, S.: Self-adaption grey DBSCAN clustering. arXiv preprint arXiv:1912.11477 (2019)
29. Mai, S.T., Assent, I., Jacobsen, J., Dieu, M.S.: Anytime parallel density-based clustering. Data Mining Knowl. Disc. **32**(4), 1121–1176 (2018). https://doi.org/10.1007/s10618-018-0562-1
30. Maxwell, A.E., Warner, T.A., Fang, F.: Implementation of machine-learning classification in remote sensing: an applied review. Int. J. Remote Sens. **39**(9), 2784–2817 (2018)
31. Pandey, S., Samal, M., Mohanty, S.K.: An SNN-DBSCAN based clustering algorithm for big data. In: Advanced Computing and Intelligent Engineering, pp. 127–137 (2020)
32. Sarma, A., et al.: μdbscan: an exact scalable DBSCAN algorithm for big data exploiting spatial locality. In: 2019 IEEE International Conference on Cluster Computing (CLUSTER), pp. 1–11. IEEE (2019)
33. Shibla, T., Kumar, K.S.: Improving efficiency of DBSCAN by parallelizing kd-tree using spark. In: 2018 Second International Conference on Intelligent Computing and Control Systems (ICICCS), pp. 1197–1203. IEEE (2018)
34. Shiqiu, Y., Qingsheng, Z.: DBSCAN clustering algorithm based on locality sensitive hashing. In: Journal of Physics: Conference Series, vol. 1314, p. 012177. IOP Publishing (2019)
35. Song, H., Lee, J.G.: RP-DBSCAN: a superfast parallel DBSCAN algorithm based on random partitioning. In: 2018 International Conference on Management of Data, pp. 1173–1187 (2018)
36. Sumbul, G., et al.: Bigearthnet-mm: a large scale multi-modal multi-label benchmark archive for remote sensing image classification and retrieval. arXiv preprint arXiv:2105.07921 (2021)
37. Tyercha, E.R., Kazmaier, G.S., Gildhoff, H., Pekel, I., Volker, L., Grouisborn, T.: Hilbert curve partitioning for parallelization of DBSCAN. uS Patent 10,318,557 (2019)
38. Wang, Y., Gu, Y., Shun, J.: Theoretically-efficient and practical parallel DBSCAN. In: 2020 ACM SIGMOD International Conference on Management of Data, pp. 2555–2571 (2020)
39. Yang, K., Gao, Y., Ma, R., Chen, L., Wu, S., Chen, G.: DBSCAN-MS: distributed density-based clustering in metric spaces. In: 2019 IEEE 35th International Conference on Data Engineering (ICDE), pp. 1346–1357. IEEE (2019)
40. Yu, H., Chen, L., Yao, J., Wang, X.: A three-way clustering method based on an improved DBSCAN algorithm. Physica A Stat. Mech. Appl. **535**, 122289 (2019)
41. Zhou, G.J.: Research on parallel design of DBSCAN clustering algorithm in spatial data mining. DEStech Trans. Eng. Technol. Res. (ecar) (2018)

Multimedia Applications - Perspectives, Tools and Applications (Special Session) and Brave New Ideas

AI for the Media Industry: Application Potential and Automation Levels

Werner Bailer[1]([✉]) [iD], Georg Thallinger[1] [iD], Verena Krawarik[2] [iD],
Katharina Schell[2] [iD], and Victoria Ertelthalner[2] [iD]

[1] JOANNEUM RESEARCH, Graz, Austria
{werner.bailer,georg.thallinger}@joanneum.at
[2] Austria Presse Agentur, Vienna, Austria
{verena.krawarik,katharina.schell}@apa.at,
victoria.ertelthalner@univie.ac.at

Abstract. Tools based on artificial intelligence (AI) are increasingly used in the media industry, addressing a potentially wide range of application areas. Based on a survey involving media professionals and technology providers, we present a taxonomy of application areas of AI in the media industry, including an assessment of the maturity of AI technology for the respective application. As many of these applications require human oversight, either due to insufficient maturity of technology or the need for editorial control, we also propose a classification of automation levels for AI in the media domain, with examples for different stages of the media value chain. Both of these aspects are strongly linked to the role of human users and their interaction with AI technologies. The results suggest that human-AI collaboration in media applications is still an unsolved research question.

Keywords: Artificial intelligence · Media · Collaborative AI · Automation levels

1 Introduction

This paper reports selected results from a study on the potential of artificial intelligence (AI) in the media industry. The study aimed at assessing the state of the use of AI in the media industry and the technology offer for this domain in Austria, and to identify the key challenges for a wider adoption of AI by the media industry. The methodology of the study consisted of a literature survey and web research, of a survey among media consumers ($n = 500$), interviews with technology providers ($n = 19$), media professionals ($n = 7$) and researchers ($n = 9$), and two half-day workshops bringing together participants from these three groups (mostly focusing on defining the challenges). In addition, a panel of three experts (IT, journalism, law) provided inputs to the work. A comprehensive report of the study has been published (in German) [8].

In this paper, we focus on two results which we consider of interest to a broader audience. One is a taxonomy of application areas of AI in the media

© Springer Nature Switzerland AG 2022
B. Þór Jónsson et al. (Eds.): MMM 2022, LNCS 13141, pp. 109–118, 2022.
https://doi.org/10.1007/978-3-030-98358-1_9

industry, including an assessment of the maturity of AI technology for the respective application. The other is a classification of automation levels for AI in the media domain (similar to those for automated driving), with examples for different stages of the media value chain. Both of these aspects are strongly linked to the role of human users and their interaction with AI technologies. This has various reasons, from AI technologies having limited maturity allowing only for semi-automatic approaches, over tasks requiring creative inputs by humans, to decisions where journalistic ethos or the reputation of a medium is at stake.

The rest of the paper is organized as follows. The remainder of this Section provides definitions and discusses related work. In Sect. 2 we present a taxonomy of application areas for AI in the media industry, and in Sect. 3 we propose automation levels for this domain. Section 4 provides conclusions.

1.1 Definitions

Both key terms of this work – media and AI – are used in various ways, and it seems worthwhile to define how we use them in this work.

Media: We consider media as social institutions and complex organizations, possibly with commercial interests. They provide communication channels or use third party channels to provide content and information they create to address needs of a large set of recipients. This definition includes a wide range of actors, but focuses on the creation of content, excluding actors that only operate platforms.

AI: We understand AI as a set of approaches and methods that, given data and an objective, are able to build a model, that allows the system to generate predictions or decisions for a particular set of tasks. This definition is similar to that used in the ISO/IEC 22989 standard under development [7], and focuses on narrow AI, which is sufficient for currently available technologies. It encompasses a wide range of approaches, including symbolic and sub-symbolic ones.

1.2 Related Work

The interest of using AI in the media industry is increasing. In a recent survey of the Reuters Institute for the Study of Journalism [11], almost 70% of media managers consider AI an important technology for their organizations. For this reasons, a number of reports and surveys have assessed the use of AI in the media industry, and have identified potential application areas. Goldhammer et al. [3] make a distinction into assistive technologies, generative technologies and distributive technologies. Chan-Olmsted [2] proposes the following eight application areas: audience content recommendations/discovery, audience engagement, augmented audience experience, message optimization, content management, content creation, audience insights, and operational automation. Nel and Milburn-Curtis [10] detail this list to 15 application areas, although some of those may be considered specializations of others. Other reports try to collect concrete evidence of the use AI in particular organizations, which provides valuable data for assessing maturity and acceptance in a particular application. One is a study commissioned by the European Parliament [13], focusing on the audiovisual sector. The probably most comprehensive work in this area is done by the Journalism AI initiative and collected in their report [1]. Like for other technology areas, technology landscapes have been published. One example, which focuses on some particular application areas is the work by Hauck et al. [4]. Another, providing a comprehensive overview on synthetic media has been published by Samsung NEXT[1].

2   Assessing Application Areas

AI applications in the media industry are diverse, and include rather generic technologies that find use across all industry domains, like data analytics or customer care, text and multimedia analysis technologies similar to those used in other domains (e.g., transportation, public safety) as well as very specific ones like virtual studios or automated news hosts.

We propose a taxonomy of application areas, that extends and details the one proposed in [10]. As the top level structure, we use three main stages of the media value chain: *sourcing* deals with collecting, organizing and assessing information, *production* is concerned with the actual creation of content and *distribution* involves publishing, monitoring impact and interaction with consumers. The next level structures these stages into tasks or applications for certain types of content, with one additional level where needed. The granularity of the taxonomy was chosen based on the heterogeneity of the task and the amount of existing AI solutions (i.e., coarser groups were formed, where the available technology is still sparse). Tables 1, 2 and 3 present the resulting taxonomy with a brief description of each application area. In addition, we provide an assessment of the maturity of AI technology for each application area. The scale of this assessment goes beyond that of technology readiness level (TRL) [6], as we also assess specifically the experimental or productive use in the media industry. However, we use a coarser scale (merging stages prior to the point when a media company could at least experimentally try the technology), classifying the assessment into research (R), prototypes (Pt), products/services (Pr) and experimental (Ue) or productive use (Up). As the current status is not reflected by a single point but rather a range on this scale, this assessment is visualized as a gradient in Tables 1, 2 and 3.

---

[1] https://www.syntheticmedialandscape.com/.

Table 1. Applications of AI in content sourcing and assessment of maturity.

Application	Description	Assessment R | Pt | Pr | Ue | Up
Text analysis		
Terms and entities	Named entities, keywords	
Classification	Including topic detection and clustering	
Sentiment	Analysis of emotion of content, user reaction or attitude towards a topic	
Summarization	Summarizing single or multiple articles	
Multimedia analysis		
Preprocessing	Temporal segmentation, proxy extraction	
Spoken language	Speech-to-text, language identification, speaker identification	
Classification	By topic, genre, age, etc.	
Sentiment	Analysis of emotion of content or user reaction	
Text in image, video, documents	Text detection and OCR, layout segmentation	
Faces	Face detection and recognition, age/gender estimation	
Similarity	Fingerprinting, copy detection, instance search	
Summarization	Summarizing videos or collections	
Technical quality	Visual/audio quality and defect analysis	
Topics & knowledge		
Semantics & knowledge	Semantic enrichment, knowledge representation, linking, reasoning	
Topic monitoring	Monitoring sources, discovering topics, assessing relevance	
Verification	Verifying content, assessing trustworthiness of sources	
License analysis	Representing and querying contracts and licenses	

The taxonomy reflects the vast range of potential AI uses in the media domain. It also shows a relatively high level of technical maturity in many applications, with products and services being available, and experimental use being reported by media organizations. However, only a small share of applications have moved into productive use beyond a few early adopters. This is mostly due

Table 2. Applications of AI in media production and assessment of maturity.

Application	Description	Assessment R	Pt	Pr	Ue	Up
Text generation	Generating text from structured or unstructured input data				■	■
Multimedia generation/improvement						
Text-to-speech	Generated speech from text (multilinguality, accessibility)				■	■
Text-to-image/video	Generating talking heads, illustrating spoken text			■	■	
Music	Background music generation (rights free, appropriate length)					■
Improvement	Super-resolution, colorization, artifact concealment				■	■
Editing & storytelling	Rough cuts, automated editing		■	■		
VFX & visualization						
VFX & virtual studios	Visual effects, camera control, keying				■	■
Data visualization	Interactive data exploration			■	■	
Inclusion and accessibility						
Subtitling	Generating closed captions from spoken text			■	■	
Sign language	Generating and visualizing sign language	■	■	■		
Image description	Generate acoustic image description for visually impaired consumers	■				
Translation	Translation to other language, including simplified language				■	■
Business decision support	Predict popularity and user acceptance of content			■	■	
Content enrichment	Consumer guidance, product placement	■	■	■		

the lack of robustness, but also due to the lack of trained models on data relevant for the particular media organization (e.g., non-English language models). Closing this gap is not feasible on short term, and human-in-the-loop approaches are required to enable the gradual introduction of AI technologies in these application areas.

Table 3. Applications of AI in media distribution and assessment of maturity.

Application	Description	Assessment R | Pt | Pr | Ue | Up
Recommendation & targeting	Including all forms of personalization and customization (e.g., version for particular target devices, content length)	▮ (Up)
Content placing & linking	Placing content, displaying linked content, adjusting paywall settings	▮ (Ue)
Encoding & streaming	Learned media coding and rate control	▮ (Pr)
Moderation	Identifying inappropriate comments	▮ (Up)
Media monitoring		
Ads, brands, sponsorship	Monitoring impact of ad-related content	▮ (Up)
IPR enforcement	Monitoring to detect rights violations	▮ (Up)
Gender & diversity	Monitoring own or others' programme for equal representation of different groups	▮ (Pt)
Reach analysis	For traditional and social media	▮ (Up)
Conversational interfaces	Chatbots for customer care and interaction with content	▮ (R)

3   Automation Levels in the Media Domain

In the different application areas, AI may take a rather supporting role, being applied to very specific tasks, or have a higher degree of autonomy and contributes to decisions or takes them alone. The acceptable degree of automation depends very much on the application area, where media creators are usually more concerned about AI technology creating content or making decisions interfacing with customers.

The automation levels for autonomous driving [14] are well known. To the best of our knowledge, no such classification exists for the media domain. We thus propose a similar framework for the media domain. Table 4 summarizes the proposed categorization into six levels, and provides examples of the role of AI for applications in sourcing, production and distribution.

AI-enhanced tools describes the case where AI technologies perform a very specific task, replacing a traditional algorithm in a specific component. This happens very often for low-level tasks and thus mostly "under the hood". In many cases users will be unaware of the particular components included and their functionalities, thus the questions of acceptance and explainability are often neglected in this setting.

AI-based assistance covers cases, where AI-based tools generate information, that is used in later process stages under human control. AI-based methods do not take any decisions in this scenario. Most of today's information extraction and content analysis tools fall into this category, as they produce information that is either reviewed by humans, or used in a process fully under human control (e.g., content search). Users are aware of the information produced by AI, and their quality, so that questions of reliability and explainability of results become relevant. As the AI-based tools mostly feed data into other process steps, there is typically no interaction between humans and AI (beyond validation of results).

Conditional automation describes a scenario where AI-based tools take over steps in a process, but the process still foresees control by a human user. This probably is the one of the automation levels, where human-AI interaction is most frequent, and thus designing this interaction is most important. As the human user needs to interact with the AI components, explainability is important to understand their behavior and provide appropriate feedback for further training.

High automation reduces the role of the human user to supervision, and interfering with the process only when necessary. This will often be the case for content or decisions that are directly addressing media consumers. While interaction between human and AI will be less frequent, explainability is very important in this scenario, as the human supervisor needs to develop an intuition in which cases they trust the AI-based components, and in which cases checking is particularly important.

Full automation covers scenarios where an AI-based system performs tasks autonomously. If the quality of AI-based tools permits, it is likely that information gathering, content versioning and targeting/personalization will use this approach. Apart from some low-profile content types most media organizations are not likely to use this automation level for content creation in the foreseeable future.

For some applications in the media industry, the higher automation levels may be entirely out of scope, or limited to specific cases. One reason is the technical feasibility, as journalism's task is to report about "the world", i.e., news may involve all possible domains and topics. Thus, the requirements for a fully automatic solution may come close to that of artificial general intelligence (AGI). Another important reason is the wish to keep human oversight over information and processes, that may have a strong impact on democracy and society, rather than leaving automated content generation and recommendation algorithms negotiate public opinion. For modifications that concern merely technical aspects, e.g., adapting content to requirements of specific consumption devices, full automation is likely to be acceptable.

Table 4. Automation levels for AI in the media domain, and examples for sourcing, production and distribution applications.

Level	Description	Sourcing	Production	Distribution
0 No automation	Humans control non-AI-based tools	Topics monitored by humans, content analyzed and verified by humans	Content created by humans, tools based on non-AI technologies	Content selection and playout by humans
1 AI-enhanced tools	Humans operate tools using AI for specific tasks in their workflows	Content quality analysis, content similarity/near duplicates, model fitting for statistical data	Content modification and enhancement tools use AI for low level tasks (e.g., color correction, spell checking, inpainting)	Media monitoring tools
2 AI-based assistance	AI-based tools generate information that is used in subsequent steps, with human verification/correction, no decision	ASR, content tagging, classification, object/logo/face detection, trustworthiness scoring, knowledge modeling	Content suggestion/completion, summarization, subtitling support	Suggestion of content and ads
3 Conditional automation	Processes including AI-based decisions, with human intervention required at some points	Selection of relevant topics and sets of source content	Text/media generation from highly structured information, preparation of accessibility content	Automated choice of encoder settings, bitrate selection, content recommendation, automated compliance checking
4 High automation	Fully AI-based processes under human supervision (in particular for consumer facing decisions)	Automatic filtering and selection of sources, automatic content verification	Automatic generation of content (with review), fully automatic generation of versions	Automated user targeting and content adaptation to user (with human checks), chatbot with handoff
5 Full automation	Fully AI-based processes directly interfacing consumer, without human supervision	Automated relevance assessment, and analysis, assessment of content	Automated content creation/adaption tools for all modalities, automatic accessibility	Automated user targeting and content adaptation to user, chatbot without handoff

4 Conclusion

We have proposed a taxonomy of application areas for AI in the media industry. Those span the entire media value chain, and range from AI technologies applied across industries to very specific solutions for media use cases. Technologies have progressed beyond research prototypes in many of these areas, and at least experimental use has commenced for some of them. It is evident, that the successful application of AI in many of these use cases will require embedding them into collaborative human-AI workflows. Also one of the specific challenges identified in the study addresses a smart assistant for journalists, supporting information collection and organization as well as content creation. The interaction between human and machine, including continuous training based on the implicit feedback by the human in the loop, is of key importance here.

Different application areas require different levels of human oversight. To this end, we have proposed automation levels for the media domain, inspired from those for automated driving. While in low automation levels AI is rather an isolated background component, in particular the mid- to high- automation levels require tight human interaction. This topic still requires further research, as currently most of the work on human AI collaboration focuses on robotics, maintenance and logistics. Existing works in the creative industries deal with other applications than media. A recent survey on collaborative AI in the creative industries [5] identified 34 publications covering applications like graphic design, urban planning, fashion and computer games, but no journalism related ones. Three archetypes of tasks in knowledge work are defined in [12], in which there is either a "human in the loop of AI" or "AI in the loop of human intelligence". As an example, the creation of a journalistic text is used. The results of a co-design workshop for a collaborative AI-based verification tool shows, that explainability and transparency are central components for collaborative use of an AI-based system [9].

Providing AI as an assistive technology in journalistic workflows, that provides support, but does not require much additional effort from users under stressful situations in order to learn, is still an open research challenge. However, given the importance of collaborative human-AI workflows in the media industry, we consider solving this challenge as a key for the successful and wider adoption of AI technologies in the media industry.

Acknowledgment. This work has received funding from the "ICT of the Future" program by the Austrian Federal Ministry of Climate Action, Environment, Energy, Mobility, Innovation and Technology (BMK) under the AI.AT.Media study, and from the European Union's Horizon 2020 research and innovation programme, under grant agreement n° 951911 AI4Media (https://ai4media.eu). The authors thank the expert panel and all interviewees of the AI.AT.Media study for their inputs.

References

1. Beckett, C.: New powers, new responsibilities: A global survey of journalism and artificial intelligence. Technical report, London School of Economics (2019)
2. Chan-Olmsted, S.M.: A review of artificial intelligence adoptions in the media industry. Int. J. Media Manag. **21**(3–4), 193–215 (2019)
3. Hildesheim, W., Michelsen, D.: Künstliche Intelligenz im Jahr 2020 – Aktueller Stand von branchenübergreifenden KI-Lösungen: Was ist möglich?, Was nicht?, Beispiele und Empfehlungen. In: Buxmann, P., Schmidt, H. (eds.) Künstliche Intelligenz, pp. 183–201. Springer, Heidelberg (2021). https://doi.org/10.1007/978-3-662-61794-6_11
4. Hauck, M., Pagel, S.: AI Media Technology Landscape - Systematisierungsinstrument für den Einsatz von KI in Medienunternehmen. In: Jahrestagung der Fachgruppe Medienökonomie der DGPUK, pp. 55–68. DEU (2020)
5. Hughes, R.T., Zhu, L., Bednarz, T.: Generative adversarial networks-enabled human-artificial intelligence collaborative applications for creative and design industries: a systematic review of current approaches and trends. Front. Artif. Intell. **4**, 24 (2021)
6. ISO 16290: Space systems – definition of the technology readiness levels (TRLs) and their criteria of assessment (2013)

7. ISO/IEC 22989: Information technology – artificial intelligence – artificial intelligence concepts and terminology. Draft of International Standard (2021)
8. Krawarik, V., Schell, K., Ertelthalner, V., Thallinger, G., Bailer, W.: AI.AT.Media - AI and the Austrian Media Sector: Mapping the Landscape, Setting a Course. Study, Austrian Federal Ministry of Climate Action, Environment, Energy, Mobility, Innovation and Technology (2021)
9. Missaoui, S., Gutierrez-Lopez, M., MacFarlane, A., Makri, S., Porlezza, C., Cooper, G.: How to blend journalistic expertise with artificial intelligence for research and verifying news stories. In: CHI (2019)
10. Nel, F.P., Milburn-Curtis, C.: World press trends 2021. WAN-IFRA (2021)
11. Newman, N., Fletcher, R., Schulz, A., Andi, S., Robertson, C.T., Nielsen, R.K.: Reuters Institute digital news report 2021. Reuters Institute for the Study of Journalism (2021)
12. Oeste-Reiß, S.: Hybride Wissensarbeit. Informatik Spektrum **44**(3), 148–152 (2021). https://doi.org/10.1007/s00287-021-01352-0
13. Rehm, G.: The use of artificial intelligence in the audiovisual sector. Technical report, European Parliament (2020)
14. SAE: Taxonomy and definitions for terms related to driving automation systems for on-road motor vehicles. J3016_202104 (2021)

Rating-Aware Self-Organizing Maps

Ladislav Peška[✉] and Jakub Lokoč

Department of Software Engineering, Faculty of Mathematics and Physics,
Charles University, Prague, Czech Republic
{ladislav.peska,jakub.lokoc}@matfyz.cuni.cz

Abstract. Self-organizing maps (SOM) are one of the prominent
paradigms for 2D data visualization. While aiming at preserving topological relations of high-dimensional data, they provide sufficiently organized view of objects and thus improve capability of users to explore
displayed information. SOMs were also extensively utilized in visualizing
results of multimedia information retrieval systems. However, for this
task, SOM lacks the ability to adapt to the relevance scores induced by
the underlying retrieval algorithm. Therefore, although exploration capability is enhanced, the capability to exploit the (best) results is severely
limited. In order to cope with this problem, we propose a rating-aware
modification of SOM algorithm that jointly optimizes for the preservation of both topological as well as relevance-based ordering of results.

Keywords: Interactive video retrieval · Relevance feedback · Deep
learning

1 Introduction

Data visualization represents a challenging but important method to better
understand information stored in data. A frequent analytical need is visualization of high-dimensional data that tries to preserve topological relations in a
low-dimensional presentation space. So far, there were various approaches proposed to tackle this challenge, each constructing the visualization space by different optimization strategies. The challenge was addressed e.g. by linear projections [16], particle models using attractive/repulsive forces [5], self-sorting maps
[1], or self-organizing maps [11]. In this work, we focus on self-organizing maps
(SOM). SOM can fit a data distribution with a 2D grid of neurons and thus provide directly topologically sorted representative database items. This principle
is often used to visualize or exploit data proximity relations for effective analysis
in various domains [2,14,19].

Nonetheless, visualizations for particular domains may obey also other criteria, not just topological ordering preservation. Let us for instance consider the
content-based interactive video retrieval domain [15,20]. In a video retrieval system, users can provide queries to specify their search needs (textual description,
example images, sketches etc.) and the task of the system is to respond with

© Springer Nature Switzerland AG 2022
B. Þór Jónsson et al. (Eds.): MMM 2022, LNCS 13141, pp. 119–130, 2022.
https://doi.org/10.1007/978-3-030-98358-1_10

the best possible collection of results to the user's query (usually depicted as a 2D grid of $w \times h$ items stretched over the majority of a viewscreen). The easiest way to address this task is to order the candidate items w.r.t. assigned relevance scores and display *Top-K* best-rated items. The main strength of *Top-K display* is its ability to exploit the best possible results (w.r.t. current retrieval model) and its placement on the most prominent areas of the display. This maximizes both the chance that relevant results are displayed and that users spot them easily. Looking at selected state-of-the-art Video Browser Showdown (VBS) systems like vitrivr [7], VIRET [17], Vireo [21], SOMHunter [12], or HTW [8], Top-K like visualizations respecting ranking of candidate items indeed prevail. However, Top-K visualizations have two principal drawbacks.

First, as was shown during recent VBS competitions, initial query results provided by video retrieval systems may be unsatisfactory [20] – either the query or the retrieval models are imprecise, or the search need is simply difficult to describe. Therefore, retrieval systems offer a wide palette of additional interactions allowing users to improve the results. These interactions could range from simple reformulations of the original query to *"more of the same"* approach (i.e. requesting further similar results to a displayed one) or relevance feedback (i.e. rating goodness of individual results in order to update the relevance model). Nonetheless, effectivity of interactive approaches greatly depends on previous result collections (e.g. ability to find a good example for *"more of the same"* strategy). In Top-K-like visualizations, displayed results usually represent only a very narrow subset of the dataset with low intrinsic diversity among displayed items. Therefore, if the query does not target the search need very precisely, it may provide completely irrelevant results and due to the low diversity, users are unable to use interactive query refinement approaches effectively. This problem is more severe for difficult tasks, where correct answers are sparse – e.g. known item search (KIS) tasks as defined in VBS [20]. The severity of the problem is illustrated by the fact that many surveyed VBS systems integrate additional exploratory types of visualizations showing semantically sorted maps of more diverse frame thumbnails (with respect to their descriptors).

The second drawback of Top-K visualizations is that the placement of individual images on the display grid does not respect inter-item similarities. The lack of topology preservation in the display makes exploration of results more challenging for users and may result into an oversight of relevant results – especially if they are placed in a less prominent area of the display.

The SOM approach is orthogonal to Top-K visualizations, as it provides a topology-preserving overview of the whole dataset, but does not exploit item's relevance in its original form. In fact, both Top-K and SOM-based visualizations are edge cases of a well known exploration-exploitation dilemma [10]: should the system provide best answers w.r.t. its current relevance model (so the user could fully exploit it), or should the system provide more speculative results with lower immediate value (which on the other hand better represent the variability of the data and allow users to fine-tune the results more effectively)?

In this paper, we aim on combining the benefits of both approaches. We start from the concept of "relevance-to-SOM" visualization [12] and develop it to a more general trade-off oriented approach denoted as Rating-aware SOM. Rating-aware SOM is essentially a multi-criteria optimization technique for grid visualizations reflecting diversity, relevance and topological constraints. To be more specific, we formulated what we believe are three principal requirements for a good collection of results, which are targeted by Rating-aware SOM.

- R1: Provide most relevant results and visualize them in such way to be easily spotted by the user (i.e. in the most prominent areas of the display).
- R2: Provide results of sufficient diversity, so users can get an overall view on possible answers to his/her query and effectively utilize interactive query refinement approaches.
- R3: Topologically organize results to enhance their explorability and allow users to easily focus their attention on a specific region of interest.

Naturally, individual requirements often contradict one another, so their importance has to be established for particular scenarios and Rating-aware SOM should be tunable to reflect this trade-off.

2   Related Work

Several related works aimed at some form of relevance-based adjustments for SOM [12,14]. Recently, SOMHunter [12] utilized an approach that combines relevance scores based on a query (or feedback) with a dynamic construction of a self-organizing map respecting the scores in its sampling procedures. The nice consequence of this combination is a self-organizing map attached around regions with the most relevant items, but the positions of best rated items within the display is arbitrary. Using a relevance score distribution to select items for the next display is a concept used already in Bayesian frameworks for relevance feedback based search [3,4]. In these works, different types of displays are considered in experiments evaluating the effectiveness of the overall interactive search process. For example, display D obtained by sampling $|D|$ items from the current distribution of relevance scores of all database items. This approach reflects both relevance and diversity, but it would require a post-processing method to organize data on the display. Even after re-organization of the display, the position of the most relevant item in the display grid may be arbitrary. It is the same problem as for SOM based displays used by SOMHunter. Hence, our motivation is to design a single method combining all three different benefits, R1–R3, to organize displays.

Note that so far we mentioned the concept of *"prominent areas of the display grid"* several times without a proper definition. It was shown by many related works from the area of eye-tracking (e.g. [6,9,22]) that users do not distribute their attention uniformly over the whole viewscreen. Instead (at least in western civilization), users tend to give more attention to objects displayed on the left rather than right and top rather than bottom parts part of the viewscreen [22]. Naturally, the most relevant items should be placed on the areas with highest expected share of user's attention, so they can be spotted more easily.

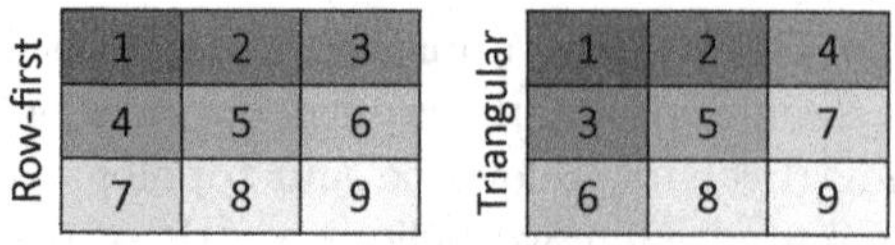

Fig. 1. Examples of nodes prominency ordering on 3 × 3 display grids: row-first (left) and triangular (right).

In this paper, we specifically considered two of the possible "prominency" ordering: row-first and triangular. Row-first approach assumes rows to be primary indicators of prominency and columns secondary. Triangular ordering aims to mimic the "golden triangle" pattern [6], which is often observed in the distribution of user's attention. As such, a sum of row ID and column ID is a primary indicator, while row ID is secondary. Examples of these orderings are depicted on Fig. 1. Throughout the rest of the paper, while referring to display nodes, we consider them to be prominency ordered. I.e. if $N = [n_1, n_2, ..., n_{w \times h}]$ is a collection of nodes for a display with width w and height h, the first node represents the most prominent position on the display and so on. $Coord(n)$ method assigns appropriate coordinates to each display node $n \in N$.

3   Rating-Aware Self-Organizing Maps

In this section we first recapitulate the Self-Organizing Maps (SOM) algorithm and then propose their rating-aware extensions. Note that for the sake of space, we only describe SOM in the context of our use-case (displaying results of retrieval systems) and ignore implications of other use-cases on SOM design.

Let us consider a 2D grid of display nodes $n \in N$, where each node is expected to depict one resulting item (image in our case). In this context, the task of SOM is to select images that should be depicted on each of the grid positions. Further assume that each candidate item $i \in I$ is described by a vector of features f_i. SOM training is depicted in Algorithm 1. Upon initialization, SOM constructs a network of neurons corresponding to the display grid and initializes all neurons with random weights w_n (line 1; note that the dimensionality of w_n is the same as those of f_i). SOM training runs in several epochs. In each epoch a random permutation of candidate items $[P(1), P(2), ..., P(|I|)]$ is considered (line 3) and permuted items are sequentially utilized as training examples. For each training example i, the best matching node (BMN_i) is selected w.r.t. Euclidean distance between w_n and f_i (line 5). Then, weights of the best matching node, as well as its neighborhood, are pulled towards f_i (line 6). Nodes further away from BMN_i (w.r.t. euclidean distance of nodes' coordinates) receive gradually decreasing updates. The learning rate linearly decreases (line 7) throughout the training to allow both major initial modifications as well as fine-tuning towards the end of training.

Once the SOM training is finished, each SOM node is assigned a list of candidate items, for which it is the best matching node. Out of these candidates, the

---

Algorithm 1. SOM training

Input: $i \in \mathcal{I}$: set candidate items and their features $\boldsymbol{f}_i$, grid dimensions w and h, volume of *epochs*, learning rate lr, neighborhood penalty σ.
Output: trained weights of SOM nodes $\boldsymbol{w}_n : n \in N$

1: $N = [n_1, n_2, ..., n_{w \times h}]$; $\forall n \in N$: initialize $\boldsymbol{w}_n$ randomly;

2: **for** $k \in [1, ..., epochs]$ **do**

3:    $candidates = \text{Permute}(I)$

4:    **for** $i \in candidates$ **do**

5:       $BMN_i = \text{argmin}_{\forall n \in N}\ L2(\boldsymbol{f}_i, \boldsymbol{w}_n)$

6:       $\forall n \in N : \boldsymbol{w}_n = \boldsymbol{w}_n + lr * e^{-\frac{L2\left(\text{Coord}(BMN_i), \text{Coord}(n)\right)}{\sigma^2}} (\boldsymbol{f}_i - \boldsymbol{w}_n)$

7:       linearly decrease lr

8:    **end for**

9: **end for**

10: **return** $[\boldsymbol{w}_n : n \in N]$

---

one with the highest relevance score is selected to be displayed. If the list of candidates for some node is empty, we greedily select the closest (w.r.t. $L2(\boldsymbol{w}_n, \boldsymbol{f}_i)$) not yet displayed candidate.[1] In results, this approach is denoted as *Plain SOM*.

3.1 Probabilistic Candidates Selection Procedure

The only way in which Plain SOM optimizes for the current query is the final selection of images to be displayed in particular node. For most cases, this does not allow users to sufficiently exploit relevant results. In order to cope with this problem, Kratochvil et al. [12] proposed a probabilistic candidates selection for SOM. Instead of permuting all candidate items (line 3 in Algorithm 1), a series of random selections[2] is performed. For each candidate i, the probability of being selected is proportional to its relevance score (r_i).

As such, probabilistic SOM (denoted as *Plain SOM+prob* in results) should primarily fit to the most relevant objects. Although there is now higher chance to display the most relevant items, *Plain SOM+prob* does not provide any guarantees on whether they will be plotted in a prominent part of the display grid (i.e., R1 is only partially supported).

3.2 Rating-Aware Extension for BMN Selection

In order to cope with the positioning problem, we propose a rating-aware extension to the best matching node selection procedure (denoted as *Rating SOM* in results). The core idea behind our proposal is that selection of the best matching

---

[1] Other options, e.g. sampling the object based on a probability distribution induced by relevance scores or employing Hungarian algorithm [13] are plausible. However, since this is not in the core of our proposal, we opted for this simple greedy approach.

[2] With repetitions; series' length is equal to the volume of candidate items.

node should not only depend on the similarity assessment, but should also reflect the need to display most relevant results in a prominent part of the display grid.

To be more formal, suppose that r@top-k is a relevance score of the k-th most relevant item. If a Top-K display is utilized, the item depicted on n-th node has the rating r@top-n. Furthermore, note that r_i is a relevance score assigned to the current candidate image i. Then the BMN selection procedure (line 5 in Algorithm 1) is modified as follows:

$$BMN_i = \operatorname*{argmin}_{\forall n \in N} \left(\alpha * L2(\boldsymbol{f}_i, \boldsymbol{w}_n) + (1 - \alpha) * \frac{abs(r_i - r@\text{top-}n)}{log_2(n + 1)} \right) \quad (1)$$

where α is a hyperparameter tuning the tradeoff between the local similarity and the rating-awareness.

The intuition behind our proposal is as follows. Imagine that we are evaluating the overall relevance of the display via Discounted Cummulative Gain: $DCG = \sum_{\forall n \in N} \frac{r@n}{log_2(n+1)}$, where $r@n$ denotes relevance score of an item displayed on n-th node. The best possible DCG is received, if items are displayed from best to worst w.r.t. relevance scores (i.e., if *Top-K* display is employed). In this case, $r@n = r@\text{top-}n$. In the rating-aware BMN procedure, we calculate how much the current item would deviate from the best possible allocation of items (w.r.t. DCG) if it was displayed on node n: $abs(r_i - r@\text{top-}n)$. Furthermore, DCG employs a relevance penalty equal to the binary logarithm of the result's rank increased by one. In another words, relevant items placed lower in the list of results has gradually decreasing impact on the metric. As a consequence, deviation from the optimal rating is a less severe problem for less prominent nodes if DCG is considered as a target metric. We reflected this by using the same penalization for ratings deviation as DCG does. As a result, the second component of Eq. 1 represents a point-wise optimization of DCG metric.

Utilization of DCG penalty during BMN selection has a nice side-effect of a smooth transition between exploitation-oriented and exploration-oriented parts of the display. For the most prominent display areas, rating-aware penalty is high, so the most relevant results should be mapped there (without too much consideration for local organization – like in a Top-K display). For the less prominent parts of display, the rating-aware penalty is smaller, which may attract more diverse, yet locally organized results to serve the explorational needs of users.

4   Evaluation

4.1   Evaluation Protocol

We evaluated the proposed *Rating SOM* approach together with several baselines in two studies. Due to its interpretability and clarity, we first focused on a color sorting problem and then evaluated the approaches on a video frames retrieval problem. In both cases, we simulate a known-item search, where user query the system to find one particular target item.

For the color sorting study, we randomly generated a set of 500 RGB colors to represent candidate items and another 100 RGB colors to represent target items. For an arbitrary target t, we simulated the relevance scores of candidate items based on a noisy target-candidate similarity: $r_i = e^{-exp*L2(f_t+b,f_i)}$, where L2 is euclidean distance, exp is a scoring hyperparameter tuning the steepness of the relevance model, f_t and f_i are vectors of red, green and blue components of target and candidate colors and b is a random noise vector selected from a normal distribution with $\mu = 0$ and $\sigma = 0.1$. Random noise was added to simulate (a moderate level of) errors caused by imperfect query construction. For each target t, five displays are generated: *Top-K* display, *Plain SOM*, *Plain SOM+prob*, *Rating SOM* and *Rating SOM+prob*. All display grids were 8×8 squares and we considered row-based and triangular ordering of node's relevance. Furthermore, all SOM variants were initialized with $\sigma = 1$, $lr = 1$ and trained for 6 epochs. The exp hyperparameter was selected from $\{5, 10, 20\}$. *Rating SOM* variants were evaluated with $\alpha \in \{0.001, 0.003, 0.01, 0.03, 0.1, 0.2, 0.5, 0.8, 0.9\}$.

For the video frames retrieval problem, we utilized a dataset of 20000 keyframes extracted from V3C1 [18]. Semantic features of the keyframes were obtained via NASnet DCNN [23] and then reduced to 128 dimensions via PCA. For evaluation, we selected 100 random keyframes as target items. Due to the differences in both datasets, the study settings were slightly adjusted: SOM networks were trained for 2 epochs only, the gaussian noise parameter was slightly increased ($\sigma = 0.2$) to account for higher distances between items. We also normalized the relevance scores before application in SOM to stabilize the α hyperparameter range.

Three metrics were evaluated for each display: normalized Discounted Cumulative Gain (nDCG), overall diversity of displayed items and the ratio between neighbors' diversity and overall diversity. NDCG evaluates R1 requirement, i.e. exploitation capability of the display. DCG of the evaluated display is divided by the DCG of ideally ordered display, so nDCG $\in [0, 1]$, where higher values indicate better results. Note that in order to account for true relevance of items, we utilize unbiased target-candidate distance ($e^{-exp*L2(f_t,f_i)}$) as a relevance score.

Overall diversity (denoted as $div(all)$) evaluates R2 requirement, i.e. coverage of the display. Diversity of displayed candidates i and j is calculated as euclidean distance of their features $L2(f_i, f_j)$) and $div(all)$ is a mean diversity w.r.t. all pairs of displayed items (higher values indicate more diverse results).

Finally, the ratio between neighbors and overall diversity (denoted as $divRatio = div(neighbors)/div(all)$) evaluates R3 requirement, i.e. orderliness of the display. For each node n in the grid, all its adjacent nodes A_n are considered as neighbors. For example, neighbors of a node with coordinates $[0, 0]$ are nodes with coordinates $[0, 1]$, $[1, 0]$ and $[1, 1]$. Let us denote the total volume of neighbors as $|A| = \sum_{\forall n \in N} |A_n|$ Then $div(neighbors)$ is calculated as mean euclidean distance between nodes and their neighbors: $div(neighbors) = \sum_{\forall n \in N, m \in A_n} (L2(f_n, f_m))/|A|$. In this case, lower values indicate more orderly results.

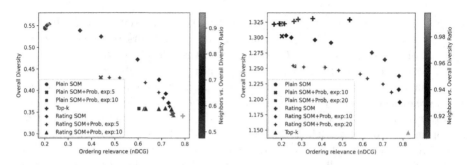

Fig. 2. Results of color sorting (left) and video retrieval (right). X-axis depicts nDCG (i.e. exploitation capability), Y-axis depicts overall nodes diversity (i.e. exploration capability) and nodes' color denotes ratio between the diversity of neighbouring vs. all nodes (i.e. orderliness feature). *A dark-blue point in top-right corner is an optimum.* (Color figure online)

Metrics were evaluated for all test items and mean values are reported. Note that for the sake of comparability, we considered $exp = 10$ while evaluating nDCG of all methods.

4.2 Results

Figure 2 depicts overall results for triangular ordering[3], color sorting scenario (left) and video retrieval scenario (right). Note that for the sake of clarity, we only depict results of $exp \in \{5, 10\}$ for color sorting and $exp \in \{10, 20\}$ for video retrieval. In both studies, we can see that variants of Rating SOM and Rating SOM+prob nicely fill the space between Plain SOM(+prob) and Top-K displays. Notably, Rating SOM(+prob) with higher α improves over Plain SOM(+prob) w.r.t. nDCG at the cost of minimal deterioration (in some cases even improvement) of $div(all)$ and $divRatio$ metrics. Also, especially the variants of Rating SOM+prob with lower α and higher exp provide close-to-best nDCG, while considerably improving both $div(all)$ and $divRatio$ metrics as compared to Top-K display. Note that in terms of absolute values, differences in $divRatio$ were much smaller for video retrieval task. This was partially caused by a smaller variance in distances distribution of video retrieval scenario. Even though, we plan to conduct a user study to determine, whether such differences in $divRatio$ are sufficiently meaningful for users.

Let us also compare individual Rating SOM variants. By utilizing probabilistic sampling and by increasing exp hyperparameter, the overall diversity of results decrease significantly, but the examples are gradually shifted towards higher nDCG. So, if lower nDCG values are sufficient, variants of Rating SOM and Rating SOM+prob with smaller exp can provide higher diversity while maintaining similar or better $divRatio$. Seemingly, probabilistic sampling indirectly defines an upper bound for possible diversity of the display. On the other

---

[3] Results of both prominence orderings (row-based and triangular) were highly similar in terms of absolute values as well as relative comparison of methods. For the sake of space, we only report results of triangular ordering.

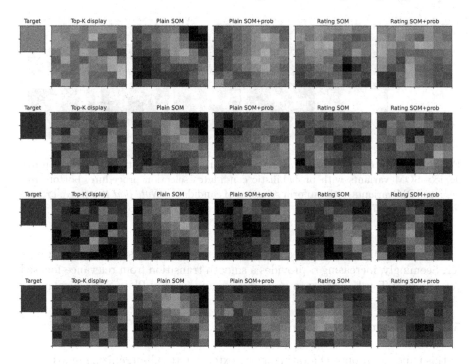

Fig. 3. Sampled display grids on RGB colors. All methods utilized $\alpha = 0.03$, $exp = 10$ settings and triangular ordering. (Color figure online)

hand, while moving towards maximal nDCG, variants of Rating SOM+prob with higher exp are able to maintain better *divRatio* for similar levels of nDCG and diversity. Therefore, the decision to (not) use probabilistic sampling as well as steepness of the sampling mainly depends on the required relevance vs. diversity tradeoff.

Overall, results indicate that Rating SOM(+prob) variants represent a favorable and tunable compromise (w.r.t. evaluated metrics) between exploration and exploitation needs of the user. Nonetheless, it is not quite clear whether the observed differences in metrics translate into better displays from the human perspective. We plan to evaluate this aspect in a dedicated user study as a part of our future work. However, we provide several examples of color sorting displays for individual comparison.

Figure 3 depicts constructed displays for several targets in color sorting scenario. Note that less prominent positions in Top-K display are rather cluttered, while Plain SOM displays only a handful of relevant objects. Plain SOM+prob displays more relevant objects than Plain SOM, but their position w.r.t. display grid is random. In contrast, Rating SOM(+prob) variants usually display the most relevant items close to the top-left corner and the relevance gradually decrease towards bottom-right corner. However, they provide much less cluttered displays than Top-K.

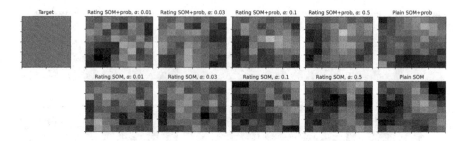

Fig. 4. The effect of α hyperparameter on resulting displays with $exp = 10$. Top row depicts SOM variants with probabilistic candidates selection procedure, bottom row depicts SOM variants with uniform selection of candidates. *Note that this figure extends the first row of* Fig. 3.

Figure 4 depicts constructed displays for several variants of α hyperparameter. Seemingly, increasing α provides a smooth transition from relevance-focused yet orderless Top-K display to more diverse and orderly Plain SOM display.

5   Discussion and Conclusions

In this paper we proposed a rating-aware extension to self-organizing maps (Rating SOM) with the aim to maintain three principal requirements of a good result collections: displaying best results on prominent spots (R1), providing sufficiently diverse results (R2) and display similar results close to each other (R3). In results, we can observe that the proposed method provides a smooth transition from Plain SOM displays to Top-K displays with beneficial trade-offs among evaluated metrics.

Nonetheless, this initial proposal has several limitations, which we plan to address in the future. First, Rating SOM was specifically designed to optimize nDCG, but other ranking-aware relevance metrics with various steepness (and therefore different exploration-exploitation tradeoff) can be considered as well.

Next, several evaluation parameters were kept fixed (display size, Gaussian noise) and their effect should be explored in a follow-up evaluation. In theory, sizes of more orderly result collections may grow larger, while maintaining similar levels of findability for displayed relevant items as compared to smaller yet orderless collections. We plan to conduct a user study focused on item's findability under the constraints of various display sizes, display construction methods and quality of the retrieval model to verify this hypothesis. For the sake of simplicity, this work utilized an artificial relevance model, where query generation was based on the knowledge of the target. However, it may be also interesting to evaluate the whole interactive retrieval process including query formulation and an effect of the displayed results on the process of interactive reformulations.

This would also require a dedicated user study on a suitable interactive retrieval testbed system.

Another question is the suitability of underlying features for similarity assessments. For color sorting, euclidean distances on RGB channels seems as a reasonable approximation of human perception of similarity. For video retrieval on the other hand, multiple options are plausible (e.g. semantic concepts, color histograms or low-resolution pixel maps). Subjectively, local similarity of SOM-generated video retrieval displays (see on-line supplementary materials for examples) was perceivable although not exactly overwhelming. Yet, considering the *divRatio* metric, SOM variants performed quite well. We hypothesize that this discrepancy may be at least partially attributed to the different perception of similarity by humans. Therefore, another direction of our future work would encompass cross-modal retrieval, where various modalities should be considered for topological preservation. Here one of the important questions is whether a static set of features is sufficient, or they should be learned e.g. from query properties or user's relevance feedback.

Acknowledgment. Source codes of Rating SOM as well as supplementary materials can be obtained from https://github.com/lpeska/RatingAwareSOM. This paper has been supported by Czech Science Foundation (GAČR) project 19-22071Y.

References

1. Barthel, K.U., Hezel, N.: Visually exploring millions of images using image maps and graphs, chap. 11, pp. 289–315. Wiley (2019). https://doi.org/10.1002/9781119376996.ch11
2. Bernard, P., Golbraikh, A., Kireev, D., Chrétien, J.R., Rozhkova, N.: Comparison of chemical databases: analysis of molecular diversity with self organising maps (SOM). Analusis **26**(8), 333–341 (1998). https://doi.org/10.1051/analusis:1998182
3. Cox, I.J., Miller, M.L., Minka, T.P., Papathomas, T.V., Yianilos, P.N.: The Bayesian image retrieval system, PicHunter: theory, implementation, and psychophysical experiments. IEEE Trans. Image Process. **9**(1), 20–37 (2000)
4. Ferecatu, M., Geman, D.: A statistical framework for image category search from a mental picture. IEEE Trans. Pattern Anal. Mach. Intell. **31**(6), 1087–1101 (2009). https://doi.org/10.1109/TPAMI.2008.259
5. Fruchterman, T.M.J., Reingold, E.M.: Graph drawing by force-directed placement. Softw. Pract. Exp. **21**(11), 1129–1164 (1991). https://doi.org/10.1002/spe.4380211102
6. Granka, L., Feusner, M., Lorigo, L.: Eye monitoring in online search. In: Hammoud, R. (ed.) Passive Eye Monitoring. Signals and Communication Technologies. Springer, Heidelberg (2008). https://doi.org/10.1007/978-3-540-75412-1_16
7. Heller, S., et al.: Towards explainable interactive multi-modal video retrieval with vitrivr. In: Lokoč, J., et al. (eds.) MMM 2021. LNCS, vol. 12573, pp. 435–440. Springer, Cham (2021). https://doi.org/10.1007/978-3-030-67835-7_41
8. Hezel, N., Schall, K., Jung, K., Barthel, K.U.: Video search with sub-image keyword transfer using existing image archives. In: Lokoč, J., et al. (eds.) MMM 2021. LNCS, vol. 12573, pp. 484–489. Springer, Cham (2021). https://doi.org/10.1007/978-3-030-67835-7_49

9. Joachims, T., Granka, L., Pan, B., Hembrooke, H., Radlinski, F., Gay, G.: Evaluating the accuracy of implicit feedback from clicks and query reformulations in web search. ACM Trans. Inf. Syst. **25**(2), 7-es (2007). https://doi.org/10.1145/1229179.1229181

10. Karimzadehgan, M., Zhai, C.: Exploration-exploitation tradeoff in interactive relevance feedback. In: 19th ACM International Conference on Information and Knowledge Management, CIKM 2010, pp. 1397–1400. ACM (2010). https://doi.org/10.1145/1871437.1871631

11. Kohonen, T.: The self-organizing map. Neurocomputing **21**(1–3), 1–6 (1998)

12. Kratochvil, M., Mejzlík, F., Veselý, P., Souček, T., Lokoć, J.: SOMHunter: lightweight video search system with SOM-guided relevance feedback. In: 28th ACM International Conference on Multimedia, MM 2020, pp. 4481–4484. ACM (2020). https://doi.org/10.1145/3394171.3414542

13. Kuhn, H.W.: The Hungarian method for the assignment problem. Nav. Res. Logist. Q. **2**(1–2), 83–97 (1955)

14. Laaksonen, J., Koskela, M., Oja, E.: PicSOM: self-organizing maps for content-based image retrieval. In: International Joint Conference on Neural Networks, IJCNN 1999, vol. 4, pp. 2470–2473 (1999). https://doi.org/10.1109/IJCNN.1999.833459

15. Lokoč, J., Bailer, W., Schoeffmann, K., Münzer, B., Awad, G.: On influential trends in interactive video retrieval: video browser showdown 2015–2017. IEEE Trans. Multimedia **20**(12), 3361–3376 (2018)

16. Metsalu, T., Vilo, J.: ClustVis: a web tool for visualizing clustering of multivariate data using Principal Component Analysis and heatmap. Nucleic Acids Res. **43**(W1), W566–W570 (2015). https://doi.org/10.1093/nar/gkv468

17. Peška, L., Kovalčík, G., Souček, T., Škrhák, V., Lokoč, J.: W2VV++ BERT model at VBS 2021. In: Lokoč, J., et al. (eds.) MMM 2021. LNCS, vol. 12573, pp. 467–472. Springer, Cham (2021). https://doi.org/10.1007/978-3-030-67835-7_46

18. Peška, L., Mejzlík, F., Souček, T., Lokoč, J.: Towards evaluating and simulating keyword queries for development of interactive known-item search systems. In: 2020 International Conference on Multimedia Retrieval, ICMR 2020, pp. 281–285. ACM (2020). https://doi.org/10.1145/3372278.3390726

19. Qian, J., et al.: Introducing self-organized maps (SOM) as a visualization tool for materials research and education. Results Mater. **4**, 100020 (2019). https://doi.org/10.1016/j.rinma.2019.100020

20. Rossetto, L., et al.: Interactive video retrieval in the age of deep learning - detailed evaluation of VBS 2019. IEEE Trans. Multimedia **23**, 243–256 (2021). https://doi.org/10.1109/TMM.2020.2980944

21. Wu, J., Nguyen, P.A., Ma, Z., Ngo, C.-W.: SQL-like interpretable interactive video search. In: Lokoč, J., et al. (eds.) MMM 2021. LNCS, vol. 12573, pp. 391–397. Springer, Cham (2021). https://doi.org/10.1007/978-3-030-67835-7_34

22. Zhao, Q., Chang, S., Harper, F.M., Konstan, J.A.: Gaze prediction for recommender systems. In: 10th ACM Conference on Recommender Systems, RecSys 2016, pp. 131–138. ACM (2016). https://doi.org/10.1145/2959100.2959150

23. Zoph, B., Vasudevan, V., Shlens, J., Le, Q.V.: Learning transferable architectures for scalable image recognition. CoRR abs/1707.07012 (2017)

Color the Word: Leveraging Web Images for Machine Translation of Untranslatable Words

Yana van de Sande$^{(\boxtimes)}$ and Martha Larson

Radboud University, Nijmegen, Netherlands
{yana.vandesande,martha.larson}@ru.nl

Abstract. Automatic translation allows people around the globe to communicate with one another. However, state-of-the art machine translation is still unable to capture fine-grained meaning. This paper introduces the idea of using Web image selections in text-to-text translation, specifically for *lacunae*, which are words that do not have a translation in another language. We asked human professional translators to rank Google translate translations of lacunae in German and Dutch. We then compared that ranking with a ranking based on color histograms of Web image data of the words. We found there is viable potential in the idea of using images to address lacunae in the field of machine translation. We publicly release a dataset and our code for others to explore this potential. Finally, we provide an outlook on research directions that would allow this idea to be used in practice.

Keywords: Machine translation · Lacunae · Semantics · Web images

1 Introduction

Translating a text requires transforming the semantics of a source language into a target language. In recent years, machine learning has made dramatic advances in text-to-text translation by exploiting huge amounts of textual training data [2]. Although today's automatic machine translation is highly advanced, the problem of *lacunae* remains unsolved. Lacunae are 'holes in meaning', or words that exist in one language, but have no direct correlate in another. Examples are the Dutch word *gezellig* and the German word *Schadenfreude*, which have no direct translations into English. In this paper, we demonstrate that image data has a potential role to play in the text-to-text translation of lacunae. We introduce the idea that Web image search has potential to extend automatic text-to-text translation in order to address the persisting challenge of lacunae.

Informally, lacunae are considered to be untranslatable words. However, this characterization does not reflect the reality of translation, which cannot simply skip difficult words, but requires the meaning of the source language to be fully and faithfully represented in the target language. When human translators

© Springer Nature Switzerland AG 2022
B. Þór Jónsson et al. (Eds.): MMM 2022, LNCS 13141, pp. 131–138, 2022.
https://doi.org/10.1007/978-3-030-98358-1_11

encounter lacunae in their source language, they are forced to choose the best fitting words in their target language. Their choice should bring the meaning of the source text across to the reader without losing the nuance expressed by original words. For this reason, the difficulty of translating lacunae can be considered to lie in the nature of the words and in the translators' knowledge of the target language, rather than in untranslatability [16].

Our proposition is that image data collected via Web search has the potential to capture knowledge of language that can complement what textual training data contributes to automatic machine translation. Specifically, we argue that images can supply information on the nuances of meaning that are necessary to identify the best fitting words of a target language that should be used to translate a lacuna in the source language. We demonstrate that color-based representations derived from sets of images naïvely collected using a general Web search engine is already surprisingly effective in picking out best-fit targets from among candidate translations.

The idea has social impact due to its potential contribution to intercultural communication. Further exploration of this idea can help improve machine translation, improve our understanding of semantic information in visual data and establish color as a feature of semantics. Improving machine translation can have positive effects for communication between people around the world. Furthermore, we hope to start a conversation on the role of multimedia data, in this research image data, in machine translation research and semantics.

The paper is organized as follows. First, we provide a brief overview of related work demonstrating why our idea can be considered both novel and brave. Next, we describe the set up of our experiment, which compares the ability of image-based features to rank translation candidates with ground truth supplied by a team of expert translators. Finally, we discuss our findings and the implications of our basic experiment for the wider use of image data for the enhancement of text-to-text translation in the future. With this paper we also publicly release a paper repository containing related resources, which will support other researchers in understanding, confirming, and extending our findings.[1] The repository includes our list of lacunae, ground truth (expert-translator rankings of translations), code, and also sets of images that illustrate particular cases.

2   Motivation and Background

2.1   Multimedia Analysis

Multimedia research has recently achieved promising results in the area of multimodal machine translation [17]. In this task, the source text is accompanied by visual content, which is leveraged to improve translation. Our idea is different because it focuses on text-to-text translation in the case of no accompanying visual input and it zeros in on the most challenging cases, lacunae. Intuitively, capturing the nuance of meaning as expressed in images could be expected to

---

[1] https://github.com/yanavdsande/ColorsOfMeaning.

require sophisticated technology capable of detailed image interpretation. For example, Borth et al. [1] pioneered research on sentiment-related visual ontologies, which directly models language nuance. Because our idea is using image data returned by a Web search engine, we can already access the nuance of image meaning. Detailed understanding of the relationship between image and text that is exploited by the search engine is not necessary.

Image retrieval research often builds on the assumption that images with similar color distributions are semantically similar [7]. Work that demonstrates the relationship between global color features and image content includes [8,13]. In this paper, we query a search engine with lacunae and represent the resulting image set as a color-based vector. Our experimental results suggest that this simple representation is enough to capture a semantic signal that discriminates different possible translations for lacunae, laying the groundwork for investigating more sophisticated image representations in the future.

2.2   Other Research Fields

The idea that image content has a contribution to make to translation is inspired by work in other fields that has indicated that visual features play a role in human translation ability. Neurological studies suggest a close cooperation between brain areas responsible for language processing and visual pathways, especially during translation [9,10]. Studies from the field of communication science show that learning a new language is easier when words are combined with pictures [12]. In addition, psychological research on memory and language proficiency reveal a better performance in remembering words when language is combined with visual stimuli [3,4]. Finally, cognitive models suggest visual information plays a role during sense-giving and language comprehension [7,14]. These studies from different fields suggest that visual information plays a role in awarding meaning to words and could, for these reason, potentially play an important role in text-to-text translation.

3   Experimental Investigation

An experiment was conducted where German and Dutch lacunae were translated by Google Translate. These translations occurred in a ranking which Google Translate considered the best to worst translation option. The translations were shuffled and human professional translators were asked to rank the translations from best to worst to their best knowledge. In addition, a new ranking was created by comparing the color histogram of the source words with color histograms of the target words. Both the Google Translate ranking and the color-based ranking were compared with the ground truth ranking.

3.1   Dataset

A dataset of lacunae with target language (English) was constructed using EUNOIA, a dictionary for lacunae. 22 German and 14 Dutch lacunae were selected. These words were translated through Google translate. Google translate is the most-used and well-known translator machine [6,11,18] using state-of-the-art algorithms, hence seemed the obvious choice. This procedure resulted in a total of 15 lacunae with translations, resulting in 52 translations for 10 German lacunae and 31 translations for 5 Dutch lacunae (N = 113). Words with a one-translation option from Google translate (N = 32) were removed from the first analysis and used as a control for the results through a comparison of the quality score of the translators and the dissimilarity score of the color histograms later. On all words of this selection a Google image search was conducted, collecting 100 images per word, using an image downloader extension.[2] N = 100 was chosen to lower the chance that image sets were lopsided in terms of factors not important for translation (such as contextual or cultural variation). The use of Google image search also allows us to demonstrate that it is not necessary to construct a carefully tailored dataset in order to measure the ability of Web images to support the translation of lacunae. Note that the search results could include both images and graphics. Also, we have no insight in whether Google translate and Google images may share common training data.

To assure search history and cookies did not affect the translations or the image selection, multiple different browsers were used, a private VPN was set up for every search, and the source language was selected prior to translation [5]. In addition, the browser was not logged in to an account to prevent personalization. Waiting 10 min before entering a new search prevented a carry-over effect from the previous search [15]. After image collection, they were resized to contain the same number of pixels per image. Of the collection of these images a color distribution was created by extracting the pixel RGB values and sum them, resulting in one color histogram per word (Fig. 1). More examples can be found on this paper's github.

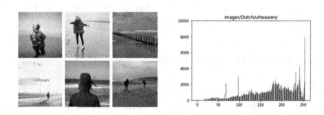

Fig. 1. A selection of images from the word "uitwaaien" and its color histogram

The dissimilarity of the different histograms was calculated using the Chi-Square of the R-channel, G-channel and B-channel between source word and translation, resulting in three measurements of dissimilarity per word-translation combination. To get one value, the three values were averaged. Note that we chose a Chi-Square measure above a KL-divergence since we are in essence not dealing with probability distribution and did not normalize to a range of $[0, 1]$.

---

[2] https://bulkimagedownloader.com.

$$\sum_{i=1}^{n} \frac{\sum_{i=1}^{n} \frac{(x_i - y_i)^2}{y_i}}{n} \tag{1}$$

In Eq. 1, x_i is the color histogram (with regards to either 'R', 'G' or 'B') of the source-word, y_i is the color histogram of the target-word, n is the number of target words by Google translate.

3.2 Survey and Expert Ground truth

A selection of human professional translators, who are assumed to be expert in the field of human translation, were asked to fill out a survey on translating lacunae. The survey consisted of two parts: part 1 ranking questions in which the translator was asked to rank translation options given by Google translate. Part 2 consisting of a scoring task to judge translation options on their quality. This quality scored will later be used in a second analysis where the score is compared with the chi-square score in regression analysis. The second part functioned as a double control of the first part and as data collection for future research. A Spearman rho test shows a high similarity $(min.Rs(26) = 0.989, p < 0.001,$ max. $Rs(26) = 1.00, p < 0.001)$ between the rankings by different translators $(n = 21)$. To create a ground truth, the rankings were summed and standardized. The resulted rankings were manually checked by the researcher to see if averaging the rankings did not result in a case of a tied ranking. This was not the case.

3.3 Results

Comparing the ground truth with the rankings of translations by the color histogram, we find that there is a significant relationship between rankings made by human translators and rankings made based on color histograms $(Rs(26) = 0.442, p = 0.024)$, demonstrating the viability of our idea. When comparing this result to the rankings created by Google Translate, we see that Google translate does outperform the color histogram with a slightly higher Spearman Rho by 0.169, which was significant as well $(p < 0.001)$. The second analysis was not significant. Taking a closer look at the data from the first analysis, we do see multiple specific cases where the color histogram translation better approached the human ranked value than did the Google translate algorithm. These specific cases can be found in the paper repository.

4   Discussion and Outlook

The results of our experimental investigation reveal the potential of Web images as a source of information complementary to the textual training material already exploited by Google Translate. We have seen that Google Translate performs already well in ranking candidate translations of lacunae but there is still much to gain. Although the Chi-Square similarity between color histograms shows not to be a good predictor for translation quality, we have seen cases in which our color-based ranking approach has outperformed Google Translate. Our observations support the main claim of our paper, that images on the Web have the potential to extend automatic text-to-text translation. In this section, we provide a discussion and mention future work that can build on our findings.

4.1 Images on the Web

A strength of our approach is that image understanding is not necessary to leverage images to support translation. However, individual cases lead us to believe that introducing additional intelligence into the selection of images could yield benefits. Specifically, when studying the collected images, we noticed that some of the images contained either textual information or depicted an instance that was named after the target-word but was less clearly related to the word itself. This could both be considered an advantage since these images bring connotations and/or related semantics to the equation as a disadvantage since it lacks the representation of a clear meaning.

To overcome this disadvantage, it would be helpful to discover how to pre-select images most suitable for supporting translation. We recommend to use a pre-checked database or to use coders to select images that are related to the words. Using a pre-checked database would also solve to problem of images that had a focus on other semantic properties. For example, an image of a butterfly in the sky. In this example the blue sky causes blue to be over-represented in the color histogram, overshadowing the colors of the butterfly that is actually the subject of the image. Example images can be found on this paper's github.

4.2 Towards the Future of Machine Translation

Regarding the future of machine translation, one can take inspiration from our idea looking at it from different fields. We believe it would be interesting to replicate this study by integrating context through word combinations; an example of this can be found in the translation of "cosy cottage" that should be translated in Dutch as "knus huisje" instead of "gezellig huisje" which is the translation Google translates raises. In addition, we suggest future work takes into account the possible relationship between the data used to train the machine translation and image search engine used, in order to understand the specific contribution of visual content in isolation.

Another direction could be taken from an engineering point of view. Our research shows the potential of making use of visual information during translation. This can, for instance, be used for the creation of an extension that includes a depiction of the target word and its translations so the user can check whether the translation covers what they try to communicate.

Concluding, exploring the potential of visual information resulted in the creation of an open access database consisting of lacunae and their translations by human translators so others could explore the potential of this idea. It showed results that indicate color could be used to enhance the translation of lacunae, and it provided research directions for the future.

References

1. Borth, D., Ji, R., Chen, T., Breuel, T., Chang, S.F.: Large-scale visual sentiment ontology and detectors using adjective noun pairs. In: Proceedings of the 21st ACM International Conference on Multimedia, MM 2013, pp. 223–232 (2013)
2. Brants, T., Popat, A.C., Xu, P., Och, F.J., Dean, J.: Large language models in machine translation. In: Proceedings of the 2007 Joint Conference on Empirical Methods in Natural Language Processing and Computational Natural Language Learning (EMNLP-CoNLL), pp. 858–867 (2007)
3. Carpenter, S.K., Geller, J.: Is a picture really worth a thousand words? Evaluating contributions of fluency and analytic processing in metacognitive judgements for pictures in foreign language vocabulary learning. Q. J. Exp. Psychol. **73**(2), 211–224 (2020)
4. Carpenter, S.K., Olson, K.M.: Are pictures good for learning new vocabulary in a foreign language? Only if you think they are not. J. Exp. Psychol. Learn. Mem. Cogn. **38**(1), 92 (2012)
5. Hannak, A., et al.: Measuring personalization of web search. In: Proceedings of the 22nd International Conference on World Wide Web, pp. 527–538 (2013)
6. Kreisha, A.M.: 3 contenders for the title of "best free online translator". https://www.fluentu.com/blog/best-free-online-translator. Accessed 10 Oct 2021
7. Lavrenko, V., Manmatha, R., Jeon, J., et al.: A model for learning the semantics of pictures. In: Advances in Neural Information Processing Systems 16 (2003)
8. Lux, M., Riegler, M., Halvorsen, P., Pogorelov, K., Anagnostopoulos, N.: LIRE: open source visual information retrieval. In: Proceedings of the 7th International Conference on Multimedia Systems, MMSys 2016 (2016)
9. Mayer, K.M., Yildiz, I.B., Macedonia, M., von Kriegstein, K.: Visual and motor cortices differentially support the translation of foreign language words. Curr. Biol. **25**(4), 530–535 (2015)
10. Oldfield, R.C.: The assessment and analysis of handedness: the Edinburgh inventory. Neuropsychologia **9**(1), 97–113 (1971)
11. Otachi, E.: 12 best online translators to translate any language. https://helpdeskgeek.com/free-tools-review/12-best-online-translators-to-translate-any-language Accessed 10 Oct 2021
12. Plass, J.L., Jones, L.: Multimedia learning in second language acquisition. In: The Cambridge Handbook of Multimedia Learning, pp. 467–488 (2005)
13. Riegler, M., Larson, M., Lux, M., Kofler, C.: How 'how' reflects what's what: Content-based exploitation of how users frame social images. In: Proceedings of the 22nd ACM international conference on Multimedia, MM 2014 (2014)
14. Roy, D.K., Pentland, A.P.: Learning words from sights and sounds: a computational model. Cogn. Sci. **26**(1), 113–146 (2002)
15. Salehi, S., Du, J.T., Ashman, H.: Examining personalization in academic web search. In: Proceedings of the 26th ACM Conference on Hypertext & Social Media, pp. 103–111 (2015)
16. Sankaravelayuthan, R.: Lexical gaps and untranslatability in translation. Lang. India **20**(5), 56 (2020)

17. Song, Y., Chen, S., Jin, Q., Luo, W., Xie, J., Huang, F.: Enhancing neural machine translation with dual-side multimodal awareness. IEEE Trans. Multimedia (2021)
18. Writtenhouse, S.: The 10 best online translators you can use in the real world. https://www.makeuseof.com/tag/best-online-translators Accessed 10 Oct 2021

Activities and Events

MGMP: Multimodal Graph Message Propagation Network for Event Detection

Jiankai Li, Yunhong Wang, and Weixin Li[✉]

IRIP Lab, School of Computer Science and Engineering, Beihang University,
Beijing 100191, China
{lijiankai,yhwang,weixinli}@buaa.edu.cn

Abstract. Multimodal event detection plays a pivotal role in social media analysis, yet remains challenging due to the large differences between images and texts, noisy contexts and the intricate correspondence of different modalities. To address these issues, we introduce a multimodal graph message propagation network (MGMP), a layer-wise approach that aggregates the multi-view context and integrates images and texts simultaneously. In particular, MGMP constructs visual and textual graphs and employs graph neural network (GNN) with an element-wise attention to propagate context and avoid transferring negative knowledge, and multimodal similarity propagation (MSP) follows to propagate complementarity for fusing images and texts. We evaluate MGMP on two public datasets, namely CrisisMMD and SED2014. Extensive experiments demonstrate the effectiveness and superiority of our method.

Keywords: Multimodal event detection · Multimodal similarity propagation · Graph neural network

1 Introduction

Event detection aims to automatically identify new and retrospective events from multimedia, such as protests, natural disasters, terrorist attacks, etc. [11,14]. In addition to responding to emergencies and minimizing the losses caused by disasters, event detection bears great significance for persons, companies and governments to search, browse and record their interesting events. However, there still exist challenges and significant space for improvements, especially in the following three aspects:

1) *Complementary information from different modalities.* Most traditional approaches on event detection merely use single modality such as image or text. In social media, images and texts typically do not appear in isolation. Using images alone cannot represent events accurately and using text alone may lack details due to character limit (e.g. Twitter). However, image-text pairs in social media sometimes contain noises, where images may be scenery unrelated to the event and texts may be meaningless symbols. Therefore, it is essential and also challenging to properly utilize complementarity from different modalities.

© Springer Nature Switzerland AG 2022
B. Þór Jónsson et al. (Eds.): MMM 2022, LNCS 13141, pp. 141–153, 2022.
https://doi.org/10.1007/978-3-030-98358-1_12

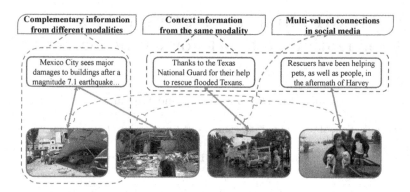

Fig. 1. Challenges of multimodal event detection in social media. Complementarity can be obtained from different and same modalities and multi-valued connections exist in social media: one piece of text may correspond to one (right) or multiple (left) images.

2) *Context information from the same modality.* As shown in Fig. 1, in social media, different images and texts may depict the same event from multiple views. Taking multi-view contexts into consideration contributes to a more accurate representation of events, which is beneficial to downstream tasks.

3) *Multi-valued connections in social media.* Also shown in Fig. 1, in social media, images and texts sometimes have multi-valued connections, i.e. one piece of text (image) may have multiple images (texts) or only one image (text) attached. It is also a challenge to take advantage of these multi-valued connections.

Motivated to make comprehensive use of images and texts, early works [10,15] concatenate features or fuse the predicted scores from different modalities in a designed manner. Recent efforts [1,13] try to embed images and texts in a common space or regularize the multimodal learning process to alleviate overfitting. But it remains unexplored to exploit complementary information from different modalities and mitigate the impact of noises. Moreover, existing methods merely focus on the multimodal fusion and ignore their multi-view contexts, and there has been very few work on multimodal event detection with multi-valued connections.

To address these issues, we propose the Multimodal Graph Message Propagation network (MGMP), a framework that regards the image or text as a vertex, and captures the complementary information of each vertex with the multimodal similarity propagation mechanism (MSP) and the graph neural network (GNN). The basic idea of MGMP is to facilitate the multimodal complementarity and multi-view contexts of each vertex propagating along the multimodal graph, where each vertex representation is promoted under the guidance of its neighbors. Specifically, we firstly develop a multimodal similarity propagation network between images and texts, where the gated fusion is applied to avoid transferring negative knowledge. Secondly, a graph neural network is introduced to exploit the multi-view context from the same modality. An attention function is added in GNN to alleviate aggregating noises from neighbors. MSP and

GNN are combined layer by layer to propagate the multimodal complementarity and multi-view contexts, thus achieving a more discriminative representation for event detection.

We perform extensive experiments on two real-world datasets, and the results demonstrate that our approach outperforms state-of-the-art baseline methods. The main contributions of this work are summarized as follow:

- We propose a multimodal message propagation network to jointly fuse images and texts with multi-valued connections.
- We propose a graph neural network (GNN) to model the multi-view contexts for event detection.
- Experimental results on two public datasets demonstrate the superiority of our approach over other state-of-the-art methods.

2   Related Work

Event Detection can be traced back to the Topic Detection and Tracking task, whose purpose is to detect the topics of online data including social media and news reports. Most previous event detection methods focus on the single text modality or visual modality. For instance, [6] introduces a hybrid neural network based on LSTM and CNN for event detection with multiple languages. Bossard et al. introduce the Stopwatch Hidden Markov model to detect events in photo collections [3].

The aforementioned methods exploit the single modality on event detection, which may bring bias when modeling events. To overcome this limitation, Lan et al. propose a double fusion method that combines features from different modalities using early fusion and late fusion to classify videos into specified classes [10]. Yang et al. propose a shared multi-view data representation model to integrate modalities from time, location, title, user, tags, description and visuals [17].

More recently, many works tend to add regularization to mitigate noise between images and texts, and report state-of-the-art performance. SSE-Cross-BERT-DenseNet [1] applies SSE to fuse images and text captions in the social media. DME [13] embeds the image and text features into the same feature space for event classification. However, the multi-view contexts in images and texts are ignored and it is still challenging to integrate images and texts due to their noises. In this work, we exploit the multi-view contexts by utilizing GNN and propose MSP to fuse images and texts simultaneously, thus obtaining a robust representations for event detection.

3   Methodology

In this section, we introduce the Mulimodal Graph Message Propagation (MGMP). As shown in Fig. 2, MGMP regards each image and text as one vertex and builds multimodal graph according to their extracted visual and textual

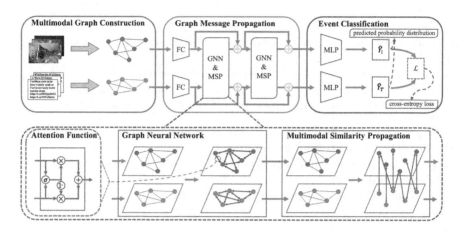

Fig. 2. Framework of MGMP. Given input images and texts, a visual-textual graph is firstly constructed. Subsequently, the Graph Neural Network and Multimodal Similarity Propagation encode context and complementary information respectively. Two multilayer perceptrons (MLPs) are finally applied to predict the label of each input node.

features. Then MGMP stacks GNN and MSP with residual connections layer by layer to pass message along the multimodal graph. Two multilayer perceptrons (MLPs) are finally applied to classify event categories.

3.1 Multimodal Graph Construction

Our multimodal graph consists of three components: a visual graph, a textual graph and their link matrices. The visual graph and textual graph are built to model the multi-view contexts, which will be detailed in the following.

Visual Graph Construction. Given the image I, we adopt DenseNet [8] as the backbone to generate features $X_I = \{\vec{f_1}, \vec{f_2}, ..., \vec{f_n}\}$, where $\vec{f_i} \in \mathbb{R}^{D_f}$ is the feature of the i-th image and D_f refers to the dimension of the extracted feature. To construct a visual graph, we regard each image as a vertex and use k-nearest neighbor (KNN) based on cosine similarity to obtain an affinity graph $G_I = \langle V_I, E_I \rangle$, where $V_I = \{v_{I_1}, v_{I_2}, ..., v_{I_n}\}$ are nodes and E_I are edges. Alternatively, G_I can also be defined as an adjacency matrix $A_I \in \mathbb{R}^{n \times n}$, where the element $a_{i,j}$ is one if v_{I_j} is one of the k nearest neighbors of v_{I_i}, otherwise it is zero.

Textual Graph Construction. Texts in social media may exist in the format of sentences (e.g. Twitter) or a set of tags (e.g. Flicker). For texts in the form of sentences, we apply BERT [5] as the backbone to extract representations $X_T = \{\vec{g_1}, \vec{g_2}, ..., \vec{g_m}\} \in \mathbb{R}^{m \times D_g}$ and take the embedding corresponding to [CLS] to represent sentences, where $\vec{g_i}$ is the feature of the i-th text, D_g is the dimension of $\vec{g}_i$. For texts in the form of tags, we choose GloVe as the backbone to extract embeddings $\{\vec{w}_{i,1}, \vec{w}_{i,2}, ..., \vec{w}_{i,d_i}\}$ of words in each text, where $\vec{w}_{i,j}$ denotes the embedding of the j-th tag in the i-th text, and d_i denotes the number of tags in the i-th text. We compute the text representations X_T by taking mean pooling on the embeddings of each word.

To construct a textual graph, we also treat each text as a vertex and take KNN to obtain an affinity graph $G_T = \langle V_T, E_T \rangle$ with an adjacency matrix $A_T \in \mathbb{R}^{m \times m}$.

3.2   Graph Message Propagation

In this subsection, we illustrate the theoretical motivation of MGMP which is a multi-layer model with a layer-wise propagation rule.

Multimodal Similarity Propagation. To address the challenge of multi-modal fusion and multi-value connections, we propose to apply multimodal similarity propagation (MSP) [16] to transfer the message between images and texts. However, the impediments to MSP is that it propagates scalars instead of vectors and it cannot avoid transferring negative knowledge. Therefore, we modify the MSP to overcome these limitations.

Consider the traditional multimodal similarity propagation mechanism, which is defined as:

$$
\begin{aligned}
P^{(l)} &= \alpha P^{(0)} + (1-\alpha)\lambda Z Q^{(l-1)} Z^T, \\
Q^{(l)} &= \beta Q^{(0)} + (1-\beta)\lambda Z^T P^{(l-1)} Z,
\end{aligned}
\tag{1}
$$

where $Z \in \mathbb{R}^{n \times m}$ is the link matrix from T (e.g. texts) to I (e.g. images) while its transpose $Z^T \in \mathbb{R}^{m \times n}$ is the link matrix from I to T. $P \in \mathbb{R}^{n \times n}$ and $Q \in \mathbb{R}^{m \times m}$ are two intra-object similarity matrices based on the content feature in modalities I and T respectively, where n is the number of nodes in modality I and m is the number of nodes in modality T.

We rewritten Eq. (1) to better observe the change of each similarity. Note that l represents the number of iterations of similarity propagation, which means that the similarity between two nodes depends only on the nodes that are at maximum l steps away. We are able to achieve similar results as Eq. (1) by stacking multiple linear layer of the form of Eq. (2).

$$
\begin{aligned}
p_{i,j}^{(l)} &= \alpha p_{i,j}^{(l-1)} + (1-\alpha)\lambda \sum_{z_{i,x} \neq 0, z_{j,y} \neq 0} q_{x,y}^{(l-1)}, \\
q_{i,j}^{(l)} &= \beta q_{i,j}^{(l-1)} + (1-\beta)\lambda \sum_{z'_{i,x} \neq 0, z'_{j,y} \neq 0} p_{x,y}^{(l-1)},
\end{aligned}
\tag{2}
$$

where $p_{i,j}$ is the (i,j)-th element of P, $q_{i,j}$ is the (i,j)-th element of Q, and $z_{i,j}$ and $z'_{i,j}$ denote whether nodes i, j are connected in the multimodal graph. Here we assume that the similarity between two nodes from the same modality can be calculated from their representations. Therefore, the propagation of similarity can be regarded as the propagation of node representation. Since Eq. (2) holds for any element in I and T, we approximate the similarity propagation mechanism at l-step as:

$$\vec{v}_i^{(l)} = \vec{\alpha} \odot \vec{v}_i^{(l-1)} + (1 - \vec{\alpha}) \odot \frac{1}{\sum_x z_{i,x}} \sum_{z_{i,x} \neq 0} \vec{u}_x^{(l-1)},$$

$$\vec{u}_j^{(l)} = \vec{\beta} \odot \vec{u}_j^{(l-1)} + (1 - \vec{\beta}) \odot \frac{1}{\sum_y z'_{j,y}} \sum_{z'_{j,y} \neq 0} \vec{v}_y^{(l-1)},$$

(3)

where $\vec{v}_i$ denotes the representation of i-th node in I, $\vec{u}_j$ denotes the representation of j-th node in T, $\vec{\alpha}$ and $\vec{\beta}$ are the weight vectors, and $\odot$ represents the element-wise product. A neural network based on multimodal similarity propagation can therefore be built by stacking multiple layers of the form of Eq. (3), where each is layer followed by a non-linear function. In practice, we further approximate λ as the mean pooling function in order to alleviate the exploding/vanishing gradients when repeating Eq. (3) in deep neural network.

In the process of similarity propagation, not only complementary information but also the noise will be transferred along the linkage between different modalities. To avoid transferring negative knowledge, it can be beneficial to calculate $\vec{\alpha}$ and $\vec{\beta}$ with a gated unit:

$$\vec{\alpha} = \sigma(\vec{v}_i^{(l-1)} W_{\alpha,1} + \frac{1}{\sum_x z_{i,x}} \sum_{z_{i,x} \neq 0} \vec{u}_x^{(l-1)} W_{\alpha,2} + \vec{b}_\alpha),$$

$$\vec{\beta} = \sigma(\vec{u}_j^{(l-1)} W_{\beta,1} + \frac{1}{\sum_y z'_{j,y}} \sum_{z'_{j,y} \neq 0} \vec{v}_y^{(l-1)} W_{\beta,2} + \vec{b}_\beta),$$

(4)

where $W_{\alpha,1}$, $W_{\alpha,2}$, $W_{\beta,1}$, $W_{\beta,2}$, $\vec{b}_\alpha$ and $\vec{b}_\beta$ are trainable parameters and $\sigma(\bullet)$ denotes the sigmoid activation function.

Graph Neural Network. As outlined in the introduction, images and texts are able to enrich their event representation through multi-view contexts from their neighbors, which is lacking in the aforementioned multimodal similarity propagation. Motivated by the message-passing mechanism in GNN, we introduce a Graph Neural Network (GNN) with an element-wise attention aggregation function to transfer the contexts from its neighbors to the center node. Considering the graph $G = \langle V, E \rangle$ with an adjacency matrix $A \in \mathbb{R}^{N \times N}$ and a feature matrix $X = \{\vec{x}_1, \vec{x}_2, ..., \vec{x}_N\} \in \mathbb{R}^{N \times D_x}$, where N represents the number of nodes and D_x denotes the dimension of $\vec{x}_i$, our GNN can be written as:

$$H^{(l+1)} = \sigma(F_{att}(H^{(l)} W_g^{(l)}, A H^{(l)} W_g^{(l)})),$$

(5)

where $H^{(0)} = X$, l denotes the propagation step, $W_g^{(l)}$ are trainable parameters, $\sigma(\bullet)$ denotes the ReLU activation function and F_{att} is an element-wise attention to avoid transferring noise, which is defined as:

$$\vec{z} = \sigma(\vec{x}W_{z,1} + \vec{y}W_{z,2} + \vec{b}_z),$$
$$F_{att}(\vec{x}, \vec{y}) = \vec{z} \odot \vec{x} + (1 - \vec{z}) \odot \vec{y}, \tag{6}$$

where $W_{z,1}, W_{z,2}, \vec{b}_z$ are trainable parameters and $\sigma(\bullet)$ denotes the sigmoid activation function. Since the neighbors are selected by the cosine similarity and KNN, it is inevitable to aggregate noise in the graph. The element-wise attention F_{att} is proposed to leverage the attention between center node feature and its neighbors feature.

3.3   Event Classification

Representations of image nodes H_I and text nodes H_T are simultaneously generated by multimodal graph message propagation. Here we employ MLPs with two fully connected layers to calculate pseudo labels. We train the whole model by minimizing the cross-entropy loss $\mathcal{L}$:

$$\mathcal{L} = CE(\hat{Y}_I, Y_I) + CE(\hat{Y}_T, Y_T), \tag{7}$$

where $\hat{Y}_I \in \mathbb{R}^{n \times c}$ and $\hat{Y}_T \in \mathbb{R}^{m \times c}$ are the predicted probability distribution of the target events, and CE denotes the cross-entropy loss function. If the event detection task is to predict the label of the image-text pairs, we will sum $\hat{Y}_I$ and $\hat{Y}_T$ as their labels, otherwise we will directly take $\hat{Y}_I$ and $\hat{Y}_T$ as the results.

4   Experiments

4.1   Datasets

CrisisMMD. CrisisMMD [2] is a dataset of crisis events collected from Twitter during seven natural disasters in 2017, which consists of tweets attached with one or more images where the images and texts from the same tweet may not share the same category. CrisisMMD contains two multimodal tasks, where the Informativeness Task is to classify whether a given image or text is related to crisis events and the Humanitarian Categorization Task is to determine the specific crisis events of images and texts.

   In this paper, we use four settings to evaluate our method. First, setting A is designed for tasks with image-text pairs. In this setting, we employ the processing method in [1] to sample tweets where the image-text pairs have the same category. The dataset is split into 7,876 training, 553 validating, and 2,821 testing for informativeness task, and 1352 training, 540 validating, and 1,467 testing for humanitarian categorization task. Secondly, we extend Setting A to Setting A+ for tasks with multi-valued data. Specifically, we relax the assumption that images and texts must be paired and add images while maintaining the data segmentation results of setting A. The split result is 8,785/601/3,163 images for informativeness task and 1,485/584/1,612 images for humanitarian categorization task, for training/validating/testing respectively. Then, setting

B is designed for multi-task experiments with paired data, where we relax the assumption that the paired images and texts must share the same category. The informativeness task for setting B is composed of 12,680/553/2,821 image-text pairs for training/validating/testing respectively. Lastly, similar to setting A+, setting B+ adds images while keeping the data segmentation results of setting B to evaluate the ability of MGMP to process multi-valued data, which is composed of 14,310/626/3,161 images and 12,680/553/2,821 texts for humanitarian categorization task, for training/validating/testing respectively.

SED2014. Each image as metadata in SED2014 [12] is accompanied by tags, timestamps, locations, etc. We follow the experimental setup in [13] which divides nearly 260k metadata into 9 common events. About ten percent of the metadata are failed to be downloaded due to invalid image links. In this paper, we take 167,020/32,707/32,799 image-text pairs from SED2014 for training, validating and testing respectively.

4.2   Implementation Details

For CrisisMMD, we employ pretrained DenseNet and pretrained BERT as the backbone and fine-tune them on training samples for a fair comparison with SSE-Cross-BERT-DenseNet (SCBD) [1]. For SED-2014, we use pretrained DenseNet and pretrained GloVe as backbone for comparisons with DME [13].

We train a two-layer Graph Message Propagation model with the 128-dim hidden units and add layer normalization after each similarity propagation layer. A dropout probability of 0.1 is employed on all layers to alleviate overfitting in MGMP. We use $k = 20$ on Informativeness Task, $k = 15$ on Humanitarian Categorization Task and $k = 15$ on SED2014 Task to construct multimodal graph due to their different categories. We train all models for 300 epochs with learning rate 0.002. MGMP are implemented based on Pytorch and Pytorch-geometric. We report the final result which has the best performance on validation set.

Table 1. Performance comparison of MGMP and other baselines on SED2014 dataset.

Method	Accuracy	Macro F1	Weighted F1
DenseNet	45.39	19.92	35.04
GloVe	66.44	53.80	65.83
Score Fusion	56.50	43.69	51.73
Feature Fusion	66.63	56.80	66.08
DME [13]	26.07	-	-
MGMP	**68.58**	**59.39**	**68.24**

- indicates that results were not reported in original paper.

Table 2. Performance comparison of MGMP and other event detection baselines on CrisisMMD dataset under Setting A.

Method	Informativeness task			Humanitarian categorization task		
	Accuracy	Macro F1	Weighted F1	Accuracy	Macro F1	Weighted F1
DenseNet	81.57	79.12	81.22	83.44	60.45	86.96
BERT	84.90	81.19	83.30	86.09	66.83	87.83
Score Fusion	88.16	83.46	85.26	86.98	54.01	88.96
Feature Fusion	87.56	85.20	86.55	89.17	67.28	91.40
CBP [7]	88.12	86.18	87.61	89.30	67.18	90.33
CBGP [9]	88.76	87.50	88.80	85.34	65.95	89.42
SCBD [1]	89.33	88.09	89.35	91.14	68.41	91.82
MGMP	**90.93**	**89.63**	**90.92**	**92.03**	**80.01**	**91.93**
MGMP*	**91.17**	**89.87**	**91.15**	**92.50**	**82.04**	**92.38**

MGMP* indicates the result of MGMP on CrisisMMD dataset under Setting A+.

4.3 Baselines

The baselines can be divided into three types: (1) *Single-modality based methods* including DenseNet, BERT and GloVe, (2) *Naive multimodal methods* including the Score Fusion and Feature Fusion which averages the predicted probability distribution and concatenates the embeddings of backbones respectively, and (3) *State-of-the-art multi-modal methods* including Compact Bilinear Pooling (CBP) [7], Compact Bilinear Gated Pooling (CBGP) [9], DME [13] and SSE-Cross-BERT-DenseNet (SCBD) and its variants [1]. CBP is a multimodal method first used in visual question answering task and CBGP is a variant which adds an attention gate on the top of CBP. DME is a recently proposed method based on GloVe and gated recurrent unit [4]. Lastly, SCBD is a strong baseline on CrisisMMD which uses a data augmentation method namely SSE and employs self-attention and co-attention to fuse images and texts.

4.4 Comparison Results

The comparison results for single task are shown in Table 1 and Table 2. To demonstrate the effectiveness of our method in dealing with multi-valued connections, we report the result of MGMP in setting A+ after setting A. It can be observed that the proposed method generally outperforms single-modality based methods, indicating that the multimodal complementarity is essential for event detection. When it comes to multimodal based method, MGMP still performs better than other methods. Benefiting from the proposed GNN which facilitates the multi-view context propagation along the multimodal graph, MGMP achieves better Macro F1 score. The performance of MGMP in setting A+ is better than setting A, indicating that our method is able to gain improvements from the multi-valued data.

Table 3. Comparison of different methods on the informativeness task of CrisisMMD under Setting B.

Method	Informativeness task @ Image			Informativeness task @ Text		
	Accuracy	Macro F1	Weighted F1	Accuracy	Macro F1	Weighted F1
DenseNet	78.30	78.30	78.31	-	-	-
BERT	-	-	-	82.63	74.93	80.87
Feature Fusion	78.37	78.15	78.21	83.63	79.01	83.22
Cross-Att [1]	77.17	77.51	77.51	83.35	**79.60**	83.41
Self-Att [1]	82.56	82.54	82.56	83.63	76.79	82.17
Self-Cross-Att [1]	81.64	81.51	81.55	83.45	78.22	82.78
MGMP	**83.55**	**83.41**	**83.55**	**84.19**	79.54	**84.05**
MGMP*	**83.87**	**83.78**	**83.90**	**84.62**	**79.67**	**84.31**

MGMP* indicates the result of MGMP on CrisisMMD dataset under Setting B+.

Table 3 shows the comparison results in multi-task experiments. The Cross-Att, Self-Att and Self-Cross-Att are three multi-task variant models in [1]. We can see that our method surpasses the single-modality based method and the state-of-the-art multimodal method, demonstrating the strong multimodal fusion ability of the proposed framework. Similarly, the performance of MGMP in setting B+ also surpasses its performance in setting B, which suggests that MGMP can still benefit from the multi-valued data in multiple tasks.

4.5   Ablation Study

To investigate the impact of each component in MGMP, we conduct an ablation study and evaluate variants of our model on CrisisMMD and SED2014.

We separately remove MSP, GNN and the attention function of GNN in our framework. The results are illustrated in Table 4. We observe better performance using GNN and MSP, which shows their effects on detecting events. Specifically, the performance of MGMP decreases a lot when we remove the MSP module, which shows the multimodal fusion effects of MSP and the improvement of MGMP over MGMP (w/o GNN) suggests the contribution of our GNN in modeling multi-view contexts. Moreover, it can be observed that the results will be boosted when we apply the element-wise attention function, indicating that the element-wise attention successfully alleviates noises from contexts.

4.6   Case Study

To provide a more intuitive understanding of MGMP, we conduct a case study on the Humanitarian Categorization Task in setting A. Part of our multimodal graph is shown in Fig. 3, where the blue arrows indicate the intra-modality edges in visual and textual graphs. Compared to DenseNet and BERT, our method leverages the multimodal contexts and predicts the right events.

Table 4. Results of ablation study. We report the results on Humanitarian Categorization Task in Setting A and the results on SED2014 dataset.

Method	Humanitarian categorization task			SED2014 task		
	Accuracy	Macro F1	Weighted F1	Accuracy	Macro F1	Weighted F1
w/o MSP	91.48	68.76	91.11	67.44	55.65	66.43
w/o GNN	91.48	68.53	91.14	68.10	53.62	67.84
w/o Attention	91.89	68.30	91.60	67.87	58.32	66.92
MGMP	**92.03**	**80.01**	**91.93**	**68.58**	**59.39**	**68.24**

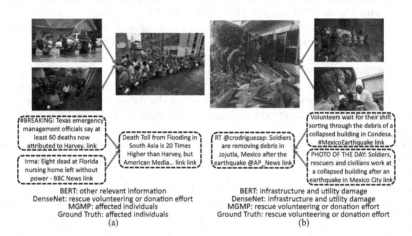

BERT: other relevant information
DenseNet: rescue volunteering or donation effort
MGMP: affected individuals
Ground Truth: affected individuals
(a)

BERT: infrastructure and utility damage
DenseNet: infrastructure and utility damage
MGMP: rescue volunteering or donation effort
Ground Truth: rescue volunteering or donation effort
(b)

Fig. 3. A case study. MGMP leverages visual and textual contexts to infer events.

5   Conclusion

In this paper, we propose a multimodal graph message propagation network (MGSP) for event detection. Specially, we propose a graph neural network (GNN) with an element-wise attention to exploit the context information. We further propose a multimodal similarity propagation (MSP) mechanism to simultaneously model the complex connections in social media data and obtain the complementary information from different modalities. Experiments on two public datasets demonstrate that our method achieves state-of-the-art performance. Besides, ablation study verifies our hypothesis and indicates the effectiveness of each module in our method.

Acknowledgement. This work is supported by the National Natural Science Foundation of China (No. 61806016).

References

1. Abavisani, M., Wu, L., Hu, S., Tetreault, J., Jaimes, A.: Multimodal categorization of crisis events in social media. In: Proceedings of the IEEE Conference on Computer Vision and Pattern Recognition (CVPR), pp. 14679–14689 (2020)
2. Alam, F., Ofli, F., Imran, M.: CrisisMMD: multimodal Twitter datasets from natural disasters. In: Proceedings of the International AAAI Conference on Web and Social Media (ICWSM), pp. 465–473 (2018)
3. Bossard, L., Guillaumin, M., Van Gool, L.: Event recognition in photo collections with a stopwatch HMM. In: Proceedings of the IEEE International Conference on Computer Vision (CVPR), pp. 1193–1200 (2013)
4. Cho, K., et al.: Learning phrase representations using RNN encoder-decoder for statistical machine translation. In: Proceedings of the 2014 Conference on Empirical Methods in Natural Language Processing (EMNLP), pp. 1724–1734 (2014)
5. Devlin, J., Chang, M.W., Lee, K., Toutanova, K.: BERT: pre-training of deep bidirectional transformers for language understanding. In: Proceedings of the 2019 Conference of the North American Chapter of the Association for Computational Linguistics: Human Language Technologies, Volume 1 (Long and Short Papers), pp. 4171–4186 (2019)
6. Feng, X., Qin, B., Liu, T.: A language-independent neural network for event detection. Sci. China Inf. Sci. **61**(9), 1–12 (2018). https://doi.org/10.1007/s11432-017-9359-x
7. Fukui, A., Park, D.H., Yang, D., Rohrbach, A., Darrell, T., Rohrbach, M.: Multimodal compact bilinear pooling for visual question answering and visual grounding. In: Proceedings of the 2016 Conference on Empirical Methods in Natural Language Processing (EMNLP), pp. 457–468 (2016)
8. Huang, G., Liu, Z., Van Der Maaten, L., Weinberger, K.Q.: Densely connected convolutional networks. In: Proceedings of the IEEE Conference on Computer Vision and Pattern Recognition (CVPR), pp. 4700–4708 (2017)
9. Kiela, D., Grave, E., Joulin, A., Mikolov, T.: Efficient large-scale multi-modal classification. In: 32nd AAAI Conference on Artificial Intelligence (AAAI), pp. 5198–5204 (2018)
10. Lan, Z., Bao, L., Yu, S.-I., Liu, W., Hauptmann, A.G.: Multimedia classification and event detection using double fusion. Multimedia Tools Appl. **71**(1), 333–347 (2013). https://doi.org/10.1007/s11042-013-1391-2
11. Li, W., Joo, J., Qi, H., Zhu, S.C.: Joint image-text news topic detection and tracking by multimodal topic and-or graph. IEEE Trans. Multimedia **19**(2), 367–381 (2016)
12. Petkos, G., Papadopoulos, S., Mezaris, V., Kompatsiaris, Y.: Social event detection at MediaEva 2014: challenges, datasets, and evaluation. In: MediaEval Workshop. Citeseer (2014)
13. Qi, F., Yang, X., Zhang, T., Xu, C.: Discriminative multimodal embedding for event classification. Neurocomputing **395**, 160–169 (2020)
14. Sakaki, T., Okazaki, M., Matsuo, Y.: Earthquake shakes Twitter users: real-time event detection by social sensors. In: Proceedings of the 19th International Conference on World Wide Web, pp. 851–860 (2010)
15. Schifanella, R., de Juan, P., Tetreault, J., Cao, L.: Detecting sarcasm in multimodal social platforms. In: Proceedings of the 24th ACM International Conference on Multimedia, pp. 1136–1145 (2016)

16. Wang, X.J., Ma, W.Y., Xue, G.R., Li, X.: Multi-model similarity propagation and its application for web image retrieval. In: Proceedings of the 12th Annual ACM International Conference on Multimedia, pp. 944–951 (2004)
17. Yang, Z., Li, Q., Liu, W., Lv, J.: Shared multi-view data representation for multi-domain event detection. IEEE Trans. Pattern Anal. Mach. Intell. **42**(5), 1243–1256 (2019)

Pose-Enhanced Relation Feature
for Action Recognition in Still Images

Jiewen Wang and Shuang Liang[(✉)]

School of Software Engineering, Tongji University, Shanghai, China
{wjwlaservne,shuangliang}@tongji.edu.cn

Abstract. Due to the lack of motion information, action recognition in still images is considered a challenging task. Previous works focused on contextual information in the image, including human pose, surrounding objects, etc. But they rarely consider the relation between the local pose and the entire human body, so that poses related to the action are not fully utilized. In this paper, we propose a solution for action recognition in still images, which makes complete and effective use of pose information. The multi-key points calculation method is carefully designed for generating pose regions that explicitly includes possible actions. The extensible Pose-Enhanced Relation Module extracts the implicit relation between pose and human body, and outputs the Pose-Enhanced Relation Feature which owns powerful representation capabilities. Surrounding objects information is also applied to strengthen the solution. Through experiments, it can be found that the proposed solution exceed the state-of-the-art performance on two commonly used datasets, PASCAL VOC 2012 Action and Stanford 40 Actions. Visualization shows that the proposed solution enables the network to pay more attention to the pose regions related to the action.

Keywords: Action recognition · Human pose · Relation networks

1 Introduction

Action recognition is a core task in the field of computer vision, and it has a number of applications in real life like video surveillance and motion sensing games. In the study of the task, still images based action recognition tends to receive less attention, since still images don't have motion or temporal information like videos, which makes it difficult to capture useful features. In order to fully dig out the information in still images, the researchers set their sights on contextual cues other than the human body. At present, poses and surrounding objects are usually used like in [12,19]. Due to the development of pose estimation and object detection technology, it's not difficult to obtain these features.

However, while applying these contextual features, the further relation between them and human body features is seldom considered in existing methods. For surrounding objects, the situation is slightly better, because the interaction between human body and objects is generally obvious; but for pose feature,

© Springer Nature Switzerland AG 2022
B. Þór Jónsson et al. (Eds.): MMM 2022, LNCS 13141, pp. 154–165, 2022.
https://doi.org/10.1007/978-3-030-98358-1_13

since its relation with the human body is not obvious, it is processed in an independent branch in most cases [4]. And addition or concatenate is performed to simply fuse it before classification. Applying these methods sometimes leads to incorrect predictions, especially when there is no object information to assist.

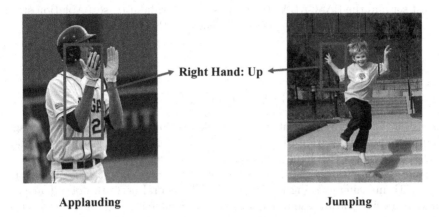

Applauding   **Jumping**

Fig. 1. An example of "similar pose, different action". The actions of the characters on the left/right are different (applauding/jumping), but the local poses (such as the right hand) show higher similarity.

An example that may lead to a false prediction is shown in Fig. 1: Although the people in two images perform different actions, the pose of a certain part may be similar. In this case, the local pose feature becomes a misleading item, and the entire body feature is needed for correct predictions. This reveals that the partial pose and the entire human body are not isolated, and the combination of the two may be able to better eliminate misleading information.

The self-attention mechanism provides a good foundation for dealing with this situation. Self-attention is widely used in deep learning works. It emerged from natural language processing [15] and soon impacted computer vision tasks like object detection [10]. Its main function is to learn the correlation between features, which is exactly what we need. In the action recognition scenario, self-attention mechanism can be applied to model the correlation between the contextual features and the human body feature.

Inspired by self-attention mechanism and its application in action recognition, we propose a solution for action recognition in still images. The contributions of this work can be summarized as follows:

- The multi-key points calculation method is designed to convert pose key points into bounding box format pose regions. The generated pose regions include the actions that may be reflected by the joints, which is helpful to establish the connection between the actual action and the pose region.
- We propose a novel Pose-Enhanced Relation Module to model the relation between the local pose and the entire human body. This relation is implicit

in the Pose-Enhanced Relation Feature output by the module. To the best of our knowledge, the proposed method is the first one to focus on this relation. Moreover, the Pose-Enhanced Relation Module can be easily extended.
- The proposed solution has obtained competitive results in experiments. The results reach new state-of-the-art performance on the Stanford 40 Actions [18] test set and the PASCAL VOC 2012 Action [3] validation set. Ablation study and visualization illustrate the effectiveness of the proposed solution.

2   Related Work

2.1   Action Recognition in Still Images

Consistent with many computer vision tasks, action recognition in still images has undergone a transition from traditional methods to deep learning methods. But what remains the same is the idea of assisting the task with contextual information. Traditional solutions usually use hand-crafted features and combine them with machine learning methods [17]. The neural network doesn't need to manually design features, so researchers pay more attention to the use of features and the mining of deep-level features. Gkioxari et al. [8] mainly captures the key areas in the image, and doesn't care about its specific meaning. Zhao et al. [19] and Fang et al. [4] use pose features explicitly to assist action recognition. New discoveries in computer vision have also been introduced to the task, such as the attention mechanism [16]. Due to the lack of motion information in still images, there is even a way to generate hallucinated motion information for images [6].

2.2   Pose Estimation

Pose estimation is an important pre-work for action recognition. It aims to obtain the key points corresponding to human joints and connect them. Pose estimation has also entered the era of deep learning, and its methods can be roughly divided into top-down methods like [2] and bottom-up methods like [13]. The former relies on the pre-generated human part, and the latter starts from the joints. Generally, the top-down methods perform better in accuracy, while the bottom-up methods control the inference time better in multi-person pose estimation.

Multi-person pose estimation is more challenging because both the inference speed and the accuracy between different people should be considered. Related method [5] is used in the pose regions generation section of this paper.

3   Approach

In this section, we will show the pose regions generation method and pose-enhanced relation module.

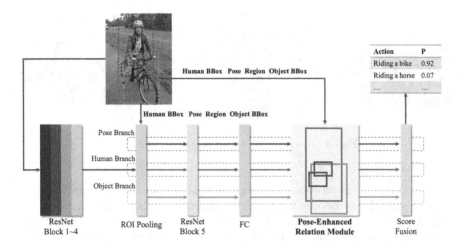

Fig. 2. The overall framework of the proposed method.

3.1 Framework Overview

The overall framework of the proposed method is presented in Fig. 2. The image, human bounding box, objects bounding boxes, and pose regions are taken as inputs, and the final output is the probabilities of each action. Among three kinds of bounding box formatted information, human body bounding box is provided by datasets, objects bounding boxes can be detected by Faster R-CNN [14], and pose regions will be generated by the method that will be introduced later.

The image will be sent to the feature extractor first. Here we choose ResNet [9] because of its efficiency. It can be replaced with other backbones since it's not the key part. ROI Pooling [7] is applied to obtain the instance feature map. Here the input includes the three kinds of bounding boxes introduced earlier. Therefore, the ROI Pooling layer will output 3 branches. They are sent to the ResNet Block5 and an FC layer, which will generate the basic features on human body, pose and objects. Then these basic features are input into the Pose-Enhanced Relation Module and the enhanced relation features will yield. Finally, the relation features are fused with the basic features and participate in the final prediction.

3.2 Pose Regions Generation

The concept of pose regions has been mentioned in Sect. 3.1. The pose estimation network can recognize the human pose, but its output format is the key points, which is difficult to use directly, so further transformation is required. In brief, it takes two steps to complete this process. First, the pose estimation network is applied to generate pose key points. Then a certain number of pose regions are calculated through the combination of key points. The final format of pose regions is the coordinate form consistent with the bounding box.

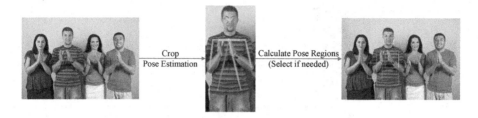

Fig. 3. The process of pose region generation.

The process of generating pose regions is shown in Fig. 3. Specifically, the first step should be cropping the required person according to its bounding box. Then AlphaPose [5] which can handle multi-person scene is applied to estimate poses, and finally 10 pose regions are calculated through key points.

There are two details to pay attention to: First, although most irrelevant characters have been removed by cropping, it is still possible to recognize multiple poses. If this happens, only the pose with the highest confidence will be chosen. In addition, AlphaPose cannot estimate the pose for a few images. There are many reasons, such as: the image is too small, the image is too blurry, or the human body is severely occluded. One solution is to use blank regions instead, but this may adversely affect the recognition results. In the proposed method, if this happens, the human bounding box will be divided into 16 parts, and then one or more (up to 4) parts will be randomly allocated to each pose region. In this way, there are always useful regions being sent to the network.

In order to better reflect the actions embodied by the pose in pose regions, when calculating the coordinates of pose regions, we try to avoid the situation where only one key point is used to calculate a region. For example, the "right elbow" region in Fig. 3 contains information about the bending of the elbow, and 3 key points are used to calculate it. We call it multi-key points calculation method. The key points for calculating each region are illustrated in Table 1.

Table 1. 10 pose regions and corresponding key points.

Region	Key points
Head	Nose, Left/Right ear
Body	Left/Right shoulder, Left/Right hip
Left hand	Left wrist, Left elbow
Right hand	Right wrist, Right elbow
Left elbow	Left wrist, Left elbow, Left shoulder
Right elbow	Right wrist, Right elbow, Right shoulder
Left foot	Left knee, Left ankle
Right foot	Right knee, Right ankle
Left knee	Left knee, Left ankle, Left hip
Right knee	Right knee, Right ankle, Right hip

3.3 Pose-Enhanced Relation Module

As mentioned in Sect. 1, the structure which deals with contextual features should be easy to extend and has strong learning capabilities. Therefore, inspired by [12], the Context-Enhanced Relation Structure shown in Fig. 4 is applied. It can be seen that the structure is symmetrical. The main advantage of such structure is that it not only considers appearance information, but also captures position information through location encoding which uses trigonometric functions to handle the relative position of the bounding boxes.

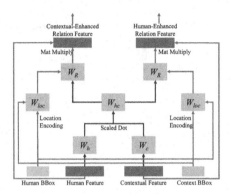

Fig. 4. Details of context-enhanced relation structure.

The final relation feature shown in Fig. 4 can be computed as follows:

$$f_R = fc(\sum(W_R \cdot f_{h\,or\,c})) \tag{1}$$

Here, W_R is the relation weight, which contains attention information from both location and appearance (reflected in W_{loc} and W_{hc} respectively). fc is a fully connected layer. h, c in the subscript represent human and context.

Context-Enhanced Relation Structure is powerful, but it can only handle two types of contextual features. In the proposed solution, the pose regions generated in Sect. 3.2 are added to enhance this module. This is different from [12].

There are two main considerations for adding pose regions:

First, which features need to be combined with the pose feature? Only combining human body feature, or combining both human body feature and objects feature? Our choice is the former. The reason is that the relation between objects and poses is not obvious, and it may have been implicit in the human-object feature. So it's redundant to repeat learning and add useless parameters.

Second, when there are only two types of relation features, the weights of them can be set to 1 for symmetry. However, the addition of the pose feature creates two more relation features. How should the ratio of these relation features be set? In the proposed solution, the final ratio for each relation feature is:

$$f_{ho} : f_{hp} : f_{oh} : f_{ph} = 1 : 1 : 2 : 2 \tag{2}$$

Here h, o, p represent human/object/pose. Larger weights are set on the latter two, mainly to force the network to pay more attention to contextual cues. The structure of the pose-enhanced relation module is shown in Fig. 5. f_{ho} and f_{hp} are merged, so the module outputs 3 types of relation features.

In addition, the idea of Multi-head Attention [15] is also applied in the proposed solution. As presented in Fig. 5, multiple pose-enhanced relation modules (the actual number is 16) are employed to accept different part of the features. The advantage is that different modules can focus on the learning of its own input part, so as to better capture the features of different part in the input.

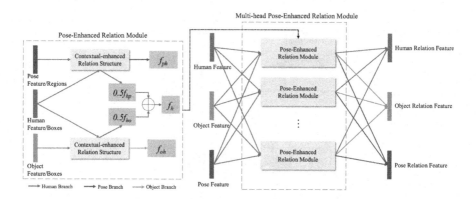

Fig. 5. Details of pose-enhanced relation module and its multi-head form.

3.4   Score Fusion and Loss Function

As shown in Fig. 5, 3 types of relation feature are generated finally. They will be added to the corresponding basic feature and then input into a fully connected layer to obtain the final classification score. For each action a, the score is:

$$Score(a) = Score_{human}^{a} + max_{object\ 1...m}^{a} + max_{pose\ 1...10}^{a} \qquad (3)$$

Here m equals to the number of the surrounding objects, and the max operation selects the highest score of multiple objects/poses for action a. After getting the classification score, $softmax$ is used to convert it to probability and compute the loss. For convenience, cross entropy loss is applied, whose expression is:

$$loss = -log(\frac{exp(Score((a^{gt})))}{\sum_a exp(Score(a))}) \qquad (4)$$

4   Experiments

In this section, we introduce some experimental details and evaluate the proposed solution on two public datasets.

4.1   Experiment Settings

Consistent with what was mentioned above, we use ResNet50 as the backbone network and, like most computer vision tasks, initialize the parameters with the pre-trained weights on ImageNet. In terms of the optimizer, we use the SGD optimizer, set the momentum to 0.9 and the weight decay to 5×10^{-4}. In terms of the learning rate, we use cosine annealing method to control the attenuation of the learning rate so that it can be reduced from 3×10^{-5} to 1×10^{-6} in 20 epochs. The collection of three kinds of bounding boxes has been introduced earlier, that is, human bounding boxes are provided by the datasets, objects bounding boxes are detected by Faster R-CNN, and pose regions are generated using the method proposed in Sect. 3.2. All experiments are done on an NVIDIA TESLA K80 GPU, and the deep learning implementation framework is MXNET [1].

4.2   Comparison with Other Methods

PASCAL VOC 2012 Action and Stanford 40 Action are two classic public datasets for action recognition in still images, and both datasets provide human bounding box annotations. Therefore, the proposed solution is evaluated on them.

PASCAL VOC 2012 Action. Due to the limitation of the test set, we choose to evaluate the proposed solution on PASCAL VOC 2012 validation set which is fully public. The results are shown in Table 2.

Table 2. Average precision (%) on the PASCAL VOC 2012 validation set.

Method	Jumping	Phoning	Playing instrument	Reading	Riding bike	Riding horse	Running	Taking photo	Using computer	Walking	mAP
R*CNN [8]	88.9	79.9	95.1	82.2	96.1	97.8	87.9	85.3	94.0	71.5	87.9
Attention [16]	87.8	78.4	93.7	81.1	95.0	97.1	**96.0**	85.5	93.1	73.4	87.1
Part action [19]	89.6	86.9	94.4	88.5	94.9	97.9	91.3	87.5	92.4	76.4	90.0
Object relation [12]	89.2	89.8	96.5	87.6	**98.2**	**99.1**	92.3	**91.6**	95.2	**79.2**	91.9
Ours	**92.3**	**91.4**	**96.9**	**89.1**	97.2	99.0	92.1	90.8	**95.5**	78.9	**92.3**

According to the results in Table 2, the proposed solution has achieved new state-of-the-art performance on the PASCAL VOC 2012 validation set. In terms of specific actions, jumping, reading and phoning gain the largest increase (at least 1.5 AP%), which directly drives the growth of the overall mAP. For the two actions of playing instrument and using computer, the proposed solution still maintains the lead, but the advantage is smaller. For the two actions of walking and riding horse, although the proposed solution is not optimal, it is extremely close to the state-of-the-art. The remaining few actions lag behind the state-of-the-art by more than 0.8 AP%. To sum up, the proposed solution obtains excellent classification results on the PASCAL VOC 2012 validation set.

Stanford 40 Action. Stanford 40 Action is a larger dataset than PASCAL VOC 2012 Action. Its training set has 4000 images while the test set has 5532. The results of the proposed solution on the Stanford 40 Action test set are shown in Table 3. Since the dataset has 40 classes, it's impossible to list them all here.

Table 3. Mean average precision (%) on the Stanford 40 Action test set.

Method	mAP
Human mask loss [11]	91.1
Part action [19]	91.2
Object relation [12]	93.1
Ours	**93.2**

In the experiment on the Stanford 40 Action test set, the proposed solution has surpassed the current state-of-the-art, and it has a more considerable increase compared with the previous method using pose features. It should be noted that we reproduced the experimental results on the source code of [12], and the best result is 92.8% mAP. The proposed solution is built on this source code, and when similar settings are employed, it can reach 93.2% mAP. Therefore, the proposed solution may be able to surpass the current state-of-the-art more if implementation differences are considered.

In addition, the above comparisons are all performed under ResNet50, and stronger backbone is not used here. According to the result of [12], applying a stronger backbone may further improve the result.

Ablation Study, Visualization and Analysis. In general, the proposed solution has added two parts compared with previous methods: one is to apply the pose regions generated by the key points, and the other is to fuse the pose regions with the human body feature through relation module. In order to verify the effectiveness of these two parts, ablation experiments were conducted on the PASCAL VOC 2012 validation set, and the results are reported in Table 4. It should be noted that the baseline of the experiment is exactly the scheme in [12]. The solution of directly adding pose features to the classifier and fusing pose features with the relation module will be verified.

Table 4. Ablation study on the PASCAL VOC 2012 validation set.

Method	Jumping	Phoning	Playing instrument	Reading	Riding bike	Riding horse	Running	Taking photo	Using computer	Walking	mAP
-	89.2	89.8	96.5	87.6	**98.2**	**99.1**	**92.3**	**91.6**	95.2	**79.2**	91.9
+pose	91.9	89.5	96.2	87.8	97.3	98.9	92.2	90.7	**95.5**	76.3	91.6
+pose, +relation	**92.3**	**91.4**	**96.9**	**89.1**	97.2	99.0	92.1	90.8	**95.5**	78.9	**92.3**

According to the results, it can be found that if the pose feature is just simply added to the classifier, the overall mAP would be lower than the group without the addition. From the perspective of a single action, the group of simply adding pose feature has a drop in the classification results of almost all actions, but jumping and using computer are exceptions. Take a look at the example in Fig. 1, we guess that pose information may be helpful for classifying actions that are not related to objects, but it is limited to certain actions, because the result of the walking action has declined. Obviously, the way of fusing pose information with human body feature through the relation module is more effective.

Fig. 6. Some visualization results on the Stanford 40 Action dataset. The green box is the human bounding box. The red box is the pose region with the highest pose relation weight. The yellow box is the pose region with the lowest pose relation weight. The relation weight value is marked on the top of the pose region. (Color figure online)

We analyze the role played by the pose through visualizing the pose relation weight. In general, the proposed solution makes a certain pose region get the focus of the network, and usually this region is the key to action classification from the perspective of human intuition. If there is no interaction with the object, the network will pay attention to the pose region where the action is performed, as shown in Fig. 6 (a)(b); if the action is associated with objects, the network will pay attention to the pose region related with the object, as shown in Fig. 6 (c)–(f). Correspondingly, the pose region which is not related to the action gets a lower pose relation weight, consistent with the expectation.

In order to further explore what type of action the proposed solution is suitable for, the top 3 and bottom 3 of the results on the Stanford 40 Action test set are listed in Table 5.

From the results, it can be seen that the classification results are generally better for images with clear objects and pose information. The result is relatively poor for actions like Waving Hands which has no surrounding objects. Such action may be confused with others. For the other two actions with poor results, we guess that it is because they don't follow a fixed action pattern. For example,

Table 5. Top 3/bottom 3 classification results on the Stanford 40 Action test set.

Top3	AP	Bottom3	AP
Playing violin	99.9	Pouring liquid	77.9
Holding an umbrella	99.7	Waving hands	79.6
Riding a horse	99.9	Taking photos	82.6

when pouring liquid, the hand movement may be upward or downward, which may cause misclassification. How to make the network adapt to such variability is still a problem that needs further exploration.

5 Conclusion

In this paper, we propose a solution that makes full use of various contextual features especially pose to assist action recognition in still images. By generating pose regions with action cues and fusing them with the human body feature in the Pose-Enhanced Relation Module, the proposed solution solves the problem of insufficient pose information usage in previous methods, and has achieved leading results on public datasets. Based on the analysis of the action classification results, adapting the solution to different action patterns may be a problem worth studying in the future.

Acknowledgments. This work was supported in part by the National Natural Science Foundation of China under Grant 62076183, Grant 61936014, and Grant 61976159; in part by the Natural Science Foundation of Shanghai under Grant 20ZR1473500 and Grant 19ZR1461200; in part by the Shanghai Innovation Action Project of Science and Technology under Grant 20511100700; in part by the National Key Research and Development Project under Grant 2019YFB2102300 and Grant 2019YFB2102301; in part by the Shanghai Municipal Science and Technology Major Project under Grant 2021SHZDZX0100; and in part by the Fundamental Research Funds for the Central Universities. The authors would also like to thank the anonymous reviewers for their careful work and valuable suggestions.

References

1. Chen, T., et al.: MXNet: a flexible and efficient machine learning library for heterogeneous distributed systems. arXiv preprint arXiv:1512.01274 (2015)
2. Chu, X., Yang, W., Ouyang, W., Ma, C., Yuille, A.L., Wang, X.: Multi-context attention for human pose estimation. In: Proceedings of the IEEE Conference on Computer Vision and Pattern Recognition, pp. 1831–1840 (2017)
3. Everingham, M., Van Gool, L., Williams, C.K., Winn, J., Zisserman, A.: The pascal visual object classes (VOC) challenge. Int. J. Comput. Vis. **88**(2), 303–338 (2010)
4. Fang, H.-S., Cao, J., Tai, Y.-W., Lu, C.: Pairwise body-part attention for recognizing human-object interactions. In: Ferrari, V., Hebert, M., Sminchisescu, C., Weiss, Y. (eds.) ECCV 2018. LNCS, vol. 11214, pp. 52–68. Springer, Cham (2018). https://doi.org/10.1007/978-3-030-01249-6_4

5. Fang, H.S., Xie, S., Tai, Y.W., Lu, C.: RMPE: regional multi-person pose estimation. In: Proceedings of the IEEE International Conference on Computer Vision, pp. 2334–2343 (2017)
6. Gao, R., Xiong, B., Grauman, K.: Im2FLow: motion hallucination from static images for action recognition. In: Proceedings of the IEEE Conference on Computer Vision and Pattern Recognition, pp. 5937–5947 (2018)
7. Girshick, R.: Fast R-CNN. In: Proceedings of the IEEE International Conference on Computer Vision, pp. 1440–1448 (2015)
8. Gkioxari, G., Girshick, R., Malik, J.: Contextual action recognition with R*CNN. In: Proceedings of the IEEE International Conference on Computer Vision, pp. 1080–1088 (2015)
9. He, K., Zhang, X., Ren, S., Sun, J.: Deep residual learning for image recognition. In: Proceedings of the IEEE Conference on Computer Vision and Pattern Recognition, pp. 770–778 (2016)
10. Hu, H., Gu, J., Zhang, Z., Dai, J., Wei, Y.: Relation networks for object detection. In: Proceedings of the IEEE Conference on Computer Vision and Pattern Recognition, pp. 3588–3597 (2018)
11. Liu, L., Tan, R.T., You, S.: Loss guided activation for action recognition in still images. In: Jawahar, C.V., Li, H., Mori, G., Schindler, K. (eds.) ACCV 2018. LNCS, vol. 11365, pp. 152–167. Springer, Cham (2019). https://doi.org/10.1007/978-3-030-20873-8_10
12. Ma, W., Liang, S.: Human-object relation network for action recognition in still images. In: 2020 IEEE International Conference on Multimedia and Expo (ICME), pp. 1–6. IEEE (2020)
13. Papandreou, G., Zhu, T., Chen, L.-C., Gidaris, S., Tompson, J., Murphy, K.: PersonLab: person pose estimation and instance segmentation with a bottom-up, part-based, geometric embedding model. In: Ferrari, V., Hebert, M., Sminchisescu, C., Weiss, Y. (eds.) Computer Vision – ECCV 2018. LNCS, vol. 11218, pp. 282–299. Springer, Cham (2018). https://doi.org/10.1007/978-3-030-01264-9_17
14. Ren, S., He, K., Girshick, R., Sun, J.: Faster R-CNN: towards real-time object detection with region proposal networks. Adv. Neural. Inf. Process. Syst. **28**, 91–99 (2015)
15. Vaswani, A., et al.: Attention is all you need. In: Advances in Neural Information Processing Systems, pp. 5998–6008 (2017)
16. Yan, S., Smith, J.S., Lu, W., Zhang, B.: Multibranch attention networks for action recognition in still images. IEEE Trans. Cogn. Dev. Syst. **10**(4), 1116–1125 (2017)
17. Yao, B., Fei-Fei, L.: Modeling mutual context of object and human pose in human-object interaction activities. In: 2010 IEEE Computer Society Conference on Computer Vision and Pattern Recognition, pp. 17–24. IEEE (2010)
18. Yao, B., Jiang, X., Khosla, A., Lin, A.L., Guibas, L., Fei-Fei, L.: Human action recognition by learning bases of action attributes and parts. In: 2011 International Conference on Computer Vision, pp. 1331–1338. IEEE (2011)
19. Zhao, Z., Ma, H., You, S.: Single image action recognition using semantic body part actions. In: Proceedings of the IEEE International Conference on Computer Vision, pp. 3391–3399 (2017)

Prostate Segmentation of Ultrasound Images Based on Interpretable-Guided Mathematical Model

Tao Peng[1], Caiyin Tang[2], and Jing Wang[1]([✉])

[1] UT Southwestern Medical Center, 2280 Inwood Road, Dallas, USA
{Tao.Peng,Jing.Wang}@UTSouthwestern.edu
[2] Taizhou People's Hospital, Taizhou, Jiangsu, China

Abstract. Ultrasound prostate segmentation is challenging due to the low contrast of transrectal ultrasound (TRUS) images and the presence of imaging artifacts such as speckle and shadow regions. In this work, we propose an improved principal curve-based & differential evolution-based ultrasound prostate segmentation method (H-SegMod) based on an interpretable-guided mathematical model. Comparing with existing related studies, H-SegMod has three main merits and contributions: (1) The characteristic of the principal curve on automatically approaching the center of the dataset is utilized by our proposed H-SegMod. (2) When acquiring the data sequences, we use the principal curve-based constraint closed polygonal segment model, which uses different initialization, normalization, and vertex filtering methods. (3) We propose a mathematical map model (realized by differential evolution-based neural network) to describe the smooth prostate contour represented by the output of neural network (i.e., optimized vertices) so that it can match the ground truth contour. Compared with the traditional differential evolution method, we add different mutation steps and loop constraint conditions. Both quantitative and qualitative evaluation studies on a clinical prostate dataset show that our method achieves better segmentation than many state-of-the-art methods.

Keywords: Ultrasound prostate segmentation · Principal curve and neural network · Interpretable-guided mathematical model

1 Introduction

One of the most common noncutaneous cancers among men worldwide is prostate cancer. Due to the cost-effectiveness and real-time nature, transrectal ultrasound images (TRUS) have become an important imaging technique for prostate cancer diagnosis and treatment. Manual delineation of the prostate boundary for medical physicians' diagnosis is tedious, time-consuming, and often depends on the experiences of radiologists [1]. Therefore, the accurate ultrasound prostate segmentation technique is highly desired to obtain consistent prostate boundary efficiently in image-guided diagnostic procedures.

© Springer Nature Switzerland AG 2022
B. Þór Jónsson et al. (Eds.): MMM 2022, LNCS 13141, pp. 166–177, 2022.
https://doi.org/10.1007/978-3-030-98358-1_14

Accurate prostate segmentation in ultrasound remains very challenging due to the low contrast of TRUS images and the presence of imaging artifacts such as speckle, micro-calcifications, and shadow artifacts. Some other issues also make prostate segmentation challenging, such as heterogeneous intensity distribution inside the prostate gland and neighboring tissues. Figure 1 shows two challenging cases in TRUS prostate automatic segmentation.

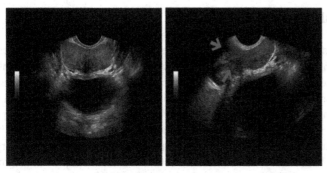

Fig. 1. The left image is an example of a TRUS image with a clear prostate boundary. The other one shows the example with weak or incomplete edge information, pointed by the red arrow.

Ultrasound prostate segmentation approaches can generally be categorized into two types: including 1) automatic methods and 2) semi-automatic methods. The DSC of most existing automatic ultrasound prostate segmentation approaches is only near 0.9 [1]. How to decrease the impact of these issues (i.e., low contrast of TRUS images and the presence of imaging artifacts) and increase the accuracy of the ultrasound segmentation methods is a challenging issue.

In this work, we propose a novel semi-automatic segmentation framework, H-SegMod, for ultrasound prostate segmentation. The proposed framework consists of three cascaded stages. In the first stage, using less than 15% points of region of interest (ROI) contour as the approximate initialization, an improved principal curve model is used to obtain the data sequences, which consists of the coordinates of points and projection indexes. In the second stage, an improved differential evolution-based model is used for preliminary searching an optimal machine learning model. Finally, an interpretable mathematical model of the prostate contour is proposed, which is denoted by the parameters of the machine learning model.

The contributions of our work are as follows:

1) We use the ability of the principal curve to automatically approaching the center of the dataset and develop a principal curve-based method to obtain the data sequence consisting of data ordinates and projection indexes.
2) Compared with other state-of-the-art principal curve models, the constraint closed polygonal segment model (CCPS) is firstly proposed by adding different normalization strategies and constraint conditions.
3) To the best of our knowledge, the improved adaptive mutation and crossover-based differential evolution model (IAMCDE) is proposed here for the first time by using

different mutation steps and loop constraint conditions as compared with other state-of-the-art differential evolution models.

4) A mathematical map function realized by learning-rate back propagation neural network (ABPNN) is proposed to generate a smooth prostate contour, which is represented by the output of ABPNN (i.e., optimized vertices) to match the ground truth contour.

2 Related Work

Currently, many different segmentation models have been investigated for medical image segmentation, including: (1) feature classification models, (2) region segmentation models, and (3) contour detection models. Yan et al. [2] have proposed the propagation-deep neural network using multi-level features for magnetic resonance imaging (MRI) prostate segmentation with good performance. However, in several cases, while the position and shape of the prostate can be precisely predicted, the prostate boundary cannot be precisely delineated due to the blurry prostate boundaries. Rundo et al. [3] have incorporated the squeeze-and-excitation blocks into the U-Net method for zonal prostate segmentation of multi-institutional MRI datasets, but the proposed model requires too many samples for proper tuning. Zhu et al. [4] proposed a cascaded Fully Convolution Network architecture for outer prostate contour and the peripheral zone contour with high efficacy in MRI. However, the method strongly relies on manual data labeling. Compared to these two methods, the contour detection method can obtain more realistic shapes of anatomical structures.

The contour detection methods can be used to denote the boundaries of the tissues based on a shape representation or curve approximation model. Shahedi et al. [5] have proposed a semi-automatic segmentation model for prostate segmentation in computed tomography (CT) images using local texture classification and statistical shape modeling. The Dice similarity coefficient (DSC) is only 88%, and the accuracy in the texture detection stage strongly depends on the image resampling results. Li et al. [6] have designed a robust active contour model using adaptive energy weight functions for medical image segmentation in different modalities, but the results of the proposed method are affected by the missing/blurry boundary and noise.

It is worth noting that among recent contour extraction models, the principal curve-based model has gained great interest for its strong ability to handle noisy input and obtains accurate results [7]. Li et al. [8] have presented an efficient coronary arteries extraction architecture based on the principal curve-based technique in computed tomography angiographies with high performance. In Ref. [9], Dai et al. have designed a novel method using the principal curve-based method and variational model with multiple energies for accurate and reliable optic disc segmentation. Furthermore, Alickovic et al. [10] have proposed a medical decision support system using a principal curve model and random forests classifier for the diagnosis of heart arrhythmia with high accuracy.

3   Model

3.1   Problem Statement

The goal of this work is to obtain a smooth and accurate contour of the arbitrary prostate ROI, where the limited manually delineated points $P_n = \{p_1, p_2,...,p_n\}$, $p_i(x_i, y_i) \subseteq R^d$ is used as a priori. We use P_n as the input of the principal curve-based method [11], then we can obtain the vertices sequences $D = \{d_1, d_2,...,d_n\} \in R^d = \{(t_i, v_i(x_i, y_i)), i = 1, 2,...,n, 0 \leq t_1 < t_2 <... < t_n \leq 1\}$, where t_i is sequence number of vertex, and x_i and y_i are the x-axis coordinate and y-axis coordinate of the vertex v_i, respectively. Meanwhile, we can also obtain prostate contour consisting of several line segments. To make the prostate contour smooth, we used an enhanced machine learning method consisting of the IAMCDE and ABPNN for training, where the sequence number of vertices t is used as the input of ABPNN, and vertices' coordinates are used to minimize the mean square error [7]. After training, we will obtain the coordinates of optimized vertices to denote the smooth prostate contour that can match the ground truth contour, shown as below,

$$f(t) = (x(t), y(t)) = \left(\frac{g(x) + 1 - \sqrt{1 - g(x)^2}}{2 \times g(x)}, \frac{g(y) + 1 - \sqrt{1 - g(y)^2}}{2 \times g(y)} \right) \quad (1)$$

where $x(t)$ and $y(t)$ denote the x-axis coordinate and y-axis coordinate of the point of the obtained prostate contour, respectively. Furthermore, $g(\bullet)$ denotes the value of the output units as follows,

$$(g(x(t)), g(y(t))) = \left(\frac{\sum\limits_{i=1}^{p} \frac{1}{1+e^{-(t\omega_i - T_i)}} v_{i,1} - b_1}{e^{\sum\limits_{i=1}^{p} \frac{1}{1+e^{-(t\omega_i - T_i)}} v_{i,1} - b_1} + e^{-(\sum\limits_{i=1}^{p} \frac{1}{1+e^{-(t\omega_i - T_i)}} v_{i,1} - b_1)}}, \frac{\sum\limits_{i=1}^{p} \frac{1}{1+e^{-(t\omega_i - T_i)}} v_{i,2} - b_2}{e^{\sum\limits_{i=1}^{p} \frac{1}{1+e^{-(t\omega_i - T_i)}} v_{i,2} - b_2} + e^{-(\sum\limits_{i=1}^{p} \frac{1}{1+e^{-(t\omega_i - T_i)}} v_{i,2} - b_2)}} \right) \quad (2)$$

Where t is the sequence number of vertices, p is the number of hidden neurons. $T_i(i = 1, 2,...,p)$ is the output threshold of the i-th hidden neuron. $b_k(k = 1, 2)$ is the output threshold of the k-th neuron at the output layer. $w_i(i = 1, 2,...,p)$ is the weight from the input layer to the i-th hidden neuron. $v_{i,k}(i = 1, 2,...,p; k = 1, 2)$ is the weight from the i-th hidden neuron to the k-th output neuron.

In principle curve-based methods, there often exist some sparse, uneven distributions and abnormal points p_j in the P_n, which may potentially impact the quality of the P_n. How to filter the unavailable and abnormal points by the appropriate principal curve-based method and obtain the optimal vertices sequence D is a challenging issue. Furthermore, after the ABPNN that has the optimal performance for training, the smooth and accurate prostate contour is achieved according to Eq. (1) and Eq. (2). The performance of the ABPNN is affected by several parameters (i.e., weights and thresholds). Hence, how to obtain the ABPNN with the optimal performance is also a challenging issue. We aim to overcome these challenging issues by developing an advanced segmentation framework detailed below.

3.2 Model Overview

The overview architecture of our model is shown in Fig. 2. In this work, our model consists of the principal curve-based method and machine learning-based method, which mainly contains the following steps:

- Generate a closed polygonal curve f consisting of several segments $S = \{s_1, s_2,..,s_n\}$ by CCPS.
- Optimize the model parameters (i.e., weights w and thresholds) of the ABPNN by IAMCDE.
- Decrease the ABPNN's global deviation $E = \sum_{k=1}^{m} E_k$ and increase the accuracy of experimental results during ABPNN's training, where E_k is the mean square error between the actual output and the expected output.
- Find mathematical map model (realized by ABPNN) to describe the smooth prostate contour represented by the output of neural network (i.e., optimized vertices) (shown in Eq. (1) and Eq. (2)).

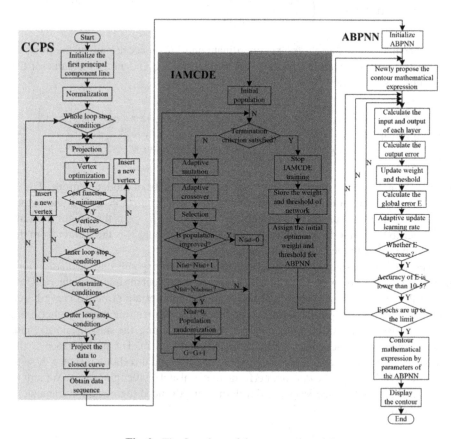

Fig. 2. The flowchart of the proposed model.

3.3 Principal Curve Based CCPS

To handle the issue that the traditional k-segments polygonal segment model (KPS) [11] cannot deal with the closed dataset, some researchers have presented the improved closed polygonal segment model (CPS) [12, 13]. However, one practical use of both works is that the model performance is always affected by abnormal data. To deal with the aforementioned issues, we design the CCPS that mainly includes two refinement parts: 1) different initialization or normalization strategies and 2) vertex filtering.

Different Initialization: Zhang *et al.* [14] used a line segment as the first principal component line and could not deal with the closed dataset well. In this work, we use a different initialization strategy by using a closed square as the first principal component line. The closed square contains all the projection points and the coordinates of each vertex of the closed square are $(0.1, 0.1)$, $(-0.1, 0.1)$, $(-0.1, -0.1)$, and $(0.1, -0.1)$, respectively.

Different Normalization: Due to the CPS using the min-max normalization method [15] with the week anti-interference ability, we used a different normalization way by using the Z-score standardization method [16].

Vertex Filtering: All the vertices' positions are updated in the vertex optimization step following the principle of the nearest distance from the data points to the principal curve [17]. However, this step can produce a distorted principal curve due to existing abnormal vertices during the optimization step. To handle this problem, we added a constraint condition to remove the abnormal vertices. The flag of removing vertices is defined as
$$Flag(v_i) = \begin{cases} 1, & if\,\{(l_{si-1} \ or \ l_{si} > r\} \\ 0, & otherwise \end{cases}$$
, where r denotes the data's radius and

satisfies $r = \max\limits_{x \in X} \left\| x - \frac{1}{n} \sum\limits_{y \in V} y \right\|$. n is the total number of vertices in generated vertices dataset V, and x and y are the x-axis and y-axis coordinate of the vertex v_i, respectively. l_{si} is the length of the i-th line segment and meets $l_{si} = \|v_{i+1} - v_i\|$ $1 \le i \le n$. Note that the P_n is the initial input dataset, and X contains generated vertices that construct the principal curve. When $Flag(v_i) = 1$, we retain the vertex v_i; otherwise, we remove the vertex v_i. A vertex v_i will be removed if it meets any of the following situations: including 1) the vertex goes outside the radius of the data, and 2) the number of data points projected onto the vertices and neighboring segments is less than five.

3.4 Differential Evolution Based IAMCDE

Due to the training results of the neural network algorithm (NN) strongly depend on the initial weights and thresholds, many studies use the differential evolution-based model (DE) for preliminarily searching parameters for NN [18].

Traditional DE: The traditional DE proposed by Storn *et al.* [19] has been used as a global search technique. The key steps of the traditional DE include initialization, mutation, crossover, and a selection step. However, both mutation factor (F) and crossover rate (CR) with a fixed value will affect the convergence speed and the quality of the solution.

Improved AMCDE Proposed by Ref. [18]: Zeng *et al.* [18] have proposed an adaptive mutation and crossover-based differential evolution model (AMCDE) and validated on the energy consumption prediction. To improve the convergence speed and the quality of the solution, the main improvements of the AMCDE are shown below,

$$F = \begin{cases} a + (1 - a) \times \sin(\frac{G}{GMax}\pi - \frac{1}{2}\pi), \text{if } G \le \frac{GMax}{2} \\ a - (1 - a) \times \cos(\frac{1}{2}\pi - \frac{G}{GMax}\pi), \text{ otherwise} \end{cases} \tag{3}$$

$$CR = \begin{cases} b + (1 - b) \times \sin(\frac{G}{GMax}\pi - \frac{1}{2}\pi), \text{if } G \le \frac{GMax}{2} \\ b - (1 - b) \times \cos(\frac{1}{2}\pi - \frac{G}{GMax}\pi), \text{ otherwise} \end{cases} \tag{4}$$

where a and b are constants within the range [0.5, 1], G is the current iteration number, and $GMax$ is the maximum iteration number.

At the beginning and end stages, both F and CR change slower, where $sin(\bullet)$ and $cos(\bullet)$ are in 1/4 cycle with a value within [1, 0], respectively. In the middle stage, they change relatively faster. Although the improvements of AMCDE have obtained good performance for searching the optimal global solution, the AMCDE is often trapped into the local optimum during training [18].

Our Newly Proposed IAMCDE: We design a new IAMCDE by adding two new improvements based on the AMCDE [18], including 1) two mutation operators and 2) a new global optimum search approach.

1) *Two mutation operators* can be used to yield the mutant vectors as follows,

$$v_i^G = \begin{cases} x_{i1}^G + r \text{ and } 1 \times (x_{i2}^G - x_{i3}^G), & \text{if } r \text{ and } [0, 1] < p_G \\ x_{i1}^G + r \text{ and } 2 \times (x_{i2}^G - x_{i3}^G) + r \text{ and } 3 \times (x_{i4}^G - x_{i5}^G), & \text{otherwise} \end{cases} \tag{5}$$

where i_k ($k = 1, 2, 3, 4, 5$) represent five random integer numbers in the range of [1, N_p], N_p is the number of solutions, and $rand(\bullet)$ is the random number in the range of [0, 1]. Random numbers are used to produce mutation factors in each cycle. During the evolution process, a mutation factor is selected in the range of [0, 1], which is useful for both global and local searches. p_G denotes the probability of using the mutation operator.

2) *Global optimum search approach* can help IAMCDE to avoid being trapped in the optimum local search, which makes the search space expanded. The execution process of the new global optimum search approach is as follows. We first set the current failure number $N_{fail} = 0$ and the max failure number $N_{failmax}$. If the current

population is improved in the *Gth* generation, we set $N_{fail} = 0$. Otherwise, $N_{fail} = N_{fail} + 1$. When $N_{fail} = N_{failmax}$, we will set $N_{fail} = 0$ and carry out the following population randomization strategy. Firstly, we sort all solutions of the population by decreasing order according to their function values. Secondly, we keep the first $N_P/2$ solutions for the next generation and delete the remaining $N_P/2$ solutions from the population. Lastly, $N_P/2$ new solutions are extended into the population.

3.5 Prostate Contour's Interpretable Mathematical Model Denoted by the Parameters of ABPNN

After determining the initial weight optimal connection weights and thresholds of ABPNN [20] by the IAMCDE, we will train the ABPNN, where the main purpose of training the ABPNN is to use its parameters to denote the mathematical model of prostate contour. Furthermore, the model error can be minimized to refine the segmentation results during ABPNN's training.

Considering that the feed-forward neural network with one hidden layer can be used to approximate any continuous function, we use the three-layer ABPNN (i.e., input, hidden, and output layers). The data sequence D obtained by the CCPS is used as the input of the ABPNN. In the forward propagation stage of the ABPNN, from the input layer to the hidden layer, we use the Sigmoid activation function $h_1 = 1/(1 + e^{-x})$. Meanwhile, the Tanh activation function $h_2 = (e^x - e^{-x})/(e^x + e^{-x})$ is used from the hidden layer to output layer. The output layer includes two units, i.e., $g(x)$ and $g(y)$, where $g(x)$ and $g(y)$ can be treated as the continuous functions $g(x(t))$ and $g(y(t))$, respectively, on the sequence number of vertices t, shown in Eq. (2). Furthermore, the smooth and accurate prostate contour can be denoted by the coordinates of optimized vertices, shown in Eq. (1).

4 Experiments

4.1 Experimental Setups

Dataset. We use a dataset containing 100 brachytherapy patients with total 295 images in the experiments. The dataset is divided into training, validation, and testing sets with 55 patients (165 images)/20 patients (55 images)/25 patients (75 images), respectively. All TRUS images were obtained using the General Electric LOGIQ E9 (LE9) system and an integrated TRUS probe with a frequency in the range of 5–8 MHz. The age of the patients ranged from 18 to 56. All images are in DICOM format, which has a matrix size of 700×615 pixels. The ground truth of each prostate contour is marked and verified by five expert radiologists. All the expert radiologists have over five years' experience in dealing with prostate anatomy, prostate segmentation, and ultrasound-guided biopsies. Each expert radiologist independently checks their own marks along with the anonymous marks of the other radiologists, and the consensus ground truth are obtained by the majority voting of five experts' annotations.

Hyper-Parameters of the Proposed H-SegMod. For all the experiments, we use the following hyper-parameters for training H-SegMod: we set 10 neurons and 1000 epochs for ABPNN to simplify the complex network model and avoid overfitting. We set the initial learning rate at 0.5.

Metrics. To demonstrate the performance of the proposed model, we use DSC [1], Jaccard Similarity Coefficient (Ω) [1], and Accuracy (ACC) [1] as the evaluation metrics.

4.2 Comparison with Hybrid Models

In this subsection, we validate the performance of our model by comparing it with three other hybrid models on our dataset, and all the models are the semi-automatic and use the same training, validation, and testing sets.

- Hybrid model 1 is the CPS-DE-BPNN, which combines the strategies proposed in Ref. [11] and Ref. [19] for prostate segmentation.
- Hybrid model 2 is the CPS-AMCDE-BPNN. On the basis of the Hybrid model 1, the Hybrid model 2 was improved by combining with the strategy proposed in Ref. [18].
- Hybrid model 3 is the CCPS-AMCDE-BPNN, which uses the improved CCPS based on Hybrid model 2.

The evaluation results of our model against three hybrid models are presented in Table 1. Meanwhile, we randomly selected four TRUS results for visual comparison, as shown in Fig. 3. The first column in Fig. 3 denotes raw prostate TRUS images. As the prostate TRUS images often contain the missing/ambiguous boundaries (shown in red arrows), the expert radiologists first mark the approximate range of the prostate with yellow and green labels (shown in raw images). The last four columns show the experimental results of the four models, where red lines show the ground truth and blue lines show the segmentation result.

As shown in Table 1, we have the following observations: 1) all the hybrid models can obtain good performance (DSC, ACC, and Ω are higher than 90%) even affected by the missing/ambiguous boundaries of the prostate in TRUS images. 2) Compared with the other three models, our proposed model outperforms them by a large margin of DSC, Ω, and ACC around 2.69~4.66%, 2.83~4.83%, and 2.59~4.57%, respectively.

Table 1. Quantitative comparison with hybrid models

Model	Method	Model	DSC (%)	Ω (%)	ACC (%)
Hybrid model 1	CPS-DE-BPNN	Hybrid	91.9	90.6	91.8
Hybrid model 2	CPS-AMCDE-BPNN	Hybrid	92.1	90.3	92
Hybrid model 3	CCPS-AMCDE-BPNN	Hybrid	93.8	92.5	93.7
Proposed model	H-SegMod	Hybrid	96.4	95.2	96.2

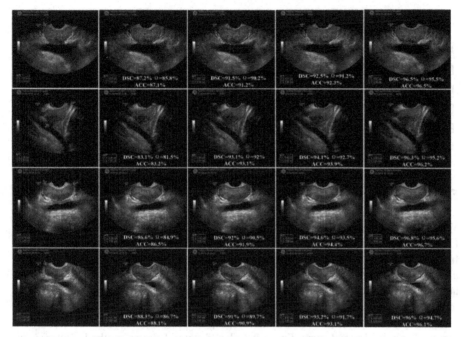

Fig. 3. Visual comparison of prostate segmentation results.

4.3 Comparison with Other State-Of-The-Art Models

This section compares the performance of our model against state-of-the-art techniques using different evaluation metrics (i.e., DSC, Ω, and ACC), where CPL-BNNM [11] and Hull-CPLM [20] are hybrid approaches, and Unet [21] and Mask-RCNN [22] are deep learning-based approaches. Two deep learning networks are automatic segmentation models, and the three hybrid models including our proposed method are semi-automatic models. The results of these experiments are presented in Table 2.

Considering that the accuracy of deep learning-based models is decreased by the limited training data, we augmented raw training data (165 slices), where each slice was rotated in the range of $[-15°, 15°]$ until they satisfied the expected number of training data (1500 slices). However, three hybrid models only used the raw training data (165 slices).

As shown in the results presented in Table 2, our proposed model has the best performance. Furthermore, all the hybrid models are principal curve-based techniques and obtain good segmentation results, which demonstrate that combining the principal curve model with the machine learning model has the ability to fit the dataset.

Table 2. Quantitative comparison with other state-of-the-art models

Paper	Method	Model	DSC (%)	Ω (%)	ACC (%)
[21]-2015	Unet	Deep learning	93	91.5	92.7
[22]-2017	Mask-RCNN	Deep learning	94.1	92.4	93.8
[11]-2018	CPL-BNNM	Hybrid	91.8	90.5	91.7
[12]-2019	Hull-CPLM	Hybrid	95.2	94.3	95
Proposed model	H-SegMod	Hybrid	96.4	95.2	96.2

5 Discussion and Conclusion

We proposed a new hybrid architecture to perform accurate ultrasound prostate segmentation. The contributions of our proposed model include: (1) an improved principal curve-based model; (2) an improved differential evolution machine learning-based model; (3) a smooth and interpretable mathematical map function (realized by ABPNN) to generate a smooth prostate contour. To demonstrate the applicability of our proposed method to prostates with various shapes, TRUS images of 100 patients were used. Experimental results show that the performance of the proposed segmentation model outperforms many other hybrid-based, curve fitting-based, and state-of-the-art methods. Future work will be focused on the evaluation of different modalities or different organs.

Acknowledgement. The authors acknowledge the funding support from the National Institute of Health (R01 EB027898).

References

1. Wang, Y., et al.: Deep attentive features for prostate segmentation in 3D transrectal ultrasound. IEEE Trans. Med. Imaging **38**, 2768–2778 (2019)
2. Yan, K., Wang, X., Kim, J., Khadra, M., Fulham, M., Feng, D.: A propagation-DNN: deep combination learning of multi-level features for MR prostate segmentation. Comput Methods Programs Biomed. **170**, 11–21 (2019)
3. Rundo, L., et al.: USE-Net: incorporating squeeze-and-excitation blocks into U-Net for prostate zonal segmentation of multi-institutional MRI datasets. Neurocomputing **365**, 31–43 (2019)
4. Zhu, Y., et al.: Fully automatic segmentation on prostate MR images based on cascaded fully convolution network. J. Magn. Reson. Imaging **49**, 1149–1156 (2019)
5. Shahedi, M., Halicek, M., Guo, R., Zhang, G., Schuster, D.S., Fei, B.: A semiautomatic segmentation method for prostate in CT images using local texture classification and statistical shape modeling. Med. Phys. **45**, 2527–2541 (2018)
6. Li, X., Wang, X., Dai, Y.: adaptive energy weight based active contour model for robust medical image segmentation. J. Sig. Proc. Syst. **90**(3), 449–465 (2017). https://doi.org/10.1007/s11265-017-1257-3
7. Peng, T., Xu, T.C., Wang, Y., Li, F.: Deep Belief Network and Closed Polygonal Line for Lung Segmentation in Chest Radiographs. Comput. J. (2020)

8. Li, Z., Zhang, Y., Gong, H., Liu, G., Li, W., Tang, X.: An automatic and efficient coronary arteries extraction method in CT angiographies. Biomed. Sig. Process Control. **36**, 221–233 (2017)

9. Dai, B., Wu, X., Bu, W.: Optic disc segmentation based on variational model with multiple energies. Pattern Recogn. **64**, 226–235 (2017)

10. Alickovic, E., Subasi, A.: Medical decision support system for diagnosis of heart arrhythmia using DWT and random forests classifier. J. Med. Syst. **40**(4), 1–12 (2016). https://doi.org/10.1007/s10916-016-0467-8

11. Peng, T., Wang, Y., Xu, T.C., Shi, L., Jiang, J., Zhu, S.: Detection of lung contour with closed principal curve and machine learning. J. Digit. Imaging **31**(4), 520–533 (2018). https://doi.org/10.1007/s10278-018-0058-y

12. Peng, T., et al.: Hybrid automatic lung segmentation on chest CT scans. IEEE Access. **8**, 73293–73306 (2020)

13. Peng, T., Wang, Y., Xu, T.C., Chen, X.: Segmentation of lung in chest radiographs using hull and closed polygonal line method. IEEE Access. **7**, 137794–137810 (2019)

14. Junping, Z., Dewang, C., Kruger, U.: Adaptive constraint K-segment principal curves for intelligent transportation systems. IEEE Trans. Intell. Transport. Syst. **9**, 666–677 (2008)

15. Chen, P.: Effects of normalization on the entropy-based TOPSIS method. Expert Syst. Appl. **136**, 33–41 (2019)

16. Kabir, W., Ahmad, M.O., Swamy, M.N.S.: A novel normalization technique for multimodal biometric systems. In: 2015 IEEE 58th International Midwest Symposium on Circuits and Systems (MWSCAS), pp. 1–4. IEEE, Fort Collins, CO, USA (2015)

17. Kégl, B., Krzyzak, A.: Piecewise linear skeletonization using principal curves. IEEE Trans. Pattern Anal. Mach. Intell. **24**, 59–74 (2002)

18. Zeng, Y.-R., Zeng, Y., Choi, B., Wang, L.: Multifactor-influenced energy consumption forecasting using enhanced back-propagation neural network. Energy **127**, 381–396 (2017)

19. Storn, R.: Differential evolution – a simple and effcient heuristic for global optimization over continuous spaces. J. Glob. Optim. **11**, 341–359 (1997)

20. Kim, D.W., Kim, M.S., Lee, J., Park, P.: Adaptive learning-rate backpropagation neural network algorithm based on the minimization of mean-square deviation for impulsive noises. IEEE Access. **8**, 98018–98026 (2020)

21. Ronneberger, O., Fischer, P., Brox, T.: U-Net: convolutional networks for biomedical image segmentation. In: Navab, N., Hornegger, J., Wells, W.M., Frangi, A.F. (eds.) MICCAI 2015. LNCS, vol. 9351, pp. 234–241. Springer, Cham (2015). https://doi.org/10.1007/978-3-319-24574-4_28

22. He, K., Gkioxari, G., Dollar, P., Girshick, R.: Mask R-CNN. In: Proceedings of the IEEE International Conference on Computer Vision, pp. 2961–2969. Venice, Italy (2017)

Spatiotemporal Perturbation Based Dynamic Consistency for Semi-supervised Temporal Action Detection

Lin Wang, Yan Song[✉], Rui Yan, and Xiangbo Shu

School of Computer Science and Engineering, Nanjing University
of Science and Technology, NanJing, China
songyan@njust.edu.cn

Abstract. Temporal action detection usually relies on huge tagging costs to achieve significant performance. Semi-supervised learning, where only a small amount of data are annotated in the training set, can help reduce the burden of labeling. However, the existing action detection models will inevitably learn inductive bias from limited labeled data and hinder the effective use of unlabeled data in semi-supervised learning. To this end, we propose a generic end-to-end framework for Semi-Supervised Temporal Action Detection (SS-TAD). Specifically, the framework is based on the teacher-student structure that leverages the consistency between unlabeled data and their augmentations. To achieve this, we propose a dynamic consistency loss by employing an attention mechanism to alleviate the prediction bias of the model, so it can make full use of the unlabeled data. Besides, we design a concise yet valid spatiotemporal feature perturbation module to learn robust action representations. Experiments on THUMOS14 and ActivityNet v1.2 demonstrate that our method significantly outperforms the start-of-the-art semi-supervised methods and is even comparable to the fully-supervised methods.

Keywords: Temporal action detection · Semi-supervised learning · Teacher-student model · Dynamic consistency

1 Introduction

Temporal action detection (TAD), which aims at detecting action categories and temporal boundaries (i.e., start and end time) of action instances occurring in untrimmed videos, is an important research direction for human behavior understanding. Recently, fully-supervised temporal action detection has made significant progresses [6,11,13,16,21]. To achieve high prediction accuracy, most of the start-of-the-art methods rely on the frame-level annotation: action category, start and end time. However, these methods have limited practical applications due to the annotation burden and the subjective bias introduced by human.

© Springer Nature Switzerland AG 2022
B. Þór Jónsson et al. (Eds.): MMM 2022, LNCS 13141, pp. 178–190, 2022.
https://doi.org/10.1007/978-3-030-98358-1_15

Semi-Supervised Learning (SSL) [1,2,17], with limited labeled data and a large amount of unlabeled data in the training set, is a more practical compromise. Recently, [8,19] have applied SSL methods based on consistency regularization in the temporal action proposal task. As a subtask of TAD, temporal action proposal only aims to localize the temporal boundaries of action instances without recognizing the action categories. Apparently, there will be new challenges to introduce the semi-supervised setting to the task of TAD which accomplishes localization and recognition simultaneously.

Under the semi-supervised setting, only part of the videos are provided with category and temporal boundary annotations for training. To make use of the unlabeled data, inspired by [8], we utilize the teacher-student two-model architecture for the SS-TAD task and face the following two issues. First, the imbalance of categories will impede the usage of the unlabeled data. Generally, the class-imbalanced data distribution in action detection datasets tend to bring in inductive bias to the model. If we treat the unbalanced pseudo soft-labels generated by a biased model for unlabeled data equally, the bias will be further aggravated through the collaborative learning of the two models and lead to a significant decrease in the utilization of the unlabeled data. Second, existing sequential perturbations are not suitable for the task of TAD. Traditional sequential perturbations, which are beneficial to the category-independent temporal action proposal, only perturb in single temporal space to help the model learn the temporal correlations of sequential data. However, these disturbances ignore the spatial semantic information, which are crucial to the learning of robust action representations for classification.

To this end, we propose a generic end-to-end framework for SS-TAD, which utilizes a dynamic consistency loss and a spatiotemporal feature perturbation module. The framework consists of a teacher-student model, where the teacher model generates pseudo soft-labels for the unlabeled data, and the student model generate predictions consistent with the teacher under the disturbances. To reduce the impact of imbalanced pseudo-labels, we propose a dynamic consistency loss, i.e., attention weighted loss for classification and improved Smooth L1 loss for localization. We adopt an attention mechanism to quantify the contribution of each sample by measuring the consistency between the teacher's and student's predictions. In addition, to enhance the spatial and temporal invariances for action classification and localization, we propose a concise yet effective spatiotemporal feature perturbation module, including time masking and noise injection. It is able to learn the temporal dependence and spatial semantic information of actions as well.

In summary, our main contributions are as follows:

- We introduce the teacher-student model into TAD to establish a generic end-to-end framework for the SS-TAD task;
- We propose a dynamic consistency loss based on an attention mechanism to solve the problem of imbalance of pseudo soft-labels in action classification and localization;
- We design a spatiotemporal feature perturbation module to enhance the spatial and temporal invariances for action classification and localization respectively.

2   Related Work

Fully-Supervised Temporal Action Detection. There are two mainstream methods: two-stage methods and one-stage methods. The two-stage methods [20,21] first extract action proposals, and then classify them into action categories. Some works [11,13] generated probability sequences to connect the start frames and the end frames to generate flexible proposals. The one-stage methods [12,16] do not depend on the proposals and can detect actions in one single stage. GTAN [16] dynamically generated action instances by learning a Gaussian kernel. BFPTAD [6] used a bidirectional feature pyramid to fuse semantics and position information for detecting actions at different levels. In this work, we adopt BFPTAD as our backbone due to its superior performance.

Semi-supervised Learning (SSL). The mainstream SSL methods usually adopt pseudo-label and consistency regularization. Pseudo-label methods [1,10] train the model to generate high-confidence pseudo labels for the unlabeled data. They usually choose the largest predicted probability to convert the output into hard labels. Consistency regularization methods [9,17] enforce a consistency loss for the same input under different data enhancement conditions. They consider the predicted output as a kind of 'pseudo soft-label'. In addition, MixMatch [2] was a holistic method that integrates a variety of SSL strategies.

Semi-supervised Action Understanding. At present, SSL methods are widely used in image recognition and object detection. Some works [2,5] integrated semi-supervised methods into the existing models to take advantage of unlabeled images. In the video field, the application of SSL has just started. Ji *et al.* [8] and SSTAP [19] took advantage of the consistency regularization under different temporal disturbances to generate action proposals, while SSTAP [19] made use of self-supervised auxiliary tasks. Lin *et al.* [15] studied the further utilization of fully labeled data based on weakly-supervised TAD, which is different from our semi-supervised setting. So far, to our knowledge, there is hardly an overall method for SS-TAD.

3   Method

3.1   Overview

Our goal is to solve the problem of TAD under a semi-supervised setting. The training set contains two parts, a subset of labeled videos $D_v = \{x_i^v, y_i^v\}_{i=1}^{N_v}$, and a subset of unlabeled videos $D_u = \{x_i^u\}_{i=1}^{N_u}$. N_v and N_u represent the number of labeled and unlabeled data respectively. For each labeled video x^v, the annotations $y^v = \{c, s, e\}$ denote the action instances contained in a video, where $c \in [1, N_c]$ indicates the action category, s and e are the corresponding start time and end time. N_c is the number of action categories. We divide a given video into clips, where the frames are split into non-overlapping snippets. Then we feed a clip into the feature encoding network to obtain snippet-wise feature $X \in \mathbb{R}^{T \times D}$, where T is the number of snippets and D is the feature dimension. An overall framework of our proposed method is illustrated in Fig. 1.

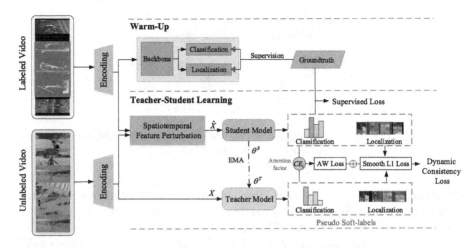

Fig. 1. Overview of our framework. Given the encoded feature sequence X, our framework goes through the following two stages. (1) In the **Warm-up** stage, the fully-supervised backbone is initialized by using the available labeled videos to train. (2) In the **Teacher-Student Learning** stage, spatiotemporal feature perturbation is utilized to obtain the perturbed feature $\hat{X}$, then the original and perturbed feature are fed into the teacher and student models respectively. The teacher model generates pseudo soft-labels for the unlabeled data, and the student model is jointly trained by the supervised loss of the labeled data and the dynamic consistency loss of the unlabeled data. Classification and localization results from the two models are aligned by the attention weighted (AW) loss and the improved Smooth L1 loss.

3.2   Network Structure

Backbone. The proposed framework is constructed upon a fully-supervised TAD model. To validate our semi-supervised framework and better illustrate our approach, we adopt BFPTAD [6] as our backbone.

BFPTAD is trained end-to-end within a unified framework and can generate detection predictions by the classification and the localization branches in one step. The classification predictions $p \in \mathbb{R}^{N \times (N_c+1)}$ represent the classification score of the anchors (including background) while the location predictions $l \in \mathbb{R}^{N \times 2}$ represent the offsets of their centers and the widths where N is the number of anchors. With the supervision D_v, the supervised loss of the model includes the classification loss $\mathcal{L}_{\text{cls}}^{\text{sup}}$ and the location regression loss $\mathcal{L}_{\text{cls}}^{\text{sup}}$,

$$\mathcal{L}^{\text{sup}} = \mathcal{L}_{\text{cls}}^{\text{sup}}(X^v) + \mathcal{L}_{\text{loc}}^{\text{sup}}(X^v), \tag{1}$$

where X^v represents the feature of the labeled clip. Please refer to [6] for more details of BFPTAD. After warming up the model, we get the initial backbone, and then we will improve it by utilizing the unlabeled data.

Teacher-Student Model. The Teacher-Student Learning stage is mainly composed of the teacher model f^T and the student model f^S. They have the same network architecture and are initialized by the backbone after the warm-up stage.

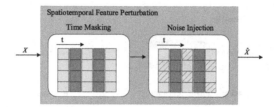

Fig. 2. Illustration of the Spatiotemporal Feature Perturbation module, which consists of two sub-modules, i.e., time masking and noise injection.

The accuracy and the stability of the teacher's predictions is significant to the student. Refer to Mean Teacher [17], we differentiate the parameter updating of the teacher from that of the student. The learnable parameters of the student model θ^S are optimized through back-propagation. The parameters of the teacher model θ^T are updated by **Exponential Moving Average(EMA)** which averages the weights from a sequence of student models of different training step,

$$\theta_t^T = \alpha\theta_{t-1}^T + (1 - \alpha)\theta_t^S, \tag{2}$$

where α is the smoothing coefficient, and t denotes the training step. With the Teacher-Student Learning, the two models keep evolving together to improve the detection accuracy.

3.3 Spatiotemporal Feature Perturbation

Many recent SSL works [2,8,17] have shown that stochastic data perturbation or enhancement is meaningful for learning a robust model. For temporal action proposal extraction, [8] proposed two sequence perturbations for sequence output. However, these disturbances only influenced data in single temporal space, ignoring the spatial semantic information.

As a result, we explore the spatiotemporal perturbations suitable to video data and propose the Spatiotemporal Feature Perturbation, which includes two effective perturbations, i.e. **Time Masking** and **Noise Injection**, as shown in Fig. 2. For the time masking, some features are randomly masked according to a certain probability along the temporal dimension. In other word, the masked features will not be passed to the next layer and the model must force itself to aggregate information from the context to learn the temporal dependence of actions. Noise injection is to inject a small amount of noise into the feature sequence. Here, we add Gaussian noise sampled from a normal distribution with a specific mean and a variance to the feature sequence. In this way, features are perturbed in the spatial dimension, and the model is prompted to learn robust spatial semantic information that is conducive to action classification. By combining the two disturbances, the model can enhance spatial-temporal invariance in action localization and classification to improve the ability of the model for action detection. And unlike some sequential perturbations, such as cropping and stretching, our method does not need to modify the original label and is suitable to any model.

In the pipeline, the original feature sequence $X \in \mathbb{R}^{T \times D}$ is subjected to time masking and noise injection successively to obtain the disturbed feature sequence $\hat{X} \in \mathbb{R}^{T \times D}$. We input the original feature X to the teacher and input the perturbed feature $\hat{X}$ to the student. Then the outputs of the two models should be consistent as the inputs have the same labels.

3.4 Dynamic Consistency

As depicted in Sect. 1, due to the prediction bias of the model, the predictions tend to be biased toward the dominant classes. In our SS-TAD framework, this will lead to the class-imbalance in the pseudo soft-labels. However, we find that the traditional consistency loss, such as Mean Square Error (MSE), holds that all samples contribute equally to the learning of the student model. As a result, a large number of easy-to-separate samples from the dominant classes will dominate the loss. Apparently, it will make the problem of imbalanced prediction worse, and make the model fail to make full use of the unlabeled data.

Based on the above observation, the perturbation-sensitive samples which have larger prediction gaps between the teacher and the student are more informative and contribute more for the student. Thus, we propose to increase the attention of these samples in a dynamic consistency loss, thereby alleviating the problem of label imbalance. Inspired by [14], we adopt an attention mechanism to propose an attention weighted loss for classification defined as:

$$CE_i = -p_i^T \log p_i^S, \quad \mathcal{L}_{\text{cls}}^{\text{cons}} = \frac{1}{M} \sum_i (1 - e^{-CE_i})^\gamma \cdot CE_i, \tag{3}$$

where p_i^S and p_i^T are the classification predictions of the i-th unlabeled sample from the teacher and the student respectively. γ is the parameter that adjusts the weight of the cross-entropy (CE) of a prediction, set to 2. M is the number of anchors of the unlabeled data. We use an attention factor $(1 - e^{-CE})^\gamma$ to weight the classification loss. When the CE of the prediction between the teacher and student is larger, it indicates that the lower the model's confidence in the sample, the more difficult the sample is. So its weight of the classification loss is close to 1 due to the attention factor. Otherwise, it is close to 0, which plays a role of attenuation. In this way, the model will pay more attention to the hard sample than the easy ones from the dominant classes. As a result, the imbalance problem of pseudo soft-labels can be alleviated.

For localization, we adopt the revised Smooth L1 inferring to [5] to mitigate the problem that the well-matching predictions between the teacher and the student dominate the regression loss. The modified Smooth L1 is formulated as follows,

$$\text{smooth}_{\text{L1}}(x) = \begin{cases} \frac{|x|^3}{3}, & |x| < \beta \\ |x| - \beta + \frac{\beta^3}{3}, & |x| \geq \beta \end{cases} \tag{4}$$

Here, the attention of the model to the location prediction difference is adjusted by controlling β. When $x < \beta$, the Smooth L1 of the over-matched samples can be reduced, and when $x > \beta$, the Smooth L1 of samples with larger prediction differences can be increased. In this way, the model will pay more attention to the samples with large prediction gaps. We select the samples with the pseudo foreground soft-labels to compute the location consistency loss $\mathcal{L}_{\text{loc}}^{\text{cons}}$, and use the corresponding confidence score to weight it.

$$\mathcal{L}_{\text{loc}}^{\text{cons}} = \frac{1}{M} \sum_{i \in Pos} \max(\boldsymbol{p}_i^T) \cdot \text{smooth}_{\text{L1}}(|\boldsymbol{l}_i^S - \boldsymbol{l}_i^T|), \tag{5}$$

where $\boldsymbol{l}^S$ and $\boldsymbol{l}^T$ are the relative location offsets output by the teacher and the student and Pos stands for the foreground sample set.

3.5   Overall loss

Training. In the teacher-student learning stage, the overall training loss includes the supervision loss of the labeled data and the dynamic consistency loss of the unlabeled data. We use the same supervision loss as [6] to stabilize the unsupervised training. The overall loss is defined as

$$\mathcal{L}^{\text{total}} = \mathcal{L}^{\text{sup}} + \lambda_u \mathcal{L}^{\text{cons}}, \tag{6}$$

where λ_u is the hyper-parameter to control the weight of consistency loss. $\mathcal{L}^{\text{cons}}$ is composed of the classification consistency loss and the location consistency loss,

$$\mathcal{L}^{\text{cons}} = \mathcal{L}_{\text{cls}}^{\text{cons}}(\boldsymbol{X}^u) + \lambda_b \mathcal{L}_{\text{loc}}^{\text{cons}}(\boldsymbol{X}^u), \tag{7}$$

where $\boldsymbol{X}^u$ is the feature of the unlabeled clip and λ_b balances the two. $\mathcal{L}_{\text{cls}}^{\text{cons}}$ is defined in Eq. (3) and $\mathcal{L}_{\text{loc}}^{\text{cons}}$ is defined in Eq. (5).

4   Experiments

4.1   Datasets and Setup

Datasets. THUMOS14 [7] is composed of 413 untrimmed videos from 20 categories related to sports actions. We follow the literature [6] to train the model on the 200 validation videos, and evaluate on the 213 test videos. **ActivityNet v1.2** [3] consists of 100 action categories. We use the 4819 training videos to train the model and the 2383 validation videos for evaluation. To construct a semi-supervised data environment, we randomly select a certain percentage of fully labeled videos from the training set as the labeled part, and treat the rest as the unlabeled part by discarding their annotations.

Evaluation Metrics. We follow the standard evaluation protocol which calculates the mean Average Precision (mAP) of temporal intersection over union (tIoU) at different thresholds. On THUMOS14, we report the performance under the tIoU thresholds of 0.1:0.1:0.7, and the average mAP is computed on

0.3:0.1:0.7. On ActivityNet v1.2, we report the performance of IoU thresholds at 0.5, 0.75, 0.9 and the average mAP on 0.5:0.05:0.95.

Implementation Details. We follow the pre- and post-processing as BFP-TAD [6], including training data construction, predefined information, confidence and NMS thresholds for fair comparison. For the feature encoding network, we use I3D [4] network pre-trained on Kinetics dataset to obtain feature $X \in \mathbb{R}^{T \times 2048}$. We use the Adam optimizer with 10^{-4} learning rate and 0.0005 weight decay to optimize the network. We adopt the ramp-up [9] strategy for λ_u with the consistency weight set to 75 and the length set to 15. The weight of λ_b is set to 4 to balance the classification and localization branches. For SSL, we set α to 0.999 for EMA decay. The masking probability of time masking is set to 0.3 and β is set to 0.5 by validation.

4.2 Comparisons with Start-of-the-Art Methods

In this section, we compare the proposed SS-TAD method with the state-of-the-art fully-supervised and semi-supervised methods to verify the effectiveness of our semi-supervised framework. We compare the temporal action detection results under two training setups: (1) For fully-supervised methods, $x\%$ of the labeled videos are employed for training without any other data; (2) For semi-supervised methods, $x\%$ of training videos are labeled and $(100-x)\%$ of training videos are unlabeled. When x is 100, the method is fully supervised. When there are no unlabeled data, we only use the student branch with the feature perturbation to compute the supervision loss in the teacher-student learning stage. Note that the teacher model and EMA are not involved here. To reduce the error caused by randomly selected labeled videos, we conduct multiple experiments with the same labeling ratio.

Comparisons with Fully-Supervised Methods. This experiment is designed to testify the benefit of using unlabeled data. The experiment results on THUMOS14 are shown in Table 1 and the results on ActivityNet v1.2 are shown in Table 2. On THUMOS14, when the proportion of labeled data is 60%, the average mAP of our semi-supervised method is about 5.0% higher than that of the fully-supervised baseline, i.e., BFPTAD. This gain mainly comes from the effective use of the 40% unlabeled data. When 100% labeled data is adopted, our method still achieves an improvement of 1.8% over BFPTAD. It is worth noting that we only use 60% of the labeled data to achieve the results of the fully-supervised baseline with 100% labeled data, as well as the existing fully-supervised TAD methods. We have similar observations on ActivityNet v1.2. The proposed semi-supervised method surpasses the baseline method by 4.6% and when the labeling proportion is 60%.

Comparisons with Semi-supervised Methods. Table 1 also compares our method with semi-supervised two-stage methods whose experimental results come from [19]. The fully-supervised method BMN is the baseline of the semi-supervised methods Ji et al. [8] and SSTAP [19]. It should be noted that they only

Table 1. Comparison between our proposed method and start-of-the-art methods on THUMOS14 in terms of mAP and average mAP.

Methods	mAP@IoU (%)							
	0.1	0.2	0.3	0.4	0.5	0.6	0.7	AVG
Fully-supervised methods								
SSN [21]	60.3	56.2	50.6	40.8	29.1	-	-	-
BSN [13]+UNet [18]	-	-	53.0	45.0	36.9	28.4	20.0	36.7
GTAN [16]	69.1	63.7	57.8	47.2	38.8	-	-	-
G-TAD [20]	-	-	54.5	47.6	40.2	30.8	23.4	39.3
BMN [11] @60%+UNet [18]	-	-	53.4	44.7	34.0	25.5	17.0	34.9
BFPTAD [6] @60%	68.5	66.4	62.4	56.8	47.0	34.7	20.2	44.3
BFPTAD [6] @100%	70.4	69.7	67.2	60.4	52.2	38.9	24.4	48.6
Semi-supervised two-stage methods								
Ji *et al.* [8] @60% +UNet [18]	-	-	55.4	47.2	37.1	28.1	19.2	37.4
SSTAP [19] @60%+UNet [18]	-	-	56.5	48.8	39.4	30.5	20.7	39.1
Ours@60%	**73.9**	**72.0**	**68.4**	**62.8**	**52.4**	**38.9**	**23.7**	**49.2**
Ours@100%	**74.4**	**72.9**	**69.2**	**63.4**	**53.2**	**40.6**	**25.8**	**50.4**

Table 2. Comparison between our proposed method with start-of-the-art methods on ActivityNet v1.2 in terms of mAP and average mAP.

Methods	mAP@IoU (%)			
	0.5	0.75	0.9	AVG
SSN-SW [21]	-	-	-	18.1
SSN-TAG [21]	-	-	-	25.9
BFPTAD [6] @60%	29.3	17.4	1.1	17.2
Ours@60%	**38.4**	**21.2**	**2.0**	**21.8**
BFPTAD [6] @100%	37.5	21.8	2.4	21.9
Ours@100%	**40.9**	**22.5**	**2.7**	**23.4**

used SSL in the temporal action proposal extraction and adopted the video-level classification results generated by UNet [18]. It is noticed that the proposed SS-TAD framework outperforms the semi-supervised two-stage methods by around 13% at mAP@IoU = 0.5.

We also compare our method with the start-of-the-art semi-supervised frameworks, i.e., Mean Teacher [17] and MixMatch [2]. For fair comparison, we implement these semi-supervised frameworks on our backbone and utilize the same video features and post-processing steps. To enhance the video feature in Mix-Match, we apply our spatiotemporal feature perturbation module as well. It can be seen in Table 3 that our method outperforms the other advanced semi-supervised baselines significantly. In addition, we investigate the impact of labeling ratio in the training set on the performance of the proposed model, as shown

Table 3. Comparison between our proposed method and semi-supervised baselines trained with 20% and 60% of the labels. We report the results of THUMOS14 in terms of mAP. Superscript '+' indicates that the method is implemented based on our backbone.

Methods	Label	mAP@IoU (%)						
		0.1	0.2	0.3	0.4	0.5	0.6	0.7
BFPTAD [6]	20%	47.3	44.7	41.6	35.1	27.1	17.4	8.6
Mean Teacher[+] [17]	20%	48.5	45.9	42.5	35.9	28.0	18.1	9.1
MixMatch[+] [2]	20%	49.4	46.7	43.2	36.9	28.9	18.8	9.6
Ours	**20%**	**53.7**	**49.8**	**45.2**	**38.8**	**29.5**	**19.9**	**10.7**
BFPTAD [6]	60%	68.5	66.4	62.7	56.8	47.0	34.7	20.2
Mean Teacher[+] [17]	60%	69.3	67.5	64.0	58.5	48.3	35.6	20.9
MixMatch[+] [2]	60%	72.4	71.0	66.9	61.1	50.7	36.8	22.1
Ours	**60%**	**73.9**	**72.0**	**68.4**	**62.8**	**52.4**	**28.9**	**23.7**

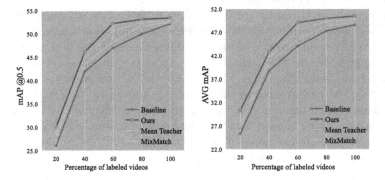

Fig. 3. We compute the mAP@0.5 and average mAP of our method, semi-supervised Mean Teacher [17], MixMatch [2] and the fully-supervised BFPTAD [6] under different labeling ratios.

in Fig. 3. Our method consistently outperforms the fully-supervised baseline and the semi-supervised methods, and the superiority over the other methods peaks at 60%.

4.3   Ablation Study

We test the impact of different components in our framework, i.e., (a) the teacher-student model denoted as "TS", (b) the spatiotemporal feature perturbation denoted as "SFP", (c) the supervision loss denoted as "SUP" and (d) the dynamic consistency loss denoted as "DCL". BFPTAD is trained on all the labeled data as the fully-supervised baseline. "TS" conducted on BFPTAD is the semi-supervised baseline. When "TS" does not use EMA, the teacher and student models share weights. For the experiments without "SFP", we add random

Table 4. Ablation study of the effectiveness of components in our framework on THU-MOS14 with 60% of the labels.

Method	0.3	0.4	0.5	0.6	0.7	AVG
BFPTAD	62.4	56.8	47.0	34.7	20.2	44.3
TS w/o EMA + SUP	63.2	57.2	47.6	35.0	20.1	44.6
TS + SUP	64.0	58.5	48.3	35.6	20.9	45.5
TS + SFP + SUP	67.8	61.3	49.9	36.9	20.6	47.3
TS + DCL + SUP	66.7	60.5	50.0	37.6	22.0	47.4
TS + SFP + DCL	65.4	61.1	50.9	37.2	22.4	47.4
ALL	**68.4**	**62.8**	**52.4**	**38.9**	**23.7**	**49.2**

numbers to the multi-layer convolution of the backbone network as perturbation instead. For the experiments without "DCL", we use MSE to measure the consistency between predictions of the two models.

The experimental results are reported in Table 4. It clearly shows that each of the basic modules in our method independently improves the performance of SS-TAD and the concurrency of these modules results in the best performance. When using EMA in "TS", the teacher model can improve the accuracy of the model by about 1%. When "SFP" and "DCL" are combined with "TS" respectively, the performance of the model is improved by 1.8% and 1.9% than the semi-supervised baseline. We experiment with the effect of "SUP" and prove the necessity of using labeled data for joint training in semi-supervised learning. Strong supervised information can make the weight of "DCL" gradually increase to stabilize the semi-supervised learning.

5   Conclusion

In this paper, we aim to solve the problem of semi-supervised temporal action detection, and propose an end-to-end semi-supervised framework for this task. Particularly, we propose an attention-based consistency regularization to constrain the consistency between the teacher and student models, in order to alleviate the problem of sample imbalance. Based on this, the two models work collaboratively and co-evolve by making use of the unlabeled data. In addition, we propose an effective spatiotemporal feature perturbation module not restricted by the input and output forms, and is able to enhance the generalization ability of the model. Extensive experiments show that our model outperforms the start-of-the-art semi-supervised methods for the task of temporal action detection.

Acknowledgments. This work is supported by the National Natural Science Foundation of China (Grant No. 61672285, 62072245, and 61932020), the Natural Science Foundation of Jiangsu Province (Grant No. BK20211520).

References

1. Arazo, E., Ortego, D., Albert, P., O'Connor, N.E., McGuinness, K.: Pseudo-labeling and confirmation bias in deep semi-supervised learning. In: Proceedings of the International Joint Conference on Neural Networks, pp. 1–8. IEEE (2020)
2. Berthelot, D., Carlini, N., Goodfellow, I., Papernot, N., Oliver, A., Raffel, C.A.: MixMatch: a holistic approach to semi-supervised learning. In: Advances in Neural Information Processing Systems (2019)
3. Caba Heilbron, F., Escorcia, V., Ghanem, B., Carlos Niebles, J.: ActivityNet: a large-scale video benchmark for human activity understanding. In: Proceedings of the Computer Vision and Pattern Recognition, pp. 961–970 (2015)
4. Carreira, J., Zisserman, A.: Quo Vadis, action recognition? A new model and the kinetics dataset. In: Proceedings of the Computer Vision and Pattern Recognition, pp. 6299–6308 (2017)
5. Chen, C., Dong, S., Tian, Y., Cao, K., Liu, L., Guo, Y.: Temporal self-ensembling teacher for semi-supervised object detection. arXiv preprint arXiv:2007.06144 (2020)
6. He, J., Song, Y., Jiang, H.: Bi-direction feature pyramid temporal action detection network. In: Palaiahnakote, S., Sanniti di Baja, G., Wang, L., Yan, W.Q. (eds.) ACPR 2019. LNCS, vol. 12046, pp. 889–901. Springer, Cham (2020). https://doi.org/10.1007/978-3-030-41404-7_63
7. Idrees, H., et al.: The THUMOS challenge on action recognition for videos "in the wild". Comput. Vis. Image Underst. **155**, 1–23 (2017)
8. Ji, J., Cao, K., Niebles, J.C.: Learning temporal action proposals with fewer labels. In: Proceedings of the International Conference on Computer Vision, pp. 7073–7082 (2019)
9. Laine, S., Aila, T.: Temporal ensembling for semi-supervised learning. arXiv preprint arXiv:1610.02242 (2016)
10. Lee, D.H., et al.: Pseudo-label: the simple and efficient semi-supervised learning method for deep neural networks. In: Workshop on Challenges in Representation Learning (ICML), vol. 3 (2013)
11. Lin, T., Liu, X., Li, X., Ding, E., Wen, S.: BMN: boundary-matching network for temporal action proposal generation. In: Proceedings of the International Conference on Computer Vision, pp. 3889–3898 (2019)
12. Lin, T., Zhao, X., Shou, Z.: Single shot temporal action detection. In: Proceedings of the Multimedia, pp. 988–996 (2017)
13. Lin, T., Zhao, X., Su, H., Wang, C., Yang, M.: BSN: boundary sensitive network for temporal action proposal generation. In: Ferrari, V., Hebert, M., Sminchisescu, C., Weiss, Y. (eds.) ECCV 2018. LNCS, vol. 11208, pp. 3–21. Springer, Cham (2018). https://doi.org/10.1007/978-3-030-01225-0_1
14. Lin, T.Y., Goyal, P., Girshick, R., He, K., Dollár, P.: Focal loss for dense object detection. In: Proceedings of the International Conference on Computer Vision, pp. 2980–2988 (2017)
15. Lin, X., Shou, Z., Chang, S.F.: Towards train-test consistency for semi-supervised temporal action localization. arXiv preprint arXiv:1910.11285 (2019)
16. Long, F., Yao, T., Qiu, Z., Tian, X., Luo, J., Mei, T.: Gaussian temporal awareness networks for action localization. In: Proceedings of the Computer Vision and Pattern Recognition, pp. 344–353 (2019)

17. Tarvainen, A., Valpola, H.: Mean teachers are better role models: weight-averaged consistency targets improve semi-supervised deep learning results. In: Proceedings of the 31st International Conference on Neural Information Processing Systems, pp. 1195–1204 (2017)
18. Wang, L., Xiong, Y., Lin, D., Van Gool, L.: UntrimmedNets for weakly supervised action recognition and detection. In: Proceedings of the Computer Vision and Pattern Recognition, pp. 4325–4334 (2017)
19. Wang, X., Zhang, S., Qing, Z., Shao, Y., Gao, C., Sang, N.: Self-supervised learning for semi-supervised temporal action proposal. In: Proceedings of the IEEE/CVF Conference on Computer Vision and Pattern Recognition, pp. 1905–1914 (2021)
20. Xu, M., Zhao, C., Rojas, D.S., Thabet, A., Ghanem, B.: G-TAD: sub-graph localization for temporal action detection. In: Proceedings of the IEEE/CVF Conference on Computer Vision and Pattern Recognition, pp. 10156–10165 (2020)
21. Zhao, Y., Xiong, Y., Wang, L., Wu, Z., Tang, X., Lin, D.: Temporal action detection with structured segment networks. In: Proceedings of the International Conference on Computer Vision, pp. 2914–2923 (2017)

Multimedia Datasets for Repeatable Experimentation (Special Session)

A Task Category Space for User-Centric Comparative Multimedia Search Evaluations

Jakub Lokoč[1(✉)] , Werner Bailer[2] , Kai Uwe Barthel[3] , Cathal Gurrin[4] ,
Silvan Heller[5] , Björn Þór Jónsson[6] , Ladislav Peška[1] , Luca Rossetto[7] ,
Klaus Schoeffmann[8] , Lucia Vadicamo[9] , Stefanos Vrochidis[10] ,
and Jiaxin Wu[11]

[1] Charles University, Prague, Czech Republic
{jakub.lokoc,ladislav.peska}@matfyz.cuni.cz
[2] JOANNEUM RESEARCH, Graz, Austria
werner.bailer@joanneum.at
[3] HTW Berlin, Berlin, Germany
barthel@htw-berlin.de
[4] Dublin City University, Dublin, Ireland
cathal.gurrin@dcu.ie
[5] University of Basel, Basel, Switzerland
silvan.heller@unibas.ch
[6] IT University of Copenhagen, Copenhagen, Denmark
bjth@itu.dk
[7] University of Zurich, Zurich, Switzerland
rossetto@ifi.uzh.ch
[8] Klagenfurt University, Klagenfurt, Austria
ks@itec.aau.at
[9] ISTI CNR, Pisa, Italy
lucia.vadicamo@isti.cnr.it
[10] Centre for Research and Technology Hellas, Thessaloniki, Greece
stefanos@iti.gr
[11] City University of Hong Kong, Hong Kong, China
jiaxin.wu@my.cityu.edu.hk

Abstract. In the last decade, user-centric video search competitions have facilitated the evolution of interactive video search systems. So far, these competitions focused on a small number of search task categories, with few attempts to change task category configurations. Based on our extensive experience with interactive video search contests, we have analyzed the spectrum of possible task categories and propose a list of individual axes that define a large space of possible task categories. Using this concept of category space, new user-centric video search competitions can be designed to benchmark video search systems from different perspectives. We further analyse the three task categories considered so far at the Video Browser Showdown and discuss possible (but sometimes challenging) shifts within the task category space.

Keywords: Multimedia retrieval · Task taxonomy · Evaluation design

© Springer Nature Switzerland AG 2022
B. Þór Jónsson et al. (Eds.): MMM 2022, LNCS 13141, pp. 193–204, 2022.
https://doi.org/10.1007/978-3-030-98358-1_16

1   Introduction

The explosion in the production and diffusion of multimedia data over the last decades has triggered a strong interest toward the development of systems for the storage, management and retrieval of large-scale multimedia archives. While Information Retrieval (IR) [26] approaches initially focused mainly on text documents, since the 1990s there has been flourishing research activity on content-based retrieval systems for other types of media, such as images and videos [9,13]. More recently, the synergy between IR and Artificial Intelligence techniques has enabled the development of retrieval systems that also support cross-modal searches and multiple query types (e.g., [12,17,20,35,36]). Furthermore, the suggestion that information retrieval is more appropriately regarded as an inherently interactive/evolving process [4,5] paved the way for the design of interactive and more user-centric systems, where the query expressing the user's information need is no longer considered as predetermined and static, but rather evolves dynamically during a search process [7,19,27,28,34].

To evaluate the effectiveness of different video retrieval systems, some benchmarking competitions have been established [8,11,28,29,31]. For example, Vide-Olympics [31] conducted assessments of interactive video retrieval systems on Ad-hoc Video Search (AVS) in 2007–2009, and the Video Browser Showdown (VBS) [28] has started to assess visual Known-Item Search (KIS) tasks since 2012. However, existing competitions focus on a small number of task categories, e.g., VBS only evaluates AVS, visual KIS, and textual KIS tasks. Moreover, the task design space is not well understood.

The main contribution of this paper is a structured description of a task category space for user-centric video search competitions. While existing evaluation initiatives are recapitulated in the related work section, a comprehensive task category space, based on our long-term experience with interactive video search competitions, is presented in Sect. 3. Three popular task categories are revisited in Sect. 4, perceiving the tasks as elements of the proposed space and discussing possible future options for designing a rich set of benchmark activities.

2   Related Work and Background

Different interactive multimedia retrieval systems naturally have distinct user interfaces, browsing, and searching functionalities, which introduce a bias in users' attitudes when formulating and refining their queries. Hence, the comparative performance of interactive retrieval systems cannot be easily evaluated and compared outside of controlled environments, set up for this specific purpose, such as benchmarking campaigns.

In this context, interactive competitions such as the Video Browser Showdown (VBS) [19,24,28] and the Lifelog Search Challenge (LSC) [10,11] provide an equitable performance assessment of interactive retrieval systems, where not only the same search tasks on the same dataset are employed, but also users with different level of knowledge of systems (i.e., expert and novice users) are involved in the evaluation process in a live real-time benchmarking activity. The VBS video search competition comprises three search tasks, namely Adhoc Video Search (AVS), visual Known-Item Search (KIS) and textual KIS. Textual KIS tasks are also evaluated in LSC but for the use case of multimodal lifelog data retrieval. Although not focusing specifically on the case of interactive systems, other evaluation campaigns have played an important role in the assessment of multimedia retrieval and analysis techniques for a wide variety of tasks (see Table 1). For example, the Benchmarking Initiative for Multimedia Evaluation (MediaEval) [8,15] has offered a large spectrum of tasks (almost 50 different tasks since 2010) related to multimedia retrieval, analysis, and exploration with a focus on the human and social aspects of multimedia. The TREC Video Retrieval Evaluation (TRECVID) [1,30] over the last two decades has spawned over twenty tasks related to content-based analysis of and retrieval from digital video, including automatic AVS, KIS, Video Hyperlinking, and the automatic detection of a variety of semantic and low-level video features [1,2,22,29]. In the context of video understanding and search, in 2020 the Video Pentathlon Workshop[1] offered an interesting challenge that tackles the task of caption-to-video retrieval, i.e. retrieving relevant videos using only natural language queries.

The task of retrieving one particular data item that satisfies a very specific information need for a user (i.e., KIS task) recurs in many benchmarking campaigns. Although there is no universally accepted definition of KIS in the multimedia domain, this concept originates in the field of library science, where it refers to the task of locating and obtaining a particular book or document of a catalogue that the searcher has in mind (e.g., the searcher knows the author, the title, or other distinguishing characteristics) [18,33]. Traditionally, there was a distinction between the concept of "Known-Item Search" (understood as the search for a particular document of which the details are known) and that of "subject search" (where the need is to locate material dealing with a particular subject or to answer a particular question) [6,32]. Walker and Janes [32] argued that the subject search is far more challenging than Known-Item Search, since it focuses on searching for what is not known, or perhaps does not exist, whereas bibliographic utilities can be employed to easily find a specific document (e.g. using the ISBN). However, arguments of this kind lose significance when the data to be handled is unstructured; in fact, searching for a specific multimedia item, say for example an image, without having a copy of the digital item at hand is hardly easier than searching for a generic image within a given topic. Lee et al. [16] made an important step toward a generalization of the KIS definition used in library and information science that could be transferred to multimedia search. They reviewed "conceptual" understandings of known-item search (e.g., looking for something the user knows exists) that are independent of the "operational" definitions designed to find the item of interest in a particular context (e.g., search a card catalogue for an item using the author or the title). In the 2010 edition of TRECVID, the KIS task category was formulated in the video search domain as one that "models the situation in which someone

---

Table 1. An overview of prominent benchmarking campaigns with multimedia retrieval and analysis tasks.

Benchmarking campaign	Evaluated tasks (years)[1]
TRECVid (since 2001)[2]	*Ad-hoc Video Search* (2003–2009, 2016–2021)[3], *Instance search* (2010–2021), *Surveillance event detection* (2008–2017), *High-level Semantic Feature Extraction* (2002–2009), *Semantic indexing (and Localization)* (2010–2016), *Shot boundary detection* (2001–2007), *Multimedia Event Detection* (2010–2017), *Activities in Extended Video* (2018–2021), *Video to Text Description* (2017–2021), *Content-based multimedia copy detection* (2008–2011), *Streaming Multimedia Knowledge Base Population task* (2018, 2019, 2021), *Video Hyperlinking*[4] (2015–2017), *Multimedia event recounting* (2012–2014), *Textual Known-item search* (2010–2012), *Rushes Exploitation and Summarization* (2006–2008), *Video Summarization* (2020, 2021), *Disaster Scene Description and Indexing* (2020, 2021), *Story segmentation* (2003, 2004), *Social-Media Video Storytelling Linking* (2018), *Low-level Feature Extraction* (2005).
VideOlympics (2007–2009)	*Ad-hoc Video Search* (2007–2009)
MediaEval (since 2010)	*Emotional Impact of Movies (including Boredom and Violent Scenes Detection)* (2010–2018), *Emotions (and Themes) in Music* (2013–2015, 2019–2021), *Multimodal geo-location prediction* (2010–2012, 2014–2016), *Medico Multimedia* (2017–2021), *Retrieving Diverse Social Images* (2013–2017), *Predicting Media Memorability* (2018–2021), *C@merata: Querying Musical Scores* (2014–2017), *Query by Example Search on Speech* (2012–2015), *Social Event Detection* (2011–2014), *Insight for Wellbeing* (2019–2021), *Sports Video* (2019–2021), *Pixel Privacy* (2018–2020), *Multimedia Satellite* (2017–2019), *Video Search and Hyperlinking* (2012–2014), *Visual Privacy* (2012–2014), *Video Genre Tagging* (2010–2012), and other 32 tasks appearing in fewer than three editions.
VBS (since 2012)	*Visual Know-Item Search* (2012–2021), *Textual Know-Item Search* (2014–2021), *Ad-hoc Video Search* (2017–2021)
LSC (since 2018)	*Known-Item search (multimodal lifelog data)* (2018–2021)
Video Pentathlon (2020)	*Video Retrieval using natural language queries (text-to-video cross-modal retrieval)* (2020)

[1] According to the information provided on the web pages of the respective evaluation campaigns: TRECVid (https://trecvid.nist.gov/), MediaEval (https://multimediaeval.github.io/), VBS (https://videobrowsershowdown.org/), LSC (http://lsc.dcu.ie), Video Pentathlon (https://www.robots.ox.ac.uk/~vgg/challenges/video-pentathlon/).
[2] Started as a video track featured in the 2001 and 2002 at the Text **RE**trieval Conference and then became an independent evaluation campaign in 2003.
[3] Since 2016 in collaboration with VBS for the evaluation of interactive systems.
[4] Previously run in MediaEval.

knows of a video, has seen it before, believes it is contained in a collection, but doesn't know where to look" [21]. However, in [21] it is also assumed that to begin a search, the user formulates a text-only description which captures what they remember about the target video. This "operational" constraint, however, is too restrictive as other search strategies may be employed to implement the Known-Item Search. For example, a user may have access to systems that support several search modes (e.g., search by sketch, search by color, etc.) that can be used alone or in combination with text-based queries.

The task of Ad-hoc Video Search (AVS) focuses on general search. The information need is formulated as a textual topic containing a person, action, object, location, etc., and a combination of them, such as *"Find shots of one or more people walking or bicycling on a bridge during daytime"* [3,14]. Given a topic, the participants need to return relevant video segments from the test collection which satisfy the need. Its history dates back to as early as 2003 when TRECVID established it as a video search task [14]. In the beginning, the task included humans in the loop to search relevant videos in manual or interactive settings (allowing users to reformulate the query). It also allows fully automatic submission since 2005. As the TRECVID AVS task was intractable, it was replaced by the Multimedia Event Detection from 2010-2017 to promote the progress of zero-example video event search [21]. However, in 2016 the AVS task has been resumed to promote a more realistic setting where not only events are used as retrieved topics [3]. While TRECVID AVS focuses on evaluating the effectiveness of the submitted search systems, VideOlympics [31] was established as a live competition from 2007 to 2010 to evaluate the influence of interaction behaviors and the visualized interface of the search systems on answering the AVS task, a similar goal to the one pursued by VBS. Since 2016, VBS has started to work with TRECVID to evaluate AVS in the interactive setting [27].

3 Task Category Space for User-Centric Video Search

Whereas related evaluation initiatives provide a large spectrum of task types for multimedia data (classification, analysis, prediction, retrieval, linking, etc.), this paper focuses on a list of options for interactive video search competitions. Nevertheless, we demonstrate that there are still many options to construct an interactive search task category and that only a negligible fraction of categories is currently addressed by evaluation campaigns.

Specifically, we present several domains describing a video search task category from different perspectives. In the following, each paragraph describes one *domain axis* A_{d_i}, constituting a particular aspect of content-based search evaluation. Their combination $A_{d_1} \times \cdots \times A_{d_n}$ forms the entire space of various task categories for user-centric video search evaluations. Elements of the space can then be selected to design a new user-centric video search campaign. Please note that there are combinations resulting in equivalent task types (e.g., for one target item in A_{CI}, all A_{SI} options request the one item), and some combinations may not model actual real-world problems.

A_{CI}: **Number of correct items satisfying a search need in a dataset**

1. One target item which is assumed to be unique (i.e., differences to near dupli-cates are considered relevant). Identical copies can be considered equivalent.
2. All near-duplicates of one target item, there is binary relevance since the near-duplicates depict the same content.
3. Many semantically related items, potentially with multi-valued relevance.

A_{SI}: **Requested number of submitted correct items**

1. One correct item is enough (e.g., searching for an evidence).
2. A limited number of correct items is sufficient, allowing variety of choices.
3. As many as possible correct items are requested, focusing on recall.

A_{PM}: **Search need presentation modality**

1. Visual and auditory experience (no recording is allowed, however, only human perception).
2. Provided text description.
3. Combined perception and text information.

A_{PT}: **Search need presentation timing**

1. Task specification is revealed a longer time (e.g., one hour) before the com-petition, some reminiscence clues may be presented during evaluation time.
2. All info about a task is revealed in the beginning of the task evaluation.
3. Search clues are gradually revealed during the task evaluation.

A_{PQ}: **Search need presentation quality**

1. Comprehensive presentation of search need (e.g., scene playback or exhaustive text description with all details present in the scene).
2. Presentation of limited information to solve a task (e.g., blurring or short abstract description with selected unique details).
3. Intentional introduction of unreliable or uncertain information.

A_{DC}: **Data collection**

1. Whole dataset is known in advance, teams search in the whole dataset.
2. Limited subset of the known dataset is specified when a task starts.
3. Completely new video is provided when task evaluation starts, fast online preprocessing is needed.

A_{TL}: **Time limit**

1. Limited time to solve a task, time limit controlled by an evaluation server.
2. Unrestricted time interval, teams search until they solve the task or give up (though the time for the whole competition can be limited).

A_{US}: **User skills**

1. Expert users who created the tool operate the system.
2. Novice users who are representative of a typical user without knowledge of how the system works and generates results operate the system.
3. Novice users who also have little experience operating computers in general operate the system.

A_{NU}: **Number of operating users**

1. One user should be able to solve a task. If there are more users per team, each user has to solve the task independently from the other team members.
2. Multiple users can cooperate to solve a task in a collaborative retrieval process.

A_{QM}: **Quality measure**

1. Time of submission, where faster systems are preferred.
2. Quantity of submitted relevant multimedia objects is important.
3. Relevance of the submitted objects is reflected, penalizing for incorrect submissions.
4. Diversity of submitted correct items is preferred.
5. Any meaningful combination of the first four options in A_{QM} can be utilized as well. The combinations are not included due to space constraints.

The presented list comprises aspects that influence a task category. The last axis A_{QM} enables to fix a competition evaluation preference, which affects the strategy that teams use to solve a task specified with the previous nine aspects. The main motivation for the task space was to analyze and present a high variety of options affecting task category design. Based on the presented list of axes and options, a large number of task categories can be identified. Whereas VBS currently uses just three of them, many other evaluation campaigns could be established for other interesting elements of the category space. For example, competitions focusing on online video preprocessing and search are definitely missing in the current pool of user-centric video search competitions.

4 Challenges of Task Categories Considered so far

In the following, the task types used in previous instances of the Video Browser Showdown are discussed in the context of the space presented in the previous section. Table 2 shows how these task types can be classified along the defined axes. The tasks represent only a small fraction of possible tasks in the space.

4.1 Visual KIS Task

The Visual Known Item Search task presents a unique video sequence of roughly 20 seconds in length and asks for the exact sequence to be retrieved from the collection within at most min. It rewards correct results which are produced quickly while penalizing incorrect results and long retrieval times.

Advantages. This relatively simple task setup has the advantage that it is easy to understand and has little ambiguity (assuming the target sequence is unique with respect to the collection). The resulting low barrier of entry makes this task type attractive for new teams or approaches, while at the same time encouraging the use of different query modes targeting different media modalities. Since there

Table 2. VBS'21 task categories represented as vectors of the task space. For each category, the value in an axis column presents the currently used axis option (specified in Sect. 3). Due to the virtual conference setting, only expert users were participating.

Task name	A_{CI}	A_{SI}	A_{PM}	A_{PT}	A_{PQ}	A_{DC}	A_{TL}	A_{US}	A_{NU}	A_{QM}
Visual KIS	1	1	1	2	1	1	1	1	2	1, 3
Textual KIS	1	1	2	3	2	1	1	1	2	1, 3
Ad-hoc search	3	3	2	2	2	1	1	1	2	2, 3

is no translation or transformation of any kind between the presented sequence and the expected result, the task does also not penalize certain teams over others as a side effect, for example based on language proficiency.

Disadvantages. The primary disadvantage of this task type is that it only roughly approximates a realistic scenario. In a situation where somebody tries to retrieve a previously observed video segment, attention and memory play a more substantial role than if the segment can be observed at the time of retrieval.

Future Options. A possible change to make the task more accurately represent a realistic scenario would be to present a number of scenes some time before the competition, and then let users search for some of them ($A_{PT} : 2 \rightarrow 1$). This would ensure only the memorized aspects are available to them. Depending on the memory prompt, this could impact A_{PM}. However, in order to adjust the experiment for the different capabilities of humans to memorize visual information, this would require a large group of searchers who are not available at VBS. Another approach would be to explicitly model attention and memory effects and modify the presented sequence to simulate them ($A_{PQ} : 1 \rightarrow 2$). While there have been some early experiments in this direction [23], it is largely unclear how such effects could be simulated realistically and further research on query representation methods modeling human visual memory is needed.

4.2 Textual KIS Task

The Textual Known Item Search task presents a textual description intended to uniquely describe a video sequence of roughly 20 s in length. The textual description becomes more detailed over time, often uniquely describing the intended sequence only in its most elaborate form. The task uses the same scoring mechanism as the previous task.

Advantages. This task models a realistic setting where a searcher has a limited recollection of a scene while having a clear search interest. It also works as a stand-in for a situation where the person with the search interest needs to verbally describe it to somebody else, who is then performing the search. Due to the inherent loss of detail in a textual description, when compared to the original sequence, the task also implicitly addresses inaccuracies in memory.

Disadvantages. The primary disadvantage of this task is its potential for ambiguity which can arise by several means. Since not all information is revealed at the start of the task, it is possible to submit sequences which match the currently available information but differ from the target sequence in a detail not yet known to participants. The limitations in textual descriptions, especially for non-native speakers, also make it difficult to establish a common understanding of the target. These problems would likely not occur to this degree in a real world setting, since there could exist a bidirectional communication channel between the person describing the search interest and the person performing the search.

Future Options. To decrease ambiguity of text descriptions, they could be complemented with visual information, such as a hand-drawn sketch of some target frame, thus turning the task into text-induced KIS ($A_{PM} : 2 \rightarrow 3$). A sketch may provide a better understanding of the composition of a scene, based on memories of the task creator. At the same time, only limited and distorted information is added to the task description and thus the task remains challenging. Currently, users browse result sets based on their own imagination of a scene; adding visual hints would make users more efficient. Further, contextual information could be provided, such as events which occur in the same video but outside of the target sequence. Another option is provide the possibility to ask questions and clarify ambiguities during the task (a specific case of $A_{PT} = 3$). While this equalizes conditions for teams, it hinders reproducibility of the task.

4.3 Ad-hoc Video Search Tasks

The Ad-hoc Video Search task provides a short textual description of a video topic. In contrast to the previously described tasks, this description is not unique to one sequence but can describe an arbitrary number of sequences. Since it is not feasible to annotate the entire dataset beforehand, submissions are assessed by human judges in a live manner.

Advantages. Several of the advantages of this task lie in its different nature compared to the previously discussed KIS tasks. In contrast to those, it models a less clearly specified search intent, where several results might satisfy an information need, which is also common in practice. The task also serves as a platform for more general text-to-video search approaches. Due to the potentially large number of relevant sequences, it also offers a non-binary outcome and lowers the burden for novel, experimental approaches.

Disadvantages. The disadvantages of this task come primarily from the need for human judges. Since the description of a task target is rather short, it is difficult to establish a common understanding on what constitutes a correct sequence. This can lead to misunderstandings between judges and participants as well as to inconsistent judgements if there is no clear understanding between judges. Another difficulty with this task type is that it is unclear how to best compare several sets of retrieved results and hence how to score them. An emphasis on pooled recall (i.e., recall established from correct submissions of all teams) discourages competitors to share their methods or extracted data, while an emphasis on precision exaggerates the previously discussed problems with a shared understanding of the task.

Future Options. The largest potential for improvement in this task lies arguably in the way correctness of retrieved results is assessed and how these assessments are aggregated into an overall score (A_{QM} : 3). To counteract possible inconsistencies in judgement, it would be possible to have multiple judges assess each retrieved sequence. Since the aggregation of multiple such assessments can not necessarily be losslessly presented in a binary format, it would be feasible to use multi-valued judgements directly. In order to better synchronize all judges and teams, clarifying questions could be allowed before the start of a task, or even during the task (A_{PT} : 2 → 3). Another possible avenue to reduce possible confusion would be to augment the description with a series of example images depicting true positives and true negatives (A_{PM} : 2 → 3). To avoid overlap with KIS tasks, these examples can be taken from outside the dataset. Similarly to Textual KIS, a paused task phase for establishing a common understanding on the scope of the query could be introduced.

5   Conclusions

This paper presented an overview of evaluation efforts in the video retrieval area and proposed a task category space covering many aspects of video search tasks. The space may inspire variations in tasks considered so far, as well as initiate novel campaigns focusing on currently missing user-centric benchmarks. We believe that in the future, interactive video search systems could be tested by multiple (even remote) evaluation campaigns using already established software tools [25]. The systems already participating at VBS and LSC, as well as many potential new systems, could prove their capabilities in a larger spectrum of tasks, ranging in various options listed in the presented task category space.

Acknowledgments. This work has been supported by Czech Science Foundation (GAČR) project 19-22071Y, by Science Foundation Ireland under grant number SFI/12/RC/2289_2, and by EU's Horizon 2020 research and innovation programs, under grant agreements n° 951911 AI4Media (https://ai4media.eu) and n° 825079 MindSpaces (https://mindspaces.eu/).

References

1. Awad, G., et al.: TRECVID 2020: a comprehensive campaign for evaluating video retrieval tasks across multiple application domains. In: Proceedings of the TRECVID, Gaithersburg, MD, USA (2020)
2. Awad, G., et al.: TRECVID 2019: an evaluation campaign to benchmark video activity detection, video captioning and matching, and video search & retrieval. In: Proceedings of the TRECVID, Gaithersburg, MD, USA (2019)

3. Awad, G., et al.: TRECVID 2016: evaluating video search, video event detection, localization, and hyperlinking. In: Proceedings of the TREC Video Retrieval Evaluation (TRECVID), Gaithersburg, MD, USA (2016)
4. Bates, M.J.: The design of browsing and berrypicking techniques for the online search interface. Online Rev. **13**(5), 407–424 (1989)
5. Belkin, N.J., Marchetti, P.G., Cool, C.: BRAQUE: design of an interface to support user interaction in information retrieval. Inf. Process. Manage. **29**(3), 325–344 (1993)
6. Buckland, M.K.: On types of search and the allocation of library resources. J. Am. Soc. Inf. Sci. **30**(3), 143–147 (1979)
7. Christel, M.G.: Carnegie Mellon University traditional informedia digital video retrieval system. In: Proceedings of the ACM Conference on Image and Video Retrieval (CIVR), Amsterdam, The Netherlands, p. 647 (2007)
8. Constantin, M.G., Hicks, S., Larson, M., Nguyen, N.T.: MediaEval multimedia evaluation benchmark: tenth anniversary and counting. ACM SIGMM Rec. **12**(2) (2020)
9. Datta, R., Joshi, D., Li, J., Wang, J.Z.: Image retrieval: ideas, influences, and trends of the new age. ACM Comput. Surv. **40**(2), 5:1–5:60 (2008)
10. Gurrin, C., et al.: Introduction to the third annual lifelog search challenge (LSC'20). In: Proceedings of the ACM International Conference on Multimedia Retrieval (ICMR), pp. 584–585 (2020)
11. Gurrin, C., et al.: Comparing approaches to interactive lifelog search at the Lifelog Search Challenge (LSC2018). ITE Trans. Media Technol. Appl. **7**(2), 46–59 (2019)
12. Heller, S., Sauter, L., Schuldt, H., Rossetto, L.: Multi-stage queries and temporal scoring in vitrivr. In: Proceedings of the IEEE International Conference on Multimedia & Expo Workshops (ICMEW), pp. 1–5 (2020)
13. Hu, W., Xie, N., Li, L., Zeng, X., Maybank, S.: A survey on visual content-based video indexing and retrieval. IEEE Trans. Syst. Man Cybern. Part C **41**(6), 797–819 (2011)
14. Kraaij, W., Smeaton, A.F., Over, P., Arlandis, J.: TRECVID 2004 - an overview. In: Proceedings of the TRECVID, Gaithersburg, MD, USA (2004)
15. Larson, M.A., Soleymani, M., Gravier, G., Ionescu, B., Jones, G.J.F.: The benchmarking initiative for multimedia evaluation: MediaEval 2016. IEEE Multimedia **24**(1), 93–96 (2017)
16. Lee, J.H., Renear, A., Smith, L.C.: Known-item search: variations on a concept. In: Proceedings of the ASIS&T Annual Meeting, Austin, TX, USA (2006)
17. Li, X., Xu, C., Yang, G., Chen, Z., Dong, J.: W2VV++: fully deep learning for ad-hoc video search. In: Proceedings of the ACM Multimedia, Nice, France (2019)
18. Li, Y., Belkin, N.J.: A faceted approach to conceptualizing tasks in information seeking. Inf. Process. Manage. **44**(6), 1822–1837 (2008)
19. Lokoč, J., Bailer, W., Schoeffmann, K., Münzer, B., Awad, G.: On influential trends in interactive video retrieval: video browser showdown 2015–2017. IEEE Trans. Multimedia **20**(12), 3361–3376 (2018)
20. Lokoč, J., et al.: A W2VV++ case study with automated and interactive text-to-video retrieval. In: Proceedings of the ACM Multimedia (Virtual Event), Seattle, WA, USA, pp. 2553–2561 (2020)
21. Over, P., et al.: TRECVID 2010 - an overview of the goals, tasks, data, evaluation mechanisms, and metrics. In: Proceedings of the TRECVID, Gaithersburg, MD, USA (2010)

22. Over, P., et al.: TRECVID 2013 - an overview of the goals, tasks, data, evaluation mechanisms and metrics. In: Proceedings of the TRECVID, Gaithersburg, MD, USA (2013)
23. Rossetto, L., Bailer, W., Bernstein, A.: Considering human perception and memory in interactive multimedia retrieval evaluations. In: Proceedings of the International Conference on Multimedia Modeling (MMM), Prague, Czech Republic, pp. 605–616 (2021)
24. Rossetto, L., et al.: On the user-centric comparative remote evaluation of interactive video search systems. IEEE Multimedia **28**, 18–28 (2021)
25. Rossetto, L., Gasser, R., Sauter, L., Bernstein, A., Schuldt, H.: A system for interactive multimedia retrieval evaluations. In: Proceedings of the International Conference on MultiMedia Modeling (MMM), Prague, Czech Republic (2021)
26. Salton, G.: Automatic Text Processing: The Transformation, Analysis, and Retrieval of Information by Computer. Addison-Wesley (1989)
27. Schoeffmann, K.: A user-centric media retrieval competition: the video browser showdown 2012–2014. IEEE Multimedia **21**(4), 8–13 (2014)
28. Schoeffmann, K.: Video browser showdown 2012–2019: a review. In: Proceedings of the International Conference on Content-Based Multimedia Indexing (CBMI), Dublin, Ireland, pp. 1–4 (2019)
29. Smeaton, A.F., Kraaij, W., Over, P.: TRECVID 2003 - an overview. In: Proceedings of the TRECVID, Gaithersburg, MD, USA (2003)
30. Smeaton, A.F., Over, P., Kraaij, W.: Evaluation campaigns and TRECVID. In: Proceedings of the ACM International Workshop on Multimedia Information Retrieval (MIR), Santa Barbara, California, USA, pp. 321–330 (2006)
31. Snoek, C.G., Worring, M., de Rooij, O., van de Sande, K.E., Yan, R., Hauptmann, A.G.: VideOlympics: real-time evaluation of multimedia retrieval systems. IEEE Multimedia **15**(1), 86–91 (2008)
32. Walker, G., Janes, J.: Online retrieval: a dialogue of theory and practice. Libraries Unlimited (1999)
33. Wildemuth, B.M., O'Neill, A.L.: The "known" in known-item searches: empirical support for user-centered design. Coll. Res. Lib. **56**(3), 265–281 (1995)
34. Worring, M., Snoek, C., de Rooij, O., Nguyen, G., van Balen, R., Koelma, D.: Mediamill: advanced browsing in news video archives. In: Proceedings of the ACM Conference on Image and Video Retrieval (CIVR), Tempe, AZ, USA, pp. 533–536 (2006)
35. Wu, J., Ngo, C.W.: Interpretable embedding for ad-hoc video search. In: Proceedings of the ACM Multimedia (Virtual Event), Seattle, WA, USA, pp. 3357–3366 (2020)
36. Wu, J., Nguyen, P.A., Ma, Z., Ngo, C.W.: SQL-like interpretable interactive video search. In: Proceedings of the International Conference on MultiMedia Modeling (MMM), Prague, Czech Republic, pp. 391–397 (2021)

GPR1200: A Benchmark for General-Purpose Content-Based Image Retrieval

Konstantin Schall[(✉)], Kai Uwe Barthel, Nico Hezel, and Klaus Jung

Visual Computing Group, HTW Berlin, University of Applied Sciences,
Wilhelminenhofstraße 75, 12459 Berlin, Germany
konstantin.schall@htw-berlin.de
http://visual-computing.com/

Abstract. Even though it has extensively been shown that retrieval specific training of deep neural networks is beneficial for nearest neighbor image search quality, most of these models are trained and tested in the domain of landmarks images. However, some applications use images from various other domains and therefore need a network with good generalization properties - a general-purpose CBIR model. To the best of our knowledge, no testing protocol has so far been introduced to benchmark models with respect to general image retrieval quality. After analyzing popular image retrieval test sets we decided to manually curate GPR1200, an easy to use and accessible but challenging benchmark dataset with a broad range of image categories. This benchmark is subsequently used to evaluate various pretrained models of different architectures on their generalization qualities. We show that large-scale pretraining significantly improves retrieval performance and present experiments on how to further increase these properties by appropriate fine-tuning. With these promising results, we hope to increase interest in the research topic of general-purpose CBIR.

Keywords: Content-based image retrieval · Image descriptors · Feature extraction · Generalization · Retrieval benchmark · Image datasets

1 Introduction

Similar to most vision related tasks, deep learning models have taken over in the field of content-based image retrieval (CBIR) over the course of the last decade [5,17,19]. More recent research has also shown that performance of retrieval models can further be enhanced by applying a more appropriate loss objective from the metric learning family which will enforce an embedding space with denser clusters and therefore will often yield better nearest neighbor search results [2,5,23]. Other publications introduce more complex pooling functions to obtain even more discriminative image features as a replacement to the commonly used

© Springer Nature Switzerland AG 2022
B. Þór Jónsson et al. (Eds.): MMM 2022, LNCS 13141, pp. 205–216, 2022.
https://doi.org/10.1007/978-3-030-98358-1_17

Fig. 1. Example images from all of the subsets of the newly introduced GPR1200 dataset. Domains from left to right, top to bottom: Landmarks, Nature, Sketches, Objects, Products and Faces

global average pooling [20,23]. However, a common denominator of these publications is that the models are trained and tested on domain specific datasets. In the large-scale settings of DELG [2] millions of landmark images are used to train a feature extractor model and the feature vectors (embeddings) are evaluated on other landmark datasets of much smaller scale. In the field of deep metric learning the most commonly used datasets are Cars196 [12], Stanford Online Products [24] and CUB200-2011 [29] which once again are very domain specific. Even though a deep learning model for general-purpose CBIR has a broad range of applications, to the best of our knowledge, no research has been conducted on how to find a suitable network which is not bound to specific domains and generalizes well to all kinds of visual data. Examples for such applications can be *visual similarity search* for stock photo agencies or *video browsing tools* as used in the Video Browser Showdown [14].

In this paper we try to manifest a protocol for testing deep learning based models for their general-purpose retrieval qualities. After analyzing the currently existing and commonly used evaluation datasets we came to the conclusion that none of the available test sets are suitable for the desired purpose and present the GPR1200 (General Purpose Retrieval) test set. This manually reviewed and well balanced dataset consists of 12000 images with 1200 classes from six different image domains. The goal of this test set is to become an easy to use and accessible benchmark for the research field of general-purpose CBIR. Evaluation code and download instructions can be found at http://visual-computing.com/project/GPR1200. Furthermore we conducted extensive experiments with a variety of pretrained models of different architectures and show how retrieval qualities can further be increased by appropriate fine-tuning with openly available data. We hope that these results will spark interest in this field and will lead to a healthy competition among researchers which will result in CBIR models with high generalization power in the future.

2   Related Work

CNNs for CBIR. Since the introduction of deep learning models for feature extraction in [1] they became the preferred modules in image retrieval systems. Performance of retrieval networks can be evaluated with metrics as *Mean Average Precision* or *Recall*. Both of these metrics will result in a perfect score, if and only if all of the positive images are retrieved and ranked before the negative ones. Retrieval qualities could further be increased by training neural networks with large scale datasets such as Google Landmarks v2 [32] and the introduction of more sophisticated pooling methods. Instead of the commonly used global average pooling of the activation maps from the last convolutional layer, approaches that aggregate regional information obtained from the activation map into a single, global descriptor have been introduced in [23,26]. Furthermore a very simple but effective pooling method has been shown to produce even better results in [20]. The generalized mean pooling (GeM) is practically parameter free and the computational costs are negligible. Additionally, multi-scale feature extraction schemes, where a given image is resized to multiple different resolutions have proven to enhance performance [2,20,23]. Usually a feature vector is computed for each scale and these vectors are L2-normalized subsequently, summed and L2-normalized again. However, all of the above approaches only have been applied to images of the landmarks domain and it is unclear if these methods will lead to the same effect in a general-purpose retrieval setting. Another caveat is that these pooling based methods are only known to be useful in the combination with CNN-architectures so far. Since models from the transformer family [4,13] do not produce conventional activation maps and encapsulate the spatial information of images through self-attention [28], pooling based methods might not be as beneficial here.

Deep Metric Learning. The two major streams in this research field can be divided into contrastive and proxy based loss functions. Contrastive loss functions often utilize sampling techniques so that a desired number of examples per class is always available in a batch and then calculate distances of positive feature vectors (from images of the same class) and compare these values to distances of negative ones. The network is harshly penalized if distances between negative feature vectors are smaller than distances between positives [24]. Proxy based loss objectives are more similar to the "traditional" Softmax Cross Entropy Loss in the sense that a linear layer is used to map feature vectors to a space where the number of dimensions equals the number of classes in the train dataset. However, the weights $W_{d,c}$ of these linear layers can be seen as class representation vectors (proxies), one for each class c. The mapping of the d-dimensional feature vectors is a computation of c dot products. Most of the loss functions from this family furthermore L2-normalize both the weight matrix $W_{d,c}$ and the feature vectors, which transforms the linear mapping to a computation of c cosine-similarities. The goal is to maximize the similarity between feature vectors and its respective class proxy vector and to minimize the similarity to proxy vectors of other classes [3,10].

3   Analysis of Available Datasets

The number of possible image combinations is almost infinite and it is therefore impossible to perfectly categorize large, web-scale image collections. However, two main categories can be observed while browsing image collections of popular stock photo agencies: photographs and planar images. While the two categories are not mutually exclusive, the major part of available images falls into one or the other. Photographs mostly consist of pictures of real life scenes showing objects such as people, animals, landmarks. Planar images are artificially created and show artworks, sketches, illustrations, book- and web pages, maps or blueprints. At the category level, the most frequently pictured objects were animals, natural and architectural landmarks, people and daily products such as clothes, electrical devices, cars, etc. All of these items are not bound to one of the main categories, since cats, for example, can also be drawn and photographed in real life. Furthermore, all of these categories can also be depicted in an isolated image with a solid color background. An evaluation benchmark dataset for general-purpose CBIR should include a large variety of images and preferably contain examples from both of the observed main categories. Furthermore, such an image collection should include several of the listed object domains.

Another important property of benchmark datasets can be summarized as unique solvability. All images of a given class should contain visual attributes that clearly distinguish them from similar images of other classes. A human annotator should be able to perfectly divide images of all classes and therefore achieve an optimal metric score without being a domain specific expert. Furthermore, the images ideally should not show several objects belonging to different classes nor should the categories have a hierarchical structure. However, as long as these two rules are respected, classes may have different intra-class variances so that a model can be tested on the ability to identify objects on instance and class level.

Table 1 analyzes a non exhaustive list of possible datasets for benchmarking general-purpose CBIR quality. Low *domain variety* indicates a small number of similar classes, while a dataset with a large number of classes from different image areas has a high domain variety. As for *unique solvability*, datasets with many labeling errors or different concepts/scenes within one class are rated as low and in the opposite case as high. The first part of the table contains the most widely used datasets in the landmarks domain. Oxford [16] and Paris[18] contain images of 11 different architectural landmarks from the respective city. Five images per class are used as a query and the remaining images serve as the

Table 1. Comparison of possible CBIR retrieval benchmark datasets

Dataset	Domain variety	Unique solvability	# Classes	# Images
Oxford [16]	Low	Low	11	5k
Paris [18]	Low	Low	11	6k
ROxford [19]	Low	Mid	11	5k
RParis [19]	Low	Mid	11	6k
Google Landmarks V2 [32]	Low	Low	200k	4.1M
Holidays [9]	Mid	High	500	1.5k
INSTRE [31]	High	Mid	250	28.5k
SOP [24]	Mid	Mid	22.6k	120k
CUB200-2011 [29]	Low	High	200	11.8k
Cars196 [12]	Low	Mid	196	16.2k
iNat Val [7]	Mid	Low	5.1k	96.8k
ImageNet1k Val [22]	Mid	High	1k	50k
ImageNet Sketch Val [30]	Mid	High	1k	50k
VGGFace [15]	Low	Mid	2.6k	2.6M
IMDB Faces [21]	Low	Low	20.3k	523k

index set. These sets have been revisited in [19] (RParis/ROxford) and it has been shown that the original sets suffered from incorrect annotations and suboptimal query selection. Regardless of the version of the datasets, these collections are not suitable to test generalization and general-purpose retrieval, since the number of classes and the domain variety is too low. Google Landmarks v2 [32] is of immense scale but has a very low solvability and domain variety, as a single landmark category can include indoor and outdoor images of the same landmark, as well as examples where the actual landmark is not visible at all. Datasets with more generic image categories are listed in the second section of the table. Even though results for the INRIA Holidays dataset [9] have been reported in the large-scale landmark retrieval field [5,23], it's popularity has declined in recent years. The INSTRE [31] set has the highest domain variety of the listed sets, as it consists of categories such as landmarks, illustrations and logos (e.g. corporate and sports). It also includes a large number of photos showing objects (toys, books, etc.) with different backgrounds and degrees of rotation. However, the main downside of this benchmark set is that most of the images do not reflect real-world scenarios and all categories have low intra-class variance. Publications in the metric learning field often use the three datasets CUB200-2011 [29] (bird species), Cars196 [12] (car models) and Stanford Online Products (SOP) [24] (images of products collected from online marketplaces). While the first two datasets have a very low domain variety, SOP is a more fitting candidate with a high number of diverse classes, although it lacks real world images of animals, people and landmarks. iNat provides a very diverse dataset and includes categories from animals, plants, fungi and insects. VGGFaces [15] is a pure faces dataset with low domain variety. We also explored the idea of using the ImageNet ILSVRC2012 [22] validation split as a retrieval benchmark, but did not consider this suitable due to the lack of some of the desired domains. However, the more important issue was that a large number of models were trained with the corresponding train split and would therefore have an unfair advantage over models trained with other class distributions. ImageNet Sketch [30] contains a collection of sketches and drawings of the same 1000 categories as in ILSVRC2012 but no photographed objects and is a more fitting candidate.

4   General-Purpose Retrieval Benchmark

The previous analysis has shown that to this day there is no suitable benchmark dataset for general-purpose CBIR. One strategy could be to introduce a protocol that involves testing with several of the listed image collections. Such a procedure would have the disadvantage that the data has to be obtained from multiple sources and that many of the datasets are not uniquely solvable and therefore have different degrees of hardness and cleanness. For these reasons, we decided to create a new dataset by manually selecting images from some of the listed collections and classes. In order to guarantee a uniform class distribution and solvability of the retrieval tasks, for each subset, 200 classes with 10 examples were selected. Manuel selection included randomization of the presentation order of images from the same class and the first 10 examples that met the solvability criteria were selected. We also took care to exclude overlapping classes in this process. Figure 1 shows some example images of the final dataset.

INSTRE. Only the first 200 classes are included since the last 50 classes show two objects from the other classes in combination. For each of the 200 classes we manually select ten representatives with different levels of difficulty.

Google Landmarks V2. Only images from the index set were considered, since those are not meant to be used for training. In addition we discarded all classes with less than twenty examples. This restriction leads to 7k possible classes. Since the original data collection process did not include any manual verification and allowed to have indoor and outdoor scenes under one category, most of the classes did not show ten clearly related examples. For this reason, we extracted embeddings with the model presented in [32] and further excluded all categories with fewer than twenty images that have a cosine similarity less than 0.5. From the remaining categories the 200 classes and corresponding ten images were manually selected as previously stated.

iNat. Classes were randomly sampled and images were manually selected according to the described criteria. We excluded some categories from plants and fungi, because they were hard to distinguish by visual characteristics without expert knowledge.

ImageNet Sketch. Images are only chosen from the validation set in this case. We observed that some of the classes only contain a very small number of unique images which were then mirrored and rotated to fill up the 50 images per class. In the manual selection process of this dataset we tried to avoid these cases and only included a maximum of two variations of the same image.

SOP. We restricted the possible categories to those with at least ten examples and chose images manually according to the specified criteria.

IMDB Faces. The *Faces* part of the original dataset was used for image selection. The celebrities were randomly selected and image instances were manually chosen.

4.1 GPR1200 Evaluation Protocol

The resulting collection will be called *GPR1200* (General-Purpose image Retrieval set with 1200 classes). It represents a compact but complex and challenging benchmarking dataset. As previously stated, the goal is to get a better understanding on how to obtain general-purpose retrieval models. As for the evaluation protocol, there is no separation into query and index splits. All of the 12k images are used as queries for robustness. Additionally, no bounding boxes or similar information is given and is not allowed to be used. The chosen evaluation metric is the full mean average precision score which is computed as follows:

$$AP(q) = \frac{1}{m_q} \sum_{k=1}^{N} P_q(k) \, \mathrm{rel}_q(k) \tag{1}$$

$$mAP = \frac{1}{N} \sum_{n=1}^{N} AP(n) \tag{2}$$

N is the number of total images (12k), m_q equals to the number of positive images (10), $P_q(k)$ represents the precision at rank k for the q-th query and $\mathrm{rel}_q(k)$ is a binary indicator function denoting the relevance of prediction k to q (1 if q and image at rank k have the same class and 0 otherwise). Additionally, the mean average precision can be calculated for each of the subsets to get a greater understanding of the models domain capabilities by averaging the 2k subset specific AP values. The remaining 10k images simultaneously act as distractors. It is also important to note that models tested with this benchmarks should not have been trained with any of the datasets used to create GPR1200. However, as for the Google Landmarks v2, the iNat and ImageNet Sketch parts, the validation splits have been used for data selection, training with the respective train splits is therefore perfectly valid. Descriptor post-processing should not be forbidden but if the method is parametrized as in [8,17], the search for parameters must be performed with other data.

5 Experiments

In this section we first present metric values according to the stated evaluation protocol for various pretrained deep learning models and discuss the importance of large-scale domain unspecific pretraining for general-purpose CBIR feature extractors. Furthermore, we conducted experiments on how to train general-purpose neural networks for CBIR. All experiments were performed on a single NVIDIA Tesla V100 GPU.

5.1   Evaluation of Pretrained Models

Table 3 shows the retrieval results for the evaluated networks which are further described in Table 2. Furthermore, the table shows ImageNet1k validation split accuracies for networks that have been trained or fine-tuned with ImageNet1k. Solely L2-normalization was used as post-processing for all of these networks. The two evaluated landmark models GLv2 and DELG, which both have been trained on the *Clean* subset of the Google Landmarks V2 dataset [2,32] show expected results: high mAPs for the landmarks subset of GPR1200, but relatively low overall mAPs. One of the main findings of the other experiments is that large-scale pretraining with ImageNet21k improves retrieval qualities for all tested network architectures. This can be seen by comparing the R101 to B-R101 (ResNets), DT-B to ViT-B (visual transformers) and the respective versions of the EfficentNetV2 models since the main differences of these pairs are that ImageNet21k pretraining was used in one and omitted in the other. Even though the stated pairs also show discrepancies in the achieved accuracies on ImageNet1k, 80.1 vs. 82.3 for the ResNets, 83.1 vs. 84.5 for the visual transformers and 85.5 vs. 86.3 for the EfficientNets. Those differences become much clearer by comparing the mean average precisions achieved on GPR1200 (42.8 vs. 55.6, 51.2 vs. 60.0 and 49.0 vs. 62.4). Consequently, extensive pretraining significantly improves the generalization of the models. Additionally, it can be seen that for the most architectures a fine-tuning on ILSVRC2012 (denoted as ++ in Table 3) yields better overall mAPs due to the large improvements in the sketches part of the set. This is not surprising since those two sets have the same classes in different representations (sketches vs. photographs). Even though the large variant of ViT achieves the highest overall GPR1200 mAP the Swin-B model seems to have the highest ratio of performance and latency. This network is also interesting, due to the fact that it achieves higher overall qualities if the ImageNet1k fine-tuning is omitted.

5.2   Training for General-Purpose CBIR

We trained two of the presented model variants with three different datasets. The *clean* subsection of the GLv2 dataset [32] is used in the first setting (denoted as *L* in Table 4), the full ImageNet21k [22] set in the second (*I*) and a combination of these two in the third case (*L+I*). Since the ImageNet part has roughly ten times more images, we oversample the landmarks part in the third setting to achieve a balance of these two datasets during training. We conducted experiments with different optimizers and loss functions and only report results for the best combination, which was a standard SGD optimizer with a starting learning rate of 5e-6 and momentum of 0.9 and the ProxyAnchor loss function [10]. Additionally, the learning rate was scaled by 0.5 after 30%, 60% and 90% of the 200k update steps and a batch size of 128 was used throughout all experiments. 10% of the train data was used for validation purposes and we present GPR1200 results for the best validation checkpoints. As for the BiT-ResNet and the Swin networks, model variants without ImageNet1k fine-tuning were used,

Table 2. Description of evaluated network architectures

Key	Network	Params (M)	Latency (ms)	Dim	ImageSize
GLv2	AF ResNet101 [32]	44.6	72.1	2048	MS*
DELG	DELG ResNet101 [2]	44.6	72.1	2048	MS*
R101	ResNet101 [6]	44.6	2.7	2048	224
B-R101	BiT ResNet101 [11]	44.5	7.7	2048	448
B-R101x3	BiT ResNet101x3 [11]	387.9	41.9	2048	448
EfN-L	EfficientNetV2-L [25]	118.5	10.9	1280	480
ViT-B	ViT-B [4]	86.6	3.9	768	224
ViT-L	ViT-L[4]	304.3	12.2	1024	224
DT-B	DeiT-B [27]	86.6	3.9	768	224
DT-B+D	Distilled DeiT-B [27]	87.3	3.9	768	224
Swin-B	Swin-B [13]	87.8	4.4	1024	224
Swin-L	Swin-L [13]	196.5	7.9	1536	224

*Landmark models employ a multi scale scheme, where images are used in its original size and resized to one smaller and one larger scale.

Table 3. GPR1200 mAPs [%] for evaluated models

Key	Train	IN1k Acc	GPR mAP	Land. mAP	Sketch mAP	iNat mAP	INST mAP	SOP mAP	Faces mAP
Glv2	−−	–	49.4	97.0	19.9	21.5	50.8	88.6	18.5
DELG	−−	–	49.6	**97.3**	20.0	21.4	51.5	88.6	18.6
R101	−+	80.1	42.8	65.4	29.6	27.4	42.6	74.9	17.8
B-R101	++	82.3	55.6	82.2	47.1	43.0	52.9	86.0	22.3
B-R101	+−	–	54.9	81.1	41.2	41.9	51.8	87.0	26.7
B-R101x3	++	84.4	57.0	83.1	52.9	40.1	55.7	87.2	22.8
B-R101x3	+−	–	56.0	83.4	40.8	40.1	55.1	90.0	26.6
EfN-L	−+	85.5	49.0	69.4	57.3	32.7	44.9	71.5	17.8
EfN-L	++	**86.3**	62.4	85.2	65.1	47.2	65.1	87.1	24.4
EfN-L	+−	–	59.2	88.2	41.5	43.8	61.4	**93.5**	26.7
ViT-B	++	84.5	60.0	83.0	64.6	43.0	58.1	87.7	24.0
ViT-B	+−	–	57.4	84.4	46.9	37.7	58.7	90.0	26.6
ViT-L	++	85.8	**63.2**	84.9	**74.8**	45.0	60.4	88.8	25.3
ViT-L	+−	–	59.9	85.7	53.0	38.1	63.5	91.2	28.3
DT-B	−+	83.1	51.2	74.7	44.6	33.4	53.9	81.5	19.0
DT-B+D	−+	83.3	55.2	79.9	48.2	38.0	58.4	86.9	19.6
Swin-B	++	85.3	61.4	84.0	65.7	41.7	63.5	86.6	24.5
Swin-B	+−	–	62.9	87.4	54.2	**45.9**	68.6	91.6	**29.1**
Swin-L	++	**86.3**	63.0	86.5	66.1	43.2	67.8	89.4	24.5
Swin-L	+−	–	63.0	88.5	50.7	44.6	**72.5**	93.1	28.5

++: Pretraining on ImageNet21k and subsequent fine-tuning on ImageNet1k,
+−: Training on ImageNet21k only, −+: Training on ImageNet1k only,
−−: Neither ImageNet21k nor ImageNet1k have been used for training.

so the effect of the loss function can be seen in the results for the I-setting. Although, exactly the same data is used as for the pretraining, the GPR1200 mAP increases in both cases. Our intuition is that the ProxyAnchor loss contracts the embeddings of positive images and therefore leads to better nearest neighbor search constellations. However, the best overall qualities are obtained with $L+I$ training. The GPR1200 mAP of the baseline model Swin-B could be improved by over 3 points in this case. Unsurprisingly, training with the highest variety of data leads to retrieval models with the highest generalization degrees.

Table 4. GPR1200 mAPs for improved models

Key	Train	GPR mAP	Land. mAP	Sketch mAP	iNat mAP	INST mAP	SOP mAP	Faces mAP
B-R101	–	55.6	82.2	47.1	43.0	52.9	86.0	22.3
B-R101	L	57.6	88.2	43.2	43.4	59.8	89.6	21.4
B-R101	I	56.4	81.6	49.4	49.2	51.8	83.6	22.8
B-R101	$L+I$	58.1	87.8	47.4	47.6	58.6	85.6	21.6
Swin-B	–	62.9	87.4	54.2	45.9	68.6	91.6	29.1
Swin-B	L	65.0	91.3	53.8	46.0	**76.8**	**93.9**	28.4
Swin-B	I	64.7	86.5	**64.9**	**50.3**	67.8	88.4	**30.0**
Swin-B	$L+I$	**66.2**	**91.7**	59.2	**50.3**	74.9	91.4	29.5

Train: Pretrained models are finetuned with either GLv2Clean L, ImageNet21k I or a combination thereof $L+I$. – shows the baseline.

6   Conclusion

This paper has three main contributions: First, the introduction of a new CBIR benchmark dataset that, unlike the existing ones, focuses on high domain diversity to test retrieval systems for their generalization ability. Images were manually selected to ensure solvability and exclude overlaps between categories of different domains. The GPR1200 dataset is easy to use and presents an evaluation protocol that is robust to errors. Secondly, this benchmark was used to evaluate modern deep learning based architectures. This showed that metrics such as ILSVRC2012 validation accuracy can be misleading in the search for general-purpose CBIR models. Lastly, we presented a retrieval-specific training scheme which utilizes a combination of two large-scale datasets to further improve retrieval qualities of two already powerful networks. However, these experiments should be considered rather preliminary, and it is subject to further research whether retrieval-specific pooling or post-processing can lead to further advances. We hope that retrieval models will therefore not only be optimized in a domain-specific setting and will be able to achieve higher levels of generalization in the future.

References

1. Babenko, A., Slesarev, A., Chigorin, A., Lempitsky, V.: Neural codes for image retrieval. In: Fleet, D., Pajdla, T., Schiele, B., Tuytelaars, T. (eds.) ECCV 2014. LNCS, vol. 8689, pp. 584–599. Springer, Cham (2014). https://doi.org/10.1007/978-3-319-10590-1_38

2. Cao, B., Araujo, A., Sim, J.: Unifying deep local and global features for image search. In: Vedaldi, A., Bischof, H., Brox, T., Frahm, J.-M. (eds.) ECCV 2020. LNCS, vol. 12365, pp. 726–743. Springer, Cham (2020). https://doi.org/10.1007/978-3-030-58565-5_43

3. Deng, J., Guo, J., Xue, N., Zafeiriou, S.: ArcFace: additive angular margin loss for deep face recognition. In: CVPR (2019)

4. Dosovitskiy, A., et al.: An image is worth 16 × 16 words: transformers for image recognition at scale. CoRR (2020)

5. Gordo, A., Almazán, J., Revaud, J., Larlus, D.: Deep image retrieval: learning global representations for image search. In: Leibe, B., Matas, J., Sebe, N., Welling, M. (eds.) ECCV 2016. LNCS, vol. 9910, pp. 241–257. Springer, Cham (2016). https://doi.org/10.1007/978-3-319-46466-4_15

6. He, K., Zhang, X., Ren, S., Sun, J.: Deep residual learning for image recognition. In: 2016 IEEE Conference on Computer Vision and Pattern Recognition (CVPR) (2016)

7. Horn, G.V., et al.: The iNaturalist species classification and detection dataset. In: CVPR (2018)

8. Iscen, A., Tolias, G., Avrithis, Y., Furon, T., Chum, O.: Efficient diffusion on region manifolds: recovering small objects with compact CNN representations. CoRR (2016)

9. Jegou, H., Douze, M., Schmid, C.: Hamming embedding and weak geometric consistency for large scale image search. In: Forsyth, D., Torr, P., Zisserman, A. (eds.) ECCV 2008. LNCS, vol. 5302, pp. 304–317. Springer, Heidelberg (2008). https://doi.org/10.1007/978-3-540-88682-2_24

10. Kim, S., Kim, D., Cho, M., Kwak, S.: Proxy anchor loss for deep metric learning. In: IEEE/CVF Conference on Computer Vision and Pattern Recognition (CVPR) (2020)

11. Kolesnikov, A., et al.: Big Transfer (BiT): general visual representation learning. In: Vedaldi, A., Bischof, H., Brox, T., Frahm, J.-M. (eds.) ECCV 2020. LNCS, vol. 12350, pp. 491–507. Springer, Cham (2020). https://doi.org/10.1007/978-3-030-58558-7_29

12. Krause, J., Stark, M., Deng, J., Fei-Fei, L.: 3d object representations for fine-grained categorization. In: 4th International IEEE Workshop on 3D Representation and Recognition (3dRR-13) (2013)

13. Liu, Z., et al.: Swin transformer: hierarchical vision transformer using shifted windows. arXiv preprint arXiv:2103.14030 (2021)

14. Lokoč, J., et al.: Is the reign of interactive search eternal? Findings from the video browser showdown 2020. ACM Trans. Multimedia Comput. Commun. Appl. **17**, 1–26 (2021)

15. Parkhi, O.M., Vedaldi, A., Zisserman, A.: Deep face recognition. In: British Machine Vision Conference (2015)

16. Philbin, J., Chum, O., Isard, M., Sivic, J., Zisserman, A.: Object retrieval with large vocabularies and fast spatial matching. In: Proceedings of the IEEE Conference on Computer Vision and Pattern Recognition (2007)

17. Philbin, J., Chum, O., Isard, M., Sivic, J., Zisserman, A.: Object retrieval with large vocabularies and fast spatial matching. In: CVPR (2007)

18. Philbin, J., Chum, O., Isard, M., Sivic, J., Zisserman, A.: Lost in quantization: improving particular object retrieval in large scale image databases. In: CVPR (2008)

19. Radenovic, F., Iscen, A., Tolias, G., Avrithis, Y., Chum, O.: Revisiting Oxford and Paris: large-scale image retrieval benchmarking. In: CVPR (2018)

20. Radenovic, F., Tolias, G., Chum, O.: Fine-tuning CNN image retrieval with no human annotation. IEEE Trans. Pattern Anal. Mach. Intell. **41**, 1655–1668 (2019)
21. Rothe, R., Timofte, R., Gool, L.V.: Deep expectation of real and apparent age from a single image without facial landmarks. Int. J. Comput. Vis. **126**, 144–157 (2018)
22. Russakovsky, O., et al.: ImageNet large scale visual recognition challenge. Int. J. Comput. Vis. (IJCV) **115**, 211–252 (2015)
23. Schall, K., Barthel, K.U., Hezel, N., Jung, K.: Deep aggregation of regional convolutional activations for content based image retrieval. In: MMSP (2019)
24. Song, H.O., Xiang, Y., Jegelka, S., Savarese, S.: Deep metric learning via lifted structured feature embedding. In: IEEE Conference on Computer Vision and Pattern Recognition (CVPR) (2016)
25. Tan, M., Le, Q.: EfficientNetV2: smaller models and faster training. In: Proceedings of the 38th International Conference on Machine Learning (2021)
26. Tolias, G., Sicre, R., Jégou, H.: Particular object retrieval with integral max-pooling of CNN activations. In: ICLR (Poster) (2016)
27. Touvron, H., Cord, M., Douze, M., Massa, F., Sablayrolles, A., Jégou, H.: Training data-efficient image transformers & distillation through attention. arXiv preprint arXiv:2012.12877 (2020)
28. Vaswani, A., et al.: Attention is all you need. In: Advances in Neural Information Processing Systems 30. Curran Associates, Inc. (2017)
29. Wah, C., Branson, S., Welinder, P., Perona, P., Belongie, S.: The Caltech-UCSD Birds-200-2011 dataset. Technical report, CNS-TR-2011-001, California Institute of Technology (2011)
30. Wang, H., Ge, S., Lipton, Z., Xing, E.P.: Learning robust global representations by penalizing local predictive power. In: Advances in Neural Information Processing Systems, pp. 10506–10518 (2019)
31. Wang, S., Jiang, S.: INSTRE: a new benchmark for instance-level object retrieval and recognition. In: ACM Transactions on Multimedia Computing, Communications, and Applications (2015)
32. Weyand, T., Araujo, A., Cao, B., Sim, J.: Google Landmarks Dataset v2 - a large-scale benchmark for instance-level recognition and retrieval. In: CVPR (2020)

LLQA - Lifelog Question Answering Dataset

Ly-Duyen Tran[1]([✉]), Thanh Cong Ho[2,3], Lan Anh Pham[2,3], Binh Nguyen[2,3], Cathal Gurrin[1], and Liting Zhou[1]

[1] Dublin City University, Dublin, Ireland
ly.tran2@mail.dcu.ie
[2] Vietnam National University,
Ho Chi Minh University of Science, Ho Chi Minh City, Vietnam
[3] AISIA Research Lab, Ho Chi Minh City, Vietnam

Abstract. Recollecting details from lifelog data involves a higher level of granularity and reasoning than a conventional lifelog retrieval task. Investigating the task of Question Answering (QA) in lifelog data could help in human memory recollection, as well as improve traditional lifelog retrieval systems. However, there has not yet been a standardised benchmark dataset for the lifelog-based QA. In order to provide a first dataset and baseline benchmark for QA on lifelog data, we present a novel dataset, *LLQA*, which is an augmented 85-day lifelog collection and includes over 15,000 multiple-choice questions. We also provide different baselines for the evaluation of future works. The results showed that lifelog QA is a challenging task that requires more exploration. The dataset is publicly available at https://github.com/allie-tran/LLQA.

Keywords: Lifelogging · Question answering

1 Introduction

Lifelogging has gained popularity within the research community in recent years with the main focus on lifelog retrieval. The term lifelogging refers to the process of capturing a personal digital diary by technologies such as body cameras and various other wearable sensors. The most extensive published lifelog data, used in the Lifelog Search Challenge workshop 2020 [12], features a collection of first-person images captured throughout the day, as well as the corresponding metadata such as time, GPS coordinates, and biometrics data. Such lifelog data can be processed in lifelog systems, which can serve as a form of 'prosthetic' memory. Lifelogs can support users in memory-related activities such as recollecting, reminiscing, retrieving, reflecting, and remembering intentions, as defined by Sellen and Whittaker's five R's [24]. Out of the five R's, retrieving lifelog data, typically lifelog photos, has been the subject of the majority of lifelog research, as seen in various workshops [11,12,21]. Recollecting details in past lifelog data, on the other hand, involves a higher level of granularity and reasoning; for example, it might involve answering

© Springer Nature Switzerland AG 2022
B. Þór Jónsson et al. (Eds.): MMM 2022, LNCS 13141, pp. 217–228, 2022.
https://doi.org/10.1007/978-3-030-98358-1_18

memory questions such as ' *What did I do, where did I go, and who did I see on [Tuesday]/[afternoon], [July 14, 2018]*?'. Thus, it becomes clear that Question Answering (QA) is an important related topic for research and this paper introduces the first QA dataset for lifelogs.

QA systems are designed to automatically answer questions posed in natural language and are considered to be one of the ultimate goals for retrieval systems [27]. For instance, users may prefer getting concise answers to specific questions instead of browsing an entire document. The same argument could be made for other types of media such as photos and videos; Visual QA systems can save the user from extraneous effort by automatically inferring a user's question regarding an image/video and producing a short and accurate answer. To produce the correct answer, the model needs to be able to interpret the question and focus on the relevant part of the image/video. Due to advances in the field of computer vision, visual QA has been a fast-growing area with various techniques for images [1,8,14] and videos [7,15,17]. Applying such visual QA techniques to lifelogs suggests that lifelog QA can be a valuable and impactful research area, since lifelog data is heavily visual-based. Having the ability to understand the whole context of a real-world event, Lifelog QA systems ultimately could provide help in human memory recollection, as well as improve traditional lifelog retrieval systems.

Despite the similarities to visual QA, the data used in Lifelog QA has several distinct aspects that render the direct application of Visual QA techniques less effective. Image QA techniques do not exploit the temporal nature of lifelog data. In the case of Video QA, standard action recognition techniques such as C3D [15] may not be useful as lifelog data are discontinuous (with an average frequency of 1 snapshot every 30 s) in the current generation of lifelog datasets. Moreover, current state-of-the-art video QA methods learn inference by relying on the appearance and motion data from a third-person point of view, which is different from the first-person photos in lifelog data. The most related work to Lifelog QA is EgoVQA [7], an egocentric video question answering dataset containing first-person perspective videos similarly to lifelog photos. However, videos still hold different characteristics compared to lifelog photos. For this reason, a novel benchmark dataset for Lifelog QA is a prerequisite to evaluate a model's ability to 'recollect' details in lifelog data.

In the field of lifelog QA, the novel dataset proposed in this paper supports the following research contributions:

1. Describing a new semi-automatic process of constructing a Lifelog QA dataset, based on an existing lifelog collection;
2. Providing 15,065 lifelog QA pairs, comprising of both multiple-choice questions and yes/no questions;
3. Presenting results of a pilot experiment to identify the gap between the human gold standard and existing QA models.

2 Related Work

2.1 Lifelogs and Personal Data Analytics

The inspiration for lifelogging dates back to Vannevar Bush's 1945 article *As We May Think* [3], which describes a blueprint personal information system which he called *Memex*. Bush considered *Memex* as 'a device in which an individual stores all his books, records, and communications, which is mechanised to be consulted with exceeding speed and flexibility. It is an enlarged intimate supplement to his memory'. However, it was not until a research project of Microsoft Research, called MyLifeBits [10] was started by Gordon Bell in 2001, that lifelogging began to gain attention from the research community. The MyLifeBits system attempted to capture every possible aspect of the daily life of Bell, including every web page visited, all Instant Message (IM) chat sessions, all telephone conversations, meetings, radio, television programs, as well as all mouse and keyboard activities and media files in his personal computers. All digitised data were stored in a SQL database to support a simple interface for different functionalities such as organising, associating metadata, assessing, and reporting information. Since then, due to advances in sensor technology and the availability of low-cost data storage, lifelogging has become an achievable activity for many. However the primarily passive nature of lifelogging means that the amount of data generated can be massive (over 1 TB of multimodal data per individual per year), and therefore effectively searching through such extensive archives of lifelog data remains an important yet challenging task.

Different lifelog benchmarking workshops/challenges have been established with distinctive evaluation metrics to assess lifelog systems, with the common objective being to facilitate the effective retrieval of specific lifelog images in an interactive or automatic manner. The standard approach taken by existing lifelog retrieval systems, such as MyScéal [26] and LifeSeeker [20], is assigning semantic context, e.g., visual concepts, to lifelog photos and applying traditional information retrieval techniques to produce a ranked list of relevant images. This approach treats each lifelog photo individually, which does not exploit the temporal and continuous nature of lifelog data. This is important because an individual snapshot of lifelog data is likely to not fully convey the whole context of an event [13].

There have been a number of lifelog datasets released since 2015 and at the most recent lifelog retrieval workshop, LSC'20 [12], the organisers published a large collection including six months of anonymised lifelog data, consisting of 50 GB of fully redacted wearable camera images at 1024 × 768 resolution, captured using OMG Autographer and Narrative Clip devices. These images were collected during periods in 2015, 2016, and 2018; some private information (for example, faces and identifiable materials) appearing in these images are anonymised in a manual or semi-manual process. The metadata for the collection consists of textual metadata representing time, physical activities, biometrics, locations, as well as visual concepts extracted from the non-redacted version of the visual dataset using a CAFFE CNN-based object detector [16]. This dataset forms the basis of the dataset augmented and released in this paper.

2.2 Video Question Answering (Video QA)

Video QA, an application of QA, is a task requiring the generation of correct answers to given questions related to a video or video archive. The questions are either in the form of fill-in-the-blank, multiple-choice, or open-ended types.

All existing Video QA datasets except for EgoVQA [7] are from third-person perspective. TGIF-QA [15] is a dataset of over 165,000 questions on 71,741 animated pictures. Multiple tasks are formulated upon this dataset, including counting the repetitions of the queried action, detecting the transitions of two actions, and image-based QA. MSVD-QA and MSRVTT-QA [28] are two datasets with third-person videos. The Video QA tasks formulated in both of these two datasets are open-ended questions of the types what, who, how, when, and where, and their answer sets are of size 1000. YouTube2Text-QA [29] is a dataset with both open-ended and multiple-choice tasks of three major question types (what, who, and other). TVQA and TVQA+ [17,18] are built on 21,793 video clips of 6 popular TV shows with 152.5K human-written QA pairs. EgoVQA [7] was proposed due to the lack of first-person point-of-view videos in these datasets; however, the size of the dataset is small, with just over 600 QA pairs.

After a comprehensive review of research on video QA, we observe that there are three unique characteristics of Lifelog QA compared with Video QA: (1) lifelog QA deals with more channels of information because of the inherent multimodality of lifelog data; (2) the collected activities in lifelog are captured in snapshots instead of being continuous, rendering the motion features ineffective; (3) unlike most video QA datasets, the point of view in lifelog visual data is first-person instead of third-person. Therefore, it is clear that the existing approaches and datasets for visual QA are not representative of the challenge posed by lifelog QA, hence it becomes necessary to investigate Lifelog QA in more detail, which is the primary motivation for this research.

3   LLQA - A Lifelog Question Answering Dataset

We define **Lifelog Question Answering (Lifelog QA)** as a task to produce correct answers to given textual representations of an individual's information needs concerning a past moment or experience from a lifelogger's daily life. In the scope of this initial research, we will consider only multiple-choice questions and yes/no questions due to the straightforward means of evaluation. It is anticipated that other types of answers will be explored at a later point.

In this section, a detailed explanation about how to build the first lifelog QA dataset is covered. This process is part of our contribution to the field of lifelog QA. To save time and effort, we applied automated steps where possible. The pipeline of the entire process is summarised in Fig. 1 and the description of each component is as follows:

3.1 Data Collection

The lifelog QA dataset for this work is based on the LSC'20 collection [12] mentioned in Sect. 2.1. Specifically, 26 d of data were selected from the year 2015

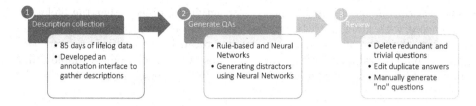

Fig. 1. The process of dataset construction.

and 59 d were selected in 2016. Each day is segmented into short events of the date based on the locations and activities of the lifelogger, which is based on the event segmentation approach of Doherty and Smeaton [6]. This encourages the annotators to focus on individual events. From the provided metadata throughout the day, whenever the location (work, home, etc.) or the activity (walking, driving, etc.) is changed, a new segment will be created. The process results in a total of 2,412 segments.

An annotation system was developed that presents annotators with all images in each segment along with the metadata such as time, GPS location, and the relative position of the segment in the whole day.

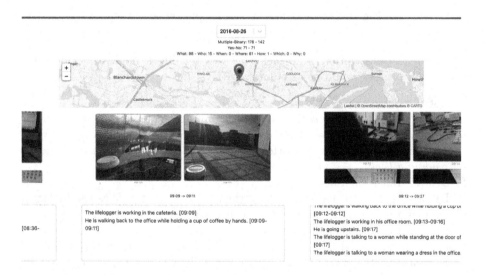

Fig. 2. Annotation Interface.

Annotators, who are volunteers from undergraduate Computer Science programmes, were asked to describe the events happening in each segment as seen in Fig. 2. Every description is annotated along with its starting and ending times.

The description should include actions or activities; objects that the lifelogger interacted with along with their properties such as size, shape, or colour; the location where the lifelogger was in, heading towards to or away from; and people (with a general identity description to preserve privacy). One example could be 'The lifelogger is reading a book in a cafe with a person in a black t-shirt.'

3.2 Generation of Question and Answers

The descriptions were converted to a list of questions by an automatic system which is summarised in Fig. 3. Entity extraction and syntax transformation were completed using hand-crafted rules based on POS tags and semantic role labels. To generate question words (who, what, where, etc.), a Seq2Seq neural network was trained on the questions and answers in the CoQA [23] dataset. False answers (distractors), are generated using RACE [9] with the gathered knowledge from ConceptNet [25] facts as context.

Fig. 3. The procedure of question-answer generation.

Given the description 'The lifelogger was reading a book in a cafe.', the generation process would be as follows:

1. Entities extraction
   The lifelogger, *reading a book*, and *in a cafe* are examples of entities in the sentence. We will choose *reading a book* in this example to illustrate further. Thus, the correct answer to this generated question-answer pair would be *reading a book*;
2. Syntax transformation - yes/no
   By moving *was* to the beginning of the sentence, we get 'Was the lifelogger reading a book in the cafe?' - 'Yes' as a yes/no question-answer pair;
3. Syntax transformation - multiple
   First, based on the POS tags, an automated process decides the entity is a *phrasal verb*, thus by replacing it with *doing* in the sentence and by applying a rule-based syntax transformation, we get '[...] was the lifelogger doing in the cafe?'
4. Wh-word generation
   Since questions in this dataset start with a Wh word, a pretrained S2S model chooses appropriate question word for this question. In this case, a sensible one would be *What*.

5. Distractor generations

So far, we get the question-answer pair as 'What was the lifelogger doing in the cafe?' - 'Reading a book'. To make this a multiple-choice question, we use RACE [9], a distractor generator for reading comprehension questions, and get the other wrong answers as 'Using his phone', 'Drinking coffee', and 'Playing football'.

Is the lifelogger in the kitchen?
Yes .
No .

What is the lifelogger doing in the living room?
He is using his laptop .
He is using his phone .
He is reading book .
He is watching television .

Fig. 4. Two example question-answer pairs in the dataset. The dataset contains both yes/no questions and multiple-choice questions.

3.3 Review

The generated questions and answers are reviewed by the annotators to correct semantics and delete duplicates, as well as ensuring constraints such as:

1. There are no duplicate answers for the same question,
2. The ratios between yes and no questions are balanced. As the automatic syntax transformation could only generate positive yes/no questions, the annotators are asked to create negative ones manually.

The dataset contains 15,065 QA pairs in total. Examples of the QA pairs can be seen in Fig. 4. On average, our questions contain 7.66 words. Correct answers tend to contain 3.57 words compared to 4.34 words in the generated wrong answers. Figure 5 and Table 1 present the breakdown of questions generated. The dataset is split into two sets: training and testing sets consisting of 10,668 (70.81%) and 4,397(29.19%) question-answer pairs, respectively. The splitting was done in a manner that ensures there are no overlapping days between the subsets, or in other words, the lifelog data in the testing set are unseen.

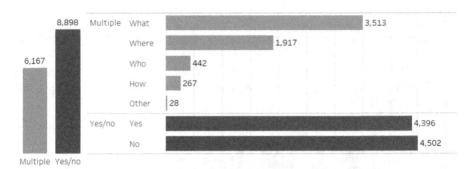

Fig. 5. Numbers of each question type in Lifelog QA dataset.

Table 1. Numbers of questions in each month in LSC'20 lifelog data collection.

Month	#Days	Days	#Images	#Questions
Feb, 2015	06	Feb 24–28	8549	941
Mar, 2015	20	Mar 01–20	28563	2745
Aug, 2016	24	Aug 08–31	32026	4871
Sep, 2016	30	Sep 01–30	51195	5595
Oct, 2016	05	Oct 01–05	7375	913
Total	**85**	–	**127708**	**15065**

4   Pilot Experiment

In order to evaluate the dataset and provide accompanying baselines for subsequent comparison, a pilot experiment has been carried out on several baselines, which are described below.

4.1   Human Gold-Standard Baseline

To determine the targeted performance (in terms of accuracy) on our dataset, we performed a user study, asking different groups of 10 volunteer students to complete the question-answering task. Each volunteer was asked to answer 20 yes/no questions and 20 multiple-choice questions chosen randomly from the testing set. Each question was accompanied by the relevant images. To avoid bias, there was no overlap between the annotators that have worked on the questions and the students participating in this study. The gold standard accuracy was found to be 0.8417 for yes/no questions and 0.8625 for multiple-choice questions. The reason that the scores are less than 1.0 is because the volunteers were presented with the relevant section for the question, rather than the lifelog data for the whole day, so in some cases, they did not fully understand the context of the event mentioned in the question. Another interesting feedback from the participants, as well as the annotators, concerns the volume of lifelog data causing issues in understanding. This is a common problem in lifelog analytics when the decisions regarding lifelog data are often made by a third party and not the original data gathering lifelogger, for example, as seen in the studies carried out by Byrne et al. [4].

4.2 Question-Only

We implement several heuristic baselines that use only the questions and their candidate answers in a similar approach to Castro et al. [5]. Specifically, *Longest answer* and *Shortest answer* choose one out of the four options with the most or the fewest number of tokens, respectively. *Word matching* chooses the answer based on the number of tokens they have in common with the question. Because yes/no answers have no difference either in length or the number of common words with the questions, we omit these models for this experiment.

Moreover, we implement *Sequence-to-sequence (S2S)* model based on the architecture of UniLMv2 [2], the state-of-the-art model in natural language understanding and generation tasks. We trained S2S on the CoQA [23] question-answer pairs. It encodes the question with a 2-layer LSTM, then encodes the candidate answers and assigns a score to each one. The text is tokenised and represented using Glove 300-D embeddings [22].

4.3 Question and Vision

Because of the similarity to Video QA task, we implemented *TVQA*, the original TVQA [17] model, trained on TVQA dataset. This is the state-of-the-art system in Video QA. To evaluate the application to lifelog data, we consider each day to be a one fps video with each image (along with the attached metadata) as one single frame in that video. We converted the annotated starting and ending times into the ordinal index of the frames in the video. Moreover, we replaced the subtitles intended for videos with a concatenation of metadata associated with the frames. While it may seem strange to treat visual lifelog data as motion video, it is temporal in nature and many of the participants in the LSC challenge [12] have modified existing Video Search systems from the VBS challenge [19] to treat lifelog data as 1 fps video.

4.4 Results

Both S2S and TVQA models have been retrained on the training set of the lifelog QA dataset and achieved a small improvement in accuracy compared to the untrained versions, as seen in Table 2. Furthermore, there is no considerable difference between the question-only models. Although the average length of the correct answers are shorter than the wrong ones, *Shortest answer* did not perform well at the lowest accuracy of 0.1717 for multiple-choice questions. Amongst the models, the retrained TVQA achieved the best performance with the accuracy of 0.6338 and 0.6136 for yes/no questions and multiple-choice questions, respectively. However, humans still significantly outperformed the models.

The results highlighted that the existing approaches are still far from the human gold standard for the lifelog QA task, so they should be optimised to improve performance. This will be a potential and promising topic for future research in lifelog domain in general, and especially in lifelog QA.

Table 2. Accuracy of different models in the pilot experiment.

Model	Yes/no	Multiple-choice
Longest answer	–	0.3202
Shortest answer	–	0.1717
Word matching	–	0.3041
S2S	0.5206	0.3148
S2S (retrained)	0.5066	0.3626
TVQA	0.4956	0.4085
TVQA (retrained)	**0.6338**	**0.6136**
Human baseline	0.8417	0.8625

5   Conclusion

In this work, we introduced Lifelog QA, a question answering dataset for lifelog data. The dataset consists of over 15,000 yes/no questions and multiple-choice questions. Through several baseline experiments, we assessed the suitability of the dataset for the task of lifelog QA. We note that there is still a significant gap between the proposed baselines and human performance on the QA accuracy, meaning that there is a significant research challenge to be addressed. Our findings suggest that a large proportion of the dataset involves the lifelogger's actions or interactions with other objects, therefore it is crucial to improve the standard action recognition mechanism. One possible approach is to sample video frames with a lower rate similarly to lifelog data and develop models based on this. Furthermore, we could develop respective sequences of features for other metadata instead of using the existing textual subtitle stream as in the TVQA model. Additionally, temporal reasoning is also essential to this task, especially for questions containing *before* or *after* actions. These three points can be integrated in future works to improve the semantic understanding of lifelog data.

The dataset is published at https://github.com/allie-tran/LLQA. We also include the annotated description with timestamps, which can be used to develop models for lifelog captioning tasks. By creating this dataset, we hope it can encourage more researchers to participate in and explore this research area further.

Acknowledgements. This work was conducted with the financial support of the Science Foundation Ireland under grant agreement 13/RC/2106_P2 and the Centre for Research Training in Digitally-Enhanced Reality (d-real) under Grant No.

18/CRT/6224. For the purpose of Open Access, the author has applied a CC BY public copyright licence to any Author Accepted Manuscript version arising from this submission.

References

1. Anderson, P., et al.: Bottom-up and top-down attention for image captioning and visual question answering, pp. 6077–6086 (2018)
2. Bao, H., et al.: Unilmv2: pseudo-masked language models for unified language model pre-training. In: International Conference on Machine Learning, pp. 642–652. PMLR (2020)
3. Bush, V., et al.: As we may think. The atlantic monthly **176**(1), 101–108 (1945)
4. Byrne, D., Kelliher, A., Jones, G.J.: Life editing: third-party perspectives on lifelog content. In: Proceedings of the SIGCHI Conference on Human Factors in Computing Systems, pp. 1501–1510 (2011)
5. Castro, S., Azab, M., Stroud, J., Noujaim, C., Wang, R., Deng, J., Mihalcea, R.: Lifeqa: a real-life dataset for video question answering. In: Proceedings of the 12th Language Resources and Evaluation Conference, pp. 4352–4358 (2020)
6. Doherty, A., Smeaton, A.: Automatically segmenting LifeLog data into events
7. Fan, C.: EgoVQA - an egocentric video question answering benchmark dataset. In: 2019 IEEE/CVF International Conference on Computer Vision Workshop (ICCVW), pp. 4359–4366 (Oct 2019), iSSN: 2473–9944
8. Fukui, A., Park, D.H., Yang, D., Rohrbach, A., Darrell, T., Rohrbach, M.: Multimodal Compact Bilinear Pooling for Visual Question Answering and Visual Grounding. arXiv:1606.01847 [cs], September 2016
9. Gao, Y., Bing, L., Li, P., King, I., Lyu, M.R.: Generating distractors for reading comprehension questions from real examinations. In: AAAI-19 AAAI Conference on Artificial Intelligence (2019)
10. Gemmell, J., Bell, C., Lueder, R.: Mylifebits: a personal database for everything. Commun. ACM **49**, 89–95 (2006)
11. Gurrin, C., et al.: Overview of the NTCIR-14 lifelog-3 task. In: Proceedings of the 14th NTCIR Conference, p. 13. NII (2019)
12. Gurrin, C., et al.: Introduction to the third annual lifelog search challenge (LSC'20). In: Proceedings of the 2020 International Conference on Multimedia Retrieval, ICMR 2020, pp. 584–585. Association for Computing Machinery
13. Gurrin, C., Smeaton, A.F., Doherty, A.R., et al.: Lifelogging: personal big data. Found. Trends Inform. Retrieval **8**(1), 1–125 (2014)
14. Hu, R., Andreas, J., Rohrbach, M., Darrell, T., Saenko, K.: Learning to reason: end-to-end module networks for visual question answering. arXiv:1704.05526 [cs], Septrmber 2017. arXiv: 1704.05526 version: 3
15. Jang, Y., Song, Y., Yu, Y., Kim, Y., Kim, G.: TGIF-QA: toward spatio-temporal reasoning in visual question answering
16. Jia, Y., et al.: Caffe: convolutional architecture for fast feature embedding
17. Lei, J., Yu, L., Bansal, M., Berg, T.L.: TVQA: localized, compositional video question answering. arXiv:1809.01696 [cs] (May 2019), arXiv: 1809.01696
18. Lei, J., Yu, L., Berg, T.L., Bansal, M.: TVQA+: spatio-temporal grounding for video question answering. arXiv:1904.11574 [cs], May 2020. arXiv: 1904.11574
19. Lokoč, J., et al.: Is the reign of interactive search eternal? findings from the video browser showdown 2020. ACM Trans. Multimedia Comput. Commun. Appl. **17**(3), July 2021

20. Nguyen, T.N., et al.: Lifeseeker 3.0: An interactive lifelog search engine for lsc'21. In: Proceedings of the 4th Annual on Lifelog Search Challenge, pp. 41–46 (2021)
21. Ninh, V.T., Le, T.K., Zhou, L., Piras, L., Riegler, M.: Overview of ImageCLE-Flifelog 2020: Lifelog moment retrieval and sport performance lifelog. In: CLEF (Working Notes), p. 17 (2020)
22. Pennington, J., Socher, R., Manning, C.D.: GloVe: global vectors for word representation. In: Empirical Methods in Natural Language Processing (EMNLP), pp. 1532–1543
23. Reddy, S., Chen, D., Manning, C.D.: CoQA: a conversational question answering challenge. Trans. Assoc. Comput. Linguist. **7**, 249–266 (2019)
24. Sellen, A.J., Whittaker, S.: Beyond total capture: a constructive critique of lifelogging 53(5), 70–77
25. Speer, R., Chin, J., Havasi, C.: Conceptnet 5.5: an open multilingual graph of general knowledge. In: Thirty-First AAAI Conference on Artificial Intelligence (2017)
26. Tran, L.D., Nguyen, M.D., Thanh Binh, N., Lee, H., Gurrin, C.: Myscéal 2.0: a revised experimental interactive lifelog retrieval system for lsc'21. In: Proceedings of the 4th Annual on Lifelog Search Challenge, pp. 11–16 (2021)
27. Trotman, A., Geva, S., Kamps, J.: Report on the sigir 2007 workshop on focused retrieval. In: ACM SIGIR Forum, vol. 41, pp. 97–103. ACM, New York (2007)
28. Xu, D., et al.: Video question answering via gradually refined attention over appearance and motion. In: Proceedings of the 25th ACM International Conference on Multimedia, MM 2017, pp. 1645–1653. Association for Computing Machinery, event-place: Mountain View, California, USA
29. Ye, Y., Zhao, Z., Li, Y., Chen, L., Xiao, J., Zhuang, Y.: Video question answering via attribute-augmented attention network learning. In: Proceedings of the 40th International ACM SIGIR Conference on Research and Development in Information Retrieval, pp. 829–832 (2017)

Learning

Category-Sensitive Incremental Learning for Image-Based 3D Shape Reconstruction

Yijie Zhong, Zhengxing Sun$^{(\boxtimes)}$, Shoutong Luo, Yunhan Sun, and Wei Zhang

State Key Laboratory for Novel Software Technology,
Nanjing University, Nanjing, China
szx@nju.edu.cn

Abstract. Recovering the three-dimensional shape of an object from a two-dimensional image is an important research topic in computer vision. Traditional methods use stereo vision or inter-image matching to obtain geometric information about the object, but they require more than one image as input and are more demanding. Recently, the CNN-based approach enables reconstruction using only a single image. However, they rely on limited categories of objects in large-scale datasets, which leads to limitations in their scope of application. In this paper, we propose an incremental 3D reconstruction method. When new interested categories are labeled and provided, we can finetune the network to meet new needs while retaining old knowledge. To achieve these requirements, we introduce the category-wise and instance-wise contrastive loss and the energy-based classification loss. They help the network distinguish between different categories, especially when faced with new ones, and the uniqueness and variability of the predictions generated for different instances. Extensive experiments demonstrate the soundness and feasibility of our approach. We hope our work can attract further research.

Keywords: 3D reconstruction · Lifelong learning · Contrastive learning

1 Introduction

Image-based 3D reconstruction is one of the most challenging problems of computer vision towards a higher level of visual understanding [9]. In real life, people have different needs to transform all kinds of 2D objects into three dimensions. And as time goes on, the number of interested objects grows. How to design a model and a convenient training strategy to adapt to changes in the input data (especially different categories) is an important issue.

The traditional methods solves the problem of shape reconstruction by using stereo or binocular vision. Shape-from-X-based methods recover sparse 3D point cloud and the camera pose of each image from motion, or infer the voxelized representation by fusing images [6] or foreground silhouettes [1]. Although they

© Springer Nature Switzerland AG 2022
B. Þór Jónsson et al. (Eds.): MMM 2022, LNCS 13141, pp. 231–244, 2022.
https://doi.org/10.1007/978-3-030-98358-1_19

Table 1. **Time** and **Size** represent for the training time and model size, respectively. An incremental 3D reconstruction method outperforms on training cost and storage.

Model	Previous model		Increment step		
	Time	Size	Strategy	Time	Size
Category-wise	$O(n)$	$O(1)$	*Retrain from scratch*	$O(n)$	$O(1)$
Category-agnostic	$O(n)$	$O(n)$	*Train a new model*	$O(1)$	$O(1)$
Category-incremental	$O(n)$	$O(1)$	*Update the old model*	$O(1)$	$O(1)$

can be applied to a wide variety of objects, the input requirements are stringent and the whole inference process is complex and time-consuming.

With the rapid development of deep learning, many works [7,10,31] can reconstruct the 3D shape with a single image input. This greatly increases the practicality of the 3D reconstruction algorithm. The current major approaches can be divided into two types. 1) **The category-sensitive approach.** The models obtained by this type of method can only handle a single category of reconstruction tasks. And it requires a complex training process on each category. When we hope to reconstruct a completely new category, these methods require an additional new model to be trained to serve the category. As the number of categories increases, the space occupied by all models will grow. 2) **The category-agnostic approach.** This type of methods combines all categories together for training, and the model does not need to know which category the input image belongs to in order to reconstruct it. They rely on large training datasets, which still have limited categories. Some of these methods can only be used for the categories that appear in the training stage. And while others claim to be usable for generic objects, they will still be constrained by the limited geometric topology types in the datasets. When coming new interested categories, the model needs to be retrained with all the data including old categories. Otherwise, the network would forget the knowledge from the previous training stage. The analysis on the different types of 3D reconstruction methods can be seen in Table 1. In order to meet new demands with a convenient training strategy and to ensure the stability of the algorithm, we introduce the **incremental 3D reconstruction method**. This type can be applied to both old and new categories by simply finetuning the original model with new data when faced with a new interested category.

To meet the above requirements, there are two problems that need to be solved: the network can distinguish between different categories of input, and can recover the 3D shape corresponding to object in the input image. Our key idea is to directly constraint the feature embedding. Contrastive learning has demonstrated its effectiveness for feature representation learning in various tasks including recognition and identification, recently. Thus, to address the first problem, we propose a category-wise contrastive loss. It establishes the category centers of the different categories in the feature embedding and constrains each sample in relation to them, so that the network could produce sufficient discrimination between categories. In addition, since the new category of subsequent inputs is unknown to the previous model, we also use a energy-based classification loss to identify unknown samples. To solve the second question, we further introduce a novel instance-wise contrastive loss. Only using the above loss, the network will map different instances of the same category to similar points in the feature embedding. This would not represent the diversity between objects. In this end, we build another contrastive loss among the instances in each category.

The key contributions of our work are:

- We introduce an incremental 3D reconstruction task, which meets the need of new interested categories.
- We develop a novel training strategy that can finetune the previous model only using the new data.
- To address the problems, we propose the category-wise contrastive loss, energy-based classification loss, and the instance-wise contrastive loss. Comprehensive experimental settings help us to measure the task and demonstrate the soundness of our method.

2 Related Work

2.1 Category-Wise 3D Reconstruction

The goal of 3D reconstruction is to recover the 3D shape of an object from the input image. For the category-wise methods, a separate model is trained for each object category for restoring the 3D structure of the instances in the category. We need extract the object mask first [15–18,30]. Tulsiani et al. [31] propose a framework for learning single-view shape and pose prediction without using direct supervision for either. However, each model can only learn the prior about a single category of shapes. Tulsiani et al. [32] also study the notion of consistency between a 3D shape and a 2D observation and propose a differentiable formulation which allows computing gradients of the 3D shape given an observation from an arbitrary view. Kato et al. [12] propose a method that can train a reconstructor using a single view or a few views for single-view 3D object reconstruction. It is limited by the fact that the collection of training images needs to be from the same category. Many works [10,19] have been devoted to improving the performance of object reconstruction or simplifying the difficulty for training. But, when we need to reconstruct multiple kinds of objects, they will be time and space consuming.

2.2 Category-Agnostic 3D Reconstruction

Unlike the above methods, there are also many other approaches that wish to learn the networks that target the reconstruction of generic objects. Fan et al. [7] firstly address the problem of 3D reconstruction from a single image, generating point cloud coordinates. Mandikal et al. [22] propose an architecture that first

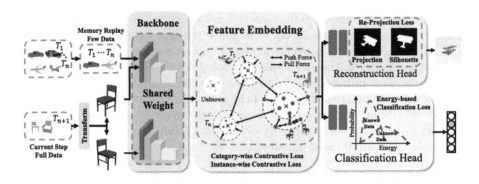

Fig. 1. An overview of the proposed network and the data preparation.

predicts a low-resolution point cloud, and then hierarchically increases the resolution by aggregating local and global point features to deform a grid. Mandikal et al. [21] propose 3D-LMNet to demonstrate the importance of learning a good prior over 3D point clouds for effectively transferring knowledge from the 3D to 2D domain. While such approaches all claim that they can handle diverse objects in life, in reality they can only accommodate shapes that share a similar topology and cannot really be used on completely new categories.

2.3   Incremental Learning

Computational systems operating in the real world are exposed to continuous streams of information and thus are required to learn the remember multiple tasks from dynamic data distributions [23]. The main issue of computational models regarding lifelong learning is that they are prone to catastrophic forgetting or catastrophic, i.e., training a model with new information interferes with previously learned knowledge [8]. Conceptually, these incremental learning approaches can be divided into methods that retrain the whole network while regularizing to prevent catastrophic forgetting with previously learned tasks, methods that selectively train the network and expand it if necessary to represent new tasks, and methods that model complementary learning systems for memory consolidation, e.g. by using memory replay to consolidate internal representations. Most incremental learning studies have been oriented towards image classification task [26]. In recent years there have also been a number of works extending incremental learning to more complex tasks like object detection [25] and semantic segmentation [3]. In this paper, to the best of our knowledge we present the first incremental learning approach for 3D reconstruction.

3   Incremental 3D Reconstruction

We first formalise the definition of the incremental 3D reconstruction in this section. At any time t, we consider the set of the shape of known categories as $\mathcal{K}^t = \{T_1, T_2, \cdots, T_n\}$. In order to realistically model the dynamics of real world, we also assume that their exists a set of the shape of unknown categories $\mathcal{U} = \{T_{n+1}, \cdots\}$, which may be encountered during inference. The known categories $\mathcal{K}^t$ are assumed to be labeled in the dataset $\mathcal{D}^t = \{X^t, Y^t\}$ where X and Y denote the input images and labels respectively. The input image set $X^t = \{I_1, \cdots, I_m\}$ consists of m training images, and associated labels for each image forms the label set $Y^t = \{Y_1, \cdots, Y_m\}$. Each Y_i can be formulated as the perspective of the camera, the corresponding shape in three-dimension, or other potential forms of supervision to help reconstruct the target object in the image.

The incremental 3D reconstruction settings considers a 3D reconstruction model $\mathcal{M}_n$ that is trained to reconstruct all the shape of previously encountered n categories. The model $\mathcal{M}_n$ is able to identify a test instance belonging to any of the known n categories. The unknown set of instances U^t can then be forwarded to a human user who can identify l new categories of interest and provide their training examples. The learner incrementally adds l new categories and updates itself to produce an updated model $\mathcal{M}_{n+l}$ without retraining from scratch on the whole dataset. The known categories set is also updated $\mathcal{K}^{t+1} = \mathcal{K}^t + \{T_{n+1}, \cdots, T_{n+l}\}$. This cycle continues over the life of the 3D shape reconstruction, where it adaptively updates itself with new knowledge.

3.1   Network Overview

The overall architecture of the proposed method is illustrated in Fig. 1. Considering at time t, the network has two parts of the input. The first part consists of few examples selected from the known categories $\{T_1, \cdots, T_n\}$ as *memory replay*, which will be described in Sect. 3.4. The second part contains all the images and their labels $\{X^t, Y^t\}$ of the categories, which are focused on this time, in the dataset. Each image of the new category will be extended into two different images of the same instance in it by data augmentations before fed into the network. This will be explained in Sect. 3.2.

Let us denote the input images as $\{I_i, i = 1 \cdots m | I_i \in \mathbb{R}^{H \times W \times 3}\}$ where H and W means the height and width of the image, respectively. Furthermore, we explicitly divide the network into a feature extractor $\mathcal{F}$ with parameters $\theta_{\mathcal{F}}$, a reconstruction head $\mathcal{R}$ with parameters $\theta_{\mathcal{R}}$ and a classification head $\mathcal{C}$ with parameters $\theta_{\mathcal{C}}$. As can be seen in Fig. 1, the features $f_i \in \mathbb{R}^d$ of the input are extracted by the feature extractor, where d is the feature dimension. And we consider that the features $(f \in F)$ are embedded into the feature embedding F. In this paper, we hope to learn a good embedding F that can receive new information about the current categories while retaining old knowledge about the known categories. Thus we introduce the contrastive learning and propose two novel contrastive loss to help build the embedding as described in Sect. 3.2.

Given the features f, the reconstruction head $\mathcal{R}$ outputs the 3D shape predictions $\{P_i\}_{i=1}^m$ of the input images and the classification head $\mathcal{C}$ projects the extracted features into a projection space $z_i \in \mathbb{R}^o$. Sect. 3.3 demonstrates that we propose an energy-based classification loss to balance the known and unknown data. More details of the network implementation can be found in Sect. 3.5.

3.2   Incremental Embedding Optimizing via Contrastive Learning

Class separation in the feature embedding would be an ideal characteristic for incremental 3D reconstruction. A natural way to enforce this would be to model it as a clustering optimizing problem, where instances of same class would be forced to remain close-by, while instances of dissimilar category would be pushed far apart. We introduce the contrastive learning to restraint the feature embedding. Different from the object classification problem which treats different instances to the same category, 3D reconstruction should preserve the unique shape and structure for every instance even if they belong to the same category. Thus in addition to the category-wise contrastive loss, we also propose loss for different instances in every category.

Category-Wise Contrastive Learning. As shown in Fig. 1, we except features that belong to the same category to be closer and features that belong to different categories to be further separated. For each known class $j \in \mathcal{K}^{t+1}$, we maintain a prototype vector w_j. Let $f_c \in \mathbb{R}^d$ be a feature vector that generated by the feature extractor $\mathcal{F}$ for an instance of category c. In order to allow the feature embedding to adapt to the incremental learning process, we add an *unknown* category ($c = 0$) to occupy a portion of the space and group all data falling outside of existing categories to *unknown*. We define the contrastive loss as follows in a triplet manner:

$$\mathcal{L}_{ccl} = \sum_{j=0}^{n} l(f_c, w_j),\tag{1}$$

where $l(f_c, w_j) = \begin{cases} \mathcal{D}(f_c, w_j), & j = c \\ max\{0, \Delta - \mathcal{D}(f_c, w_j)\}, & otherwise \end{cases}$ where $\mathcal{D}$ is any distance function and Δ defines how close a similar and dissimilar item can be. Minimizing this loss would ensure the desired class separation in the feature embedding.

The set of category prototypes $\mathcal{W} = \{w_0, \cdots, w_n\}$ can be generated from mean of feature vectors corresponding to each category. Maintaining each prototype vector is a crucial component of incremental 3D reconstruction. As the whole network is trained end-to-end, the category prototypes should also gradually evolve, as the constituent features change gradually. So we maintain a fixed-length queue v_j, per category for storing the corresponding features. A feature store $\mathcal{V} = \{v_0, \cdots, v_n\}$, stores the category-specific features in the corresponding queues. This is a scalable approach for keeping track of how the feature vectors evolve with training, as v_j can be denoted as $v_j \in \mathbb{R}^{Q \times d}$, where Q is the size of the queue.

After every iteration, we compute the category-wise contrastive loss and $\{v_j\}_{j=0}^{n}$ is updated by the extracted features f_i. After every S iterations, a set of new category prototypes $\mathcal{W}_{new}$ is computed by: $w_j = \frac{1}{Q}\sum_{k=1}^{Q} v_{j,k}, \quad j = 1\cdots n$, where $v_{j,k} \in \mathbb{R}^d$. Then the existing prototypes $\mathcal{W}$ are updated by weighting $\mathcal{W}$ and $\mathcal{W}_{new}$ with a momentum parameter η: $\mathcal{W} = \eta\mathcal{W} + (1-\eta)\mathcal{W}_{new}$. This allows the category prototypes to evolve gradually keeping track of previous context and the loss can be back-propagated to learn the network end-to-end.

Instance-Wise Contrastive Learning. The category-wise contrastive loss can increase the discrimination between samples from different categories. However for the classification task we only need to map different instances belonging to the same category to the same point in the feature embedding. The 3D reconstruction task is different and more demanding. The prediction of 3D shape must correspond to the object in the input image, i.e. the different instances have their own uniqueness. Thus we introduce an instance-wise contrastive loss to identify different instances. We pre-define a set of data augmentation as image transformation, including undergoes random color jittering, random horizontal flip, random gray scale conversion, and so on. For every input image I_i, it is firstly transformed to two different images I_i^1 and I_i^2. Although they are not identical in appearance, they still represent the same instance and the network should produce the same predictions for them. Naturally, the network needs to be separated from the other samples in its category. Formulally, the instance-wise contrastive loss can be defined as:

$$\mathcal{L}_{icl} = \sum_{i=1}^{m} -log\frac{exp(\text{sim}(I_i^1, I_i^2)/\tau)}{exp((\text{sim}(I_i^1, I_i^2) + \sum_{j=1}^{Q}\text{sim}(I_i^2, v_{c,j}))/\tau)}, \quad (2)$$

where $\text{sim}(\mathbf{e}_1, \mathbf{e}_2) = \mathbf{e}_1^T\mathbf{e}_2/\|\mathbf{e}_1\|\|\mathbf{e}_2\|$, τ is a temperature hyper-parameter per, and c means the category I_i belongs to. This loss encourages positive distances between instances of the same class.

3.3 Energy-Based Classification

Given the projected features $z_i \in Z$ from the classification head $\mathcal{C}$ and their corresponding category labels $l_i \in Y_i$, we seek to learn a function $E(Z,Y)$. Generally, other methods use the cross-entropy loss with a softmax operation. However, in this manner, the responses from the network will not fit into the categories that are currently unlabelled and those that will be labelled soon. Thus our formulation is based on the Energy based models that learn a function $E(\cdot)$ to estimates the compatibility between observed variables Z and possible set of output variables Y using a single output scalar i.e., $E(z) : \mathbb{R}^o \to \mathbb{R}$. The intrinsic capability of this to assign low energy values to in-distribution data and vice-versa motivates us to use an energy measure to characterize whether a sample is from an unknown category.

Specifically, we use the Helmholtz free energy formulation where energies for all values in Y are combined,

$$E(z) = -\alpha_e log \int_{l'} exp(-\frac{E(z,l')}{\alpha_e}), \qquad (3)$$

where α_e is the temperature parameter. There exists a simple relation between the network outputs after softmax layer and the Gibbs distribution of category specific energy values [20]. This can be formulated as,

$$p(l|z) = \frac{exp(\frac{z_i}{\alpha_e})}{\sum_{j=1}^{n} exp(\frac{z_j}{\alpha_e})} = \frac{exp(-\frac{E(z,l)}{\alpha_e})}{exp(-\frac{E(z_j)}{\alpha_e})}, \qquad (4)$$

where $p(l|z)$ is the probability density for a label l. Using this correspondence, we define free energy of our classification models in terms of their logits as follows:

$$\mathcal{L}_{energy} = E(z) = -\alpha_e log \sum_{j=1}^{n} exp(\frac{z_j}{\alpha_e}). \qquad (5)$$

Due to the separation that we enforce in the feature embedding with contrastive learning, we see a clear separation in the energy level of the known category and unknown data-points. We model the energy distribution of the known and unknown energy values $\xi_{kn}(z)$ and $\xi_{un}(z)$, with a set of shifted Weibull distributions. The learned distributions can be used to label a prediction as unknown if $\xi_{kn}(z) < \xi_{un}(z)$.

3.4 Reducing Forgetting

An important requisite for incremental 3D reconstruction is to be able to learn new categories, when the images and their labels of the unknown categories of the interest are provided. Importantly, the training data for the previous tasks will not be present at this stage since retraining from scratch is not a feasible solution. Training with only the new categories instances will lead to catastrophic forgetting [8] of the previous categories. We note that a number of involved approaches have been developed to alleviate such forgetting, including methods based on parameter regularization [13], memory replay [2], dynamically expanding networks [28], and meta-learning [11].

We build on the recent insights from [14] which compare the importance of example replay against other more complex solutions. Specifically, Prabhu *et al.* [27] retrospects the progress made by the complex continual learning methodologies and show that a greedy exemplar selection strategy for replay in incremental learning consistently outperforms the state-of-the-art methods by a large margin. The effectiveness of storing few examples and replaying has been found effective in the related few-shot object detection setting by Wang *et al.* [33]. These motivates us to use a relatively simple methodology for incremental 3D reconstruction to mitigate forgetting i.e., we randomly select a balanced set of examples and jointly train the model with current data at each incremental step. At each point, we ensure that a minimum of N_{mr} instances for each category $\{T_j\}_{j=1}^n$ are present in the memory replay set.

3.5   Implementation Details

Loss Functions. To supervise the reconstruction head, we apply a more convenient way and require the camera viewpoint as input. Obviously, our network can be adapted to an unsupervised manner or other forms of supervision. As given the 3D shape predictions $\{P_i\}_{i=1}^m$ and camera viewpoints $\{A_i\}_{i=1}^m$, we can acquire the projections B using a differentiable projection approach Φ: $B_i = \Phi(P_i, A_i)$. And the re-projection loss for reconstruction head can be calculated by the mean square error (MSE): $\mathcal{L}_{proj} = \frac{1}{m}\frac{1}{H}\frac{1}{W}\sum_{i=1}^m \sum^H \sum^W MSE(B_i, G_i)$, where G_i means the ground-truth silhouettes generated from input images. In summary, the total loss can be defined as: $\mathcal{L} = \lambda_1\mathcal{L}_{ccl}+\lambda_2\mathcal{L}_{icl}+\lambda_3\mathcal{L}_{ce}+\lambda_4\mathcal{L}_{energy}+\lambda_5\mathcal{L}_{proj}$. $\mathcal{L}_{ce}$ is the common used cross-entropy loss.

Hyper-Parameters. Since there are many adjustable parameters in our method, here we elaborate on the default settings. If not specially mentioned, the experiments are under this settings. In order to balance the different losses to obtain a stable training, we allocate different weights to the different terms. Specifically, we set $\lambda_1 = 1, \lambda_2 = 0.5, \lambda_3 = 2, \lambda_4 = 0.5$ and $\lambda_5 = 3$. The temperature τ of the instance-wise contrastive loss is 0.5 and the temperature α_e of the energy loss is set to 1. For the dimensions of the feature embedding F and projection space Z, we set $d = 512$ and $o = 128$. For the feature store $\mathcal{V}$, each category has $Q = 64$ memory feature samples. The update momentum parameter η is set to 0.999. The number of memory replay instances is set to $N_{mr} = 50$.

Training Details. We use the PyTorch framework to implement our method. We apply the ResNet18 as our feature extractor. We use the Adam optimizer with $\beta_1 = 0.5$ and $\beta_2 = 0.999$. The weight decay is set to 5e−4 for loss optimization. The learning rate is initialized to 1e−4. It drops to half at 20 epochs, and is set to 1e−5 after 40 epochs (overall 50 epochs for each learning task). During the training stage, the batch size is set to 32.

Table 2. Quantitative comparison on the ShapeNet. We first train the model on 6, 9, and 12 categories from the dataset. Then each model are trained on the other categories (show in blue background). Our method is able to perform favourably on all the settings. The smaller chamfer distance and larger IoU are better.

6+7 setting	Chamfer Distance / IoU													
	Airplane	Bench	Cabinet	Car	Chair	Lamp	Monitor	Rifle	Sofa	Speaker	Table	Telephone	Vessel	Mean
All 13	1.17	1.63	4.45	1.61	1.67	3.53	3.92	0.51	2.91	4.43	1.69	3.24	1.02	2.44
	0.513	0.376	0.591	0.701	0.444	0.425	0.422	0.596	0.479	0.574	0.436	0.595	0.485	0.51
First 6	0.85	1.89	4.92	1.12	2.07	4.62	9.59	8.02	10.36	9.74	7.23	10.77	9.34	6.19
	0.521	0.331	0.565	0.712	0.439	0.376	0.029	0.021	0.013	0.033	0.022	0.009	0.018	0.24
New 7	9.03	8.74	9.12	9.88	9.06	9.97	3.22	0.51	2.89	4.47	1.79	2.98	1.06	5.59
	0.021	0.023	0.018	0.017	0.022	0.018	0.433	0.582	0.475	0.568	0.424	0.603	0.479	0.28
Ours	2.02	1.84	4.87	1.78	1.98	3.71	3.34	0.52	3.05	4.51	2.08	3.16	1.14	**2.62**
	0.483	0.358	0.557	0.688	0.424	0.381	0.379	0.581	0.464	0.542	0.411	0.597	0.425	**0.48**

9+4 setting	Chamfer Distance / IoU													
	Airplane	Bench	Cabinet	Car	Chair	Lamp	Monitor	Rifle	Sofa	Speaker	Table	Telephone	Vessel	Mean
First 9	1.51	1.54	4.84	1.15	1.78	3.52	3.25	0.55	2.87	10.76	10.31	9.92	10.08	4.78
	0.509	0.368	0.582	0.711	0.443	0.428	0.434	0.579	0.483	0.008	0.009	0.012	0.011	0.35
New 4	9.12	8.69	0.26	10.24	9.02	10.05	9.76	8.82	9.37	4.36	1.87	2.77	1.03	6.57
	0.015	0.017	0.021	0.007	0.019	0.008	0.012	0.014	0.581	0.433	0.625	0.482	0.17
Ours	1.86	1.74	5.12	1.77	2.01	3.66	2.89	0.59	3.02	4.38	2.06	3.11	1.34	**2.58**
	0.504	0.359	0.549	0.664	0.416	0.398	0.426	0.553	0.467	0.573	0.414	0.597	0.427	**0.49**

12+1 setting	Chamfer Distance / IoU													
	Airplane	Bench	Cabinet	Car	Chair	Lamp	Monitor	Rifle	Sofa	Speaker	Table	Telephone	Vessel	Mean
First 12	1.75	1.71	5.02	1.93	1.92	3.68	2.01	0.53	3.02	4.41	2.28	2.79	11.83	3.30
	0.502	0.362	0.551	0.652	0.441	0.381	0.465	0.586	0.468	0.578	0.428	0.612	0.006	0.46
New 1	8.91	8.06	9.35	9.67	8.72	10.14	9.31	9.58	9.93	10.66	11.82	12.07	1.01	9.17
	0.018	0.022	0.014	0.012	0.023	0.009	0.013	0.014	0.011	0.008	0.008	0.006	0.466	0.05
Ours	1.98	1.69	4.96	1.87	1.93	3.62	2.45	0.61	2.96	4.39	2.03	2.98	1.31	**2.52**
	0.495	0.371	0.562	0.684	0.448	0.403	0.437	0.545	0.472	0.575	0.431	0.604	0.432	**0.50**

4 Experiments and Results

4.1 Experiment Settings

Datasets and Data Split. We train and test our method on the public dataset ShapeNet [4]. Each object in it is rendered from 24 viewpoints by [5]. We use a subset of them, which contains the commonly used 13 categories. The '$A + B$ setting' means a two step training strategy on two tasks with the 13 categories. During the first step, the network is trained for Task 1 which contains A categories. Then we finetune the network on the new B categories as Task 2. It is worth note that the models from Task 1 and Task 2 are both evaluated on all the $A + B$ categories.

Evaluation Metrics. We use the 3D intersection-over-union (IoU) and the chamfer distance (CD for evaluation. The IoU is computed in 32 voxel resolution, and the chamfer distance is computed on 2048 points which are randomly sampled from the surface. The chamfer distance has been shown to be well correlated with human judgment of shape similarity [29].

4.2 Incremental 3D Reconstruction Results

As shown in Table 2, we could find that our method has the ability to distinctly model unknown category shapes. The whole network performs favourably well

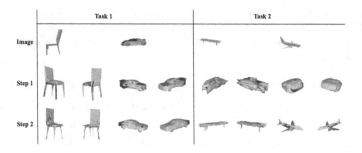

Fig. 2. Visualization comparison of the two reconstruction tasks between two steps.

on the incremental 3D reconstruction task against the baseline network. This is because, our method reduces the confusion of a specific shape being classified as other categories, which lets the reconstruction head incrementally learn the true structure of the shape in the real world. We use the standard protocol [24] used in the incremental learning domain to evaluate our method.

We also report qualitative results in Fig. 2. Step 1 means that the network is only trained on the data from Task 1. And we finetune our model with data from Task 2 in Step 2. We can notice in the first step that we cannot get a good prediction for the images in Task 2, because those categories are unknown at this point. When we train our network incrementally with new categories of data, our model is able to adapt to all categories in multiple tasks simultaneously.

4.3 Ablation Study

Ablation for Proposed Components. To study the contribution of each of the components in incremental 3D reconstruction, we design careful ablation experiments. The results can be seen in Table 3. We apply the $5 + 5$ setting, where Task 1 is introduced to the model with 5 categories and the model is trained on the next 5 categories in Task 2. Compared between Line 1 and Line 2, we could find that the category-wise contrastive loss guarantes variability between categories allows the model to identify shapes from different categories. From Line 4, it demonstrates that the use of instance-wise contrastive loss alone does not result in effective enhancement. Because even though the network distinguishes between instances, it cannot reconstruct them using the correct geometric prior. Line 5 shows that the network has better performance when it first identifies the category of objects and ensures the differences between instances. We can also see how energy-based classification loss can help us in Line 3 and Line 6.

Sensitivity on Memory Replay Size. Our balanced fine-tuning strategy for the new task requires storing example images with at least N_{mr} instances per category as memory replay. We vary N_{mr} while learning Task 2 and report the results in Table 3. We find that the fine-tuning step on the original model is very effective in improving the accuracy of previously known categories, even

Table 3. We carefully ablate each of the constituent component of category-wise contrastive loss (**CCL**), instanec-wise contrastive loss (**ICL**), energy-based classification loss (**Energy**), and memory replay (**MR**). To the number of examples in memory replay, we also show the sensitivity analysis.

ICL	CCL	Energy	CD↓	IoU↑	N_{mr}	Previous		Current		Both	
						CD↓	IoU↑	CD↓	IoU↑	CD↓	IoU↑
✗	✗	✗	9.34	0.02							
✓	✗	✗	3.09	0.36	0	7.46	0.03	2.37	0.43	4.91	0.23
✓	✗	✓	2.85	0.40	20	4.58	0.37	2.29	0.47	3.44	0.42
✗	✓	✗	3.56	0.31	50	2.79	0.51	2.41	0.46	2.61	0.48
✓	✓	✗	2.67	0.44	100	2.77	0.52	2.41	0.48	2.59	0.50
✓	✓	✓	2.61	0.48	250	2.74	0.55	2.43	0.49	2.58	0.52

just having minimum 20 instances per category. However, we find that increasing N_{mr} to large values does-not help too much. Hence by validation, we set N_{mr} to 50 in our all experiments, which is a sweet spot that balances performance on known and new coming categories.

5 Conclusion

The various 3D reconstruction methods has pushed the performance benchmarks on standard datasets by a large margin. To accommodate the need of reconstruction of new interested categories of object shape in life, we introduce the task of incremental 3D reconstruction, and the whole network gradually learns the new knowledge as the model gets exposed to images and their labels from new categories. For this purpose, we propose the category-wise contrastive loss to discriminate different categories and the instance-wise contrastive loss to increase the difference among instances belonging to the same category. We hope that our work will kindle further research along this important and open direction.

Acknowledgment. This work is supported by the National Natural Science Foundation of China No. 42075139, 42077232, 61272219; the National High Technology Research and Development Program of China No. 2007AA01Z334; the Science and technology program of Jiangsu Province No. BE2020082, BE2010072, BE2011058, BY2012190; the China Postdoctoral Science Foundation No. 2017M621700 and Innovation Fund of State Key Laboratory for Novel Software Technology No. ZZKT2018A09.

References

1. Broadhurst, A., Drummond, T., Cipolla, R.: A probabilistic framework for space carving. In: ICCV, pp. 388–393 (2001)
2. Castro, F.M., Marín-Jiménez, M.J., Guil, N., Schmid, C., Alahari, K.: End-to-end incremental learning. In: Ferrari, V., Hebert, M., Sminchisescu, C., Weiss, Y. (eds.) ECCV 2018. LNCS, vol. 11216, pp. 241–257. Springer, Cham (2018). https://doi.org/10.1007/978-3-030-01258-8_15

3. Cermelli, F., Mancini, M.: Modeling the background for incremental learning in semantic segmentation. In: CVPR, pp. 9230–9239. IEEE (2020)
4. Chang, A.X., Funkhouser, T.A., Guibas, L.J., Hanrahan, P., Huang, Q.: Shapenet: an information-rich 3d model repository. CoRR abs/1512.03012 (2015)
5. Choy, C.B., Xu, D., Gwak, J.Y., Chen, K., Savarese, S.: 3D-R2N2: a unified approach for single and multi-view 3D object reconstruction. In: Leibe, B., Matas, J., Sebe, N., Welling, M. (eds.) ECCV 2016. LNCS, vol. 9912, pp. 628–644. Springer, Cham (2016). https://doi.org/10.1007/978-3-319-46484-8_38
6. Curless, B., Levoy, M.: A volumetric method for building complex models from range images. In: SIGGRAPH, pp. 303–312. ACM (1996)
7. Fan, H., Su, H., Guibas, L.J.: A point set generation network for 3d object reconstruction from a single image. In: CVPR, pp. 2463–2471 (2017)
8. French, R.M.: Catastrophic interference in connectionist networks: Can it be predicted, can it be prevented? In: NIPS, pp. 1176–1177. Morgan Kaufmann (1993)
9. Han, X., Laga, H., Bennamoun, M.: Image-based 3d object reconstruction: state-of-the-art and trends in the deep learning era. IEEE TPAMI (2021)
10. Insafutdinov, E., Dosovitskiy, A.: Unsupervised learning of shape and pose with differentiable point clouds. In: NeurIPS, pp. 2807–2817 (2018)
11. Joseph, K.J., Balasubramanian, V.N.: Meta-consolidation for continual learning. In: NeurIPS (2020)
12. Kato, H., Harada, T.: Learning view priors for single-view 3d reconstruction. In: CVPR, pp. 9778–9787 (2019)
13. Kirkpatrick, J., Pascanu, R., Rabinowitz, N.C., Veness, J., Desjardins, G.: Overcoming catastrophic forgetting in neural networks. CoRR abs/1612.00796 (2016)
14. Knoblauch, J., Husain, H., Diethe, T.: Optimal continual learning has perfect memory and is np-hard. In: ICML (2020)
15. Li, B., Sun, Z., Guo, Y.: Supervae: superpixelwise variational autoencoder for salient object detection. In: AAAI (2019)
16. Li, B., Sun, Z., Tang, L., Hu, A.: Two-b-real net: two-branch network for real-time salient object detection. In: ICASSP (2019)
17. Li, B., Sun, Z., Tang, L., Sun, Y., Shi, J.: Detecting robust co-saliency with recurrent co-attention neural network. In: IJCAI (2019)
18. Li, B., Sun, Z., Xu, J., Wang, S., Yu, P.: Saliency based multiple object cosegmentation by ensemble MIML learning. MTAP (2020)
19. Lin, C., Kong, C., Lucey, S.: Learning efficient point cloud generation for dense 3d object reconstruction. In: AAAI, pp. 7114–7121. AAAI Press (2018)
20. Liu, W., Wang, X.: Energy-based out-of-distribution detection. In: NeurIPS (2020)
21. Mandikal, P., L., N.K.: 3d-lmnet: latent embedding matching for accurate and diverse 3d point cloud reconstruction from a single image. In: BMVC (2018)
22. Mandikal, P., Radhakrishnan, V.B.: Dense 3d point cloud reconstruction using a deep pyramid network. In: WACV, pp. 1052–1060. IEEE (2019)
23. Parisi, G.I., Kemker, R., Part, J.L., Kanan, C., Wermter, S.: Continual lifelong learning with neural networks: a review. Neural Netw. 113, 54–71 (2019)
24. Peng, C., Zhao, K., Lovell, B.C.: Faster ILOD: incremental learning for object detectors based on faster RCNN. Pattern Recognit. Lett. 140, 109–115 (2020)
25. Pérez-Rúa, J., Zhu, X., Hospedales, T.M., Xiang, T.: Incremental few-shot object detection. In: CVPR, pp. 13843–13852. IEEE (2020)
26. Pfülb, B., Gepperth, A.: A comprehensive, application-oriented study of catastrophic forgetting in DNNs. In: ICLR (Poster). OpenReview.net (2019)

27. Prabhu, A., Torr, P.H.S., Dokania, P.K.: GDumb: a simple approach that questions our progress in continual learning. In: Vedaldi, A., Bischof, H., Brox, T., Frahm, J.-M. (eds.) ECCV 2020. LNCS, vol. 12347, pp. 524–540. Springer, Cham (2020). https://doi.org/10.1007/978-3-030-58536-5_31

28. Rusu, A.A., Rabinowitz, N.C., Desjardins, G.: Progressive neural networks. CoRR abs/1606.04671 (2016)

29. Sun, X., et al.: Pix3d: dataset and methods for single-image 3d shape modeling. In: CVPR, pp. 2974–2983 (2018)

30. Tang, L., Li, B.: CLASS: cross-level attention and supervision for salient objects detection. In: ACCV (2020)

31. Tulsiani, S., Efros, A.A., Malik, J.: Multi-view consistency as supervisory signal for learning shape and pose prediction. In: CVPR, pp. 2897–2905 (2018)

32. Tulsiani, S., Zhou, T., Efros, A.A., Malik, J.: Multi-view supervision for single-view reconstruction via differentiable ray consistency. In: CVPR, pp. 209–217 (2017)

33. Wang, X., Huang, T.E., Gonzalez, J., Darrell, T., Yu, F.: Frustratingly simple few-shot object detection. In: ICML (2020)

AdaConfigure: Reinforcement Learning-Based Adaptive Configuration for Video Analytics Services

Zhaoliang He[1,4], Yuan Wang[2], Chen Tang[3], Zhi Wang[3(✉)], Wenwu Zhu[1], Chenyang Guo[5], and Zhibo Chen[5]

[1] Department of Computer Science and Technology, Tsinghua University, Beijing, China
hezl19@mails.tsinghua.edu.cn, wwzhu@tsinghua.edu.cn
[2] Tsinghua-Berkeley Shenzhen Institute, Tsinghua University, Shenzhen, China
wangyuan19@mails.tsinghua.edu.cn
[3] Tsinghua Shenzhen International Graduate School, Tsinghua University, Shenzhen, China
tc20@mails.tsinghua.edu.cn, wangzhi@sz.tsinghua.edu.cn
[4] Peng Cheng Laboratory, Shenzhen, China
[5] Tencent Youtu Lab, Shanghai, China
{chenyangguo,ruibobchen}@tencent.com

Abstract. The configuration in video analytics defines parameters including frame rate, image resolution, and model selection for video analytics pipeline, and thus determines the inference accuracy and resource consumption. Traditional solutions to select a configuration are either fixed (i.e., the same configuration is used all the time) or periodically adjusted using a brute-force search scheme (i.e., periodically trying different configurations and selecting the one with the best performance), and thus suffer either low inference accuracy or high computation cost to find a proper configuration timely. To this end, we propose a video analytical configuration adaptation framework called AdaConfigure that dynamically selects video configuration without resource-consuming exploration. First, we design a reinforcement learning-based framework in which an agent adaptively chooses the configuration according to the spatial and temporal features of the current video stream. In particular, we use a video segmentation strategy to capture the characteristics of the video stream with much-reduced computation cost: profiling uses only 0.2–2% computation resources as compared to a full video. Second, we design a reward function that considers both the inference accuracy and computation resource consumption so that the configuration achieves good accuracy and resource consumption trade-off. Our evaluation experiments on an object detection task show that our approach outperforms the baseline: it achieves 10–35% higher accuracy with a similar amount of computation resources or achieves similar accuracy with only 10–50% of the computation resources.

Keywords: Adaptive configuration · Reinforcement learning · Video analytics services

© Springer Nature Switzerland AG 2022
B. Þór Jónsson et al. (Eds.): MMM 2022, LNCS 13141, pp. 245–257, 2022.
https://doi.org/10.1007/978-3-030-98358-1_20

(a) Static configuration solution: fixed configuration for video analytics services.

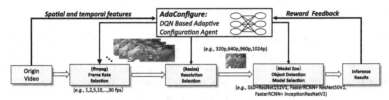

(b) AdaConfigure solution: reinforcement learning-based adaptive configuration framework.

Fig. 1. Comparing to the static solution, our solution can adaptively update the configuration strategy based on the reward feedback.

1   Introduction

With the increasing demand for continuous video analytics in public safety and transportation, more and more cameras are being deployed to various locations. The video analytics are based on classical computer vision techniques as well as deep convolutional neural networks. A video analytics application consists of a *pipeline* of several video processing modules, typically including a decoder, a selective sampling frame application, and a target detector. Such a pipeline always has multiple *knobs*, such as frame rate, resolution, detector model selection and so on. A combination of the knob values is video analytics *configuration*, and the configuration space grows *exponentially* with the number of knobs and their values [10].

Different configurations directly affect accuracy and resource consumption. The best configuration is the one with the lowest resource demand whose accuracy is over the desired threshold, which can optimize the *trade-off* between accuracy and energy consumption. The *best* configuration for video analysis services often varies in minutes or even seconds [10]. As shown in Fig. 1(a), if one uses an expensive static configuration (e.g., only profiles the processing pipeline *once* to choose the high frame rate and image resolution) can be precise, but it can also be a huge drain on resources. Similarly, specifying a cheap static configuration (e.g., low resolution and small model) will significantly reduce accuracy. The framework of our solution is shown in Fig. 1(b), and we tackle the following design challenges.

Choosing the Best Configuration is a Complicated Decision-Making Problem that is Challenging to be Solved by Rules. The best configuration for video analytics services changes significantly because the exact context of the videos varies over time and across space. For instance, tracking vehicles when traffic moves quickly requires a higher frame rate than when traffic moves slowly. Spatially, the characteristics of video content are different in different locations. For instance, cameras in downtown areas show more cars than the other cameras deployed in the suburbs. It is hard to make an exact rule to choose a configuration for the current context by profiling such complicated video characteristics.

Adaptive Configuration Would Cause a Huge Extra Overhead. The number of possible configurations grows exponentially, and thousands of configurations can be combined with just a few knobs [10]. So exhaustive periodically (e.g., profile once per 4 s) configuration to find the best configuration is a highly unrealistic approach because it causes a huge extra overhead, which may exceed the benefits of adaptive configurations. To significantly reduce the resource cost for adaptive configuration requires one solution that automatically chooses a configuration instead of manually trying to use various configurations, which is challenging to previous studies including [10, 20], since their approaches pay attention to reduce search space algorithm, and try various configurations in the search space to find the best configuration.

In our solution, AdaConfigure can adaptively and automatically select the best configuration according to intrusive dynamics of video context, thus solving this difficult optimal configuration decision problem in a low-cost way. To the best of our knowledge, we are the first to propose an adaptive video configuration solution to automatically choose a configuration instead of manually trying to use various configurations. The main contributions of this paper are summarized as follows.

We propose a Deep Q-learning Network-based [14] agent to adaptively pick the best video analytics configuration according to the characteristics of the video stream. For the agent's state, we extract the spatial and temporal features of the video context, so that the agent can adaptively update configuration over time and achieve a superior performance in the multi-camera situation.

We leverage agent's automatic selection characteristic and the video segmentation strategy to reduce profiling cost. In particular, we divide the video into T-second intervals as video chunks and use the agent to choose the best configuration for the first t seconds of the video chunk. It then sticks with the chosen configuration for the rest of the video chunk ($T - t$ seconds) to reduce profiling number. In the evaluation, the profiling cost is about 0.2–2% of the overall video analytics resource consumption.

We design a reward function that considers both inference accuracy and computation resources to assess each configuration's impact. Also, to meet different accuracy-demand services, we leverage the balance factor in the reward function to train different agents. Our evaluation experiments on an object detection task show that our approach outperforms the baseline: it achieves 10–35% higher accuracy with a similar amount of computation resources or achieves similar accuracy with only 10–50% of the computation resources.

2   Related Works

2.1   Static Configuration Optimization

Several previous papers have considered optimizing video analytics services by either adjusting the configuration knobs or training specialized NN models. VideoStorm [21] profiles thousands of video analytics queries on live video streams over large clusters, achieving resource-quality tradeoff with multidimensional configurations. VideoEdge [9] introduces *dominant demand* to identify the best tradeoff between multiple resources and accuracy. MCDNN [4] provides a heuristic scheduling algorithm to select model variants for deep stream processing under resource constraints. Focus [7] deconstructs video analytics into two phases (i.e., video ingests and video query), achieving an effective and flexible tradeoff of video analytics's latency and accuracy. These algorithms all profile and optimize video analytics only once at the beginning of the video. In their works, video is divided into pictures at a constant frame rate, and the work of video analysis is regarded as a fixed task either. In other words, they do not handle changes in video stream context. But the optimal configurations do change over time because of the complex and changing video stream context.

2.2   Dynamic Configuration Optimization

Some classic works study dynamic optimization problems. INFaaS [17] automatically selects a model, hardware architecture, and any compiler optimizations and makes scaling and resource allocation decisions. QuickAdapt [19] uses fuzzy rules to enable a Big Data Cyber Security Analytics (BDCA) system to adapt to the changes in security events data quickly. These algorithms do not apply to video configuration.

Some papers study how to dynamically optimize the configuration for video analytics when the video stream context changes. JCAB [20] jointly optimizes configuration adaption, and bandwidth allocation to address several critical challenges in edge-based video analytics systems, including edge capacity limitation, unknown network variation, intrusive dynamics of video context. Chameleon [10] leverages temporal and spatial correlation to decrease the cost of profiling, and exploits the knob independence to reduce the search space from exponential to linear.

Notice these reduce search space algorithms still trying various configurations to find the best configuration. Using different configurations lead to extra expensive profiling costs. To significantly reduce the cost of profiling, we propose an automatic and adaptive configuration algorithm. In particular, we leverage agent's automatic selection characteristic instead of manually trying to use various configurations, achieving an enormous reduction in profiling cost.

3   Reinforcement Learning-Based Adaptive Configuration

Figure 2 summarizes how Reinforcement Learning (RL) can be applied to the adaptive configuration. Briefly, it is a reinforcement learning-based system to

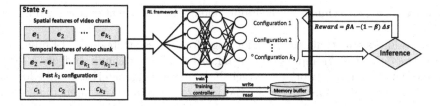

Fig. 2. Applying reinforcement learning to adaptive configuration.

train an agent to choose a proper configuration c for one video chunk for inference. We discuss the formulation, agent design, reinforcement learning-based framework, reward feedback in the following subsections. We provide experimental details of all the hyperparameters in Sect. 4.

3.1 Problem Formulation

To adaptively choose different configurations for a video stream, we divide the video into T-second intervals as video chunks, and profiles configurations for each video chunk. Without loss of generality, we denote the object detection service as $y_i = M(x_i)$ that provides a predicted result list y_i for each input video chunk x_i. It has a baseline output $y_{\text{ref}} = M(x_{\text{ref}})$ for each input video chunk $x \in X_{\text{ref}}$ using *reference configuration* (the most expensive configuration). We use this y_{ref} as the ground truth label. For each video chunk x_c that uses a configuration c, the output is $y_c = M(x_c)$. Therefore, we have an accuracy metric $\mathcal{A}_c$ by comparing y_{ref} and y_c. In general, we use the F1 score as the accuracy $\mathcal{A}$ and average GPU processing time per frame as the metric of resource consumption, detailed described in Sect. 4.2. We also denote the metric of resource consumption as $\hat{s}_{ic}$ that for an input video chunk x_i and a given configuration c. For a reference configuration c_{ref}, the reference resource consumption is $\hat{s}_{\text{ref}}$.

Initially, the agent tries different configurations c to obtain inference results y_c from input video chunk x. To obtain object detection results $\{y_{\text{ref}}, y_c\}$, the agent uses the choosen configuration c and the reference configuration x_{ref}. Comparing the two object detection results $\{y_{\text{ref}}, y_c\}$ and two resource consumptions $\{\hat{s}_{\text{ref}}, \hat{s}_c\}$, the agent computes the resource consumption ratio $\Delta s = \frac{\hat{s}_c}{\hat{s}_{\text{ref}}}$ and accuracy metric $\mathcal{A}_c$.

3.2 RL Agent Design and Video Characteristic Extraction

The RL agent is expected to give a proper configuration c for minimizing the resource consumption $\hat{s}_c$ while keeping the accuracy $\mathcal{A}$. For the RL agent, the input features are continuous numerical vectors, and the expected output is discrete video configuration c. Therefore we can use the Deep Q-learning Network [14] as the RL agent. But the naive Deep Q-learning Network can not work well in this task because the state space of reinforcement learning is too large if we directly treat video chunks as the input, making the RL agent extremely difficult to converge.

To address this challenges, we leverage frame loss strategies of FFmpeg [2] to extract the top k_1 representative images from each chunk and use a pretrained small neural network to extract the structural characteristics embeddings $\{e_1, e_2, ..., e_{k_1}\}$ of the images as spatial features to reduce the input dimension and accelerate the training procedure. This is a commonly used strategy in training a deep neural network [3,15]. In this work, we use the early convolution layers of MobileNetV2 [6] as the image feature extractor $\mathcal{E}(\cdot)$ for its efficiency in image recognition. To extract the temporal features of the video chunk, we obtain $\{\hat{e}_1, \hat{e}_2, ..., \hat{e}_{k_1-1}\}$ by each embedding subtracting previous embedding. Besides, we record the last k_2 configurations $\{c_1, c_2, ..., c_{k_2}\}$. To solve that vectors of different lengths are not conducive to input to the neural network, we use the fully connected layer to transform the spatial embedding $\{e_1, e_2, ..., e_{k_1}\}$, temporal embedding $\{\hat{e}_1, \hat{e}_2, ..., \hat{e}_{k_1-1}\}$, and recent configuration $\{c_1, c_2, ..., c_{k_2}\}$ to the fixed length vector, similar to the work [13]. We formulate the fixed length vector s as *states* and the configuration c as discrete *actions*.

We update the RL agent's policy by changing the parameters of the Deep Q-learning Network ϕ while fixing the feature extractor $\mathcal{E}$.

3.3   Reinforcement Learning-Based Framework

In our system, we define k_3 discrete actions to indicate k_3 configuration, and the specific configurations are provided in Sect. 4.1. We denote the *action-value function* as $Q(s, c; \theta)$ and the optimal configuration at time t as $c_t = \text{argmax}_c Q(s, c; \theta)$ where θ indicates the parameters of the Deep Q-learning Network ϕ. In such reinforcement learning formulation, the training phase is to minimize the loss function $L_i(\theta_i) = \mathbb{E}_{s, c \sim \rho(\cdot)} \left[(y_i - Q(s, c; \theta_i))^2 \right]$ that changes at each iteration i where target $y_i = \mathbb{E}_{s' \sim \{\mathcal{X}, M\}} \left[r + \gamma \max_{c'} Q(s', c'; \theta_{i-1}) \mid s, c \right]$. Especially, r is the reward feedback, and $\rho(s, c)$ is a probability distribution over state s and the configuration c [14]. When minimizing the distance of *action-value function*'s output $Q(\cdot)$ and target y_i, the *action-value function* $Q(\cdot)$ outputs a more accurate estimation of an action.

In the training phase, the RL agent firstly uses a ϵ-greedy method to take some random trials to observe the environment's reaction and decreases the randomness when training afterward. In iteration t, we input state s_t to neural network ϕ. The RL agent ϕ generates a specific configuration c_t. The framework processes the video chunk x_t using configuration c_t to infer object detection services and obtains reward r_t. Then the framework obtains the next video chunk x_{t+1} and generates the next state s_{t+1}. The framework stores transition (s_t, c_t, r_t, s_{t+1}) in a memory buffer $\mathcal{D}$. All transitions are saved into a memory buffer $\mathcal{D}$, and the agent learns to optimize its *action* by minimizing the loss function L on a mini-batch from $\mathcal{D}$. The training procedure would converge when the agent's randomness keeps decaying. Finally, the agent's actions are based on its historical "optimal" experiences. The training procedure is presented in Algorithm 1.

Algorithm 1. Training RL agent ϕ

1: Initialize action-value function Q with random weights θ, replay memory buffer $\mathcal{D}$
   and state s_1
2: **for** $t \in 1, 2, \cdots, K$ **do**
3:    **1) Exploration**
4:    With probability ϵ:
5:       $c_t \leftarrow$ a random valid value
6:    Otherwise:
7:       $c_t \leftarrow \text{argmax}_c Q(s_t, c; \theta)$
8:    **2) Reward calcuation**
9:    Process video chunk x_t using configuration c_t for inference
10:   Obtain $(\boldsymbol{y}_{\text{ref}}, \boldsymbol{y}_c)$ from the object detection service
11:   Compute reward $r \leftarrow R(\Delta s, \mathcal{A}_c)$ according to 3.4 Reward Feedback
12:   **3) Gradient descent**
13:   Obtain next video chunk x_{t+1}
14:   Generate next state s_{t+1}
15:   $\mathcal{D} \leftarrow \mathcal{D} \bigcup \{(s_t, c_t, r_t, s_{t+1}\}$
16:   Sample a randomly mini-batch of transitions (s_j, c_j, r_j, s_{j+1}) from memory buffer
      $\mathcal{D}$
17:   $y_j \leftarrow r_j + \gamma \max_{c'} Q(s_{j+1}, c'; \theta)$
18:   Perform a gradient descent step on $\left(y_j - Q(s_j, c_j; \theta)\right)^2$ according to [14]
19: **end for**

3.4 Reward Feedback

In our solution, the agent is trained by the reward feedback. In the above formulation, we define resource consumption rate $\Delta s = \frac{\hat{s}_c}{\hat{s}_{\text{ref}}}$ and accuracy metric $\mathcal{A}_c$ at configuration c. Basically, we want the agent to choose a proper configuration for minimizing the resource consumption while remaining acceptable accuracy. Therefore the overall reward r should be positively correlated with the accuracy $\mathcal{A}$ while negatively with the resource consumption ratio Δs. We introduce a balance factor β to form a linear combination $r = \beta \mathcal{A} - (1 - \beta)\Delta s$ as the *reward function* $R(\Delta s, \mathcal{A})$ so that the configuration achieves good accuracy and resource consumption trade-off.

4 Evaluation

4.1 Experiment Setup

We carry out real-world experiments on the object detection task (basic computer vision services) to verify our solution's performance. We use a desktop PC (Intel Xeon E5-2650 v4 CPU) with four NVIDIA 1080ti graphic card as the server infrastructure, and simulate the environment [8] with three pretrained object detection models in Tensorflow, which are SSD [12] + ResNet152V1 [5], FasterRCNN [16] + ResNet50V1, FasterRCNN + InceptionResNetV2 [18]. For each model, two kinds of image resolutions, which is 1024×1024 and 640×640, can be chosen. In our experiment, we set the choices space of fps as {1, 2, 5, 10, 15, 20, 25, 30}. We use FFmpeg to switch the frame rate and image resolution, which decide which frames and in what size they should be fed to the object detection model. The configuration space comprises all possible combinations of values of these knobs, so the environment has 48 configurations in total.

4.2 Datasets and Metric

Most public datasets cannot fully satisfy all configuration choices, they provide only a fraction of the requirements for configuration. For example, some can only guarantee 30 frames but cannot guarantee 1024p resolution. In contrast, others can ensure resolution but cannot provide a sufficient frame rate.

In recent years, most of traffic cameras can provide enough resolution and frame rate, so we try to search keywords (e.g., "highway traffic") on Youtube and download videos that meet the resolution and frame rate requirements. We select three datasets: M6, Duke, and Multi-Camera Dataset. M6 is taken from a traffic camera on the longest motorway in Britain. Duke is a video from a fixed camera placed at an intersection, and the traffic flow in the video increases or decreases periodically with the traffic light change. Since the first two datasets were sourced from a fixed camera, in order to ensure that AdaConfigure performs better in multi-camera inference, we combine three videos collected from different locations into one video dataset, Multi-Camera Dataset. The exact content of this dataset varies significantly over time and across space.

For metric, we use the F1 score as the accuracy and average GPU processing time per frame as the resource consumption because GPU is the dominant resource for most video processing workloads [10]. F1 score is the harmonic mean of precision and recall, where the precision is true positives divided by the detected objects, and the recall is true positives divided by the ground truth objects. We identify true positives using two conditions, a bounding box-based condition (only check the classified label) and a label-based condition (check the classified label and spatial overlap [1]), consistent with prior work [10,11]. Both accuracy metrics are useful in real video analytics services and used in our experiments. Besides, to compute the accuracy of a frame that is not sampled by exact configuration, we use the location of objects from the previous sampled frame.

4.3 Experiment Parameters

In the training procedure, we build up to eight independently identical environments for each data set to speed up the training and decrease the data's dependency. For each dataset, we train the agent 5 epochs and 600 steps (5 min) per epoch. Some important hyperparameters in our experiments are given in Table 1.

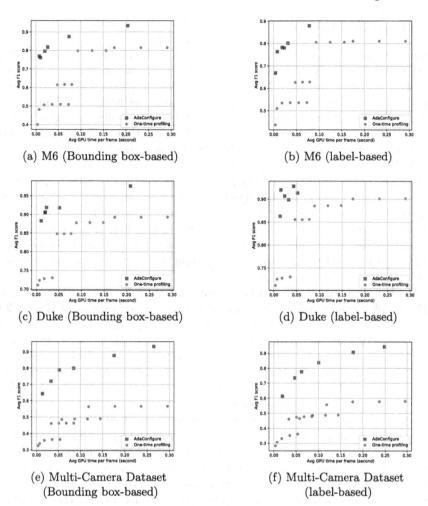

(a) M6 (Bounding box-based)

(b) M6 (label-based)

(c) Duke (Bounding box-based)

(d) Duke (label-based)

(e) Multi-Camera Dataset
(Bounding box-based)

(f) Multi-Camera Dataset
(label-based)

Fig. 3. AdaConfigure (blue) consistently outperforms the baseline of one-time profiling (magenta) across different metrics on different datasets. Each dot represents the results of running each solution. (Color figure online)

Table 1. Experiment parameters.

Notation	Value	Notation	Value
ϵ	0.8	k_1	3
γ	0.9	k_2	3
β	0.2,0.3,...,0.7	$T(train)$	1
t	1	$T(inference)$	4

4.4   Experiment Results

Figure 3 shows that AdaConfigure consistently outperforms the static configuration baseline (only profiling configurations once) along with resource consumption and two accuracy metrics on different datasets. Each magenta dot represents one static configuration solution (one-time profiling). These static configuration solutions include some fixed expensive configurations and fixed cheap configurations. These static configuration solutions include some expensive configurations, such as {FasterRCNN+InceptionResNetV2, 640p, 30fps}, {FasterRCNN+ResNet50V1, 1024p, 25fps}, and some cheap configurations, such as {SSD+ResNet152V1, 640p, 1fps}, {SSD+ResNet152V1, 640p, 5fps}. Each blue dot represents one AdaConfigure configuration solution, which is dependent on the balance factor β in reward function, presented in Sect. 3.4. The detailed discussion about different AdaConfigure solutions is in Sect. 4.4. Note that AdaConfigure's resource consumption includes both running the best configuration to get inference results and profiling cost of adaptive configuration, which is detailed discussed in Sect. 4.4.

As shown in Fig. 3(a)(b), AdaConfigure achieves 10–30% higher accuracy with a similar amount of resources, or achieves a similar accuracy with only 20–50% of the resources on the M6 dataset. As shown in Fig. 3(c)(d), AdaConfigure achieves 10–20% higher accuracy with a similar amount of resources, or achieves a similar accuracy with only 10–20% of the resources on a Duke dataset. As shown in Fig. 3(e)(f), AdaConfigure achieves 25–35% higher accuracy with a similar amount of resources, or achieves higher accuracy with only 15–25% of the resources on Multi-Camera Dataset.

In a word, AdaConfigure achieves a high accuracy of 10–35% with the same amount of computing resources, which benefits from the adaptive selection of relatively expensive configuration when the video content is complex (e.g., traffic congestion, high-speed vehicles). Also, AdaConfigure achieves a 50–90% reduction in resource consumption while achieving almost the same precision as the baseline, which benefits from the adaptive selection of relatively cheap configurations when the video content is simple (e.g., low-traffic flow).

4.4.1 Low Profiling Cost of Adaptive Configuration

In our solution, the video chunk is passed to the AdaConfigure firstly to estimate the configuration, bringing profiling cost (extra resource consumption) to the whole system. The profiling cost, including the resource of extract k_1 embeddings and the cost of agent choosing actions. We test the average time on 30 h video of Multi-Camera Dataset, and conclude that the average time of extract one embedding is 0.02 s, and the average time of agent choosing action is 0.0006 s, which can be ignored. We compute the ratio by dividing profiling time into total inference time as metric of profiling cost. The profiling cost is about 0.2–2% of the overall video analytics resource consumption. The concrete ratio depends on the concrete AdaConfigure configuration solutions, such as the solutions listed in Table 2. For instance, when using the solution of $\beta = 0.7$, the profiling cost

Table 2. Resource consumption and bounding box-based F1 for different AdaConfigure solutions.

Balance factor β	Avg GPU time per frame (second)	Avg F1 score
0.2	0.01384	0.64307
0.3	0.03314	0.72008
0.4	0.05203	0.79096
0.5	0.08479	0.80056
0.6	0.17570	0.87731
0.7	0.26511	0.93262

is only 0.2% of overall resource consumption on this solution; when using the solution of $\beta = 0.2$, the profiling cost is 1.5%.

4.4.2 Different AdaConfigure Solutions to Meet Different Services

In the training phase, when using different balance factors β in the reward function, we would obtain different agents (different adaptive configuration strategies). In general, if the β is bigger, we indicate that the accuracy is more important relatively, and the agent would choose a more expensive configuration. In our experiment, we set β is 0.2,0.3,...,0.7, and the results of different AdaConfigure solutions on Multi-Camera Dataset are listed in Table 2.

Table 2 shows that when the β increases, the resource consumption and the accuracy of the corresponding solution would increase, indicating the AdaConfigure solutions of big β would choose the more expensive configuration for inference. We can leverage this to train proper configuration strategy for different service demands, for example, using big β for high-accuracy demand services and using small β for low-accuracy demand services.

5   Conclusion

This paper proposes a reinforcement learning-based adaptive video analytics configuration framework, AdaConfigure. Our solution can adapt the best configuration to intrusive dynamics of video contexts, meaning that it can adaptively choose the proper configuration for the current video chunk according to the spatial and temporal features of video contexts. Therefore, our solution can adaptively update configuration strategy over time, and it adaptive to different location-camera inferences and various accuracy-demand services. In the evaluation, AdaConfigure achieves 10–35% higher accuracy with a similar amount of resources or achieves similar accuracy with only 50–90% of the resources. AdaConfigure proves to be more efficient than static solutions and only creates an overhead of 0.2–2% to the overall video analytics services.

Acknowledgements. This work is supported in part by NSFC (Grant No. 61872215), and Shenzhen Science and Technology Program (Grant No. RCYX202007 14114523079). We would like to thank Tencent for sponsoring the research.

References

1. Everingham, M., Van Gool, L., Williams, C.K., Winn, J., Zisserman, A.: The pascal visual object classes (voc) challenge. Int. J. Comput. Vision **88**(2), 303–338 (2010)
2. FFmpeg: Ffmpeg (2000–2018). http://ffmpeg.org/
3. Ge, W., Yu, Y.: Borrowing treasures from the wealthy: deep transfer learning through selective joint fine-tuning. In: CVPR, pp. 1086–1095 (2017)
4. Han, S., Shen, H., Philipose, M., Agarwal, S., Wolman, A., Krishnamurthy, A.: Mcdnn: an approximation-based execution framework for deep stream processing under resource constraints. In: MobiSys, pp. 123–136 (2016)
5. He, K., Zhang, X., Ren, S., Sun, J.: Deep residual learning for image recognition. In: CVPR, pp. 770–778 (2016)
6. Howard, A.G., et al.: Mobilenets: efficient convolutional neural networks for mobile vision applications. arXiv preprint arXiv:1704.04861 (2017)
7. Hsieh, K., et al.: Focus: querying large video datasets with low latency and low cost. In: OSDI, pp. 269–286 (2018)
8. Huang, J., et al.: Speed/accuracy trade-offs for modern convolutional object detectors. In: CVPR, pp. 7310–7311 (2017)
9. Hung, C.C., et al.: Videoedge: Processing camera streams using hierarchical clusters. In: SEC, pp. 115–131. IEEE (2018)
10. Jiang, J., Ananthanarayanan, G., Bodik, P., Sen, S., Stoica, I.: Chameleon: scalable adaptation of video analytics. In: SIGCOMM, pp. 253–266 (2018)
11. Kang, D., Emmons, J., Abuzaid, F., Bailis, P., Zaharia, M.: Noscope: optimizing neural network queries over video at scale. arXiv preprint arXiv:1703.02529 (2017)
12. Liu, W., et al.: SSD: single shot MultiBox detector. In: Leibe, B., Matas, J., Sebe, N., Welling, M. (eds.) ECCV 2016. LNCS, vol. 9905, pp. 21–37. Springer, Cham (2016). https://doi.org/10.1007/978-3-319-46448-0_2
13. Mao, H., Netravali, R., Alizadeh, M.: Neural adaptive video streaming with pensieve. In: SIGCOMM, pp. 197–210 (2017)
14. Mnih, V., et al.: Playing atari with deep reinforcement learning. arXiv preprint arXiv:1312.5602 (2013)
15. Radford, A., Narasimhan, K., Salimans, T., Sutskever, I.: Improving language understanding by generative pre-training (2018). https://s3-us-west-2.amazonaws.com/openai-assets/research-covers/languageunsupervised/languageunderstandingpaper.pdf
16. Ren, S., He, K., Girshick, R., Sun, J.: Faster r-cnn: towards real-time object detection with region proposal networks. In: NIPS, pp. 91–99 (2015)
17. Romero, F., Li, Q., Yadwadkar, N.J., Kozyrakis, C.: Infaas: a model-less inference serving system. arXiv preprint arXiv:1905.13348 (2019)
18. Szegedy, C., Ioffe, S., Vanhoucke, V., Alemi, A.: Inception-v4, inception-resnet and the impact of residual connections on learning. arXiv preprint arXiv:1602.07261 (2016)
19. Ullah, F., Babar, M.A.: Quickadapt: scalable adaptation for big data cyber security analytics. In: ICECCS, pp. 81–86. IEEE (2019)

20. Wang, C., Zhang, S., Chen, Y., Qian, Z., Wu, J., Xiao, M.: Joint configuration adaptation and bandwidth allocation for edge-based real-time video analytics. In: INFOCOM, pp. 1–10 (2020)
21. Zhang, H., Ananthanarayanan, G., Bodik, P., Philipose, M., Bahl, P., Freedman, M.J.: Live video analytics at scale with approximation and delay-tolerance. In: NSDI, pp. 377–392 (2017)

Mining Minority-Class Examples
with Uncertainty Estimates

Gursimran Singh[1]([✉]), Lingyang Chu[2], Lanjun Wang[3], Jian Pei[4], Qi Tian[5],
and Yong Zhang[1]

[1] Huawei Technologies Canada, Burnaby, Canada
{gursimran.singh1,yong.zhang3}@huawei.com
[2] McMaster University, Hamilton, Canada
chul9@mcmaster.ca
[3] Tianjin University, Tianjin, China
[4] Simon Fraser University, Burnaby, Canada
jpei@cs.sfu.ca
[5] Huawei Technologies China, Shenzhen, China
tian.qi1@huawei.com

Abstract. In the real world, the frequency of occurrence of objects is naturally skewed forming long-tail class distributions, which results in poor performance on the statistically rare classes. A promising solution is to mine tail-class examples to balance the training dataset. However, mining tail-class examples is a very challenging task. For instance, most of the otherwise successful uncertainty-based mining approaches struggle due to distortion of class probabilities resulting from skewness in data. In this work, we propose an effective, yet simple, approach to overcome these challenges. Our framework enhances the subdued tail-class activations and, thereafter, uses a one-class data-centric approach to effectively identify tail-class examples. We carry out an exhaustive evaluation of our framework on three datasets spanning over two computer vision tasks. Substantial improvements in the minority-class mining and fine-tuned model's task performance strongly corroborate the value of our method.

Keywords: Minority-class example mining · Class-imbalanced datasets

1 Introduction

A majority of powerful machine learning algorithms are trained in a supervised fashion [10,18,24]. Hence, the quality of the model depends heavily on the quality of data. However, in many real-life applications, the distribution of occurrence of examples is heavily skewed, forming a long tail. This has a detrimental effect on training machine learning models and results in sub-optimal performance on underrepresented classes, which is often critical [4,13]. For instance, in medical

---

G. Singh and L. Chu—Contribute equally in this work.

© Springer Nature Switzerland AG 2022
B. Þór Jónsson et al. (Eds.): MMM 2022, LNCS 13141, pp. 258–271, 2022.
https://doi.org/10.1007/978-3-030-98358-1_21

diagnosis the inherent data distribution contains a majority of examples from a *common-disease* (head-class) and only a minority from a *rare-disease* (tail-class, a.k.a. minority-class). Similarly, this problem naturally occurs in many domains like fraud detection, spam detection, autograding systems, and is so pervasive that even carefully crafted research datasets like ImageNet, Google Landmarks, and MS-CELEBS-1M are all class-imbalanced [1,10,14,25].

In order to balance these datasets, we need to augment them by procuring additional labeled examples from the tail classes. However, any pool of data sampled uniformly at random is similarly skewed and contains few desired tail-class examples [2]. Consequently, human workers will spend most of their time labeling useless majority-class examples, wasting time and resources. To address these disproportions, we must design intelligent algorithms to actively mine minority-class examples. Such an algorithm has immense practical value in balancing skewed datasets by procuring statistically rare labeled examples in a cost-effective manner. As a result, we can train effective machine learning models in all the above-mentioned cases. *How can we mine minority-class examples from unlabeled datasets automatically?* Given a biased model trained with a pool of skewed data, this work addresses the problem of mining (or active sampling) of minority-class examples from unlabeled data.

Despite being extremely useful, minority-class mining, unfortunately, is a very challenging task. The difficulty is three-fold. First, although tail-class examples are semantically distinct from head-class examples, it is not easy to separate them in high-dimensional input spaces. Often, examples lie on complex manifolds that are not amenable to unsupervised density-based modeling [26]. Second, even in the output space, the bias in the trained model due to class imbalance subdues tail-class activations, resulting in distortion of the model's uncertainty estimates. This effect is aggravated in deep neural networks where due to pervasive overfitting of the final softmax layer [12,20], head-class activations completely eclipse tail-class activations. Hence, the otherwise successful informative-sample mining methods in active learning literature, which rely on the model's uncertainties in the output space, are well-known to perform poorly in mining tail-class examples [1–3,6]. Third, many of these approaches, like max score [8], and entropy [23], aggregate the information-rich class-probability distribution into a scalar, rendering it unable to model relationships among individual values. These metrics are fixed formulae (like $-\sum_{k}^{C} p_k^i \log(p_k^i)$ for entropy), having no parameters, and unlike a learning process, are unable to adapt to identifying and discriminating patterns in a particular dataset. However, in reality, head-class and tail-class examples exhibit myriad characteristic patterns in the model's output space, which needs to be *learned* using an expressive modeling technique.

In this paper, we address these challenges and propose a simple, yet effective, technique to mine minority-class examples. There are two key ideas of our approach. First, we propose to use pen-ultimate layer activations of the trained model, which, unlike the input or output space, are not afflicted by the high-dimensionality, miscalibration, or overfitting problem. We use these activations to obtain re-calibrated head-class and tail-class probabilities, which retain their distinctive patterns and are more amenable to the learning process. Second, we formulate the minority-class mining problem as a one-class learning algorithm. The resultant data-centric method, unlike a fixed formula, helps to *learn* characteristic activation patterns corresponding to majorly present head-class examples and flags aberrant tail-class examples as anomalies. As shown in the experiments section, both of these simple ideas lead to a *substantial improvement* in the minority-class mining performance.

Contributions: Our contributions are three-fold. **1)** We identified the key challenges and presented a novel framework to effectively mine minority-class examples using the uncertainties in the model's output probabilities. This is in contrast to the previous line of thought that uncertainty-based approaches alone are not effective in mining minority-class examples [1,2,6]. **2)** Our approach can be easily extended to many machine learning tasks since it only relies on the trained model's output activations. We demonstrate the effectiveness of the proposed method on two different computer vision tasks, namely classification, and object detection. In doing so, we device a methodology to extend tail-class mining to object detection, which, to the best of our knowledge, is the first attempt in this direction. **3)** We devise a new experimental setup to analyze the minority-class mining performance based on the individual class's skewness. We show that our approach has a desirable property of mining a greater number of direly-needed examples from the most skewed classes.

2   Related Works

Imbalanced data is a major problem in machine learning [13,16,28]. Among many possible approaches, a promising direction is to mine tail-class examples with an aim to balance the dataset. In this direction, although uncertainty sampling [8,9,23] is an effective method for mining generic informative examples [8,22,23], they are known to be ineffective in mining minority-class examples [1–3,6]. This has been attributed to the fact that uncertainty sampling, being biased on previously seen examples, ignores regions that are underrepresented in the initially labeled dataset [14]. Several approaches [7,11,15,27] propose to account for the skewness by using prior information about class imbalance to boost query scores corresponding to tail classes. For instance, [15] proposes to weight Shannon's entropy by the inverse of class-proportion ratios in the training dataset. Similarly, [7] proposes to boost the vote score corresponding to tail classes of a query-by-committee strategy. However, boosting tail-class activations does not help in high-skew environments (especially in overfit neural networks) where tail-class probabilities are very weak or non-existent.

As a workaround, recent approaches [5,14] propose augmenting uncertainty sampling with an exploration/geometry/redundancy criteria in the input space. The key insight is to allow exploration to new uncertain areas in the input space. They either use bandit algorithms [14] or linear programming formulation [5] as an optimization objective to choose among different criteria. However, the exploration/geometry/redundancy criteria in the input space perform poorly in high-dimensional spaces. Moreover, they incur additional computational or memory overhead (quadratic in the number of examples and classes), making them unscalable to large datasets. Another set of techniques [2,6] proposes to use generation queries (tasking crowd workers to create examples of tail classes), and claim better performance than mining-based methods. However, these techniques have limited applicability (not possible in the medical domain) and are financially expensive due to increased human effort [6].

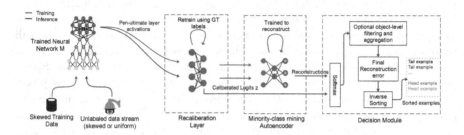

Fig. 1. Overall framework of the proposed method.

In contrast to the above-mentioned workarounds, we do not rely on any additional input like exploration or example generation by humans. Hence, our method does not suffer from the above-mentioned shortcomings. Instead, our method takes a more heads-on approach and addresses the key challenges of uncertainty sampling (see Sect. 1) in skewed settings. Further, most of the approaches (except [5]) mentioned above assume a binary classification setting, with a single minority and majority class. Additionally, these are designed with classification in mind and, in many cases, are not easily extendable to other learning tasks. Our approach, on the other hand, directly handles multi-class settings (multiple minority and majority classes) and can be easily extended to other tasks, like object detection.

3   Our Method

Consider a machine-learning task where a model is trained using a pool of finite labeled dataset D_L. Each instance in D_L is mapped to one or more elements of a set of classes C. Additionally, we are given that there is a class imbalance in dataset D_L, such that a subset of classes $C_M \subset C$ are relatively under-represented (a.k.a minority classes or tail-classes). Given a pool of unlabelled data D_U, sampled from a space of instances $\mathcal{X}$, the *minority-class example mining* algorithm aims to learn a ranking function $\Omega_\beta(x) : \mathcal{X} \to \mathbb{R}$, such that higher scores indicate a high likelihood of a sample x belonging to one of the minority-classes. In this work, we learn the parameters β in a one-class setting using the training dataset D_L. Specifically we expect the function $\Omega_\beta(x)$ to overfit the majorly-present head-class data in D_L so that unfamiliar minority-class samples can be flagged as anomalies. Once the tail-class examples are mined, they are sent for labeling. The labeled tail-class examples aid in balancing the dataset and, thereafter, train effective machine learning models in real-life applications with skewed long-tail class distributions.

The proposed minority-class hard example mining framework (shown in Fig. 1) consists of three major components: (a) the re-calibration layer (RC layer), (b) the minority-class mining autoencoder (MCM-AU), and (c) the decision module. First, we use the re-calibration layer to recalibrate the final layer probabilities which are distorted due to class imbalance and overfitting. Specifically, the recalibration layer takes pen-ultimate layer activations of model M as input and outputs the calibrated logits $z \in R^C$. Second, we model the calibrated logits z using an autoencoder which acts as an anomaly detector to help separate tail-class examples due to their anomalous activation patterns. Specifically, the calibrated logits z, obtained from the recalibration layer, is passed into the autoencoder and a potential reconstruction $\hat{z}$ is obtained as the output. Finally, based on the quality of the reconstruction, instances are flagged as minority-class examples by the decision module. Specifically, it takes the original calibrated logit z and its reconstruction $\hat{z}$ as input, computes the reconstruction error for each example. The examples with the highest reconstruction error are selected for labeling. We describe these components in more detail as follows.

The Recalibration Layer: The Recalibration layer (RC-Layer) aims to solve the problem of distorted class-probability distribution for tail-class examples. As explained earlier, this problem occurs due to two main reasons: overfitting in the final softmax layer and subdued tail-class activations. The overfitting and the resulting miscalibration in softmax probabilities is a known phenomenon observed in many modern multi-class classification networks [12,20]. This has been attributed to prolonged training to minimize the negative log-likelihood loss on a network with a large capacity. Subdued activations for tail classes are a result of skewness and insufficient data due to the class imbalance. Lack of sufficient data causes the weak tail-class activations to be dominated by stronger head-class activations.

To mitigate these problems, the overfit softmax layer of the model f_θ is replaced with a structurally similar newly-initialized layer (recalibration layer). The intuition behind replacing only the last layer is based on the idea that overfitting and miscalibration are mainly attributed to weight magnification particularly in the last layer of the neural network [20]. The new layer is trained with early stopping and focal loss which help solve the problem of overfitting and subdued activations, respectively. Early stopping does not allow the layer to overfit the negative log-likelihood loss and hence results in better calibration. Note that any loss of performance due to early stopping is not important as it is not supposed to be used for inference. Focal loss, which is a dynamically weighted variant of the negative log-likelihood loss, helps the network to focus on statically-rare tail-class examples, and hence mitigate the problem of subdued activations. Additionally, focal loss also acts as an entropy-maximizing regularisation which has an added benefit further preventing the model to become overconfident on head-classes [20].

Formally, we denote a truncated copy of the model $f_\theta(x)$ with the removed softmax-layer as $\tilde{f}_\theta(x)$, and the newly-initialized recalibration layer, with learnable parameters ϕ, as g_ϕ. For an instance x in dataset D_L or D_U, the recalibrated activations are obtained as $z = g_\phi(\tilde{f}_\theta(x))$. The parameters θ are frozen to prevent any update to the model. The parameters ϕ are learned by backpropagation using the focal loss [18] which can be written as $FL(p_t) = -\alpha_t(1 - p_t)^\gamma \log(p_t)$; where p_t is the probability corresponding to the ground truth class t, $\alpha_t \in [0, 1]$ is the weighting factor for the tth class, usually set equal to the inverse class frequencies, and $\gamma \geq 0$ is the tunable focussing parameter. Refer to [18] for more details. For each example x, the probabilities p_t are obtained by taking a softmax over the logits z.

The Minority-Class Mining Autoencoder: Minority-class mining autoencoder (MCM-AU) aims to solve the problem of information loss due to the aggregation of class-probability distribution in typical uncertainty sampling (§5.1). For instance, the entropy baseline aggregates information-rich probability distribution into a scalar metric ($\sum_k^C p_k^i \log p_k^i$). Hence, it fails to capture vital information about the pattern, relationships, and interactions among individual probability values. Further, these mathematical formulae are fixed (without any parameters), which, unlike a learning process, do not allow it to adapt to identifying and discriminatory patterns in data. MCM-AU, on the other hand, is a parametric function that learns the characteristic patterns and relationships among individual class-activation values. Specifically, the autoencoder, trained using a skewed training dataset, is expected to overfit the activation pattern of majorly occurring head-class examples. During inference, the activation pattern of a rarely occurring tail-class example acts as an anomaly and is flagged as a minority-class example. The key idea is that a tail-class activation pattern is not expected to be reconstructed accurately by an autoencoder trained majorly on head-class data.

Formally, we denote $A_E : Z \to W$ as encoder and $A_D : W \to Z$ as decoder. Given a logit vector $z \in Z$, the encoder maps it to a latent representation $w \in W$, which acts as a bottleneck. The decoder maps the latent representation w to output a potential reconstruction $\hat{z} = A_D(A_E(z; \psi_E); \psi_D)$ where ψ_E and ψ_D denote the learnable parameters, trained by optimising the mean-squared error loss, which can be written as MSE= $||z - \hat{z}||_2^2$.

The Decision Module: The main job of the decision module is to rank examples based on their likelihood of belonging to one of the minority classes. As explained earlier, minority-class examples are less likely to be reconstructed well using an autoencoder trained on majorly present head-class examples. For each example x, the decision module computes the reconstruction error (MSE) between the softmax of the calibrated logits z and their reconstruction $\hat{z}$. The softmax helps to accentuate the difference and works better in practice. Finally, it sorts all the examples based on their score as:

$$S_x = ||\sigma(z) - \sigma(\hat{z})||_2^2, \tag{1}$$

$$\text{Rank List} := invsort_{\forall x \in D_U}(S_x). \tag{2}$$

However, in the case of object detection, each example x can have multiple candidate detections. Hence we have multiple sets of logits z_j, reconstructed logits $\hat{z}_j$, and an additional score s_j, quantifying the confidence of a particular detection d_j. We use aggregation and filtering to obtain a single example-level score for each example x. Specifically, we obtain a set of most-confident (topK) detections. Then, for each topK detection, we compute the reconstruction error (Eq. 1) and aggregate them by averaging.

4   Evaluation

4.1   Datasets and Setup

We conduct experiments on three different datasets, covering two computer vision tasks. The details and relevant summary statistics are presented in Table 1. The COCO-11 and SIFAR-10 are derived from benchmark object detection and classification datasets, namely MS-COCO [19] and CIFAR-10 [17], respectively. CakeDet is a real-application dataset, on cake detection, sourced from one of our high-end clientele, who is struggling to gather labeled images for a rare item in their inventory, i.e. *chocolate*. For each dataset, the tail classes are identified as poorly-performing classes with skewness-ratio less than 0.30, where *skewness-ratio* (s) is defined as the ratio between the number of samples in the particular class divided by the mean number of samples across all classes. While COCO-11 and CakeDet have a similar skewness, SIFAR-10, on the other hand, is designed to be significantly more skewed (see Table 1).

Table 1. Statistics of the various datasets used in our experiments. Tail-class skewness-ratio (Sect. 4.1) is based on the train sub-dataset. COCO-11 (11/80 categories) and SIFAR-10 are sub-samples of MS-COCO [19] and CIFAR-10 [17] datasets, respectively.

Dataset	#Class	Tail class names (skewness-ratio)	#Train	#Pool	#Test
COCO-11	11	Car (0.05), chair (0.14), bottle (0.23)	4594	7445	3723
SIFAR-10	10	Airplane (0.003), automobile (0.04)	14398	24000	12000
CakeDet	31	Chocolate (0.04)	4091	11877	650

The sub-datasets Train, Pool, and Test (Table 1) correspond to different sub-samples of a particular data, where the set Train is used to train various models (the initial skewed target model, re-calibration layer, and autoencoder), the Pool is used to mine minority-class examples and evaluate the mining algorithm's performance, and lastly, the Test is used to test the final performance of the final finetuned model. Unlike CakeDet, CIFAR-10 and MSCOCO datasets are not naturally skewed. To simulate the skewed experimental setup, we obtain the above-mentioned three separate stratified subsets. We artificially induce a long-tail pattern of skewness in the Train set (corresponding datasets and tail-classes are shown in Table 1). We keep the Pool and Test to be uniform distributions. This allows better analysis, interpretation, and comparison of results among individual classes. However, in the case of real-application CakeDet, all subsets Train, Pool, and Test are similarly skewed.

Evaluation: In order to evaluate, each mining algorithm draws candidate examples from the pool set, which are expected to belong to one of the minority classes (Table 1). To quantify the mining performance, we use Precision, Precision-Recall (PR) curve, Area Under Precision-Recall curve (AUC-PR), and average F-score. Precision P, computed as $\frac{TP}{TP+FP}$, quantifies the percentage of minority-class examples in a queried sample of a certain size. Another quantity of interest is recall, computed as $\frac{TP}{TP+FN}$, and since there is a trade-off, we can visualize precision at various recalls in the PR curve. Finally, we summarise the PR characteristics in a single metric using AUC-PR, which is the area under the PR curve, and average F-score, which is the average of F-score, computed as $\frac{2P \cdot R}{P+R}$ for all points in the PR curve. TP represents true positive, FP is false positive and FN is false negative.

After mining minority-class examples, we finetune the model with the new training dataset and measure improvement in performance on the minority classes. In the case of SIFAR-10, we use classification accuracy (CAcc), and in the case of COCO-11 and CakeDet we use MS-COCO object-detection metrics [19] (Average Precision(AP) and Average Recall(AR)). Since our algorithm performs significantly better than all the baselines, for better interpretation and conciseness, we also report relative percentage improvement, which is computed as $\frac{(R_{our}-R_{baseline})}{R_{baseline}} * 100$, where R_{our} and $R_{baseline}$ represent performance of our approach and a particular baseline, respectively. This quantifies the percentage improvement of our approach with respect to other baselines.

Baselines: We compare our approach with multiple state-of-the-art baselines. 1) Random (samples randomly), 2) MaxScore ($\phi^i_{MS} = 1 - \max_k p^i_k$) [8], 3) Entropy ($\phi^i_{ENT} = -\sum_k^C p^i_k \log p^i_k$) [23], 4) Weighted Shannon Entropy ($\phi^i_{WENT} = -\sum_k^C \frac{p^i_k}{b_k \cdot C} \log \frac{p^i_k}{b_k \cdot C}$) [15], and 5) HAL (exploration based) [14]. p^i_k is softmax probability for example i and b_k is the proportion of samples corresponding to the kth class among C total classes. Additionally, we tried USBC [7], which is a query-by-committee based approach geared towards skewed datasets and a recent approach designed for multi-class imbalance problems [5]. However, the former performed significantly worse than random, possibly due to large skew across multiple classes and the latter did not scale to the size of our datasets due to the huge memory overhead of solving Eq. 7 in [5]. Note that all of these baselines are designed primarily for classification and some are not easily extendable to other tasks. Hence, in the case of object detection datasets, we did not try some of these baselines like [7] and [5].

Implementation Details: We implement our models and design our experiments in PyTorch. For classification, we used a vanilla 4-layered Convolutional Neural Network (CNN), followed by a Fully-Connected (FC) layer. For object detection, we used a RetinaNet detector with a ResNet18/50 backbone. These networks are trained for 20 epochs with batch sizes of 64 and 6, respectively. Similar to the respective final layer, the re-calibration layer is an FC layer in the case of classification and a CNN layer for object detection. Auto-encoder is composed of a two-layered (with hidden dimensions 10 and 9) fully connected encoder and a similar decoder with ReLU activations. It is trained for 10-40 epochs using MSE loss and a learning rate of $1e^{-3}$. During finetuning, the models are trained using the training dataset augmented with the mined minority-class examples for another 20 epochs. All results are averaged over multiple runs to rule out the effect of randomness. The code of our work is accessible at https://tinyurl.com/yckvyyre.

4.2 Experiments

Minority-Class Mining Performance: In this experiment, we analyze the minority-class mining performance of our approach in comparison to start-of-the-art baselines. Specifically, we generate a rank-list (Eq. 2) of being a minority-class example (column 3 of Table 1) for the entire pool set. Then, we compute the precision of minority-class mining for sets of various sizes, sampled from the top of the rank list. The corresponding precision-recall curves are provided in Fig. 2. In terms of relative percentage improvement, for COCO-11 (left), our approach (red) beats all baselines by **16–44%** on average F-Score and **40–200%** on AUC-PR, depending on the baseline. These figures are **133–233%** and **409–692%** for SIFAR-10 (middle), and **17–64%** and **21–87%** for CakeDet (right). Significantly improved performance of our approach demonstrates the value of our autoencoder-based approach. Notice that, the percentage improvement is significantly higher for the highly-skewed SIFAR-10. We suspect this is due to the fact that usual uncertainty sampling baselines degrade under high skewness and perform as worse as random, as concluded in the previous research [2,3]. Our approach, on the other hand, does not suffer from any such degradation. Slightly worse performance of all baselines on COCO-11, we believe, is due to

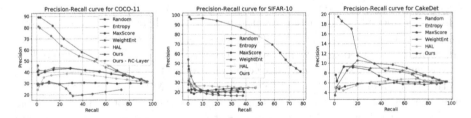

Fig. 2. Precision-recall characteristics of minority-class mining for different datasets. Our approach outperforms all baselines. Curves towards the top-right are better.

noise introduced by filtering and aggregation (§3) for object detection problems. Also for CakeDet, all methods perform relatively poorly since here, unlike the other two datasets, the Pool set is also class-imbalanced.

Robustness of Hypothesis: In this experiment, we simulate different settings by varying the number of minority classes and also changing the actual minority classes for SIFAR-10 dataset. As shown in Fig. 3 (left), our approach continues to outperform all baselines, which eventually becomes less significant as the number of minority classes increases. This is expected as the odds of an example falling into one of the minority classes eventually takes over as the proportion of minority classes rises. Similarly, as shown in Fig. 3 (right), the trend generalizes for different sets of minority classes than the one used in the experiment above.

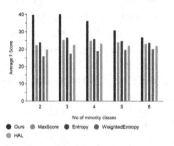 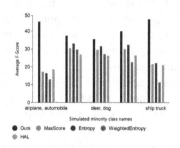

(a) Trend of F-Score vs No of minority classes   (b) Trend of F-Score vs Different minority classes

Fig. 3. Shows average F-Score of different baselines on SIFAR-10 as we vary (instead of what is shown in Table 1) *(a)* number of minority classes, and *(b)* choosing different classes. Our approach consistently outperforms all baselines across all settings.

Fine-Tuned Performance: In this experiment, we demonstrate the effectiveness of our approach in terms of the performance of the fine-tuned model on minority classes. Here we only compare with MaxScore and Entropy since they show competitive performance in comparison to all other baselines, an observation consistent with previous research [3,21]. Table 2 shows the relative-percentage improvement of our method over the baselines for various sample sizes, datasets, and tail classes. Our approach beats all the baselines by a significant margin, which is up to **18–21%** for COCO-11, **88–117%** for SIFAR-10, and **3%** for CakeDet. For CakeDet, although, our approach mines 10–20% more tail-class examples , we suspect the modest 3% rise is due to low variance of images (top-view with similar cakes and backgrounds), resulting in diminishing returns after a point.

Table 2. Relative % increase in the finetune performance of our approach in comparison to the baselines for *(left)* various sample sizes and *(right)* for tail classes, arranged by decreasing skewness. Results are averaged over multiple runs and sample sizes.

Dataset	#Sample	Random	Entropy	MaxSc.
COCO-11	300	46.94%	18.62%	21.80%
	744	29.64%	9.63%	8.37%
	1500	23.79%	9.20%	9.36%
SIFAR-10	212	82.56%	88.97%	117.3%
	2000	51.21%	47.68%	46.19%
	5000	9.56%	31.91%	24.74%
CakeDet	200	7.38%	3.38%	3.31%
	800	4.36%	3.38%	3.24%

Dataset	ClassName	Random	Entropy	MaxSc.
SIFAR-10	airplane	305.2%	66.34%	155.5%
	automobile	30.57%	74.67%	69.86%
COCO-11	car	34.31%	3.39%	5.34%
	chair	26.73%	37.34%	36.07%
	bottle	7.93%	10.47%	10.66%

Further Analysis: Here, we demonstrate the two desirable properties of the rank list generated by our approach. *First*, the proportion of minority-class examples increases as we move up in the rank list. Figure 4 (a), shows percentage improvement (mining and finetuning) of our approach over the random baseline with different sample sizes for COCO-11. As shown, the mining performance (red) rises rapidly with a lower sample size. Similarly, this trend also generalizes to all baselines and datasets and can also be observed in Table 2 (left). *Second*, our approach ranks a greater number of examples belonging to the most skewed classes (hardest examples), up in the rank list. In other words, the most-needed examples (most skewed classes) are prioritized over less-needed examples (less skewed classes). For COCO-11, we show in Fig. 4 (b), *car* which is the most skewed class, shows the highest percentage of improvement (mining and finetuning) over the random baseline, which gradually reduces for *chair* and *bottle* as the skewness becomes less severe. The same trend can also be observed in fine-tuned model's performance (with a few exceptions, marked with underline) for individual minority classes in Table 2 (right), where the classes are arranged with decreasing skewness (from *airplane* to *bottle*). Observing these trends, we

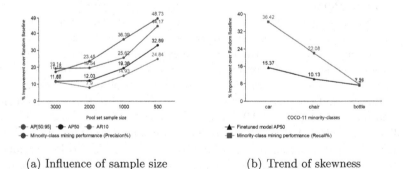

(a) Influence of sample size   (b) Trend of skewness

Fig. 4. % improvement for *(a)* various sample sizes and *(b)* tail classes (skewness-ordered). Shows that performance is better for smaller sample and higher skewness.

conclude that a higher proportion and high quality (corresponding to most skewed classes) of minority-class examples are ranked higher in our approach in comparison to other baselines. This is a very desirable property for finetuning the model with baby steps, like in active learning, instead of one large step.

Ablation Study: Finally, we conduct an ablation study to clearly understand the value addition of individual components of our framework (i.e. RC-layer and the one-class autoencoder). In the PR-curve for COCO-11 (Fig. 2 left), *Ours* (red) represents the performance of our approach and *Ours - RC-Layer* (purple) represents the performance of our approach without the RC-Layer. The importance of recalibrating activations is established by the significant drop in performance after ablating the RC-Layer. Further, note that the only difference between Ours - RC-Layer (purple) and uncertainty baselines (green and orange) is the use of autoencoder instead of uncertainty metrics. Substantial improvement (purple vs. green and orange) demonstrates the importance of using an autoencoder instead of a fixed formula.

5   Conclusion

This study presents a novel, simple, and effective framework to mine minority-class examples using uncertainty estimates. We identified key challenges due to which earlier works struggled to mine minority-class examples. We addressed these challenges using one-class modeling of re-calibrated activations. Consequently, we demonstrate the effectiveness of our method by a significant improvement in minority-class mining and fine-tuned model performance. Additionally, we demonstrated two desirable properties of our approach to mine better samples, both in terms of quality and quantity, up in the rank list.

References

1. Aggarwal, U., Popescu, A., Hudelot, C.: Active learning for imbalanced datasets. In: The IEEE WACV, pp. 1428–1437 (2020)
2. Attenberg, J., Provost, F.: Why label when you can search? alternatives to active learning for applying human resources to build classification models under extreme class imbalance. In: Proceedings of the 16th ACM SIGKDD, pp. 423–432 (2010)
3. Attenberg, J., Provost, F.: Inactive learning? difficulties employing active learning in practice. ACM SIGKDD Explor. **12**(2), 36–41 (2011)
4. Bengio, S.: The battle against the long tail. In: Talk on Workshop on Big Data and Statistical Machine Learning, vol. 1 (2015)
5. Bhattacharya, A.R., Liu, J., Chakraborty, S.: A generic active learning framework for class imbalance applications. In: BMVC, p. 121 (2019)
6. C Lin, M.: Active learning with unbalanced classes & example-generated queries. In: AAAI Conference on Human Computation (2018)
7. Chen, Y., Mani, S.: Active learning for unbalanced data in the challenge with multiple models and biasing. In: Active Learning and Experimental Design workshop In conjunction with AISTATS 2010, pp. 113–126. JMLR Workshop and Conference Proceedings (2011)

8. Culotta, A., McCallum, A.: Reducing labeling effort for structured prediction tasks. In: AAAI, vol. 5, pp. 746–751 (2005)

9. Dagan, I., Engelson, S.P.: Committee-based sampling for training probabilistic classifiers. In: Machine Learning Proceedings 1995, pp. 150–157. Elsevier (1995)

10. Deng, J., Dong, W., Socher, R., Li, L.J., Li, K., Fei-Fei, L.: Imagenet: a large-scale hierarchical image database. In: 2009 IEEE Conference on Computer Vision and Pattern Recognition, pp. 248–255. IEEE (2009)

11. Ertekin, S., Huang, J., Bottou, L., Giles, L.: Learning on the border: active learning in imbalanced data classification. In: Proceedings of the Sixteenth ACM Conference on Conference on Information and Knowledge Management, pp. 127–136 (2007)

12. Guo, C., Pleiss, G., Sun, Y., Weinberger, K.Q.: On calibration of modern neural networks. arXiv preprint arXiv:1706.04599 (2017)

13. He, H., Garcia, E.A.: Learning from imbalanced data. IEEE Trans. Knowl. Data Eng. **21**(9), 1263–1284 (2009)

14. Kazerouni, A., Zhao, Q., Xie, J., Tata, S., Najork, M.: Active learning for skewed data sets. arXiv preprint arXiv:2005.11442 (2020)

15. Kirshners, A., Parshutin, S., Gorskis, H.: Entropy-based classifier enhancement to handle imbalanced class problem. Procedia Comput. Sci. **104**, 586–591 (2017)

16. Krawczyk, B.: Learning from imbalanced data: open challenges and future directions. Progress Artif. Intell. **5**(4), 221–232 (2016). https://doi.org/10.1007/s13748-016-0094-0

17. Krizhevsky, A., Hinton, G., et al.: Learning multiple layers of features from tiny images (2009)

18. Lin, T.Y., Goyal, P., Girshick, R., He, K., Dollár, P.: Focal loss for dense object detection. In: Proceedings of the IEEE ICCV, pp. 2980–2988 (2017)

19. Lin, T.-Y., et al.: Microsoft COCO: common objects in context. In: Fleet, D., Pajdla, T., Schiele, B., Tuytelaars, T. (eds.) ECCV 2014. LNCS, vol. 8693, pp. 740–755. Springer, Cham (2014). https://doi.org/10.1007/978-3-319-10602-1_48

20. Mukhoti, J., Kulharia, V., Sanyal, A., Golodetz, S., Torr, P.H., Dokania, P.K.: Calibrating deep neural networks using focal loss. arXiv preprint arXiv:2002.09437 (2020)

21. Ramirez-Loaiza, M.E., Sharma, M., Kumar, G., Bilgic, M.: Active learning: an empirical study of common baselines. Data Mining Knowle. Discov. **31**(2), 287–313 (2016). https://doi.org/10.1007/s10618-016-0469-7

22. Settles, B.: Active learning literature survey. Technical report, UW-Madison Dept. of Computer Sciences (2009)

23. Shannon, C.E.: A mathematical theory of communication. ACM SIGMOBILE Mob. Comput. Commun. **5**(1), 3–55 (2001)

24. Singh, G., Sigal, L., Little, J.J.: Spatio-temporal relational reasoning for video question answering

25. Singh, G., Srikant, S., Aggarwal, V.: Question independent grading using machine learning: the case of computer program grading. In: Proceedings of the 22nd ACM SIGKDD International Conference on Knowledge Discovery and Data Mining, pp. 263–272 (2016)

26. Thudumu, S., Branch, P., Jin, J., Singh, J.J.: A comprehensive survey of anomaly detection techniques for high dimensional big data. J. Big Data **7**(1), 1–30 (2020). https://doi.org/10.1186/s40537-020-00320-x

27. Tomanek, K., Hahn, U.: Reducing class imbalance during active learning for named entity annotation. In: Proceedings of the Fifth International Conference on Knowledge Capture, pp. 105–112 (2009)

28. Zhu, X., Anguelov, D., Ramanan, D.: Capturing long-tail distributions of object subcategories. In: IEEE CVPR, pp. 915–922 (2014)

Conditional Context-Aware Feature Alignment for Domain Adaptive Detection Transformer

Siyuan Chen[(⊠)]

University of Science and Technology of China, Hefei, China
csy0407@mail.ustc.edu.cn

Abstract. Detection transformers have recently gained increasing attention, due to its competitive performance and end-to-end pipeline. However, they suffer significant performance drop when the test and training data are drawn from different distributions. Existing domain adaptive detection transformer methods adopt feature distribution alignment to alleviate the domain gaps. While effective, they ignore the class semantics and rich context preserved in attention mechanism during adaptation, which leads to inferior performance. To tackle these problems, we propose Conditional Context-aware Feature Alignment (CCFA) for domain adaptive detection transformer. Specifically, a context-aware feature alignment module is proposed to map the high-dimensional context into low-dimensional space, so that the rich context can be utilized for distribution alignment without optimization difficulty. Moreover, a conditional distribution alignment module is adopted to align features of the same object class from different domains, which better preserves discriminability during adaptation. Experiments on three common benchmarks demonstrate CCFA's superiority over state-of-the-arts.

Keywords: Unsupervised domain adaptation · Object detection · Detection transformer

1 Introduction

With the development of deep learning, recent years have witness remarkable progress of object detection. Representative detection methods include Faster RCNN [17], YOLO [16], SSD [14], FCOS [20], and so on. Recently, Detection Transformer [2] has received increasing attention, due to its end-to-end pipeline and competitive performance. Although significant progress has been made in constrained scenarios, where the test data is sampled from the same distribution as the training data, real-world scenarios are much more complex and the performance of object detectors can degrade significantly, due to domain shift.

Domain adaptive object detection (DAOD) aims to solve this problem by training an object detector that can generalize to the target domain, based on samples from labeled source domain data and unlabeled target data. Although progresses have been made, most of the existing DAOD methods rely on specific

© Springer Nature Switzerland AG 2022
B. Þór Jónsson et al. (Eds.): MMM 2022, LNCS 13141, pp. 272–283, 2022.
https://doi.org/10.1007/978-3-030-98358-1_22

object detector structures, such as RPN in Faster RCNN [3], centerness branch in FCOS [9], and thus cannot be directly applied to the Detection Transformer [2].

Recently, SFA [23] proposes domain-query-based feature alignment and bipartite matching consistency regularization to improve detection transformers' cross-domain performance. While effective, the sequence feature alignment in SFA perform solely based on the current token, while ignoring contextual information contained in the sample locations and the attention weights of deformable attention [28]. Moreover, SFA aligns the marginal distribution between the source and target domains, without considering the class semantics, which may cause losses in discriminability and performance degradation.

To address the above issues, we propose conditional context-aware feature alignment (CCFA) to exploit context information and align feature representations of the same object class from different domains. Concretely, our CCFA consists of two parts: firstly, a context-aware feature alignment module is proposed to utilize the attention weights and sampled features in deformable attention as an additional context in addition to token feature. Instead of directly utilizing these high-dimensional contexts, we perform feature alignment base on the context feature projected in low-dimensional space, which eases the optimization and avoids mode collapse. Secondly, we propose a conditional feature alignment module, specifically, a category-aware domain discriminator is utilized to align instances of objects of the same category on different domains, thus alleviating the loss of discriminability caused by mismatch, and improve detection transformers' cross-domain performance. Experiments on three common domain adaptation scenarios, including weather adaptation, synthetic to real adaptation, and scene adaptation, validates the effectiveness of our methods. Our main contribution can be summarized as follows:

- We propose a novel context-aware feature alignment module to utilizes the rich context preserved in the attention mechanism for feature alignment. Moreover, it maps the high-dimensional context feature to low-dimensional space, which eases optimization, and avoids mode collapse.
- We develop a conditional feature alignment module to exploit class semantics for feature alignment. It aligns features of the same object class from different domains, which alleviates the negative impact caused by mismatching objects from different classes.
- Experiments and analyses on three common domain adaptation scenarios validate the effectiveness of our methods.

2   Related Works

2.1   Object Detection

Object detection is a fundamental task in computer vision and is essential for many multimedia applications, including image caption, person re-identification, etc. Representative object detection algorithms can be broadly classified into two categories: one-stage, e.g., YOLO, SSD, and two-stage, e.g., Faster RCNN. One-stage detectors tend to have faster inference, while two-stage detectors generally enjoy higher accuracy. Despite the great progress of these object detection algorithms, they are not end-to-end and rely on specific post-processing, such as NMS. Recently, Detection Transformer proposes to view object detection as a set prediction problem and adopt transformer and bipartite graph matching to achieve end-to-end object detection, achieve promising results. Since then, Detection Transformer has drawn increasing attention due to its simplicity and effectiveness, and many detection transformer variants are proposed, e.g., Deformable DETR, SMCA, and conditional DETR.

2.2   Unsupervised Domain Adaptation

Unsupervised domain adaptation aims at training models on a labeled source domain such that it can generalize to an unlabeled target domain. Early domain adaptation methods, e.g., DANN [7] and ADDA [22], align marginal distribution of source and target domains. By contrast, MADA [15] and IDDA [13] align conditional distribution to alleviate the negative effect caused by the mismatch between samples from different domains.

While these methods concentrate on domain adaptive classification tasks, DA-Faster [3] is the first to handle the domain adaptive object detection task. Specifically, instance- and image-level feature alignment modules are proposed to alleviate the domain gap. EPM [9] proposes a center-aware feature alignment method built on FCOS [20]. Although significant improvement has been achieved, these methods are designed for detection transformer and rely on specific designs like RoI extraction [17] and centerness branch [20]. Recently, SFA [23] propose the first domain adaptive detection transformer method, by exploring sequence feature alignment. While impressive performance has been achieved, SFA ignores the context information preserved in the attention mechanism. Moreover, class semantics are not taken into consideration during feature alignment, which may lead to misalignment between different object classes. By contrast, our method exploits both context information and class semantics to achieve better domain adaptation.

3   Methodology

Domain adaptation object detection aims at training an object detector on a labeled source domain such that it is generalizable to an unlabeled target domain. The labeled source domain can be denoted as $\mathcal{D}_s = \{(x_i^s, y_i^s)\}_{i=1}^{N_s}$, where x_i^s is an image from the source domain, y_i^s is the corresponding label, and N_s is the total number of training images on the source domain. Similarly, the unlabeled target domain can be written as $\mathcal{D}_t = \{(x_i^t)\}_{i=1}^{N_t}$, where x_i^t is a sample image from the target domain and N_t is the number of target images.

3.1   Preliminaries on Detection Transformer

Detection transformers generally consist of a CNN backbone, a transformer encoder, a transformer decoder, and a lightweight prediction head. Specifically,

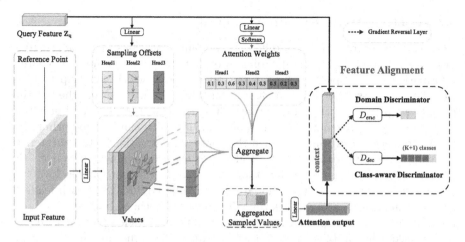

Fig. 1. Diagram of our Conditional Context-aware Feature Alignment Method. It contains a context-aware feature alignment module for both transformer encoder and decoder, and a conditional feature alignment module for the transformer decoder.

the transformer encoder takes features extracted by the CNN backbone for context modeling, and the transformer decoder aggregates object-related context from the sequence feature output by the encoder for final prediction. While our method is broadly applicable to multiple detection transformers, e.g. DETR [2], Deformable DETR [28], and conditional DETR [6], we built our method on top of Deformable DETR, due to its efficiency and fast convergence.

Given an input image x, Deformable DETR proposes multi-scale deformable attention (MDA) to explores multi-scale feature $\{x^l\}_{l=1}^L$ of L different feature levels. The MDA with M different heads and P sample points for each head can be formulated as:

$$\text{MDA}\left(\mathbf{z_q}, \hat{p}, \mathbf{x}\right) = \sum_{m=1}^{M} \boldsymbol{W}_m \left[\sum_{l=1}^{L} \sum_{k=1}^{P} A_{mlqk} \boldsymbol{W}'_m \boldsymbol{x}^l\left(\phi_l\left(\hat{\boldsymbol{p}}\right) + \Delta\boldsymbol{p}_{mlqk}\right)\right], \quad (1)$$

where $\mathbf{z}_q$ and $\mathbf{x} = \{\boldsymbol{x}^l\}_{l=1}^L$ are the query and key features, respectively, $\hat{\boldsymbol{p}}_q$ is the reference point, ϕ_l is a scale normalizer, $\boldsymbol{W}_m$ and $\boldsymbol{W}'_m$ are learnable projection weights, A_{mlqk} and $\Delta\boldsymbol{p}_{mlqk}$ are attention weights and learned sampling offset, respectively, both of which are obtained by applying linear projection on the query feature $\mathbf{z}_q$. For deformable self-attention in transformer encoder, the query feature $\mathbf{z}_q$ is equivalent to the key features $\mathbf{z}$, while for the deformable cross-attention in the decoder, the query features are object queries, denoted as $\boldsymbol{q}$. The supervised object detection loss on the labeled source domain is denoted as

$$\mathcal{L}_{det} = \frac{1}{N_s} \sum_{i=1}^{N_s} \mathcal{L}\left(x_i^s, y_i^s\right), \quad (2)$$

where $\mathcal{L}$ is the detection loss defined in [28]. Readers are encouraged to refer to their paper for more details.

3.2   Context-Aware Feature Alignment

The features extracted from different sampling locations, i.e. $\{x^l(\phi_l(\hat{p}) + \Delta p_{mlqk})\}_{l=1}^L$ and their corresponding attention weights contain rich context information with respect to the current query token, which can help to identify the domain-specific features for better adaptation. However, the existing domain adaptive detection transformer [23] ignores such context, and only uses the current query token z_q for feature alignment, which can be sub-optimal.

A straightforward way to utilize the context information is to concatenate the context feature with the query feature for feature alignment. However, the context information is extracted from $M \times P \times L$ different sample locations ($M = 8, P = 4, L = 4$ for the standard Deformable DETR [28], which leads to 128 sampling feature vectors). Feature alignment on such a high-dimensional representation is hard to optimize, thus often results in degraded performance [21].

To tackle this problem, we propose to project the high-dimensional context feature to a low dimensional representation space, before concatenating it with the query feature for distribution alignment. Fortunately, the attention weights aggregate the sampled features, and the projection weight W_m further maps the aggregated context feature to a low dimensional representation in the output space. This allows us to directly utilize this low-dimensional representation for feature alignment without additional project modules. Mathematically, our context-aware feature alignment can be written as:

$$\mathcal{L}_{enc} = -\frac{1}{N}\frac{1}{N_z}\sum_{i=1}^{N}\sum_{j=1}^{N_z} \text{CE}\left(D_{enc}\left([z_{i,j}, \text{MDA}(z_{i,j}, \hat{p}_{i,j}, \mathbf{x}_i)]\right), d_i\right), \qquad (3)$$

where CE denotes the cross-entropy loss, $[\cdot, \cdot]$ indicates the concatenate operation, D_{enc} is a lightweight domain discriminator, i and j are the indexes for image and the token in the encoder, respectively, N_z is the number of tokens in the transformer encoder layer, d_i is the domain label. We set $d_i = 0$ when $x_i \in \mathcal{D}_s$, and $d_i = 1$ when $x_i \in \mathcal{D}_t$.

In addition to the low-dimensional context information, the class semantics can be further exploited in the decoder layers to facilitate better adaptation, based on the class prediction made by Deformable DETR. We will detail this in the next section.

3.3   Conditional Feature Alignment

The existing domain adaptive detection transformer method [23] aligns the marginal distribution of source and target domains, without considering the category semantics. As a result, the instances from different classes can be mismatched for distribution alignment, e.g. an instance of "person" in the source domain could be matched be an instance of "car", leading to reduced discriminability and dropped detection performance.

To alleviate this problem, we propose a conditional feature distribution alignment module, where class probability predicted by the model is utilized to align

Table 1. Comparison with state-of-the-arts on weather adaptation, *i.e.*, Cityscapes to Foggy Cityscapes. FRCNN and DD are abbreviations for Faster RCNN and Deformable DETR, respectively.

Method	Detector	Person	Rider	Car	Truck	Bus	Train	Mcycle	Bcycle	mAP
FRCNN (Source)	FRCNN	26.9	38.2	35.6	18.3	32.4	9.6	25.8	28.6	26.9
DAF [3]	FRCNN	29.2	40.4	43.4	19.7	38.3	28.5	23.7	32.7	32.0
DivMatch [11]	FRCNN	31.8	40.5	51.0	20.9	41.8	34.3	26.6	32.4	34.9
SWDA [18]	FRCNN	31.8	44.3	48.9	21.0	43.8	28.0	28.9	35.8	35.3
SCDA [27]	FRCNN	33.8	42.1	52.1	26.8	42.5	26.5	29.2	34.5	35.9
MTOR [1]	FRCNN	30.6	41.4	44.0	21.9	38.6	40.6	28.3	35.6	35.1
CR-DA [24]	FRCNN	30.0	41.2	46.1	22.5	43.2	27.9	27.8	34.7	34.2
CR-SW [24]	FRCNN	34.1	44.3	53.5	24.4	44.8	38.1	26.8	34.9	37.6
GPA [25]	FRCNN	32.9	46.7	54.1	24.7	45.7	**41.1**	32.4	38.7	39.5
FCOS (Source)	FCOS	36.9	36.3	44.1	18.6	29.3	8.4	20.3	31.9	28.2
EPM [9]	FCOS	44.2	46.6	58.5	24.8	45.2	29.1	28.6	34.6	39.0
DD (Source)	DD	39.0	40.9	45.3	18.8	33.7	3.5	24.6	37.6	30.4
SFA [23]	DD	47.1	46.4	62.2	**30.0**	**50.2**	35.8	30.0	41.2	42.6
CCFA (Ours)	DD	**48.2**	**47.3**	**63.9**	23.7	47.8	39.0	**33.6**	**42.8**	**43.3**

instances representation of the same object class from different domains. Inspired by IDDA [13], we adopt a class-aware domain discriminator, which performs fine-grained domain classification by categorizing features into the target domain or one of the object classes in the source domain. Since only tokens in the decoder are matched to object instances, our class-aware classifier is only applied to the tokens in the decoder layers. The classification loss can be formulated as:

$$\mathcal{L}_{\text{dec}} = -\frac{1}{N}\frac{1}{N_q}\sum_{i=1}^{N}\sum_{i=1}^{N_q} \text{CE}\left(D_{dec}\left([q_{i,j}, \text{MDA}(q_{i,j}, p_{i,j}, x_i)]\right), y_{i,j}\right), \quad (4)$$

where i and j are the indexes for the image and the query token in the decoder, respectively, N_q is the number of object queries, D_{dec} is the class-aware domain discriminator, $y_{i,j}$ is the class-aware domain label. Specifically, it is defined as:

$$y_{i,j} = \begin{cases} y_{i,j}^s, & \text{if } x_i \in \mathcal{D}_s \\ K+1, & \text{if } x_i \in \mathcal{D}_t \end{cases}, \quad (5)$$

where $y_{i,j}^s$ is the semantic label for the j-th object query, which can be generated from y_i^s by bipartite matching [2].

The class-aware discriminator is required to perform accurate classification. At the same time, our detector tries to mislead the discriminator by extracting domain-ambiguous features, so that the domain discriminator mis-classifies the target domain instances as a specific class in the source domain. In this way, the target instance features are aligned with the most related class in the source domain, without losing discriminability.

Table 2. Comparison with state-of-the-art methods on synthetic to real adaptation, *i.e.*, Sim10k to Cityscapes.

Methods	Detector	*car* AP
Faster RCNN (Source)	FRCNN	34.6
DAF [3]	FRCNN	41.9
DivMatch [11]	FRCNN	43.9
SWDA [18]	FRCNN	44.6
SCDA [27]	FRCNN	45.1
MTOR [1]	FRCNN	46.6
CR-DA [24]	FRCNN	43.1
CR-SW [24]	FRCNN	46.2
GPA [25]	FRCNN	47.6
FCOS (Source)	FCOS	42.5
EPM [9]	FCOS	47.3
Deformable DETR (Source)	DD	50.4
SFA [23]	DD	54.5
CCFA (Ours)	DD	**55.1**

3.4   Total Loss

To summarize, the training objective of our CCFA can be written as:

$$\min_{G} \max_{D} \mathcal{L}_{det}(G) - \lambda_{enc}\mathcal{L}_{enc}(G, D) - \lambda_{dec}\mathcal{L}_{dec}(G, D), \tag{6}$$

where G denotes the Deformable DETR object detector and D indicates one of the discriminators: D_{enc} or D_{dec}. λ_{enc} and λ_{dec} are hyper-parameters that balance the loss terms. The min-max loss function is implemented by gradient reverse layers [7].

4   Experiments

4.1   Datasets

The experiment involves four datasets, i.e., Cityscapes [4], Foggy Cityscapes [19], Sim10k [10], and BDD100k [26]. Specifically, Cityscapes [4] contains 2048 ×1024 images from real-world traffic scenes, split into 2975 images for training and 500 for validation. The bounding box annotations and obtained by drawing the tightest rectangles on object masks. Foggy Cityscapes [19] is a synthetic foggy dataset that simulates fog in real scenes. The annotations can be directly inherited from the Cityscapes dataset. BDD100K [26] uses a 2D rectangular frame to annotate a total of 100,000 images collected from diverse scenes and weather. We use the daytime subset of the BDD100k dataset, following [24] and [23]. The

Table 3. Comparison with state-of-the-art methods on scene adaptation, *i.e.*, Cityscapes to BDD100k daytime subset.

Methods	Detector	Person	Rider	Car	Truck	Bus	Mcycle	Bcycle	mAP
FRCNN (Source)	FRCNN	28.8	25.4	44.1	17.9	16.1	13.9	22.4	24.1
DAF [3]	FRCNN	28.9	27.4	44.2	19.1	18.0	14.2	22.4	24.9
SWDA [18]	FRCNN	29.5	**29.9**	44.8	20.2	20.7	15.2	23.1	26.2
SCDA [27]	FRCNN	29.3	29.2	44.4	20.3	19.6	14.8	23.2	25.8
CR-DA [24]	FRCNN	30.8	29.0	44.8	20.5	19.8	14.1	22.8	26.0
CR-SW [24]	FRCNN	32.8	29.3	45.8	**22.7**	20.6	14.9	**25.5**	27.4
FCOS [20] (Source)	FCOS	38.6	24.8	54.5	17.2	16.3	15.0	18.3	26.4
EPM [9]	FCOS	39.6	26.8	55.8	18.8	19.1	14.5	20.1	27.8
DD (Source)	DD	41.0	28.2	58.9	12.7	14.3	15.4	16.5	26.7
SFA [23]	DD	41.8	28.4	59.6	17.8	21.3	16.5	18.9	29.2
CCFA (Ours)	DD	**42.2**	28.6	**60.2**	18.4	**21.1**	**16.9**	19.4	**29.5**

Table 4. Ablation studies on the Cityscapes to Foggy Cityscapes scenario. TDA, CTX, and CON represents token-wise feature alignment [23], context-aware feature alignment, and conditional feature distribution alignment, respectively.

Methods	TDA	CTX	CON	Person	Rider	Car	Truck	Bus	Train	Mcycle	Bcycle	mAP
DD (Source)				39.0	40.9	45.3	18.8	33.7	3.5	24.6	37.6	30.4
Proposed	✓			47.2	47.1	**63.9**	**30.0**	45.3	25.1	28.3	42.4	40.7
	✓	✓		45.2	47.1	58.4	27.3	44.7	**43.0**	30.3	44.1	42.5
	✓		✓	46.1	47.1	62.1	26.3	44.7	30.6	**34.6**	41.5	41.6
CCFA (Ours)	✓	✓	✓	**48.2**	**47.3**	**63.9**	23.7	**47.8**	39.0	33.6	**42.8**	**43.3**

SIM10k dataset is a synthetic dataset generated by the Grand Theft Auto V (GTA5) game engine, containing 10,000 images. To verify the effectiveness of our method, we set up three-domain adaptation scenarios as follows:

- Weather adaptation, i.e., Cityscapes to Foggy Cityscapes adaptation.
- Synthetic to real adaptation, i.e., Sim10k to Cityscapes adaptation.
- Scene Adaptation, i,e, Cityscapes to the daytime subset of BDD100k.

Following the common practice [3,23], we use mean average precision (mAP) with a threshold of 0.5 as the evaluation metric.

4.2   Implementation Details

Our CCFA is built on top of Deformable DETR with iterative bound box refinement [28]. ResNet-50 [8] pretrained on ImageNet-1k [5] is adopted as the backbone and AdamW [12] is adopted as the optimizer. The learning rate is initialized as 2×10^{-4}, and decay by 10 after 40 epochs. All models are trained for 50 epochs in total, with a batch size of 4. Both D_{enc} and D_{dec} are implemented as

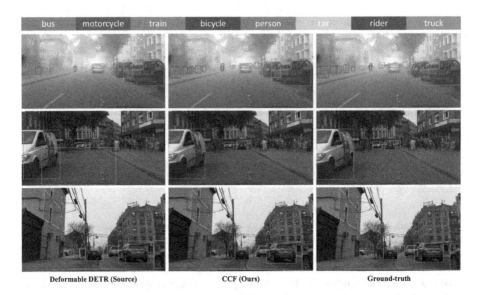

| bus | motorcycle | train | bicycle | person | car | rider | truck |

Deformable DETR (Source)   CCF (Ours)   Ground-truth

Fig. 2. Qualitative detection result. From top to bottom are samples from weather adaptation, synthetic to real adaptation, and scene adaptation, respectively.

simple three-layer MLP. Following [23], we adopt hierarchical feature alignment by averaging the domain loss calculated from each encoder/decoder layer. We set λ_{enc} and λ_{dec} as 1 for weather adaptation, and 0.01 for other adaptation scenarios.

4.3 Main Results

Table 1, Table 2, and Table 3 show the results of our CCFA compared with other state-of-the-art domain adaptive object detection methods. As can be seen, our CCFA outperforms existing methods either they are Faster RCNN based, FCOS based, or Deformable DETR based. Especially, CCFA shows systematic improvement over another domain adaptive detection transformer–SFA, where it obtains better results not only on the overall mAP, but also AP on most individual object classes. Moreover, noticeable improvements have been made on all three benchmarks compared to the source-only baseline, where CCFA brings an improvement of 12.9, 5.1, and 2.8 mAP, respectively.

4.4 Ablation Study

To better understand the proposed CCFA, we perform ablation studies on weather adaptation scenarios by isolating each component of our method. The results are shown in Table 4, as can be seen from the second and the third row, context-aware feature alignment improves the vanilla token-wise feature alignment in SFA [23] by 1.8 mAP. Our conditional feature distribution alignment

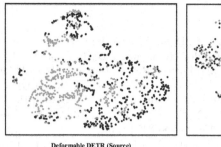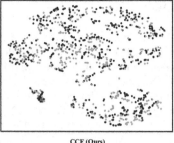

Deformable DETR (Source)   CCF (Ours)

Fig. 3. T-SNE visualization. Blue and red dots represents source and target samples, respectively. (Color figure online)

improves the vanilla TDA by 0.9 mAP. Moreover, the context-aware feature alignment and the conditional feature alignment are complementary to each other, combining them together brings further performance gain, achieving 43.3 mAP.

4.5 Further Analysis

Qualitative Demo Results. We provide demo detection results in Fig. 2. As shown in the first row, the source only Deformable DETR overlooked many object instances, especially the small ones, due to the heavy fog. By contrast, our CCFA detected those neglected instances. Moreover, the source-only model produces false-negative detection results, as can be seen in the second and the third row, while our CCFA successfully avoided these false negatives, and produces accurate detection results.

T-SNE Visualization. We visualize the token features extracted by the last transformer decoder in both the source-only baseline and our CCFA, via T-SNE. As can be seen from Fig. 3, the features extracted by our CCFA, though from two different domains, are indeed mixed. By comparison, the source and target features extracted by the source only Deformable DETR distribute to different clusters, and they can easily be separated by domain. The T-SNE visualization demonstrates that our CCFA can significantly suppress the domain shift between source and target domains.

5 Conclusion

In this paper, we propose a novel conditional context-aware feature alignment method for domain adaptive detection transformer. It contains a context-aware feature alignment module that utilizes context information for feature alignment and a conditional feature alignment module that aligns objects of the same class from different domains. Both quantitative and qualitative experimental results show the superiority of our method. In future work, we will extend our CCFA to improve the cross-domain instance segmentation tasks.

References

1. Cai, Q., Pan, Y., Ngo, C.W., Tian, X., Duan, L., Yao, T.: Exploring object relation in mean teacher for cross-domain detection. In: Proceedings of the IEEE/CVF Conference on Computer Vision and Pattern Recognition, pp. 11457–11466 (2019)
2. Carion, N., Massa, F., Synnaeve, G., Usunier, N., Kirillov, A., Zagoruyko, S.: End-to-end object detection with transformers. In: Vedaldi, A., Bischof, H., Brox, T., Frahm, J.-M. (eds.) ECCV 2020. LNCS, vol. 12346, pp. 213–229. Springer, Cham (2020). https://doi.org/10.1007/978-3-030-58452-8_13
3. Chen, Y., Li, W., Sakaridis, C., Dai, D., Van Gool, L.: Domain adaptive faster r-cnn for object detection in the wild. In: Proceedings of the IEEE Conference on Computer Vision and Pattern Recognition, pp. 3339–3348 (2018)
4. Cordts, M., et al.: The cityscapes dataset for semantic urban scene understanding. In: Proceedings of the IEEE Conference on Computer Vision and Pattern Recognition, pp. 3213–3223 (2016)
5. Deng, J., Dong, W., Socher, R., Li, L.J., Li, K., Fei-Fei, L.: Imagenet: a large-scale hierarchical image database. In: 2009 IEEE Conference on Computer Vision and Pattern Recognition, pp. 248–255. IEEE (2009)
6. Depu, M., et al.: Conditional detr for fast training convergence. In: Proceedings of the IEEE International Conference on Computer Vision (2021)
7. Ganin, Y., et al.: Domain-adversarial training of neural networks. J. Mach. Learn. Res. **17**(1), 2030–2096 (2016)
8. He, K., Zhang, X., Ren, S., Sun, J.: Deep residual learning for image recognition. In: Proceedings of the IEEE Conference on Computer Vision and Pattern Recognition, pp. 770–778 (2016)
9. Hsu, C.-C., Tsai, Y.-H., Lin, Y.-Y., Yang, M.-H.: Every pixel matters: center-aware feature alignment for domain adaptive object detector. In: Vedaldi, A., Bischof, H., Brox, T., Frahm, J.-M. (eds.) ECCV 2020. LNCS, vol. 12354, pp. 733–748. Springer, Cham (2020). https://doi.org/10.1007/978-3-030-58545-7_42
10. Johnson-Roberson, M., Barto, C., Mehta, R., Sridhar, S.N., Rosaen, K., Vasudevan, R.: Driving in the matrix: can virtual worlds replace human-generated annotations for real world tasks? In: 2017 IEEE International Conference on Robotics and Automation (ICRA), pp. 746–753. IEEE (2017)
11. Kim, T., Jeong, M., Kim, S., Choi, S., Kim, C.: Diversify and match: a domain adaptive representation learning paradigm for object detection. In: Proceedings of the IEEE/CVF Conference on Computer Vision and Pattern Recognition, pp. 12456–12465 (2019)
12. Kingma, D.P., Ba, J.: Adam: a method for stochastic optimization. In: International Conference on Learning and Representations (2015)
13. Kurmi, V.K., Namboodiri, V.P.: Looking back at labels: a class based domain adaptation technique. In: 2019 International Joint Conference on Neural Networks (IJCNN), pp. 1–8. IEEE (2019)
14. Liu, W., et al.: SSD: single shot MultiBox detector. In: Leibe, B., Matas, J., Sebe, N., Welling, M. (eds.) ECCV 2016. LNCS, vol. 9905, pp. 21–37. Springer, Cham (2016). https://doi.org/10.1007/978-3-319-46448-0_2
15. Pei, Z., Cao, Z., Long, M., Wang, J.: Multi-adversarial domain adaptation. In: Thirty-Second AAAI Conference on Artificial Intelligence (2018)
16. Redmon, J., Divvala, S., Girshick, R., Farhadi, A.: You only look once: unified, real-time object detection. In: Proceedings of the IEEE Conference on Computer Vision and Pattern Recognition, pp. 779–788 (2016)

17. Ren, S., He, K., Girshick, R., Sun, J.: Faster R-CNN: towards real-time object detection with region proposal networks. IEEE Trans. Pattern Anal. Mach. Intell. **39**(6), 1137–1149 (2016)
18. Saito, K., Ushiku, Y., Harada, T., Saenko, K.: Strong-weak distribution alignment for adaptive object detection. In: Proceedings of the IEEE/CVF Conference on Computer Vision and Pattern Recognition, pp. 6956–6965 (2019)
19. Sakaridis, C., Dai, D., Van Gool, L.: Semantic foggy scene understanding with synthetic data. Int. J. Comput. Vision **126**(9), 973–992 (2018)
20. Tian, Z., Shen, C., Chen, H., He, T.: Fcos: fully convolutional one-stage object detection. In: Proceedings of the IEEE/CVF International Conference on Computer Vision, pp. 9627–9636 (2019)
21. Tsai, Y.H., Hung, W.C., Schulter, S., Sohn, K., Yang, M.H., Chandraker, M.: Learning to adapt structured output space for semantic segmentation. In: Proceedings of the IEEE Conference on Computer Vision and Pattern Recognition, pp. 7472–7481 (2018)
22. Tzeng, E., Hoffman, J., Saenko, K., Darrell, T.: Adversarial discriminative domain adaptation. In: Proceedings of the IEEE Conference on Computer Vision and Pattern Recognition, pp. 7167–7176 (2017)
23. Wen, W., Yang, C., Jing, Z., Fengxiang, H., Zheng-Jun, Z., Yonggang, W., Dacheng, T.: Exploring sequence feature alignment for domain adaptive detection transformers. In: Proceedings of the 29th ACM International Conference on Multimedia (2021)
24. Xu, C.D., Zhao, X.R., Jin, X., Wei, X.S.: Exploring categorical regularization for domain adaptive object detection. In: Proceedings of the IEEE/CVF Conference on Computer Vision and Pattern Recognition, pp. 11724–11733 (2020)
25. Xu, M., Wang, H., Ni, B., Tian, Q., Zhang, W.: Cross-domain detection via graph-induced prototype alignment. In: Proceedings of the IEEE/CVF Conference on Computer Vision and Pattern Recognition, pp. 12355–12364 (2020)
26. Yu, F., Xian, W., Chen, Y., Liu, F., Liao, M., Madhavan, V., Darrell, T.: Bdd100k: a diverse driving video database with scalable annotation tooling. arXiv preprint arXiv:1805.04687 2(5), 6 (2018)
27. Zhu, X., Pang, J., Yang, C., Shi, J., Lin, D.: Adapting object detectors via selective cross-domain alignment. In: Proceedings of the IEEE/CVF Conference on Computer Vision and Pattern Recognition, pp. 687–696 (2019)
28. Zhu, X., Su, W., Lu, L., Li, B., Wang, X., Dai, J.: Deformable detr: deformable transformers for end-to-end object detection. In: International Conference on Learning and Representations (2020)

Multimedia for Medical Applications
(Special Session)

Human Activity Recognition with IMU and Vital Signs Feature Fusion

Vasileios-Rafail Xefteris[1]([⊠])[ID], Athina Tsanousa[1], Thanassis Mavropoulos[1],
Georgios Meditskos[2], Stefanos Vrochidis[1], and Ioannis Kompatsiaris[1]

[1] Centre for Research and Technology Hellas, Information Technologies Institute, 6th
Km Charilaou -Thermi, 57001 Thessaloniki, Greece
{vxefteris,atsan,mavrathan,stefanos,ikom}@iti.gr
[2] School of Informatics, Aristotle University of Thessaloniki, Thessaloniki, Greece
gmeditsk@csd.auth.gr

Abstract. Combining data from different sources into an integrated
view is a recent trend taking advantage of the Internet of Things (IoT)
evolution over the last years. The fusion of different modalities has
applications in various fields, including healthcare and security systems.
Human activity recognition (HAR) is among the most common applications of a healthcare or eldercare system. Inertial measurement unit
(IMU) wearable sensors, like accelerometers and gyroscopes, are often
utilized for HAR applications. In this paper, we investigate the performance of wearable IMU sensors along with vital signs sensors for HAR.
A massive feature extraction, including both time and frequency domain
features and transitional features for the vital signs, along with a feature selection method were performed. The classification algorithms and
different early and late fusion methods were applied to a public dataset.
Experimental results revealed that both IMU and vital signs achieve
reasonable HAR accuracy and F1-score among all the classes. Feature
selection significantly reduced the number of features from both IMU
and vital signs features while also improved the classification accuracy.
The rest of the early and late level fusion methods also performed better
than each modality alone, reaching an accuracy level of up to 95.32%.

Keywords: Human activity recognition · Wearable sensors · Vital
signals · Sensor fusion · Feature selection

1 Introduction

The development of computer systems and the Internet of Things (IoT) over the
last decades have led to the emergence of the research field of recognizing daily
activities using sensors and mobile devices, finding use in the healthcare, mili-
tary and security applications [8]. Systems analyze sensor readings to recognize
various activities, like walking, sitting, lying and other Activities of Daily Living
(ADL) [3]. Such systems can also be utilized in fall detection problems. Different
sensor modalities can be utilized in these applications, including vision-based

© Springer Nature Switzerland AG 2022
B. Þór Jónsson et al. (Eds.): MMM 2022, LNCS 13141, pp. 287–298, 2022.
https://doi.org/10.1007/978-3-030-98358-1_23

sensors, ambient sensors and wearable sensors [19]. Among the most common sensors deployed in such applications are wearable sensors, like accelerometers and gyroscopes, also known as Inertial Measurement Units (IMU).

When applying this type of sensor, a time window is typically used to extract useful features from the data. The feature extraction is a crucial process in Human activity recognition (HAR) systems since the extracted features determine the overall performance of the HAR systems. Usually, some features may be redundant, not providing any new information to the HAR systems, or even mislead the systems, thus worsening their performance. In these cases, a commonly used technique is to perform Feature Selection (FS). This task is responsible for extracting only the more useful features out of the total of the extracted feature set, thus improving the HAR system's performance and making it more robust [20].

Currently, smartwatches and wearables have been deployed with a lot of sensors including IMU and sensors measuring vital signs, like heart rate and temperature. The availability of all of these sensors allows for more sophisticated solutions of HAR by combining information from both IMU and vital signs sensors. Sensor fusion can benefit from multiple unrelated sources to develop more reliable and robust HAR systems [11]. The different fusion methods can generally be divided into early or feature level and late or decision level fusion. Since each fusion method has its advantages and disadvantages, comparative research is important for providing the optimal method for HAR applications based on IMU and vital signs.

In this work, we performed an IMU and vital sign fusion for HAR on the PAMAP2 dataset [12], which is a well-known publicly available dataset for HAR based on IMU and vital signs. We extracted statistical features from the whole data and structural and transient features from the vital sign data. Apart from the transient features introduced in [9], we computed two additional features, the starting trend and ending trend. We tested multiple well-known early and late level fusion techniques and also different FS algorithms. We selected to test five classifiers to assess the performance of eight different fusion and seven different FS methods in this work. Our goal is to reveal the early or late fusion technique performing the best on a publicly available HAR dataset and also examine the performance of different FS methods in such applications. The main contribution of this paper could be summarized in the following: (i) performing different feature extraction methods for IMU and vital signs data on a publicly available dataset, (ii) comparing different well-known early and late fusion methods applied on a publicly available dataset and (iii) applying FS algorithms on the extracted features to assess their performance on HAR applications.

This research was conducted during the REA project[1] and the methodologies demonstrated in the paper are also applicable to the xR4DRAMA project[2]. The REA project seeks to use state-of-the-art technologies, such as dialogue agents, semantic services and multimodal sensor analysis to assist in the rehabilitation

---

[1] https://rea-project.gr/en/home-en/.
[2] https://xr4drama.eu.

of people with motor disorders. Considering the mobility issues that these users are facing, a critical requirement sourced from user feedback revolves around the fall detection task, since having a relevant notification system in place is of paramount importance to timely perform patient interventions. The proposed solution leverages the abovementioned sensor data analysis and along with the respective data analysis of a computer vision-based system [6], presents a robust HAR-focused framework towards this objective. Since the wearable sensors used in this work are the same as those deployed in the REA project, the proposed solutions and analysis methods will be utilized in the project implementation as well. IMU and vital sensors are also employed in xR4DRAMA for activity recognition and stress detection of first responders employed in disaster management scenarios.

The rest of the paper is organized as follows. In Sect. 2 the current state-of-the-art on FS and IMU and vital signs fusion in HAR systems is presented. In Sect. 3 we describe the feature extraction methods and the different early and late fusion techniques and FS algorithms for the fusion of IMU and vital signs. In Sect. 4 we present the results of the different fusion methods and FS techniques tested on five classifiers, followed by the conclusion of the paper in Sect. 5.

2   Related Work

HAR applications by means of wearable sensors have been extensively proposed in the literature. The most common type of wearable sensor deployed is accelerometers, either alone [14] or in combination with other IMU sensors [16]. In [13] the authors extracted two different feature sets, one including simple time, frequency and time-frequency domain features and the other including only features of the time-domain analysis of the signal, from 3-axis accelerometer, gyroscope and magnetometer to perform HAR. Applying a genetic algorithm (GA) based technique for FS and classifier parameter tuning, they managed to reach an accuracy score of over 96% for each dataset. The authors in [21] focused on the feature extraction from 3-axis accelerometer, gyroscope, magnetometer and quaternion data. They also introduced various normalization methods for scenarios with different subjects in the training and testing of the system. When combining all the sensors and using time-domain features they achieved an accuracy score of up to 99.1%.

FS techniques have been utilized to reduce the total number of extracted features, maintaining only the more useful ones for the final HAR. In [4] the authors performed FS using minimum Redundancy Maximum Relevance (mRMR) algorithm on a feature set of 561 features. Applying accuracy thresholds of 95% they managed to reduce the number of features while maintaining a high accuracy score and also reduce the runtime of the system. In [20], Zhang et al. introduced a set of features named physical features and performed two different FS techniques on IMU data. They resulted in an increased accuracy score of 93.1% when applying FS techniques in HAR applications.

Several researchers have attempted to utilize the combination of IMU and vital signs in HAR systems. In [1] the authors proposed the fusion of accelerometer, gyroscope, surface Electromyogram (EMG) and joint angle for HAR. They performed a genetic algorithm-based FS to discard redundant features and tested six different classifiers. The authors in [9] developed Centinela, a HAR system combining accelerometer and vital sign data. They introduced a new feature set for vital sign data processing including structural and transient features. Comparing eight different classifiers they suggest that combining acceleration data with vital signs improves the overall HAR performance. Chen et al. [2] proposed a deep neural network method to extract automated features for IMU and vital signs fusion to perform HAR with complex activities. Even though the results were promising, the system had relatively low performance in similar activities, indicating that the system is not able to fully describe the complex structure of such activities.

3   Methods

The selected dataset (PAMAP2 [12]) consists of IMU and vital sign data. Since the IMU and the vital signs sensors have different sampling rates, we resampled the data to include only timestamps that have both IMU and vital signs measurements. We perform a feature extraction applying a 10-s window with 50% overlap. Regarding the IMU sensors, the features extracted were time and frequency domain features from every axis and from the signal vector magnitude which can be computed with Eq. 1:

$$Signal\ Vector\ Magnitude = \sqrt{x^2 + y^2 + z^2} \qquad (1)$$

Using Eq. 1 we computed the acceleration magnitude (MAG) from the accelerometer and the angular velocity magnitude (AVM) from the gyroscope.

The statistical features extracted can be seen in Table 1.

Table 1. Statistical features for classification.

	Time-domain		Frequency-domain
Mean	Standard deviation	25% quartile	Energy
Median	Minimum	75% quartile	Dominant frequencies (1–5)
Variance	Maximum	Interquartile range	
Skewness	Kurtosis	Entropy	

For the vital signs, following [9] we also extracted structural features and transient features. Structural features are computed by using a function f with a set of parameters $[a_0, a_1, \ldots, a_n]$ to fit the given time series S (Table 2). For our experiments, we chose a 3rd order polynomial function (n=3) and an exponential function.

Table 2. Structural features for vital signs.

Feat function	Equation	Feature set
Polynomial	$F(t) = a_0 + a_1 t + a_2 t^2 + \cdots + a_n t^n$	$a_0, a_1, a_2, \ldots, a_n$
Exponential	$F(t) = ae^t + b$	a, b

The transient features are used to describe the behavior of the vital signs in the window. Apart from the trend (τ, Eq. 2) and the Magnitude of Change (MoC, Eq. 3) which are proposed in [9] we also computed two other features; the starting trend and the ending trend. These features provide information on the behavior of the signal (increasing, decreasing, constant) at the start and the end of the window, giving a more detailed view of the direction of the signal.

$$\tau = \begin{cases} 1 & \text{if } m >= r \\ -1 & \text{if } m <= r \\ 0 & \text{if } |m| < |r| \end{cases} \qquad (2)$$

$$MoC = max\{|max(S_p^+) - min(S_p^-)|, |max(S_p^-) - min(S_p^+)|\} \qquad (3)$$

where S_p^+ is the subset of the time series S in the upper p percentage of the total time window and S_p^- is the subset of the time series S in the lower p percentage of the total time window (Fig. 1).

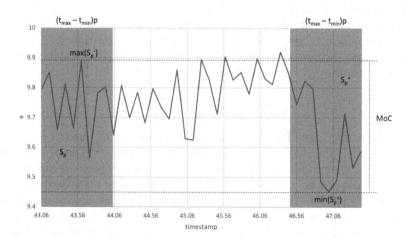

Fig. 1. Calculation of MoC. Data generated from PAMAP2 dataset.

18 statistical features were computed from both the IMU and vital sign modalities (180 in total) and 6 structural (12 in total) and 4 transient (8 in total) features were computed only from the vital sign modalities. A total number of 200 features were extracted, 180 of which were statistical features.

After computing the features, we split the data into training and testing data with a 70/30 ratio and trained five different classifiers, namely bagged Classification and Regression Tree (CART), Random Forest (RF), k-Nearest Neighbors (kNN), Linear Discriminant Analysis (LDA) and Support Vector Machines (SVM) on the IMU and the vital sign data separately. The classifiers were trained using 10-fold cross-validation. We tested two feature level fusion techniques, concatenation and principal component analysis (PCA) and six different decision level fusion techniques, averaging, product, accuracy weighted average, GA based weighted average, SVM stacking and Gradient Boosting Machine (GBM) stacking, to fuse the IMU and vital signs for every classifier.

For the early or feature level fusion, we used concatenation and PCA. For the concatenation, we simply fed all the computed features of the different modalities directly to one classifier. For the PCA-based fusion, we computed the principal components of the extracted features and then kept only the principal components that describe the 95% of the features' variance.

The averaging fusion technique is one of the simplest forms of late fusion [10] that uses the average of the predicted class probabilities of different classification algorithms and the class with the highest final probability is assigned to each case in the data. The final probability of each class is computed in Eq. 4:

$$\hat{P}_j = \frac{\sum_{i=1}^{M} P_{i,j}}{\sum_{j=1}^{N} \sum_{i=1}^{M} P_{i,j}} \tag{4}$$

where $P_{i,j}$ is the probability of the j class of the i_{th} classifier, M is the total number of classifiers and N the total number of classes.

Another class of late fusion algorithms is the ones that use weights. A very well-known algorithm is the weighted accuracy fusion algorithm [10], where the weights express the performance of each of the algorithms that will be combined, in terms of accuracy, an evaluation metric calculated by Eq. 5.

$$accuracy = \frac{TP + TN}{TP + FP + TN + FN} \tag{5}$$

In the above, TP (True Positives) indicates the number of cases of a class correctly identified, TN (True Negatives) indicates the number of cases not belonging in a class that was correctly identified, FP (False Positives) indicates the number of cases not belonging to a class that was wrongly identified and finally, FN (False Negatives) indicates the number of cases belonging to a class that was erroneously identified.

Then, a weighted sum is performed on the probabilities of each class and the class with the highest probability is chosen as the decision. Generally, in the weighted fusion techniques, the probability of each class is given by Eq. 6.

$$\hat{P}_j = \sum_{i=1}^{M} P_{i,j} W_{i,j} \tag{6}$$

In the above, $P_{i,j}$ denotes the probability of the j class of the $i_t h$ classifier and $W_{i,j}$ the weight of the j class of the i_{th} classifier, while corresponding to the respective accuracy.

For the GA-based weighted average, we performed a GA optimization of the different weights for the weighted average technique. The GA algorithm is an optimization algorithm based on the process of natural selection to maximize a fitness function. In our study, the fitness function is the prediction's accuracy.

The stacking method is based on training a new classifier on the probabilities of the classes as they are computed from the best fit of the cross-validation for each classifier. For training, the SVM and GBM classifiers were selected. From the cross-validation process, we extracted the out-of-fold probabilities for each class for the IMU and the vital sign data. These probabilities along with their class label were used to train the stacking classifiers. For the final prediction firstly we computed the probabilities of each class using the testing data and the initial classifiers and then these probabilities were fed to the stacking classifiers.

For the feature selection, we used seven different methods on the concatenated IMU and vital signs features. For the first method, we computed the correlation of all the extracted features and selected only the features with correlation values below 0.75. For the second method, we computed the importance of the different features for each classifier and selected the top 20 features with the higher value of importance. For the third method, we performed a Recursive Feature Elimination (RFE) feature selection technique with the estimator algorithm being the classifier used for the final classification each time. We also applied a Simulated Annealing (SA) optimization method for the selection of the optimal subset of the features per classification algorithm. The rest of the feature selection techniques are based on the computation of Mutual Information (MI) between the feature set and the different activity classes. The first technique computes the MI of the features and then chooses the 20 features with the highest MI scores. The next technique uses the joint MI (JMI) of the features and again chooses the top 20 features. Finally, the last feature selection technique is the mRMR technique, which is based on MI to assess relevance and redundancy. Again the top 20 features were selected.

4   Results

4.1   Dataset

The PAMAP2 dataset [12] includes data originating from 3 IMU worn in the wrist, the chest and the dominant side's ankle, a heart rate sensor and a temperature sensor. We chose to use the heart rate and temperature sensors and the accelerometer and the gyroscope from the wrist-worn IMU. The dataset includes measurements from 9 subjects performing a series of 12 different activities. These activities were *lying, sitting, standing, walking, running, cycling, Nordic walking, ascending stairs, descending stairs, vacuum cleaning, ironing and rope jumping.*

4.2   Fusion Results

The accuracy results of the different fusion methods of our experiments are presented in Table 3. Each modality on its own manages to achieve a relatively high accuracy score, the highest being at 86,64%. This classification accuracy, even though it is not considered as bad, definitely needs improvement.

As is evident in Table 3, the fusion methods applied in this paper manage to improve this classification accuracy score, especially RF and CART which outperform the other classifiers. These 2 classifiers are the only ones to achieve an accuracy score of around 95%, with the RF classifier using the GBM stacking late fusion method achieving the highest accuracy, that being 95,32%. In 3 out of 5 classifiers, the fusion method achieving the best accuracy score is the GBM stacking method. Also, in all of the classifier cases, most of the fusion methods perform better than each modality alone, meaning that the fusion methods offer added value to the overall HAR system.

Table 3. Accuracy results from different fusion methods. Max values from each classifier are in bold.

	RF	LDA	kNN	Bagged CART	SVM
IMU	0.8664	0.8164	0.5191	0.8555	0.4286
vital signs	0.8359	0.4305	0.4759	0.8109	0.3564
Concatenation	0.9177	0.8473	0.6218	**0.9423**	0.4964
PCA	0.8277	0.7236	0.6191	0.8055	0.4282
Max probability	0.9395	0.8368	0.6473	0.9300	0.4691
Product	0.9527	0.8455	0.6373	0.9364	0.5205
Accuracy weighted	0.9395	0.8264	0.6445	0.9291	0.4714
GA weighted	0.9391	0.8368	0.6477	0.9295	0.4814
SVM stack	0.4264	0.4927	0.4282	0.5105	**0.5241**
GBM stack	**0.9532**	**0.8900**	**0.6914**	0.9409	0.4727

For illustrative purposes, we only provide the graph of the F1-score of the classifier performing the best, that being RF. Figure 2 depicts the F1-score of every different activity and all different fusion methods applied. In Fig. 2 it can be seen that the GBM stack method and Product method are the only methods that have an F1-score over 90% in all of the different classes. These are also the only two methods with an accuracy score over 95%. It can also be seen that the methods performing the worst are PCA and SVM stack, with the SVM stack having the worst performance. This is in line with the accuracy score in Table 3 where the SVM stack has the lowest accuracy score.

4.3   Feature Selection Results

In Table 4 the accuracy scores of the different feature selection methods are presented. Feature selection methods improve the classification accuracy in all

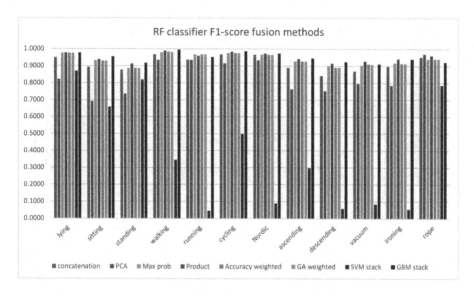

Fig. 2. F1-score of RF classifier with different fusion methods.

Table 4. Accuracy results from different feature selection methods. Max values from each classifier are in bold.

	RF	LDA	kNN	Bagged CART	SVM
IMU	0.8664	0.8164	0.5191	0.8555	0.4286
Vital signs	0.8359	0.4305	0.4759	0.8109	0.3564
Correlation FS	0.9155	0.8205	0.6200	0.8995	0.5114
VarImp FS	0.8877	0.7418	0.6259	0.9086	0.4809
RFE	**0.9532**	**0.8495**	**0.7232**	**0.9423**	**0.5850**
SA	0.9123	0.7591	0.3436	0.8995	0.5736
MI	0.8395	0.7155	0.4100	0.8295	0.5559
JMI	0.9086	0.7700	0.4395	0.8936	0.5736
mRMR	0.9200	0.7841	0.4491	0.9055	0.5673

classifiers, compared to each modality alone. Between all classifiers, the feature selection method performing the best is the RFE. With regards to feature selection methods, again the best performing classifiers are RF and CART, with RF having the highest score. The RFE method used with the RF classifier also reduced the number of features from a total of 200 to only 24 features. These features include 7 statistical features from the IMU data and 12 statistical and 4 structural features from vital sign data.

Similarly, we present only the F1-scores of the classifier performing the best, that being again RF. In Fig. 3 the F1-scores for all the different activities for RF classifier using different feature selection methods can be seen, where it is

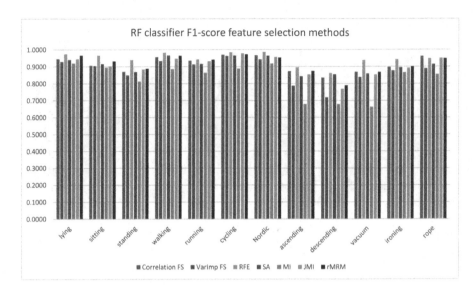

Fig. 3. F1-score of RF classifier with different feature selection methods.

Table 5. Comparison of our accuracy results with other studies

Study	Accuracy	Method used
Wu et al. [18]	61.28%	Zero-shot learning with neural networks
Kasnesis et al. [7]	84.41%	One-shot learning with deep neural network features
Wan et al. [17]	91.00%	Convolutional neural network on the IMU data
Spara et al. [15]	94.36%	Piecemeal Training on convolutional neural network
Dua et al. [5]	95.27%	Convolutional neural network with Gated recurrent unit layers
Our work	**95.32%**	Statistical, structural and transient features, RFE technique

evident that the RFE feature selection method performs better than the rest of the feature selection methods in most cases. It is important to mention that even though the RFE accuracy score is the same as the GBM stack fusion method, that is 95,32%, the RFE F1-score reveals that the RFE method performs worse than the GBM stack method, especially in the *ascending* and *descending* classes. In these classes, the RFE method does not manage to have an F1-score over 90%, while the GBM stack method has an F1-score over 90% in all cases.

Our work shows very promising results in HAR using the PAMAP2 dataset. In Table 5 a comparison of our accuracy results with results from other studies using the PAMAP2 dataset is presented, indicating that our approach outperforms other methods in terms of accuracy. However, it should be stated that the method described in [5] achieves comparable results to ours without dealing with the massive handcrafted feature extraction, selection and fusion procedures, but lacks in explainability, because of the neural networks' black box nature. In contrast, the proposed approach is fully transparent, which is of paramount importance when dealing with the healthcare domain.

5   Conclusion

In this work, we applied various early and late fusion techniques and feature selection methods to combine IMU and vital signs from a publicly available dataset on HAR. We also extracted structural and transient features for the vital signs, apart from the statistical features that were extracted from both the IMU and vital signs. Our fusion experiments revealed that the RF classifier with the GBM stack late fusion method performs the best, with an accuracy score of 95,32%. In our FS experiments, the RFE FS method outperformed the rest with the RF classifier having the highest accuracy, which is again 95,32%. Nevertheless, since the features extracted are handcrafted and there are multiple configurations tested, the methods described in the paper need to be tested on other datasets as well to validate the uniformity of our results.

Acknowledgment. This research was supported by the xR4DRAMA project (grant agreement No 952133), which is funded by the European Union's Horizon 2020 research and innovation programme and by the REA project (project code: T1EDK-00686), co-financed by the European Regional Development Fund of the European Union and Greek national funds through the Operational Program Competitiveness, Entrepreneurship, and Innovation, under the call RESEARCH - CREATE - INNO-VATE.

References

1. Chen, J., Sun, Y., Sun, S.: Improving human activity recognition performance by data fusion and feature engineering. Sensors **21**(3), 692 (2021)
2. Chen, L., Liu, X., Peng, L., Wu, M.: Deep learning based multimodal complex human activity recognition using wearable devices. Appl. Intell. **51**(6), 4029–4042 (2020). https://doi.org/10.1007/s10489-020-02005-7
3. Cornacchia, M., Ozcan, K., Zheng, Y., Velipasalar, S.: A survey on activity detection and classification using wearable sensors. IEEE Sens. J. **17**(2), 386–403 (2016)
4. Doewes, A., Swasono, S.E., Harjito, B.: Feature selection on human activity recognition dataset using minimum redundancy maximum relevance. In: 2017 IEEE International Conference on Consumer Electronics-Taiwan (ICCE-TW), pp. 171–172. IEEE (2017)
5. Dua, N., Singh, S.N., Semwal, V.B.: Multi-input CNN-GRU based human activity recognition using wearable sensors. Computing **103**(7), 1461–1478 (2021). https://doi.org/10.1007/s00607-021-00928-8
6. Giannakeris, P., et al.: Fusion of multimodal sensor data for effective human action recognition in the service of medical platforms. In: Lokoč, J., et al. (eds.) MMM 2021. LNCS, vol. 12573, pp. 367–378. Springer, Cham (2021). https://doi.org/10.1007/978-3-030-67835-7_31
7. Kasnesis, P., Chatzigeorgiou, C., Patrikakis, C.Z., Rangoussi, M.: Modality-wise relational reasoning for one-shot sensor-based activity recognition. Pattern Recogn. Lett. **146**, 90–99 (2021)
8. Lara, O.D., Labrador, M.A.: A survey on human activity recognition using wearable sensors. IEEE Commun. Surv. Tutor. **15**(3), 1192–1209 (2012)

9. Lara, O.D., Pérez, A.J., Labrador, M.A., Posada, J.D.: Centinela: a human activity recognition system based on acceleration and vital sign data. Pervasive Mob. Comput. **8**(5), 717–729 (2012)

10. Maghsoudi, Y., Alimohammadi, A., Zoej, M.V., Mojaradi, B.: Weighted combination of multiple classifiers for the classification of hyperspectral images using a genetic algorithm. In: ISPRS Commission I Symposium From Sensors to Imagery (2006)

11. Nweke, H.F., Teh, Y.W., Mujtaba, G., Al-Garadi, M.A.: Data fusion and multiple classifier systems for human activity detection and health monitoring: review and open research directions. Inf. Fusion **46**, 147–170 (2019)

12. Reiss, A., Stricker, D.: Introducing a new benchmarked dataset for activity monitoring. In: 2012 16th International Symposium on Wearable Computers, pp. 108–109. IEEE (2012)

13. Rosati, S., Balestra, G., Knaflitz, M.: Comparison of different sets of features for human activity recognition by wearable sensors. Sensors **18**(12), 4189 (2018)

14. Saha, J., Chowdhury, C., Biswas, S.: Two phase ensemble classifier for smartphone based human activity recognition independent of hardware configuration and usage behaviour. Microsyst. Technol. **24**(6), 2737–2752 (2018). https://doi.org/10.1007/s00542-018-3802-9

15. Sapra, D., Pimentel, A.D.: Constrained evolutionary piecemeal training to design convolutional neural networks. In: Fujita, H., Fournier-Viger, P., Ali, M., Sasaki, J. (eds.) IEA/AIE 2020. LNCS (LNAI), vol. 12144, pp. 709–721. Springer, Cham (2020). https://doi.org/10.1007/978-3-030-55789-8_61

16. Steven Eyobu, O., Han, D.S.: Feature representation and data augmentation for human activity classification based on wearable IMU sensor data using a deep LSTM neural network. Sensors **18**(9), 2892 (2018)

17. Wan, S., Qi, L., Xu, X., Tong, C., Gu, Z.: Deep learning models for real-time human activity recognition with smartphones. Mob. Netw. Appl. **25**(2), 743–755 (2020)

18. Wu, T., Chen, Y., Gu, Y., Wang, J., Zhang, S., Zhechen, Z.: Multi-layer cross loss model for zero-shot human activity recognition. In: Lauw, H.W., Wong, R.C.-W., Ntoulas, A., Lim, E.-P., Ng, S.-K., Pan, S.J. (eds.) PAKDD 2020. LNCS (LNAI), vol. 12084, pp. 210–221. Springer, Cham (2020). https://doi.org/10.1007/978-3-030-47426-3_17

19. Xefteris, V.R., Tsanousa, A., Meditskos, G., Vrochidis, S., Kompatsiaris, I.: Performance, challenges, and limitations in multimodal fall detection systems: a review. IEEE Sens. J. **21**, 18398–18409 (2021)

20. Zhang, M., Sawchuk, A.A.: A feature selection-based framework for human activity recognition using wearable multimodal sensors. In: BodyNets, pp. 92–98 (2011)

21. Zhu, J., San-Segundo, R., Pardo, J.M.: Feature extraction for robust physical activity recognition. HCIS **7**(1), 1–16 (2017). https://doi.org/10.1186/s13673-017-0097-2

On Assisting Diagnoses of Pareidolia by Emulating Patient Behavior

Zhaohui Zhu[1,2]([✉]) [iD], Marc A. Kastner[2] [iD], and Shin'ichi Satoh[1,2] [iD]

[1] The University of Tokyo, Tokyo, Japan
[2] National Institute of Informatics, Tokyo, Japan
{zhzhu,mkastner,satoh}@nii.ac.jp

Abstract. The pareidolia phenomenon is a discriminating characteristic of psychiatric disorders, expressed through visual illusions seen by patients. Typically, it can be diagnosed through the noise pareidolia test, which is time-consuming to both patients and experts. In this research, we propose a novel computer-assisted method to identify pareidolia phenomenon. The idea is to emulate patient behavior in face detection models to get a similar behavior in noise pareidolia tests as patients. Unlike most medical image analysis methods, for psychiatric disorders the ground-truth varies from patient to patient, making this challenging. For a set of training patients, we fine-tune reference models to detect noise pareidolia test responses in the same way as each individual patient. Then, a new test patient is identified by comparing their behavior to the reference models using a distance function in a trained embedding space. In the experiments, the effectiveness of the proposed method is demonstrated. Further, we can show that our method can improve the efficiency of the clinical noise pareidolia test by reducing the number of necessary test images while reaching a comparable high accuracy.

Keywords: Psychiatric disorders · Emulating patient behavior · Medical multimedia · Computer-assisted diagnosis

1 Introduction

The pareidolia phenomenon is a medical condition, where patients see visual illusions from ambiguous patterns, perceiving them as objects or faces. It is observed as an important clinical feature in a psychiatric disorder called dementia with Lewy bodies (DLB) [2,16], but similar illusions can also be seen in others such as Alzheimer's Disease (AD) [19]. The so-called *noise pareidolia test* [10,19] is used to diagnose the pareidolia phenomenon in patients. In this test, a medical expert shows a set of black-and-white noise-like images to a patient, asking them whether they sees a face in the ambiguous patterns. Figure 1 shows examples of such test images. While most healthy people would identify face patterns as shown in Fig. 1a as a face, patients with pareidolia phenomenon might also misunderstand patterns as shown in Fig. 1b as a face.

A medical expert can make a diagnosis whether the patient is suffering from a psychiatric disorder using this test. However, in order to get meaningful results, the test needs to be repeated with a large number of images, resulting in a time-consuming burden for both the patients and the experts [10,19]. Furthermore, while the test is designed

© Springer Nature Switzerland AG 2022
B. Þór Jónsson et al. (Eds.): MMM 2022, LNCS 13141, pp. 299–310, 2022.
https://doi.org/10.1007/978-3-030-98358-1_24

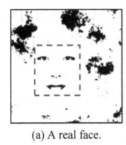 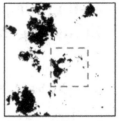

(a) A real face.   (b) Only random noise.

Fig. 1. Noise pareidolia test images [10]. The red box in (a) shows a region with a real face, which most people would understand as a face. In contrast, (b) just consists of noise, which only a patient might misunderstand it as a face. (Color figure online)

for DLB patients, patients suffering from AD might also see similar illusions in the test, making it harder to conclusively diagnose one disease or another [19]. To solve these issues, in this research, we want to get a better understanding of the noise pareidolia test. First, we aim to improve the efficiency of the clinical diagnosis by reducing the number of needed images. Second, we aim to get a better understanding of the disease and patient types and use this for a computer-assisted diagnosis.

Machine-learning based approaches have provided promising ways for automated or assisted diagnosis [14,15]. In particular, medical image analysis has shown great improvement, advancing fields like cancer detection [17] through anomaly detection. However, psychiatric phenomena can not easily be identified through common methods for anomaly detection. In the case of psychiatric disorders, medical conditions are mainly found in behavioral changes rather than physical changes, and the *ground-truth* greatly varies from patient to patient, making it challenging to design a computer-assisted method for this task.

In this paper, we propose a method to diagnose and better understand pareidolia phenomenon by emulating the behavior of patients. To achieve this, we first prepare a set of models, each behaving similarly to an individual known patient. As the noise pareidolia test is based on facial misunderstandings in noise images, we fine-tune a pretrained face detection model to force a similar kind of face misunderstanding on noise pareidolia test images, as a patient would have. In collaboration with a laboratory for psychiatry, we obtained noise pareidolia test images marked with regions misunderstood as faces by patients, as annotated by medical experts. Using this data, we prepare a set of reference models for each patient, fine-tuning towards a detection behavior closely emulating the responses of that patient. Next, given a new patient with an unknown type of behavior, we prepare a query model and compare it to the behavior of the known reference models using a proposed distance function. It allows us to detect the type of the patient, and which combination of existing reference patient their behavior most closely resembles. We can also show promising performance in whether the patient would behave more similarly to DLB patients or more similarly to AD patients and healthy people. Lastly, we propose a sampling method which can be used to reduce the number of necessary test images, in order to improve the efficiency of clinical testing while keeping the diagnosis accuracy comparable. An evaluation of the proposed method with a selected number of baseline methods shows promising performance for this novel task.

To summarize, our main contributions are as follows:

- We propose a method for the novel task to identify pareidolia phenomenon in patients through emulating patient behavior. This is a step towards a computer-assisted diagnosis for psychiatric conditions.
- Using a dataset annotated by medical experts, we can show promising performance for discerning real pareidolia (in DLB) from similar visual illusions (such as AD).
- We provide a way to reduce the number of needed test images in clinical noise pareidolia tests, by sampling for the most decisive test images.

2 Related Work

In the following, we discuss existing research on noise pareidolia tests and other machine-learning based tasks in medical diagnosis.

Noise Pareidolia Test. There have been a number of researches on pareidolia phenomenon in medical science. Ballard et al. [2] and Uchiyama et al. [16] show that the pareidolia phenomenon is occurring in psychiatric disorders, mainly dementia with lewy bodies (DLB). Zhou et al. [20] explain individual differences in pareidolia phenomenon including sex differences, developmental factors, personality traits, and neurodevelopmental factors. The noise pareidolia test [19] uses black-and-white noise-like images to evaluate facial pareidolia symptoms. In the test process, the images are shown to patients and they are asked whether they see a face. The individual responses are used for diagnosing pareidolia. Mamiya et al. [10] discuss the effectiveness of the noise pareidolia test, showing that the test results correlate with clinical visual hallucinations. There has been research [1,11] which defines face pareidolia in a more open sense of seeing face-like patterns in daily life objects and trying to discern them from real human faces. However, these works have not been working with the medical definition of pareidolia phenomenon in psychiatric disorders and did not target to diagnose them. Furthermore, they do not use noise pareidolia tests or patient data for analysis. To the best of our knowledge, there is no existing research on medical imaging for noise pareidolia tests.

Machine Learning for Medical Diagnosis. Machine learning algorithms have been applied for medical diagnosis and analysis [14,15], helping medical experts in analyzing data. In medical image analysis, many works propose deep neural network-based methods for computed tomography (CT) scans, magnetic resonance imaging (MRI) scans, and retinal photography [6]. Xu et al. [17] perform classification, segmentation, and visualization in large-scale tissue histopathology images to help experts diagnose tumor and cancer subtypes. Kermany et al. [7] develop an effective transfer learning algorithm to process retinal image for classifying macular degeneration and diabetic retinopathy, which are related to blindness. Another use for machine learning for medical applications is clinical psychology and psychiatry [4]. Klöppel et al. [8] use support

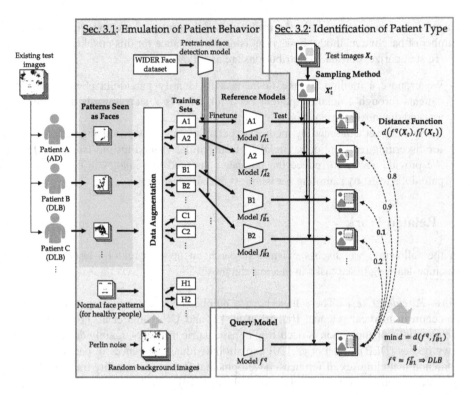

Fig. 2. Flowchart of the proposed method. The left part shows the emulation of patient behavior (details in Sect. 3.1). The right part describes the proposed method for identifying pareidolia phenomenon (details in Sect. 3.2).

vector machines to assist diagnosing AD by structural neuroimaging data. Pettersson-Yeo et al. [13] propose a multimodal approach which include genetic data to identifying psychosis. However, these existing works mostly rely on physically observed data of the patient, such as image, genetic and conversational data. In the case of pareidolia phenomenon, the medical condition is mainly observed through the behavior of a patient, and can often vary based on daily condition. Furthermore, the characteristics of seen visual illusions greatly vary from patient to patient, making a training and optimization for single pattern difficult. As such, a better approach for identifying this psychiatric phenomenon is needed.

3   Proposed Method

In this section, we describe the proposed method of identifying pareidolia phenomenon by modelling patients. The proposed method consists of two stages: First, the patient behavior in the noise pareidolia test is emulated by retraining face detection models. As the clinical noise pareidolia test is based on confusing noise patterns with faces, we use face detection models fine-tuned towards misunderstanding noise in the same way as individual patients. With this, we gain a set of *reference models*, each emulating an individual patient. Second, the type of an unknown patient is identified by comparing it with all reference models. We consider the unknown patient to be a *query model*. The difference between the query model and each reference model is described using a distance function. This way, the method can identify which models have a similar behavior and decide the type of the query model. The two stages are discussed in Sect. 3.1 and 3.2, respectively. The full method is depicted in Fig. 2.

3.1 Emulation of Patient Behavior

In the first step, face detection models are trained to emulate healthy people and patients, with regards to how they would respond to the noise pareidolia test. We first prepare pareidolia test data which is then used for training the reference models.

Pareidolia Patient Data. Previous work [10] provided 43 black-and-white noise pareidolia images, including both real face patterns and random noise misidentifiable by patients. Using these images, medical experts from the Integrated Innovation Lab for Psychiatry, Keio University School of Medicine helped us to annotate a dataset using real patient responses for use in this paper. As the number of the existing images is not enough for training face detection models to emulate human behavior, we extend the data using data augmentation. We first generate new random background images based on Perlin noise [12]. Next, patterns mistakenly identified as faces by each patients are randomly embedded, using rotation, flipping and resizing, in order to increase the amount of images.

Training Method for Reference Models. For training the reference models, we use a two-step process: First, a face detection model based on Single Shot Multi-Box Detector (SSD) [9] is pretrained on the WIDER FACE dataset [18]. This ensures that it detects faces closely approximating a healthy human. Second, the pretrained face detection model is fine-tuned on the training set consisting the noise pareidolia test images prepared by data augmentation. This second step fine-tunes the behavior of the model to resemble each individual patient. This step is repeated for each patient individually, using different subsets of annotated data. For instance, to emulate Patient A, only the patterns identified as faces by Patient A and the real face patterns are labeled as positive samples. In order to emulate small deviations even within the same patient type (e.g., a same patient giving slightly different responses on different time of the day), we train a set of models for each patient, introducing some random noise, shuffled subsets of training data, and different random seeds.

3.2 Identification of Patient Type

In the previous section, we prepared a number of reference models $f_i^r, i \in \{1, 2, ...M_r\}$. To identify if a given query model f^q has pareidolia phenomenon, first, N test images X_t are input to the reference models and the query model. The test data X_t include random background images without any appended patterns, as well as images containing real faces and some patterns misidentified by the patients. Then, the distance between

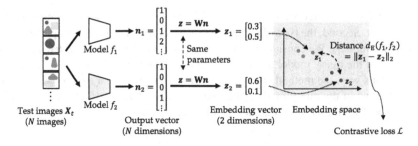

Fig. 3. Definition of distance in embedding space d_E. Two models are tested with N images, and mapped into a 2-dimensional embedding space using a linear mapping.

the outputs of the query model f^q and each reference models f_i^r is measured using a designed function $d(\cdot, \cdot)$. Finally, the query model is considered to have the same type of behavior with the reference models close to it. In this procedure, the key to distinguish if the query model is similar to the model with pareidolia phenomenon is the distance function. We propose a distance function that makes the models of same pareidolia phenomenon closer to each other. In addition, a sampling method is proposed to reduce the number of necessary test image from N to N', making it more feasible and efficient in practice.

Distance Function and Embedding Space. To compute distances, we first embed the models into a low-dimensional space. The embedding is trained in a metric learning way, pushing similar patients close to another while pushing different types of disorder apart. Then, the Euclidean distance in the embedding space d_E is used to compute the distance between two models f_m, $m \in \{1, 2\}$, as shown in Fig. 3. Each model f_m is tested with the test data $\boldsymbol{X}_t$ with N images, and the number of detected objects in each test images are listed as an output vector $\boldsymbol{n}_m = \{n_m^{(i)}\}_{i=1}^N$, where $n_m^{(i)}$ is the number of object detected in the i-th image. Then, $\boldsymbol{n}_m$ is mapped into a 2-dimensional embedding vector $\boldsymbol{z}_m$ in the embedding space using a linear mapping $\boldsymbol{z}_m = \mathbf{W}\boldsymbol{n}_m$, $\mathbf{W} \in \mathbb{R}^{2 \times N}$. Finally, the Euclidean distance between the embedding vector $\boldsymbol{z}_m$ of the two models is calculated as $d_E(f_1(\boldsymbol{X}_t), f_2(\boldsymbol{X}_t)) = \|\boldsymbol{z}_1 - \boldsymbol{z}_2\|_2$, where $\|\cdot\|_2$ is ℓ^2 norm.

In this process, the weight matrix $\mathbf{W}$ is learned to optimize this distance function. Contrastive loss [3,5], a distance-based loss function commonly used for metric learning is adopted. We compute the contrastive loss over pairs of samples in a training model set $\{f_i^{tr}\}_{i=1}^{M_{tr}}$, which consists of some of the reference models. In our method, we can defined the contrastive loss on two levels: type-level and patient-level. The type-level contrastive loss $\mathcal{L}_t$ is positively correlated with the distance d_E for a pair of models with the same type, for instance, both having pareidolia phenomenon. In contrast, for models of different types, it is negatively correlated with d_E. Similarly, the patient-level contrastive loss $\mathcal{L}_p$ is positively correlated with d_E between a pair of models emulating the same patient, and negatively correlated with d_E between models emulating different patients. Then, the weight $\mathbf{W}$ is updated by gradient descent in order to minimize the contrastive loss, and other reference models can be used as a test model set to perform identification with the optimized distance function.

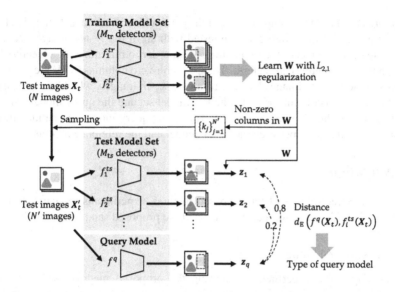

Fig. 4. Identifying models using sampling method. Test images are sampled using the information of the training model set, reducing the number of needed tests.

Sampling Methods. The key idea of sampling method is to reduce the number of test results necessary for calculating the embedding vector. It is achieved by involving a regularization term while training the embedding for the distance function. Concretely, during the training process of the embedding, the parameter $\mathbf{W}$ is optimized to minimize the contrastive loss. In the sampling method, a regularization term is added to the objective function $\arg\min_{\mathbf{W}} (\mathcal{L}(\mathbf{W}) + \lambda \|\mathbf{W}\|_{2,1})$, where λ is a regularization parameter, $\|\mathbf{W}\|_{2,1}$ is the $L_{2,1}$ norm of the weight matrix $\mathbf{W}$, defined as $\|\mathbf{W}\|_{2,1} = \sum_{i=1}^{N} \|\mathbf{w}_i\|_2$, where $\mathbf{w}_i \in \mathbb{R}^2$ is each column of $\mathbf{W}$.

After training with the training model set, the objective function is minimized, the $L_{2,1}$ norm of the weight will be smaller, and there will be more zero columns $\mathbf{w}_i = 0$ in the weight $\mathbf{W}$. It can be assumed that there are N' non-zero columns ($N' \leq N$) and the set of non-zero columns is $K = \{k_j\}_{j=1}^{N'} \subseteq \{1, \ldots, N\}$. When the embedding vector of each model f_m is calculated, the linear mapping is

$$z_m = \mathbf{W} n_m = \sum_{i=1}^{N} w_i n_m^{(i)} = \sum_{j=1}^{N'} w_{k_j} n_m^{(k_j)}. \tag{1}$$

Here, the test result on the i-th test image $n_m^{(i)}$ is multiplied with the corresponding column w_i. If w_i is zero, $w_i n_m^{(i)}$ will always be zero, and the corresponding test results $n_m^{(i)}$ have no effect to the embedding vector z_m of the model. Thus, the embedding vector is only related to N' items $w_{k_j} n_m^{(k_j)}$ where $k_j \in K$. By using this, unimportant test images which are corresponding to the zero columns in $\mathbf{W}$ can be omitted, and the number of the test images can be reduced to N'.

Identifying Patients. The complete flow of the patient identification is depicted in Fig. 4. First, the models in the training set are tested with all of the N test images. Next, the embedding of the distance function is trained, in order to minimize the objective function with the $L_{2,1}$ regularization term. Then, N' non-zero columns in $\mathbf{W}$ are found, and we can sample the test images by only using the k_j-th images, which are corresponding to the non-zero columns. Finally, the test model set and the query model only need to be tested with the N' images, and the type of the query model can be identified by comparing the distances between the query model and the reference models.

4 Evaluation

To verify the effectiveness of the proposed method, experiments are carried out. We evaluate patient identification performance and the proposed sampling method.

4.1 Experimental Setup

Preprocessing. The experiments are using the proposed method as introduced in Sect. 3. We were provided a closed dataset with noise pareidolia test images, consisting of annotated visual illusion regions for five patients (four DLB and one AD). We call the AD patient *Patient A*, and the DLB patients *Patient B-E*. Using this, we extract four to twenty-one isolated visual illusion regions for each patient. Then, we use data augmentation to generate a high number of noise images with embedded annotated regions for each patient. In total, we end up with 2520 images: First, there are 2100 training images, consisting of seven subsets with different embedded patterns (five patients, healthy, and no patterns) with 300 images each. Using these training images, we train 50 reference models for each of the five patients and the healthy people (i.e., 300 models in total), by annotating corresponding patterns to closely emulating their characteristics. Second, there are 420 test images X_t, consisting of 60 images each for every subset. These are used for testing the identification of patient types.

While the dataset contains annotated visual illusions for both DLB and AD patients, medically speaking, the pareidolia phenomenon only describes the condition for DLB patients [2, 16, 19]. Because of this, we group the reference models into two: pareidolia (DLB patients) and non-pareidolia (AD and healthy people). Lastly, the target is to identify whether a query model (i.e., a new unknown patient model) is a pareidolia or a non-pareidolia model.

Embedding Space. In order to identify the type of models using the distance function, we train the embedding with the training model set. The experiment is repeated for four times: For each time, 50 models for one of the four DLB patients (Patient B, C, D and E) are used as query models, and 60 models are randomly selected as the training model set. After training the embedding and sampling the test images, the remaining 190 models are used as reference models. For each of the query models, the distances from the reference models are calculated. By ranking the type of reference models by distance, the average precision of identifying the query model is calculated. Repeating the evaluation on each query model, the mean average precision (mAP) of identifying all models is obtained as the evaluation metric.

4.2 Comparison Methods and Ablation Studies

Our paper is, to the best of our knowledge, the first research to tackle pareidolia diagnosis as a multimedia task. Because of this, we do not have proper comparison methods to compare to. Therefore, we propose a variety of comparison methods as ablation studies in order to verify our choice of approaches. Furthermore, we can show a promising performance in getting a better understanding of this disease, further discussed in Sect. 4.4.

Distance Functions. To verify the effectiveness of the proposed distance function, comparison experiments are carried out for different distance functions. We compare the proposed method d_E to two baseline distance functions: d_N (Baseline 1) is defined as the difference between the numbers of the images with patterns detected as faces by the two models. d_H (Baseline 2) is the Hamming distance of the test results. For each model f_m, there is a N-dimension output vector n_m. The distance d_H between f_1 and f_2 is defined as the Hamming distance between n_1 and n_2.

Loss Functions. The embedding for the proposed distance function is trained with a contrastive loss. We evaluate two types of loss functions: The *one-way loss* is to use only the type-level loss $\mathcal{L}_t$. In this case, models for different patients with the same type are not discriminated. The *two-way loss* is defined as the sum of the type-level loss $\mathcal{L}_t$ and the patient-level $\mathcal{L}_p$. Using two-way loss can make the models separated on the embedding space by both the type and the patient.

Sampling Methods. To evaluate the efficiency of the proposed sampling, a random sampling method is also used in the experiment as a baseline. After the experiment using the proposed sampling method, we sample the same number of test images totally randomly. Then, we train the embedding and conduct identification again, using only the randomly sampled test images. The mAP of using this random sampling method is compared with the performance of the proposed sampling method.

4.3 Results

First, we look at the distribution of the embedding space. Two examples are plotted in Fig. 5, where Fig. 5a shows an embedding trained with one-way loss and Fig. 5b is trained with two-way loss. The models of *Healthy* and *Patient A* (called *A* onwards) are non-pareidolia models, and the others are pareidolia models. Both show that *Healthy* and *A* type models are relatively far from those of *B*, *C*, *D*, and *E* in the embedding space. The result indicates that the embedding can successfully separate the pareidolia phenomenon, which is only found in those of the latter. Moreover, Fig. 5b indicates that, by training with two-way loss, the models of each patient can also be successfully separated from another.

Second, we evaluate the performance of the patient identification, as shown in Table 1. Baseline distance functions are used without training and sampling. The results show that the proposed distance function d_E reaches a higher mAP compared to the baseline distance functions. For both the two-way loss and the one-way loss, the proposed sampling method outperforms the random sampling by having a higher mAP

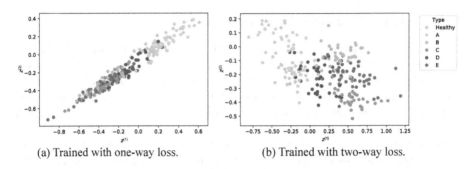

(a) Trained with one-way loss.   (b) Trained with two-way loss.

Fig. 5. Distribution of the models on the embedding space. Each color indicates a different patient. Models of *Healthy* and *A* are medically non-pareidolia, while those of *B, C, D* and *E* have pareidolia phenomenon.

Table 1. Performance of identifying type of the models. The proposed method outperforms baseline comparisons for both the distance functions and the sampling functions.

Distance function	Loss function	Sampling method ($N = 420$)	Avg. mAP
Baseline 1 (d_N)	–	None ($N' = 420$)	0.6565
Baseline 2 (d_H)	–	None ($N' = 420$)	0.5322
Proposed (d_E)	One-way loss	Proposed ($N' = 68.5$)	**0.9014**
		Random ($N' = 68.5$)	0.6472
	Two-way loss	Proposed ($N' = 78.5$)	**0.8736**
		Random ($N' = 78.5$)	0.7438

while using the same number of test images. The mAP of one-way loss is slightly higher than that of two-way loss. In the process of training the embedding, the proposed sampling method is used to reduce the number of test images. Before sampling, the number of test images is $N = 420$. However, using the sampling method, the number can be reduced to N', when the number of zero columns in $\mathbf{W}$ is N'. In average, our proposed method reaches an N' of 68.5 for the one-way loss and one of 78.5 for the two-way loss, resulting in a significant reduction compared to the original method.

4.4 Discussion

The results show promising performance for identifying the type of new patients. The embedding separates different types of models, and the proposed distance function outperforms the two baseline distance functions. Furthermore, the proposed sampling method reduces the number of test image to a more feasible value for a diagnosis, while still reaching higher accuracy than random sampling. Therefore, the study provides a novel approach to a computer-assisted diagnosis of psychiatric disorders.

Comparing the loss functions, the method using one-way loss can reach a slightly higher accuracy. However, as Fig. 5 shows, one-way loss makes the models of *B, C, D* and *E* mixed with each other in the embedding space, while two-way loss can separate models of different patient. This result indicates that using two-way loss may provide more information for medical analysis of patients and classification of pareidolia phenomenon, while keeping a high accuracy for identification.

We found some models showing a lower-than-average performance. For example, in Fig. 5, the models of D is distributed closer to non-pareidolia models. In discussion with medical experts, we believe this outlier may be due to a characteristic of patient behavior not yet well understood. Some DLB patients like D may also see some illusions which are more likely to be seen by AD patients. As such, this finding could be further studied using the embedding trained with the proposed method.

5 Conclusion

In this paper, we proposed a novel method for computer-assisted noise pareidolia test by emulating patient behavior. We train per-patient reference models, incorporating individual behavior differences of each patient. Using a distance function, we can then identify the characteristics of unknown patients by comparing them to the existing reference models. A sampling method is designed to reduce the number of needed tests, providing promising performance for improving efficiency of the clinical noise pareidolia test. The experimental results show that the proposed method can reach a promising performance. To the best of our knowledge, this is the first work to apply machine learning in computer-assisted diagnosis of pareidolia phenomenon for patients. The understanding of patient behavior gained through this research could yield new insights for a better understanding of the psychiatric disorder.

Currently, we use individual patients as reference models due to the low number of patients in our dataset. In future, with a larger amount of patient data, it may be possible to use patient clusters as reference. Furthermore, data augmentation for extending the training data is based on the assumption that the patient always tend to see face in similar patterns of different scales. Future study can explore other possible methods of data augmentation for a more clinical coherent emulation of patient behavior.

Acknowledgments. We would like to thank researchers at the Integrated Innovation Lab for Psychiatry, Keio University School of Medicine for providing us expert knowledge and dataset annotations for pareidolia phenomenon. This work was supported by JST, CREST Grant Number JPMJCR1686, Japan.

References

1. Abbas, A., Chalup, S.: From face recognition to facial pareidolia: analysing hidden neuron activations in CNNs for cross-depiction recognition. In: 2019 International Joint Conference on Neural Networks, pp. 1–8 (2019)
2. Ballard, C., et al.: A detailed phenomenological comparison of complex visual hallucinations in dementia with Lewy bodies and Alzheimer's disease. Int. Psychogeriatr. **9**(4), 381–388 (1997)
3. Chopra, S., Hadsell, R., LeCun, Y.: Learning a similarity metric discriminatively, with application to face verification. In: 2005 IEEE Computer Society Conference on Computer Vision and Pattern Recognition, vol. 1, pp. 539–546 (2005)

4. Dwyer, D.B., Falkai, P., Koutsouleris, N.: Machine learning approaches for clinical psychology and psychiatry. Annu. Rev. Clin. Psychol. **14**, 91–118 (2018)
5. Hadsell, R., Chopra, S., LeCun, Y.: Dimensionality reduction by learning an invariant mapping. In: 2006 IEEE Computer Society Conference on Computer Vision and Pattern Recognition, vol. 2, pp. 1735–1742 (2006)
6. Ker, J., Wang, L., Rao, J., Lim, T.: Deep learning applications in medical image analysis. IEEE Access **6**, 9375–9389 (2017)
7. Kermany, D.S., et al.: Identifying medical diagnoses and treatable diseases by image-based deep learning. Cell **172**(5), 1122–1131 (2018)
8. Klöppel, S., et al.: Accuracy of dementia diagnosis-a direct comparison between radiologists and a computerized method. Brain **131**(11), 2969–2974 (2008)
9. Liu, W., et al.: SSD: single shot MultiBox detector. In: Leibe, B., Matas, J., Sebe, N., Welling, M. (eds.) ECCV 2016. LNCS, vol. 9905, pp. 21–37. Springer, Cham (2016). https://doi.org/10.1007/978-3-319-46448-0_2
10. Mamiya, Y., et al.: The pareidolia test: a simple neuropsychological test measuring visual hallucination-like illusions. PLoS ONE **11**(5), e0154713 (2016)
11. Natsume, R., Inoue, K., Fukuhara, Y., Yamamoto, S., Morishima, S., Kataoka, H.: Understanding fake faces. In: Leal-Taixé, L., Roth, S. (eds.) ECCV 2018. LNCS, vol. 11131, pp. 566–576. Springer, Cham (2019). https://doi.org/10.1007/978-3-030-11015-4_42
12. Perlin, K.: An image synthesizer. ACM SIGGRAPH Comput. Graph. **19**(3), 287–296 (1985)
13. Pettersson-Yeo, W., et al.: Using genetic, cognitive and multi-modal neuroimaging data to identify ultra-high-risk and first-episode psychosis at the individual level. Psychol. Med. **43**(12), 2547–2562 (2013)
14. Rajkomar, A., Dean, J., Kohane, I.: Machine learning in medicine. N. Engl. J. Med. **380**(14), 1347–1358 (2019)
15. Sajda, P.: Machine learning for detection and diagnosis of disease. Annu. Rev. Biomed. Eng. **8**, 537–565 (2006)
16. Uchiyama, M., et al.: Pareidolias: complex visual illusions in dementia with Lewy bodies. Brain **135**(8), 2458–2469 (2012)
17. Xu, Y., et al.: Large scale tissue histopathology image classification, segmentation, and visualization via deep convolutional activation features. BMC Bioinform. **18**(1), 1–17 (2017)
18. Yang, S., Luo, P., Loy, C.C., Tang, X.: Wider face: a face detection benchmark. In: Proceedings of the IEEE Conference on Computer Vision and Pattern Recognition, pp. 5525–5533 (2016)
19. Yokoi, K., Nishio, Y., Uchiyama, M., Shimomura, T., Iizuka, O., Mori, E.: Hallucinators find meaning in noises: pareidolic illusions in dementia with Lewy bodies. Neuropsychologia **56**, 245–254 (2014)
20. Zhou, L.F., Meng, M.: Do you see the "face"? Individual differences in face pareidolia. J. Pac. Rim. Psychol. **14**, e2 (2020)

Using Explainable AI to Identify Differences Between Clinical and Experimental Pain Detection Models Based on Facial Expressions

Pooja Prajod[✉], Tobias Huber, and Elisabeth André

Chair for Human-Centered Artificial Intelligence, Augsburg University,
Augsburg, Germany
{pooja.prajod,tobias.huber,elisabeth.andre}@uni-a.de

Abstract. Most of the currently available pain datasets use two types
of pain stimuli - people with clinically diagnosed conditions (e.g. surgery)
performing tasks that cause them pain (we call this clinical pain) and
pain caused by external stimuli such as heat or electricity (we call this
experimental pain). In high-risk domains like healthcare, understanding
the decisions and limitations of various types of pain recognition models
is pivotal for the acceptance of the technology. In this paper, we present
a process based on Explainable Artificial Intelligence techniques to investigate the differences in the learned representations of models trained on
experimental pain (BioVid heat pain dataset) and clinical pain (UNBC
shoulder pain dataset). To this end, we first train two convolutional neural networks - one for each dataset - to automatically discern between
pain and no pain. Next, we perform a cross-dataset evaluation, i.e., evaluate the performance of the heat pain model on images from the shoulder
pain dataset and vice versa. Then, we use Layer-wise Relevance Propagation to analyze which parts of the images in our test sets were relevant
for each pain model. Based on this analysis, we rely on the visual inspection by a human observer to generate hypotheses about learned concepts that distinguish the two models. Finally, we test those hypotheses
quantitatively utilizing concept embedding analysis methods. Through
this process, we identify (1) a concept which the *clinical* pain model is
more strongly relying on and, (2) a concept which the *experimental* pain
model is paying more attention to. Finally, we discuss how both of these
concepts are involved in known pain patterns and can be attributed to
behavioral differences found in the datasets.

Keywords: Automatic pain detection · Explainable Artificial
Intelligence · Cross-database evaluation · Facial expression recognition

This work has received funding from the European Union's Horizon 2020 research and
innovation programme under grant agreement No 847926 MindBot and from the DFG
under project number 392401413, DEEP.

B. Þór Jónsson et al. (Eds.): MMM 2022, LNCS 13141, pp. 311–322, 2022.
https://doi.org/10.1007/978-3-030-98358-1_25

1 Introduction

Expressing pain is an important social component as it triggers social reactions such as empathy and care [3]. In clinical practice, recognizing pain facial expression helps in pain diagnosis and eliminates the need for verbalization. This is especially important for patients who cannot provide verbal pain reports like people with dementia, infants, and ventilated patients [3]. So, assessing facial expressions is crucial for many healthcare applications and also a valuable skill for medical staff [3,18]. In many of these cases, caregivers have to routinely monitor the pain levels of a patient for optimal pain management. However, this is often not possible due to practical issues like a lack of available clinical staff. As a consequence, there has been an increasing interest in developing methods to automatically detect pain from facial expressions.

Many works [22,26] have proposed models for automatic pain recognition. These models are shown to achieve good performances but are usually trained and tested on the same dataset. Cross-database evaluations are not very common. According to Othman et al. [16], this could be because well-trained models tend to perform poorly on other databases. This was observed in [6], where the authors found that a model trained using one pain dataset performed poorly on another dataset. Real-world scenarios like hospitals or nursing homes will inevitably be different from the settings used to collect the training datasets. Therefore, cross-database evaluation is important to ensure the robustness of the models and verify that they are not learning database-specific patterns.

Another drawback of many state-of-the-art pain recognition models is that they come in the form of deep neural networks whose decisions are usually incomprehensible to humans. The research area of Explainable Artificial Intelligence (XAI) aims to make such "black-box" models more understandable. Explainability is crucial for deploying pain recognition models to support therapy, as patients and therapists should be able to understand the system's decisions in order to achieve successful treatment [3]. Petyaeva et al. [17], for instance, showed that briefly training medical staff on pain observation scales and therefore increasing the staff's understanding of the scales, led to more frequent and more confident use of the scales in everyday care. This indicates that similar improvements can be expected from increasing the comprehensibility of automatic pain recognition models. A second benefit of increasing the explainability of pain recognition models is that it can help to mitigate some of the problems of the models that do not perform well on cross-database evaluations. On the one hand, understanding the reasoning and biases of models trained on different datasets can help to create less biased models and datasets in the future. On the other hand, pain recognition models are often employed in ensembles of several pain recognition models. Here, it is crucial to understand the reasoning and biases of each model to judge which models can be trusted in a given situation.

As a first step to solve the aforementioned problems, we study two pain recognition models in this paper - one trained on clinical pain images from the UNBC shoulder pain database and the other on experimental pain images from the BioVid heat pain database. In addition to the typical within-database evaluation, we perform cross-database evaluation of these models. Furthermore, we utilize XAI techniques to find more detailed differences between the models' reasoning and biases. As far as we know, this is the first time that XAI is used for cross-database evaluation of pain models. First, we generate saliency maps that highlight which areas of input images were important for the decision of each model. Based on a manual inspection of these saliency maps, we formulate hypotheses about the concepts learned by the models. Then, we use concept embedding analysis to test our hypotheses. Finally, we discuss our results in light of underlying behavioral differences between the datasets.

2 Related Work

2.1 Cross-database Evaluation of Pain Datasets

Cross-database evaluations involve evaluating a model on samples from different databases than the one used for training. Such evaluations are crucial for building robust models and testing the generalization capabilities of a model. In [16], the authors used the BioVid heat pain database and the X-ITE pain database (thermal pain) to train pain recognition models. They trained pairs of pain recognition models using facial activity descriptors based on random forest classifiers and CNNs. They performed cross-database evaluation of the models using the two datasets. They found that models trained using both methods performed well in cross-database evaluations. It can be noted that both BioVid and X-ITE databases use the same stimuli (varying temperatures) to induce pain.

Dai et al. [6] studied various combinations of emotion datasets and the UNBC shoulder pain dataset to train a real-time pain detection model. They also tried CNNs and SVMs based on Action Units (AUs) - visible indicators of the activity of individual facial muscles. In addition to the within-dataset evaluations, they tested the models on datasets consisting of posed emotion and pain expressions. They found that even though the CNN models performed extremely well in within-database evaluations, all posed pain images were classified as no-pain. They concluded that CNNs learned database-specific features which enabled them to predict pain in subjects from the UNBC database. The only model that performed well in real-time posed pain recognition was an AU-based SVM trained on AffectNet and UNBC shoulder pain images. They tested this model on images of 20 randomly chosen participants from the BioVid heat database. The model performed poorly which prompted the authors to examine their test images. They found that many of the participants closed their eyes for most parts of the experiment. Some even had closed eyes for the entire experiment. Since closed eyes are an indicator of pain in the UNBC dataset, they attribute the poor performance of the model to this difference in behavior between datasets.

2.2 Explainable Artificial Intelligence

In scenarios where neural networks are used to support medical therapy, patients and therapists must be able to understand the system's decisions in order to achieve successful treatment. A common way of analyzing the predictions of neural networks trained on images is the creation of so-called *saliency maps* that highlight how important each pixel of an input image was for the prediction. For the specific use-case of pain recognition, Weitz et al. [23] applied and compared two different saliency map methods: Layer-wise Relevance Propagation (LRP) [15] and Local Interpretable Model-agnostic Explanations (LIME) [19]. While the authors found that the salience maps generated in their work provide some initial insights into the reasoning of the network, they concluded that saliency maps in their current form are often ambiguous and hard to interpret for end-users. Besides saliency maps, another promising explanation approach is the generation of counterfactual images that show how an input image could be modified to change the network's prediction. For medical applications, Mertes et al. [13] generated such counterfactual explanations for a pneumonia detection network and found in a user study that those counterfactual explanations were easier to interpret than LRP and LIME saliency maps. However counterfactual explanations still heavily rely on the final interpretation by human users.

To reduce the amount of interpretation that has to be done by the user, recent work on *concept embedding analysis* investigates which human-comprehensible concepts were learned by a given network. Bau et al. [4] show that semantic concepts are often embedded in individual neurons of the latent space of a neural network. For example, Khorrami et al. [8] demonstrate that certain neurons in the final convolutional layer of a network trained to analyze facial expressions learned to recognize specific AUs. To extend this method to concepts that might be embedded in multiple neurons within the latent space, Kim et al. [9] trained a binary linear classifier that takes as input the output of an intermediate layer of the network and learns to recognize a predefined concept. If the linear classifier can recognize the concept, then it is likely that the concept is embedded in the intermediate layer that acts as input to the linear classifier. They tested their approach on multiple image classification networks and a network for predicting diabetic retinopathy. A common challenge for the aforementioned concept embedding analysis techniques is that the potential concepts have to be externally identified by human experts. To mitigate this effort, Prajod et al. [18] utilized LRP saliency maps to facilitate the identification of potential concepts.

3   Approach

3.1   Datasets

UNBC-McMaster Shoulder Pain Expression Database [12] - This database contains image sequences of 25 participants with shoulder pain performing a range of arm movements. Each image is annotated with a Prkachin and Solomon Pain Intensity(PSPI) score on a scale of 0 (no pain) to 15 (extreme pain). Since these images are from a video, many of them are similar. We remove the redundant images through the approach followed in [26]. For each image sequence, whenever the pain intensity doesn't change for more than five consecutive images, we keep only the first image. From the down-sampled dataset, we reserve images belonging to four participants, who gave consent to publish their images, as test set. The images belonging to one randomly chosen participant are used for validation and the images of the remaining 20 participants for training.

BioVid Heat Pain Database [21] - We use the part A of this database that contains short videos showing facial expressions of 87 participants reacting to heat pain stimuli. Each participant has 20 short videos (5.5s long) for each of five conditions (no pain + four pain intensities). In [25], the authors found that the initial two pain intensities failed to trigger a facial response in many participants and use only the highest intensity for discerning pain vs. no pain. Based on their findings, we only consider videos that are labeled as baseline (no-pain) and highest pain level. The authors also found that the facial activity for the highest pain level starts at around 2s and peaks around the 4s mark. So, we choose the frame at 4s in the video as a representative image. As suggested by the creators of the BioVid dataset [1], we exclude 20 participants who did not have a visible reaction to the stimuli. Among the remaining 67 participants, 15 participants were reserved for testing, five participants were used for validation and the images of the remaining participants formed the training set.

3.2   Pain Training

After selecting representative images from the videos or image sequences (see Sect. 3.1), the resulting datasets are relatively small with around 1000–2000 images. This is typical for pain datasets [22], but deep learning usually requires larger amounts of training data. To mitigate this problem, deep learning models are often trained using *transfer learning*. This involves re-using the knowledge that the model learned for a specific task A, for training an adjacent task B. In this paper, we adopt the transfer learning process from [18]. The idea is to fine-tune an emotion recognition model to discern between pain and no-pain images. We use the same emotion recognition model as Prajod et al. [18] which is a VGG-16 based convolutional neural network (CNN) trained on the Affect-Net dataset [14]. This dataset consists of 420299 face images that are manually annotated with 11 emotions. As described by Prajod et al. [18] we remove images belonging to 'None', 'Uncertain' and 'Non-face'. Afterward, we modify the prediction layer of the model to predict pain vs. no-pain. To train the model for pain recognition, we fine-tune all layers of this model. We train two pain models - one trained on clinical pain images (UNBC shoulder pain dataset) and one on experimental pain images (BioVid heat pain dataset). Both models are trained using SGD optimizer (learning rate = 0.01) and focal loss [11] given by:

$focal\_loss = (1 - p_t)^\gamma \times cross\_entropy\_loss$. The variable p_t is the predicted probability of a sample belonging to its true class (t) and we set the hyperparameter $\gamma = 2$.

Before passing an image through our models, we detect and crop the face using OpenCV. We also scale them to the default VGG16 input dimensions (224×224). While training both the models, we use Keras data augmentation options: rotation ($[-25°, 25°]$), height shift ($[-10\%, 10\%]$), width shift

([−10%, 10%]), shear ([−10%, 10%]), zoom ([−10%, 10%]) and horizontal flip. We train the models using NVIDIA GeForce GTX 1060 6GB GPU.

Unlike the BioVid dataset, the UNBC dataset is imbalanced. So, for the clinical pain model, we use weighted focal loss. We follow the weighting scheme proposed in [5], where weights of classes are computed as (we set the hyperparameter $\beta = 0.99$): $weighted\_loss = \frac{1-\beta}{1-\beta^{samples\_per\_cls}} \times focal\_loss$.

3.3   Cross-database Evaluation

Many works propose automatic pain recognition models that achieve good performances on the datasets they are trained on. However, cross-dataset evaluations are less explored. One reason for this might be that well-trained models may not perform well on other datasets [16]. So, in addition to the typical performance evaluation, we perform a cross-dataset evaluation of both our models and determine the generalization capabilities of these models. The generalizability of a model is particularly important when deploying it in real-world applications. First, we evaluate the performance of the models in terms of f1-score, recall, precision, and accuracy. Since the UNBC dataset is not balanced, we compute the macro-average of these metrics - compute the metric for each class and average them. In this step, the evaluation is within-database i.e., training and test images come from the same database. After the within-database evaluation, we perform the cross-database evaluation. Here we compute the same performance metrics as before, but for the test set derived from the other database. If the model's cross-database performance is comparable to its initial performance, we say the model learned generic pain features and not dataset-specific features.

3.4   Visual Analysis

After determining if the models learned generic pain features, we explore the differences in the features that were relevant for each model. We follow the technique proposed in [18] to visually inspect these differences. To this end, we generate saliency maps highlighting the areas of the input image which, according to each model, are indicators of pain (i.e. were important for the pain prediction neuron). For generating the saliency maps, we use the iNNvestigate [2] implementation of LRP with the z-rule for fully connected layers and the z^{+}-rule for convolution layers. This composite LRP method is relatively robust to sanity checks [20] and retains the conservation property of LRP which states that the relevance values of all pixels sum up to the prediction value. The conservation property is important for an accurate comparison of different saliency maps. We use our test sets from both the UNBC and BioVid datasets as input images. For each input image, we obtain two saliency maps - one from the clinical pain model and the other from the experimental pain model. To better highlight the differences between these models, we subtract the raw saliency maps from each other and normalize the differences between 0 and 1. With this method, we obtain saliency maps that highlight the areas that the experimental pain model payed more attention to than the clinical pain model and vice versa. We manually inspect these images to derive hypotheses about potential differences in the concepts that were relevant for the clinical and experimental pain models.

3.5 Concept Embedding Analysis

In this section, we describe our method of verifying the hypothesis that the concepts identified with the method described in Sect. 3.4 actually distinguish the models trained on clinical and experimental pain. To this end, we follow the approach of Prajod et al. [18] and Kim et al. [9] and train binary linear classifiers on the output of an intermediate layer of each model to investigate how well these concepts are embedded. We use our test sets of both UNBC and BioVid datasets as training data for the linear classifiers. For each image in the combined test set, two of the authors manually annotate whether the concept is present or not. Afterward, we check where the two annotators disagree. Those images are additionally labeled by a third annotator, who is not involved with the paper, and the final label is chosen by majority vote.[1] The authors have experience with facial affect recognition models which was sufficient for annotating the specific concepts we identified in our experiment. By computing the output of the last pooling layer of each pain model for all images within our combined test set, we obtain an experimental pain and a clinical pain feature-set that represent the latent space of the respective pain recognition models. We then train a linear Support Vector Machine (SVM) on the task of detecting the concept candidate on each of those two feature sets. For this training, we use 2-fold cross-validation and compute the average f1-score of the two folds. This training process is repeated for 500 iterations using different random seeds for fold image selection and weight initialization. Finally, we run a paired t-test between the 500 averaged F1 scores of each feature-set. This comparison method is suggested in [7] for five iterations as 5×2 cross validation paired t-test and we extend it to 500 iteration as suggested by Kim et al. [9]. The result of this test shows whether there is a significant difference between the performance of SVMs trained on the clinical pain feature-set and the SVMs trained on the experimental pain feature-set. If there is a significant difference then it is likely that there is a difference in the quality of the embedding of the concept candidate between the latent spaces of the two pain models.

4 Results

As described in Sect. 3.2, we train two pain recognition models based on a clinical pain dataset (UNBC shoulder pain) and an experimental pain dataset (BioVid heat pain). Tables 1 and 2 show the results of within-database and cross-database evaluations of the clinical pain model and the experimental pain model, respectively. The within-database accuracy of both our models are comparable to other papers (clinical pain: 85% [6], experimental pain: 66% [16]).

---

[1] The final annotations are available upon request to the authors.

Table 1. Performance of clinical pain model

Test images	Precision			Recall			F1-score			Accuracy
	No pain	Pain	Avg.	No pain	Pain	Avg.	No pain	Pain	Avg.	
Clinical pain	0.74	0.87	0.80	0.71	0.88	0.80	0.72	0.88	0.80	0.83
Experimental pain	0.74	0.56	0.65	0.28	0.90	0.59	0.41	0.69	0.55	0.59

Table 2. Performance of experimental pain model

Test images	Precision			Recall			F1-score			Accuracy
	No pain	Pain	Avg.	No pain	Pain	Avg.	No pain	Pain	Avg.	
Clinical pain	0.48	0.87	0.68	0.80	0.61	0.71	0.60	0.72	0.66	0.67
Experimental pain	0.65	0.80	0.73	0.87	0.54	0.70	0.74	0.64	0.69	0.70

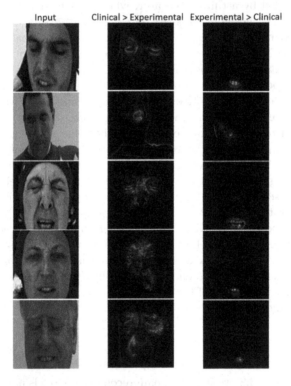

Fig. 1. Saliency maps of some images belonging to our experimental pain (BioVid) and clinical pain (UNBC) test sets. Each row shows the original input image and the result of subtracting the saliency maps generated for both models. The images under 'Clinical > Experimental' highlight the areas that the clinical pain model pays more attention to than the experimental pain model. The images under 'Experimental > Clinical' highlight the areas that are more relevant for the experimental pain model than for the clinical pain model.

Looking at the within-database evaluation, the clinical pain model yields better overall performance and seems better at recognizing pain images. However, the performance of the clinical pain model is considerably lower in cross-database evaluation. The experimental pain model has comparable performance on both datasets. To draw insights about the differences in the features that were relevant for the two models, we generate saliency maps for both models and manually analyze them as described in Sect. 3.4. Figure 1 shows some of the input images and the corresponding saliency map differences. We noticed that the clinical pain model pays more attention to the eye area, especially on closed eyes. In contrast, the experimental pain model pays attention to the mouth area, especially on visible teeth. So, we hypothesize that the clinical pain model is more biased towards closed eyes whereas, the experimental pain model is biased towards detecting visible teeth. We use concept embedding analysis (see Sect. 3.5) to test our hypothesis. We choose closed eyes and visible teeth as the concepts for our analysis. For analyzing the concept of closed eyes, we divide the images from test sets into two sets - images where the participants closed both their eyes and images where they did not. We use the clinical pain model and experimental pain model as feature extractors. We trained pairs of SVMs (one on clinical pain features and the other on experimental pain features) to recognize the concept of closed eyes. We found that the SVMs trained using clinical pain model features significantly outperformed the ones trained on experimental pain model features (clinical mean $F1 = 81.6\%$, experimental mean $F1 = 78.38\%$, t-statistic: 92.2, p-value: < 0.001). We follow the same procedure to analyze the concept of visible teeth. This time the images are divided into two sets based on whether the teeth were at least partially visible or not. In this case, the SVMs trained using experimental pain features were significantly better in discerning visible teeth images (clinical mean $F1 = 73.47\%$, experimental mean $F1 = 82.54\%$, t-statistic: -131.43, p-value: < 0.001).

To ensure that our findings are indeed based on differences in the datasets and not due to our specific models, we repeated fined-tuning the models and the concept embedding analysis four more times (using different seeds). In all the iterations, the models differed significantly on closed eyes and visible teeth.

5   Discussion

One interesting finding is that the clinical pain model doesn't perform well in cross-database evaluation, although it performs well on the clinical pain dataset. In contrast, the experimental pain model performs well on both datasets. It can be seen from Table 1 that misclassification of no-pain images from the experimental pain dataset is a key reason for the drop in performance of the clinical pain model. As the results of our concept analysis show, the clinical pain model pays more attention to the eye area, especially the closed eyes. In [24], the authors studied various facial activity descriptors from the BioVid database to predict pain. They found that eye closure is less relevant in predicting pain than other features. They attributed this to their observation that some participants close their eyes even during no-pain videos. When we annotated the test sets for concept embedding analysis, we noticed that around 20% of the no-pain images from the experimental pain test set were annotated as closed eyes. This could be a plausible reason for the misclassification of no-pain images by the clinical pain model. Our result is also in line with [6], where the authors observed that it was difficult for a model trained on the UNBC dataset to recognize pain in inputs from the BioVid dataset. They chose the videos of 20 random participants from the BioVid database and found that many of them closed their eyes for most of the experiment. In contrast, the participants from UNBC database look at the camera and usually close their eyes while in pain. The authors attribute the poor performance of their model to this difference in behavior. Our results reinforce their hypothesis by, for the first time, analyzing the trained models themselves through XAI and empirically showing that the model trained on the UNBC dataset is paying more attention to closed eyes.

The experimental pain model pays more attention to the mouth area, especially the visibility of teeth (see Fig. 1). This concept can be associated with the pain pattern of 'open mouth' - one of the four facial pain patterns identified in [10]. They associate AUs 25, 26, 27 with the open mouth pattern. However, as noted in [24], these AUs are absent in the calculation of PSPI scores. The clinical pain dataset (UNBC database) is annotated based on PSPI scores whereas the experimental pain dataset (BioVid database) is annotated based on the temperature applied. Therefore, it is plausible that an image in the clinical pain dataset with an open mouth is labeled as no-pain (if PSPI AUs are absent). Moreover, from our manual annotations, we found that around 90% of visible teeth images were from the experimental pain dataset. While the total number of images with visible teeth is low our results show that this bias is reflected in the trained models. Hence, future works that use the BioVid dataset and medical personal that employ models based on this dataset should be aware of this bias.

6   Conclusion

In this paper, we explored the differences between models trained on clinical and experimental pain datasets. We used the UNBC shoulder pain database for clinical pain facial expressions and the BioVid heat pain database for experimental pain expressions. Using these datasets, we trained a clinical pain and an experimental pain model. In addition to the typical within-database evaluations, we evaluated the models on cross-database test sets. We found that the clinical pain model performed poorly on cross-database evaluation whereas the experimental pain model performed similarly on both datasets. This prompted us to use XAI techniques to explore the features that each model prioritizes in its predictions. We found that the concept of closed eyes is more important for clinical pain models and an open mouth with visible teeth is important for experimental pain models. We also found that these differences are rooted in the difference in the behavior of the participants in these datasets. Knowing these biases will aid researchers and medical personal when working with these datasets or when they employ models trained on those datasets.

The insights from this work show the potential merits of cross-database evaluations of pain recognition models with both performance metrics as well as XAI techniques. However, one limitation of our work is that we only tested one specific pair of pain datasets. People in real-life scenarios express various emotions other than pain. Therefore, our next step is to train models that can recognize other emotions like anger, fear, etc., along with pain and investigate those models in XAI-assisted cross-database evaluations based on different pain and emotion datasets. It will also be interesting to study the generalization performance of the models for different levels of pain (e.g. trace, weak, and strong pain).

References

1. The biovid heat pain database. http://www.iikt.ovgu.de/BioVid.html. Accessed 18 July 2021
2. Alber, M., et al.: iNNvestigate neural networks! J. Mach. Learn. Res. **20**(93), 1–8 (2019)
3. André, E., Kunz, M.: Digitale gesichts- bzw. schmerzerkennung und ihr potential für die klinische praxis. In: Digitalisierung und Gesundheit. G.IP - Gesundheitsforschung. Interdisziplinäre Perspektiven, Nomos Verlagsgesellschaft mbH & Co. KG (to appear)
4. Bau, D., Zhou, B., Khosla, A., Oliva, A., Torralba, A.: Network dissection: quantifying interpretability of deep visual representations. In: IEEE Conference on Computer Vision and Pattern Recognition, CVPR, pp. 3319–3327. IEEE Computer Society (2017)
5. Cui, Y., Jia, M., Lin, T.Y., Song, Y., Belongie, S.: Class-balanced loss based on effective number of samples. In: Proceedings of the IEEE Conference on Computer Vision and Pattern Recognition, pp. 9268–9277 (2019)
6. Dai, L., Broekens, J., Truong, K.P.: Real-time pain detection in facial expressions for health robotics. In: 2019 8th International Conference on Affective Computing and Intelligent Interaction Workshops and Demos (ACIIW), pp. 277–283. IEEE (2019)
7. Dietterich, T.G.: Approximate statistical tests for comparing supervised classification learning algorithms. Neural Comput. **10**(7), 1895–1923 (1998)
8. Khorrami, P., Paine, T., Huang, T.: Do deep neural networks learn facial action units when doing expression recognition? In: Proceedings of the IEEE International Conference on Computer Vision Workshops, pp. 19–27 (2015)
9. Kim, B., Wattenberg, M., Gilmer, J., Cai, C., Wexler, J., Viegas, F., et al.: Interpretability beyond feature attribution: quantitative testing with concept activation vectors (TCAV). In: International Conference on Machine Learning, pp. 2668–2677. PMLR (2018)
10. Kunz, M., Lautenbacher, S.: The faces of pain: a cluster analysis of individual differences in facial activity patterns of pain. Eur. J. Pain **18**(6), 813–823 (2014)
11. Lin, T.Y., Goyal, P., Girshick, R., He, K., Dollár, P.: Focal loss for dense object detection. In: Proceedings of the IEEE International Conference on Computer Vision, pp. 2980–2988 (2017)
12. Lucey, P., Cohn, J.F., Prkachin, K.M., Solomon, P.E., Matthews, I.: Painful data: the UNBC-McMaster shoulder pain expression archive database. In: Proceedings of the International Conference on Automatic Face & Gesture Recognition and Workshops, pp. 57–64. IEEE (2011)

13. Mertes, S., Huber, T., Weitz, K., Heimerl, A., André, E.: Ganterfactual - counterfactual explanations for medical non-experts using generative adversarial learning. CoRR abs/2012.11905 (2021)
14. Mollahosseini, A., Hassani, B., Mahoor, M.H.: AffectNet: a database for facial expression, valence, and arousal computing in the wild. IEEE Trans. Affect. Comput. **10**(1), 18–31 (2019)
15. Montavon, G., Binder, A., Lapuschkin, S., Samek, W., Müller, K.-R.: Layer-wise relevance propagation: an overview. In: Samek, W., Montavon, G., Vedaldi, A., Hansen, L.K., Müller, K.-R. (eds.) Explainable AI: Interpreting, Explaining and Visualizing Deep Learning. LNCS (LNAI), vol. 11700, pp. 193–209. Springer, Cham (2019). https://doi.org/10.1007/978-3-030-28954-6_10
16. Othman, E., Werner, P., Saxen, F., Al-Hamadi, A., Walter, S.: Cross-database evaluation of pain recognition from facial video. In: 2019 11th International Symposium on Image and Signal Processing and Analysis (ISPA), pp. 181–186. IEEE (2019)
17. Petyaeva, A., et al.: Feasibility of a staff training and support programme to improve pain assessment and management in people with dementia living in care homes. Int. J. Geriatr. Psychiatry **33**(1), 221–231 (2018)
18. Prajod, P., Schiller, D., Huber, T., André, E.: Do deep neural networks forget facial action units?-exploring the effects of transfer learning in health related facial expression recognition. arXiv preprint arXiv:2104.07389 (2021)
19. Ribeiro, M.T., Singh, S., Guestrin, C.: "Why should I trust you?": explaining the predictions of any classifier. In: Proceedings of the 22nd ACM SIGKDD International Conference on Knowledge Discovery and Data Mining, pp. 1135–1144 (2016)
20. Sixt, L., Granz, M., Landgraf, T.: When explanations lie: why many modified BP attributions fail. In: Proceedings of the 37th International Conference on Machine Learning, ICML 2020, 13–18 July 2020, Virtual Event, pp. 9046–9057 (2020)
21. Walter, S., et al.: The biovid heat pain database data for the advancement and systematic validation of an automated pain recognition system. In: 2013 IEEE International Conference on Cybernetics (CYBCO), pp. 128–131. IEEE (2013)
22. Wang, F., et al.: Regularizing face verification nets for pain intensity regression. In: 2017 IEEE International Conference on Image Processing (ICIP), pp. 1087–1091. IEEE (2017)
23. Weitz, K., Hassan, T., Schmid, U., Garbas, J.U.: Deep-learned faces of pain and emotions: Elucidating the differences of facial expressions with the help of explainable AI methods. tm-Technisches Messen **86**(7–8), 404–412 (2019)
24. Werner, P., Al-Hamadi, A., Limbrecht-Ecklundt, K., Walter, S., Gruss, S., Traue, H.C.: Automatic pain assessment with facial activity descriptors. IEEE Trans. Affect. Comput. **8**(3), 286–299 (2016)
25. Werner, P., Al-Hamadi, A., Walter, S.: Analysis of facial expressiveness during experimentally induced heat pain. In: 2017 Seventh International Conference on Affective Computing and Intelligent Interaction Workshops and Demos (ACIIW), pp. 176–180. IEEE (2017)
26. Zhao, R., Gan, Q., Wang, S., Ji, Q.: Facial expression intensity estimation using ordinal information. In: Proceedings of the IEEE Conference on Computer Vision and Pattern Recognition, pp. 3466–3474 (2016)

Applications 2

Double Granularity Relation Network with Self-criticism for Occluded Person Re-identification

Xuena Ren[1,3], Dongming Zhang[2(✉)], Xiuguo Bao[2], and Lei Shi[2]

[1] Institute of Information Engineering, Chinese Academy of Sciences, Beijing, China
renxuena@iie.ac.cn
[2] The National Computer Network Emergency Response Technical Team
Coordination Center of China, Beijing, China
zhdm@cert.org.cn
[3] School of Cyber Security, University of Chinese Academy of Sciences,
Beijing, China

Abstract. Occluded person Re-identification is still a challenge. Most existing methods capture visible human parts based on external cues, such as human pose and semantic mask. In this paper, we propose a double granularity relation network with self-criticism to locate visible human parts. We learn the region-wise relation between part and whole and pixel-wise relation between pixel and whole. The relations find non-occluded human body parts and exclude noisy information. To guide the relation learning, we introduce two relation critic losses, which score the parts and maximize the performance by imposing higher weights on large parts and lower ones on small parts. We design the double branch model based on the proposed critic loss and evaluate it on the popular benchmarks. The experimental results show the superiority of our method, which achieves mAP of 51.0% and 75.4% respectively on Occluded-DukeMTMC and P-DukeMTMC-reID. Our codes are available at DRNC.

Keywords: Occluded person re-identification · Relationships learning · Relation critic loss

1 Introduction

Person Re-Identification (Re-ID) aims at identificating the same person across different cameras with various backgrounds, poses, and positions. We can roughly divide research works into two categories of feature learning and metric learning. Recently, these two methods have achieved excellent performance on standard benchmarks by using Convolutional Neural Networks (CNN) and excellent optimization strategies. But their performance degrade in occlusion cases, and

This work is supported in part by the National Key Research and Development Plan of China(No.2018YFB0804202) and in part by the National Natural Science Foundation of China (No. 61672495, No. U1736218 and No.2019YFB1005201).

B. Þór Jónsson et al. (Eds.): MMM 2022, LNCS 13141, pp. 325–338, 2022.
https://doi.org/10.1007/978-3-030-98358-1_26

occluded person Re-ID is still a challenging task despite its great value in practical application.

To address the occlusion problem, existing approaches mostly leverage local features extracted from human body parts to improve representations of the pedestrian. They roughly work in the following streams: 1) Hand-crafted partitioning methods. They manually design grids [7,30] or horizontal stripes [16,23] of the feature maps. But they need strict person alignment and tend to produce mismatches when they can not distinguish human bodies from obstacles properly. 2) Methods based on human pose estimation [3,16,25], or human parsing results [12]. They extract and align body part features based on the external cues. They, however, heavily depend on the accuracy of the off-the-shelf human parsing or pose estimation models, which are error-prone in serious occlusion cases.

To deal with the mentioned issues, we present a novel network, named Double-granularity Relation Network with Self-Criticism (DRNC). It mines visible human parts without needing extra external cues even on heavy occlusion occasions. Specially, we first model the pixel-wise relevance among pixels to suppress the influence of background. For each pixel, we take the pair-wise relations of one pixel on all the other pixels to represent the pixel-wise global relevance. Besides, we also study channel relations to get the pure feature. However, the pixel-wise relevance alone cannot avoid the interference of occluded information in the cases of heavy occlusion. We then develop the region-wise relationship, which exploits part-level impact and assigns different scores to different feature parts. We also design two relation critic losses to learn probability maps based on ID prediction performance. These losses maximize the performance by assigning the discriminative parts with larger relation weights and the occlusion parts with smaller relation weights. We summarize the major contributions of our work as follows:

We propose a novel double granularity relation learning architecture for occluded person Re-ID, which includes a pixel-wise relation(PWR) and region-wise relation (RWR) learning blocks. It utilizes double relevance to extract the non-occluded feature. Unlike previous methods, it does not need external cues.

We design two novel relation critic losses that facilitates adjusting the relation learning process by assigning the helpful parts with larger weights and the other parts with smaller weights based on the Re-ID performance. The losses maximize the contribution of the target-related features and suppress that of unrelated objects.

Experimental results show the proposed approach achieves impressive results on Occluded-DukeMTMC [16] and P-DukeMTMC-reID [33]. Additionally, DRNC achieves competitive results on multiple benchmark person datasets including Market1501 [31] and DukeMTMC [13].

2   Related Work

Various methods have been proposed to solve the problem of Re-ID in recent years, which can be grouped into feature extraction methods [5,12,14,18,19,21,

26] and metric learning strategies [11,27,32]. These deep models, which focus on matching holistic images, are yet not invariable to uncontrollable variations like pose, low resolution, illumination, and occlusion. Among the factors, occlusion has been considered the most challenging. The performances of existing Re-ID methods, which are based on global features, degrade on occluded or partial data. Several methods have been proposed for processing non-full body images.

2.1 Part-Based Scheme

The Occluded Re-ID task is to identify the same person from non-overlap cameras when given a detected target person with occlusions. Generally speaking, the previous methods to solve this problem are to use data augmentation strategies or use external cues (such as masks and poses) or use part-based methods.

The strategy of data enhancement is to enrich the data set by adding simulated occlusion images [33,34]. Artificial occlusion images are employed in model training. The simulated occlusion image can indeed alleviate the problem of insufficient data set to a certain extent. However, the simulated occlusion images cannot reflect the complexity of the obstacles in the actual scene.

Part-based models, which use a part-to-part matching strategy, are employed to handle occlusion. VPM (Visibility-aware part model) [22] learns to perceive the visibility of regions through self-supervision. DSR (Deep Spatial Feature Reconstruction) [7] and its improvements of SFR (Spatial Feature Reconstruction) and FPR (Foreground-aware Pyramid Reconstruction) [9] sparsely reconstruct the feature map of a partial query from the feature map of gallery images. Part-based approaches can flexibly match local features across person images, which often require complicated extra operations and often fail to distinguish human bodies from obstacles reliably, leading to a mismatch in the complex environment.

2.2 External Cues

Approaches with external cues leverage semantic partition or pose estimation to tackle the occlusion problem. PGFA (Pose-Guided Feature Alignment) [16] applies a pose-guided feature alignment method to match the local non-occluded person parts based on the human semantic key-points, and use a pre-defined threshold of keypoints confidence to decide the part visibility. HOReID (High-Order Information Matters) [25] uses key-points estimation to learn high-order relation information and PVPM (Pose-guided Visible Part Matching) [3] learns the distinguishing features through pose-guided attention and self-mines the part visibility in an end-to-end framework. By introducing extra semantic information, these methods can accurately locate and align body parts, and can address occlusion problem, however, the success of such approaches heavily depends on accurate pedestrian partition, they inevitably cost much time to infer these external cues.

2.3   Relation Learning

To alleviate reliance on external cues, attention and relation learning are introduced into Re-ID. RGA (Relation-Aware Global Attention) [29] stacks the pairwise relation with the original feature to create an attention map. DAAF (Deep Attention Aware Feature Learning) [2] extracts global and local attention-aware features with the weakly supervision of human body masks and key points. The weight learning of attention comes from supervising semantic information. DAAF does not explore the non-local relation in detail. The relation module in [17] build a part-level relation to exploits the relevance within image features.

In this paper, we also focus on relation learning to deal with occlusion problem. Different from the mentioned methods, DRNC addresses the occluded Re-ID by exploring a double granularity global relation within feature maps. It studies both the pixel level and part level relevance and further uses them to weight the human parts and non-human parts. To reduce the influence of noisy information, DRNC excludes the original feature map. Besides, the proposed critic blocks measure the gain on the performance and evaluate the quality of the relation blocks. Furthermore, critic losses dynamically adjust the learning of relation. Those are the major differences between our method and RGA [29], ABD-NET (Attentive but Diverse) [1], etc.

3   Proposed Approach

In this section, we elaborate on the proposed semantic-free occluded person Re-identification approach. We first introduce the network architecture. After that, we present our pixel-wise and region-wise relation learning for images with occlusion. Then we define the critic loss. Finally, we explain the training strategy of our model.

3.1   Architecture of the Proposed Model

Our proposed occluded Re-ID model is shown in Fig. 1, which consists of three parts: the Pixel-Wise Relation(PWR) Block, the Region-Wise Relation(RWR) Block, and the Critic Block. Giving an image, we first feed into the backbone network (our model uses ResNet-50 [6] as the backbone), and we obtain the feature mappings. Then, we utilize the PWR block to achieve the pixel-wise relation maps. Afterforwards, the pixel-wise feature map is fed into the RWR block to obtain region-wise relations. The critic block is applied for the outputs of PWR and RWR to guide the relation learning. In the following, we introduce them in detail respectively. And the strong model [15] is our baseline. The backbone network is $\mathcal{F}$ and the input image is x, the features from $\mathcal{F}$ is formulated as $F = \mathcal{F}(x|\theta_b)$.

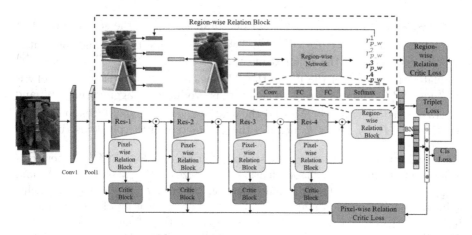

Fig. 1. The framework of DRNC. The feature masks go through pixel-wise relation blocks and region-wise relation blocks in turn. The relation critic loss adjusts the relationship scores. The improved triplet loss, cross-entropy loss, and two kinds of critic loss, i.e., pixel-wise relation critic loss and region-wise relation critic loss, jointly guide the learning process.

3.2 Double Granularity Relation

Pixel-Wise Relation. The PWR is important for estimating the relevance of pixels pairs. We try to learn relation maps from the raw data without semantic guidance. The relation maps base on the correspondence among pixels and provide a coarse estimation of both the human body and non-human parts. Traditional CNNs have a local receptive field, which results in the generation of local feature representations. Since long-range contextual information is not properly encoded, local feature representations may lead to potential differences between features with the same label. Therefore, we build the relations globally and measure the correlation by the dot product between pixels.

One-vs.-All and All-vs.-One Relational Module. To accurately find the non-occluded part, we explore the one-vs.-all and all-vs.-one relation among pixels. For a feature vector with length N, the one-vs.-all relation expresses as $r_i^{o-a} = [r_{i,1}^{o-a}, r_i^{o-a}, ..., r_{i,N}^{o-a}]$, The all-vs.-one relation is formulated as $r_i^{a-o} = [r_{1,i}^{a-o}, r_{2,i}^{a-o}, ..., r_{N,i}^{a-o}]$, where $r_{i,j} = elements_i \times elements_j$. Then the global pairwise relation maps are extracted. The pixel-wise blocks consist of a stack of spatial and channel relation blocks. The stack of relation blocks will help gradually filter noise out and highlight relevantly information.

Global Spatial Relation. The feature $F \in R^{C \times H \times W}$ from the convolution layers go through the pixel-wise blocks, where C, W, H represent the channel, width, and height. First, F passes a convolutional layer to reduce the number of channels, and the number of channels changes from C to C', resulting in a feature map $F' \in R^{C' \times H \times W}$. Then F' enters two conversion branches separately. F' is reshaped as $F^{SR}_{size\_1} \in R^{C' \times (H \times W)}$ in one branch, and in the second branch it is converted to $F^{SR}_{size\_2} \in R^{(H \times W) \times C'}$. Two maps are multiplied, and the spatial relation map is from the resulted matrix $F^{SR} \in R^{(H \times W) \times (H \times W)}$, where $F^{SA}_{i,j}$ evaluates the impact of the ith on the jth element. The pairwise relation of i is $F^{SR}_{i,:}$ and $F^{SR}_{:,i}$. The relation of all elements is produced by aggregating F^{SR} and its transposed matrix $(F^{SR})'$. And the spatial relation map R^{SR} is formulated as $R^{SR} = \mathcal{F}(F|\theta_r)$, where θ_r denotes the parameters of the pixel-wise blocks.

Global Channel Relation. Like the spatial relation, the $F \in R^{C \times H \times W}$ performs a flattening to get two reshaped features with size of $F^c_{size\_1} \in R^{C \times (H \times W)}$ and $F^c_{size\_2} \in R^{(H \times W) \times C}$. Then, a multiplication between $F^c_{size\_1}$ and $F^c_{size\_2}$ helps gain the channel relation map $F^{CR} \in C \times C$. The correlation of each channel is $(c_i, c_j)((c_i, c_{j+1}), ..., (c_c, c_c))$. Where the impact of the ith channel on the jth is $F^{CR}_{i,j}$. The pair-wise relation of channel i is $F^{CR}_{i,:}$ and $F^{CR}_{:,i}$. The pair-wise relation of all channels F^C is to aggregate F^{CR} and its transposed matrix $(F^{CR})'$. The F^C goes through a dimensionality reduction block, which consists of two 1×1 convolutional layer, then passes batch normalization (BN) layer and a ReLU activation layer. After the dimensionality reduction, the feature finally passes through the Sigmoid layer to get the final attention map. And the final attention map R expresses as $R = \mathcal{F}(R^{CR}|\theta_r)$.

Both spatial and channel relations include dimensionality reduction blocks. The features first go through the spatial relation module, and then the features with different weights enter the channel relation module, and finally the refined feature is obtained. The overall pixel-wise relation block is shown in Fig. 2.

Region-Wise Relation. The PWR may fail to avoid the interference from contaminated regions when the person is in heavy occlusion. For example, if a car occupies more than half of the entire image, most elements in the image have high scores with the pixels of the car. Motivated by this observation, we design the RWR block to considers the relation among the parts and the whole to weight different parts.

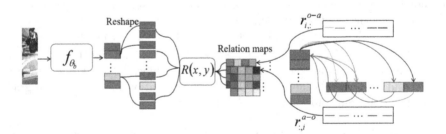

Fig. 2. Details of the relationship blocks. The input images pass the backbone f_{θ_b} to get the original feature, and then the original feature is subjected to a series of matrix transformations, $R(x, y)$ is the dot product of the vector. The relationship maps are learned in both the channel and the spatial dimension.

Specifically, the RWR consists of one convolution embedding function, two fully connected layers, and a softmax layer, as seen in the top part of Fig. 1. The output F first goes through the embedding function which is implemented by a 1×1 convolutional layer followed by batch normalization (BN) and ReLU activation to reduce its channel from C to $C/8$ and then reshapes to $R^{(C/8) \times (H/4) \times (4 \times W)}$. Then the feature is split into four parts P by a uniform partition. $P = \{p_i\}_{i=1}^{4}, p_i \in \mathbb{R}^{1 \times d}$. In order to reduce computational complexity, each part is normalized to a 256-dimensional feature. Then all part feature are concatenated with the global representation g. The network takes in four pairs of feature vectors, and the Softmax layer outputs four normalized relation weights. Finally, the relation weights are multiplied with their corresponding part feature to get the final representation.

3.3   Relation Critic Mechanism

Pixel-Wise Relation Critic. Existing methods usually use the off-the-shelf semantic masks to remove the occlusion or as the attention guides. It takes extra consumed computation to obtain the masks. On the other hand, strong supervision cannot be obtained when semantic information is unavailable.

To increase the representation ability, we propose the relation critic loss, which evaluates the relation performance gain through the prediction results. Specifically, the classification results of the model adjust the relation learning. The details about critic loss are as follows. The features from different layers are first dimensionally reduced through a 1×1 convolutional layer, as shown in Fig. 1. And then the relation map and the reduced feature map are aggregated together. Finally, the concatenated features go through two fully connected layers and get a value. The value is formulated as $ac = \mathcal{C}(A, F | \theta_c)$, where $\mathcal{C}$ is the critic block and θ_c stands for the parameters of the critic blocks. The predicted classification results compare with the ground-truth. The detail of the evaluation value is:

$$e = \begin{cases} 1 & y_i^c = y_i^p \\ 0 & y_i^c \neq y_i^p \end{cases} \tag{1}$$

where y_i^p denotes the prediction label by the relation-based features about person i and the y_i^c is the ground-truth classification label. The evaluation value is used to adjust the relation maps. Formally, the pixel-wise relation critic loss expresses as $L_{rc}^{pw} = \sum_{i=1}^{4} \|ac_i - e\|_2^2$, where ac_i is the value from the i th residual blocks. L_{rc}^{pw} constrains the model to focus on the helpful pixels (vectors).

Region-Wise Relation Critic. To train the relation network, we employ a part-whole critic loss. Each image has four local parts and one global feature. The corresponding label $y = 1$ if the predicted label is the same as the ground-truth classification label. Then the loss function is as follows.

$$L_{rc}^{rw} = \sum_{j=1}^{N} \sum_{i=1}^{4} \left\| max(ac_{j,i}) - 1(y_j^c == y_j^p)) \right\|_2^2 + \left\| min(ac_{j,i}) - (1 - 1(y_j^c == y_j^p)) \right\|_2^2, \tag{2}$$

where y_j^p is the prediction, y_j^c is the ground-truth, $ac_{j,i}$ is the value from p_i part of the j th sample. When the prediction is correct, this loss term makes the relational weight of the useful part larger and that of the irrelevant part smaller, forcing the model to focus more on the future that contributes the most to performance.

3.4   Optimization

We apply the classification loss L_{cls} with the label smoothing and the batch hard triplet loss L_{tri} to jointly supervise the training of CNN model DRNC.

where N is the size of training batch, ε is 0.1, y is truth ID label and p_i is ID prediction logits of class i. As for the pixel-wise relation learning, our task is to enforce the pixels of target-related to suppress the noisy information and improve the discriminative ability of features, so we apply the relation critic loss $L_{cr^{pw}}$. As for the region-wise relation learning, we employ the $L_{cr^{rw}}$ to maximize the performance gain by increasing the maximum relation weight and decreasing the minimum relation weight continuously. In summary, the total loss of DRNC is formulated as:

$$L_{loss} = \lambda(L_{rc}^{pw} + L_{rc}^{rw}) + (1 - \lambda)(L_{tri} + L_{cls}), \tag{3}$$

where λ is the hyperparameter and it is experimentally set to 0.5.

4   Experiments

To evaluate the proposed method, experiments were conducted on holistic (Market-1501 [31], DukeMTMC-reID [13]) and two large occluded (Occ-DukeMTMC [16], P-DukeMTMC-reID [33]) datasets. We adopt standard metrics that are currently used in most literature, namely Cumulative Matching Characteristic (CMC) and mean average precision (mAP) to evaluate our method. Rank-1, rank-5, rank-10, and mAP results are reported. Euclidean Distance is used to measure dissimilarities of image pairs. All results reported in this paper are under a single query setting.

4.1   Implementation and Training Details

The images are resized to 256 × 128. The margin of batch hard triplet loss is 0.3. The batch size is 64. There are 16 identities in each mini-batch and 4 images for each identity. The initial learning rate for the backbone network is 0.0008, decreases by 0.1 at 40, 70, 150,200 epochs. Our model is trained on 240 epochs. The model is implemented on the Pytorch platform and trained with one NVIDIA 3080Ti GPU.

4.2   Experimental Results

Results on Occluded Datasets. We evaluate our proposed framework on two occluded datasets, which includes DukeMTMC-reID [13], P-DukeMTMC-reID [33]. In P-DukeMTMC-reID [33], we use the occluded images as the probe. The comparison results with the existing methods on Occluded-DukeMTMC [16] are listed in Table 1. The results of other methods either from its papers or from the official codes. DRNC gets the top mAP among the compared approaches, and gains 59.6%/51.0% in rank-1/mAP. DRNC surpasses HOReID and MoS by +6.2% and 0.8% mAP, which is a large margin. From Table 1, we can find the occluded methods always perform better than those holistic approaches by a large margin. This result certifies that to propose a specifically designed network for the occluded Re-ID task is essential. The comparable performance of DRNC also displays that without semantic clues, it can also get the target person. This property is attributed to these aspects: 1) Relation-aware attention module, which focuses on these regions with high correlation. The noise data has low relevance with the person, resulting in low concern. 2) Relation constraints, on the one hand, adjust the weights based on model predictions, and on the other hand, restrict inter layer attention.

For the large-scale dataset P-DukeMTMC-ReID [33], we further run experiments to evaluate the performance with the target training set. DRNC achieves 87.6% at rank-1 in Table 2. This result shows the superiority of our model under the supervised setting for occluded person Re-ID.

Table 1. Performance comparison on Occluded-DukeMTMC [16]

Method	rank1	rank5	rank10	mAP
Adver Occluded [10] (CVPR18)	44.5	–	–	32.2
FD-GAN [4] (NIPS 18)	40.8	–	–	–
PCB [23] (ECCV 18)	42.6	57.1	62.9	33.7
DSR [7] (CVPR 18)	40.8	58.2	65.2	30.4
SFR [8] (ArXiv 18)	42.3	60.3	67.3	32.0
PGFA [16] (ICCV 19)	51.4	68.6	74.9	37.3
RGA [29] (CVPR 20)	54.6	–	–	42.9
HOReID [25] (CVPR 20)	55.1	–	–	43.8
MoS [11] (AAAI 21)	**61.0**	–	–	49.2
DRNC(Ours)	59.6	**75.2**	**80.1**	**51.0**

Results on Holistic Datasets. Although methods for occlusion has greatly improved the performance, some strategies cannot achieve satisfactory results on the holistic dataset. Thus, we also apply our method on holistic person Re-ID datasets, Market-1501 [31] and DukeMTMC-ReID [13]. As shown in Table 3, our method achieves comparative performances on both datasets, which suggests the fine generality of our approach.

5   Analyses

5.1   Varying Trade-Off Coefficients

To evaluate the impact of λ and find the value that makes the model optimal, we conduct a test with different trade-off coefficients of λ, which is defined in Eq. 3. The results of the rank-1 accuracy and mAP are shown in Fig. 3 and Fig. 4. We change λ from 0.1 to 0.9. The reason that 1 is not included is that the attention constraints information is from ID prediction, if $\lambda = 1$, we can not get the prediction from the model. As can be seen from Fig. 3 and Fig. 4, when the value of λ increases, the performance of the model first increases and then declines. The model works better when λ is 0.5 or 0.6. When λ is greater than 0.6, the performance decreases dramatically.

Table 2. Performance on the P-DukeMTMC-reID [33] dataset.

Model	Under unsupervised setting				Under supervised setting			
	rank-1	rank-5	rank-10	mAP	rank-1	rank-5	rank-10	mAP
PCB [23] (ECCV 18)	43.6	57.1	63.3	24.7	79.4	87.1	90.0	63.9
Teacher-S [34] (arXiv 19)	18.8	24.2	32.2	22.4	51.4	50.9	–	–
PVPM [3] (arXiv 20)	50.1	63.0	68.6	29.4	85.1	91.3	93.3	69.9
DRNC (Ours)	**52.5**	**64.4**	**69.5**	**31.5**	**87.6**	**93.3**	**94.5**	**75.4**

Table 3. Performance comparisons on holistic datasets

Method	Market-1501		DukeMTMC-reID	
	rank-1	mAP	rank-1	mAP
DSR [7] (CVPR 18)	83.5	64.2	–	–
Adver Occluded [10] (CVPR 18)	86.5	78.3	79.1	62.1
SSP-ReID [19] (arXiv 18)	89.3	75.9	80.1	66.1
PGFA [16] (ICCV 19)	91.2	76.8	82.6	65.5
MGCAM [21] (CVPR 18)	83.8	74.3	46.7	46.0
PCB [23] (ECCV 18)	92.4	77.3	81.9	65.3
PCB+RPP [23] (ECCV 18)	93.8	81.6	83.3	69.2
SPreID [12] (CVPR 18)	92.5	81.3	85.9	73.3
AlignedReID [28] (ArXiv18)	92.6	82.3	–	–
AANet [24] (CVPR 19)	93.9	82.5	86.4	72.6
RGA [29] (CVPR 20)	**95.8**	**88.1**	86.1	74.9
HOReID [25] (CVPR 20)	94.2	84.9	86.9	75.6
MoS [11] (AAAI 21)	94.7	86.8	**88.7**	77.0
DRNC (Ours)	95.0	87.5	88.4	**77.9**

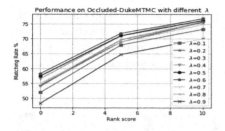

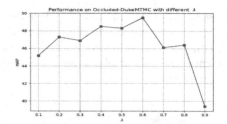

Fig. 3. Rank-r comparision on Occluded-DukeMTMC with different λ

Fig. 4. MAP curve on Occluded-DukeMTMC with different λ

5.2 The Contribution of Each Component

We conduct extensive ablation studies on Occluded-DukeMTMC to analyze each component of DRNC.

The comparison results in Table 4 shows that the performance of the model on the two data sets gradually increases with adds each component. PWR exceeds the baseline by more than 5.0% rank-1 accuracy (0.6% rank-1 accuracy for holistic Re-ID). It can be learned that our proposed DRNC improves much more performance in occluded Re-ID than holistic Re-ID. As shown in Table 4, the proposed relation critic loss outperforms baseline significantly (7.3% and 0.8% gap on Occluded-DukeMTMC and Market-1501), which implies it has learned to extract pure feature and is more robust to occlusions and appearance variation. Combined with RWR, DRNC exceeds PWR by more than 1.8% and 0.3% mAP accuracy on Occluded-DukeMTMC [16] and Market-1501 [31].

Table 4. Influence of different components on Market-1501 [31] and Occluded-DukeMTMC [16].

Method	Occluded-DukeMTMC				Market-1501			
	rank-1	rank-5	rank-10	mAP	rank-1	rank-5	rank-10	mAP
base	49.9	64.9	70.7	42.8	94.1	–	–	85.7
base+PWR	54.9	71.5	77.4	46.5	94.7	–	–	86.8
base+PWR+L_{rc}^{rw}	57.2	72.1	77.2	47.4	94.9	98.4	98.9	87.2
base+PWR+ RWR+L_{rc}^{rw}	57.5	72.9	78.0	49.2	95.0	98.2	98.9	87.5

5.3 Visualization

We apply the Grad-CAM [20] tool to the baseline model and DRNC for the qualitative analysis. Grad-CAM tool can identify the regions that the network considers important.

As Fig. 5 and Fig. 6 show, our network can locate target human subjects without explicit guidance of semantic masks. This nice property is largely attributed to the double granularity relation blocks, which pay more attention to these identity-related pixels or parts and suppress occlusion and noise data to a certain extent.

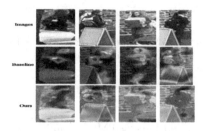

Fig. 5. Illustration of activation maps.   **Fig. 6.** Mask map on different stages

6   Conclusion

In this paper, we deal with the Occluded Person Re-ID Problem with relation learning. We propose a novel Re-ID network DRNC, which utilizes the double granularity relation to suppress the noisy information from the occluded regions and focus on human body rather than occlusions. Besides, DRNC heightens the identity-related pixels or parts by using the relation critic loss. Critic loss uses the performance gain as guidance to adjust the relevance learning, and avoids the time cost caused by the external semantic information. Extensive experiments show that DRNC achieves superior performance for occluded Re-ID.

References

1. Chen, T., et al.: ABD-Net: attentive but diverse person re-identification. In: 2019 IEEE/CVF International Conference on Computer Vision (ICCV), pp. 8350–8360 (2019)
2. Chen, Y., Wang, H., Sun, X., Fan, B., Tang, C.: Deep attention aware feature learning for person re-identification. arXiv abs/2003.00517 (2020)
3. Gao, S., Wang, J., Lu, H., Liu, Z.: Pose-guided visible part matching for occluded person ReID. arXiv abs/2004.00230 (2020)
4. Ge, Y., et al.: FD-GAN: pose-guided feature distilling GAN for robust person re-identification. In: NeurIPS (2018)
5. Guo, J., Yuan, Y., Huang, L., Zhang, C., Yao, J.G., Han, K.: Beyond human parts: dual part-aligned representations for person re-identification. In: Proceedings of the IEEE International Conference on Computer Vision, pp. 3642–3651 (2019)
6. He, K., Zhang, X., Ren, S., Sun, J.: Deep residual learning for image recognition. In: 2016 IEEE Conference on Computer Vision and Pattern Recognition (CVPR), pp. 770–778, June 2016. https://doi.org/10.1109/CVPR.2016.90

7. He, L., Liang, J., Li, H., Sun, Z.: Deep spatial feature reconstruction for partial person re-identification: alignment-free approach. In: Proceedings of the IEEE Conference on Computer Vision and Pattern Recognition, pp. 7073–7082 (2018)
8. He, L., Sun, Z., Zhu, Y., Wang, Y.: Recognizing partial biometric patterns. arXiv preprint arXiv:1810.07399 (2018)
9. He, L., et al.: Foreground-aware pyramid reconstruction for alignment-free occluded person re-identification. In: 2019 IEEE/CVF International Conference on Computer Vision (ICCV), pp. 8449–8458 (2019)
10. Huang, H., Li, D., Zhang, Z., Chen, X., Huang, K.: Adversarially occluded samples for person re-identification. In: 2018 IEEE/CVF Conference on Computer Vision and Pattern Recognition, pp. 5098–5107 (2018)
11. Jia, M., et al.: Matching on sets: conquer occluded person re-identification without alignment. In: Proceedings of the AAAI Conference on Artificial Intelligence, vol. 35, pp. 1673–1681 (2021)
12. Kalayeh, M.M., Basaran, E., Gökmen, M., Kamasak, M.E., Shah, M.: Human semantic parsing for person re-identification. In: Proceedings of the IEEE Conference on Computer Vision and Pattern Recognition, pp. 1062–1071 (2018)
13. Ristani, E., Solera, F., Zou, R., Cucchiara, R., Tomasi, C.: Performance measures and a data set for multi-target, multi-camera tracking. In: Hua, G., Jégou, H. (eds.) ECCV 2016. LNCS, vol. 9914, pp. 17–35. Springer, Cham (2016). https://doi.org/10.1007/978-3-319-48881-3_2
14. Liu, J., Ni, B., Yan, Y., Zhou, P., Cheng, S., Hu, J.: Pose transferrable person re-identification. In: Proceedings of the IEEE Conference on Computer Vision and Pattern Recognition, pp. 4099–4108 (2018)
15. Luo, H., Gu, Y., Liao, X., Lai, S., Jiang, W.: Bag of tricks and a strong baseline for deep person re-identification. In: Proceedings of the IEEE/CVF Conference on Computer Vision and Pattern Recognition Workshops, pp. 0–0 (2019)
16. Miao, J., Wu, Y., Liu, P., Ding, Y., Yang, Y.: Pose-guided feature alignment for occluded person re-identification. In: Proceedings of the IEEE International Conference on Computer Vision, pp. 542–551 (2019)
17. Park, H., Ham, B.: Relation network for person re-identification. In: AAAI (2020)
18. Qian, X., et al.: Pose-normalized image generation for person re-identification. In: Ferrari, V., Hebert, M., Sminchisescu, C., Weiss, Y. (eds.) ECCV 2018. LNCS, vol. 11213, pp. 661–678. Springer, Cham (2018). https://doi.org/10.1007/978-3-030-01240-3_40
19. Quispe, R., Pedrini, H.: Improved person re-identification based on saliency and semantic parsing with deep neural network models. Image Vis. Comput. 92, 103809 (2019)
20. Selvaraju, R.R., Das, A., Vedantam, R., Cogswell, M., Parikh, D., Batra, D.: Grad-CAM: visual explanations from deep networks via gradient-based localization. Int. J. Comput. Vis. 128, 336–359 (2019)
21. Song, C., Huang, Y., Ouyang, W., Wang, L.: Mask-guided contrastive attention model for person re-identification. In: Proceedings of the IEEE Conference on Computer Vision and Pattern Recognition, pp. 1179–1188 (2018)
22. Sun, Y., et al.: Perceive where to focus: learning visibility-aware part-level features for partial person re-identification. In: 2019 IEEE/CVF Conference on Computer Vision and Pattern Recognition (CVPR), pp. 393–402 (2019)

23. Sun, Y., Zheng, L., Yang, Y., Tian, Q., Wang, S.: Beyond part models: person retrieval with refined part pooling (and a strong convolutional baseline). In: Ferrari, V., Hebert, M., Sminchisescu, C., Weiss, Y. (eds.) ECCV 2018. LNCS, vol. 11208, pp. 501–518. Springer, Cham (2018). https://doi.org/10.1007/978-3-030-01225-0_30

24. Tay, C., Roy, S., Yap, K.: AANet: attribute attention network for person re-identifications. In: 2019 IEEE/CVF Conference on Computer Vision and Pattern Recognition (CVPR), pp. 7127–7136 (2019)

25. Wang, G., et al.: High-order information matters: learning relation and topology for occluded person re-identification. arXiv abs/2003.08177 (2020)

26. Xu, J., Zhao, R., Zhu, F., Wang, H., Ouyang, W.: Attention-aware compositional network for person re-identification. 2018 IEEE/CVF Conference on Computer Vision and Pattern Recognition, pp. 2119–2128 (2018)

27. Ye, M., et al.: Person reidentification via ranking aggregation of similarity pulling and dissimilarity pushing. IEEE Trans. Multimedia 18(12), 2553–2566 (2016)

28. Zhang, X., et al.: AlignedReID: surpassing human-level performance in person re-identification. arXiv preprint arXiv:1711.08184 (2017)

29. Zhang, Z., Lan, C., Zeng, W., Jin, X., Chen, Z.: Relation-aware global attention for person re-identification. In: 2020 IEEE/CVF Conference on Computer Vision and Pattern Recognition (CVPR), pp. 3183–3192 (2020)

30. Zheng, W.S., Li, X., Xiang, T., Liao, S., Lai, J., Gong, S.: Partial person re-identification. In: Proceedings of the IEEE International Conference on Computer Vision, pp. 4678–4686 (2015)

31. Zheng, L., Shen, L., Tian, L., Wang, S., Wang, J., Tian, Q.: Scalable person reidentification: A benchmark. In: 2015 IEEE International Conference on Computer Vision (ICCV), pp. 1116–1124 (2015)

32. Zhong, Z., Zheng, L., Cao, D., Li, S.: Re-ranking person re-identification with k-reciprocal encoding. In: Proceedings of the IEEE Conference on Computer Vision and Pattern Recognition, pp. 1318–1327 (2017)

33. Zhuo, J., Chen, Z., Lai, J., Wang, G.: Occluded person re-identification (2018)

34. Zhuo, J., Lai, J., Chen, P.: A novel teacher-student learning framework for occluded person re-identification. arXiv abs/1907.03253 (2019)

A Complementary Fusion Strategy for RGB-D Face Recognition

Haoyuan Zheng, Weihang Wang, Fei Wen[✉], and Peilin Liu

Brain-Inspired Application Technology Center, School of Electronic Information and Electrical Engineering, Shanghai Jiao Tong University, Shanghai, China
{zhenghaoyuan980108,weihangwang,wenfei}@sjtu.edu.cn

Abstract. RGB-D Face Recognition (FR) with low-quality depth maps recently plays an important role in biometric identification. Intrinsic geometry properties and shape clues reflected by depth information significantly promote the FR robustness to light and pose variations. However, the existing multi-modal fusion methods mostly lack the ability of complementary feature learning and establishing correlated relationships between different facial features. In this paper, we propose a *Complementary Multi-Modal Fusion Transformer* (CMMF-Trans) network which is able to complement the fusion while preserving the modal-specific properties. In addition, the proposed novel tokenization and self-attention modules stimulate the Transformer to capture long-range dependencies supplementary to local representations of face areas. We test our model on two public datasets: Lock3DFace and IIIT-D which contain challenging variations in pose, occlusion, expression and illumination. Our strategy achieves the state-of-the-art performance on them. Another meaningful contribution in our work is that we have created a challenging RGB-D FR dataset which contains more kinds of difficult scenarios, such as, mask occlusion, backlight shadow, etc.

Keywords: RGB-D face recognition · Complementary multi-modal fusion · Transformer · Long-range dependencies

1 Introduction

Face representation is an important component of human identifiable features. Currently, 2D face recognition (FR) based on RGB images has been relatively mature, but its performance will be significantly reduced for unconstrained environmental changes such as lighting condition, partial occlusion, pose variation and complex backgrounds [1]. Compared with RGB images, the semantic information provided by depth sensors reflects the inherent shape property and convexity [2] of facial representation and is demonstrated to have good robustness to external changes in illumination and viewpoint [3, 4]. The emergence of consumer-level depth sensors (e.g., Microsoft Kinect [5], Intel RealSense [6]) provides feasibility for low-cost RGB-D face recognition.

However, the research community of RGB-D FR has long been limited by three major problems:

© Springer Nature Switzerland AG 2022
B. Þór Jónsson et al. (Eds.): MMM 2022, LNCS 13141, pp. 339–351, 2022.
https://doi.org/10.1007/978-3-030-98358-1_27

1. How to integrate the multi-media information between RGB and depth maps is always an active topic in FR. Existing methods mostly use independent pipelines to handle individual modality [7] or directly concatenate the multi-modal feature maps [8] without considering the modal-specific characteristics and implicit correlations.
2. Face is identified by the combined features of eyes, nose, and mouth. Therefore, each region should establish an interdependent relationship with others for better representation. However, CNN-based methods are limited by their fixed local reception field to establish such long-range dependencies [9, 10].
3. RGB-D FR datasets [11–13] contain a limited number of identities compared with RGB FR datasets [14, 15]. To bridge this gap, previous training approaches [16, 17] typically pre-train on large RGB datasets and then transfer the weights directly to the depth branch. However, due to the difference in semantic meaning between the two modalities, such approaches will lead to an imbalanced generalization.

Our work makes the following contributions to address the above issues:

1. We firstly use the signal-level fusion encoding of depth maps, composed of Surface Normal and ColorJet, to enhance the discrimination of depth representation.
2. We propose a *complementary multi-modal fusion Transformer* (CMMF-Trans) model to embed different modalities in a complementary fusion approach. A series of convolutional based tokenization and self-attention modules effectively enhance both locality and global representation of facial features.
3. We introduce a novel challengeable dataset SmartToFFace, which contains a wide variety of complex scenarios in order to simulate the real-life situations of FR. Moreover, we construct a large-scale 3D-VGGFace2 dataset to deal with the imbalanced transfer learning due to insufficient depth samples. The simulated depth data are generated by the depth face estimation approach [18].

The performance of our strategy has been evaluated on three datasets: Lock3DFace [13], IIIT-D [19] and the proposed SmartToFFace. Compared with other solutions, experimental results demonstrate that our model shows superior ability in dealing with pose changes, partial occlusions, and illumination variations, thereby improving the state-of-the-art.

2 Related Work

2.1 CNN-Based Multi-modal Feature Learning in RGB-D FR

Due to the strong ability in image characterization, CNNs have been widely used to solve RGB-D FR problems in recent years. Zhang et al. [4] propose a complementary fusion network which is built up with two separate modal-specific CNN branches for early stage feature learning. Then a joint loss architecture is introduced to capture the interferences between RGB & Depth. Jiang et al. [8] introduce a novel attribute-aware loss function which takes auxiliary information, such as gender, ethnicity and age, into consideration. The proposed loss function stimulates the model to learn more discriminative features that are correlated to the attributes. In [17], the LSTM model is firstly applied to obtain the relationships between the modal-specific features. Then a spatial attention layer is used for identifying the inter-channel salient information. A depth-guided attention mechanism for RGB-D FR is proposed in [16]. The depth features extracted from VGG-16 architecture are applied for establishing an attention map that induces the model to focus on the most significant person-specific parts in RGB.

2.2 Transformers in Vision

Motivated by the exemplary performance of Transformer models in a wide range of natural language processing tasks, there emerge some remarkable attempts to apply Transformer in computer vision. In particular, ViT [10] reshapes the image into a sequence of flattened patches with fixed size, and then feed the tokens into sequential Transformer encoders. However, the pure Transformer based models always face the problem of not being able to generalize well when the size of the training set is not sufficient [10]. In order to alleviate the dependence of large amount of data, CEiT [20] extracts the low-level features using shallow convolution layers, and then inputs the feature map patches into Transformers. Wu et al. [21] combine the advantages of CNN's locality with Transformer's long-range dependency modeling to give birth to a novel hybrid architecture CvT. They use depth-separable convolution instead of linear projection in ViT [10] to improve the Transformer's local feature embedding ability.

2.3 Transformers for Multi-modal Tasks

Multi-modal Transformers are extensively used for dealing with vision-language tasks. The Vision and Language BERT [22] model is a two-stream architecture where each stream separately encodes the visual and language input. Then the modal-specific features are input to a co-attention block where the Key-Value pairs of one modality are correlated with the Query matrix of another modality. Unicoder-VL [23] concatenates the visual and textual features and puts the fused representation to self-attention blocks. Prakash et al. [24] develop a TransFuser network for autonomous driving. Several standard transformer modules are used to fuse the intermediate feature maps generated from the ResNet branches of RGB and LiDAR representations.

3   Facial Depth Map Enhancement

In [26], they have demonstrated that a combination of the depth encoding methods can enhance the recognition performance. In this work, we use the signal-level fusion of the SurFace Normal and ColorJet encoding outputs to generate a 6-channel depth representation. After following the pre-process steps proposed in [25], two kinds of depth encoding algorithms (Surface Normal & ColorJet) are then applied to highlight the geometry attributes and shape clues. Given the depth map D, $D(x, y)$ refers to its depth values. The surface normal vector $\mathbf{n} = \langle n_x, n_y, n_z \rangle$ of $D(x, y)$ can be expressed as:

$$\mathbf{n} = (-\frac{\partial D(x, y)}{\partial x}, -\frac{\partial D(x, y)}{\partial y}, 1), \tag{1}$$

Based on the 1st order differential approximation, we calculate the normal vector for discrete images as follows:

$$n_x = \frac{\partial D(x, y)}{\partial x} \approx D(x + 1, y) - D(x, y), \tag{2}$$

$$n_y = \frac{\partial D(x, y)}{\partial y} \approx D(x, y + 1) - D(x, y), \tag{3}$$

The normalized surface normal vector $\hat{\mathbf{n}}$ can then be calculated as:

$$\hat{\mathbf{n}} = (n_x, n_y, 1)/\sqrt{n_x^2 + n_y^2 + 1}, \tag{4}$$

ColorJet allocates the depth values into the RGB domain. The highest value is mapped to the red channel, the lowest value is mapped to the blue channel and the value in the middle is mapped to green. The intermediate values are arranged accordingly [26].

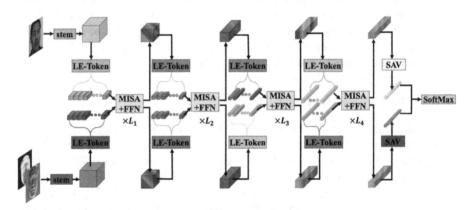

Fig. 1. Illustration of the proposed CMMF-Trans framework. CMMF-Trans contains a convolutional stem block and a 4-stage Transformer architecture. Each stage consists of a LE-Token module for tokenization, and a series of MISA + FFN encoders.

4 Complementary Multi-modal Fusion Transformer

4.1 Overall Architecture

The proposed *complementary multi-modal fusion transformer* (CMMF-Trans) aims to model long-range dependencies of the local enhanced representations from an RGB-D image pair. The overall structure of CMMF-Trans is shown in Fig. 1. The RGB and the 6-channel depth encodings are separately input to the stem blocks in order to obtain the low-level features. The stem block consists of a 7 × 7 convolutional layer with the kernel size of 7, the stride size of 2. Then the modal-specific feature maps are input to our proposed 4-stage Transformer architecture. Each stage is built up with a *locally enhanced tokenization* (LE-Token) module and a series of *mutually interacted self-attention* (MISA) modules connected with *feed-forward networks* (FFN). We take the output feature maps from the last stage into the spatial average vectorization (SAV) layer for embedding vectorization. In the remaining parts of this section we will focus on the principle of LE-Token, MISA and SAV modules.

4.2 LE-Token: Locally Enhanced Tokenization

Motivation. Previous vision Transformers [10, 20] mostly perform the tokenization by splitting the original image or features maps into fixed-size local patches and then reshaping them into a 1D token. These methods lead to uneven distribution of effective information and low robustness to translation and rotation. In addition, large patch size leads to high computational cost. Therefore, we design a novel tokenization method by using convolutional aggregation of multi-scale local regions based on the basic module of MobileNet V2 [27]. We consider each pixel of the convolutionally processed feature map as a token, i.e. $x \in \mathbb{R}^{H \times W \times C}$ is a token map, $x_i \in \mathbb{R}^{1 \times 1 \times C}$ is a token. The proposed LE-Token module is shown in Fig. 2.

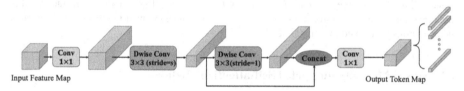

Fig. 2. Illustration of the proposed *locally enhanced tokenization* (LE-Token) module, s denotes the stride size of the first 3×3 Depth-wise separable convolutional layer.

Implementation Details. Given a 3D-shaped output feature map from a previous stage $x_{i-1} \in \mathbb{R}^{H_{i-1} \times W_{i-1} \times C_{i-1}}$ as the input for tokenization in stage i. Similar to the Inverted Residuals in [27], the 1×1 convolution layer is applied to expand the feature dimension with an expansion parameter e (is set to 4 in our work). Then we use two sequential 3×3 depth-wise separable convolutional layers to encode the multi-scale local regions around the pixels. The strides of the layers are separately set to $(s, 1)$ and the paddings are set to $(p, 1)$. We concatenate the output of the two convolutional layers, and then apply the 1×1 convolution layer to project the multi-scale fused feature map to dimension C_i. Finally, the locally enhanced token map $x_i \in \mathbb{R}^{H_i \times W_i \times C_i}$ has height and width:

$$H_i = \left\lfloor \frac{H_{i-1} + 2p - 3}{s} + 1 \right\rfloor, W_i = \left\lfloor \frac{W_{i-1} + 2p - 3}{s} + 1 \right\rfloor \tag{5}$$

x_i is then flattened into sequences and normalized by layer normalization for input into the subsequent MISA blocks of stage i. In the 4 stages, parameter s is separately set to $(1, 2, 2, 2)$, parameter p is set to $(1, 1, 1, 1)$, the output dimension of each token in the 3D token map is set to $(64, 128, 256, 512)$.

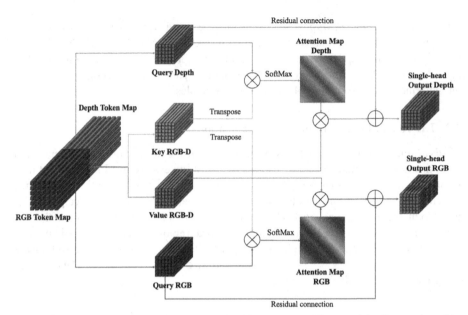

Fig. 3. Illustration of the *mutually interacted self-attention* (MISA) module. In practice, this module is a multi-head architecture where all heads are arranged in parallel, this figure illustrates the operations performed in a single head.

4.3 MISA: Mutually Interacted Self-attention Module

Motivation. Uppal et al. [16] use the features extracted from the depth map as attention of RGB faces to locate the most relevant regions to the identity, which has achieved the latest SOTA accuracies on several databases. However, their model lacks the ability of learning the mutual interaction between different modalities. Thus, we aim to explore a novel fusion approach that can complement the fusion while preserving the unique properties of the modalities. We propose a *mutually enhanced self-attention* (MISA) module, which differs from standard self-attention in that we generate two modality-specific Queries, then generate Key-Value pairs using the fused modality features. The modal-specific Queries are separately correlated with the Key matrix to generate the attention score matrix. Finally, a residual connection is adopted to fuse the modal-specific Queries and the weighted Value matrix. The structure is shown in Fig. 3.

Implementation Details. Given the RGB & Depth token sequences from the previous tokenization module in stage i, we firstly reshape them into 3D as $x_{RGB} \in \mathbb{R}^{H_i \times W_i \times C_i}$, $x_{Dep} \in \mathbb{R}^{H_i \times W_i \times C_i}$. Then we concatenate the RGB and Depth token maps in channels. Next, the 1×1 convolutional projection is separately implemented to generate the modality-specific Queries, and fused Key-Value pairs. This can be formulated as:

$$Q_{RGB} = Conv_{1 \times 1}(x_{RGB}) \in \mathbb{R}^{H_i \times W_i \times C_i}, \quad Q_{Dep} = Conv_{1 \times 1}(x_{Dep}) \in \mathbb{R}^{H_i \times W_i \times C_i}, \quad (6)$$

$$K_{fusion} = Conv_{1 \times 1}(Concat(x_{RGB}, x_{Dep})) \in \mathbb{R}^{H_i \times W_i \times C_i}, \quad (7)$$

$$V_{fusion} = Conv_{1 \times 1}(Concat(x_{RGB}, x_{Dep})) \in \mathbb{R}^{H_i \times W_i \times C_i}, \tag{8}$$

Then we split the dimension of the Q, K, V matrices by h number of heads with a token dimension of C_i/h in a single head. Then we reshape the multi-head Q, K, V into 2D sequences. The single head attention score maps of RGB & depth are computed by:

$$Attn\_Score_{RGB} = Softmax(Q_{RGB}K_{fusion}^T/\sqrt{C_i/h}), \tag{9}$$

$$Attn\_Score_{Dep} = Softmax(Q_{Dep}K_{fusion}^T/\sqrt{C_i/h}), \tag{10}$$

The mutually interacted Value matrices are separately calculated by:

$$V_{RGB} = Attn\_Score_{RGB}V_{fusion}, \quad V_{Dep} = Attn\_Score_{Dep}V_{fusion}, \tag{11}$$

We then adopt a residual connection between the modality-specific Queries and the complimentarily fused Value matrix:

$$Output_{RGB} = Q_{RGB} + V_{RGB}, \quad Output_{RGB} \in \mathbb{R}^{(H_i \times W_i) \times (C_i/h)}, \tag{12}$$

$$Output_{Dep} = Q_{Dep} + V_{Dep}, \quad Output_{Dep} \in \mathbb{R}^{(H_i \times W_i) \times (C_i/h)}, \tag{13}$$

Finally, we reshape the mutually interacted tokens into a 3D token map. The output token map produced by the multi-head architecture is obtained by concatenating the results from each single head. In the 4 stages, the head numbers are set to (2, 4, 8, 16), the encoder numbers are set to (2, 4, 4, 16).

4.4 Classification Layer

Different from ViT [10] where a separate classification token is applied, we generate the modal-specific embeddings by vectorizing the feature maps from the MISA module at stage 4. In this work, we adopt the Spatial Attention Vectorization (SAV) layer proposed in [25], which is demonstrated to be more efficient than global average pooling. The essence of the SAV module is a separable convolutional layer, which assigns an equally sized weight matrix to the feature maps on each channel. The RGB & Depth feature vectors are then concatenated as the input to the SoftMax classification layer.

5   SmartToFFace Dataset

We use the SmartToF [28] camera to capture a novel RGB-D database SmartToFFace[1] under a wide variety of complex scenarios from a total of 42 volunteers.

The images of each person in the database are organized in 5 video sequences corresponding to neutral frontal, pose variation, expression change, illumination and partial occlusion. In addition, 10 subjects are selected to capture an additional backlight

---

[1] https://bat.sjtu.edu.cn/zh/smart-tof-face/.

shadow video sequence. Each capturing sequence contains 150 synchronized RGB-D image pairs, resulting in 33000 samples in total.

With the current epidemic of Coronavirus, it is important to perform accurate face recognition under the scenario of wearing masks. Compared with the current publicly available RGB-D FR [13] dataset, we add a large number of samples of volunteers wearing masks in different postures in the occlusion subset. In addition, we also add more challenging scenarios to our database, such as backlight shadows, extreme illumination, etc. Figure 4 presents the backlight shadow scenario in SmartToFFace.

Fig. 4. Illustration of the backlight shadow scenario in SmartToFFace dataset

6   Experimental Analysis

6.1   Public Dataset Description

Lock3DFace [13] – contains 5671 short video re cordings from 509 volunteers. All samples are captured in two sessions. In the first session, all volunteers are required to present neutral-frontal, expression variation, pose variation and partial occlusion with natural light. In the second session, 169 volunteers are selected under different attire after a 7-month interval using the same acquisition configuration as the first session, which forms the time-lapse subset.

IIIt-D [19] – contains 4605 co-registered RGB-D image pairs from 106 subjects under a normal lighting condition. For face recognition, four image pairs per subject are used as galleries, the remaining image pairs for each subject are used as probes.

6.2   Implementation Details

In the following experiments, we pre-train the models on the proposed 3D-VGGFace2 dataset for 30 epochs with a learning rate of 0.001. We use the depth face estimation method proposed in [18] to generate the 3D-VGGFace2 dataset containing simulated face depth maps. After rejecting the bad samples, this dataset contains 9131 individuals with 3.17 million RGB-D images. 70% images of each individual are used for training, and the remaining samples are used for testing and validating. The pre-training stage significantly improves the generalization ability and adaptability for feature representation of our Transformer-based model in small datasets. For the evaluation in Lock3DFace [13], the neutral-frontal subset is used as the training set, the remaining 4 subsets are used as the testing sets. For the evaluation in IIIT-D [19], the gallery set is used for training and the probe set is used for testing. For the evaluation in SmartTofFace, the neural-frontal set is used for training and the remaining five subsets are used for testing. In addition, extensive data augmentation processes based on the depth map in [25] are replicated in the RGB-D image pairs in our work.

6.3 Performance on Public Datasets

The evaluation performance on Lock3DFace [13] is shown in Table 1. Our model achieves the highest recognition accuracy in three subsets, except for the expression variation subset. In particular, for the subset of pose changes, our accuracy improves by 4.5% compared to [20]. This improvement demonstrates that since our Transformer network can model the sensitive parts of the face over a long distance, it is possible to authenticate the identity when only a limited area of the human face is exposed. While for the time-elapse test set, our solution achieves 84.5% accuracy, +3.4% higher than the depth-guided attention mechanism in [20]. In addition, our approach achieves higher (+0.4%) accuracy of 86.2% for the partial occlusion scenario.

Table 1. Evaluation performance on Lock3DFace [13] dataset, P E O T separately denotes to the pose, expression, occlusion and time-lapse test set.

Year	Authors	Input	Accuracy			
			P	E	O	T
2018	Cui et al. [29]	RGB-D	54.5%	97.3%	69.6%	66.1%
2019	Mu et al. [25]	Depth	70.4%	98.2%	78.1%	65.3%
2020	Uppal et al. [16]	RGB-D	70.6%	**99.4%**	85.8%	81.1%
2021	Proposed approach	RGB-D	**75.1%**	98.4%	**86.2%**	**84.5%**

Table 2. Evaluation performance on IIIT-D [19] dataset.

Year	Authors	Input	Accuracy
2018	Zhang et al. [4]	RGB-D	98.6%
2018	Cui et al. [29]	RGB-D	96.5%
2020	Uppal et al. [16]	RGB-D	99.7%
2021	Proposed approach	RGB-D	**99.74%**

Table 2 shows the results on IIIT-D [19]. Our method achieves the same best performance of 99.7% as the method proposed in [16]. Since IIIT-D is a small-scale database, such experimental result fully demonstrates the improvement in model generalization ability that results from fusing convolutional neural networks with the self-attention mechanism. It also shows the effectiveness of our pre-train protocol on 3D-VGGFace2.

6.4 Comparison to Other Cross Modal Self-attention Mechanisms

Existing cross modal Transformers applied in computer vision consists of two categories: one is to generate Key-Value pairs of both modalities, and correlate with the Query matrix by co-attention blocks, the other is to directly input the multi-modal tokens into self-attention module. In this part we compare our Transformer model with the TransFuser model [24], the CrossViT model [30] and a two-stream ViT-based model combined with the co-attention block proposed in [22]. Table 3 demonstrates that the performance of our model on SmartToFFace dataset is superior to the other three Transformer-based multi-modal fusion approaches on all the five test sets of SmartToFFace.

Table 3. Evaluation performance compared with other cross modal self-attention mechanisms on SmartToFFace dataset. P, E, O, I, B separately denotes to the pose, expression, occlusion, illumination and backlight shadow test set.

Model Name	Accuracy				
	P	E	O	I	B
TransFuser [24]	59.4%	94.6%	72.3%	83.0%	49.7%
CrossViT [30]	47.0%	81.3%	40.1%	65.6%	21.4%
Co-Attention [22]	49.8%	88.9%	47.4%	77.3%	23.5%
Proposed approach	**63.8%**	**97.1%**	**75.4%**	**89.5%**	**57.4%**

6.5 Ablation Study to the Depth Encoding Algorithm

Using the proposed Transformer network as backbone, we compare the performance of RGB, RGB & original depth map, and RGB & proposed depth encoding on SmartToFFace. From the results presented in Table 4, we can see that the encoded depth map significantly improves the recognition accuracy compared to other input types. In addition, the poor recognition results when only using RGB in backlight shadow and occluded environments illustrate the significance to use depth data for face recognition.

Table 4. Ablation study to the effectiveness of our proposed depth encoding on SmartToFFace. P, E, O, I, B separately denotes to the pose, expression, occlusion, illumination and backlight shadow test set. We use a separate branch in CMMF-Trans for single RGB evaluation.

Input type	Accuracy				
	P	E	O	I	B
RGB	41.5%	89.0%	41.1%	75.6%	14.2%
RGB + Depth Original	61.3%	95.3%	74.8%	87.1%	55.6%
RGB + Depth Encoding	**63.8%**	**97.1%**	**75.4%**	**89.5%**	**57.4%**

7 Conclusion

In this paper, we have introduced a Transformer based multi-modal fusion network for RGB-D based face recognition. Our model is able to capture the correlations between different modality representations by applying the proposed MISA modules. Through the experimental analysis, we find that our model outperforms than the current state-of-the-art methods on Lock3DFace and IIIT-D datasets. In particular, under some unconstrained environmental variations, our model has a huge improvement relative to the CNN-based models, which demonstrates that the combination of locality and long-range dependency is more robust to extreme conditions. Furthermore, we have compared our strategy against other cross modal self-attention mechanisms in our proposed SmartToFFace, the evaluation results show the superiority of our method.

References

1. Goswami, G., Vatsa, M., Singh, R.: RGB-D face recognition with texture and attribute features. IEEE Trans. Inf. Forensics Secur. **9**(10), 1629–1640 (2014)
2. Lee, Y.C., Chen, J., Tseng, C.W., Lai, S.H.: Accurate and robust face recognition from RGB-D images with a deep learning approach. In: BMVC, pp. 123.1–123.14 (Sep 2016)
3. Chowdhury, A., Ghosh, S., Singh, R., Vatsa, M.: RGB-D face recognition via learning-based reconstruction. In: 2016 IEEE 8th International Conference on Biometrics Theory, Applications and Systems (BTAS), pp. 1–7. IEEE (Sep 2016)
4. Zhang, H., Han, H., Cui, J., Shan, S., Chen, X.: RGB-D Face Recognition via Deep Complementary and Common Feature Learning. In: 13th IEEE International Conference on Automatic Face & Gesture Recognition (FG), pp. 8–15 (May 2018)
5. Zhang, Z.: Microsoft Kinect sensor and its effect. IEEE Multimedia Mag. **19**(2), 4–10 (2012)
6. Keselman, L., Woodfill, J.I., Grunnet-Jepsen, A., Bhowmik, A.: Intel(R) RealSense (TM) Stereoscopic Depth Cameras. In: 2017 IEEE Conference on Computer Vision and Pattern Recognition Workshops (CVPRW), pp. 1–10 (Jul 2017)
7. Lin, T.Y., Chiu, C.T., Tang, C.T.: RGB-D based multi-modal deep learning for face identification. In: ICASSP 2020–2020 IEEE International Conference on Acoustics, Speech and Signal Processing (ICASSP), pp. 1668–1672. IEEE (May 2020)
8. Jiang, L., Zhang, J., Deng, B.: Robust RGB-D face recognition using attribute-aware loss. IEEE Trans. Pattern Anal. Mach. Intell. **42**(10), 2552–2566 (2020)
9. Khan, S., Rahmani, H., Shah, S.A.A., Bennamoun, M.: A guide to convolutional neural networks for computer vision. Synth. Lect. Comput. Vision **8**(1), 1–207 (2018)

10. Dosovitskiy, A., Beyer, L., Kolesnikov, A., Weissenborn, D., Houlsby, N.: An image is worth 16x16 words: transformers for image recognition at scale. In: International Conference on Learning Representations, pp. 1–7 (2021)
11. Chhokra, P., Chowdhury, A., Goswami, G., Vatsa, M., Singh, R.: Unconstrained Kinect video face database. Inf. Fusion **44**, 113–125 (2018)
12. Min, R., Kose, N., Dugelay, J.L.: KinectFaceDB: A Kinect database for face recognition. IEEE Trans. Syst. Man Cybern. Syst. **44**(11), 1534–1548 (2014)
13. Zhang, J., Huang, D., Wang, Y., Sun, J.: Lock3DFace: aA large-scale database of low-cost Kinect 3D faces. In: 2016 International Conference on Biometrics, pp. 1–8. IEEE (2016)
14. Cao, Q., Shen, L., Xie, W., Parkhi, O.M., Zisserman, A.: Vggface2: aA dataset for recognising faces across pose and age. In: 2018 13th IEEE international conference on automatic face & gesture recognition (FG 2018), pp. 67–74. IEEE (May 2018)
15. Guo, Y., Zhang, L., Yuxiao, H., He, X., Gao, J.: Ms-celeb-1m: a dataset and benchmark for large-scale face recognition. In: Leibe, B., Matas, J., Sebe, N., Welling, M. (eds.) Computer Vision – ECCV 2016: 14th European Conference, Amsterdam, The Netherlands, October 11-14, 2016, Proceedings, Part III, pp. 87–102. Springer International Publishing, Cham (2016). https://doi.org/10.1007/978-3-319-46487-9_6
16. Uppal, H., Sepas-Moghaddam, A., Greenspan, M., Etemad, A.: Depth as attention for face representation learning. IEEE Trans. Inf. Forensics Secur. **16**, 2461–2476 (2021)
17. Uppal, H., Sepas-Moghaddam, A., Greenspan, M., Etemad, A.: Two-level attention-based fusion learning for RGB-D face recognition. In: 2020 25th International Conference on Pattern Recognition (ICPR), pp. 10120–10127. IEEE (Jan 2021)
18. Zhu, X., Liu, X., Lei, Z., Li, S.Z.: Face alignment in full pose range: a 3d total solution. IEEE Trans. Pattern Anal. Mach. Intell. **41**(1), 78–92 (2017)
19. Goswami, G., Bharadwaj, S., Vatsa, M., Singh, R.: On RGB-D face recognition using Kinect. In: 2013 IEEE Sixth International Conference on Biometrics: Theory, Applications and Systems (BTAS), pp. 1–6. IEEE (Sep 2013)
20. Yuan, K., Guo, S., Liu, Z., Zhou, A., Yu, F., Wu, W.: Incorporating convolution designs into visual transformers. *arXiv preprint arXiv:2103.11816* (2021)
21. Wu, H., Xiao, B., Codella, N., Liu, M., Dai, X., Yuan, L.: Cvt: introducing convolutions to vision transformers. *arXiv preprint arXiv:2103.15808* (2021)
22. Lu, J., Batra, D., Parikh, D., Lee, S.: ViLBERT: pretraining task-agnostic visiolinguistic representations for vision-and-language tasks. In: Proceedings of the 33rd International Conference on Neural Information Processing Systems, pp. 13–23 (Dec 2019)
23. Li, G., Duan, N., Fang, Y., Gong, M., Jiang, D.: Unicoder-VL: a universal encoder for vision and language by cross-modal pre-training. In: Proceedings of the AAAI Conference on Artificial Intelligence, vol. 34, no. 1, pp. 11336–11344 (2020)
24. Prakash, A., Chitta, K., Geiger, A.: Multi-modal fusion transformer for end-to-end autonomous driving. In: Proceedings of the IEEE/CVF Conference on Computer Vision and Pattern Recognition, pp. 7077–7087 (2021)
25. Mu, G., Huang, D., Hu, G., Sun, J., Wang, Y.: Led3D: a lightweight and efficient deep approach to recognizing low-quality 3D faces. In: Proceedings of the IEEE/CVF Conference on Computer Vision and Pattern Recognition, pp. 5773–5782 (2019)
26. Rahman, M.M., Tan, Y., Xue, J., Lu, K.: RGB-D object recognition with multimodal deep convolutional neural networks. In: 2017 IEEE International Conference on Multimedia and Expo (ICME), pp. 991–996. IEEE (July 2017)
27. Sandler, M., Howard, A., Zhu, M., Zhmoginov, A., Chen, L.C.: Mobilenetv2: Inverted residuals and linear bottlenecks. In: Proceedings of the IEEE Conference on Computer Vision and Pattern Recognition, pp. 4510–4520 (2018)
28. Data Miracle Intelligent Technology Homepage. https://www.smarttof.com. Accessed 20 Aug 2021

29. Cui, J., Zhang, H., Han, H., Shan, S., Chen, X.: Improving 2D face recognition via discriminative face depth estimation. In: 2018 International Conference on Biometrics (ICB), pp. 140–147. IEEE (Feb 2018)
30. Chen, C.F., Fan, Q., Panda, R.: Crossvit: Cross-attention multi-scale vision transformer for image classification. *arXiv preprint arXiv:2103.14899* (2021)

Multi-scale Cross-Modal Transformer Network for RGB-D Object Detection

Zhibin Xiao[1,2] , Pengwei Xie[1] , and Guijin Wang[1](✉)

[1] Department of Electric Engineering, Tsinghua University, Beijing, China
{xzb18,xpw18}@mails.tsinghua.edu.cn, wangguijin@tsinghua.edu.cn
[2] Tsinghua Shenzhen International Graduate School,
Tsinghua University, Shenzhen, China

Abstract. RGB-D object detection is a fundamental yet challenging task due to the inherent difference between the RGB and Depth information. In this paper, we propose a Multi-scale Cross-modal Transformer Network (MCTNet) consisting of two well-designed components: the Multi-modal Feature Pyramid module (MFP), and the Cross-Modal Transformer (CMTrans). Specially, we introduce the MFP to enrich the high-level semantic features with geometric information and enhance low-level geometric clues with semantic features, which is demonstrated facilitating the further cross-modal feature fusion. Furthermore, we develop the CMTrans to effectively exploit the long-range attention between the enhanced RGB and depth features, enabling the network to focus on regions of interest. Extensive experiments show our MCTNet surpasses state-of-the-art detectors by **1.6%** mAP on SUN RGB-D and **1.0%** mAP on NYU Depth v2, which demonstrates the effectiveness of the proposed method.

Keywords: Object detection · Multi-scale feature fusion · Cross-modal attention

1 Introduction

Object detection, a fundamental computer vision task, aims to locate and classify objects from input images. Remarkable progress has been made in the past few years, which benefits many intelligent tasks, including autonomous driving, vision navigation, and scene understanding. With the rapid development of commercial depth sensors, depth images can be readily collected, which are also expected to complement RGB images to promote object detection performance. Consequently, RGB-D object detection, which detects objects from RGB images and depth maps simultaneously, begins to attract attention.

In recent years, many RGB-D Object detection algorithms have been proposed. Early works [1–3] mainly focus on the RGB modality. They take depth maps as an extra channel of the three-channel RGB images, and leverage hand-

© Springer Nature Switzerland AG 2022
B. Þór Jónsson et al. (Eds.): MMM 2022, LNCS 13141, pp. 352–363, 2022.
https://doi.org/10.1007/978-3-030-98358-1_28

designed features such as SIFT and multiple shape features from the depth channel. Since the RGB and depth information is inherently different, it is not easy to directly extract features from the concatenated data. Some recent works [9,14,15,17,29] have been dedicated to improving object detection performance by paying more attention to the depth features. R-CNN-Depth [14] generalize the R-CNN detector into a two streams network for RGB and depth modalities, respectively. They utilize large-scale CNNs pre-trained on RGB images to extract depth features. To further facilitate the depth feature extraction, Gupta et al. [14] propose a geocentric embedding to convert single-channel depth maps into three-channel depth images (HHA). Though it is time-consuming as a hand-designed conversion, the HHA format is adopted by some following works [17,29]. But multi-scale features, which have been certified beneficial for object detection, don't receive enough attention. Super Transfer network [15] supervises the depth backbone with the mid-level semantic representations learned from corresponding well-labeled RGB images, to initialize the depth network with better parameters. To learn the correlated information from the two modalities. Li et al. [17] propose a cross-modal attentional context framework. However, these methods have an insufficient ability to build the long-range attention between RGB-D features, which limits their performance.

Aiming to address the above-mentioned issues in RGB-D object detection, we propose a novel Multi-scale Cross-modal Transformer Network (MCTNet) to extract multi-modal features efficiently. It consists of two well-designed components. Firstly, we introduce the Multi-modal Feature Pyramid module (MFP) to effectively fuse the high-level semantic information and low-level geometric clues, which facilitates the further cross-modal feature fusion; Secondly, motivated by the recent success of Transformer on computer vision tasks, we develop the Cross-Modal Transformer (CMTrans) to learn the long-range attention of the two modalities and perform cross-modal feature fusion. Embedded with the two modules, MCTNet surpassing state-of-the-art detectors by **1.6%** mAP on SUN RGB-D and **1.0%** mAP on NYU Depth v2. The effectiveness of our method is certified by its outstanding performance.

2   Related Work

2.1   Depth Feature Extraction

Benefiting from the steady development of commercial 3D sensors, depth maps are more accessible than ever before. Unlike RGB images that depict visual perception, depth maps are related to the distance from specified viewpoints to the surfaces of scene objects. They provide an opportunity to obtain the geometric information of the natural world, which is complementary to the appearance representation. To this end, depth maps have attracted much attention from the computer vision community. Unfortunately, it still remains a challenging task to effectively extract features from the distance-related modality.

Hand-designed operators such as SIFT are firstly adopted to extract features from the depth modality by early works [1–3]. They generally take depth maps as the fourth channel of the corresponding three-channel RGB images-the inherent difference between the two modalities leading to the poor performance of these methods.

With the development of deep learning, recent methods [9,14,15,17,29] adopt large-scale pretrained CNNs to extract features from depth data. To bridge the gap between the RGB-pretrained CNN and input depth data, Super Transfer et al. [15] train the depth backbone by teaching the network to reproduce the mid-level semantic representations learned from well-labeled RGB counterparts. Gupta et al. [14] convert the single-channel depth maps into three-channel HHA format (i.e., Horizontal disparity, Height above ground, and Angle for the gravity direction), which facilitates the depth feature extraction. This geocentric embedding is adopted by some following works [17,29], though the conversion process is time-consuming [16].

Different from them, the proposed MCTNet achieves state-of-the-art performance with both raw depth format and the converted HHA format, proving that the handcrafted conversion is not necessary.

2.2 Multi-modal Feature Fusion

Many successful methods have been proposed to explore the effective fusion between multi-modal data in the past few years. RGBD R-CNN [14] first propose to fuse RGB images and depth maps at a late stage, i.e., conducting feature fusion instead of raw data, and they build a two-stream network extended from R-CNN [12], to extract RGB-D features separately. To alleviate the disagreements between the results from the two modalities, Xu et al. [29] introduce a third subnet to learn modality-correlated representations from the modality-specific RGB and depth backbone features at early stages. However, multi-scale features, which have been proven crucial for RGB-based object detection tasks, are neglected by these methods. To this end, we introduce the Multi-scale Feature Pyramid (MFP) module to utilize multi-modal multi-scale features. By generalizing Fast R-CNN [11], Li et al. [17] propose a cross-modal attentional context network and introduce LSTM [13] to recurrently generate contextual information from both RGB and depth data. But the ability to exploit long-range attention between the multi-modal features is far from sufficient in these methods. Consequently, we develop the Cross-Modal Transformer (CMTrans) module, utilizing the Multi-Head Self-Attention mechanism to model global and local attention, to fuse multi-modal features effectively.

3 MCTNet

3.1 Network Overview

Figure 1 illustrates the architecture of the proposed MCTNet. It takes RGB images and the corresponding depth maps as input. RGB images and depth maps are fed into two different backbone networks to extract their multi-scale features, respectively. Then the proposed MFP module first fuses the multi-scale features to facilitate the further feature fusion between the two modalities, and then reduces the dimension of fused features into a fixed small value to lessen the computational cost. CMTrans takes the slimmed features as input at each stage to capture their long-range attention and conduct cross-modal feature fusion. Output features of each level in CMTrans are fed into a weight-shared head to locate and classify objects in the images. After a post-processing procedure (Non-Maximum Suppression, NMS), we get the final detection results.

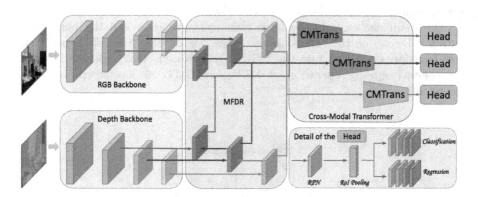

Fig. 1. Network architecture of the proposed MCTNet. The blue dotted frame indicates the structure of the Multi-modal Feature Pyramid module. Features from each *CMTrans* are fed into a weight-shared *Head* to get the location and classification results. For simplicity, we only show the detail of one *Head*, instead of demonstrating the full structures. (Color figure online)

3.2   Multi-modal Feature Pyramid (MFP)

Due to the gap between sensed photometric (RGB) and geometry information, it's tricky to fuse RGB-D features directly. Thus we introduce the MFP module to enrich the high-level semantic features with low-level geometric information and enhance the geometric clues with semantic information. To this end, it facilitates the further cross-modal feature fusion conducted by CMTrans. Besides, MFP reduces the feature channel into a small fixed dimension. Notice that the computational cost (floating-point operations, or FLOPs) of CMTrans is quadratic in terms of the channels of input features. MFP can significantly cut down the time complexity and memory occupation. For the features of the last stage of the backbone network, MFP reduces the computational complexity to $1/64$.

The proposed MFP can be formulated as:

$$\mathcal{F}_i^{RGB} = Conv_{3\times3}(\mathcal{F}_i^{RGB} + \mathbb{N}(Conv_{1\times1}(\mathcal{F}_{i+1}^{RGB}))) \tag{1}$$

$$\mathcal{F}_i^{Depth} = Conv_{3\times3}(\mathcal{F}_i^{Depth} + \mathbb{N}(Conv_{1\times1}(\mathcal{F}_{i+1}^{Depth}))) \tag{2}$$

where $\mathcal{F}_i$ denotes features from the i_{th} layer, $Conv$ indicates convolution, and $\mathbb{N}$ represents the bilinear interpolation operation to ensure different-level feature maps at the same size.

3.3   Cross-Modal Transformer (CMTrans)

Inspired by the recent success of Transformer [27] on computer vision tasks (image classification [8,26], object detection [5,31], video processing [20], *etc.*), we find Transformer [27] is naturally suitable for RGB-D feature fusion as its strong ability to capture long-range attention.

The main challenge is the large memory occupation and the huge computational cost of the Transformer. Thus we develop the CMTrans from Self-Transformer [31] to fuse the RGB-D features effectively. Benefiting from the channel squeeze operation of MFP, our CMTrans has acceptable time complexity.

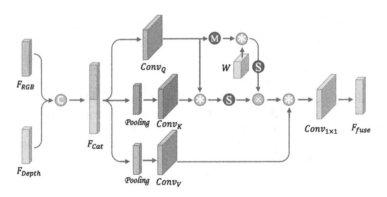

Fig. 2. Schematic diagram of the proposed CMTrans, where C means the concatenation operation, S indicates the Softmax function, $*$ represents the outer product, $\times$ denotes the element-wise product, and M denotes the average pooling operation on the flattened spatial dimension.

As illustrated in Fig. 2, RGB and Depth features are first flattened in the height and width dimensions, and concatenated together as the input sequence. With average pooling and convolution, the concatenated feature $\mathcal{F}_{Cat}$ is converted into the Query $\mathcal{F}_Q$, Key $\mathcal{F}_K$, and Value $\mathcal{F}_V$. Here we implement the convolution with a large kernel size to enhance the ability to capture spatial attention. By multiplying Query and Key, we can get the primitive attention matrix $\mathcal{A}ttn$. Mixture of Softmaxes (MoS) [30] is introduced to get the final attention matrix for the Value $\mathcal{F}_V$. After a 1×1 convolution, we get the fused feature, which is reduced to the original dimension as $\mathcal{F}_{RGB}$.

In detail, we divide the Query and Key into N parts and calculate the primitive attention matrix for every pair (*i.e.*, Q_i and K_i), which is widely known as the Multi-Head Self-Attention mechanism. Following [31] we deploy the Mixture of Softmaxes (MoS) [30] function to calculate the final attention matrix for the Value, which has been demonstrated more effective than the standard Softmax function on images in Self-Transformer. Inside the MoS, we further segment each Q_i and K_i into m particles. A learnable parameter matrix $\mathcal{W}$ (implemented by torch.nn.Parameter) is introduced to learn the importance of each particle. The reweighted matrix π is multiplied by the primitive attention matrix $Attn$ to get the final attention for the Value $\mathcal{F}_V$.

The proposed CMTrans can be simply formulated as:

$$Attn = Softmax(\mathcal{F}_Q * \mathcal{F}_K) \tag{3}$$

$$\pi = Softmax(\mathcal{W} * \mathcal{Mean}(\mathcal{F}_Q)) \tag{4}$$

$$\mathcal{F}_{fuse} = \mathcal{C}onv_{1 \times 1}(Attn \times \pi * \mathcal{F}_V) \tag{5}$$

where $\mathcal{F}_Q, \mathcal{F}_K, \mathcal{F}_V$ denotes the Query, Key, and Value matrix respectively. $\mathcal{W}$ denotes the learnable parameter matrix. $\mathcal{Mean}$ represents the average pooling on the flattened spatial dimension. $*$ denotes the outer product, $\times$ denotes the element-wise product, and $\mathcal{F}_{fuse}$ indicates the fused features of the CMTrans.

3.4 Loss Function

The loss function of the proposed MCTNet is composed of four terms:

$$Loss = \alpha \mathcal{L}_{RPN}^{reg} + \beta \mathcal{L}_{RPN}^{cls} + \eta \mathcal{L}_{reg} + \gamma \mathcal{L}_{cls}, \tag{6}$$

where $\mathcal{L}_{RPN}^{reg}$ and $\mathcal{L}_{reg}$ are the regression loss of the Region Proposal Network (RPN) and the regression head respectively, implemented as the L1 loss; $\mathcal{L}_{RPN}^{cls}$ and $\mathcal{L}_{cls}$ are the classification loss of the RPN network and the classification head respectively, implemented as the Cross-Entropy Loss; α, β, η and γ are the balancing parameters, by default they are set equal to 1.

4 Experimental Results

We evaluate our model on SUN RGB-D [24] and NYU Depth v2 [22] dataset, which contain 10,335 and 1,449 RGB-D images, respectively. The train and test split keep the same as official.

The evaluation metrics we use for object detection are Average Precision (AP) and mean Average Precision (mAP), the same as those proposed by PASCAL VOC [10]. AP is calculated by sampling the precision-recall curve at all unique recall values, and mAP is the average value of AP on N classes:

$$AP = \int_0^1 P(R)dR \tag{7}$$

$$mAP = \sum_{i=1}^{N} AP_i \tag{8}$$

where P and R are the precision and recall value on the precision-recall curve of specified class; N denotes the number of object classes.

4.1   Implementation Details

We implement our model with MMDetection toolbox [6] based on PyTorch framework. Faster R-CNN head proposed by Ren *et al.* [21] is adopted as the classification and regression head. It can be replaced by almost all the object detection heads, and with a better head MCTNet can achieve better performance. Our idea of MFP is generic, it can be instantiated with different multi-scale feature fusion strategies and get improvements on detection capacity. VGG-16 [23] pre-trained on ImageNet [7] is the default backbone to extract features from RGB images. As for depth modality, we adopt VGG-11 [23] pre-trained on ImageNet [7] to extract features. For a fair comparison, no model is pre-trained on other public datasets for object detection. Following previous works [17,29], we only work with 19 major furniture categories available in the two datasets: bathtub, bed, bookshelf, box, chair, counter, desk, door, dresser, garbage bin, lamp, monitor, nightstand, pillow, sink, sofa, table, television, and toilet.

On SUN RGB-D [24], models are trained with stochastic gradient descent (SGD) optimizer with the initial learning rate 0.01 and batch size as 4. The linear warm-up strategy is used for all experiments with 500 warm-up iters. Weight decay and momentum are set as 0.0001 and 0.9, respectively. During training, images are horizontally flipped with a probability of 0.5 for data augmentation, and no other augmentation is used. The input images are resized to make their shorter sides equal to 600, and longer sides are computed to keep the aspect ratio. All models are trained with 24 epochs. Same as previous works [17,29], we finetune the SUN RGB-D [24] pre-trained model On NYU Depth v2 [22] to get the detection results.

4.2   Results on SUN RGB-D and NYU Depth V2

We compare the proposed MCTNet against current state-of-the-art RGB-D object detection methods and RGB-based algorithms. For RGB-D methods, we adopt the results reported in their published papers. As for RGB-based networks, we train and test them on the corresponding datasets following the above-mentioned pipeline with the default configuration implemented by the MMDetection toolbox [6].

As shown in Table 1, MCTNet achieves the best performance on SUN RGB-D [24]. The VGG-based MCTNet promotes *mAP* to 53.9, surpassing state-of-the-art VGG-based RGB-D detectors at least **6.4%**. The ResNet-based MCTNet further improving the *mAP* to 55.9, indicates the great potential of the proposed method. Since Xu *et al.* [29] leave out the RGB-D images captured by Intel RealSense and adopt the remaining standard splits in experiments, we don't take their results into account, though MCTNet performs better.

Compared with previous RGB-D algorithms, the ResNet-based RGB detection methods perform better on SUN RGB-D [24], due to their deeper and better backbone (*i.e.*, ResNet-50). But they are still not as good as our MCTNet. As can be seen in Table 1, the VGG-based MCTNet surpasses SOTA RGB-based

Table 1. Experimental results on SUN RGB-D [24]. The results in bold and italics represent the first and second best performances.

Method	Reference	Input modality	RGB backbone	Depth backbone	mAP
RGB-D R-CNN [14]	ECCV 2014	RGB-D	AlexNet	AlexNet	35.2
Super Transfer [15]	CVPR 2016	RGB-D	VGG-16	AlexNet	43.8
AC-CNN [18]	TMM 2016	RGB-D	VGG-16	AlexNet	45.4
CMAC [17]	TIP 2018	RGB-D	VGG-16	AlexNet	47.5
Sparse R-CNN [25]	CVPR 2021	RGB	ResNet-50	–	43.4
ATSS [33]	CVPR 2020	RGB	ResNet-50	–	47.3
GFL [19]	NeurIPS 2020	RGB	ResNet-50	–	47.5
SABL [28]	ECCV 2020	RGB	ResNet-50	–	50.4
Cascade R-CNN [4]	CVPR 2018	RGB	ResNet-50	–	51.5
Dynamic R-CNN [32]	ECCV 2020	RGB	ResNet-50	–	52.2
Faster R-CNN [21]	NeurIPS 2015	RGB	ResNet-50	–	*52.3*
MCTNet (Ours)	–	RGB-D	VGG-16	VGG-11	**53.9**$^{(+1.6)}$
MCTNet (Ours)	–	RGB-D	ResNet-50	ResNet-18	**55.7**$^{(+3.5)}$

methods at least 1.6%, even with a more shallow backbone network. The ResNet-based MCTNet exceeds RGB-based methods more than 3.5%.

Table 2 shows the detection results on NYU Depth v2 [22] of the pre-trained models, the VGG-based MCTNet boosts mAP to 53.3, substantially suppressing all the VGG-based RGB-D detectors and ResNet-based RGB detection methods. The ResNet-based MCTNet steadily improves mAP to 54.8, surpassing SOTA methods at least 2.5%.

The outstanding performance on both datasets evidently demonstrates the effectiveness of the proposed method.

Table 2. Experimental results on NYU Depth v2 [22]. The results in bold and italics represent the first and second best performances.

Method	Reference	Input modality	RGB backbone	Depth backbone	mAP
RGB-D R-CNN [14]	ECCV 2014	RGB-D	AlexNet	AlexNet	32.5
Super Transfer [15]	CVPR 2016	RGB-D	VGG-16	AlexNet	49.1
AC-CNN [18]	TMM 2016	RGB-D	VGG-16	AlexNet	50.2
CMAC [17]	TIP 2018	RGB-D	VGG-16	AlexNet	*52.3*
Sparse R-CNN [25]	CVPR 2021	RGB	ResNet-50	–	40.2
ATSS [33]	CVPR 2020	RGB	ResNet-50	–	44.4
GFL [19]	NeurIPS 2020	RGB	ResNet-50	–	44.2
SABL [28]	ECCV 2020	RGB	ResNet-50	–	48.6
Cascade R-CNN [4]	CVPR 2018	RGB	ResNet-50	–	49.3
Dynamic R-CNN [32]	ECCV 2020	RGB	ResNet-50	–	49.2
Faster R-CNN [21]	NeurIPS 2015	RGB	ResNet-50	–	49.7
MCTNet (Ours)	–	RGB-D	VGG-16	VGG-11	**53.3**$^{(+1.0)}$
MCTNet (Ours)	–	RGB-D	ResNet-50	ResNet-18	**54.8**$^{(+2.5)}$

4.3 Ablation Studies

Extensive ablation studies are executed to reveal the characteristics of the proposed method. Since NYU Depth v2 [22] is a subset of SUN RGB-D [24], we only conduct experiments on the latter dataset.

Table 3. Ablation Studies on SUN RGB-D [24].

Method	RGB backbone	Depth backbone	MFP	CMTrans	mAP
Baseline	VGG-16	VGG-11			41.9
Baseline+CMTrans	VGG-16	VGG-11		✓	46.7
Baseline+MFP	VGG-16	VGG-11	✓		50.4
MCTNet	VGG-16	VGG-11	✓	✓	**53.9**

Table 3 illustrates the effect of each component of the proposed MCTNet. The baseline method is extended from Faster R-CNN [21]. RGB-D features extracted from backbones are fused by directly element-wise addition. Only the final output feature of the backbone is used for object detection. It achieves 41.9 mAP, which is lower than existing methods [15,17,18]. When adopting the CMTrans, the baseline method gains a 4.8% improvement in mAP, and integrating MFP into the baseline method promotes mAP by 8.5%. This demonstrates that both modules are effective for RGB-D object detection. Once we combine these two modules to build MCTNet, it can surpass the baseline method by 12.0%, which is the best result and surpassing existing methods with a large margin.

Table 4. Performance of different kernel size of the proposed Cross-modal Transformer on SUN RGB-D [24].

Method	RGB backbone	Depth backbone	kernel size	mAP
MCTNet	VGG-16	VGG-11	1	53.2
MCTNet	VGG-16	VGG-11	3	53.4
MCTNet	VGG-16	VGG-11	5	53.6
MCTNet	VGG-16	VGG-11	7	**53.9**

We further explore the effect of different kernel size in CMTrans ($Conv_Q$, $Conv_K$, $Conv_V$ in Fig. 2). As shown in Table 4, the performance increases with the enlarging of the kernel size. When setting a larger kernel size, CMTrans has a stronger ability to capture spatial attention, which is beneficial for RGB-D object detection. When setting kernel size as 1, the detection capability also suppresses existing methods, indicates the proposed CMTrans can effectively fuse the features of two modalities.

Table 5. Performance of different depth formats (*i.e.*, HHA and raw depth) of the MCTNet on SUN RGB-D [24].

Method	RGB backbone	Depth backbone	depth format	mAP
MCTNet	VGG-16	VGG-11	HHA [14]	53.5
MCTNet	VGG-16	VGG-11	Raw depth	**53.9**

Finally, we executed experiments on different formats of depth information. As illustrated in Tabel 5, the performance of the two formats is similar. The proposed MCTNet is robust for the format of depth data. It proves that MCTNet can effectively extract and fuse multi-modal features from raw depth data, handcrafted conversion (*i.e.*, HHA [14]) is not necessary (Table 5).

5 Conclusion

In this paper, we propose a Multi-scale Cross-modal Transformer Network (MCTNet) to fuse multi-modal features efficiently. Two well-designed components are introduced. The MFP is introduced to extract and enrich high-level semantic information with low-level geometric clues and vice versa. It reduces the difficulty of conducting cross-modal feature fusion between the two modalities. The CMTrans is developed to enable the effective exploitation of long-range attention between the two modalities. Extensive experiments show our MCTNet surpasses state-of-the-art detectors with a large margin in RGB-D object detection.

Acknowledgement. This paper is partially supported by National Key R&D Program of China (2019YFB1600400). This paper is partially supported by Sichuan Science and Technology Program (2020GZYZF0006). This work is partially supported by Beijing Advanced Innovation Center for Future Chip (ICFC) and Huachuang Aima Information Technology (Chengdu) Co., Ltd.

References

1. Blum, M., Springenberg, J.T., Wülfing, J., Riedmiller, M.: A learned feature descriptor for object recognition in RGB-D data. In: 2012 IEEE International Conference on Robotics and Automation, pp. 1298–1303. IEEE (2012)
2. Bo, L., Lai, K., Ren, X., Fox, D.: Object recognition with hierarchical kernel descriptors. In: IEEE Conference on Computer Vision and Pattern Recognition, pp. 1729–1736 (2011)
3. Bo, L., Ren, X., Fox, D.: Depth kernel descriptors for object recognition. In: 2011 IEEE/RSJ International Conference on Intelligent Robots and Systems, pp. 821–826. IEEE (2011)
4. Cai, Z., Vasconcelos, N.: Cascade R-CNN: delving into high quality object detection. In: IEEE Conference on Computer Vision and Pattern Recognition, pp. 6154–6162 (2018)

5. Carion, N., Massa, F., Synnaeve, G., Usunier, N., Kirillov, A., Zagoruyko, S.: End-to-end object detection with transformers. arXiv preprint arXiv:2005.12872 (2020)
6. Chen, K., et al.: MMDetection: open MMLab detection toolbox and benchmark. arXiv preprint arXiv:1906.07155 (2019)
7. Deng, J., Dong, W., Socher, R., Li, L.J., Li, K., Fei-Fei, L.: ImageNet: a large-scale hierarchical image database. In: IEEE Conference on Computer Vision and Pattern Recognition, pp. 248–255. IEEE (2009)
8. Dosovitskiy, A., et al.: An image is worth 16x16 words: transformers for image recognition at scale. arXiv preprint arXiv:2010.11929 (2020)
9. Eitel, A., Springenberg, J.T., Spinello, L., Riedmiller, M., Burgard, W.: Multimodal deep learning for robust RGB-D object recognition. In: 2015 IEEE/RSJ International Conference on Intelligent Robots and Systems (IROS), pp. 681–687. IEEE (2015)
10. Everingham, M., Eslami, S.A., Van Gool, L., Williams, C.K., Winn, J., Zisserman, A.: The pascal visual object classes challenge: a retrospective. Int. J. Comput. Vis. **111**(1), 98–136 (2015)
11. Girshick, R.: Fast R-CNN. In: Proceedings of the IEEE International Conference on Computer Vision, pp. 1440–1448 (2015)
12. Girshick, R., Donahue, J., Darrell, T., Malik, J.: Rich feature hierarchies for accurate object detection and semantic segmentation. In: Proceedings of the IEEE Conference on Computer Vision and Pattern Recognition, pp. 580–587 (2014)
13. Greff, K., Srivastava, R.K., Koutník, J., Steunebrink, B.R., Schmidhuber, J.: LSTM: a search space odyssey. IEEE Trans. Neural Netw. Learn. Syst. **28**(10), 2222–2232 (2016)
14. Gupta, S., Girshick, R., Arbeláez, P., Malik, J.: Learning rich features from RGB-D images for object detection and segmentation. In: Fleet, D., Pajdla, T., Schiele, B., Tuytelaars, T. (eds.) ECCV 2014. LNCS, vol. 8695, pp. 345–360. Springer, Cham (2014). https://doi.org/10.1007/978-3-319-10584-0_23
15. Gupta, S., Hoffman, J., Malik, J.: Cross modal distillation for supervision transfer. In: Proceedings of the IEEE Conference on Computer Vision and Pattern Recognition, pp. 2827–2836 (2016)
16. Hazirbas, C., Ma, L., Domokos, C., Cremers, D.: FuseNet: incorporating depth into semantic segmentation via fusion-based CNN architecture. In: Lai, S.-H., Lepetit, V., Nishino, K., Sato, Y. (eds.) ACCV 2016. LNCS, vol. 10111, pp. 213–228. Springer, Cham (2017). https://doi.org/10.1007/978-3-319-54181-5_14
17. Li, G., Gan, Y., Wu, H., Xiao, N., Lin, L.: Cross-modal attentional context learning for RGB-D object detection. IEEE Trans. Image Process. **28**(4), 1591–1601 (2018)
18. Li, J., et al.: Attentive contexts for object detection. IEEE Trans. Multimedia **19**(5), 944–954 (2016)
19. Li, X., et al.: Generalized focal loss: learning qualified and distributed bounding boxes for dense object detection. In: NeurIPS (2020)
20. Liu, Z., et al.: ConvTransformer: a convolutional transformer network for video frame synthesis. arXiv preprint arXiv:2011.10185 (2020)
21. Ren, S., He, K., Girshick, R., Sun, J.: Faster R-CNN: towards real-time object detection with region proposal networks. In: Advances in Neural Information Processing Systems, pp. 91–99 (2015)
22. Silberman, N., Hoiem, D., Kohli, P., Fergus, R.: Indoor segmentation and support inference from RGBD images. In: Fitzgibbon, A., Lazebnik, S., Perona, P., Sato, Y., Schmid, C. (eds.) ECCV 2012. LNCS, vol. 7576, pp. 746–760. Springer, Heidelberg (2012). https://doi.org/10.1007/978-3-642-33715-4_54

23. Simonyan, K., Zisserman, A.: Very deep convolutional networks for large-scale image recognition. arXiv preprint arXiv:1409.1556 (2014)
24. Song, S., Lichtenberg, S.P., Xiao, J.: Sun RGB-D: a RGB-D scene understanding benchmark suite. In: IEEE Conference on Computer Vision and Pattern Recognition, pp. 567–576 (2015)
25. Sun, P., et al.: Sparse R-CNN: end-to-end object detection with learnable proposals. In: Proceedings of the IEEE/CVF Conference on Computer Vision and Pattern Recognition, pp. 14454–14463 (2021)
26. Touvron, H., Cord, M., Douze, M., Massa, F., Sablayrolles, A., Jégou, H.: Training data-efficient image transformers & distillation through attention. arXiv preprint arXiv:2012.12877 (2020)
27. Vaswani, A., et al.: Attention is all you need. arXiv preprint arXiv:1706.03762 (2017)
28. Wang, J., et al.: Side-aware boundary localization for more precise object detection. In: Vedaldi, A., Bischof, H., Brox, T., Frahm, J.-M. (eds.) ECCV 2020. LNCS, vol. 12349, pp. 403–419. Springer, Cham (2020). https://doi.org/10.1007/978-3-030-58548-8_24
29. Xu, X., Li, Y., Wu, G., Luo, J.: Multi-modal deep feature learning for RGB-D object detection. Pattern Recogn. **72**, 300–313 (2017)
30. Yang, Z., Dai, Z., Salakhutdinov, R., Cohen, W.W.: Breaking the softmax bottleneck: a high-rank RNN language model. arXiv preprint arXiv:1711.03953 (2017)
31. Zhang, D., Zhang, H., Tang, J., Wang, M., Hua, X., Sun, Q.: Feature pyramid transformer. In: Vedaldi, A., Bischof, H., Brox, T., Frahm, J.-M. (eds.) ECCV 2020. LNCS, vol. 12373, pp. 323–339. Springer, Cham (2020). https://doi.org/10.1007/978-3-030-58604-1_20
32. Zhang, H., Chang, H., Ma, B., Wang, N., Chen, X.: Dynamic R-CNN: towards high quality object detection via dynamic training. arXiv preprint arXiv:2004.06002 (2020)
33. Zhang, S., Chi, C., Yao, Y., Lei, Z., Li, S.Z.: Bridging the gap between anchor-based and anchor-free detection via adaptive training sample selection. In: IEEE/CVF Conference on Computer Vision and Pattern Recognition, pp. 9759–9768 (2020)

Joint Re-Detection and Re-Identification for Multi-Object Tracking

Jian He[1], Xian Zhong[1,2]($\boxtimes$) (iD), Jingling Yuan[1], Ming Tan[1], Shilei Zhao[1], and Luo Zhong[1]

[1] School of Computer and Artificial Intelligence,
Wuhan University of Technology,Wuhan, China
zhongx@whut.edu.cn
[2] School of Electronics Engineering and Computer Science, Peking University,
Beijing, China

Abstract. Within the tracking-by-detection framework, multi-object tracking (MOT) has always been plagued by missing detection. To address this problem, existing methods usually predict new positions of the trajectories first to provide more candidate bounding boxes (BBoxes), and then use non-maximum suppression (NMS) to eliminate the redundant BBoxes. However, when two BBoxes belonging to different objects have a significant intersection over union (IoU) due to occlusion, NMS will mistakenly filter out the one with lower confidence score, and these methods ignore the missing detection caused by NMS. We propose a joint re-detection and re-identification tracker (JDI) for MOT, consisting of two components, trajectory re-detection and NMS with re-identification (ReID). Specifically, the trajectory re-detection could predict new position of the trajectory in detection, a more reliable way than motion model (MM), based on feature matching. Furthermore, we propose to embed ReID features into NMS and take the similarity of the ReID features as an additional necessary condition to determine whether two BBoxes are the same object. Based on the "overlap degree" calculated by IoU and the similarity of ReID features, accurate filtering can be achieved through double-checking. We demonstrate the effectiveness of our tracking components with ablative experiments and surpass the state-of-the-art methods on the three tracking benchmarks **MOT16, MOT17**, and **MOT20**.

Keywords: Multi-Object tracking · Trajectory re-detection · Re-identification non-maximum suppression · Missing detection

1 Introduction

Multi-object tracking aims to locate objects while maintain their identities to form trajectories across video frames. It has attracted significant attention because of its broad applications, such as robotics, and autonomous driving.

© Springer Nature Switzerland AG 2022
B. Þór Jónsson et al. (Eds.): MMM 2022, LNCS 13141, pp. 364–376, 2022.
https://doi.org/10.1007/978-3-030-98358-1_29

Most of the existing approaches follow the paradigm of tracking-by-detection, which divides the MOT task into two separate steps. Objects are firstly detected as bounding boxes in each frame and then associated with existing tracks. This paradigm benefits from the rapid progress in the field of object detection [10,19,27] meanwhile is also limited by object detection as detection result is not always reliable, especially missing detection. There are two situations of the missed objects. The first is that the missed object appears in the video sequence for the first time, and it should be initialized as a new track. The other is that the missed object has already appeared in the previous frame. The latter situation has a more significant impact on tracking performance, making the corresponding trajectory unable to be successfully updated and increasing identity switches (IDSW). Furthermore, because the matching between tracks and detections is one-to-one, once the track corresponding to the missed object is incorrectly matched with other detection, it will inevitably cause other tracks to be unsuccessfully updated.

To address missing detection, most works predict the positions of the trajectories to obtain more candidate BBoxes based on motion model. As a result of the change of the object's motion, the candidates provided by this method are not always reliable. So We propose that the extra candidates should be provided by detection, a more reliable way. Inspired by [11], we propose the trajectory re-detection (T-ReDet) network, a lightweight detection module based on feature matching for a specific object in a local area. The T-ReDet exploits depth-wise cross correlation to realize the feature matching to find the most likely new track position and then employs a regression sub-network to regress the BBoxes at the pixel level.

On the other hand, the detection given by the detector combines with the predicted BBoxes is extremely noisy with strange false positives (FP). Existing trackers employ NMS to eliminate the redundant detections. The standard NMS only relies on IoU to determine whether two detections belong to the same object. However, in MOT, especially in crowded scenes, there are often occlusions between objects, which means that even two BBoxes belong to different objects, there will be a large IoU, and the NMS will eliminate the true positives (TP) BBoxes by mistake. This creates another type of missing detection outside the detector, as shown in Fig. 1(a). Consequently, we further propose to embed ReID feature into NMS as a necessary condition for filtering BBoxes, and we named it ReID-NMS. Combined with the ReID feature, ReID-NMS can accurately filter out those BBoxes that locate the same object and achieve accurate filtering as shown in Fig. 1(b). Under the cooperation of T-ReDet and ReID-NMS, we can provide much more reliable detection for data association during tracking.

In summary, we propose a novel online multi-object tracker that joint re-detection and re-identification (JDI), containing two components T-ReDet and ReID-NMS. Our contributions can be threefold, as follows:

- We design a T-ReDet module to predict new positions of the trajectories in re-detection way to address the missing detection of detector.

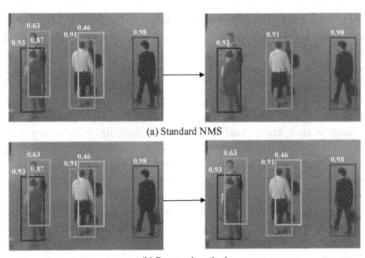

(a) Standard NMS

(b) Proposed method

Fig. 1. Qualitative comparison between standard NMS (a) and our proposed method (b). Standard NMS and our method correctly filter out false positives (FP) (dashed line), but standard NMS also deletes occluded true positives (TP) (solid line). Our method achieves accurate filtering.

- We propose to embed ReID feature into NMS, under the double checking of IoU and ReID, our method can accurately filter out redundant BBoxes and address the missing detection caused by NMS.
- Our proposed tracker achieves a considerable improvement, and the experiments conducted on three MOT challenge benchmarks demonstrate competitive results compared with the state-of-the-arts.

2   Related Work

2.1   Tracking-by-Detection

The tracking-by-detection paradigm has been commonly adopted in most modern online multi-object trackers [3,6,16,18,23,25,26,31]. Within this framework, the tracking performance depends heavily on the detection results. However, the detector cannot accurately detect all objects in each frame, mainly on missing and spurious detections. Missing detection is a widespread problem of object detectors, especially in crowded scenes. To deal with the missing detection, different solutions have been proposed. In the earlier works [1,6,25], the Kalman filter has been widely used to estimate the new position of each existing track as candidates. DPCNet [29] introduced backward tracking to run the tracker in both temporal directions to generate more candidate BBoxes. In recent years, the latest trackers [2,12,21] turned detector into tracker by exploiting the motion model and regression head, which was proposed in the Faster R-CNN [19], to predict and refine the new position based on the assumption that object movement between two adjacent frames is very slight. As for spurious detections, most trackers [2,12,21,29] filter these BBoxes based on the confidence score provided by the classification head of Faster R-CNN and the "overlap degree" measured by IoU. Despite this, missing and spurious detection still affects tracking performance, which is indicated by relatively large false negative (FN) and FP numbers in evaluation results.

2.2 Appearance Models and ReID

A robust similarity model is crucial for data association based MOT trackers, and most recent works [2,22,28,29,31] utilize the appearance embedding feature of individual objects extracted by the Convolutional Neural Network based ReID network to compute the similarity between existing tracks and detections detected in the current frame. The tracker LMP [22] proposed a ReID model that combines holistic representations and body pose layout obtained with a pose estimation model. DMAN [31] used spatial and temporal attention mechanisms to extract the feature of tracks. Since the ReID model is only a module in the tracker, and it should not be designed to be too complicated, Tracktor [2] proposed to use only a simple ResNet as the feature extractor. More recently, UMA [28] proposed to integrate ReID feature generation into its position prediction with a triplet structure, while DeepMOT [26] adopted an embedding head to produce identity embeddings simultaneously with regression-based position prediction. These works have used additional costs to generate appearance embedding, making the tracker more complicated, and there is no further use of ReID feature.

2.3 Non-Maximum Suppression

Usually, NMS is a post-processing module in the object detection framework and is used to delete highly redundant BBoxes. The human detector [9] proposed a greedy NMS algorithm that a BBox with the maximum detection score is selected and its neighboring boxes are suppressed using a pre-defined IoU threshold. Since then, greedy NMS has been the general algorithm used in object detection and other fields as standard NMS. There is a dilemma that a relative low threshold of IoU leads to missing highly overlapped BBoxes, while a higher one brings in plenty of FP, especially in crowded scenes. Some works had proposed improved NMS. For example, Soft-NMS [4] lowers the detection scores of neighbors by an increasing function of their overlaps with the most confident one instead of setting the score to zero as in standard NMS. Adaptive NMS [17] proposed to predict a density map and sets adaptive IoU thresholds for different BBoxes according to the predicted density. R^2NMS [14] exploits an extra RPN to generate visible-body proposals, based on the visible regions, a relative low IoU threshold sufficiently removes the redundant BBoxes locating the same object.

3   Proposed Method

3.1   Overview

As shown in Fig. 2, based on the latest regression tracker TADAM [12], the tracker we proposed is mainly composed of three modules, namely, trajectory re-Detection, ReID-NMS, and data association. T-ReDet network aims to obtain more detection candidates as a supplement to public detection to address missing detection, while ReID-NMS try to accurately eliminate spurious detection. Data association realizes the matching between the existing tracks and the detections, and we adopt the same matching strategy as our baseline TADAM [12]. Based on the much more reliable detections, the tracking performance is boosted.

3.2   Trajectory Re-Detection Network

To solve the missing detection of the detector, especially the case that the object that matches the current trajectory is missed, we propose a trajectory re-Detection network. It predicts the new position of the trajectory in the way of detection. As a detector, it only detects a specific object in a local area and can be divided into two stages, as shown in Fig. 2. The first stage is feature matching, this sub-network takes ResNet as backbone to extract appearance feature and consists of two branches: a branch which takes the tracks at frame t-1

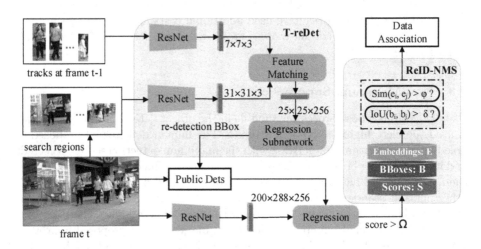

Fig. 2. The overall framework of our proposed method. The two modules in gray background represent T-ReDet and ReID-NMS, respectively. T-ReDet takes the tracks at frame t-1 and search regions in frame t as input, based on feature matching, it predicts the BBox in detection. In addition, we use the similarity between the appearance embedding features of BBoxes as an additional necessary condition to determine whether two BBoxes belong to the same object. With this double-checked method, redundant BBoxes can be filtered out more accurately. δ, φ, and Ω are the thresholds.

as input, and a search branch which takes the search regions, crops corresponding to the track in frame t, as input. We reshape the tracks to a size of 127×127, while the search region is 255×255. Note that the center of the search region is consistent with the corresponding track and the parameters of these two branches are shared, also known as Siamese architecture. Then exploit the depth-wise cross correlation to achieve feature matching based on the extracted features and get a $25 \times 25 \times 256$ multi-channel response map. In the subsequent regression sub-network, we decode the response map to obtain the location and scale information of the track and outputs the predicted BBox. Finally, all these predicted BBoxes are imported into public detection.

Algorithm 1. ReID-NMS

Input:

    Initial detection BBoxes: B $= \{b_1, b_2, \ldots, b_n\}$;

    Corresponding detection scores: S $= \{s_1, s_2, \ldots, s_n\}$;

    Corresponding detection appearance embeddings: E $= \{e_1, e_2, \ldots, e_n\}$;

    IoU overlap threshold: δ;

    ReID similarity threshold: φ.

Output:

    Detection and embedding pairs: P $= \{\{b_I, e_I\}, \{b_{II}, e_{II}\}, \ldots, \{b_N, e_N\}\}$

  1: Removed BBoxes index list: R $\leftarrow \{\}$
  2: According to S, rank B and E in descending order
  3: P $\leftarrow \{\}$
  4: **for** b_i in B **do**
  5:     **if** b_i in R or i = n **then**
  6:         pass
  7:     **else**
  8:         j $\leftarrow$ i + 1
  9:         **for** b_j in B **do**
10:             overlap $\leftarrow$ IoU(b_i, b_j)
11:             **if** overlap $> \delta$ **then**
12:                 similarity $\leftarrow$ Sim(e_i, e_j)
13:                 **if** similarity $> \varphi$ **then**
14:                     add j to R
15:                 **end if**
16:             **end if**
17:         **end for**
18:     **end if**
19: **end for**
20: **for** $\{b_i, e_i\}$ in $\{$B,E$\}$ **do**
21:     **if** i not in R **then**
22:         add $\{b_i, e_i\}$ to P
23:     **end if**
24: **end for**
25: **return** P

3.3   ReID-NMS

Appearance Embedding. Most of the works take an additional ReID module to extract appearance embedding features. Considering that the cost of calculating the ReID feature is relatively high, the ReID feature is extracted after BBoxes are preprocessed in these works. However, this is only a limited optimization, and it does not fundamentally solve the high overhead caused by the introduction of ReID. When using Faster R-CNN [19] to perform regression operation on BBoxes, the backbone (ResNet) will first extract global feature for the current frame, on the other hand, the BBoxes are contained in the frame, which means that the backbone has extracted features for BBoxes, and these features are stored in the global feature. As a consequence of this observation, we propose using the spatial relationship between BBoxes and frame to crop the global feature, also known as RoI pooling, and then use the convolutional layer to further extract it as the appearance embedding features of BBoxes. Our tracker does not require an additional ReID module through feature reuse, which solves the problem of high ReID cost and obtains the appearance embedding earlier.

Standard NMS with ReID Feature. To address the deficiencies in standard NMS and filter out redundant BBoxes more accurately, we propose to embed the appearance embedding into standard NMS by taking full advantage of ReID feature. The critical difference between our ReID-NMS and standard NMS lies in the conditions for deleting BBoxes. Specifically, we adopted a double-checked method, instead of first calculating the IoU of two BBoxes and then directly deleting the one with the lower confidence score, we introduced the similarity between their appearance embeddings as an additional necessary condition. We apply cosine similarity to measure ReID similarity as follows:

$$\text{Sim}(e_i, e_j) \;=\; \frac{e_i e_j}{\max(\|e_i\|_2 \|e_j\|_2, \epsilon)} \in [-1, 1] \tag{1}$$

where e_i and e_j denote the appearance embedding feature of two BBoxes respectively, ϵ is a small value to avoid division by zero, and we set it 10^{-8}. Only when two BBoxes, b_i and b_j, meet the condition that both the IoU and the ReID similarity reach their corresponding threshold can the BBoxes be regarded as locating the same object and then the BBox with the lower score, assumed to be b_j, is removed. The specific process can be abstracted as function Φ as follows:

$$\Phi(b_i, b_j) \;=\; \begin{cases} 1, \; IoU(b_i, b_j) > \delta \;\wedge\; \text{Sim}(e_i, e_j) > \varphi \\ 0, \; else \end{cases} \tag{2}$$

If the output of function Φ is 1, then b_j will be deleted.

Such a double-checked method is based on the following observations. When two BBoxes locate different objects, even if the IoU between the BBoxes is large, there will be enough differences between their appearance embeddings. In contrast, the BBoxes would have a large IoU, and their appearance embeddings would also be close if two BBoxes locate the same object. As a result, with the help of appearance embedding, a relative low IoU threshold sufficiently removes the redundant BBoxes locating the same object and avoids many FP. The detailed algorithm of our ReID-NMS is described in Algorithm 1.

4   Experiments

4.1   Implementation Details

We turn the Faster R-CNN into a tracker like our baseline [12], and employ ResNet as the backbone. Note that, in the test phase, we discard the RPN network and only keep the RoI head sub-network. We set IoU overlap threshold $\delta = 0.3$, ReID similarity $\varphi = 0.9$, and min BBox confidence score $\Omega = 0.2$.

4.2   Datasets and Metrics

At present, the main datasets used in multi-object tracking are **MOT16**, **MOT17**, and **MOT20**, which focus on pedestrian tracking. **MOT16** and **MOT17** contain the same video sequences, and the main difference between them is the public detection. In **MOT16**, the detection is obtained by the DPM [10] detector, whereas in **MOT17** also detections from Faster R-CNN [19] and SDP [27] are given. **MOT20** is designed to test the tracking performance in extreme crowded scenes, which makes it more challenging compared to **MOT16** and **MOT17**. We adopt multiple metrics to evaluate the performance of our tracker, including FP, FN, IDSW, identification F1 score (IDF1), and multiple object tracking accuracy (MOTA). Note that MOTA is the most critical metric for evaluating tracker's performance, which is defined as follows:

$$\text{MOTA} = 1 - \frac{(\text{FN} + \text{FP} + \text{IDSW})}{\text{GT}} \in (-\infty, 1] \tag{3}$$

where GT is the number of ground-truth BBoxes.

4.3   Evaluation Results on Test Set

We use the public detection sets for a fair comparison, and the official website of MOT challenge provides the results. As demonstrated in Table 1, the benchmark results show the superior performance of our tracker over other trackers, and our tracker achieves the best MOTA and FN on all **MOT16**, **MOT17** and **MOT20** datasets, especially the most important metric MOTA. Specifically, for MOTA, the second-best tracker is beaten by 0.7% on **MOT16**, 0.4% on **MOT17** and 1.1% on **MOT20**. In addition, compared with our baseline, our tracker improves MOTA by 4.8%, 2.8% and 0.8%, improves IDF1 by 2.6%, 0.5% and 0.8%, and decreases FN, the main error source of MOT, by 17.0%, 14.9%, and 9.5% on **MOT16**, **MOT17**, and **MOT20**, respectively. Generally, our proposed tracker achieves a higher tracking accuracy compared with state-of-the-arts by producing a small FN.

Table 1. Comparison of our proposed tracker with the state-of-the-art trackers on **MOT16**, **MOT17**, and **MOT20** test set. The arrows indicate low or high optimal metric values. The best result in each metric is marked in **bold**.

Tracker	Venue	MOTA↑	IDF1↑	FP↓	FN↓	IDSW↓
MOT16						
Tracktor++v2 [2]	ICCV'19	56.2	54.9	**2,394**	76,844	617
DPCNet [29]	ICIP'20	57.0	54.2	4,446	73,258	688
GSM [16]	IJCAI'20	57.0	58.2	4,332	73,573	475
Lif-TsimInt [13]	ICML'20	57.5	64.1	4,249	72,868	**335**
MPNTrack [5]	CVPR'20	58.6	61.7	4,949	70,252	354
CSTracker [23]	MMM'21	42.0	48.5	19,056	85,855	917
LPC-MOT [8]	CVPR'21	58.8	**67.6**	6,167	68,432	435
TMOH [21]	CVPR'21	63.2	63.5	3,122	63,376	635
TADAM (Baseline) [12]	CVPR'21	59.1	59.5	2,540	71,542	529
JDI (Ours)		**63.9**	62.1	5,619	**59,372**	917
MOT17						
FAMNet [7]	ICCV'19	52.0	48.7	14,138	253,616	3,072
Tracktor++v2 [2]	ICCV'19	56.3	55.1	**8,866**	235,449	1,987
UAM [28]	CVPR'20	53.1	52.8	22,893	239,534	2,251
DPCNet [29]	ICIP'20	55.1	52.8	15,489	235,694	2,119
GSM [16]	IJCAI'20	56.4	57.8	14,379	230,174	1,485
MPNTrack [5]	CVPR'20	58.8	61.7	17,413	213,594	1,185
CTTrack [30]	ECCV'20	61.5	59.6	14,076	200,672	2,583
LPC-MOT [8]	CVPR'21	59.0	**66.8**	23,102	206,948	**1,122**
TMOH [21]	CVPR'21	62.1	62.8	10,951	201,195	1,897
TADAM (Baseline) [12]	CVPR'21	59.7	58.7	9,697	216,029	1,930
JDI (Ours)		**62.5**	59.2	22,443	**186,088**	2,953
MOT20						
Tracktor++v2 [2]	ICCV'19	52.6	52.7	6,930	236,680	**1,648**
UnsupTrack [15]	arXiv'20	53.6	50.6	**6,439**	231,298	2,178
TBC [20]	TIP'20	54.5	50.1	37,937	195,242	2,449
Sp-Con [24]	arXiv'21	54.6	53.4	9,486	223,607	1,674
LPC-MOT [8]	CVPR'21	56.3	**62.5**	11,726	213,056	1,865
TADAM (Baseline) [12]	CVPR'21	56.6	51.6	39,407	182,520	2,690
JDI (Ours)		**57.4**	52.4	52,019	**165,198**	3,125

4.4   Ablation Studies

Impact of Our Tracking Components. To demonstrate the effectiveness of our method, we ablate the two main components: trajectory re-Detection

Table 2. Ablation study of components on **MOT17** train set. "MM" stands for motion model, "T-ReDet" stands for trajectory re-Detection, "ReID-NMS" for NMS with ReID feature.

Base	MM	T-ReDet	ReID-NMS	MOTA↑	IDF1↑	FP↓	FN↓	IDSW↓
✓	×	×	×	68.0	71.2	**2,671**	104,327	**718**
✓	✓	×	×	68.7	**72.4**	3,859	100,846	742
✓	×	✓	×	70.9	71.8	5,374	91,734	1,004
✓	×	×	✓	69.2	71.0	3,439	99,342	963
✓	×	✓	✓	**72.8**	71.3	7,706	**82,583**	1,376

Table 3. Ablation study of the parameter φ denoting the similarity threshold between the appearance embedding features of two BBoxes.

φ	MOTA↑	IDF1↑	FP↓	FN↓	IDSW↓
0.1	71.7	72.4	7,884	86,167	1,241
0.2	71.7	72.4	7,884	86,167	1,241
0.3	71.7	72.4	7,884	86,167	1,241
0.4	71.8	**72.5**	7,332	86,524	**1,235**
0.5	71.5	72.1	8,380	86,310	1,247
0.6	71.6	71.8	8,378	86,031	1,297
0.7	72.0	72.1	**7,256**	85,742	1,287
0.8	72.5	71.5	7,425	83,991	1,309
0.9	**72.8**	71.3	7,706	**82,583**	1,376

network and ReID-NMS on the **MOT17** train set. For a fair comparison, we use the same parameter settings as our baseline and set the IoU threshold in NMS to 0.3. We first add the proposed ReID-NMS and T-ReDet module to the baseline tracker, respectively, as shown in Table 2, our ReID-NMS improves MOTA by 1.2% and reduces FN by 4,985, but FP only increases by 768. So, ReID-NMS meets the expectation of accurately filtering BBoxes. In order to verify the performance of T-ReDet more intuitively, we introduced the motion model proposed in tracktor [2] as a horizontal comparison. Compared with the motion model, T-ReDet significantly reduces the FN and greatly improves the MOTA, while the motion model is only more advantageous for improving IDF1, which means that providing candidate BBoxes through detection is indeed a more effective missing detection solution. And then, we add both T-ReDet and ReID-NMS to the baseline as our whole model, MOTA is further improved to 72.8%. From the results of the ablation experiment, it can be seen that both T-ReDet and ReID-NMS can improve tracking performance on their way, and the improvement is more significant when they work together.

Impact of Parameter φ. Referring to (1), the similarity value is between −1 and 1. Since in ReID-NMS only the two BBoxes whose IoU is greater than the threshold will be calculated for similarity, we conduct experiments when the parameter φ is greater than 0. Note that, when $\varphi = -1$, our ReID-NMS degenerates to the standard NMS, when $\varphi = 1$, ReID-NMS will not filter out any BBox. As can be seen in Table 3, when we set φ to 0.1, 0.2, 0.3, the tracking results are the same. In addition, MOAT metric fluctuates very little for $\varphi \in [0.1, 0.6]$ and then quickly increases for $\varphi > 0.6$. It is worth noting that the IDF1 reaches its maximum for $\varphi = 0.4$, and then with the decline in the number of FN, IDF1 is on a downward trend as a whole. This is because we provide more BBoxes when solving missing detection, which inevitably increases the probability of IDSW.

5   Conclusion

In this paper, we propose a trajectory re-Detection network to predict the position of the trajectory in the next frame through local detection to solve the problem of missing detection of detector. Furthermore, we also propose to embed the ReID feature into the NMS to filter out redundant BBoxes accurately. In our experiments, we have demonstrated the remarkable performance of our tracker and the effectiveness of proposed components with extensive analyses.

Acknowledgement. This work was supported in part by the Department of Science and Technology, Hubei Provincial People's Government under Grant 2021CFB513, in part by the Hubei Key Laboratory of Transportation Internet of Things under Grant 2020III026GX, and in part by the Fundamental Research Funds for the Central Universities under Grant 191010001.

References

1. Andriyenko, A., Schindler, K., Roth, S.: Discrete-continuous optimization for multi-target tracking. In: CVPR, pp. 1926–1933 (2012)
2. Bergmann, P., Meinhardt, T., Leal-Taixé, L.: Tracking without bells and whistles. In: ICCV, pp. 941–951 (2019)
3. Bewley, A., Ge, Z., Ott, L., Ramos, F.T., Upcroft, B.: Simple online and realtime tracking. In: ICIP, pp. 3464–3468 (2016)
4. Bodla, N., Singh, B., Chellappa, R., Davis, L.S.: Soft-NMS - improving object detection with one line of code. In: ICCV, pp. 5562–5570 (2017)
5. Brasó, G., Leal-Taixé, L.: Learning a neural solver for multiple object tracking. In: CVPR, pp. 6246–6256 (2020)
6. Chen, L., Ai, H., Zhuang, Z., Shang, C.: Real-time multiple people tracking with deeply learned candidate selection and person re-identification. In: ICME, pp. 1–6 (2018)
7. Chu, P., Ling, H.: FAMNet: joint learning of feature, affinity and multi-dimensional assignment for online multiple object tracking. In: ICCV, pp. 6171–6180 (2019)
8. Dai, P., Weng, R., Choi, W., Zhang, C., He, Z., Ding, W.: Learning a proposal classifier for multiple object tracking. In: CVPR, pp. 2443–2452 (2021)

9. Dalal, N., Triggs, B.: Histograms of oriented gradients for human detection. In: CVPR, pp. 886–893 (2005)
10. Felzenszwalb, P.F., Girshick, R.B., McAllester, D.A., Ramanan, D.: Object detection with discriminatively trained part-based models. IEEE Trans. Pattern Anal. Mach. Intell. **32**(9), 1627–1645 (2010)
11. Guo, D., Wang, J., Cui, Y., Wang, Z., Chen, S.: SiamCAR: siamese fully convolutional classification and regression for visual tracking. In: CVPR, pp. 6268–6276 (2020)
12. Guo, S., Wang, J., Wang, X., Tao, D.: Online multiple object tracking with cross-task synergy. In: CVPR, pp. 8136–8145 (2021)
13. Hornáková, A., Henschel, R., Rosenhahn, B., Swoboda, P.: Lifted disjoint paths with application in multiple object tracking. In: ICML, pp. 4364–4375 (2020)
14. Huang, X., Ge, Z., Jie, Z., Yoshie, O.: NMS by representative region: towards crowded pedestrian detection by proposal pairing. In: CVPR, pp. 10747–10756 (2020)
15. Karthik, S., Prabhu, A., Gandhi, V.: Simple unsupervised multi-object tracking. arXiv 2006.02609 (2020). https://arxiv.org/abs/2006.02609
16. Liu, Q., Chu, Q., Liu, B., Yu, N.: GSM: graph similarity model for multi-object tracking. In: Proceedings of the Twenty-Ninth International Joint Conference on Artificial Intelligence (IJCAI), pp. 530–536 (2020)
17. Liu, S., Huang, D., Wang, Y.: Adaptive NMS: refining pedestrian detection in a crowd. In: CVPR, pp. 6459–6468 (2019)
18. Nie, W., Liu, A., Su, Y., Gao, Z.: An effective tracking system for multiple object tracking in occlusion scenes. In: MMM, pp. 206–216 (2013)
19. Ren, S., He, K., Girshick, R.B., Sun, J.: Faster R-CNN: towards real-time object detection with region proposal networks. IEEE Trans. Pattern Anal. Mach. Intell. **39**(6), 1137–1149 (2017)
20. Ren, W., Wang, X., Tian, J., Tang, Y., Chan, A.B.: Tracking-by-counting: using network flows on crowd density maps for tracking multiple targets. IEEE Trans. Image Process. **30**, 1439–1452 (2021)
21. Stadler, D., Beyerer, J.: Improving multiple pedestrian tracking by track management and occlusion handling. In: CVPR, pp. 10958–10967 (2021)
22. Tang, S., Andriluka, M., Andres, B., Schiele, B.: Multiple people tracking by lifted multicut and person re-identification. In: CVPR, pp. 3701–3710 (2017)
23. Wang, F., Luo, L., Zhu, E.: Two-stage real-time multi-object tracking with candidate selection. In: MMM, pp. 49–61 (2021)
24. Wang, G., Wang, Y., Gu, R., Hu, W., Hwang, J.: Split and connect: a universal tracklet booster for multi-object tracking. arXiv 2105.02426 (2021). https://arxiv.org/abs/2105.02426
25. Wojke, N., Bewley, A., Paulus, D.: Simple online and realtime tracking with a deep association metric. In: ICIP, pp. 3645–3649 (2017)
26. Xu, Y., Osep, A., Ban, Y., Horaud, R., Leal-Taixé, L., Alameda-Pineda, X.: How to train your deep multi-object tracker. In: CVPR, pp. 6786–6795 (2020)
27. Yang, F., Choi, W., Lin, Y.: Exploit all the layers: Fast and accurate CNN object detector with scale dependent pooling and cascaded rejection classifiers. In: CVPR, pp. 2129–2137 (2016)
28. Yin, J., Wang, W., Meng, Q., Yang, R., Shen, J.: A unified object motion and affinity model for online multi-object tracking. In: CVPR, pp. 6767–6776 (2020)
29. Zhong, X., Tan, M., Ruan, W., Huang, W., Xie, L., Yuan, J.: Dual-direction perception and collaboration network for near-online multi-object tracking. In: ICIP, pp. 2111–2115 (2020)

30. Zhou, X., Koltun, V., Krähenbühl, P.: Tracking objects as points. In: ECCV, pp. 474–490 (2020)
31. Zhu, J., Yang, H., Liu, N., Kim, M., Zhang, W., Yang, M.: Online multi-object tracking with dual matching attention networks. In: ECCV, pp. 379–396 (2018)

Multimedia Analytics for Contextual Human Understanding (Special Session)

An Investigation into Keystroke Dynamics and Heart Rate Variability as Indicators of Stress

Srijith Unni, Sushma Suryanarayana Gowda, and Alan F. Smeaton[✉][iD]

Insight Centre for Data Analytics, Dublin City University,
Glasnevin, Dublin 9, Ireland
alan.smeaton@dcu.ie

Abstract. Lifelogging has become a prominent research topic in recent years. Wearable sensors like Fitbits and smart watches are now increasingly popular for recording one's activities. Some researchers are also exploring keystroke dynamics for lifelogging. Keystroke dynamics refers to the process of measuring and assessing a person's typing rhythm on digital devices. A digital footprint is created when a user interacts with devices like keyboards, mobile phones or touch screen panels and the timing of the keystrokes is unique to each individual though likely to be affected by factors such as fatigue, distraction or emotional stress. In this work we explore the relationship between keystroke dynamics as measured by the timing for the top-10 most frequently occurring bigrams in English, and the emotional state and stress of an individual as measured by heart rate variabiity (HRV). We collected keystroke data using the Loggerman application while HRV was simultaneously gathered. With this data we performed an analysis to determine the relationship between variations in keystroke dynamics and variations in HRV. Our conclusion is that we need to use a more detailed representation of keystroke timing than the top-10 bigrams, probably personalised to each user.

Keywords: Keystroke dynamics · Heart rate variability · Lifelogging

1 Introduction

There are multiple ways in which we can capture aspects of our lives to record our activities and even our state of mind. Typically this requires wearable devices for measuring aspects of our physiology (heart rate, respiration rate), our activities (step counters and location trackers) or our environment (wearable cameras, bluetooth detectors). The dependency is on using wearable devices but the body is a hostile environment for wearables and we are not always comfortable wearing them, such as when we sleep for example. Thus environmental sensing can substitute for wearables and *in situ* sensing in a home environment can tell as much about occupants' activities as wearables can.

In this work we use another form of environmental sensing – keystroke dynamics – to explore what we can infer about the mental state and mental

© Springer Nature Switzerland AG 2022
B. Þór Jónsson et al. (Eds.): MMM 2022, LNCS 13141, pp. 379–391, 2022.
https://doi.org/10.1007/978-3-030-98358-1_30

stress on a user at a point in time. Keystroke dynamics or typing dynamics refers to the detailed timing information which describes exactly when each key was pressed and when it was released, as a person is typing on a keyboard. Keystroke dynamics are unique to each individual and is known to vary according to factors including fatigue, stress, and emotional state [4]. We capture information on user state using keystroke dynamics as a form of contextual data. As a ground truth against which to measure, we use heart rate variability (HRV), a measure of timing variations between two consecutive heartbeats known as an indicator of mental strain, stress and mental workload [10]. If we can correlate data drawn from keystroke dynamics with variations in HRV then we will demonstrate that using keystroke dynamics we can measure some aspects of a user's mental state or stress.

Research on keystroke dynamics applications has been increasing, especially in the last decade. The main motivation behind this is the uniqueness of the patterns to an individual person and the ease of data collection. Keystroke events can now be measured up to milliseconds precision by software [16]. In contrast to traditional physiological biometric systems such as palm print, iris and fingerprint recognition that rely on dedicated device and hardware infrastructure, keystroke dynamics recognition is entirely software implementable. The benefit of low dependency on specialised hardware not only can significantly reduce deployment cost but also creates an ideal scenario for implementation in remote authentication environments [18].

The approach we take here is to collect keystroke data from subjects using a simple keystroke logging application called Loggerman. Loggerman [9] is an application which collects data generated from normal usage of a computer system including keystrokes data and it operates passively in the background. For the collection of physiological data we use heart rate variability, which we use as a proxy for emotional state and which we introduce in the next section.

In the next section we review related literature on uses of keystroke dynamics and the section following that presents an overview of heart rate variability. We then describe the data we have gathered from participants and how this was prepared and analysed, and the results we have obtained.

2   Literature Review

The earliest noted use of keystroke dynamics was to identify individual telegraph operators in late 19th century by listening to the patterns of their taps on the device [18]. Analysis of keystroke dynamics was explored in the 1970s with the study of time intervals between keystrokes and other keying rate information [14], with further research focusing on how this information can be applied for practical purposes. One of the main aspects in which prospective applications were researched was user authentication and interpreting how different users can be identified from their typing patterns [3].

The behavioural biometrics of Keystroke Dynamics uses the manner and rhythm in which an individual types characters on a keyboard or keypad [6].

The keystroke rhythms of a user can be measured to develop a unique biometric template of a user's typing patterns for future authentication [15]. Keystrokes are separated into static and dynamic typing, which are used to help distinguish between authorised and unauthorised users. Additionally, integration of keystroke dynamics biometrics leaves random password guessing attacks obsolete [5].

In [12], Leijten et al. described keystroke logging as an instrumental method in determining writing strategies and established how cognitive actions are performed and correlate with keystroke timings. One reason for this that has been identified is that keystroke timing data reveals various ebbs and flows in the fluency of writing which can be interpreted and can help further understand the cognitive process going on as we write. Gunetti et al. [8] concluded in their research that "typing dynamics is the most natural kind of biometrics that stems from the use of computers, it is relatively easy to sample, and it is available throughout the entire working session."

The ability to recognise emotions is an important part of building intelligent computers. Emotionally-aware systems have a rich context from which to make appropriate decisions about how to interact with the user or adapt their system response [7]. Various algorithms like facial emotional analysis, auditory emotional analysis, sentiment analysis, and emotional body gesture recognition are currently used to determine human emotions. The problem with these approaches for identifying emotions that limit their applicability is that they are invasive and can require costly equipment [7].

Teh et al. [18] discussed in their paper that although there certain advantages such as uniqueness, transparency and non-invasiveness, keystroke dynamics can reveal variations in typing rhythm caused by external factors such as injury, fatigue or distractions. Hence there is an opportunity to investigate keystroke dynamics to indicate the mental state of a person at a point in time. For example, a person might compose an email quicker when s/he realises they would get off work right after that action, compared to a person who knows s/he must work hours after that mail has been composed. Such differences in the timing of typing, if logged, would indirectly enable us to identify certain models to determine the emotional state or stress levels in a more generalised manner. We believe that this could help us observe how emotion correlates with the keystroke data. Vizer et al. [19] confirmed in their research "the potential of monitoring keyboard interactions for an application other than security and highlighted the opportunity to use keyboard interaction data to detect the presence of cognitive or physical stress."

Some previous research has been reported to determine the emotions of a user using keystroke dynamics. In [7], Epp et al. determine user emotions by comparing the rhythm of typing patterns on a standard keyboard with emotional state as collected via self-report. They claim that the results include 2-level classifiers for confidence, hesitance, nervousness, relaxation, sadness, and tiredness with accuracy ranging from 77 to 88%. In addition, they show promise for anger and excitement, with accuracy of 84%. One problem with this approach is that the emotional state of their subjects is collected using self-reporting. This is not completely reliable since humans have a tendency to mis-report, for various reasons. More recently, [17], analysed variations in keystroke dynamics with respect to the previous day's sleep score for participants but could not find any significant relationship between the two.

3   Heart Rate Variability (HRV)

Heart rate variability (HRV) is a measure of variations observed between two consecutive heartbeats. HRV originates in the autonomic nervous system that is responsible for involuntary aspects of our physiology. The autonomic nervous system has two branches, the parasympathetic system (deactivating/rest) which handles inputs from internal organs and causes decrease in heart rate, and the sympathetic system (activating/fight or flight) which handle inputs from external factors like fatigue, stress, exercise and increases the heart rate. If our nervous system is balanced, the heart is constantly told to beat faster by the sympathetic system and slower by the parasympathetic system. Thus there is a fluctuation caused in the heart rate and this is HRV [10].

A high measure of heart rate variability means that our body is responsive to both sets of inputs (parasympathetic and sympathetic). This is a sign that our nervous system is balanced, and that our body is very capable of adapting to its environment and performing at its best. On the other hand, if we have a low heart rate variability, one branch is dominating (usually the sympathetic) and sending stronger signals to our heart than the other branch. However, if we are not doing something active and we have a low heart rate, then a low HRV at such periods indicates that our body is working hard for some other reason, perhaps fatigue, dehydration, stress, or we are ill and need to recover, and that leaves fewer resources available to dedicate towards other activities like exercising, competing, giving a presentation at work, etc.

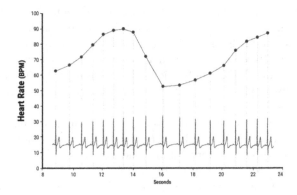

Fig. 1. Heart Rate Variability derived from Heart Rate measurements

In Figure 1, we observe an electrocardiogram (ECG) which is shown as the bottom graph, and the instantaneous heart rate is shown at the top. If we examine the time taken between each of the heartbeats (the blue line) between 0 and approximately 13 seconds, we notice that they become progressively shorter as heart rate accelerates and start to decelerate at around 13 seconds. Such a pattern of heart-rate acceleration and deceleration is the basis of the heart's rhythms [13].

Acharya *et al.* in [2] explained that there is a clear relationship between HRV and gender and age and that physically active young and old women have higher HRV whereas lower HRV is observed in alert new-born males compared to females. In a study among healthy subjects between 20 and 70 years of age, it was observed that HRV decreases with age and that variations in HRV are less in the case of men.

The method for calculating HRV is as follows. A time domain index uses statistical measures to quantify the amount of variance in the inter-beat interval (IBI) of a heart beat. The three most important and frequently reported time-domain metrics are SDNN, SDNN index, and RMSSD [13]. SDNN is the standard deviation of the NN intervals of normal sinus beats as measured in milliseconds where normal involves removing abnormal beats like ectopic beats. The NN interval, sometimes known as the R-R interval, is the time difference between successive heartbeats measured from the point of peak voltage amplitude. The standard short-term recording of HRV is of 5 minutes duration.

HRV is known as an indicator of mental strain, stress, and mental workload [11] and thus as a quantitative metric is has strong value. The traditional method of collecting data from short-term (5-minute) heart rate series involves a dedicated electrocardiograph (ECG) running from a computer or micro-controller and connected to a single participant in a laboratory environment. The HRV value is calculated based on the R wave time series provided by the ECG, which is the signal history of ventricular depolarisation over time. This collection procedure is common in published studies but this experimental setup does not suit our needs.

Reliable HRV calculation outside the laboratory faces many challenges, though recently the quality of wearable sensing has made this feasible. Optical sensors for measuring heart rate are inexpensive, portable, computationally efficient, non-invasive, reusable, and have low power consumption so as wearable devices they have a long time between charges. Thus optically derived pulse rate is an ideal choice for wearables to collect a good estimation of HRV value.

For our work we use a Scosche RHYTHM24 fitness band to capture heartbeat data for our test subjects. Data recorded by the band is passed to the SelfLoops HRV mobile app for further analysis. In the next section we describe our data collection.

4   Data Gathered

Ethical approval for this work was granted by the Ethics Committee of the School of Computing at Dublin City University and consisted of a *Plain Lan-*

guage statement and an *Informed Consent Form* signed by participants indicating their understanding and approval. Participants were provided with an instruction manual for collecting both their keystroke data with the Loggerman application on their Mac and HRV data collected via the Scosche RHYTHM24 fitness band. Participants were asked to wear the band at the appropriate position on their arm and to start recording their HRV data at least 30 minutes before they start using their laptop.

Participants used Loggerman and HRV data collection while using their laptops for planned typing "episodes" of long duration. For example, just quickly checking email or news first thing in the morning would not be recorded as it would not require much typing. A planned work session to work on a paper, or write a blog, or process and respond to a stack of emails are examples of planned typing sessions which are of long enough duration and involve typing. Watching a movie on a laptop would not be recorded as there is no user typing involved.

While recording, users proceeded with their work as usual for as long as they wanted to on their Macs but the typing was not continuous as breaks would be taken for rest or refreshment, interruptions would happen because people are working from home, and thinking time for reflection or interaction with others would be interspersed with actual typing. Thus while HRV recording is continuous, the recording of keystroke dynamics during the recording sessions is scattered and bursty, which is normal typing behaviour for most people.

After every recorded session, participants shared their keystrokes and HRV files and the data they gathered is shown in Table 1. This shows the total number of keystrokes pressed, the number of typing episodes or instances and the number of hours of heart rate and typing data that was gathered. The duration of the recorded sessions varied from 33 minutes to almost 7 hours for participant 1 and 25 minutes to 2 hours 45 minutes for participant 2.

Table 1. Details of keystroke and heart rate data logged by participants

Participant	Keystrokes	Typing 'episodes'	Hours of HR	Hours of typing
1	33,583	17	48	23
2	16,286	5	8	2.5

5   Data Preparation

Keystroke dynamics data gathered by Loggerman is in the form of a code for each key pressed, and a Unix timestamp measured in milliseconds. A major challenge was to extract features from this raw time series data so we can identify variations in keystroke dynamics across time, for each participant.

Peter Norvig published results of an analysis of the letters, words and n-gram frequencies extracted from the Google Books collection of 743,842,922,321 word occurrences in the English Language. In this, Norvig observed the top 10 most frequently occurring bigrams in the English language to be the following - TH,

HE, IN, ER, AN, RE, ON, AT, EN and ND.[1] Given that these 10 bigrams are likely to occur frequently in the text typed by our participants we use the time taken to type these 10 bigrams, the number of milliseconds between typing the two characters, as features for characterising a typing episode.

Our data pre-processing was performed using Python libraries on Google Colab. As our analysis focused on the top 10 bigrams observed by Norvig's analysis, we identified instances of each bigram for recorded sessions but only where the characters were typed within a 1000ms window. Our reasoning is that if it takes longer than 1 second between typing these bigram characters then there is an interruption to the flow of typing and we are interested in episodes of continuous typing.

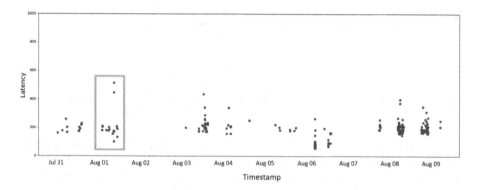

Fig. 2. Sample of typing episodes observed for typing of the ER bigram

Figure 2 shows a snapshot of some of the typing episodes for the ER bigram chosen as an illustration, which were observed over 10 days for one participant. The graph shows observed typing episodes of differing durations with gaps removed, so it does not display 24 hours per day. We observe distinct episodes where the bigram was used considerably rather than rarely. The red box on Aug 01 highlights 17 occurrences (blue dots in the figure) of an "ER" during one typing session with the timing for this, i.e. the latency between the keystrokes, varying from about 100ms to 550 ms. We represent this typing episode as the mean of the 17 instances, a value of around 220 ms, and repeat this computation for the other 9 of the top-10 bigrams but as we see when we look at HRV values, there can be a lot of variety of HRV and thus of stress and mental workload within a typing session thus we need more temporally fine-grained analysis of keystrokes within each typing episode.

---

[1] http://norvig.com/mayzner.html

Figure 3 presents a schematic of how we do this. Using the highlighted typing episode from Figure 2 which we see is of 15 minutes duration, we divide this into 5 overlapping 5-minute windows shown as green bars labelled A, B, C, D, E and for each we compute the average latency for ER within that window. If any 5-minute windows have no ER bigrams, they are removed from the analysis. In the case of this example we have 5 mean latencies for the typing of ER and we repeat this for all top-10 bigrams.

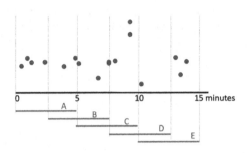

Fig. 3. Calculating keystroke timing for ER bigram in 5-minute overlapping windows

As outlined earlier, to calculate HRV we used short term HRV calculated from the RR-intervals, for a duration of 5 minutes. Outlier HRV values, also called ectopic beats, were removed using Malik's rule [1] with the help of the HRV-analysis library in Python. A number of 5-minute HRV values were calculated for each of the typing sessions using the same 5-minute sliding windows with 2.5 minutes overlap for correlation with the keystroke dynamics for the same 5-minute windows.

Using data for all recorded sessions, for each participant we calculated their average HRV that acts as a their HRV baseline. Figure 4 shows some of those (non-overlapping) HRV values for 2 participants with the dotted line showing their average HRV value. This indicates that participant 1 has a lot of variability from a low of about 20 ms to a high of almost 250 ms whereas the variations are almost flat for Participant 2 whose range is 25 ms to about 75 ms. In turn this suggests that participant 1 was, at the times of logging, experiencing a range of stress levels which made their HRV values vary considerably.

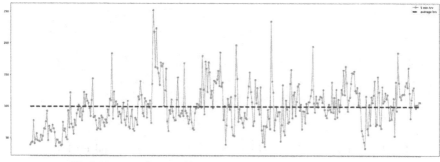

30.6 Hours of HRV data recorded for Participant 1

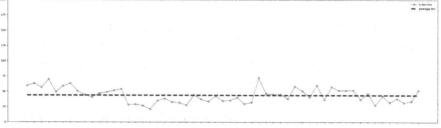

5 Hours of HRV of participant 2

Fig. 4. A sample of the 5-minute cumulative and contiguous HRV values for 2 participants showing how HRV varies from person-to-person and within an individual person.
The top graph shows 30.6 hours and the lower shows only 5 hours.

6   Data Analysis and Results

We processed keystroke timing data by using only the non-empty 5-minute windows within each of the typing episodes where at least one of the top-10 bigrams
had been typed within 1,000ms. For each window we calculated the mean latency
for each, for each of the ten bigrams. We then computed the difference between
those values for each bigram and the mean bigram latencies for the whole recording for each participant which we define as their baseline, to compute the deviation from the baseline, for each window. We then used the simple average of all
the deviation ratios of all bigrams for the same 5-minute window as the observed
change in keystroke dynamics, which we can measure against observed changes
in HRV.

We can see the cumulative variations in latencies for all bigrams in Figure 5
and this illustrates how participants' typing speeds for the same top-10 bigrams
vary within and across multiple typing sessions. Table 2 shows the baseline timings for the top-10 bigrams for both users. In practice only 44% of the 645
5-minute windows for participant 1 had any typing of any of the top-10 bigrams
and on average those windows had 4.4 of those top-10. For user 2, 71% of the
5-minute windows had at least 1 of the top-10 bigram, on average 7.1.

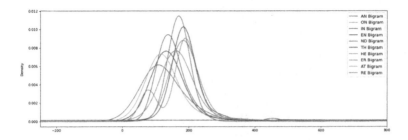

Fig. 5. Cumulative Density Plots for top 10 bigrams for collected data

Table 2. Baseline top-10 bigram timings (in ms)

Bigram	TH	HE	IN	ER	AN	RE	ON	AT	EN	ND	Average
User 1	88.9	69.5	89.0	56.1	78.6	475.6	58.4	65.4	83.4	103.9	117 ms
User 2	124.0	118.7	141.3	130.3	122.9	51.8	82.0	112.1	76.0	131.9	109 ms

We then calculated the HRV values for the same 5-minute overlapping windows for each of the typing sessions, for each participant. For User 1 there were 275x overlapping 5-minute windows with HRV recorded and those HRV values varied from 46ms to 240ms with an overall average of 106.3ms. For user 2 there were 86x overlapping 5-minute windows with HRV recorded and those HRV values varied from 21ms to 67ms with an overall average of 40.9ms, considerably lower than for user 1.

With baseline HRV values and observed HRV values for each 5-minute window we can compare these against the variance between observed and baseline keystroke timing data for each user and a scatterplot of this for user 1 is shown in Figure 6.

Figure 6 shows there is little correlation between deviations in HRV and deviations in keystroke dynamics when all of the top-10 occurring bigrams are considered and combined, for either user. We know user 1 has a higher baseline HRV compared to user 2 (106.3ms vs. 40.9ms) and from Figure 6 we see user 1 also has a greater HRV range, shown by the ranges in the y-axes of the two graphs. User 1 also has a grater range of timings for keystroke typing than user 2.

In terms of bigram usage, not all of the top-10 bigrams are used equally by any individual in any 5-minute typing window. We observe in Table 2 that user 1 has an obvious timing peculiarity when typing the RE bigram, taking an average of 475ms across all recorded typing compared to less than 100ms for almost all other top-10 bigrams. When we removed the RE bigram from calculating keystroke dynamic deviations this improved the correlation but only marginally. A similar observation was made when removing other top-10 bigrams individually from the overall keystroke timing representation. Even for using just 1 of the bigrams, for both users, the correlation between HRV variance and keystroke timing variance against respective baselines, was weak. What this

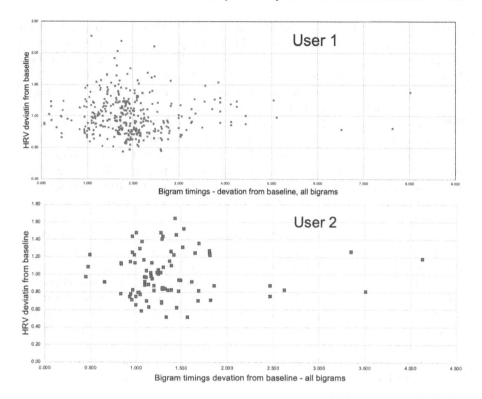

Fig. 6. Correlation between latency for timing of top-10 bigrams vs. mean HRV for each 5-minute window, for user 1 and user 2

tells us is that we cannot take the observed timing information compared against the baselines of only the top-10 most frequently occurring bigrams or even any group of them as the sole feature for characterising typing information and that we need a richer representation of timing information drawn from across more of the bigrams.

7   Conclusions

In this paper, we explored the relationship between keystroke dynamics and heart-rate variability to find a relationship between a person's stress level as represented by changes in their HRV compared to their baseline, with variations in their keystroke timing information. We used the Loggerman application to collect keystroke data for 2 participants and the Scosche RHYTHM24 band to collect HRV data for the same participants for approximately the same amount of time. We presented the speed or latency at which each of the top-10 most frequently occurring bigrams from the English language were typed and how short-term HRV values measured over 5 minute windows which is the standard used for HRV, differed over a period of time for the users.

We observed from our analysis that there is little correlation between keystroke timing latency as represented by the top-10 bigrams, and HRV value changes yet we know from work elsewhere that keystroke timing information does correlate with user stress and cognitive load, as do variations in HRV. This suggests there is scope for extracting alternative features from keystroke timing, other than timing of top-10 bigrams, which might allow us to correlate with HRV data. We are severely constrained here because whatever keystroke timing information is extracted from raw timing data, can only be from within a 5-minute window as that is the standard duration for calculating short-term HRV values [13]. We know that each individual has unique timing habits for their typing [17] and it may be that instead of choosing the same top-10 most frequently used bigrams from Norvig's analysis, a different subset might be appropriate for each user.

For future work, there is a spectrum of different platforms on which we could look into for collecting keystroke data. In this work we were limited to Apple Mac users due to limitations of the Loggerman application being available only on OS/X. So as to increase the participant base, we are capturing keystroke data from mobile devices. HRV data could also be recorded for longer durations if even lesser intrusive wearable devices are used with longer battery life. Finally, of course we would like to get more participants to record for longer periods and possibly to have some of this in controlled environments. For example we could indirectly measure stress levels from keystroke dynamics for people working from home vs. working in an office environment, or we could measure mental state as students get closer to examination time.

Acknowledgements. We are grateful to our participants for sharing their data with us. This work was partly supported by Science Foundation Ireland (SFI) under Grant Number SFI/12/RC/2289_P2, co-funded by the European Regional Development Fund

References

1. Acar, B., Savelieva, I., Hemingway, H., Malik, M.: Automatic ectopic beat elimination in short-term heart rate variability measurement. Computer Methods and Programs in Biomedicine 63(2), 123–131 (2000)
2. Acharya, U.R., Joseph, K.P., Kannathal, N., Lim, C.M., Suri, J.S.: Heart rate variability: a review. Medical and Biological Engineering and Computing 44(12), 1031–1051 (2006)
3. Bergadano, F., Gunetti, D., Picardi, C.: User authentication through keystroke dynamics. ACM Transactions on Information and System Security (TISSEC) 5(4), 367–397 (2002)
4. Crawford, H.: Keystroke dynamics: Characteristics and opportunities. In: 2010 Eighth International Conference on Privacy, Security and Trust. pp. 205–212. IEEE (2010)
5. De Ru, W.G., Eloff, J.H.: Enhanced password authentication through fuzzy logic. IEEE Expert 12(6), 38–45 (1997)
6. Deng, Y., Zhong, Y.: Keystroke dynamics user authentication based on Gaussian mixture model and deep belief nets. International Scholarly Research Notices 2013 (2013)

7. Epp, C., Lippold, M., Mandryk, R.L.: Identifying emotional states using keystroke dynamics. In: Proc. SIGCHI Conference on Human Factors in Computing Systems. pp. 715–724 (2011)

8. Gunetti, D., Picardi, C.: Keystroke analysis of free text. ACM Transactions on Information and System Security (TISSEC) 8(3), 312–347 (2005)

9. Hinbarji, Z., Albatal, R., O'Connor, N., Gurrin, C.: Loggerman, a comprehensive logging and visualization tool to capture computer usage. In: International Conference on Multimedia Modeling. pp. 342–347. Springer (2016)

10. Hjortskov, N., Rissén, D., Blangsted, A.K., Fallentin, N., Lundberg, U., Søgaard, K.: The effect of mental stress on heart rate variability and blood pressure during computer work. European Journal of Applied Physiology 92(1), 84–89 (2004)

11. Kaur, B., Durek, J.J., O'Kane, B.L., Tran, N., Moses, S., Luthra, M., Ikonomidou, V.N.: Heart rate variability (hrv): an indicator of stress. In: Independent Component Analyses, Compressive Sampling, Wavelets, Neural Net, Biosystems, and Nanoengineering XII. vol. 9118, p. 91180V. International Society for Optics and Photonics (2014)

12. Leijten, M., Van Waes, L.: Keystroke logging in writing research: Using inputlog to analyze and visualize writing processes. Written Communication 30(3), 358–392 (2013)

13. McCraty, R.: Science of the Heart : Exploring the Role of the Heart in Human Performance, An Overview of Research Conducted by the HeartMath Institute : Chapter 03: Heart Rate Variability. HeartMath Institute (2016)

14. Neal, A.S.: Time intervals between keystrokes, records, and fields in data entry with skilled operators. Human Factors 19(2), 163–170 (1977)

15. Panasiuk, P., Saeed, K.: A modified algorithm for user identification by his typing on the keyboard. In: Image Proc. and Communications Challenges 2. pp. 113–120. Springer (2010)

16. Senk, C., Dotzler, F.: Biometric authentication as a service for enterprise identity management deployment: a data protection perspective. In: 2011 Sixth International Conference on Availability, Reliability and Security. pp. 43–50. IEEE (2011)

17. Smeaton, A.F., Krishnamurthy, N.G., Suryanarayana, A.H.: Keystroke dynamics as part of lifelogging. In: Intnl. Conference on Multimedia Modeling. pp. 183–195. Springer (2021)

18. Teh, P.S., Teoh, A.B.J., Yue, S.: A survey of keystroke dynamics biometrics. The Scientific World Journal 2013 (2013)

19. Vizer, L.M., Zhou, L., Sears, A.: Automated stress detection using keystroke and linguistic features: An exploratory study. Intnl. J. of Human-Computer Studies 67(10), 870–886 (2009)

Fall Detection Using Multimodal Data

Thao V. Ha[1,2], Hoang Nguyen[1,2], Son T. Huynh[1,2,3], Trung T. Nguyen[4],
and Binh T. Nguyen[1,2,3(✉)]

[1] University of Science, Ho Chi Minh City, Vietnam
ngtbinh@hcmus.edu.vn
[2] Vietnam National University in Ho Chi Minh City, Ho Chi Minh City, Vietnam
[3] AISIA Research Lab, Ho Chi Minh City, Vietnam
[4] Hong Bang International University, Ho Chi Minh City, Vietnam

Abstract. In recent years, the occurrence of falls has increased and
has had detrimental effects on older adults. Therefore, various machine
learning approaches and datasets have been introduced to construct an
efficient fall detection algorithm for the social community. This paper
studies the fall detection problem based on a large public dataset, namely
the UP-Fall Detection Dataset. This dataset was collected from a dozen
of volunteers using different sensors and two cameras. We propose several
techniques to obtain valuable features from these sensors and cameras
and then construct suitable models for the main problem. The experimental results show that our proposed methods can bypass the state-of-
the-art methods on this dataset in terms of accuracy, precision, recall,
and F1-score.

Keywords: Fall detection · Extreme gradient boosting ·
Convolutional neural networks

1 Introduction

Falling is one of the most common dangers that the elderly usually face during
their daily lives, and the potential of death after falling might increase if they
live alone. As reported by the Center for Diseases and Controls (CDC)[1], the
percentage of deaths after falling in the U.S went up 30% from 2007 to 2016
for older adults. In case we do not find an appropriate way to stop these rates
from continuing to grow, there may be approximately seven deaths per hour
by 2030. Among persons above 65 years of age or older, more than one-third of
them fall each year, and remarkably, in half of such cases, the falls are recurrent
[1]. The corresponding risk may double or triple with the occurrence of cognitive
impairment or history of previous falls [2]. Typically, there are various costly
consequences that fall incidents lead to, including:

1. Causing serious injuries for the elderly such as broken bones e.g. wrist, arm,
   ankle, and hip fractures.

---

[1] https://www.cdc.gov/homeandrecreationalsafety/falls/adultfalls.html.

© Springer Nature Switzerland AG 2022
B. Þór Jónsson et al. (Eds.): MMM 2022, LNCS 13141, pp. 392–403, 2022.
https://doi.org/10.1007/978-3-030-98358-1_31

2. Causing head injuries for people who are who are taking certain medicines could make their situations worse. Furthermore, when fall incident result in damage to an elderly person's head, the people need to go to the hospital right away to inspect for any brain injuries.
3. Causing many people the fear of falling and making them less active. As a result, they become weaker and have a higher percentage of getting the same incident again.

Understanding the fearful outcomes that falling leads to, developing a fall detection system is essential than ever before. In addition, when an incident occurs, the time that the elderly remain to lie on the floor after the fall is one of the critical factors for determining the severity of the fall [3]. Timely detection of falls can quickly help older people to receive immediate assistance by caregivers and then reduce the adverse consequences from the incident [4]. Consequently, a robust fall detection system to monitor the fall and provide alerts or notifications is necessary to lighten the burden of caregivers and resource-strained health care systems [5].

This paper aims to investigate the falling detection problem based on a public dataset, namely the UP-Fall Detection dataset, provided by Martinez and colleagues [6]. This dataset contains sensor data and images collected by various devices and sensors, including wearable sensors, ambient sensors, and vision devices, from different healthy young volunteers. They performed six daily activities and simulated five different falls, with three attempts for each activity. The wearable sensors include an accelerometer, gyroscope, and ambient light sensors. On the other hand, they used one electroencephalograph (EEG) headset, six infrared sensors, and two cameras to acquire data. Furthermore, we present an improved method for the fall detection problem in this dataset and compare the proposed approach with previous techniques. The experimental results show that our method could bypass the state-of-the-art techniques and obtain better accuracy, precision, recall, and F1-score.

2   Related Work

There have been recent works related to the research of building fall detection systems. For example, Vallabh et al. [7] introduced their fall detection system using different classifiers, which are: Naïve Bayes, K-nearest neighbor, neural network, and support vector machine. Furthermore, they measured the corresponding performance of these methods based on two well-known datasets (FDD and URFD). In the experiments, Support Vector Machine achieved the best performance with 93.96% accuracy.

Delgado and colleagues [8] presented a new deep learning-based approach for the fall detection problem using four datasets recorded under different conditions. They utilized sensor data and subject information (accelerometer device, sampling rate, sequence length, age of the subjects, etc.) for feature extraction and obtained more than 98% of accuracy in these datasets. Furthermore, the proposed platform could get a low false positive (less than 1.6% on average) and handle simultaneously two tasks: fall detection and subject identification.

Tsai et al. [9] presented a fall detection system by combining both traditional and deep neural methods. First, for extracting relevant features for the main problem, they initialized a skeleton information extraction algorithm that could transform depth information into skeleton information and extract the important joints related to fall activity. Then, they pulled seven highlight feature points and employed deep convolution neural networks to implement the fall detection algorithm based on the approach. As a result, they could obtain high accuracy on a popular dataset NTU RGB+D with 99.2% accuracy. One can find more details at [10, 11].

3   Methodology

This section introduces our approach to the fall detection problem. First, we describe the feature extraction step with sensor and camera data and then present various models for the fall detection problem based on features extracted. We also provide the list of performance metrics used in our experiments.

3.1   UP-Fall Detection Dataset

All volunteers set up different devices to collect the UP-Fall Detection dataset, including wearables, context-aware sensors, and cameras. They collected these multimodal data at the same time. During the data collection process, these volunteers stayed in a controlled laboratory room, having the same light intensity, and the context-aware and cameras remained in the same position.

Five Mbientlab MetaSensor wearable sensors were put in the five different places (the left wrist, below the neck, in the right trouser pocket, in the middle of the waist (in the belt), and at the left ankle) to collect raw data (the 3-axis accelerometer, the 3-axis gyroscope, and the ambient light value). In addition, each volunteer used one electroencephalograph (EEG) NeuroSky Mind-Wave headset to measure the associated EED signals from the head. Six other infrared sensors were placed as a grid 0.40 m above the room floor to track all changes in interruption of the optical devices. In addition, the authors installed two Microsoft LifeCam Cinema cameras at 1.82 m above the floor for two different views: lateral view and frontal view (as depicted in Fig. 1). One can find further details at [6] (Tables 1 and 3).

3.2   Data Processing

Related to the sensor data, we dropped all duplicate records and removed rows having missing values. Finally, to combine the sensor data with all images extracted from a camera, we carefully checked the timestamp information from the sensor data and selected the most relevant mapping to associated images. As a result, the total number of samples for sensor data is 258,113 with 28 different

Table 1. Activities duration in the UP-Fall detection dataset [6]

Activity ID	Description	Duration (s)
1	Falling forward using hands	10
2	Falling forward using knees	10
3	Falling backwards	10
4	Falling sideward	10
5	Falling sitting in empty chair	10
6	Walking	60
7	Standing	60
8	Sitting	60
9	Picking up an object	10
10	Jumping	30
11	Laying	60

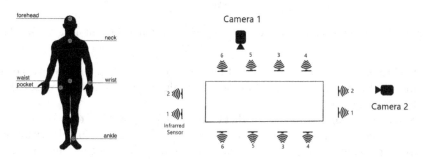

Fig. 1. Location of different sensors and camera devices in the UP-fall detection dataset [6]

attributes and one label. When extracting useful features for sensor data, we applied the standardization technique for the sensor dataset by normalizing the mean of attributes to zero and the corresponding standard deviation to one.

We ensured all images extracted from Camera 1 and Camera 2 could have the same size and sorting order for the camera data by removing redundant photos of both cameras. We also carefully reviewed the timestamp of both images and sensor data for the most relevant mapping. We scaled each image by dividing each pixel's value to 255 to guarantee those entire photos' pixels were in the range [0,1].

3.3   Feature Extraction and Modeling

As described in the previous section, two data sources are collected in the UP-Fall Detection dataset, sensor and camera data. Therefore, we employ different feature extraction steps for these data after doing necessary data processing.

3.3.1   Sensor Data

With a given list of 28 attributes from the sensor data, we present the following neural network only using sensor features for the fall detection algorithm: one fully connected layer of 2000 units with Relu activation function, one batch normalization layer, one fully connected layer of 600 units using the Relu activation function, another batch normalization layer, a dropout layer of the rate 0.2, and the final Softmax layer for the output size as 12. One can see more detailed in Fig. 2.

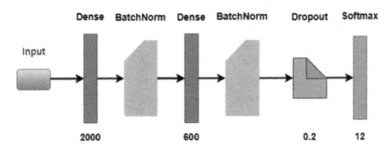

Fig. 2. Our proposed neural network for the fall detection algorithm using sensor data.

Besides using the proposed neural network above, we also consider two other techniques to create a suitable fall detection algorithm using only sensor data: XGBoost and CatBoost.

XGBoost is an optimized gradient tree boosting system that enables the design of decision trees in a sequential form [12]. Moreover, this algorithm can compute relevant calculations relatively faster in all computing environments. As a result, XGBoost is widely used for its performance in modeling newer attributes and classification of labels [13].

At the same time, CatBoost is a strong gradient boosting machine learning technique that achieves state-of-the-art results in various practical tasks. Despite the original aim of designing this algorithm being to deal with categorical features, it is still plausible to run CatBoost over a dataset with continuous features [14]. We will show the corresponding results in our experiments.

Table 2. Parameters of 2 ML models

Models	Parameters
XGBoost	Objective="multi:softprob",
	Learning rate = 0.5,
	Random state = 42,
	Use label encoder = False,
	# Of estimators = 100
CatBoost	# Of estimators = 500,
	Random seed = 42,
	Learning rate = 0.25,
	Max depth = 12

3.3.2   Camera Data

We employed convolutional neural networks (CNNs) to extract features from camera data. It is worth noting that CNN has been performing outstanding results for understanding contents presented in an image better and achieving state-of-the-art results in different applications, including image recognition, segmentation, detection, and retrieval [15].

It is worth noting that there are two cameras installed in the UP-Fall Detection dataset: Camera 1 and Camera 2. As a result, we consider three different cases for constructing an appropriate fall detection model for the main problem.

For only using Camera 1 or Camera 2, we selected the input size of images collected as (32,32). Then, we pushed the input data to the same CNN architecture having the following layers: a two-dimensional convolutional layer with 16 filters of size (3,3), one batch normalization layer, one Max-pooling layer of size (2,2), one Flatten layer, a fully-connected layer of 200 units, one Dropout layer of the rate 0.2, and the final Softmax layer with 12-dimensional output. We depicted this CNN in Fig. 3.

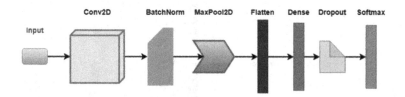

Fig. 3. Our proposed CNN for constructing a suitable fall detection model only using one camera (Camera 1 or Camera 2).

Finally, we study the remaining case when combining images collected from Camera 1 and Camera 2. Typically, we extracted features from each camera for given input data. As a result, the input data from Camera 1 and Camera 2 shifted through the same CNN architecture: one two-dimensional convolutional later with the number of filters as 15 and the kernel size as (3,3), one Max pooling layer with the pool size as (2,2), one batch normalization later, and one flattened layer. After this step, all two features extracted from Camera 1 and Camera 2 could be concatenated and then go through two consecutive fully-connected layers with the corresponding number of units as 400 and 200 using the Relu activation function. We used another dropout after that for regularization, and this could help us reduce the percentage of overfitting problems during the training step. Subsequently, we put the computed vector into the final layer using the Softmax activation function to obtain the 12-dimensional output. One can see more details in Fig. 4.

3.3.3   Fusion Data

For fusing multimodal data from both sensors and cameras, we designed the following neural network architecture. First, two input data from two cameras were passed through the same CNN architectures as mentioned above. Then,

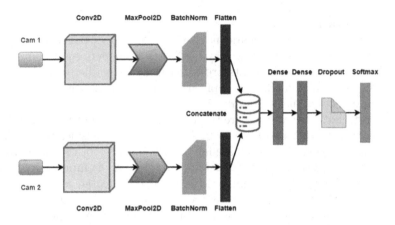

Fig. 4. Concatenated CNN model for Cam 1 + Cam 2

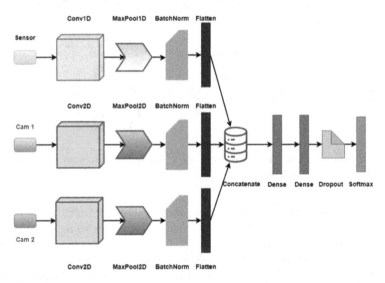

Fig. 5. Our proposed deep neural network using all sensor data and two cameras.

on the other hand, sensor data are passed through one convolutional 1D layer with ten filters and the size of the kernel as three, and the Relu activation function. Next, these computed vectors from sensors and two cameras continue passing through one max pooling 1D layer with the pool size as two, one batch normalization layer, and a flattened layer. Subsequently, these three flattened layers are concatenated as a final feature vector before going through two fully connected layers with units 600 and 1200. Next, the dropout layer with a rate of 0.2 is added for regularization, and the final result can be computed via a Softmax layer at the end for classifying fall detection. One can find more information related to this architecture in Fig. 5.

3.4   Performance Metrics

For comparing the performance of different approaches, we use the following metrics in our experiments: accuracy, precision, recall, and F1 scores.

4   Experiments

This paper runs all experiments on a computer with Intel(R) Core (TM) i7-7700K 4 CPUs running at 4.2 GHz with 16 GB of RAM and 48 GB of virtual memory. During the processing step, with the help of some essential libraries: **numpy, pandas, cv2**, we can work through the operation easily. In the modeling procedure, the **scikit-learn** package provides a powerful tool for us to run some algorithms like XGBoost and CatBoost. On the other hand, the **Tensorflow** and **Keras** libraries are crucial tools to train deep learning models. In the end, the package **ModelCheckpoint** is utilized to save deep learning models and **joblib** for **scikit-learn** models.

4.1   Data Collection

We used the UP-Fall Detection dataset for all experiments. This dataset was published by Martinez et al. [6] at the following link[2]. There are two types of datasets in this link: Consolidated Dataset and Feature Dataset. We decided to use the Consolidated Dataset because it is the core dataset to make further extractions more accessible. We concatenate all the CSV files together for the sake of easiness in the training process. After combining all the files, we get a CSV file with 294,678 samples and 45 features.

All images are converted to gray-scale images and resized to the shape of (32,32) by the following equation:

$$Gray = 0.299 * Red + 0.587 * Green + 0.114 * Blue$$

4.2   Previous Methods

In the previous work proposed by Martinez et al. [6], the authors did not give the information about a random seed for the dataset to reproduce the result with their techniques. As a result, we decided to split the dataset into training, test, and validation sets with the ratio of 60/20/20 and run experiments with our proposed models for both sensor and camera data. Likewise, the models in the article [6] are implemented again to compare the performance with our proposed model. From that, we can find a better fall detection system.

Related to the sensor data, Martinez and colleagues used Random Forest[16], Support Vector Machines [17], Multi-Layer Perceptron [18], and K-Nearest Neighbors [19]. One can find more information about in their paper [6] as well as their hyperparameter configuration in Table 2.

---

[2] https://sites.google.com/up.edu.mx/har-up.

For using camera data, they implemented one model using a Convolutional layer with eight filters size 3 × 3, one ReLu activation function, and then one Max Pooling layer of size 2 × 2. These consecutive layers repeated twice in that architecture with minor changes in filter sizes of the Convolution layer: 16 in the second and 32 in the third time. Finally, this model ended with one flatten layer and a Softmax layer with size 12 for obtaining the final prediction. It is worth noting that they trained this system using the stochastic gradient descent algorithm with an initial learning rate of 0.001, regularization coefficient 0.004, a maximum number of epochs 5, and a mini-batch size of 100. This architecture can be shown in Fig. 6.

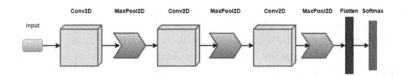

Fig. 6. The CNN model adapted from [6]

4.3 Experimental Results

In experiments, we analyze the performance of three different methods: using the sensor dataset (S), only using two cameras that are Camera 1 (C1) and Camera 2 (C2), a combination of two cameras (C1+C2), and a compound of these features (S+C1+C2). Then we measure all results using four metrics, including Accuracy, Precision, Recall, and F1-Score. One can see more details in our experimental results in Tables 4, 5, and 6.

First, we compare models and techniques on the sensor dataset without using any Camera information. The experiment shows that three of our algorithms, including XGBoost, CatBoost, and Multi-Layers Perceptron (MLP), can achieve exhilarating results in terms of Accuracy, Precision, Recall and F1-Score greater than 99%. Interestingly, our methods could bypass all techniques that Martinez et al. [6] which consists of Random Forest, Support Vector Machines, Multi-Layer Perceptron, and K-Nearest Neighbors. Significantly, in our methods, we increase the number of layers and units in the MLP model. As a result, the critical metric, F1-Score, can reach 99.03% with the modified MLP, while the best result of the previous work barely gained 97.28%.

For the approach using Camera information, we modify the CNN model, proposed by Martinez et al. [6] by eliminating two Conv2D layers and adding BatchNormalization and Dropout. Our proposed method reduces the time training and increases the performance in Accuracy, Precision, Recall higher than 99.1% in Camera 1 and 99.3% in Camera 2. Furthermore, the F1-Score of Camera 1 and Camera 2 can achieve 99.16% and 99.40% respectively. In comparison, model CNN of the previous author group [6] has the results of F1-Score value in Camera 1 and Camera 2 are 76.69% and 86.96% in that order. From this result,

Table 3. Parameters of ML models in [6]

Models	Parameters
Random forest	Estimators = 10, Min. samples split = 2, Min. samples leaf = 1, bootstrap = true
Support vector machines	C = 1.0, Kernel = Radical basis function, Kernel coefficient = 1/features, Shrinking = true, Tolerance = 0.001
Multi-layer perceptron	Hidden layer size = 100, Activation function = ReLU, Solver = stochastic gradient, Penalty parameter = 0.0001, Batch size = min(200,samples) , Initial learning rate = 0.001, Shuffle = true, Tolerance = 0.0001 , Exponential decay (first moment) = 0.9, Exponential decay (second moment) = 0.999, Regularization coefficient = 0.000000001, Max. epochs = 10
k-Nearest neighbors	Neighbors = 5 , Leaf size = 30, Metric = Euclidean

using multiple Convolutional layers as the previous work [6] in a consecutive sequence does not always give good results. One possible reason is that more information can be lost for each time passing through a Convolutional layer. In this case, using a convolutional layer is enough to extract information from the input image. In addition, BatchNormalization layers make the model easier to converge and overfit in the training set. Finally, adding Dropout classes helps the model avoid overfitting, thereby providing high performance on the test set.

Interestingly, using both the information of the sensor and two Cameras can help improve our approach's performance. In the case of the concatenation models in Table 6, the results are far better in all metrics that we mentioned above. At first, we try to combine Camera 1 and Camera 2 to train with this model, and it gets 99.46% in F1-Score compared to the best model we acquired with CNN, which is 99.40% F1-Score. Furthermore, it is worth noting that a training model with the combination of sensors and two Cameras can outperform using each feature. The corresponding Accuracy, Precision, Recall, and F1-Score are 99.56%, 99.56%, 99.56%, 99.55%, which is most dominant than the using Sensor, one Camera, and the combination of two Cameras on each metric.

Table 4. Performance of our proposed models

Data	Model	Accuracy	Precison	Recall	F1-Score
S	XGBoost	99.21	99.19	99.21	99.20
	Catboost	99.05	99.02	99.05	99.02
	MLP	99.04	99.05	99.03	99.03
C1	CNN	99.17	99.24	99.12	99.16
C2	CNN	99.39	99.40	99.39	99.40

Table 5. Performance of models of Martinez et al. [6]

Data	Model	Accuracy	Precison	Recall	F1-Score
S	RF	97.46	97.29	98.46	97.28
	SVM	96.96	96.82	96.96	96.61
	KNN	97.24	97.07	97.24	97.05
	MLP	90.21	88.36	90.21	88.43
C1	CNN	78.92	84.80	70.97	76.69
C2	CNN	88.24	90.32	86.13	86.96

Table 6. The performance when combining different features: C1+C2 and S+C1+C2.

Data	Model	Accuracy	Precison	Recall	F1-Score
C1+C2	Combination	99.46	99.47	99.46	99.46
S+C1+C2	Combination	99.56	99.56	99.56	99.55

5   Conclusion and Future Works

In the future, we aim to focus more on feature extractions work on this dataset
to have a deeper understanding of falling. In addition, we will also apply other
recent techniques in this data to improve the performance of the fall detection
problem.

References

1. Al-Aama, T.: Falls in the elderly: spectrum and prevention. Can. Fam. Physician
   57(7), 771–776 (2011)
2. Tinetti, M.E., Speechley, M., Ginter, S.F.: Risk factors for falls among elderly
   persons living in the community. New England J. Med. **319**(26), 1701–1707 (1988)
3. Igual, R., Medrano, C., Plaza, I.: Challenges, issues and trends in fall detection
   systems. Biomed. Eng. Online **12**(1), 1–24 (2013)
4. Bagala, F., et al.: Evaluation of accelerometer-based fall detection algorithms on
   real-world falls. PLoS ONE **7**(5), e37062 (2012)

5. Xu, T., Zhou, Y., Zhu, J.: New advances and challenges of fall detection systems: a survey. Appl. Sci. **8**(3), 418 (2018)
6. Martínez-Villaseñor, L., Ponce, H., Brieva, J., Moya-Albor, E., Núñez-Martínez, J., Peñafort-Asturiano, C.: Up-fall detection dataset: a multimodal approach. Sensors **19**(9), 1988 (2019)
7. Vallabh, P., Malekian, R., Ye, N., Bogatinoska, D.C.: Fall detection using machine learning algorithms. In: 24th International Conference on Software, Telecommunications and Computer Networks (SoftCOM), vol. 2016, pp. 1–9, IEEE (2016)
8. Delgado-Escaño, R., Castro, F.M., Cózar, J.R., Marín-Jiménez, M.J., Guil, N., Casilari, E.: A cross-dataset deep learning-based classifier for people fall detection and identification. Comput. Methods Program. Biomed. **184**, 105265 (2020)
9. Tsai, T.-H., Hsu, C.-W.: Implementation of fall detection system based on 3d skeleton for deep learning technique. IEEE Access **7**, 153 049–153 059 (2019)
10. Sadreazami, H., Bolic, M., Rajan, S.: Tl-fall: contactless indoor fall detection using transfer learning from a pretrained model. In: IEEE International Symposium on Medical Measurements and Applications (MeMeA), vol. 2019, pp. 1–5, IEEE (2019)
11. Keskes, O., Noumeir, R.: Vision-based fall detection using ST-GCN. IEEE Access **9**, 28 224–28 236 (2021)
12. Zhao, P., Lee, C.: Assessing rear-end collision risk of cars and heavy vehicles on freeways using a surrogate safety measure. Accid. Anal. Prev. **113**, 149–158 (2018)
13. Bhattacharya, S., et al.: A novel PCA-firefly based XGBoost classification model for intrusion detection in networks using GPU. Electronics **9**(2), 219 (2020)
14. Al-Sarem, M., Saeed, F., Boulila, W., Emara, A.H., Al-Mohaimeed, M., Errais, M.: Feature selection and classification using CatBoost method for improving the performance of predicting Parkinson's disease. In: Saeed, F., Al-Hadhrami, T., Mohammed, F., Mohammed, E. (eds.) Advances on Smart and Soft Computing. AISC, vol. 1188, pp. 189–199. Springer, Singapore (2021). https://doi.org/10.1007/978-981-15-6048-4_17
15. Sharma, N., Jain, V., Mishra, A.: An analysis of convolutional neural networks for image classification. Procedia Comput. Sci. **132**, 377–384 (2018)
16. Ho, T.K.: Random decision forests. In: Proceedings of 3rd International Conference on Document Analysis and Recognition, vol. 1, pp. 278–282, IEEE (1995)
17. Hearst, M.A.: Support vector machines. IEEE Intell. Syst. **13**(4), 18–28 (1998). https://doi.org/10.1109/5254.708428
18. Popescu, M.-C., Balas, V.E., Perescu-Popescu, L., Mastorakis, N.: Multilayer perceptron and neural networks. WSEAS Trans. Cir. Sys. **8**(7), 579–588 (2009)
19. Silverman, B.W., Jones, M.C., Fix, E., hodges, J.L.: An important contribution to nonparametric discriminant analysis and density estimation: commentary on fix and hodges (1951). International Statistical Review/Revue Internationale de Statistique **57**(3), 233–238 (1989). http://www.jstor.org/stable/1403796

Prediction of Blood Glucose Using Contextual LifeLog Data

Tenzin Palbar, Manoj Kesavulu, Cathal Gurrin$^{(\boxtimes)}$, and Renaat Verbruggen

Dublin City University, Dublin, Ireland
{manoj.kesavulu,cathal.gurrin}@dcu.ie

Abstract. In this paper, we describe a novel approach to the prediction of human blood glucose levels by analysing rich biometric human contextual data from a pioneering lifelog dataset. Numerous prediction models (RF, SVM, XGBoost and Elastic-Net) along with different combinations of input attributes are compared. An efficient ensemble method of stacking of multiple combination of prediction models was also implemented as our contribution. It was found that XGBoost outperformed three other models and that a stacking ensemble method further improved the performance.

Keywords: Blood glucose · Lifelogging · Human context

1 Introduction

Blood Glucose (BG) level also known as Blood Sugar level, is the concentration of glucose present in the blood. BG value is an important health indicator and when it is in high or low range for a long duration can lead to serious health conditions. There are different human contextual and environmental factors that influence BG level, such as diet, physical activity, emotional state, and other environmental factors. Analysing these parameters and including them in a prediction model can provide valuable insights into the life activities and health context of an individual. Lifelogging [10] and the Quantified Self [15] practice has led to the gathering of vast varieties of contextual human data in different forms, such as PoV images, personal biometrics, physical activity logs, and various other sources [10]. Using such data for personalized prediction models supporting health behaviour recommendations are not yet widely explored in the healthcare and wellness domains. Prior work explores prediction model using limited pre-defined attributes or continuous data from blood glucose monitors, whereas in this paper we use a rich multimodal contextual lifeLog dataset from two LifeLoggers which includes data from various sources and types such as physical activity logs, food consumption images, locations, heart rate and blood glucose monitors. The contribution of this paper is in the evaluation of prediction models such as RF, SVM, XGBoost and Elastic Net Regression along with a novel stacking ensemble approach in the first study of BG prediction using lifelog data.

© Springer Nature Switzerland AG 2022
B. Þór Jónsson et al. (Eds.): MMM 2022, LNCS 13141, pp. 404–415, 2022.
https://doi.org/10.1007/978-3-030-98358-1_32

2   Background and Related Research

The quantified-self movement supports the individual to monitor and enhance their wellness using data [18] and typically such data is gathered with a health and wellness goal. A lifelog [10] on the other hand, aims to gather a rich multimodal archive of the totality of an individual's life experience, and consequently, data from various sources are combined to form the lifelog, which promises to bring health benefits and lifestyle benefits. One such source of quantified self or lifelog data is BG level. In past work, a variety of approaches has been employed to predict BG values from various wearable sensor sources [21]. Examining only historical BG data, Marcus et al. [13], performed Kernel Ridge Regression (KRR) on Continuous Glucose Monitor (CGM) data and Martinsson et al. [14], presented a BG prediction model based on a Recurrent Neural Network (RNN) with a prediction horizon of 60 min. Alfian et al. [2], utilized time-domain features as additional attributes for the proposed Artificial Neural Networks (ANN) based prediction model to improve accuracy with CGM as the single input.

Recently, we have seen the that various other sensor sources, such as food intake, physical activity, and stress levels have been demonstrated effective in studies [12,25]. Takeuchi et al. [19], used time-series blood-sugar level data to analyse the relationship to lifestyle events (food ingestion, alcohol intake, and exercise) using manual logging and wearable sensors. El Idrissi et al. [11], presented a deep learning neural network (NN) model for BG prediction using a Long-Short-Term Memory (LSTM) layer with two fully connected dense layers showing promising results. Zecchin et al. [24], proposed a jump neural network prediction algorithm with a 30-minute horizon that exploits historical CGM data and consumed carbohydrate information. The prediction model showed accurate and comparable results to those obtained by the previously proposed feed-forward neural network (FNN) and first-order polynomial model approach [26]. Zarkogianni et al. [23], performed a comparative assessment of four glucose prediction models based on FNN, SOM, a neurofuzzy network with wavelets as activation functions (WFNN), and a linear regression model (LRM), using BG and physical activity data, with SOM demonstrating best performance. Munoz-Organero et al.[16], used simulated and real datasets consisting of CGM, meals and insulin boluses (slow and fast acting insulin). LSTM based RNN was applied to learn the carbohydrate digestion and insulin absorption processes from each parameter. Finally Georga et al. [6], used multiple input variables such as glucose concentration, the energy expenditure, the time of the day, meal, and insulin intake. Summarising past work, NNs and Auto Regression (AR) are the most popular techniques.

In this paper, we will evaluate the effect on BG prediction of employing a wide set of multimodal features from a lifelog dataset, which we consider to be the ultimate form of user context at present. We will evaluate the significance of the input variables and perform comparison of prediction models such as RF, SVR, XGBoost, Elestic-Net Regression and our own contribution in terms of a stacked ensemble model. To the best of our knowledge, this is first BG prediction study using LifeLog data.

3   Dataset

In this work we use the NTCIR-14 dataset, which is a rich multimodal lifelog dataset that was created for the NTCIR-14 Lifelog Retrieval challenge in 2019. The NTCIR-14 Lifelog dataset [9] consists of multimodal lifelog data over 42 d from two active lifeloggers. The data consists of multimedia data with wearable camera PoV images (two per minute, about 1,500 images per day). It includes a time-stamped record of music listened to and an archive of all conventional digital photos of food consumed (for examples, see Fig. 1). Additionally all-day time-aligned biometric data (heart rate, calorie burn, steps taken and distance moved) was provided using FitBit fitness trackers, continuous blood glucose monitoring (CGM) with readings of every 15 min was captured using a wearable sensor. Additionally daily activities of the lifeloggers were captured in terms of the semantic locations visited and time-stamped diet log of all food and drink consumed by the lifeloggers throughout the day were manually annotated. This dataset has been widely used for tasks such as activity detection, semantic event retrieval and analysis to gain insights into the lifelogger daily life routine. Some outliers and missing values were observed in the dataset, which are described in the next section. Both univariate and multivariate imputation approaches were used to estimate features with missing values. Ordinary Least Squares (OLS) was used to analyse the significance of each attribute to the missing data containing attribute.

Fig. 1. Examples of wearable camera images of food from the NTCIR-14 dataset [9].

4   Data Processing

As the dataset consists of a rich number of attributes that could have high influence on BG variability, we will be using a variety data sources to bring new insights on the factors influencing BG level and possible improvements of prediction models.

4.1 Data Understanding and Cleaning

As the dataset consists of real-world data gathered from a LifeLogger wearable devices and manual records, it contains some missing values. Multiple techniques were compared and used to handle missing data in the dataset. Univariate and Multivariate imputation techniques were applied in this work. Multivariate imputation strategy imputes missing values by modelling each feature with missing values as a function of other features. A univariate approach, which utilizes the attribute itself, was used for location name feature imputation. The following imputation methods were used to handle the observed missing values.

Heart Rate. The heart rate attribute in LifeLogger 1 dataset had 26% missing values. We split the non-missing heart-rate values into training (70%) and test set (30%), and used the test portion to compare multiple imputation techniques (Bayesian Ridge, Linear interpolation, Decision Tree, Extra Trees and k-Nearest Neighbors).

Table 1. Heart rate imputation methods.

Imputation method	MSE	RMSE	R-Squared
Bayesian ridge	176.09	13.27	0.22
k-Nearest neighbors	41.69	6.46	0.81
Decision tree regressor	34.01	5.83	0.85
ExtraTrees regressor	**32.44**	**5.69**	**0.86**

We evaluated the performance of four imputation methods using non-missing features (heart rate, steps, calories, distance and carbohydrate intake) and found that Extra Trees Regressors performed best, which aligns with similar efforts [17]. Table 1 shows the four approaches and we used an Extra Trees method to impute heart rate missing values.

As the historic glucose attribute was recorded on average every 15 min, the remaining attributes with continuous variables were averaged according to historic glucose except for carbohydrate intake. The sum of carbohydrate intake in grams (g) every 15 min were considered.

4.2 Carbohydrate Estimation

Images with time stamp for everyday meal intake were used to extract information about carbohydrate intake in grams (g). To calculate the carbohydrate values of each meal in the dataset, we consulted the Food and Nutrient Database for Dietary Studies (FNDDS) 2017–2018 issued by U.S. Department of Agriculture, Agricultural Research Service [1]. The database consists of the nutrient amount per 100g of edible portion for 64 nutrients, for more than 7,000 main food descriptions. The food portion estimation was performed using portions and weights estimate guidelines provided in the FNDDS database. Figure 2, outlines the food annotation and Table 2 presents the food description and other variables used from the FNDDS database for carbohydrate estimation. In future work, acquiring a food intake dataset with accurate portion and food class information can provide better estimation of carbohydrate values.

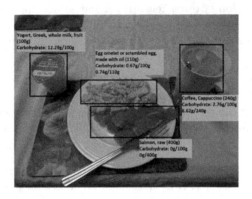

Fig. 2. Diet log image food annotation for carbohydrate estimation [9].

Table 2. Carbohydrate intake estimation variable.

Variable	Description	Example values
Main_food_description	Identified from diet log image	Coffee, Potato, Chocolate
Amt_g	Food amount in grams	240, 400
Amt_consumed	Amount consumed (%)	80, 100
Carbs_100g	Carbohydrate per 100 grams	2.76, 12.29
Total_carbs	Total carbohydrate (grams)	12.29, 6.62

4.3   Additional Feature Extraction

For physical activity metadata, activities were segmented the data into three categories, 'physical activity' which represented physical activities and transport activities, 'sedentary', which was derived from distance and step features, and a sleep category which was derived from motion and (lack-of) camera features. Additionally, each minute of each day was used to derive three categorical features, 'day of the week', 'time of the day' and 'day of the month' to capture the potential daily and weekly periodicity of BG level. Binarization of all categorical features were performed with the one hot encoding technique. The features such as heart rate, calories burned, steps, distance, carbohydrate intake, location, physical activity, time of the day, day of the week, day of the month were used as predictor variables for the models.

5   Prediction Methods

As mentioned earlier, we employ four basic (pre-existing) models from the related literature to represent and we also propose our own new ensemble technique (Stacked BG Detector).

5.1   State-of-the-Art Prediction Methods

Random Forest. There may be potentially irrelevant and redundant features in the proposed dataset either from raw data (distance and steps count) or derived features (day of the week and time of the day). Moreover, the relevant features set may differ from individual to individual, so feature selection with pre-defined rules would not advisable. Hence Random Forest (RF), which has been proved to be robust with redundant and irrelevant features [4] was employed. RF is an ensemble learning method that creates a forest with multiple decision trees. It averages the prediction of the individual tree, providing a better result compared to single decision trees, which are prone to over-fitting to the training set.

Support Vector Regression. Support Vector Regression (SVR) uses the same principle as Support Vector Machine (SVM), which is a margin-based classifier that uses a hyperplane to separate feature classes. SVR helps in deciding a decision boundary at some distance away from the hyperplane where the data points within the decision boundary has least error rate are considered. SVR acknowledges the presence of non-linearity in the data and provides a proficient prediction model. We choose SVR kernel-based method as one of our prediction models as they have been shown to perform well over the full range of glucose values in previous studies [6,7].

XGBoost. XGBoost (XGB) is short for eXtreme Gradient Boosting. It implements the gradient boosting decision tree algorithm, an ensemble technique where new models are added to correct the errors made by the prior models [5]. Gradient Boosting uses a gradient descent algorithm to minimize the loss when adding new models. Alfian et al. [3] developed a model based on XGB to predict BG. The model was shown to outperform Multi-Layer Perceptron (MLP), KNN, DT, SVR, RF, and AdaBoost models.

Elastic-Net. Elastic-Net Regression uses regularization to reduce the magnitude of coefficients of features in a regression model to avoid prediction dependency on specific features with extreme coefficient values, and is especially useful at dealing with the presence of correlation between features. Zanon et al. [22] used regularization-based techniques such as Lasso, Ridge, and Elastic-Net regression, which proved effective at predicting BG levels. Thus, we used Elastic-Net in this work with hyper parameter tuning using 10-fold cross validation on the training set. Cost functions of the regularization techniques are calculated as follows.

Elestic-Net Regression:

$$min\left(\left|\left|Y-X\theta\right|\right|_2^2+\lambda_1||\theta||_1+\lambda_2||\theta||_2^2\right) \tag{1}$$

Ridge Regression:

$$min\left(\left|\left|Y-X\theta\right|\right|_2^2+\lambda||\theta||_2^2\right) \tag{2}$$

Lasso Regression:

$$min\left(\left|\left|Y-X\theta\right|\right|_2^2+\lambda||\theta||_1\right) \tag{3}$$

Stacked BG Detector. Stacking or Stacked Generalization is an ensemble machine learning algorithm which involves using a meta learner which is a machine learning model to learn how best to combine the output of the base learners [20]. A stacking implementation is not widely used in previous BG prediction studies, thus this paper introduces stacking ensemble approach as the primary contribution of this work.

Preprocessing pipelines were designed for each prediction model that included one-hot encoding for categorical data and standardization for numeric data where applicable. Hyperparameter tuning was performed on each model with girdSearch 10-fold cross validation with repetition on the training dataset. In this study, we compared multiple combinations of base models and observed the model performance. Out of all combinations, two stacking models comprised of a combination of basic models are outlined in this paper. We decided to use the above mentioned four models as base models for the stacking model. The first stacking model with simple Linear Regression (LR) model as meta-model because most of the work is already done by the base learners and simple linear model usually works well as meta-learners [20]. For the second stacking model, we used Ridge Regression, a variant of LR as a meta-model because Ridge Regression can restrict the influence of predictor variables (output of base-model) over the output variable by compressing their coefficients.

5.2   Evaluation

The dataset was partitioned such that 80% of the data was used for training, and the rest of the data (20%) was used for testing. The training set was used to perform hyperparameter tuning on each predictive model using 10-fold cross-validation. The developed models were then utilized to predict the test data. Two performance metrics were used in this study to evaluate each model. Root mean square error (RMSE) and mean square error (MSE) were used as evaluation metrics. RMSE is better in terms of reflecting performance when dealing with large error values and when dealing with domains where slight increase in fall in error can have a huge impact. MSE score was used for hyperparameter tuning evaluation on the training dataset. It is widely accepted in the diabetes research community. [3,22].

6   Results Analysis and Discussion

This section presents the evaluation results for both the basic models and stacking systems. For each prediction model, grid search was performed to tune the hyperparameters. The hyperparameters rendering the model with the lowest MSE across all 10-fold cross-validated training dataset was then saved, and the corresponding model was used later to perform prediction on the testing dataset. In the below discussion we present the average performance of each model as well as considering the performance for each of the two lifeloggers separately, since BG prediction can differ across individuals.

Base Methods. The results of the RMSE and MAE of the basic predictive models for the prediction on both validation and test sets are displayed in Table 3 In addition to model performance on the individual LifeLogger dataset, the average of RMSE and MSE of both L-1 and L-2 are outlined. XGBoost showed the best performance among the basic models as it combines the advantages from both RF and gradient boosting. XGBoost was also observed to outperform other models in literature [22]. RF model showed better result with L-2 dataset due to lesser number of features and samples available compared to L-1.

Table 3. Evaluation table of the basic prediction models.

Life logger	Basic model	Evaluation			
		MSE(mmol/L)		MSE(mmol/L)	
		Validation	Test	Validation	Test
L1	RF	0.56	0.56	0.75	0.75
	SVR	0.77	0.83	0.88	0.91
	XGBoost	**0.51**	**0.5**	**0.72**	**0.71**
	Elastic-Net	1.08	1.07	1.04	1.03
L2	RF	**0.55**	**0.39**	**0.74**	**0.63**
	SVR	0.73	0.67	0.85	0.82
	XGBoost	0.61	0.47	0.78	0.68
	Elastic-Net	0.99	0.94	0.99	0.97
Average	RF	**0.56**	**0.48**	**0.75**	**0.69**
	SVR	0.75	0.75	0.86	0.86
	XGBoost	0.56	0.49	0.75	1
	Elastic-Net	1.04	1	1.02	0.69

Novel Stacking Model. In Table 4, we can observe that the evaluation result of the stacking ensemble method shows a performance improvement compared to individual base models. As the stacked regressor combines the strength of different base regressors, there was a decrease in both MSE, the average squared difference between the predicted and the actual value and RMSE, the squared root of MSE. Lower MSE and RMSE score indicates better performance of our model with unseen test data. We have used k-fold cross validation to handle possible overfitting. Figure 3, illustrates the MSE and RMSE values for all four base model and stacked model 2 on both LifeLogger datasets.

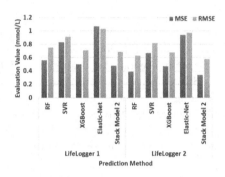

Fig. 3. Evaluation result.

The overall performance was further improved by considering the predictions from all base models as features to train a meta-learner L-1 (MSE: 0.48, RMSE: 0.69) and L-2 (MSE: 0.34, RMSE: 0.58). Thus, the combined learner was able to make more accurate predictions on the test set compared to individual basic models. Figure 3 shows the results of all models for each lifelogger.

Observations on Performance. We observed that three readily available data sources from off-the-shelf fitness trackers (heart rate, calories burned and step count) to have highest contribution to model performance and therefore are the most useful features. Carbohydrate intake also (unsurprisingly) has a very high influence on BG variation. Since we had performed food and portion classification and used the FNDDS database [1] for carbohydrate estimation, there is a significant opportunity to fully-automate this process using wearable cameras.

Table 4. Model evaluation table for stacked system.

Life logger	Stacking system	Evaluation			
		MSE(mmol/L)		MSE(mmol/L)	
		Validation	Test	Validation	Test
L1	Stack model 1	**0.50**	**0.48**	**0.71**	**0.69**
	Stack model 2	**0.50**	**0.48**	**0.71**	**0.69**
L2	Stack Model 1	0.49	0.34	0.71	0.58
	Stack model 2	**0.49**	**0.34**	**0.70**	**0.58**
Average	Stack Model 1	0.49	0.41	0.71	0.64
	Stack model 2	0.49	0.41	0.70	0.64

7 Conclusion and Future Work

In this work we compared the effectiveness of various basic BG predictor models
to a new ensemble model when operating over the rich contextual lifelog data
from two lifeloggers. The LifeLog dataset includes many forms of multimodal
data captured continuously during 42 d. To the best of our knowledge, this is
the first BG prediction study on a rich contextual LifeLog dataset. Unlike previous studies that used predefined attributes or only CGM, we have performed
statistical analysis on a multimodal attributes available in the LifeLog dataset
and enriched the dataset by extracting features from LifeLog images. Multiple
prediction models were implemented on the LifeLog extracted attributes and
their performance were compared using RMSE and MSE evaluation metrics. Initially, four regression models were trained and validated on the training dataset
using 10-fold cross validation, resulting in selection of hyperparameters for each
model. The four models were then used to make final predictions on the test set.
Predictions from the basic models were fed as features to a regression to build
two stacked ensemble approaches, which improved BG prediction and forms the
main contribution of this paper.

This work has some limitations, such as a small dataset, but it is the only
one available which has such rich contextual data. Data from multiple participants could provide us better insight on intra-individual variability of influence
of attributes on individual BG. Another issue is the lack of a well-defined approach to estimate carbohydrate intake, which can reduce the performance of the
models, and lead to errors, as was also found in [21]. In future work, inclusion
of richer contextual features and a larger dataset can give us more scope to
perform analysis. In addition, stress is known to have a high correlation to BG
variation [8], so it can be included as another feature. Finally, a better approach
for carbohydrate estimation adoption can improve predictive performance [21]
and recent advances in wearable cameras (from Facebook) can facilitate more
data for better carbohydrate estimation.

References

1. U.S. Department of Agriculture, A.R.S.: Food and nutrient database for dietary studies (fndds). In: FoodData Central. Food Surveys Research Group, Beltsville Human Nutrition Research Center (2017). http://www.ars.usda.gov/nea/bhnrc/fsrg
2. Alfian, G., et al.: Blood glucose prediction model for type 1 diabetes based on artificial neural network with time-domain features. Biocybernetics Biomed. Eng. **40**(4), 1586–1599 (2020). https://doi.org/10.1016/j.bbe.2020.10.004, https://www.sciencedirect.com/science/article/pii/S0208521620301248
3. Alfian, G., Syafrudin, M., Rhee, J., Anshari, M., Mustakim, M., Fahrurrozi, I.: Blood glucose prediction model for type 1 diabetes based on extreme gradient boosting. In: IOP Conference Series: Materials Science and Engineering, vol. 803, p. 012012, May 2020. https://doi.org/10.1088/1757-899x/803/1/012012
4. Breiman, L.: Random forests. Mach. Learn. **45**(1), 5–32 (2001). https://doi.org/10.1023/A:1010933404324, http://dx.doi.org/10.1023/A%3A1010933404324
5. Chen, T., Guestrin, C.: Xgboost: A scalable tree boosting system. In: Proceedings of the 22nd ACM SIGKDD International Conference on Knowledge Discovery and Data Mining, KDD 2016, pp. 785–794. Association for Computing Machinery, New York (2016). https://doi.org/10.1145/2939672.2939785
6. Georga, E.I., Protopappas, V.C., Polyzos, D., Fotiadis, D.I.: Evaluation of short-term predictors of glucose concentration in type 1 diabetes combining feature ranking with regression models. Med. Biol. Eng. Comput. **53**(12), 1305–1318 (2015). https://doi.org/10.1007/s11517-015-1263-1
7. Georga, E.I., Protopappas, V.C., Ardigò, D., Polyzos, D., Fotiadis, D.I.: A glucose model based on support vector regression for the prediction of hypoglycemic events under free-living conditions. Diab. Technol. Ther. **15**(8), 634–643 (2013). https://doi.org/10.1089/dia.2012.0285
8. Goetsch, V.L., Wiebe, D.J., Veltum, L.G., van Dorsten, B.: Stress and blood glucose in type ii diabetes mellitus. Behav. Res. Ther. **28**(6), 531–537 (1990). https://doi.org/10.1016/0005-7967(90)90140-E, https://www.sciencedirect.com/science/article/pii/000579679090140E
9. Gurrin, C., et al.: Advances in lifelog data organisation and retrieval at the NTCIR-14 lifelog-3 task. In: Kato, M.P., Liu, Y., Kando, N., Clarke, C.L.A. (eds.) NTCIR 2019. LNCS, vol. 11966, pp. 16–28. Springer, Cham (2019). https://doi.org/10.1007/978-3-030-36805-0_2
10. Gurrin, C., Smeaton, A.F., Doherty, A.R.: Lifelogging: personal big data. Found. Trends® Inf. Retrieval **8**(1), 1–125 (2014). https://doi.org/10.1561/1500000033, http://dx.doi.org/10.1561/1500000033
11. Idriss, T.E., Idri, A., Abnane, I., Bakkoury, Z.: Predicting blood glucose using an LSTM neural network. In: 2019 Federated Conference on Computer Science and Information Systems (FedCSIS), pp. 35–41 (2019). https://doi.org/10.15439/2019F159
12. Manohar, C., et al.: The effect of walking on postprandial glycemic excursion in patients with type 1 diabetes and healthy people. Diabetes Care **35**(12), 2493–2499 (2012)
13. Marcus, Y., et al.: Improving blood glucose level predictability using machine learning. Diabetes/Metab. Res. Rev. **36**(8), e3348 (2020). https://doi.org/10.1002/dmrr.3348, https://onlinelibrary.wiley.com/doi/abs/10.1002/dmrr.3348

14. Martinsson, J., Schliep, A., Eliasson, B., Mogren, O.: Blood glucose prediction with variance estimation using recurrent neural networks. J. Healthcare Inf. Res. 4(1), 1–18 (2019). https://doi.org/10.1007/s41666-019-00059-y

15. Meyer, J., Simske, S., Siek, K.A., Gurrin, C.G., Hermens, H.: Beyond quantified self: data for wellbeing. In: CHI 2014 Extended Abstracts on Human Factors in Computing Systems, CHI EA 2014, pp. 95–98. Association for Computing Machinery, New York (2014)

16. Munoz-Organero, M.: Deep physiological model for blood glucose prediction in t1dm patients. Sensors 20(14) (2020). https://doi.org/10.3390/s20143896 ,https://www.mdpi.com/1424-8220/20/14/3896

17. Suresh, M., Taib, R., Zhao, Y., Jin, W.: Sharpening the BLADE: missing data imputation using supervised machine learning. In: Liu, J., Bailey, J. (eds.) AI 2019. LNCS (LNAI), vol. 11919, pp. 215–227. Springer, Cham (2019). https://doi.org/10.1007/978-3-030-35288-2_18

18. Swan, M.: The quantified self: fundamental disruption in big data science and biological discovery. Big data 1(2), 85–99 (2013)

19. Takeuchi, H., Kodama, N., Tsurumi, K.: Time-series data analysis of blood-sugar level of a diabetic in relationship to lifestyle events. In: 2009 Annual International Conference of the IEEE Engineering in Medicine and Biology Society, pp. 5195–5198 (2009). https://doi.org/10.1109/IEMBS.2009.5334582

20. Witten, I.H., Frank, E.: Data mining: practical machine learning tools and techniques with java implementations. SIGMOD Rec. 31(1), 76–77 (2002). https://doi.org/10.1145/507338.507355

21. Woldaregay, A.Z., et al.: Data-driven modeling and prediction of blood glucose dynamics: machine learning applications in type 1 diabetes. Artif. Intell. Med. 98, 109–134 (2019)

22. Zanon, M., Sparacino, G., Facchinetti, A., Talary, M.S., Caduff, A., Cobelli, C.: Regularised model identification improves accuracy of multisensor systems for non-invasive continuous glucose monitoring in diabetes management. J. Appl. Math. 2013(SI05), 1 – 10 (2013). https://doi.org/10.1155/2013/793869

23. Zarkogianni, K., et al.: Comparative assessment of glucose prediction models for patients with type 1 diabetes mellitus applying sensors for glucose and physical activity monitoring. Med. Biol. Eng. Comput. 53(12), 1333–1343 (2015). https://doi.org/10.1007/s11517-015-1320-9

24. Zecchin, C., Facchinetti, A., Sparacino, G., Cobelli, C.: Jump neural network for online short-time prediction of blood glucose from continuous monitoring sensors and meal information. Comput. Methods Program. Biomed. 113(1), 144–152 (2014). https://doi.org/10.1016/j.cmpb.2013.09.016, https://www.sciencedirect.com/science/article/pii/S0169260713003234

25. Zecchin, C., et al.: Physical activity measured by physical activity monitoring system correlates with glucose trends reconstructed from continuous glucose monitoring. Diabetes Tech. Ther. 15(10), 836–844 (2013). https://doi.org/10.1089/dia.2013.0105, pMID: 23944973

26. Zecchin, C., Facchinetti, A., Sparacino, G., De Nicolao, G., Cobelli, C.: Neural network incorporating meal information improves accuracy of short-time prediction of glucose concentration. IEEE Trans. Biomed. Eng. 59(6), 1550–1560 (2012). https://doi.org/10.1109/TBME.2012.2188893

Multimodal Embedding for Lifelog Retrieval

Liting Zhou[✉][iD] and Cathal Gurrin[iD]

Dublin City University, Dublin, Ireland
{becky.zhou,cathal.gurrin}@dcu.ie

Abstract. Nowadays, research on lifelog retrieval is attracting increasing attention with a focus on applying machine learning, especially for data annotation/enrichment which is necessary to facilitate effective retrieval. In this paper, we propose two annotation approaches that apply state-of-the-art text/visual and joint embedding technologies for lifelog query-text retrieval tasks. Both approaches are evaluated on the commonly used NTCIR13-lifelog dataset and the results demonstrate embedding techniques show improved retrieval accuracy over conventional text matching methods.

Keywords: Lifelog · Visual-semantic retrieval · Information retrieval

1 Introduction

The challenge of contextual human understanding usually relies on analysing single, or multi-modal data to infer knowledge about the context of the individual in an automated process. The recent popularity of lifelogging [8] as a concept has presented a new source of continuous contextual data about the individual, which has been utilised to support various applications. Specifically lifelog retrieval and has been the focus of numerous benchmarking efforts [9,10] in recent years. Lifelog are rich multimodal continuous archives of life activity data, and can include thousands of wearable camera images per day, along with other sensor data, such as location, physical activity. In this paper we consider lifelogs to be a source of contextual human data, which, if indexed appropriately can support effective personal search engines.

Most lifelog retrieval has focused on creating accurate textual annotations via extracted concepts from visual data and thereby facilitated conventional textual information needs, but has ignored the capabilities for understanding human relations in queries and images, i.e. contextual information and human interactions in different scenarios. This is because of an underlying assumption that categories or tags are known in advance, which does not hold for many real world complex lifelog scenes. To improve the retrieval accuracy for realistic and complex scenes, we need to drop the assumption mentioned above and reduce the "semantic gap" between query and image features of lifelog data. This "semantic gap" problem is especially important for lifelog retrieval when

© Springer Nature Switzerland AG 2022
B. Þór Jónsson et al. (Eds.): MMM 2022, LNCS 13141, pp. 416–427, 2022.
https://doi.org/10.1007/978-3-030-98358-1_33

single modality information needs (usually text) must match with multimodal lifelog data. Hence lifelog retrieval is difficult due to multi-modality and the semantic gap problem. A lifelog retrieval system should be able to judiciously determine what modalities (from images, activity, location and biometric data) to use and combine them to make search more efficient. The question is posed as how one can multimodal (especially visual) data from lifelogs which have the same semantics as the text without modality exchange? In this paper, we will address this challenge by proposing two novel approaches to lifelog retrieval based on deep learning architectures. Such visual-semantic retrieval enables flexible retrieval across different modes, and the key aspect of the retrieval process is measuring similarity between different types of data. Visual-semantic retrieval has been proven to be an effective solution when searching over enormous and multi-varied data.

The first approach is built on a pre-trained image captioning in Sect. 3. In this caption-based retrieval, we focus on predicting the image captions and matching the query with the predicted captions. The second approach is the visual-semantic embedding for lifelog retrieval, described in Sect. 4. Visual-Semantic embedding mainly aims to find a common latent space where the related visual and textual documents are close to each other, and it is popular approach to cross-model retrieval [13,14]. In our visual-semantic retrieval, we employ deep learning methods for both images and text to facilitate cross-modal matching. In our experiment, both approaches use BERT [4], which is currently a state-of-the-art word embedding model.

The main contribution of this paper are thus summarized:

- To the best of our knowledge, this is the first work to explore visual-semantic embedding learning in lifelog retrieval problem.
- A proposal for an approach utilizing trained image captioning model and state-of-the-art NLP technique to learn and match the lifelog query and images.
- The application of a joint representations model to learn the visual-text matching and retrieving the queried related images.

2 Related Work

2.1 Feature Learning

Feature learning refers to techniques that learn to transform raw data input to an effective representation for further higher-level processing such as classification, automatic detection, and segmentation. Feature learning approaches provide a natural way to capture cues by using a large number of code words (sparse coding) or neurons (deep networks), while traditional computer vision features, designed for basic-level category recognition, may eliminate many useful cues during feature extraction [25]. Deep neural networks are multi-layered and they are used to learn feature representations in the hidden layer(s). These representations are subsequently used for classification or regression at the output layer, and feature learning is an integral part of deep learning [17].

Text Feature Representation in NLP. The process of transforming text into numeric features, is usually performed by building a language model. These models typically assign probabilities, frequencies or some calculated numbers to words, sequences of words, group of words, section of documents or whole documents. The most common techniques are: one-hot encoding, N-grams, bag-of-words, vector semantics (TF-IDF), distributional semantics (Word2vec [2] and GloVe [20]). Recently, very powerful language models have been developed such as BERT [4], which is Google's neural network-based technique for natural language processing (NLP) pre-training. In this work, one-hot Encoding and BERT are the two main approaches we used for textual embedding transformation.

Image Feature Representation in Computer Vision. In the computer vision domain, the image representations derived from pre-trained Convolutional Neural Networks (CNNs) [21] have become the preferred technique for computer vision tasks such as instance retrieval from image archives. Convolutional Neural Networks (ConvNet/CNN) is a deep Learning algorithm which can take in an input image, assign importance (learnable weights and biases) to various aspects/objects in the image and be able to differentiate one from the other. The pre-processing required in a ConvNet is much lower as compared to other classification algorithms. While in primitive methods filters are hand-engineered, with enough training, ConvNets have the ability to learn these filters/characteristics. In machine learning, deep learning networks have multiple non-linear hidden layers and can represent the data in a hierarchical way from lower to higher abstraction. CNNs are a variant of the multilayer perceptron, which are inspired by the visual cortex and have deep architectures.

2.2 Deep Learning in Text-Image Retrieval

This refers to the application of text-based image retrieval with text description as an input matched against image archives. Although text-image retrieval has a wide application in semantic search, it still poses a challenge. Text-based image retrieval systems can be divided into two categories: single-direction retrieval and bi-directional retrieval. In single-direction retrieval, similar images to the text query are retrieved from the training set based on their similarities with the query in a trained visual space [18,19]. In bi-directional retrieval, most approaches [7,12] are building a common multimedia embedding space for the visual and textual data based on a training a set of image-description pairs. This matching visual data and natural language has been a challenging problem for multimedia and it has facilitated large-scale applications, including, image and video captioning [1,3].

Image Captioning. Image captioning has became an active research topic in recent years and its main contribution is that it translates multimodal data from unstructured image data to structured text data. Currently, automatic image and video captioning is extremely important, as well as challenging, because it connects the domain of computer vision and natural language processing. The current existing image captioning methods include sentence-template based [6], retrieval based [15], neural-network based [3]. The neural-network framework with the encoder-decoder structure is widely used in image caption generation, in which the encoder extracts the image features by Convolutional Neural Network (CNN), and the decoder adopts Recurrent Neural Network (RNN) to generate the image description.

3 Text Embedding for Semantic Retrieval Based on Captions

The first approach is to use pre-trained image captioning. The automatic understanding of semantic correlations between text queries and associated lifelog images as well as their interaction has a great potential for enhanced multimodal lifelog retrieval systems. The semantic correlations represent the actual intention of the user who makes the query. When intention cannot be interpreted by the machine, a semantic gap arises. For instance, if the query is 'Nike', the user may be looking for the shoes of 'Nike' brand, but the system cannot capture this intention. Rather, images of 'Nike' brand are returned by the system. To reduce this semantic gap, extracting the semantic features becomes necessary. A typical method resorts to the image captioning, which translates the visual content to text, to bridge the semantic gap between vision and language in lifelog retrieval. Extracting the complete detail of individual object, related attributes and their interaction relationship from image is main path for image captioning.

3.1 Object Detection

Extracting objects and corresponding attributes (e.g. blue bag, large room) in images are important in image captioning. The bottom-up attention model [1] provides the localization of labeled objects from images with complex backgrounds, such as lifelog images, therefore in this chapter we use the bottom-up attention model which is built upon Faster-RCNN [23] to extract semantic concepts, object labels and object attributes to describe the visual content of lifelog images. Each region proposal in Faster R-CNN has an associated feature vector and the corresponding weights are determined by a top-down mechanism. The model generates bounding boxes as regions of objects and feature vectors as object descriptors. In our image captioning, Faster-RCNN is adopted to detect and encode image regions at the object level. Image-text similarity is then obtained by aggregating similarity scores from all word-region pairs.

3.2 Captioning Model

The image captioning process takes visual content and represents it in natural language; this has attracted increasing interest in the computer vision community. It generally describes visual content based on the semantic relations and relative positions of objects in an image. Predicted image captioning needs to describe the implicit attributes of the item which are extracted using a bottom-up attention model and cannot be easily localized by object detectors. Commonly, the approach is to use a nearest neighbor algorithm. This takes two or more vectors, and calculates the distance (or similarity) between them in an efficient manner. The M2 (Meshed-Memory Transformer) model [3], a state-of-the-art transformer based image captioning model, uses a transformer encoder for self-attention on visual features and a transformer decoder for masked self-attention on caption tokens and encoder-decoder attention. A linear layer projects visual features into the usually lower-dimensional representation space of the encoder. Noticeably, the M2 model can exploit prior knowledge by incorporating a region encoding approach and a meshed connectivity between encoding and decoding modules. Our captioning generation is built based on the M2 model. The input of the M2 model is visual features from images and text features of captions and then output is the probability between the image and caption. We choose the highest probability as our prediction result.

3.3 Semantic Similarity

Finally we need to consider how to rank results. The most general method to address such semantic search is to map the each encoded document vector into a single vector space and determine which semantically similar sentences are close via calculating the distance between the vectors. After selecting and interactive computation, we choose to use the Sentence-BERT [24] to calculate the semantic similarity. Sentence-BERT is a modification of the pretrained BERT network that uses siamese and triplet network structures to derive semantically meaningful sentence embeddings that can be compared using cosine-similarity. The reason we choose Sentence-BERT is its higher efficiency for finding the most similar pair than BERT while maintaining the accuracy of BERT.

In our experiment, the cosine-similarity distance is employed to calculate the similarity between the captioning result and text query. These similarity measures can be performed efficiently on semantic similarity search as well as for clustering. Given an captions and query denoted as Q and C, and fed them into the Sentence-BERT model. The cosine function are used to calculate the relevance score. The formula are shown below:

$$\cos(\mathbf{q}, \mathbf{c}) = \frac{\mathbf{q}\mathbf{c}}{\|\mathbf{q}\|\|\mathbf{c}\|} = \frac{\sum_{i=1}^{n} \mathbf{q}_i \mathbf{c}_c}{\sqrt{\sum_{i=1}^{n} (\mathbf{q}_i)^2}\sqrt{\sum_{i=1}^{n} (\mathbf{c}_i)^2}} \tag{1}$$

4 Joint Embedding for Cross-Modal Retrieval in Lifelog Retrieval

The second approach is the visual-semantic embedding based lifelog retrieval. The main challenge in this image-text retrieval task is semantic matching data from different modalities. Visual-semantic retrieval is designed for such scenarios where the queries and retrieval results are from different media types. Currently most recent image-text retrieval methods show promise by learning deep representations aligned across modalities. In our work, we follow the state-of-the-art techniques to learn robust Visual-Semantic joint representation which is used to match the text query to lifelog images. There are two types of challenges we must consider: how to learn two projection matrices to map multimodal data into a common feature space, in which cross-modal data matching can be performed, and how to design a deep neural network that can project the query into a visual feature space by vectoring the query. In our approach, the text query and image are encoded as text and visual embeddings using different encoders firstly and then pass them to a learned common latent space to calculate the relevance.

4.1 Visual Representation

Given an lifelog image, how to encode the image to the representation is a first task we should consider. Deep Neural Networks (DNNs) are a popular and powerful technique for learning representations from data in a hierarchical and compositional manner. We choose to use Resnet152 [11] to extract visual features due to its high-degree of accuracy. Resnet introduced a new architecture called Residual Network which is a powerful deep neural network that has achieved excellent performance results in the computer vision domain. Resnet152 is trained on the ImageNet dataset and the residual nets with a depth of up to 152 layers. In our work, we applied the resnet152 to extract the visual representation of lifelog images. We take the input of the classification layer as a feature, which has a dimensionality of 2,048.

4.2 Unsupervised Cross-modal Common Vector Space Learning

After the text and visual embedding are extracted, how to match the visual and text embedding is the third point we should consider. The image features and the text features can be transformed to the same joint features, in the same space for retrieval. Common vector space learning based on methods are currently the mainstream in cross-modal retrieval. Among many choice of common vector space learning algorithm, the (Visual-Semantic Embedding) VSE++ [5] has shown impressive performance in image classification and text-based image retrieval tasks. The VSE++ models explicitly maps images into a rich semantic space, with the goal that images of the same category are mapped to nearby location and text descriptions are embedded in such a common vector space with respect to some measure of similarity. The VSE++ model has trained on MS-COCO and Flickr30K dataset and performed well in mapping images to text descriptions. The prototype of this assumption is shown in 1. Given a text query expressed by a natural-language sentences of $Q\{w1, w2, ..., wl\}$, we aim to match the sentence and retrieve lifelog images relevant with respect to the query from a collection of n unlabeled images $I\{i1, i2, ..., in\}$. We focus on query representation learning that predicts s from the query. Meanwhile, v can be instantiated using either deep CNN features or concept vectors as used in previous works.

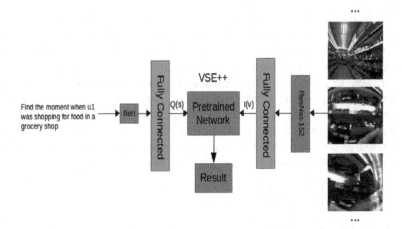

Fig. 1. The left to VSE++ is using BERT to extract text embedding. The right to VSE++ is applying resnet152 to extract 2048 dimensions visual features. The results is calculated using the cosine-similarity

5   Experimental Analysis

We now examine the performance of both approaches (only text embedding and visual-semantic joint embedding) and compare both against a standard baseline. It is the first time these techniques have been applied to lifelog data.

5.1   Baseline

For the baseline tool we choose LIFER [26] system which is a concept-based filter using semantic concepts and has been shown to perform well in the LSC benchmarking workshop [26]. It is an example of a state-of-the-art conventional approach. Semantic concepts are automatically extracted from lifelog images content to represent their visual information. Users are able to filter images content using a concept faceted filtering technique. This tool could help users to speed up the validation process by providing a list of related images candidates.

5.2   Setting 1 - Text Embedding

We use the following steps to perform the experiments:

- Visual embedding: The bottom-up attention model is used to extract visual features with attributes from a given image.
- Captions and query embedding: We choose M2-based image captioning model [3] to predict the corresponding captions.
- Matching: Sentence-BERT [24] vectorized the sentences and captions to calculate and rank the similarity between them.

5.3   Setting 2 - Visual-Semantic Embedding

We use the following steps to perform the experiments:

- Visual Embedding: Resnet152 predicts the CNN feature of ResNet-152 for a given image.
- Query Embedding: Sentence-BERT decodes the text feature to text embedding which will be used to calculate the similarity in next step.
- Matching: Project the visual and query embedding into the learned latent space to match them.

In order to test the approaches to semantic retrieval based on the image captioning model and cross-modal retrieval model, we applied this method on NTCIR13-lifelog LSAT task (Dateset:90 d, 114,547 images with associated metadata; Topics: 23 topics). Also, we evaluate the performance improvement of our proposed approach by comparing the search results to the baseline approach.

Results Comparison

The evaluation results from the approaches described are shown in Table 1. As can be seen both proposed approaches clearly outperform baseline and the joint embedding technique achieves a highest score among these three approaches. There is a classification step to turn the image into captions in the first approach, which could cause the retrieval accuracy to be lower than second approach. Table 2 shows the comparison of two approaches on P@10 score. As all LSAT lifelog queries are finding the moment of lifelogger's behavior, the ground-truth of the these queries are the top 10 images. So the cut-off at 10 will be better to compare the performance of our two approaches. We found that the captioning-based approach could accurately detect specific concepts and scene recognition in a query sentence. On the other hand, in the visual-semantic embedding approach, we found that phrases including verbs, prepositions, and relationships between objects (e.g. people and objects) were captured relatively well.

Table 1. Overall comparison of different approaches on NTCIR13 dataset

Approach	MAP@10	CR@10	F1
Baseline(interactive) [26]	0.37	0.3	0.29
Caption	0.6	0.45	0.41
Joint Embedding	0.71	0.66	0.57

Table 2. The P@10 of 10 query sentences evaluated in the LSAT sub-task NTCIR13-Lifelog and comparison of video retrieval performance (average precision) between caption-based and visual-semantic joint embedding approaches

Query-id	Description	Caption	Joint embedding
001	Find the moments when I was eating lunch	0.65	0.88
002	Find moments when I was gardening in my home	0.12	0.23
003	Find the moment when I was visiting a castle at night	0.51	0.67
004	Find the moments when I was drinking coffee in a cafe	0.6	0.7
005	Find the moments when I was outside at sunset	0.56	0.64
006	Find the moments when I visited a graveyard	0.54	0.43
007	Find the moments when I was lecturing to a group of people in a classroom environment	0.35	0.55
008	Find all the moments when I was grocery shopping	0.62	0.68
009	Find the moments when I worked at home late at night	0.67	0.71
010	Find the moments when I was working on the computer at my office desk	0.57	0.85

Fig. 2. Selected example of Top 5 retrieved results on caption based retrieval (text embedding)

5.4   Discussion and Contribution

Figure 2 and Fig. 3 illustrate the selected results using caption based retrieval and the visual-semantic retrieval respectively. In these two figures, the text queries are shown on the left side and the retrieved images are shown on the right side. The comparison of the top 5 results retrieved using two approaches

Fig. 3. Selected example of Top 5 retrieved result using the visual-semantic based retrieval (visual-semantic embedding)

clearly demonstrates that our proposed semantic-visual embedding approaches can increase the performance of lifelog moment retrieval.

The approach using visual-semantic joint embedding outperforms the caption-based approach when tested on a popular lifelog dataset. As shown in Table 1, with the support of the embedding techniques, the performance of lifelog moment retrieval is improved by 34% when compared to Baseline(interactive). Therefore we can conclude that our approach could help to reduce "semantic gap" between text query and images, and also boost the retrieval performance because it provides more reliable feature matching after applying the embedding model on lifelog moment retrieval task.

6   Conclusion

Given that lifelogs currently provide the ultimate source of continuous human contextual data, it is important to be able to provide retrieval models over such rich contextual data. In this paper, we proposed two novel approaches of applying the state-of-the-art caption extraction model and visual-semantic embedding model to facilitate effective lifelog retrieval systems. This is the fist time that such models have been used for human contextual data from lifelogs. We compared our proposed text and visual-semantic embedding model approaches in performing lifelog moment retrieval task between text query and images. We also compared the results with our previous baseline search engine and causality-based retrieval approach. Our experiments show that the visual-semantic embedding model outperforms the state-of-the-art caption extraction model, and both outperform a conventional retrieval model. This result highlights new opportunities for researchers to consider such text and multimodal embedding models to support retrieval from contextual human lifelog data. Future work involves refining and improving both approaches and integrating them into a custom interactive interface. However, there are limitations to this initial work:

- The models we employed are trained on existing visual datasets, but not lifelog datasets, due to a lack of annotated data.
- We focused on only visual lifelog data. Lifelog contextual data includes many other sources, so these also need to be considered in future work. Therefore it is expected that learning a joint image-text embedding with spatial-aware, location-aware, temporal-aware should lead to better performance.

Acknowledgements. This work was conducted with the financial support of the Science Foundation Ireland under grant numbers 13/RC/2106_P2 and S12/RC/2289_P2.

References

1. Anderson, P., et al.: Bottom-up and top-down attention for image captioning and visual question answering. In: Proceedings of the IEEE Conference on Computer Vision and Pattern Recognition (2018)
2. Church, K.W.: Word2Vec. Nat. Lang. Eng. **23**(1), 155–162 (2017)
3. Cornia, M., et al.: Meshed-memory transformer for image captioning. In: Proceedings of the IEEE/CVF Conference on Computer Vision and Pattern Recognition (2020)
4. Devlin, J., et al.: Bert: pre-training of deep bidirectional transformers for language understanding. arXiv preprint arXiv:1810.04805 (2018)
5. Faghri, F., et al.: Vse++: Improving visual-semantic embeddings with hard negatives. arXiv preprint arXiv:1707.05612 (2017)
6. Farhadi, A., et al.: Every picture tells a story: generating sentences from images. In: Daniilidis, K., Maragos, P., Paragios, N. (eds.) ECCV 2010. LNCS, vol. 6314, pp. 15–29. Springer, Heidelberg (2010). https://doi.org/10.1007/978-3-642-15561-1_2
7. Gong, Y., et al.: A multi-view embedding space for modeling internet images, tags, and their semantics. Int. J. Comput. Vis. **106**(2), 210–233 (2014)
8. Gurrin, C., Smeaton, A.F., Doherty, A.R.: Lifelogging: personal big data. Found. Trends Inf. Retrieval **8**(1), 1–125 (2014)
9. Gurrin, C., et al.: Introduction to the Fourth Annual Lifelog Search Challenge, In: Proceedings of the 2021 International Conference on Multimedia Retrieval, LSC 2021 (2021)
10. Gurrin, C., et al.: Overview of NTCIR-13 Lifelog-2 task (2017)
11. He, K., et al.: Deep residual learning for image recognition. In: Proceedings of the IEEE Conference on Computer Vision and Pattern Recognition (2016)
12. Hodosh, M., Young, P., Hockenmaier, J.: Framing image description as a ranking task: data, models and evaluation metrics. J. Artif. Intell. Res. **47**, 853–899 (2013)

13. Karpathy, A., Li, F.F.: Deep visual-semantic alignments for generating image descriptions. In: Proceedings of the IEEE Conference on Computer Vision and Pattern Recognition (2015)
14. Kiros, R., Salakhutdinov, R., Zemel, R.S.: Unifying visual-semantic embeddings with multimodal neural language models. arXiv preprint arXiv:1411.2539 (2014)
15. Kuznetsova, P., et al.: Treetalk: composition and compression of trees for image descriptions. Trans. Assoc. Comput. Linguist. **2**, 351–362 (2014)
16. Lample, G., Alexis, C.: Cross-lingual language model pretraining. arXiv preprint arXiv:1901.07291 (2019)
17. Lee, H.: Unsupervised feature learning via sparse hierarchical representations. Stanford University (2010)
18. Mason, R., Eugene, C.: Nonparametric method for data-driven image captioning. In: Proceedings of the 52nd Annual Meeting of the Association for Computational Linguistics (Volume 2: Short Papers) (2014)
19. Ordonez, V., Kulkarni, G., Berg, T.: Im2text: describing images using 1 million captioned photographs. Adv. Neural Inf. Process. Syst. **24**, 1143–1151 (2011)
20. Pennington, J., Socher, R., Manning, C.D.: Glove: global vectors for word representation. In: Proceedings of the 2014 Conference on Empirical Methods in Natural Language Processing (EMNLP) (2014)
21. Prasoon, A., Petersen, K., Igel, C., Lauze, F., Dam, E., Nielsen, M.: Deep feature learning for knee cartilage segmentation using a triplanar convolutional neural network. In: Mori, K., Sakuma, I., Sato, Y., Barillot, C., Navab, N. (eds.) MICCAI 2013. LNCS, vol. 8150, pp. 246–253. Springer, Heidelberg (2013). https://doi.org/10.1007/978-3-642-40763-5_31
22. Radford, A., et al.: Improving language understanding by generative pre-training (2018)
23. Ren, S., et al.: Faster R-CNN: towards real-time object detection with region proposal networks. Adv. Neural Inf. Process Syst. **28**, 91–99 (2015)
24. Reimers, N., Iryna, G.: Sentence-bert: sentence embeddings using siamese bert-networks. arXiv preprint arXiv:1908.10084 (2019)
25. Yang, S.: Feature engineering in fine-grained image classification. Diss. (2013)
26. Zhou, L., et al.: Lifer: an interactive lifelog retrieval system. In: Proceedings of the 2018 ACM Workshop on The Lifelog Search Challenge (2018)

Applications 3

A Multiple Positives Enhanced NCE Loss for Image-Text Retrieval

Yi Li, Dehao Wu, and Yuesheng Zhu[✉]

Shenzhen Graduate School, Peking University, Beijing, China
{li_yi,wudehao,zhuys}@pku.edu.cn

Abstract. Image-Text Retrieval (ITR) enables users to retrieve relevant contents from different modalities and has attracted considerable attention. Existing approaches typically utilize contrastive loss functions to conduct contrastive learning in the common embedding space, where they aim at pulling semantically related pairs closer while pushing away unrelated pairs. However, we argue that this behaviour is too strict: these approaches neglect to address the inherent misalignments from potential semantically related samples. For example, it commonly exists more than one positive samples in the current batch for a given query and previous methods enforce them apart even if they are semantically related, which leads to a sub-optimal and contradictory optimization direction and then decreases the retrieval performance. In this paper, a Multiple Positives Enhanced Noise Contrastive Estimation learning objective is proposed to alleviate the diversion noise by leveraging and optimizing multiple positive pairs overall for each sample in a mini-batch. We demonstrate the effectiveness of our approach on MS-COCO and Flickr30K datasets for image-to-text and text-to-image retrieval.

Keywords: Image-text retrieval · Contrastive learning · Noise contrastive estimation

1 Introduction

With the rapid growth of multimedia data, Image-Text Retrieval(ITR) has received considerable attention. One major theoretical issue of ITR lies in how to enforce comprehensive learning of two different modalities, which is so-called *bridging the heterogeneity gap*.

Recently, many works have been proposed and achieve promising performance in ITR task. Existing works usually adopt contrastive losses, such as triplet loss, Noise Contrastive Estimation (NCE) loss, and their variants [1–4], which enable semantically related inputs (*i.e.*, positives) from two domains mapped into close locations in the latent common embedding space, while unrelated inputs (*i.e.*, negatives) are pushed apart. Extensive research has validated the effectiveness [4–7], mostly based on one positive and other negatives or one (hardest) negative in each iteration.

© Springer Nature Switzerland AG 2022
B. Þór Jónsson et al. (Eds.): MMM 2022, LNCS 13141, pp. 431–442, 2022.
https://doi.org/10.1007/978-3-030-98358-1_34

However, we posit that negatives are not necessarily all unrelated pairs. One image will form several positive pairs with all annotated captions, for example, 5 for Flickr30K [8] and MS-COCO [9] datasets. Specifically, in these datasets, each image is annotated with 5 different captions, hence there are 5 aligned pairs for each image or text query. Meanwhile, random batch formation makes it possible that more than one aligned pairs attend in the current mini-batch. Therefore, as illustrated in the left of Fig. 1, in one mini-batch, sampled negatives possibly include other aligned pairs from the same query. Previous methods neglect to explore these distractors, and try to push these *false-negative* pairs apart either, hence these false negatives not only fail to contribute commonalities but also raise a contradiction that these potential multiple positives work as positive and negative simultaneously.

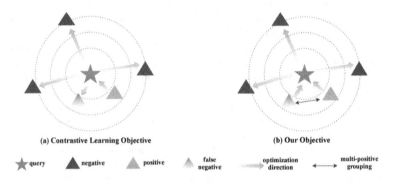

Fig. 1. Previous contrastive learning objective vs. our learning objective. Previous works try to push all negatives away from current query, including potential aligned positives (*i.e.* false negatives), while our method eliminated this noise by positive sample mining and multiple positives enhancement strategy.

We propose a **M**ultiple **P**ositives **E**nhanced - **N**oise **C**ontrastive **E**stimation loss (MPE-NCE) for ITR task to tackle the above problem. In one mini-batch, we gather all aligned positive pairs and adopt multiple positives grouping strategy to compute the discrimination overall against other negatives for each query, as is shown in the right of Fig. 1. More specifically, we introduce two strategies to form our proposed MPE-NCE learning objective. Firstly, we explicitly combine all positive pairs in a mini-batch and compute NCE loss for discriminating several positives against other negatives. Besides, in order to directly pulling semantically related images and texts closer, we introduce additional similarity scores of all positive pairs. These two strategies establish a more robust and informative representation learning.

The advantages of MPE-NCE are in two-fold. Firstly, it can be considered as a positive reuse strategy inside one mini-batch. The commonality learning for one sample is strengthened and compensated by several diverse positives. Secondly, all positives contribute to the learning procedure in cooperation and the contradiction caused by false negatives is eliminated, hence revise the diversion noise and achieve sufficient semantic learning.

In addition, we also conduct sufficient experiments and prove that our method achieves better performance than regular contrastive learning even in a manual batch formation where no false negatives are contained in each mini-batch. It gives further evidence of the effectiveness of multiple positives enhancement learning.

Our main contributions can be summarized as follows:

- A novel Multiple Positives Enhanced Noise Contrastive Estimation learning objective is proposed to alleviate the influence of false negatives in the Image-Text Retrieval task. Our objective can be used as a general and incremental objective for contrastive learning tasks. This work will generate fresh insight into the use of more positive pairs.
- Our experiments demonstrate that our method outperforms previous works by a large margin on MS-COCO and Flickr30K datasets.
- Contrast to an ideal experimental condition that no false negatives for all samples in the training process, we achieve better performance and prove the enhancement effect from multiple positive grouping strategy.

2   Related Works

Image-Text Retrieval. Extensive works [4,6,10,11] have been published for ITR task, which heavily rely on precise matching between the two modalities. Existing works exploit various networks to encode two modalities into a common latent space and then compute visual-language correlations by simple measurement such as cosine similarity.

For image modeling, early works adopt Convolutional Neural Networks(CNN) to obtain representation for whole image such as VGGs [12,13], ResNet [4,14–16], while concerning text input, GRU or LSTM takes in a series of natural sentence and the last hidden state is considered as semantic representation [1,4,15,17]. This line of studies suffers from the lack of explicit grounding in segment-level and imposes limits on generating dense descriptions.

Recent works propose to exploit a fine-grained grounding methodology in region and word level for discovering latent alignments, which is a human-like matching pipeline. Thanks to powerful object detectors such as Faster-R-CNN [18] with Bottom-Up attention [19], region-level image features can be provided for detailed descriptions. As for sentences, BERT-like architectures are widely used for word-level self-supervision, producing context-aware representations [20]. Inspired by the outstanding performance in contextual modeling of BERT, some works process both visual and textual contents using transformer or BERT architecture [21,22]. After encoding these segment features, the score between an image-text pair is defined as the summation of dot product from all region-word fragments in [23]. DVSA [1] proposes a structured and interpretable similarity measurement, grounding each word with the most related image region and vice versa, preventing matching confusion from misaligned segments. Different from previous methods, we put emphasis on eliminating the common contradiction caused by false negatives in the learning procedure.

Metric Learning. Recently, different types of metric learning have been explored to find latent alignments in ITR task. Hinge-based triplet ranking loss is the most popular manner for joint visual-semantic embedding learning [2]. Given a query, if the similarity score of a positive pair does not exceed that of a negative pair by a preset margin, the model will be optimized. Instead of summing over all negatives in the training set, Karpathy et $al.$ [1] define triplet loss over negatives from one mini-batch for computational efficiency. Some works [4,6] incorporate the hardest negative in the ranking loss function, $i.e.$, the negative pair that has the highest alignment score in a mini-batch. NCE [3] establishes a remarkable manner to discriminate between true value and noise data, as well as between aligned and misaligned pairs in ITR task. In contrast to these contrastive learning manners above, we explore the potential of positive pairs, which has so far been ignored.

3   Method

3.1   Problem Definition and Notations

ITR task is based on the principle of learning discriminative representation for two modalities lying in a common space. To verify the effectiveness of our proposed objective, we build a transformer-based architecture that has been proved effective in many vision and language tasks. The detailed architecture used in this process is shown in Fig. 2. For images, a pre-trained Faster-R-CNN [18] with Bottom-Up attention [19] takes the first step to extract m significant image regions, and the concatenation of region features and positions forms initial position-sensitive image tokens for the subsequent transformer model. Besides, we use BERT [20] as the text encoder and obtain the textural representations with contextual semantic relations for a sentence with n words. After a linear projection to match the dimension of region and word embeddings, every image and sentence is thus represented as delicate context-aware vectors as $I = \{i_0, i_1, \ldots, i_m\}$ and $T = \{t_0, t_1, \ldots, t_n\}$.

We follow [1] to measure pair similarity. Specifically, the word t_l that has the maximum cosine similarity with image region i_k contributes to the k-th region-word similarity. This behaves in a human-like semantic matching manner as the most related entity should support the alignment process, naturally filtering out a series of semantically isolated segments.

As a result, image-text similarity can be formulated as follows:

$$S\left(I, T\right) = \sum_{i_k \in I} \max_{t_l \in T} sim(i_k, t_l), \tag{1}$$

where $sim(i_k, t_l)$ denotes the cosine similarity between the k-th region and the l-th word.

Text-image similarity is formed in a similar manner:

$$S\left(T, I\right) = \sum_{t_l \in T} \max_{i_k \in I} sim(t_l, i_k). \tag{2}$$

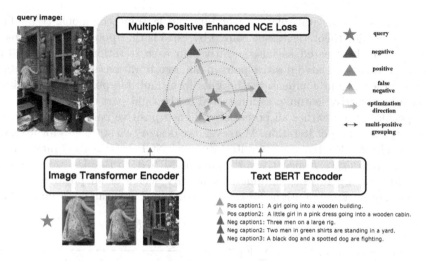

Fig. 2. The pipeline of our Multiple Positive Enhanced Noise Contrastive Estimation Loss (MPE-NCE). Image regions and words are processed through transformer-based and BERT encoders respectively. Take image-to-text retrieval for example, in a random mini-batch, other than the original positive pair, false negative comes with the occurrence of another aligned caption for the query. Our proposed MPE-NCE aims to eliminate the noise caused by false negatives and achieves further improvement through a multiple positives grouping strategy.

3.2 Noise Contrastive Estimation: A Revisit

Noise Contrastive Estimation (NCE) has demonstrated its superiority in self-supervised learning from computer vision [24,25] to natural language processing [26]. Given a query, NCE measures the discrimination of each positive pair from other negatives. Actually, optimizing NCE loss is maximizing the lower bound of the mutual information between query and corresponding positive sample [27]. Take image-to-text retrieval as an example, we define our proposed objective based on NCE loss:

$$
L_{NCE}(I,T) = -\sum_I \log\left(\frac{e^{S(I,T^+)/\tau}}{e^{S(I,T^+)/\tau} + \sum_{i=1}^{K} e^{S(I,T_i^-)/\tau}}\right), \tag{3}
$$

where T^+ denotes the positive sample and T^- denotes other K negatives in a mini-batch. τ is a temperature hyperparameter.

3.3 Multiple Positive Enhanced NCE: Our Approach

In this section, we introduce the proposed Multiple Positives Enhanced Noise Contrastive Estimation (MPE-NCE) learning objective.

Positives play a vital role in grounding and learning commonality for ITR task. One major theoretical issue caused by Eq. 3 is that potential aligned pairs will possibly be treated as false negatives in each iteration. To address this problem, we reuse related positive pairs in different iterations and take advantage of strengthened and compensated insights from multiple positives to facilitate efficient contrastive learning, as illustrated in the right part in Fig. 1.

Specifically, we gather all potentially aligned positive pairs to enforce commonality learning per iteration. Moreover, we design two strategies for utilizing these positives. Firstly, we compute improved NCE loss as discriminating P positives from other K negatives, denoted as MP-NCE. Besides, we design an MP-SIM strategy to take account of similarity scores of all positive pairs to enforce similar representations for related contents. These can be formulated as:

$$L_{MP-NCE}(I,T) = -\sum_{I} \log \left(\frac{\sum_{j=1}^{P} e^{S(I,T_j^+)/\tau}}{\sum_{j=1}^{P} e^{S(I,T_j^+)/\tau} + \sum_{i=1}^{K} e^{S(I,T_i^-)/\tau}} \right). \quad (4)$$

$$L_{MP-SIM}(I,T) = -\sum_{j=1}^{P} S\left(I,T_j^+\right). \quad (5)$$

We use a balance parameter controlling the relative importance of two strategies, denoted as α. The final objective for both image-to-text and text-to-image retrieval is defined as:

$$L_{MPE-NCE} = L_{MP-NCE}(I,T) + L_{MP-NCE}(T,I) \\ + \alpha(L_{MP-SIM}(I,T) + L_{MP-SIM}(T,I)). \quad (6)$$

Our proposed positive sampling strategy is superior for two reasons. 1) Several positives strengthen and compensate with each other hence enable integration of aligned semantics in each iteration, and this can be treated as a positive reuse strategy. 2) We seek out all aligned positives and compute NCE loss in a manner of multiple positive versus other negatives, thus the contradiction caused by false negatives is solved and achieve sufficient semantic learning.

4   Experiment

4.1   Experimental Settings

Datasets. We conduct experiments on MS-COCO [9] and Flickr30K [8] datasets. Both of them are annotated manually for 5 reference sentences for each image. For the MS-COCO dataset, we follow the splits in [1] with 113,287 images in the training set and both 5,000 images for validation and test set. MS-COCO 1k test is performed by a 5-fold cross-validation manner on the 5k test split. Flickr30K consists of 31,000 images and over one and a half million sentences, of which 29,000 are used for training, 1,000 for validation and 1,000 for test following [1].

Table 1. Results on the Flickr30K dataset.

Model	Text-to-image			Image-to-text			rsum
	R@1	R@5	R@10	R@1	R@5	R@10	
VSE++ [4]	39.6	70.1	79.5	52.9	80.5	87.2	409.8
TIMAM [28]	42.6	71.6	81.9	53.1	78.8	87.6	415.6
SMAN [10]	43.4	73.7	83.4	57.3	85.3	92.2	435.3
M3A-Net [29]	44.7	72.4	81.1	58.1	82.8	90.1	429.2
AAMEL [30]	49.7	79.2	86.4	68.5	91.2	95.9	470.9
VSRN [5]	53.0	77.9	85.7	70.4	89.2	93.7	469.9
CAMERA [7]	58.9	84.7	90.2	76.5	95.1	**97.2**	502.6
TERN [11]	41.1	71.9	81.2	53.2	79.4	86.0	412.8
TERAN [6]	59.5	84.9	90.6	75.8	93.2	96.7	500.7
Ours	**62.4**	**86.7**	**91.9**	**78.4**	**94.6**	97.0	**511.0**

Evaluation Metrics. We evaluate the retrieval performance by Recall@k (R@k, k = 1,5,10) which is the standard metric in ITR task. Recall@k is the portion of queries that correctly retrieval corresponding sentences in the top K ranking list. We also report rsum as the sum of all Recall@k including image-to-text and text-to-image retrieval. Larger R@k indicate better retrieval performance.

Implementation Details. We initialize image region features extracted by Faster-R-CNN with Bottom-Up attention [19]. We use pre-extracted features provided by [19] and [17] for MS-COCO and Flickr30K dataset respectively. They both include 36 top confident semantic regions for each image, and each region is represented by a 2048-dimensional feature vector and a 4-d position vector including coordinates of top-left and bottom-right bounding box corners. We concatenate these two kinds of vectors to form position-sensitive region features following [31], and the resulting features are transformed through a linear projection to ensure the dimension is the same as that of word token embedding. All region features are processed through a stack of 6 transformer layers for visual reasoning. For the textual pipeline, we use a pre-trained 12-layer BERT model and a succeeding 2-layer transformer. Finally, we use linear projections to transform region and word features into 1024-dimensional vectors in the common space. The model is trained for 40 epochs using Adam optimizer with a batch size of 32 and a learning rate of 1e−5 for the first 20 epochs and 1e−6 for the rest. For NCE loss, we set the temperature parameter to 0.07. In our objective, we set the balance parameter α to 0.1.

4.2 Comparison to Prior State-of-the-Arts

We compare our method with several representative ITR methods. Table 1 presents the quantitative results on the Flickr30K dataset. Experimental results show that our learning objective achieves a new state-of-the-art in rsum metric and outperforms the best baseline by 4.87% and 3.43% on the Recall@1 metric in text-to-image and image-to-text task respectively.

Table 2. Results on the MS-COCO dataset

Dataset	Model	Text-to-image			Image-to-text			rsum
		R@1	R@5	R@10	R@1	R@5	R@10	
1k-test	VSE++ [4]	52.0	84.3	92.0	64.6	90.0	95.7	478.6
	SMAN [10]	58.8	87.4	93.5	68.4	91.3	96.6	496.0
	M3A-Net [29]	58.4	87.1	94.0	70.4	91.7	96.8	498.4
	AAMEL [30]	59.9	89.0	95.1	74.3	95.4	98.2	511.9
	VSRN [5]	60.8	88.4	94.1	74.0	94.3	97.8	509.4
	CAMERA [7]	62.3	90.1	95.2	75.9	95.5	98.6	517.6
	TERN [11]	51.9	85.6	93.6	63.7	90.5	96.2	481.5
	TERAN [6]	65.0	91.2	96.4	77.7	95.9	98.6	524.8
	Ours	**66.0**	**92.1**	**96.7**	**79.5**	**96.2**	**98.6**	**529.1**
5k-test	VSE++ [4]	30.3	59.4	72.4	41.3	71.1	81.2	355.7
	AAMEL [30]	39.9	71.3	81.7	51.9	84.2	91.2	420.2
	VSRN [5]	37.9	68.5	79.4	50.3	79.6	87.9	403.6
	CAMERA [7]	39.0	70.5	81.5	53.1	81.3	89.8	415.2
	TERN [11]	28.7	59.7	72.7	38.4	69.5	81.3	350.3
	TERAN [6]	42.6	72.5	82.9	55.6	83.9	91.6	429.1
	Ours	**44.1**	**73.9**	**84.1**	**58.1**	**85.6**	**92.4**	**438.2**

Table 2 shows further analysis on the MS-COCO 1K and 5K test sets. We see 1.54% improvements for 1K-test and 3.52% for 5K-test on Recall@1 in text-to-image task and 2.32% improvements for 1K-test and 4.50% for 5K-test on Recall@1 in image-to-text task.

In Table 3, we also report the results of ensemble models following [17], which is indicated as "(ens.)" at the end of the model name. As for our model, we use two models trained with MP-NCE only and the full MPE-NCE objective respectively. Our ensemble model shows consistent improvement over others on all indicators and all three datasets.

Compared to these baseline methods with margin loss or triplet loss [4–7], the superiority of our model comes from that the proposed learning objective prevents the model from being stuck into a contradiction caused by false negatives, and boosts performance further through a multiple positive commonality learning.

4.3 Ablation Studies

In this section, we conduct experiments with several batch formation methods on Flickr30K dataset (see Table 4). P denotes the number of positives in a mini-batch. $P = random$ indicates that we do not control the batch formation process, which simulates a natural ITR baseline and means P in Eq. 4 is different for each sample in one mini-batch. Then we form batches strictly with 2 positives

Table 3. Results of ensemble models.

Dataset	Model	Text-to-image			Image-to-text			rsum
		R@1	R@5	R@10	R@1	R@5	R@10	
Flickr30K	SCAN(ens.) [17]	48.6	77.7	85.2	67.4	90.3	95.8	465.0
	VSRN (ens.) [5]	54.7	81.8	88.2	71.3	90.6	96.0	482.6
	CAMERA (ens.) [7]	60.3	85.9	91.7	78.0	95.1	97.9	508.9
	TERAN (ens.) [6]	63.1	87.3	92.6	79.2	94.4	96.8	513.4
	Ours (ens.)	**65.5**	**88.7**	**93.3**	**81.6**	**95.5**	**98.0**	**522.6**
MS-COCO 1k-test	SCAN (ens.) [17]	58.8	88.4	94.8	72.7	94.8	98.4	507.9
	VSRN (ens.) [5]	62.8	89.7	95.1	76.2	94.8	98.2	516.8
	CAMERA (ens.) [7]	63.4	90.9	95.8	77.5	96.3	98.8	522.7
	TERAN (ens.) [6]	67.0	92.2	96.9	80.2	96.6	99.0	531.9
	Ours (ens.)	**67.8**	**93.0**	**97.2**	**82.6**	**97.0**	**99.1**	**536.7**
MS-COCO 5k-test	VSRN (ens.) [5]	40.5	70.6	81.1	53.0	81.1	89.4	415.7
	CAMERA (ens.) [7]	40.5	71.7	82.5	55.1	82.9	91.2	423.9
	TERAN (ens.) [6]	45.1	74.6	84.4	59.3	85.8	92.4	441.6
	Ours (ens.)	**46.8**	**75.9**	**85.4**	**62.5**	**87.7**	**93.6**	**451.9**

Table 4. The ablation results on Flickr30K dataset.

P	Loss	Text-to-image			Image-to-text			rsum
		R@1	R@5	R@10	R@1	R@5	R@10	
Random	L_{NCE}	61.7	86.3	92.0	78.1	93.4	96.3	507.8
1	L_{NCE}	61.7	86.6	**92.1**	**78.6**	93.7	96.5	509.1
2	L_{NCE}	52.2	81.5	88.8	66.0	86.5	93.7	468.7
2	$L_{MP-NCE} + L_{MP-SIM}$	61.8	86.1	91.6	77.7	93.8	96.6	507.5
Random	L_{MP-NCE}	61.6	**86.8**	92.0	77.9	94.3	**97.6**	510.1
Random	$L_{MP-NCE} + L_{MP-SIM}$	**62.4**	86.7	91.9	78.4	**94.6**	97.0	**511.0**

for each query, as a result of one false negative for each pair, denoted as $P = 2$. Relatively, $P = 1$ forms an ideal experimental condition that no false negative for all samples in the training process.

The first three rows of the table give intuitive evidence that the existence of false negatives will reduce retrieval performance. Besides, from the second and the last two rows, despite the inherent decrease of negative pairs in random batch contrast to $P = 1$ formation, we can still boost performance by MPE-NCE strategy since some pairs benefit from more than one insights contributed by other positive samples. We conduct two experiments under $P = 2$, and the results give a straight verification for the harm of false negatives and the superiority of our method. Note that $P = 2$ condition implicitly reduces the number of valid negatives to half of that in $P = 1$, and less than that in $P = random$, hence the fourth row shows a performance decline than the last row. Moreover, the three experiments under $P = random$ show the effectiveness of our two strategies.

4.4 Qualitative Analysis

In Fig. 3, we visualize some examples to validate the effectiveness of our method. We choose TERAN [6] for comparison, which is the best previous method. In the image-to-text retrieval, our model succeeds to match two ground-truth captions with lower rank, while TERAN failed to find the most accurate alignments. Note that the captions retrieved by our model are all highly related to the query image, and the top 2 caption gives a fine-grained alignment with more details.

Fig. 3. Our qualitative result versus TERAN in image-to-text retrieval. The top-5 retrieved results are shown. Green and red color denote ground-truth and wrong alignments respectively. Best viewed in color. (Color figure online)

5   Conclusion

In this paper, we put emphasis on the false negatives noise in contrastive learning and propose a Multiple Positives Enhanced Noise Contrastive Estimation learning objective for Image-Text Retrieval task by grouping the commonalities from several positives together. Our method not only yields a unified insight for each query through a positive reuse manner, but eliminates the contradiction caused by potential false negatives. This proposed objective guides comprehensive and informative representation learning and we demonstrate its effectiveness on sufficient experiments. For future work, we will delve into the superiority of our method in other contrastive learning tasks.

References

1. Karpathy, A., Fei-Fei, L.: Deep visual-semantic alignments for generating image descriptions. In: Proceedings of the IEEE Conference on Computer Vision and Pattern Recognition, pp. 3128–3137 (2015)

2. Zhu, Y., et al.: Aligning books and movies: towards story-like visual explanations by watching movies and reading books. In: Proceedings of the IEEE International Conference on Computer Vision, pp. 19–27 (2015)
3. Gutmann, M., Hyvärinen, A.: Noise-contrastive estimation: a new estimation principle for unnormalized statistical models. In: Proceedings of the Thirteenth International Conference on Artificial Intelligence and Statistics, pp. 297–304. JMLR Workshop and Conference Proceedings (2010)
4. Faghri, F., Fleet, D.J., Kiros, J.R., Fidler, S.: VSE++: improving visual-semantic embeddings with hard negatives. In: BMVC, p. 12. BMVA Press (2018)
5. Li, K., Zhang, Y., Li, K., Li, Y., Fu, Y.: Visual semantic reasoning for image-text matching. In: Proceedings of the IEEE/CVF International Conference on Computer Vision, pp. 4654–4662 (2019)
6. Messina, N., Amato, G., Esuli, A., Falchi, F., Gennaro, C., Marchand-Maillet, S.: Fine-grained visual textual alignment for cross-modal retrieval using transformer encoders. ACM Trans. Multimed. Comput. Commun. Appl. (TOMM) 17(4), 1–23 (2021)
7. Qu, L., Liu, M., Cao, D., Nie, L., Tian, Q.: Context-aware multi-view summarization network for image-text matching. In: Proceedings of the 28th ACM International Conference on Multimedia, pp. 1047–1055 (2020)
8. Young, P., Lai, A., Hodosh, M., Hockenmaier, J.: From image descriptions to visual denotations: new similarity metrics for semantic inference over event descriptions. Trans. Assoc. Comput. Linguist. 2, 67–78 (2014)
9. Lin, T.-Y., et al.: Microsoft COCO: common objects in context. In: Fleet, D., Pajdla, T., Schiele, B., Tuytelaars, T. (eds.) ECCV 2014. LNCS, vol. 8693, pp. 740–755. Springer, Cham (2014). https://doi.org/10.1007/978-3-319-10602-1_48
10. Ji, Z., Wang, H., Han, J., Pang, Y.: SMAN: stacked multimodal attention network for cross-modal image-text retrieval. IEEE Trans. Cybern. (2020)
11. Messina, N., Falchi, F., Esuli, A., Amato, G.: Transformer reasoning network for image-text matching and retrieval. In: 2020 25th International Conference on Pattern Recognition (ICPR), pp. 5222–5229. IEEE (2021)
12. Eisenschtat, A., Wolf, L.: Linking image and text with 2-way nets. In: Proceedings of the IEEE Conference on Computer Vision and Pattern Recognition, pp. 4601–4611 (2017)
13. Klein, B., Lev, G., Sadeh, G., Wolf, L.: Associating neural word embeddings with deep image representations using fisher vectors. In: Proceedings of the IEEE Conference on Computer Vision and Pattern Recognition, pp. 4437–4446 (2015)
14. Gu, J., Cai, J., Joty, S.R., Niu, L., Wang, G.: Look, imagine and match: improving textual-visual cross-modal retrieval with generative models. In: Proceedings of the IEEE Conference on Computer Vision and Pattern Recognition, pp. 7181–7189 (2018)
15. Huang, Y., Wu, Q., Song, C., Wang, L.: Learning semantic concepts and order for image and sentence matching. In: Proceedings of the IEEE Conference on Computer Vision and Pattern Recognition, pp. 6163–6171 (2018)
16. Liu, Y., Guo, Y., Bakker, E.M., Lew, M.S.: Learning a recurrent residual fusion network for multimodal matching. In: Proceedings of the IEEE International Conference on Computer Vision, pp. 4107–4116 (2017)
17. Lee, K.H., Chen, X., Hua, G., Hu, H., He, X.: Stacked cross attention for image-text matching. In: Proceedings of the European Conference on Computer Vision (ECCV), pp. 201–216 (2018)

18. Ren, S., He, K., Girshick, R., Sun, J.: Faster R-CNN: towards real-time object detection with region proposal networks. Adv. Neural Inform. Process. Syst. **28**, 91–99 (2015)
19. Anderson, P., et al.: Bottom-up and top-down attention for image captioning and visual question answering. In: Proceedings of the IEEE Conference on Computer Vision and Pattern Recognition, pp. 6077–6086 (2018)
20. Devlin, J., Chang, M., Lee, K., Toutanova, K.: BERT: pre-training of deep bidirectional transformers for language understanding. In: NAACL-HLT, pp. 4171–4186 (2019)
21. Lu, J., Batra, D., Parikh, D., Lee, S.: ViLBERT: pretraining task-agnostic visiolinguistic representations for vision-and-language tasks. In: Advances in Neural Information Processing Systems, pp. 13–23 (2019)
22. Sun, C., Myers, A., Vondrick, C., Murphy, K., Schmid, C.: VideoBERT: a joint model for video and language representation learning. In: Proceedings of the IEEE International Conference on Computer Vision, pp. 7464–7473 (2019)
23. Karpathy, A., Joulin, A., Fei-Fei, L.F.: Deep fragment embeddings for bidirectional image sentence mapping. Adv. Neural Inform. Process. Syst. **27** (2014)
24. He, K., Fan, H., Wu, Y., Xie, S., Girshick, R.: Momentum contrast for unsupervised visual representation learning. In: Proceedings of the IEEE/CVF Conference on Computer Vision and Pattern Recognition, pp. 9729–9738 (2020)
25. Chen, T., Kornblith, S., Norouzi, M., Hinton, G.: A simple framework for contrastive learning of visual representations. In: International Conference on Machine Learning, pp. 1597–1607. PMLR (2020)
26. Gao, T., Yao, X., Chen, D.: Simcse: Simple contrastive learning of sentence embeddings. In: EMNLP (1). pp. 6894–6910. Association for Computational Linguistics (2021)
27. Oord, A.V.D., Li, Y., Vinyals, O.: Representation learning with contrastive predictive coding. arXiv preprint arXiv:1807.03748 (2018)
28. Sarafianos, N., Xu, X., Kakadiaris, I.A.: Adversarial representation learning for text-to-image matching. In: Proceedings of the IEEE/CVF International Conference on Computer Vision, pp. 5814–5824 (2019)
29. Ji, Z., Lin, Z., Wang, H., He, Y.: Multi-modal memory enhancement attention network for image-text matching. IEEE Access **8**, 38438–38447 (2020)
30. Wei, K., Zhou, Z.: Adversarial attentive multi-modal embedding learning for image-text matching. IEEE Access **8**, 96237–96248 (2020)
31. Li, X., et al.: OSCAR: object-semantics aligned pre-training for vision-language tasks. In: Vedaldi, A., Bischof, H., Brox, T., Frahm, J.-M. (eds.) ECCV 2020. LNCS, vol. 12375, pp. 121–137. Springer, Cham (2020). https://doi.org/10.1007/978-3-030-58577-8_8

SAM: Self Attention Mechanism for Scene Text Recognition Based on Swin Transformer

Xiang Shuai[1], Xiao Wang[1,2(✉)], Wei Wang[1,2], Xin Yuan[1], and Xin Xu[1,2]

[1] School of Computer Science and Technology, Wuhan University of Science and Technology, Wuhan 430065, Hubei, China
wangxiao2021@wust.edu.cn
[2] Hubei Province Key Laboratory of Intelligent Information Processing and Real-time Industrial System, Wuhan 430065, Hubei, China

Abstract. Scene text recognition, which detects and recognizes the text in the image, has engaged extensive research interest. Attention mechanism based methods for scene text recognition have achieved competitive performance. For scene text recognition, the attention mechanism is usually combined with RNN structures as a module to predict the results. However, RNN attention-based methods are sometimes hard to converge on account of gradient vanishing/exploding during training, and RNN cannot be computed in parallel. To remedy this issue, we propose a Swin Transformer-based encoder-decoder mechanism, which relies entirely on the self attention mechanism (SAM) and can be computed in parallel. SAM is an efficient text recognizer that is only formed by two components: 1) an encoder based on Swin Transformer that gets the visual information of input image, and 2) a Transformer-based decoder gets the final results by applying self attention to the output of encoder. Considering that the scale of scene text has a large variation in images, we apply the Swin Transformer to compute the visual features with shifted windows, which permits self attention computation to cross-window connections and limits for non-overlapping local window. Our method has improved in accuracy over previous methods at ICDAR2003, ICDAR2013, SVT, SVT-P, CUTE and ICDAR2015 by 0.9%, 3.2%, 0.8%, 1.3%, 1.7%, 1.1% respectively. Especially, our method achieved the fastest predict time of 0.02s per image.

Keywords: Scene text recognition · Swin transformer · Attention

1 Introduction

In the area of computer vision, scene text recognition is always an important task because text serves as an important cue to provide more accurate information for computer vision tasks. Scene text recognition has been used in a wide range of life scenarios, such as text CAPTCHA applications [1], screen-rendered text image recognition [2] and video subtitle recognition [3]. However, scene text recognition

© Springer Nature Switzerland AG 2022
B. Þór Jónsson et al. (Eds.): MMM 2022, LNCS 13141, pp. 443–454, 2022.
https://doi.org/10.1007/978-3-030-98358-1_35

is still a challenging task on account of the different font sizes, colors, and styles of characters in scene text.

Recently, some scene text recognition methods have offered remarkable performances based on deep learning. The attention [4] and connectionist temporal classification(CTC) [5] are the most popular approaches at present. Especially, Cong et al. [6] conducted a comprehensive comparison of these two prediction methods in the scene text recognition. The attention-based methods have higher recognition accuracy compared to CTC-based methods based on the extensive experiments.

Initially, Bahdanau et al. [4] proposed the attention mechanism to solve the neural machine translation problem. Because of its powerful modeling ability, it is widely used in deep learning areas such as visual categorization [7], music recommendation [8] and emotion recognition [9], *etc.* Lee et al. [10] used it to deal with scene text recognition and Shi et al. [11] did the same. Since then, it has dominated the scene text recognition neighborhood with more developments [12–14]. Although the methods mentioned before have achieved significant performance, there are still two crucial problems: 1) both encoder or decoder use RNN units, which are time-consuming to predict, 2) RNN units are sometimes hard to converge because of the gradient vanishing/exploding problem in the training process.

To solve the aforementioned challenges, we presented a new deep learning method named SAM, which completely discards the RNN units based on Swin Transformer [15], for scene text recognition. Especially, SAM follows an encoder-decoder framework and converts 2-dimension input images into 1-dimension feature representation sequences by using a hierarchical attention network, then the decoder outputs the predicted character sequences by using the stacked self attention network.

We summarised the contributions of our work as follows:

- We proposed an efficient method that applies the Swin Transformer structure to scene text recognition, discarding the RNN units. This can adequately represent the contextual information and greatly reduce the predicted time.
- A hierarchical attention scheme is presented in the encoder stage to accelerate the prediction process for the scene text recognition. The experiment shows that our method achieved the fastest predicted speed of 0.02s per image.
- Our method achieved an accuracy of 95.2% in ICDAR 2003, 96.0% in ICDAR2013, 90.0% in SVT, 83.9% in SVT-P, 86.1% in CUTE and 82.0% in ICDAR2015. All of them surpassed the previous methods.

2   Related Work

In recent years, deep learning has been widely used in various areas [16–20]. As for the scene text recognition, it also has entered a new era. A detailed description of the current progress is given in the excellent survey [21]. In this paper, we focus on the parts that are most relevant to our work. Recently, researchers have proposed many text recognition methods for scenes. These methods include two types: segmentation-free methods and segmentation-based methods.

Segmentation-Based Methods. These methods attempt to locate each character from the input image and identify each character with a character classifier, then group the characters into text sequences to output the result. A segmentation-based method was presented by Wang et al. [22], which applied the histogram of gradient (HOG) to split the characters in the image. Then, researchers explored the presentation of word images to improve the performance, such as SIFT [23]. However, the methods mentioned before require a lexicon, and the time spent is related to the magnitude of the lexicon. For a very large lexicon, these methods are time-consuming on account of the search space. So some researchers used larger scale data [24] or more complex neural networks [25] to recognize the scene text in a lexicon-free way. Recently, Wan et al. [26] established a semantic segmentation-based recognition system to improve the performance. Although segmentation-based methods perform well in scene text recognition, such methods have a major drawback in that they all need to split each character precisely, which is considered one of the most challenging problems.

Segmentation-Free Methods. Such methods focus on mapping the cropped image instance directly to the character sequences through the encoder-decoder framework, thus avoiding character segmentation. As stated in Sect. 1, attention mechanism and connectionist temporal classification are used most in the segmentation-free methods. Inspired by the connectionist temporal classification, Shi et al. [27] applied the connectionist temporal classification to scene text recognition. From then on, many CTC-based algorithms [28–30] have shown good performance. But, Liu et al. [31] believe that CTC tends to produce peak distribution, which can lead to over-fitting. To solve this problem, a regularization method was presented by them to enhance the generalization and exploration capability of CTC. Besides, CTC is used for the sequence-to-sequence model, which is difficult to apply to 2D prediction problems, where the characters are distributed in a spatial space of the input image. To remedy this problem, Wan et al. [32] proposed the 2D-CTC by adding another dimension along the height direction for the traditional CTC. But this method did not completely solve the problem.

Attention Mechanism. Bahdanau et al. [4] presented the attention mechanism for the machine translation problems. For scene text recognition, the attention mechanism is usually combined with the RNN to predict the text sequences. As a pioneering work, Lee et al. [10] presented a network named R2AM by combining RNN with an attention mechanism. Cheng et al. [33] used an arbitrary orientation network(AON) to directly capture the vision features of scene text and combine them into an attention-based decoder to output the results. Despite the great performance achieved by these methods, as stated in Sect. 1, these methods use RNN units in the network where predict is time-consuming. Existing work had introduced the Transformer [34] to alleviate this problem. The Transformer was used in the field of natural language processing, and then first used in scene text recognition by Sheng et al. [35]. They presented a no-recurrence network that greatly improved the speed of the network. Later, this work was extended by Yang et al. [36].

Swin Transformer. Liu et al. [15] presented the network for object detection and semantic segmentation. Inspired by Swin Transformer, we use the hierarchical self attention network as our fundamental module to get the feature representation of the image. Benefit by the mechanism, our method has linear computational complexity for input image size, which is suited for scene text recognition to get a faster prediction performance.

3   Methodology

The overall framework of SAM is shown in Fig. 1. SAM is a very efficient method and only composed of two branches: the encoder and the decoder.

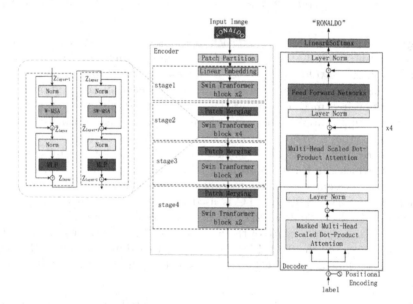

Fig. 1. The overall network of SAM. SAM was composed of only an encoder and a decoder. The encoder uses four Swin Transformer-based blocks to extract the hierarchical features of the input image, which is then used as the input to the decoder. The decoder will decode the output of the encoder by using the multi-head self attention mechanism combined with the positional encoding information. The result of the decoder is outputted after a linear and softmax layer. (Color figure online)

3.1   Encoder

In our SAM network, we encode an input image as feature vectors. The encoder has four stages. Firstly, we split the image into the non-overlapping patches from a patch partition block. A patch size of $4 \times 4 \times 3 = 48$ was used in the implementation. A linear embedding block has been applied to the features of this original value to project to an arbitrary dimension. And we applied two Swin Transformer blocks to these patches. The Swin Transformer blocks keep the number of patches $\frac{H}{4} \times \frac{W}{4}$. It is projected to any dimension(expressed as C) on the feature of the original value, which is called as "stage 1".

Aiming to generate a layered representation, a patch merging block was used to reduce the number of patches. The role of patch merging is used to downsample the image, similar to the pooling layer in CNN. The difference is that the most commonly used pooling layer in CNN tends to discard some information. For example, maximum pooling discards low response values within a window, while the patch merging strategy does not discard any responses. The first patch block connects the features of each group of 2×2 adjacent patches, and a linear layer was applied to the 4C dimensional connection features. This will reduce the number of patches by a multiple of $2 \times 2 = 4$ and set the output dimension to 2C. The Swin transformer block is applied to the feature transformation with the resolution maintained at $\frac{H}{8} \times \frac{W}{8}$. The first block of patch merging and the Swin Transformer block is represented as "stage2". This process is repeated twice, as "stage 3" and "stage 4", with the output resolutions $\frac{H}{16} \times \frac{W}{16}$ and $\frac{H}{32} \times \frac{W}{32}$, respectively.

Swin Transformer Block is the core point of the algorithm, which consists of window multi-head self attention (W-MSA) and shifted-window multi-head self attention (SW-MSA). Therefore, the number of layers for Swin Transformer is to be an integer multiple of 2. One layer is provided to W-MSA and another is provided to SW-MSA. As shown in Fig. 1 (green dashed box), the structure of the SW-MSA layer is similar to the W-MSA layer, with the difference that the SW-MSA and W-MSA are used in the computed features section, respectively. This part can be expressed as the equations:

$$
\begin{aligned}
\overline{Z}_{layer} &= \text{W-MSA}(\text{NORM}(Z_{layer-1})) + Z_{layer-1}, \\
Z_{layer} &= \text{MLP}(\text{NORM}(\overline{Z}_{layer})) + \overline{Z}_{layer}, \\
\overline{Z}_{layer+1} &= \text{SW-MSA}(\text{NORM}(Z_{layer})) + Z_{layer}, \\
Z_{layer+1} &= \text{MLP}(\text{NORM}(\overline{Z}_{layer+1})) + \overline{Z}_{layer+1}
\end{aligned}
\tag{1}
$$

where $\overline{Z}_{layer}$ and Z_{layer} represent the output features of the W-MSA and the MLP for block layer, and $\overline{Z}_{layer+1}$ and $Z_{layer+1}$ for next layer by SW-MSA and MLP. More information can be found in Swin Transformer [15].

3.2   Decoder

The decoder generates text sequences based on encoder outputs and the input labels. For each input label, a positional encoding was applied to convert per character to a D_{model}-dimension vector.

$$Pos(p, i) = \begin{cases} sin(p/10000^{2i/D_{model}}) & 0 \leq i \leq D_{model}/2 \\ cos(p/10000^{2i/D_{model}}) & D_{model}/2 \leq i \leq D_{model} \end{cases} \quad (2)$$

where p denotes the location in the label and i is the dimension.

As shown in Fig. 1, The decoder stacked 4 identical blocks(pink block). Each block consists of 4 base modules: masked multi-head scaled dot-product attention, multi-head scaled dot-product attention, feed forward networks, and layer norm. First, a masked multi-head scaled dot-product attention is applied to guarantee that the predictions for position i can only rely on the outputs before i. Then, the multi-head scaled dot-product attention has keys $\mathbf{K}$ and values $\mathbf{V}$ by the input from the encoder, and queries $\mathbf{Q}$ from the previous block of the decoder. Eventually, the final results are obtained by connecting the outputs and applying a layer norm to the outputs. The formulation of multi-head attention can be described as below:

$$\text{MultiHeadAtten}(\mathbf{Q}, \mathbf{K}, \mathbf{V}) = \text{Concat}(\text{head}_1, ..., \text{head}_h)\mathbf{W}^O \quad (3)$$

where $\text{head}_i = \text{Atten}(\mathbf{Q}\mathbf{W}_i^Q, \mathbf{K}\mathbf{W}_i^K, \mathbf{V}\mathbf{W}_i^V)$. And $\mathbf{W}_i^Q \in \mathbf{U}^{D_{model} \times D_q}$, $\mathbf{W}_i^K \in \mathbf{U}^{D_{model} \times D_k}$, $\mathbf{W}_i^V \in \mathbf{U}^{D_{model} \times D_v}$, $\mathbf{W}_i^O \in \mathbf{U}^{D_c \times D_{model}}$, where $D_c = \text{h} \times D_v$ and $D_q = D_k = D_v = D_{model}$. As for the feed forward networks, there are two linear layers with an activation function.

$$F(x) = \max(0, x\mathbf{W}_1 + c_1)\mathbf{W}_2 + c_2 \quad (4)$$

where $\mathbf{W}_1 \in \mathbf{U}^{D_{model} \times D_{ff}}$ and $\mathbf{W}_2 \in \mathbf{U}^{D_{ff} \times D_{model}}$, the bias are $c_1 \in \mathbf{U}^{D_{ff}}$ and $c_2 \in \mathbf{U}^{D_{model}}$.

Finally, through a linear layer and a function of softmax, the results are converted to the probabilities for characters.

4   Experiments

Since recent methods are trained with Synth90K [37] and SynthText [38], for fair comparison, we also train SAM on two synthetic datasets. Then as the same, without any fine-tuning, we evaluated our method on six standard benchmarks. The examples of benchmarks have been shown in Fig. 2. For all experiments, we use the word recognition accuracy metric to measure the performance of methods. As shown in Eq. 5, the evaluation protocol is:

$$acc = Word_c/Word \quad (5)$$

where the $Word$ means the overall of words in the dataset, and $Word_c$ is the number of words that have been recognized correctly.

4.1   Benchmarks

ICDAR2003 [39] was created for the ICDAR2003 Scene Text Recognition Contest. It contains 1110 images for evaluation.

Fig. 2. Example images of different datasets.

ICDAR2013 [40] inherited most of the images from ICDAR2003, which was also created for the ICDAR2013 text recognition competition. It contains 1095 images for evaluation.

SVT [22] includes 647 outdoor street images for evaluation collected by Google glasses.

ICDAR2015 [41] was created for the ICDAR2015 text recognition competition. It contains 2077 images for evaluation.

SVT-P [23] was collected from Google glasses and contains 645 images for evaluation.

CUTE [42] was collected from natural scenes and contains 288 cropped images for evaluation.

The above datasets are divided into regular text datasets and irregular text datasets. And the ICDAR2003, ICDAR2013, and SVT are the regular scene text. As for the other three datasets, they are irregular scene text, which includes scene text images that are distorted or blurred, *etc.*

4.2   Implementation Details

SAM is implemented by PyTorch and all the experiments are conducted on a TITAN Xp GPU with 12 GB memory. In our network, the input images are resized to a uniform height and width: 32 × 96. Then the model has trained 19

Table 1. The parameters of the Swin Transformer for each stage.

Parameter	Patch	Dimension	Depths	Heads	Window	Down scaling
Setting	2	64	[2,4,6,2]	[4,8,16,32]	4	[4,2,2,2]

Table 2. The accuracy(%) of regular scene text datasets.

Method	Year	ICDAR2003	ICDAR2013	SVT
R2AM [10]	2016	88.7	90.0	80.7
RARE [11]	2016	90.1	88.6	81.9
CRNN [27]	2017	89.4	86.7	80.8
MAAN [44]	2018	92.2	91.1	83.5
CCL [29]	2019	93.5	92.8	85.9
SEED [45]	2020	81.4	83.6	80
MBAN [46]	2021	94.3	92.8	89.2
Ours	2021	**95.2**	**96.0**	**90.0**

Table 3. The accuracy(%) of the irregular scene text datasets.

Method	Year	SVT-P	CUTE	ICDAR2015
AON [33]	2018	73.0	76.8	68.2
EPAN [47]	2019	79.4	82.6	73.9
ReELFA [48]	2019	–	82.3	68.5
HATN [49]	2019	73.5	75.7	70.1
DAN [50]	2020	80.0	84.4	74.5
SEED [45]	2020	81.4	83.6	80
MBAN [46]	2021	82.6	82.6	80.9
Ours	2021	**83.9**	**86.1**	**82.0**

epochs on synthetic datasets and evaluated on benchmarks. For encoder block in our network, to adapt to scene text recognition task, the parameters of the Swin Transformer for each stage are set as shown in Table 1. As for the attention dropout rate and residual dropout rate, we set them to 0.0 and 0.1 respectively.

4.3   Performance on Benchmarks

We first assess our method on the regular text images, and the results were shown in Table 2. Our method improves the accuracy over the previous optimal methods by 0.9%, 3.2%, and 0.8% on the ICDAR2003, ICDAR2013, and SVT, respectively. As can be seen from Fig. 3, even for the image that includes complex background: London, our method can recognize it correctly.

As a general scene text recognition method, we also verify the robustness of our method on irregular scene text datasets. The results were shown in Table 3, our method achieved the state-of-the-art over the previous methods, which improves the accuracy of SVT-P, CUTE, and ICDAR2015 by 1.3%, 1.7%, and 1.1%, respectively. Since RNN units are completely discarded in this network and a multi-headed self attention mechanism is used to avoid attention drift. Our model achieves very good results in heavily distorted scene texts, *i.e.*, "RONALDO" and "DONOVAN".

As for the speed, only a few methods report their predict time. Experiments show that our method has the fastest predict speed in these methods. The predict speed of SAM is 0.02 s per image, faster than 0.03 s in [35], 0.11 s in [43] and 0.2 s in [11].

As shown in Fig. 3, there are some challenges for our method. Some characters have similar visual information, such as 'C' and 'G', 'V' and 'Y', which are difficult to distinguish even for human beings when they are scribbled. And the image resolution is too low to affect the recognition effect, such as "wahlen", "PARK". In the future work, we will focus on how to solve these challenges.

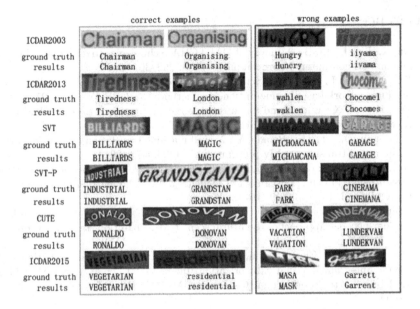

Fig. 3. Example images of recognition results.

5   Conclusion

In this paper, firstly, we analyze the limitations in current methods for scene text recognition. Then, in response to the limitations, we proposed an efficient and strong method, named SAM for scene text recognition inspired by Swin Transformer. And as a non-recurrent network, SAM achieved the fastest predict speed of 0.02 s per image. Especially, SAM uses a encoder based on Swin Transformer to produce a hierarchical representation for the input image. The hierarchical representation is better suited to convey visual information in high-resolution images, which is important for scene text recognition. Finally, to verify the superiority and effectiveness of SAM, we conduct comparative experiments on six public benchmarks. The Experiments demonstrate superiority in the accuracy of our model. SAM not only improves 0.9%, 3.2%, and 0.8% on the regular scene text datasets ICDAR2003, ICDAR2013, and SVT, respectively, over the previous best method, but also improves 1.3%, 1.7%, and 1.1% on the irregular scene text datasets SVT-P, CUTE, and ICDAR2015. For future work, we will focus on how to solve the effect of low resolution.

Acknowledgement. The work described in this paper was supported by National Natural Science Foundation of China (U1803262, 61602349), Key Project of Scientific Research Plan of Hubei Provincial Department of Education (No. D20211106), and Opening Foundation of Key Laboratory of Fundamental Science for National Defense on Vision Synthetization, Sichuan University, China (No. 2021SCUVS003).

References

1. Xu, X., Liu, L., Li, B.: A survey of CAPTCHA technologies to distinguish between human and computer. Neurocomputing **408**, 292–307 (2020)
2. Xu, X., Zhou, J., Zhang, H.: Screen-rendered text images recognition using a deep residual network based segmentation-free method. In: ICPR, pp. 2741–2746 (2018)
3. Yan, H., Xu, X.: End-to-end video subtitle recognition via a deep residual neural network. Pattern Recognit. Lett. **131**, 368–375 (2020)
4. Bahdanau, D., Cho, K., Bengio, Y.: Neural machine translation by jointly learning to align and translate. arXiv preprint arXiv:1409.0473 (2014)
5. Graves, A., Fernández, S., Gomez, F.J., Schmidhuber, J.: Connectionist temporal classification: labelling unsegmented sequence data with recurrent neural networks. In: ICML, vol. 148, pp. 369–376 (2006)
6. Cong, F., Hu, W., Huo, Q., Guo, L.: A comparative study of attention-based encoder-decoder approaches to natural scene text recognition. In: ICDA), pp. 916–921 (2019)
7. Zhang, F., Li, M., Zhai, G., Liu, Y.: Multi-branch and multi-scale attention learning for fine-grained visual categorization. In: Lokoc, J., et al. (eds.) MultiMedia Modeling - 27th International Conference, MMM 2021, vol. 12572, pp. 136–147 (2021)
8. Fu, Y., Guo, L., Wang, L., Liu, Z., Liu, J., Dang, J.: A sentiment similarity-oriented attention model with multi-task learning for text-based emotion recognition. In: Lokoc, J., et al. (eds.) MultiMedia Modeling - 27th International Conference, MMM 2021, vol. 12572, pp. 278–289 (2021)
9. Feng, W., Li, T., Yu, H., Yang, Z.: A hybrid music recommendation algorithm based on attention mechanism. In: Lokoč, J., Skopal, T., Schoeffmann, K., Mezaris, V., Li, X., Vrochidis, S., Patras, I. (eds.) MMM 2021. LNCS, vol. 12572, pp. 328–339. Springer, Cham (2021). https://doi.org/10.1007/978-3-030-67832-6_27
10. Lee, C., Osindero, S.: Recursive recurrent nets with attention modeling for OCR in the wild. In: CVPR, pp. 2231–2239 (2016)
11. Shi, B., Wang, X., Lyu, P., Yao, C., Bai, X.: Robust scene text recognition with automatic rectification. In: CVPR, pp. 4168–4176 (2016)
12. Luo, C., Jin, L., Sun, Z.: MORAN: a multi-object rectified attention network for scene text recognition. Pattern Recognit. **90**, 109–118 (2019)
13. Zhan, F., Lu, S.: ESIR: end-to-end scene text recognition via iterative image rectification. In: CVPR, pp. 2059–2068 (2019)
14. Zhang, Y., Nie, S., Liu, W., Xu, X., Zhang, D., Shen, H.T.: Sequence-to-sequence domain adaptation network for robust text image recognition. In: CVPR, pp. 2740–2749 (2019)
15. Liu, Z., et al.: Swin transformer: hierarchical vision transformer using shifted windows. CoRR abs/2103.14030 (2021)
16. Xu, X., Liu, L., Zhang, X., Guan, W., Hu, R.: Rethinking data collection for person re-identification: active redundancy reduction. Pattern Recognit. **113**, 107827 (2021)
17. Xu, X., Wang, S., Wang, Z., Zhang, X., Hu, R.: Exploring image enhancement for salient object detection in low light images. ACM Trans. Multimedia Comput. Commun. Appl. **17**(1s), 1–19 (2021)
18. Xie, P., Xu, X., Wang, Z., Yamasaki, T.: Unsupervised video person re-identification via noise and hard frame aware clustering. In: 2021 IEEE International Conference on Multimedia and Expo (ICME), pp. 1–6 (2021)

19. Wang, X., Wang, Z., Liu, W., Xu, X., Chen, J., Lin, C.: Consistency-constancy bi-knowledge learning for pedestrian detection in night surveillance. In: MM 2021: ACM Multimedia Conference, pp. 4463–4471. ACM (2021)

20. Jiang, K., et al.: Rain-free and residue hand-in-hand: a progressive coupled network for real-time image deraining. IEEE Trans. Image Process. 30, 7404–7418 (2021)

21. Chen, X., Jin, L., Zhu, Y., Luo, C., Wang, T.: Text recognition in the wild: a survey. ACM Comput. Surv. 54(2), 42:1–42:35 (2021)

22. Wang, K., Babenko, B., Belongie, S.J.: End-to-end scene text recognition. In: Metaxas, D.N., Quan, L., Sanfeliu, A., Gool, L.V. (eds.) ICCV, pp. 1457–1464 (2011)

23. Phan, T.Q., Shivakumara, P., Tian, S., Tan, C.L.: Recognizing text with perspective distortion in natural scenes. In: ICCV, pp. 569–576 (2013)

24. Bissacco, A., Cummins, M., Netzer, Y., Neven, H.: PhotoOCR: reading text in uncontrolled conditions. In: ICCV, pp. 785–792. IEEE Computer Society (2013)

25. Guo, Q., Wang, F., Lei, J., Tu, D., Li, G.: Convolutional feature learning and hybrid CNN-HMM for scene number recognition. Neurocomputing 184, 78–90 (2016)

26. Wan, Z., He, M., Chen, H., Bai, X., Yao, C.: TextScanner: reading characters in order for robust scene text recognition. In: AAAI, pp. 12120–12127 (2020)

27. Shi, B., Bai, X., Yao, C.: An end-to-end trainable neural network for image-based sequence recognition and its application to scene text recognition. IEEE Trans. Pattern Anal. Mach. Intell. 39(11), 2298–2304 (2017)

28. Gao, Y., Chen, Y., Wang, J., Tang, M., Lu, H.: Reading scene text with fully convolutional sequence modeling. Neurocomputing 339, 161–170 (2019)

29. Qi, X., Chen, Y., Xiao, R., Li, C., Zou, Q., Cui, S.: A novel joint character categorization and localization approach for character-level scene text recognition. In: Second International Workshop on Machine Learning, pp. 83–90. IEEE (2019)

30. Hu, W., Cai, X., Hou, J., Yi, S., Lin, Z.: GTC: guided training of CTC towards efficient and accurate scene text recognition. In: AAAI, pp. 11005–11012 (2020)

31. Liu, H., Jin, S., Zhang, C.: Connectionist temporal classification with maximum entropy regularization. In: NeurIPS, pp. 839–849 (2018)

32. Wan, Z., Xie, F., Liu, Y., Bai, X., Yao, C.: 2D-CTC for scene text recognition. CoRR abs/1907.09705 (2019)

33. Cheng, Z., Xu, Y., Bai, F., Niu, Y., Pu, S., Zhou, S.: AON: towards arbitrarily-oriented text recognition. In: CVPR, pp. 5571–5579 (2018)

34. Vaswani, A., et al.: Attention is all you need. In: NeurIPS, pp. 5998–6008 (2017)

35. Sheng, F., Chen, Z., Xu, B.: NRTR: a no-recurrence sequence-to-sequence model for scene text recognition. In: ICDAR, pp. 781–786 (2019)

36. Yang, L., Wang, P., Li, H., Li, Z., Zhang, Y.: A holistic representation guided attention network for scene text recognition. Neurocomputing 414, 67–75 (2020)

37. Jaderberg, M., Simonyan, K., Vedaldi, A., Zisserman, A.: Synthetic data and artificial neural networks for natural scene text recognition. CoRR abs/1406.2227 (2014)

38. Gupta, A., Vedaldi, A., Zisserman, A.: Synthetic data for text localisation in natural images. In: CVPR, pp. 2315–2324 (2016)

39. Lucas, S.M., et al.: ICDAR 2003 robust reading competitions: entries, results, and future directions. Int. J. Document Anal. Recognit. 7(2–3), 105–122 (2005)

40. Karatzas, D., et al.: ICDAR 2013 robust reading competition. In: ICDAR, pp. 1484–1493 (2013)

41. Karatzas, D., et al.: ICDAR 2015 competition on robust reading. In: ICDAR, pp. 1156–1160 (2015)

42. Risnumawan, A., Shivakumara, P., Chan, C.S., Tan, C.L.: A robust arbitrary text detection system for natural scene images. Expert Syst. Appl. **41**(18), 8027–8048 (2014)
43. Bai, F., Cheng, Z., Niu, Y., Pu, S., Zhou, S.: Edit probability for scene text recognition. In: 2018 IEEE/CVF Conference on Computer Vision and Pattern Recognition, pp. 1508–1516 (2018)
44. Wang, C., Yin, F., Liu, C.: Memory-augmented attention model for scene text recognition. In: ICFHR, pp. 62–67 (2018)
45. Qiao, Z., Zhou, Y., Yang, D., Zhou, Y., Wang, W.: SEED: semantics enhanced encoder-decoder framework for scene text recognition. In: CVPR, pp. 13525–13534 (2020)
46. Wang, C., Liu, C.: Multi-branch guided attention network for irregular text recognition. Neurocomputing **425**, 278–289 (2021)
47. Huang, Y., Sun, Z., Jin, L., Luo, C.: EPAN: effective parts attention network for scene text recognition. Neurocomputing **376**, 202–213 (2020)
48. Wang, Q., Jia, W., He, X., Lu, Y., Blumenstein, M., Huang, Y., Lyu, S.: ReELFA: a scene text recognizer with encoded location and focused attention. In: Second International Workshop on Machine Learning, pp. 71–76 (2019)
49. Zhu, Y., Wang, S., Huang, Z., Chen, K.: Text recognition in images based on transformer with hierarchical attention. In: ICIP, pp. 1945–1949 (2019)
50. Wang, T., et al.: Decoupled attention network for text recognition. In: AAAI, pp. 12216–12224 (2020)

JVCSR: Video Compressive Sensing Reconstruction with Joint In-Loop Reference Enhancement and Out-Loop Super-Resolution

Jian Yang, Chi Do-Kim Pham, and Jinjia Zhou[✉]

Graduate School of Science and Engineering, Hosei University, Tokyo, Japan
zhou@hosei.ac.jp

Abstract. Taking advantage of spatial and temporal correlations, deep learning-based video compressive sensing reconstruction (VCSR) technologies have tremendously improved reconstructed video quality. Existing VCSR works mainly focus on improving deep learning-based motion compensation without optimizing local and global information, leaving much space for further improvements. This paper proposes a video compressive sensing reconstruction method with joint in-loop reference enhancement and out-loop super-resolution (JVCSR), focusing on removing reconstruction artifacts and increasing the resolution simultaneously. As an in-loop part, the enhanced frame is utilized as a reference to improve the recovery performance of the current frame. Furthermore, it is the first time to propose out-loop super-resolution for VCSR to obtain high-quality images at low bitrates. As a result, JVCSR obtains an average improvement of 1.37 dB PSNR compared with state-of-the-art compressive sensing methods at the same bitrate.

Keywords: Video compressive sensing reconstruction · Low bitrate · Super-resolution · Reference enhancement

1 Introduction

Compressive sensing (CS) reconstructs the signal at a rate that is lower than the Nyquist-Shannon Sampling Criterion [6]. In the encoder, N-length signal x will be transformed to a specific domain. The transformation of x is a sparse signal and obtains $M \times 1$ measurement y by multiplying the measurement matrix, such as binary matrix, random matrix, and structure matrix. In the decoder, the signal x is reconstructed given the transmitted measurement y and measurement matrix by different reconstruction algorithms, e.g., OMP, SPGL, and SAMP [17]. CS is one of effective coding methods that can achieve the rival performance of full sampling by using a few pieces of information. Therefore, it is also gradually applied in various practical fields such as Magnetic Resonance Imaging (MRI), medical scanners, and surveillance camera sensors.

© Springer Nature Switzerland AG 2022
B. Þór Jónsson et al. (Eds.): MMM 2022, LNCS 13141, pp. 455–466, 2022.
https://doi.org/10.1007/978-3-030-98358-1_36

Traditional CS algorithms achieve acceptable reconstruction performance but have not sufficiently exploit the spatial and temporal correlations. Deep convolution neural networks (CNN) are well-known for outstanding performance in representing, extracting, and learning features compared to the design handcraft filters. Therefore, CNNs have been widely applied to CS for enhancing the visual quality or optimizing the reconstruction. The authors of [18] propose an ISTA-Net for image CS reconstruction. Nonlinear transform is used to solve the proximal mapping associated with the sparsity-inducing regularizer and dramatically promotes the results of traditional approaches while maintaining fast run time. Similar to ISTA-Net, Zhang et al. [20] develop a deep model (AMP-Net) by unfolding the iterative denoising process of the well-known approximate message passing algorithm. An additional deblocking module and training sampling matrix strategy are also utilized in AMP-Net, leading to state-of-the-art reconstructed performance.

These image-level CS algorithms can be directly applied to compress video but fail to utilize the temporal and spatial correlations, such as neighboring frames in video sequences. The research [16] presents a novel recurrent convolutional neural network (CNN) called CSVideoNet for extracting spatial-temporal correlation features, and proposes a synthesizing Long Short Term Memory (LSTM) network for motion estimation. CSVideoNet can enhance the recovered video quality when compared to other iterative algorithms. Huang et al. [10] introduce a learning-based CS algorithm (CS-MCNet) with multi-hypothesis motion compensation (MC) to extract correlation information, and improves the reconstruction performance by reusing the similarity between adjacent frames. Although remarkable results was performed, some artifacts and noises still remain in the reconstructed videos, resulting in an unpleasant visual effect, especially at low bitrates.

To further improve the quality of the reconstructed video, this work proposes a novel VCSR framework employing two additional modules. Low-resolution videos are sampled by the CS encoder and utilize motion compensation to improve the coding performance. Our in-loop reference enhancement module is designed to remove the artifacts and provide a superior frame to motion compensation cyclically. The reconstructed outputs are fed to our out-loop super-resolution module to obtain a higher-resolution and higher-quality video at the lower bitrates. The contributions of our work can be described as follows:

- We design an in-loop reference enhancement to remove the artifacts and noises of current frame before providing reference to the next frame, which significantly improves CS reconstruction performance.
- We propose degradation-aware out-loop super-resolution for the video compressive sensing reconstruction and obtain state-of-the-art performance with lower bitrates.
- Our proposal finally improves the rate-distortion performance of the existing compressive sensing algorithms in a wide bitrate range.

2 Related Technologies

The paper of [3] investigates three compression architectures, including using super-resolution (SR). Their experimental results demonstrate that super-resolution can achieve superior rate-distortion performance that compares to BPG compression images. In [2], the authors present an end-to-end SR algorithm (CISRDCNN) for JPEG images that improves image resolution and reduces compression artifacts jointly. Plenty of researches indicate that it is beneficial to exploit super-resolution methods with compressed images or videos. Nevertheless, there are not many studies that conduct super-resolution base on compressive sensing. On the other hand, such as transform and quantization in HEVC, AVC, and limited measurements in CS, all of them split the image into non-overlapping blocks, and each block is performed by lossy compression. Images can not be fully reconstructed and lead to signal distortion. Therefore, recovering the original signal requires a method to achieve quality enhancement with fewer artifacts and more precise structures. In the past few years, several CNN-based algorithms present powerful potentiality of denoising and artifacts removal [4,19]. Dong [4] demonstrate that their 3-layer convolutional neural network is efficient in reducing various compression artifacts. They also mention that reusing shallow features can help learn deeper models for artifact removal. Similar to other compression methods, some blocking artifacts and blurs are generated after compressive sensing reconstructing, especially at low sampling rates.

Due to the limited bandwidth and storage capacity, videos and images are down-sampled at the encoder and up-sampled at the decoder, which can effectively save data in storing and transmission. On the other hand, super-resolution, where high-resolution images are obtained from low-resolution ones, offers higher resolution for images and videos captured and recorded in the low-resolution. With the rapid development of CNN methods recently, the algorithms for normal image super-resolution and some CNN-based compressed image super-resolution methods are also proposed. However, for the compressed images or videos, directly performing super-resolution would magnify the artifacts and noises simultaneously. To address this issue, the authors in [9], and [8] present a restoration-reconstruction deep neural network (RR-DnCNN), which solves degradation from down-sample and compression by using the degradation-aware method. The technique of degradation-aware consists of restoration and reconstruction. Restoration removes the compression artifacts, and reconstruction leverages up-sampled features from restoration to generate high-resolution video.

3 Proposed JVCSR

3.1 Overall Framework

Our proposed framework consists of three main parts: Compressive sensing with motion compensation (CS-MC), in-loop reference enhancement (I-RE), and out-loop super-resolution (O-SR). The overall architecture is shown in Fig. 1. As

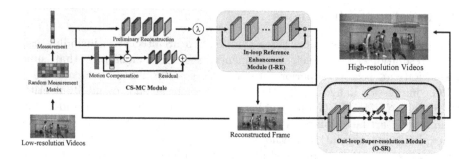

Fig. 1. The proposed JVCSR framework. Our JVCSR includes three main stages. First, low-resolution video is recovered by CS-MC module. Second, reconstructed frames are then fed to the I-RE net before feeding back to the CS-MC nodule as the reference frame. Finally, enhanced video frames are fed to the proposed O-SR to obtain the high-resolution video.

the input of CS-MC, the measurement is acquired by multiplying the pixels of low-resolution videos with a random measurement matrix. After being reconstructed, the video frame is stored in a buffer and continues being used as the reference for the later frame. It is noteworthy that the images restored through CS-MC would generate black spots in some specific cases, which are caused by block-based MC. To address this problem, we design an I-RE module for removing noises and blocking artifacts on reference frames. The recovery frame with higher quality is utilized for motion compensation of CS decoder to reconstruct superior next frame cyclically and as the input of super-resolution. After the in-loop enhancement section, we present an out-loop super-resolution module to increase the resolution of sequences to achieve satisfying visual results and compare performance with other CS algorithms. In our JVCSR framework, low-resolution videos are sampled by the CS encoder and finally up-sample after decoding, which means a lower bitrate in transmission. This allows us to have the coding advantage in saving data while comparing to other off-the-shelf compressive sensing algorithms.

3.2   Network Architectures

In-loop Reference Enhancement (I-RE). In [10], the recovered result of current frame can provide a reference for reconstructing next frame. However, there are still artifacts that remain in the reconstructed image, especially in the high compression ratio, which makes it difficult to provide the instrumental reference. Therefore, it is more significant to conduct post-processing enhancement. As shown in Fig. 2, we design our architecture base on the work of [19], which demonstrates that combining residual learning and batch normalization can achieve the outstanding visual performance of denoise models. Residual learning aims to obtain noisy images, and batch normalization focuses on improving denoising and accelerating the training. The enhanced image without noises and blocking artifacts can be obtained by subtracting the reconstructed image. As aforementioned, the compression ratio (CR), also well-known as sampling rate is defined as $CR = \frac{M}{N}$. Since lower CR indicates fewer signals are sampled, a deep neural network can not play its role completely. To simplify the network and reduce the size of parameters, we appropriately delete some hidden layers when CR is set to low. For hidden layers, we use 64 filters of size $3 \times 3 \times 64$ to get feature maps, and batch normalization is also connected after each convolution layer. Except for the last layer, all convolutional layers are followed by rectified linear units (ReLU) layers. The experiments demonstrate that our I-RE module is able to achieve presentable performance with fewer layers and fewer network parameters.

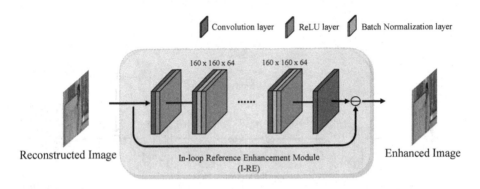

Fig. 2. In-loop Reference Enhancement (I-RE) architecture. Enhanced image is obtai ned after subtracting the learning result from the reconstructed image.

Out-Loop Super-Resolution (O-SR). In the work of [11], the authors propose a novel feedback block module, which effectively reuses feature and feedback information to achieves state-of-the-art SR performance. Inspired by [11], we present a CNN-based super-resolution module to obtain the ultimate high-resolution videos by using the reconstructed and enhanced frames. The architecture is shown in Fig. 3. We define a cyclical block in our network to reuse the extracted information recurrently. The cyclical block is composed of four groups with dense skip connections between them. Each group comprises two point-wise layers. The point-wise layer is followed a deconvolutional and a convolutional layer, which refers to the up-sample and down-sample operation. The extracted shallow features are maintained and reused in the cyclical block to produce the refined features. Except the final layer, PReLU is the activation function of all convolutional and deconvolutional layers in the main out-loop super-resolution network.

Besides, we design an additional attention module for the cyclical block to refine the feature adaptively. In [15], the authors introduce a convolutional block attention module (CBAM), which is extensively applied in various learning-based tasks such as image recognition and classification. This attention module has two parts: The channel attention module utilizes both average-pool and max-pool synchronously to boost the representation power of the network. On the other hand, the spatial attention module works to find an informative part to supplement channel attention. It is worth noting that this attention module also performs well in our task. We also explored the connection way of these two modules by adjusting the order in our network: sequential channel attention module then add spatial attention module, sequential spatial attention module then add channel attention, parallel spatial attention module and channel attention. In the experiments, we finally decided to use sequential channel attention module then add spatial attention module since it performs better.

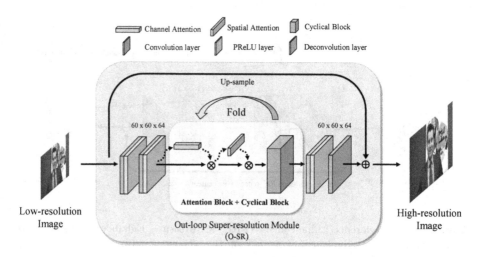

Fig. 3. The architecture of out-loop super-resolution (O-SR). Attention block is connected in each cyclical block for adaptive feature refinement. The final output high-resolution image is obtained by adding the up-sampled low-resolution image and learning results. The up-sample kernel is set to bicubic here.

4   Experiments

4.1   Experimental Settings

Training Dataset. We use Ultra Video Group (UVG) [12] to build the training dataset of training super-resolution. The UVG comprises 16 versatile 4K (3840 * 2160) video sequences and is commonly used in video-based works. These natural sequences were captured at 50 or 120 frames per second (fps) and stored online in different formats. We choose videos from the UVG dataset and get around 1050 pairs of images for training and validation in total. For training compressive sensing model, as there is not standard dataset designed for video CS, we randomly pick 15% UCF-101 dataset with 100 frames for training. All the video sequences are converted to one channel and only extracted the luminance signal.

Testing Dataset. It might be difficult to distinguish the quality difference between two video sequences of the identical content with a close compressed ratio. The MCL-JCV dataset [14] is designed to measure this phenomenon for each test subject. Moreover, since surveillance is ubiquitous in practical and requires high-resolution videos, we also use the VIRAT dataset [1] obtained from various surveillance camera viewpoints to demonstrate the robustness of our method.

Training Setting. The experiments of our framework are implemented with Pytorch 1.2.0 on Ubuntu 16.04, and NVIDIA GeForce RTX2080Ti GPUs are supported for our training. We use Adam optimization to refine the parameters while training. We separate the training into three modules, a super-resolution module, an enhancement module, and a compressive sensing module but finally connect them to an end-to-end trainable network. To demonstrate the robustness of our framework, four models are trained for each module with different compression ratio videos.

In the training of super-resolution, the scale factor is set to 2. We initialize the learning rate to 1×10^{-4}, and multiplies by $\frac{1}{2}$ every 250 epochs with total 1000 epochs. For training the enhancement module, the network depth depends on the compression ratio. The model of the largest CR we used (0.75) has 17 hidden layers, and CR = 0.5 has 16 layers, and so on. For compressive sensing, training for 200 epochs with a batch size of 400 and 0.01 learning rate yield the best reconstruction performance in our case.

4.2 Experimental Results

The results of experiments are evaluated by two standards, signal-to-noise ratio (PSNR) and structural similarity (SSIM). Visual performance is also shown in the following sections.

Results on In-Loop Reference Enhancement. Higher-quality video frames are generated before upsampling in our JVCSR framework since we have the enhancement for motion compensation in compressive sensing. To demonstrate the performance of our in-loop reference enhancement module, we show some visual examples of reconstructed images and enhanced results in Fig. 4. It can be seen that most of the noises are removed by our enhancement module successfully.

Ablation Study on the Proposed Components. To analysis the effect and perform the superiority of each module in our work, we conduct the comparison with other state-of-the-art super-resolution approaches as follows: 1) Delete I-RE and O-SR module then directly up-sample the images by bicubic interpolation. 2) Keep I-RE but delete O-SR module then up-sample the images by bicubic interpolation. 3) Replaced O-SR module with SRCNN [5]. 4) Replaced O-SR module with DRRN [13]. 5) Replaced O-SR module with DBPN [7]. 6) Both I-RE and O-SR are utilized. As shown in Table 1, it is easy to judge our work achieves superior performance by these ablation experiments.

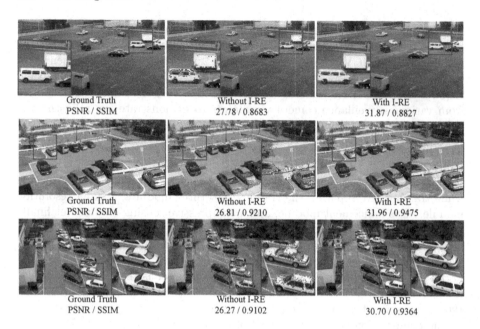

Fig. 4. The enhancement visual results of VIRAT dataset. Noises and artifacts reconstructed by compressive sensing are effectively alleviated by our I-RE module. Please zoom in for better views and comparisons.

Table 1. The average PSNR and SSIM performance comparison between I-RE + O-SR and other super-resolution algorithms at different CRs.

CR	0.125	0.25	0.5	0.75
Bicubic	24.20/0.6793	25.90/0.7391	26.99/0.8168	27.91/0.8575
I-RE + Bicubic	25.64/0.7253	27.44/0.7822	28.83/0.8504	30.03/0.8873
I-RE + SRCNN [5]	25.95/0.7532	28.03/0.8141	29.47/0.8721	30.93/0.8998
I-RE + DRRN [13]	26.79/0.7784	28.97/0.8345	30.14/0.8823	31.68/0.9074
I-RE + DBPN [7]	27.24/0.7882	29.32/0.8492	31.07/0.8942	32.59/0.9169
I-RE + O-SR (Ours)	**27.75/0.8053**	**29.91/0.8610**	**31.98/0.9020**	**33.31/0.9238**

Overall Bitrate Reduction and Comparison. To perform the coding advantage of our proposal, Fig. 6 shows the rate-distortion results at different bitrates obtained by our test dataset. We compare with ISTA-Net [18], SAMP [17], CS-MCNet [10], and AMP-Net [20], the curves demonstrate that our proposal outperforms other compressive sensing algorithms over a wide range of bitrates. We show PSNR and SSIM results of some test examples (9 sequences from MCL-JCV) at two bitrates comparison with different compressive sensing algorithms in Table 2. For a fair comparison, we choose appropriate sampling rates for these algorithms to make them have different compression ratios, but the same bitrates

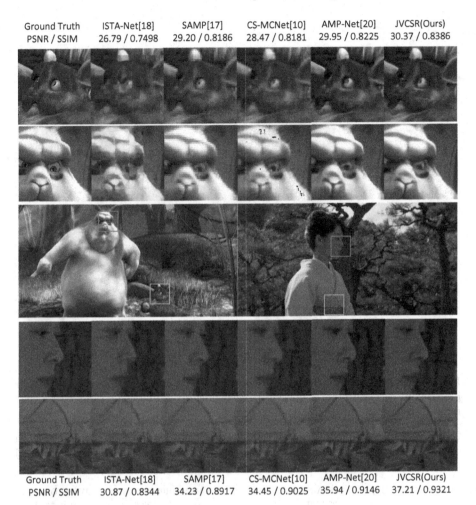

| Ground Truth | ISTA-Net[18] | SAMP[17] | CS-MCNet[10] | AMP-Net[20] | JVCSR(Ours) |
| PSNR / SSIM | 26.79 / 0.7498 | 29.20 / 0.8186 | 28.47 / 0.8181 | 29.95 / 0.8225 | 30.37 / 0.8386 |

| Ground Truth | ISTA-Net[18] | SAMP[17] | CS-MCNet[10] | AMP-Net[20] | JVCSR(Ours) |
| PSNR / SSIM | 30.87 / 0.8344 | 34.23 / 0.8917 | 34.45 / 0.9025 | 35.94 / 0.9146 | 37.21 / 0.9321 |

Fig. 5. The visual results of some examples at the same bitrate. The original images are also presented in the figure. Please zoom in for better views and comparisons.

as ours work. Obviously, our proposed JVCSR can outperform almost all comparative methods. Moreover, Fig. 5 shows the visual results of some examples at the same bitrate to further prove the superiority of our framework. As we can see, our proposal retains the most details, suffers minimal block effect, and removes noises dramatically.

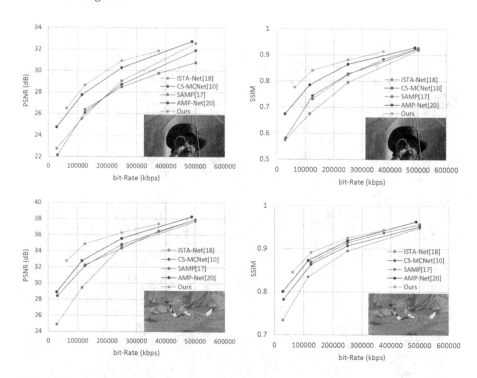

Fig. 6. The PSNR and SSIM rate-distortion curves of two test video sequences. Our proposal outperforms other compressive sensing algorithms for comparison over a wide range of bitrates.

Table 2. PSNR and SSIM results of test examples at two bitrates comparison with different compressive sensing algorithms. The best performance is indicated as Bold and second best as Italic.

bitrate (kbps)	Sequence	ISTA-Net [18]	SAMP [17]	CS-MCNet [10]	AMP-Net [20]	JVCSR(Ours)
	Park	22.57/0.6019	24.64/0.7157	23.68/0.7109	**26.32**/*0.7254*	*25.89*/**0.7394**
	Cartoon 01	26.79/0.7498	29.20/0.8186	28.47/0.8181	*29.95*/*0.8225*	**30.37**/**0.8386**
	Cartoon 02	29.28/0.8583	*30.97*/*0.9011*	30.51/0.8948	29.43/0.9079	**33.59**/**0.9273**
	Telescope	30.54/0.7769	32.92/0.8282	32.84/0.8228	*33.49*/*0.8295*	**34.50**/**0.8369**
1.2×10^5	Kimono	30.87/0.8344	34.23/0.8917	34.45/0.9025	*35.94*/*0.9146*	**37.21**/**0.9321**
	Car	33.98/0.8909	39.04/*0.9708*	*39.06*/0.9630	37.63/0.9506	**38.85**/**0.9782**
	Building	28.76/0.8328	31.36/0.9014	31.63/0.8998	*31.77*/*0.9104*	**34.35**/**0.9308**
	Beach	29.59/0.8506	32.17/0.9001	32.74/0.9103	*33.47*/*0.9180*	**35.39**/**0.9377**
	Parrot	32.51/0.8870	35.46/0.9114	*35.58*/*0.9172*	33.99/0.9191	**37.30**/**0.9275**
	Park	26.76/0.7539	26.71/*0.8335*	25.80/0.8073	**30.23**/**0.8491**	*27.01*/0.8048
	Cartoon01	30.30/0.8331	31.11/*0.8817*	30.97/0.8662	**33.06**/**0.8871**	*31.52*/0.8679
	Cartoon02	33.14/0.9273	32.94/0.9431	31.99/0.9298	*33.47*/*0.9462*	**33.75**/**0.9475**
	Telescope	33.94/0.8280	34.24/*0.8652*	*34.74*/0.8503	33.28/0.8483	**35.61**/**0.8522**
2.5×10^5	Kimono	36.25/0.9106	36.93/*0.9380*	*37.94*/0.9348	36.82/0.9364	**39.22**/**0.9451**
	Car	41.46/0.9639	41.88/0.9701	42.02/0.9718	*43.37*/*0.9733*	**44.73**/**0.9823**
	Building	34.53/0.9173	33.06/0.9469	*34.77*/*0.9380*	34.21/0.9474	**36.21**/**0.9511**
	Beach	34.83/0.9223	34.78/0.9505	36.03/0.9471	*36.93*/*0.9565*	**37.58**/**0.9570**
	Parrot	36.51/0.9167	37.08/0.9341	37.67/0.9308	*37.84*/**0.9378**	**38.48**/*0.9351*

5   Conclusions

In this paper, we propose a video compressive sensing reconstruction framework with joint in-loop reference enhancement and out-loop super-resolution (JVCSR). First, an in-loop enhancement module is designed to enhance the pixel information and realize the optimization of the reference frame for CS. Experimental results show that the artifacts and noises are removed effectively, leading to better CS recovery results. Taking the advantage of downsampling-based video coding concept, we propose an out-loop super-resolution module to increase the resolution for low-resolution videos at different compression ratios. By comparing to other state-of-the-art algorithms, our proposal delivers the comparative performance. Moreover, we obtain better rate-distortion performance in a wide range than other CS algorithms to show the merit of our framework in low bitrate video coding. To the best of our knowledge, it is the first time to exploit degradation-aware super-resolution for video compressive sensing reconstruction. We believe that our work can be integrated to simple hardware cameras and is able to provide higher higher-quality videos while sending the low compressed data.

References

1. Virat description. http://www.viratdata.org/
2. Chen, H., He, X., Ren, C., Qing, L., Teng, Q.: CISRDCNN: super-resolution of compressed images using deep convolutional neural networks. Neurocomputing **285**, 204–219 (2018)
3. Cheng, Z., Sun, H., Takeuchi, M., Katto, J.: Performance comparison of convolutional autoencoders, generative adversarial networks and super-resolution for image compression. In: CVPR Workshops, pp. 2613–2616 (2018)
4. Dong, C., Deng, Y., Loy, C.C., Tang, X.: Compression artifacts reduction by a deep convolutional network. In: Proceedings of the IEEE International Conference on Computer Vision, pp. 576–584 (2015)
5. Dong, C., Loy, C.C., He, K., Tang, X.: Learning a deep convolutional network for image super-resolution. In: Fleet, D., Pajdla, T., Schiele, B., Tuytelaars, T. (eds.) ECCV 2014. LNCS, vol. 8692, pp. 184–199. Springer, Cham (2014). https://doi.org/10.1007/978-3-319-10593-2_13
6. Duarte, M.F., et al.: Single-pixel imaging via compressive sampling. IEEE Sign. Process. Mag. **25**(2), 83–91 (2008)
7. Haris, M., Shakhnarovich, G., Ukita, N.: Deep back-projection networks for super-resolution. In: Proceedings of the IEEE Conference on Computer Vision and Pattern Recognition, pp. 1664–1673 (2018)
8. Ho, M.M., Zhou, J., He, G., Li, M., Li, L.: SR-CL-DMC: P-frame coding with super-resolution, color learning, and deep motion compensation. In: Proceedings of the IEEE/CVF Conference on Computer Vision and Pattern Recognition Workshops, pp. 124–125 (2020)
9. Ho, M.-M., He, G., Wang, Z., Zhou, J.: Down-sampling based video coding with degradation-aware restoration-reconstruction deep neural network. In: Ro, Y.M., et al. (eds.) MMM 2020. LNCS, vol. 11961, pp. 99–110. Springer, Cham (2020). https://doi.org/10.1007/978-3-030-37731-1_9

10. Huang, B., Zhou, J., Yan, X., Jing, M., Wan, R., Fan, Y.: CS-MCNet: a video compressive sensing reconstruction network with interpretable motion compensation. In: Proceedings of the Asian Conference on Computer Vision (2020)
11. Li, Z., Yang, J., Liu, Z., Yang, X., Jeon, G., Wu, W.: Feedback network for image super-resolution. In: Proceedings of the IEEE Conference on Computer Vision and Pattern Recognition, pp. 3867–3876 (2019)
12. Mercat, A., Viitanen, M., Vanne, J.: UVG dataset: 50/120fps 4K sequences for video codec analysis and development. In: Proceedings of the 11th ACM Multimedia Systems Conference, pp. 297–302 (2020)
13. Tai, Y., Yang, J., Liu, X.: Image super-resolution via deep recursive residual network. In: Proceedings of the IEEE Conference on Computer Vision and Pattern Recognition, pp. 3147–3155 (2017)
14. Wang, H., et al.: MCL-JCV: a JND-based h. 264/AVC video quality assessment dataset. In: 2016 IEEE International Conference on Image Processing (ICIP), pp. 1509–1513. IEEE (2016)
15. Woo, S., Park, J., Lee, J.Y., Kweon, I.S.: CBAM: convolutional block attention module. In: Proceedings of the European Conference on Computer Vision (ECCV), pp. 3–19 (2018)
16. Xu, K., Ren, F.: CSVideoNet: a real-time end-to-end learning framework for high-frame-rate video compressive sensing. In: 2018 IEEE Winter Conference on Applications of Computer Vision (WACV), pp. 1680–1688. IEEE (2018)
17. Yao, S., Guan, Q., Wang, S., Xie, X.: Fast sparsity adaptive matching pursuit algorithm for large-scale image reconstruction. EURASIP J. Wirel. Commun. Netw. **2018**(1), 1–8 (2018). https://doi.org/10.1186/s13638-018-1085-6
18. Zhang, J., Ghanem, B.: ISTA-NET: interpretable optimization-inspired deep network for image compressive sensing. In: Proceedings of the IEEE Conference on Computer Vision and Pattern Recognition, pp. 1828–1837 (2018)
19. Zhang, K., Zuo, W., Chen, Y., Meng, D., Zhang, L.: Beyond a gaussian denoiser: residual learning of deep CNN for image denoising. IEEE Trans. Image Process. **26**(7), 3142–3155 (2017)
20. Zhang, Z., Liu, Y., Liu, J., Wen, F., Zhu, C.: AMP-NET: denoising-based deep unfolding for compressive image sensing. IEEE Trans. Image Process. **30**, 1487–1500 (2020)

Point Cloud Upsampling
via a Coarse-to-Fine Network

Yingrui Wang, Suyu Wang[✉], and Longhua Sun

Faculty of Information Technology, Beijing University of Technology, Beijing, China
{wangyingrui,suyuwang,islhua}@emails.bjut.edu.cn

Abstract. Point clouds captured by 3D scanning are usually sparse and noisy. Reconstructing a high-resolution 3D model of an object is a challenging task in computer vision. Recent point cloud upsampling approaches aim to generate a dense point set, while achieving both distribution uniformity and proximity-to-surface directly via an end-to-end network. Although dense reconstruction from low to high resolution can be realized by using these techniques, it lacks abundant details for dense outputs. In this work, we propose a coarse-to-fine network PUGL-Net for point cloud reconstruction that first predicts a coarse high-resolution point cloud via a global dense reconstruction module and then increases the details by aggregating local point features. On the one hand, a transformer-based mechanism is designed in the global dense reconstruction module. It aggregates residual learning in a self-attention scheme for effective global feature extraction. On the other hand, the coordinate offset of points is learned in a local refinement module. It further refines the coarse points by aggregating KNN features. Evaluated through extensive quantitative and qualitative evaluation on synthetic data set, the proposed coarse-to-fine architecture generates point clouds that are accurate, uniform and dense, it outperforms most existing state-of-the-art point cloud reconstruction works.

Keywords: 3D point cloud reconstruction · Point cloud upsampling · Transformer · Coarse-to-fine

1 Introduction

As a compact representation of 3D data, point cloud data are gaining increasing popularity in many application areas [1–3]. However, due to the hardware and computational constraints, raw point clouds captured by 3D sensors are often sparse and noisy which heavily limits its application. Hence, point cloud data must be enhanced before it was effectively used for other application. An example is shown in Fig. 1. The goal of point cloud upsampling is to convert sparse, incomplete, and noisy point clouds (Fig. 1(a)) into dense, complete, and clean ones, in which points faithfully locate on the underlying surface and cover the surface with a uniform distribution. As for the limited information available in the sparse input and the sparse input points might be non-uniform and noisy,

© Springer Nature Switzerland AG 2022
B. Þór Jónsson et al. (Eds.): MMM 2022, LNCS 13141, pp. 467–478, 2022.
https://doi.org/10.1007/978-3-030-98358-1_37

(a) Input   (b) PU-GCN[14] (c) $\mathcal{P}_{coarse}$(Our)   (d) Our   (e) Ground-truth

Fig. 1. Visual comparison at 4× upsampling for image *Horse* with different methods.

the input may not well represent fine structures on the underlying surface, which makes the goals of point cloud upsampling being extremely challenging.

The existing methods for point cloud upsampling can be roughly classified into two categories: optimization-based methods and deep learning-based methods. The optimization-based methods [4,5] usually work well for smooth areas with less features. However, various shape priors are needed to constrain the point generation. Deep learning methods now achieve state-of-the-art performance in point cloud upsampling [12,13]. The general framework for existing learning-based methods is that they first design a feature extraction module, then an upsampling module is used to expand the number of points in feature space. Finally, various loss functions are used to constrain the output points. However, it is the major challenge of current research that how to generate the points meeting all the requirements that is denseness, distribution uniformity, and proximity-to-surface, while maintaining rich details of the geometric shape via a whole end-to-end network. In Fig. 1(b), some phenomena, such as loss of details, still persist even though the reconstruction results of the existing method PU-GCN [14] can describe the overall shape of the object to a certain extent. Especially, the geometric details cannot be effectively reconstructed in the cropped area.

Therefore, in this paper, we propose a novel network to overcome the limitations in the existing deep learning methods. In summary, the main contributions of this work are as follows:

1) We design a novel coarse-to-fine network PUGL-Net, which achieves the point cloud upsampling task using two steps: The first step is global dense reconstruction, which aims to generate dense points by using global features and roughly describe the geometric shape of point cloud (Fig. 1(c) denoted as $\mathcal{P}_{coarse}$). The second step is local refinement, which complementarily improves the point distribution in local feature space.
2) We design a global dense reconstruction module which aims to encode the input points into a higher dimensional global feature space, and then achieve the dense reconstruction via feature expansion. An improved transformer scheme is proposed for characterizing the semantic affinities between points and effectively promoting the global feature extraction.
3) We propose a local refinement module to learn coordinates offset by aggregating local point features which aims to further rectify the points to locate closely to surface and distribute uniformly.

The rest of this paper is organized as follows: Sect. 2 reviews the most related work. Section 3 describes the proposed method, and Sect. 4 introduces the experimental details. Section 5 concludes the paper.

2 Related Work

In the following, we briefly review the related point cloud upsampling methods. The related point cloud upsampling methods are divided into two categories: i)Optimization-based upsampling. This kind of methods typically rely on hand-crafted priors to generate new points from the inputs. ii)Deep learning-based upsampling. These methods recovery a dense point cloud via end-to-end network with paired dataset.

2.1 Optimization-Based Upsampling.

Alexa et al. [4] introduced an early work that generates new points at the vertices of the Voronoi diagram, which is computed based on the moving-least squares surface. Lipman et al. [6] proposed a locally optimal projection operator in which points are resampled based on the L1 norm. To up-sample point cloud in an edge-aware manner, Huang et al. [5] proposed to upsample points away from the edges and progressively move points towards the edge singularities to upsample point cloud in an edge-aware manner. Wu et al. [7] introduced a point-set consolidation method by augmenting surface points into deep points that lie on the meso-skeleton of the shape. Preiner et al. [8] proposed improved weighted LOP and continuous LOP. These methods assume that points are sampled from smooth surfaces, which degrades the upsampling quality towards sharp edges and corners.

2.2 Deep Learning-Based Upsampling

Deep learning methods achieve a promising improvement over optimization-based methods [4–6]. For the point cloud upsampling task, Yu et al. proposed PU-Net [9] for the point cloud upsampling, which used deep learning to learn multi-scale features and expand a point set via a multi-branch convolution in the feature space. Yu et al. also proposed EC-Net [10], an edge-aware network for point set consolidation. They used an edge-aware joint loss to encourage the network to learn to consolidate points for edges. Wang et al. [11] proposed MPU, a network that gradually upsamples point patches gradually. Li et al. [12] proposed PUGAN by leveraging the generative adversarial network to learn to synthesize points with a uniform distribution in the latent space. They also proposed Dis-PU [15] for point cloud upsampling task by combining a disentangled refinement with a global and local refiner. Qian et al. [13] proposed PUGeoNet to first generate samples in a 2D domain and then use a linear transform to lift up the samples to 3D. Recently, Qian et al. [14] proposed PU-GCN to upsample points by leveraging a new inception-based module to extract multi-scale information.

3   Proposed Approach

3.1   Overview

Point cloud upsampling is a prediction problem that involves using a given sparse point cloud to generate more denser points on the underlying original surface. To address the problem of geometric details loss in reconstructed point cloud by existing methods, we propose a novel coarse-to-fine upsampling framework, including a global dense reconstruction module and a local refinement module, called PUGL-Net as shown in Fig. 2

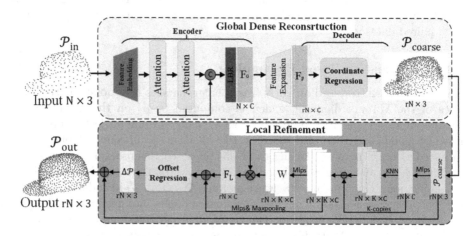

Fig. 2. An illustration of our framework PUGL-Net. The training pipeline consists of first predicting a dense point cloud, and then enhancing the spatial geometric details by local refinement module. Given a sparse input $\mathcal{P}_{in}$ of N points, the global dense reconstruction module first extracts global feature $\mathbf{F}_G$ from the input, then produces a coarse but dense point set $\mathcal{P}_{corase}$ with rN points, where r is the upsampling rate. Meanwhile, the local refinement module is used to obtain a offset feature map $\triangle \mathcal{P}$, finally output the refined dense points $\mathcal{P}_{out} = \mathcal{P}_{corase} + \triangle \mathcal{P}$. LBR module combines Linear, BatchNorm and ReLU layers.

Figure 2 shows the overall framework of our proposed coarse-to-fine framework, in which we first generate a coarse but dense point set and then refine these points over the underlying surface and improve the distribution uniformity. We first feed a sparse point set $\mathcal{P}_{in}$ into our global dense reconstruction module to generate the dense output $\mathcal{P}_{coarse}$ with rN points. This dense output $\mathcal{P}_{coarse}$ may still be somewhat non-uniform and noisy as shown in the Fig. 2. Then, we feed it into our local refinement module to learn a per-point coordinate offset using its KNN features. It can effectively adjust the location of each point in $\mathcal{P}_{coarse}$, to ensure that the refined dense points $\mathcal{P}_{out}$ can uniformly locate on the underlying surface. In the following, we will present the details of the global dense reconstruction module and local refinement module in Sect. 3.2 and Sect. 3.3, respectively.

3.2   Global Dense Reconstruction

The global dense reconstruction module aims to transform the input points into a new higher dimensional global feature space, extend the points in feature space, and regress the output from the feature space into a 3D coordinate space.

Transformer for Point Cloud Global Feature Representation. Inspired by the application of transformers [16,19] in the image domain, we propose to use an improved transformer scheme to extract the global feature in point cloud. This can effectively represent the semantic affinities between points. The encoder of designed transformer starts by embedding the input coordinates into a new feature space. The embedded features are later fed into two stacked offset-attention (OAT) modules instead of self-attention (SA) layers in original transformers. This OAT module learns a semantically rich and discriminative representation for each point, which aggregates global information and is followed by a linear layer to generate the output feature. The transformer scheme ends by MLPs of coordinate regression module, which decodes the points from the feature space into a 3D coordinate space after point expansion.

Specifically, given an input point cloud $\mathcal{P}_{in} \in \mathcal{R}^{N \times d}$ with N points each having d-dimensional feature description, usually, the d is 3 of the input point cloud. A d_e-dimensional embedded feature $\mathbf{F}_e \in R^{N \times d_e}$ is first learned via the feature embedding module as shown in Fig. 2. To extract an effective global feature vector $\mathbf{F}_G \in R^{N \times C}$ representing the point cloud, the designed transformer is formed by concatenating the OAT output of each attention layer through the feature dimension, and followed by a linear transformation (LBR module in Fig. 2). This process can be written as follows:

$$\mathbf{F}_1 = OAT^1(\mathbf{F}_e), \mathbf{F}_2 = OAT^2(F_1), \mathbf{F}_G = LBR(concat(\mathbf{F}_1, \mathbf{F}_2) \cdot \mathbf{W}_0) \qquad (1)$$

where OAT^i represents the i-th OAT layer, and each has the same output dimension as its input, and $\mathbf{W}_0$ is the learned weights of the LBR layer. Specifically, the proposed offset-attention (OAT) layer is an improved self-attention (SA) layer of the transformer scheme. It calculates the offset (difference) between SA features and input features by element-wise subtraction. Specifically, let the input and output of OAT layer be $\mathbf{F}_{in}$ and $\mathbf{F}_{out}$, respectively. The equation of the OAT module is as follows:

$$\mathbf{F}_{out} = OAT(\mathbf{F}_{in}) = LBR(\mathbf{F}_{in} - SA(\mathbf{F}_{in})) + \mathbf{F}_{in} \qquad (2)$$

Feature Expansion. Given that points can be regressed from features space, we expand the number of features in order to expand the number of points. As previously mentioned above, the dimension of global feature is $N \times C$, where N is the number of input points, and C is the feature dimension. The feature expansion operation would output a feature $\mathbf{F}_p$ with dimension $rN \times C$, where r is the upsampling rate. In this step, we use a sub-pixel convolution layer [17] for an efficient feature expansion operation. This operation can be represented as follows:

$$\mathbf{F}_p = \mathcal{RS}([Conv_1^2(Conv_1^1(\mathbf{F}_G)), ..., Conv_r^2(Conv_r^1(\mathbf{F}_G))]) \tag{3}$$

where $Conv_i^1(\cdot)$ and $Conv_i^2(\cdot)$ are two sets of separate 1×1 convolutions, and $\mathcal{RS}(\cdot)$ is a reshape operation to convert an $N \times rC$ tensor to a $rN \times C$ tensor.

Coordinate Regression. In this part, we reconstruct the 3D coordinates of the output points from the expanded feature with the size of $rN \times C$. Specifically, we regress the 3D coordinates via a series of fully connected layers on the feature of each point, and the final output is the up-sampled point coordinates $rN \times 3$.

3.3 Local Refinement

As shown in Fig. 2, the local refinement module aims to promote $\mathcal{P}_{coarse}$ by using a local geometric structure in feature space. In this part, we adopt residual learning to regress the per-point offset combining effective local features instead of directly regressing the refined point coordinates. Specifically, we first use MLPs to covert the coarse output $\mathcal{P}_{coarse}$ to a high dimension feature space. Then, KNN is applied to group the feature to obtain K-nearest neighbors of each point, which forms a stacked $rN \times K \times C$ feature tensor. Moreover, we obtain a residual tensor by applying a subtraction operation on the K copies of this MLP feature and the grouped feature tensor. The residual tensor will contribute to the generation of local feature. On the one hand, we employ a common routine using MLPs and max-pooling along the C-dimension of residual tensor to obtain a basic local point feature. On the other hand, a spatial weight tensor W from the residual tensor is learned to measure the relative importance among KNN neighbors. Then, the initial local feature $\mathbf{F}_L$ is obtained by a convolution of the learned weight W and the grouped feature tensor. Finally, We employ a summation of these two parts to obtain a final enhanced $rN \times C$ feature map, which will be fed to the offset regression module to learn a coordinates offset for each point. This learned coordinate offset will be employed as a modifier to adjust the coarse output $\mathcal{P}_{coarse}$. Finally, a refined point cloud $\mathcal{P}_{out}$ will be generated.

4   Experiments

In this section, we compare our method with state-of-the-art point upsampling methods from both quantitative and qualitative perspectives, and evaluate various aspects of our model.

4.1   Experimental Settings

Datasets. In our experiments, we employ the challenging PU1K dataset, proposed by PU-GCN [14]. PU1K consists of 1,147 3D models split into 1020 training samples and 127 testing samples. It covers a large semantic range of 3D objects and includes simple, as well as complex shapes.

For training and testing, PU1K dataset generates pairs of input and ground-truth point clouds using Poisson disk sampling from original meshes. Specifically, 50 patches are cropped from each 3D model as inputs to the network for training. There are 51,000 training patches in PU1K in total. Each patch consists of 256 points as low resolution inputs and 1024 points as ground truth. In terms of data for testing, the PU1K dataset generate pairs of input point cloud (2048 points) and ground truth(8096 points). In testing, we use farthest point sampling at first to sample overlapping patches (patch size is 256) of the input point cloud and ensure the coverage of entire input. The final results are obtained by first merging the overlapping patch outputs, and then re-sampling with farthest point sampling.

Loss Function. We propose to use a joint Chamfer distance loss to optimize the network, which includes minimizing the distance between the coarse point cloud and the ground truth, and minimizing the distance between predicted refined point cloud and the ground truth in our experiments:

$$Loss = L_{CD}(\mathcal{P}_{coarse}, \mathcal{P}_{gt}) + L_{CD}(\mathcal{P}_{out}, \mathcal{P}_{gt}) \tag{4}$$

where $\mathcal{P}_{coarse}$ is the coarse recovered point cloud output by global dense reconstruction module, $\mathcal{P}_{out}$ is the finally refined point cloud, $\mathcal{P}_{gt}$ is the ground-truth. $L_{CD}(\cdot)$ means Chamfer distance(CD) measuring the average closest point distance between two point sets.

Evaluation Metrics. We employ the Chamfer distance (CD), Hausdorff distance (HD), and point-to-surface distance (P2F) as the evaluation metrics in accordance with previous work. The smaller the metrics, the better the performance. All models are tested on the same computer with one NVIDIA GeForce RTX 2080Ti.

Comparison Methods. We compare our method with other five state-of-the-art point cloud upsampling methods, including PU-GAN [12], PU-Net [9], MPU [11], Dis-PU [15], and PU-GCN [14], to demonstrate its effectiveness. We use their released public codes and follow the same setting in the original papers to retrain their networks using PU1K point cloud dataset.

Implementation Details. We train our network with a batch size of 32 for 300 epochs on TensorFlow platform. The Adam [20] optimizer is used with the learning rate of 0.001.

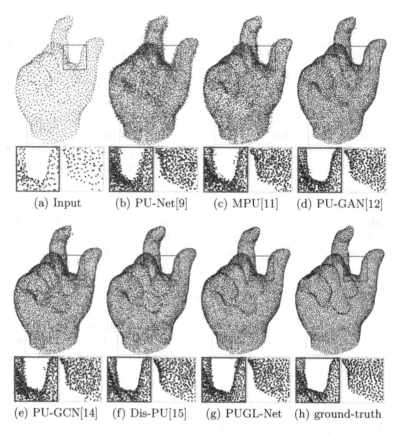

(a) Input   (b) PU-Net[9]   (c) MPU[11]   (d) PU-GAN[12]

(e) PU-GCN[14]   (f) Dis-PU[15]   (g) PUGL-Net   (h) ground-truth

Fig. 3. Visual comparison at 4× upsampling for image *Hand* with different methods.

4.2 Results on PU1K Dataset

Quantitative Results. Table 1 compares our proposed PUGL-Net against other five state-of-the-art methods on PU1K dataset in terms of upsampling factor of 4×. We can see that our method achieves the lowest values on all evaluation metrics. Moreover, PU-Net [9], an early work in point cloud upsampling task, did not produce particularly promising results when trained and evaluated on PU1K. MPU [11] proposed to progressively upsample point patches and finally promote the metrics results compared with PU-Net [9]. Dis-PU [15] disentangled the upsampling task into two parts, namely, Dense Generator and Spatial Refiner. As the feature extraction in Dense Generator is too sample, it is unable to effectively extract the geometric feature, resulting in not very promising metric results finally. PU-GAN [12] outputs promoted upsampling results but has somewhat instability, because of the instability of generative adversarial network (GAN) [18]. PU-GCN [14] uses graph convolution for point cloud upsampling joint local features by KNN algorithm which finally achieves better results.

Table 1. Quantitative comparisons (4×) with the state-of-the-arts.

Methods	CD (10^{-3})	HD (10^{-3})	P2F (10^{-3})
PU-Net2018 [9]	1.120	15.261	4.248
MPU2019 [11]	0.925	13.327	3.551
PU-GAN2019 [12]	0.622	13.556	2.511
Dis-PU2021 [15]	0.925	12.121	2.846
PU-GCN2021 [14]	0.585	7.577	2.499
PUGL-Net (Our)	**0.526**	**6.586**	**2.080**

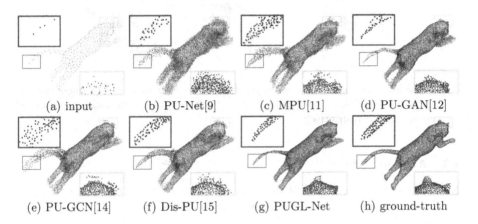

(a) input   (b) PU-Net[9]   (c) MPU[11]   (d) PU-GAN[12]

(e) PU-GCN[14]   (f) Dis-PU[15]   (g) PUGL-Net   (h) ground-truth

Fig. 4. Visual comparison at 16× upsampling for image **Tiger** with different methods.

Qualitative Results. Figure 3 shows the qualitative comparison results with upsampling factor of 4×. All compared models are trained on PU1K dataset for a fair comparison. We further show more visual comparison results in Fig. 4 with an upsampling factor of 16×. Specifically, two cropped patches are displayed at the bottom of corresponding images to clearly show the details. It is worth noting that there are 2048 points and 512 points of each input point cloud for the 4× and 16× upsampling factors, respectively. Each ground-truth point cloud has 8196 points.

As shown in the highlighted regions, our proposed method effectively suppresses the visual artifacts in the edge areas and produces more accurate geometric structures. Our method enables to produce uniform dense points with uniform points and low deviations to the underlying object surface. The reconstructed upsampled points can well describe the geometric structures both in 4× and 16× upsampling factors. PU-Net [9] and MPU [11] are prone to produce artifacts with many discrete points. PU-GAN [18] obtained clear geometric structure in some local areas, however, the points distribution is not much uniform. PU-GCN [14] and Dis-PU [15] can achieve better visual results in terms of 4× upsampling factor, however, they have a serious geometric structural loss in the 16× upsampling factor.

Fig. 5. Visual comparison between the results with or without local refinement module at 4× upsampling. The top row and the second row are the results without/with local refinement module respectively.

4.3   Ablation Study

To evaluate the effectiveness of the main components in our model, we designed two ablation studies by adjusting the model structure.

Number of Offset-Attention(OAT) Module. We tested different numbers of OAT layers in the encoder to explore the effect of the transformer encoder on feature extraction. The experimental results are shown in Table 2. When there is no OAT layer, all three evaluation metrics (CD, HD, and p2f) are relatively high. However, the offset-attention module may also be overused. When four layers of OAT are used, the metrics can not achieve the best results.

Table 2. Results comparisons with different numbers of OAT layers.

Number of OAT layers	CD (10^{-3})	HD (10^{-3})	P2F (10^{-3})
0	1.120	9.805	4.248
1	0.57	7.021	2.387
2	**0.526**	**6.586**	**2.080**
3	0.541	6.662	2.182
4	0.556	6.865	2.533

Local Refinement Module. The local refinement module is an important part of our coarse-to-fine structure. We conducted upsampling experiments without local refinement module to test its effectiveness. The experimental results are shown in Table 3. Without local refinement module, the CD, HD, and P2F values increased by 0.08, 0.1, and 1.14, respectively. Moreover, obvious visual changes have been shown in Fig. 5.

Table 3. The results with/without local refinement module.

Local Refinement Module	CD (10^{-3})	HD (10^{-3})	P2F (10^{-3})
Without	0.608	6.681	3.22
With	**0.526**	**6.586**	**2.080**

5 Conclusions

In this work, we present a novel framework PUGL-Net for point cloud upsampling using a coarse-to-fine architecture. It first predicts a coarse high-resolution point cloud via a global dense reconstruction module, and then modifies the coarse output by a local refinement module aggregating the local features. The global dense reconstruction module aims to encode the input points into a new higher dimensional global feature space and achieve the dense reconstruction by feature expansion. Considering the importance of feature extraction, we propose a transformer-based global feature extractor with an offset-attention(OAT) module. We adopt residual learning for the local refinement module to regress the per-point offset. This further adjusts the coarse output to have detail geometric features and more uniformly distributed points. The experimental results demonstrate the superiority of our method over other existing state-of-the-art approaches.

References

1. Chen, X., Ma, H., Wan, J., Li, B., Xia, T.: Multi-view 3D object detection network for autonomous driving. In: IEEE Conference on Computer Vision and Pattern Recognition (CVPR) 2017, pp. 6526–6534 (2017). https://doi.org/10.1109/CVPR. 2017.691
2. Cole, D.M., Newman, P.M.: Using laser range data for 3D SLAM in outdoor environments. In: Proceedings 2006 IEEE International Conference on Robotics and Automation, 2006, ICRA 2006, 2006, pp. 1556–1563 (2006). https://doi.org/10. 1109/ROBOT.2006.1641929
3. Orts-Escolano, S., et al.: Holoportation: virtual 3D teleportation in real-time. In: Proceedings of the 29th Annual Symposium on User Interface Software and Technology, pp. 741–754, January 2016
4. Alexa, M., Behr, J., Cohen-Or, D., Fleishman, S., Levin, D., Silva, C.T.: Computing and rendering point set surfaces. IEEE Trans. Vis. Comput. Graph. **9**(1), 3–15 (2003). https://doi.org/10.1109/TVCG.2003.1175093
5. Huang, H., Wu, S., Gong, M., Cohen-Or, D., Ascher, U., (Richard) Zhang, H.: Edge-aware point set resampling. ACM Trans. Graph. **32**(1), Article 9 (2013)

6. Lipman, Y., Cohen-Or, D., Levin, D., Tal-Ezer, H.: Parameterization-free projection for geometry reconstruction. In: ACM SIGGRAPH 2007 Papers (SIGGRAPH 2007) (2007)
7. Wu, S., Huang, H., Gong, M., Zwicker, M., Cohen-Or, D.: Deep points consolidation. ACM Trans. Graph. **34**(6), Article 176 (2015)
8. Preiner, R., Mattausch, O., Arikan, M., Pajarola, R., Wimmer, M.: Continuous projection for fast L1 reconstruction. ACM Trans. Graph. **33**(4), Article 47 (2014)
9. Yu, L., Li, X., Fu, C.-W., Cohen-Or, D., Heng, P.-A.: EC-net: an edge-aware point set consolidation network. In: Ferrari, V., Hebert, M., Sminchisescu, C., Weiss, Y. (eds.) ECCV 2018. LNCS, vol. 11211, pp. 398–414. Springer, Cham (2018). https://doi.org/10.1007/978-3-030-01234-2_24
10. Yu, L., Li, X., Fu, C., Cohen-Or, D., Heng, P.: PU-Net: point cloud upsampling network. In: IEEE/CVF Conference on Computer Vision and Pattern Recognition 2018, pp. 2790–2799 (2018). https://doi.org/10.1109/CVPR.2018.00295
11. Yifan, W., Wu, S., Huang, H., Cohen-Or, D., Sorkine-Hornung, O.: Patch-based progressive 3D point set upsampling. In: IEEE/CVF Conference on Computer Vision and Pattern Recognition (CVPR) 2019, pp. 5951–5960 (2019). https://doi.org/10.1109/CVPR.2019.00611
12. Li, R., Li, X., Fu, C., Cohen-Or, D., Heng, P.: PU-GAN: a point cloud upsampling adversarial network. In: IEEE/CVF International Conference on Computer Vision (ICCV) 2019, pp. 7202–7211 (2019). https://doi.org/10.1109/ICCV.2019.00730
13. Qian, Y., Hou, J., Kwong, S., He, Y.: PUGeo-Net: a geometry-centric network for 3D point cloud upsampling. In: Vedaldi, A., Bischof, H., Brox, T., Frahm, J.-M. (eds.) ECCV 2020. LNCS, vol. 12364, pp. 752–769. Springer, Cham (2020). https://doi.org/10.1007/978-3-030-58529-7_44
14. Qian, G., Abualshour, A., Li, G., Thabet, A., Ghanem, B.: PU-GCN: point cloud upsampling using graph convolutional networks. In: Proceedings of the IEEE/CVF Conference on Computer Vision and Pattern Recognition (CVPR), pp. 11683–11692, June 2021
15. Li, R., Li, X., Heng, P.-A., Fu, C.-W.: Point cloud upsampling via disentangled refinement. In: Proceedings of the IEEE Conference on Computer Vision and Pattern Recognition (CVPR) (2021)
16. Guo, M.-H.: PCT: point cloud transformer. Computational Visual Media, pp. 187–199 (2021)
17. Shi, W., et al.: Real-time single image and video super-resolution using an efficient sub-pixel convolutional neural network. In: IEEE Conference on Computer Vision and Pattern Recognition (CVPR) 2016, pp. 1874–1883 (2016). https://doi.org/10.1109/CVPR.2016.207
18. Goodfellow, I.J., et al.: Generative Adversarial Networks (2014). arXiv:1406.2661 [stat.ML]
19. Vaswani, A.: Attention is all you need. In: Advances in Neural Information Processing Systems, pp. 5998–6008 (2017)
20. Kingma, D., Ba. Adam, J.: A method for stochastic optimization. In: International Conference on Learning Representations (ICLR) (2015)

Image Analytics

Arbitrary Style Transfer with Adaptive Channel Network

Yuzhuo Wang and Yanlin Geng[(✉)]

State Key Laboratory of ISN, Xidian Univeristy, South Taibai Road 2, Xi'an 710071,
Shaanxi, China
ylgeng@xidian.edu.cn

Abstract. Arbitrary style transfer aims to obtain a brand new stylized image by adding arbitrary artistic style elements to the original content image. It is difficult for recent arbitrary style transfer algorithms to recover enough content information while maintaining good stylization characteristics. The balance between style information and content information is the main difficulty. Moreover, these algorithms tend to generate fuzzy blocks, color spots and other defects in the image. In this paper, we propose an arbitrary style transfer algorithm based on adaptive channel network (AdaCNet), which can flexibly select specific channels for style conversion to generate stylized images. In our algorithm, we introduce a content reconstruction loss to maintain local structure invariance, and a new style consistency loss that improves the stylization effect and style generalization ability. Experimental results show that, compared with other advanced methods, our algorithm maintains the balance between style information and content information, eliminates some defects such as blurry blocks, and also achieves good performance on the task of style generalization and transferring high-resolution images.

Keywords: Arbitrary style transfer · Adaptive channel network · Local structure invariance · Style consistency loss

1 Introduction

Style transfer [8] refers to a technique that uses algorithms to learn artistic styles, which can transform an image into another artistic style while maintaining local structure invariance of the content image. Gatys et al. [8] creatively propose the use of deep convolutional neural networks to complete the transformation from the real image to the stylized image, and call the procedure "style transfer". Following the work of Gatys et al., some researchers propose different style transfer algorithms [3,7,13,17,19]. These methods have a limitation that each model can only convert one style, and thus the model needs to be retrained for other art categories.

Arbitrary style transfer removes this limitation, and can complete any type of real-time conversion through one training session. Some methods [18,21,23]

© Springer Nature Switzerland AG 2022
B. Þór Jónsson et al. (Eds.): MMM 2022, LNCS 13141, pp. 481–492, 2022.
https://doi.org/10.1007/978-3-030-98358-1_38

adjust the statistics of content feature maps to match style features. The WCT [18] proposed by Li et al. uses the whitening transformation method on the feature map extracted from the content image to remove the style information while retaining the content information. Avatar-Net [23] uses the method based on style patches, which maps content features to style patches while maintaining the content structure. AdaIN [10] realizes the transformation of style features by matching the variance and mean of the content feature map.

There are some other methods besides these parametric methods. SANet [21] introduces a self-attention mechanism to learn the semantic relationship between content features and style features by rearranging the feature space. Kotovenko et al. [14] proposed a method to resolve the entanglement of style features and content features, using fixpoint triplet loss and disentanglement loss to complete the control of artistic image generation. The TPFR algorithm [27] proposed by Svoboda et al. uses metric learning to separate content information and style information in the feature space, so as to exchange styles between input and target styles while retaining semantic information, similar to StyleSwap [4]. These methods can usually synthesize images with obvious stylized characteristics, but it is difficult to balance the content structure and style information, and there are some defects in the local structure of the image, such as fuzzy blocks.

In this paper, we propose an arbitrary style transfer algorithm based on an adaptive channel network (AdaCNet). By introducing the AdaCNet module, a new content reconstruction loss to maintain local structure invariance, and a style consistency loss to improve stylized performance, we reduce the appearance of blurry blocks and other bad phenomena. And our algorithm also performs well on style generalization and high-resolution images.

By decoupling the relationship between feature channels and style information through the AdaCNet module, we match the statistical parameters of the specific channel in the content feature map with the style feature map. Our model is based on a generative adversarial network (using InfoGAN [5]): the generator is composed of an encoder, AdaCNet and a decoder, and the discriminator uses the Patch-GAN structure [11]. The training uses adversarial training method (WassersteinGAN-Div [30]) to obtain more realistic stylized pictures. The main contributions of this paper are as follows:

- We propose an arbitrary style transfer algorithm based on AdaCNet, which can select specific channels for style transfer to generate stylized images.
- We design a new content reconstruction loss to maintain the local structure invariance, and a style consistency loss to improve the stylized performance and ability of style generalization. In addition, auxiliary style classification loss is used to enhance the performance of style features.
- Experiments show that our algorithm can flexibly synthesize stylized images, maintain the content structure in the local details of the image, and have rich stylized texture features. Compared with other advanced methods, our algorithm eliminates some defects such as fuzzy blocks and color blocks, and has good performance on style generalization and high-resolution images.

2 Related Work

Arbitrary Style Transfer. The goal of arbitrary style transfer is to convert content images to any given style category, and to balance content information and style information. The current methods can be divided into parametric methods and non-parametric methods. The AdaIN [10] proposed by Huang and Belongie is a typical parameterization method. They found that the mean and variance of the feature map on each channel can represent the style information of the image. By adjusting the mean and variance of the content feature map and matching it to the style feature map, stylized images can be generated flexibly. WCT [18] uses a pair of feature transformations, whitening and coloring to complete the embedding of style information, which has similar characteristics to optimizing the Gram matrix. ETNet [26], SANet [21], disentanglement of content and style [14], and TPFR [27] are recent non-parametric methods. ETNet uses a self-correcting model to predict the current style of errors, and iteratively improve it accordingly. SANet introduces a self-attention mechanism, which uses a learnable similarity core to represent content feature maps to decorate style images. D. The content and style disentanglement method proposed by Kotovenko et al. uses fixpoint triplet loss and disentanglement loss to control the characteristics of stylized images, thereby transforming arbitrary style information. The TPFR algorithm uses metric learning to force the separation of different style information, and uses a two-stage peer-to-peer regularized feature reorganization method in style conversion. And this method can not use pre-trained feature extraction network. In this paper, we use the AdaCNet module based on the parameterization method to decouple the relationship between feature map channels and style features, and select specific channels for statistical parameter matching to generate stylized images.

Generative Adversarial Network. Goodfellow et al. [9] first propose the generative adversarial networks (GAN). The adversarial training between the generator and the discriminator, the generator can generate extremely realistic images, and the discriminator has a strong ability to distinguish between true and false. In this paper, we use the InfoGAN [5] and WGAN-Div [30] structures to make the model converge stably, and at the same time utilizes the prior classification information of the style image to enhance the characteristics of the style image.

3 Our Method

In this paper, we propose an arbitrary style transfer algorithm based on adaptive channel network. The generative adversarial network is used as the overall structure of the network, which is composed of a generator (G) and a discriminator (composed of discriminant network D and auxiliary classification network Q).

In the model, the generator is trained to learn a mapping from content domain to style domain, using training data $P_{data,c} = \{c_i | i = 1 \ldots N\} \subset \mathcal{C}$, $P_{data,s} = \{s_i | i = 1 \ldots M\} \subset \mathcal{S}$ and $P_{data,a} = \{a_i | i = 1 \ldots M\} \subset \mathcal{A}$. Where c_i

and s_i represent the content image and style image respectively, a_i represents the style category information where s_i is located, and N and M are the number of content images and style images in the training set.

Here we use $\mathcal{L}$ to represent the loss function, G^*, D^* and Q^* to represent the weight of G, D and Q. The proposed generative adversarial network is trained by solving the following minimax problem:

$$(G^*, D^*, Q^*) = \arg \min_{G,Q} \max_{D} \mathcal{L}(G, D, Q). \tag{1}$$

In the following, the overall structure of the network and the design of the loss function are described in detail.

3.1   Network Architecture

The overall network framework uses the InfoGAN network structure, combined with the WGAN-Div strategy in training in Fig. 1.

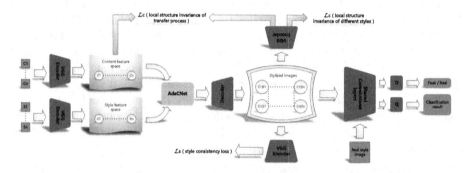

Fig. 1. The structure of the GAN model. **Generator** consists of a pre-trained VGG-19 network, AdaCNet and decoder. **Discriminator** is composed of convolutional layers sharing weights, a discriminating network D and an auxiliary classification network Q.

GAN Architecture. The generator consists of three parts: encoder, AdaCNet and decoder. The encoder (Enc) uses the fixed pre-trained VGG-19 network [25]. The generator takes a content image and an arbitrary style image as input to obtain feature maps, and then the AdaCNet module maps the two feature maps to obtain the target feature map: $t = AdaCNet(Enc(c), Enc(s))$.

The decoder (Dec) generates the target image through the convolutional layers and the up-sampling layers: $G(c, s) = Dec(t)$.

The discriminator part is composed of the discriminant network D and the auxiliary network Q, which are used to distinguish the authenticity of the input image and classify the art category. D uses Patch-GAN structure [11] and does not use sigmoid activation. G shares part of the convolutional layers of D and uses a fully connected network for classification at the end.

AdaCNet Structure. The structure of the AdaCNet module is shown in Fig. 2. In the AdaCNet module, we define a variable $\beta \in \mathbb{R}^c(\beta_i \in \{0, 1\})$, which is adaptively adjusted with the training of the network. By multiplying β and the content feature map, the model will select some specific channels to convert between variance and mean. The AdaCNet module can be expressed by the following formula:

$$t = \sigma(t_s) \cdot \frac{\beta \otimes t_c - \mu(\beta \otimes t_c)}{\sigma(\beta \otimes t_c)} + \mu(t_s) + (1 - \beta) \otimes t_c. \qquad (2)$$

In the above formula, t_s and t_c are used to represent the feature maps $Enc(s)$ and $Enc(c)$ of the style image and content image, respectively. μ and σ represent the variance and mean value of the feature map according to each channel.

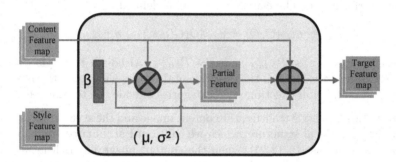

Fig. 2. AdaCNet. The adaptive variable β is used to select a specific channel of the content feature map to complete the conversion of style information.

After the image is convolved, each channel can represent some abstract features. In the previous algorithm [10], the style transfer transformation is performed on each channel of the content image feature map. But in fact, only the features represented by part channels are related to style information.

We select specific channels of the feature map by an adaptive vector parameter β, and update β through the constraints of loss function during training. In fact, AdaCNet decouples the style information and content information of the content feature map, which uses the adaptive parameter β to separate the features represented by each channel of the feature map. Experimental results show that the use of AdaCNet significantly improves the effect of style transfer, while maintaining rich content details, it also has better stylization characteristics.

3.2 Loss Function

In order to make the generative adversarial network converge better and generate more realistic stylized images with rich image details, we define the following loss function $\mathcal{L}(G, D, Q)$:

$$\mathcal{L} = \lambda_{gan}\mathcal{L}_{gan}(G, D) + \lambda_{cla}\mathcal{L}_{cla}(G, Q) + \lambda_{con}\mathcal{L}_{con}(G) + \lambda_{sty}\mathcal{L}_{sty}(G), \qquad (3)$$

where $\mathcal{L}_{gan}(G, D)$ represents the adversarial loss of the WGAN-Div network [30], $\mathcal{L}_{con}(G)$ represents content reconstruction loss, $\mathcal{L}_{sty}(G)$ represents style loss, and $\mathcal{L}_{cla}(G, Q)$ represents auxiliary classification loss.

GAN Loss. For the WGAN-Div network, the loss function is defined as follows:

$$\mathcal{L}_{gan}(G, D) = \mathbb{E}_{c \sim P_{data,c}, s \sim P_{data,s}}[D(G(c, s))] + \mathbb{E}_{s \sim P_{data,s}}[D(s)]$$
$$+ k \cdot \mathbb{E}_{x \sim P_u}[\|\nabla_x D(x)\|^p], \tag{4}$$

where P_u represents the interpolation sampling between the real style image and the generated fake image. Similar to the parameter setting in WGAN-Div, we set the parameters k and p in $\mathcal{L}_{gan}$ as $k = 2$ and $p = 6$.

Classification Loss. We design an auxiliary style classification loss to improve stylized performance. The classification loss is defined as follows:

$$\mathcal{L}_{cla}(G, Q) = \mathbb{E}_{c,s}\|Q(G(c, s_i)) - a_i\|_2, \tag{5}$$

where $c \sim P_{data,c}, s \sim P_{data,s}$ and $a \sim P_{data,a}$. Although the style categories used in training are limited, the experimental results show that the model still has a good conversion effect on style categories outside the training set.

Content Loss. In style transfer, the content image and the stylized image should be consistent in local structure, which we call **local structure invariance**. In previous algorithms [10,18,21], when the content image has rich local details, the generated stylized image loses this local structure invariance and exhibits some bad phenomena such as blurred blocks, color patches and smears. In order to solve these problems, we construct new content reconstruction loss:

$$\mathcal{L}_{con}(G) = \mathbb{E}_{c,s}\|Enc_{relu4\_1}(G(c, s)) - t\|_2 + \mathbb{E}_{c,s}\sum_i \|\overline{Enc_i(G(c, s))} - \overline{Enc_i(c)}\|_2$$
$$+ \mathbb{E}_{c,s}\sum_i \sum_{j \neq k} \|\overline{Enc_i(G(c, s_j))} - \overline{Enc_i(c, s_k)}\|_2, \tag{6}$$

where $t = AdaIN(Enc(c), Enc(s))$, $c \sim P_{data,c}$, $s \sim P_{data,s}$, and $\overline{Enc_i(c)}$ denotes normalized $Enc_i(c)$ on each channel. And each Enc_i denotes a layer in VGG-19, $relu1\_1$, $relu2\_1$, $relu3\_1$ and $relu4\_1$ layers are used in experiments.

The first part of $\mathcal{L}_{con}(G)$ is AdaIN content loss [10]. The second and third parts of $\mathcal{L}_{con}(G)$ are **local structure invariance loss of transfer process** and **local structure invariance loss of different styles**. From the existing methods [2,12,15,20,29], in the task of style transfer, the variance and mean of the image feature map on each channel and the Gram matrix of the image can well represent the style information of the image. From the work of [1, 16,24,28,31] et al., AdaIN style information has a better performance in the optimization process and transfer results. Therefore, after the image is encoded, the normalization operation on the channel of the feature map can effectively remove the style information, so as to better measure the difference in the content structures.

Style Consistency Loss. In addition to using AdaIN style loss, we also define a new style consistency loss, as shown in the following formula:

$$\mathcal{L}_{sty}(G) = \mathbb{E}_{c,s} \sum_i \|\mu(Enc_i(G(c,s))) - \mu(Enc_i(s))\|_2$$

$$+ \mathbb{E}_{c,s} \sum_i \|\sigma(Enc_i(G(c,s))) - \sigma(Enc_i(s))\|_2$$

$$+ \mathbb{E}_{c,s} \sum_i \sum_{j \neq k} \|\mu(Enc_i(G(c_j,s))) - \mu(Enc_i(c_k,s))\|_2$$

$$+ \mathbb{E}_{c,s} \sum_i \sum_{j \neq k} \|\sigma(Enc_i(G(c_j,s))) - \sigma(Enc_i(c_k,s))\|_2, \quad (7)$$

where $c \sim P_{data,c}, s \sim P_{data,s}$.

Intuitively, when different content images are converted into the same style, they should have the same style information. For example, whether it is an oil painting depicting a landscape or an oil painting of a person, it should have the same texture of oil painting. Therefore, we define the **style consistency loss**, as shown in the last two terms of Eq. 7. The style consistency loss enables different content images to have as much common style information as possible when they are converted into one style.

4 Experiments

4.1 Experiments Setting

The model structure of the generative adversarial network proposed in the paper is shown in Fig. 1. The ImageNet dataset [6] is used as the content images and the Wikiart dataset [22] is used as the style images. In the experiment, nearly 100 categories of images are randomly selected as content images in ImageNet, a total of about 130,000 images. After processing the Wikiart dataset, it is divided into 27 categories according to art genres. 21 categories are randomly selected as the style pictures during training, and the remaining 6 categories are used as tests. In the training process, we first resize the content image and style image to 256×256, and then randomly crop an area of 224×224 pixels.

For the parameters in the loss function, we set $\lambda_{gan} = 1$, $\lambda_{cla} = 1$, $\lambda_{con} = 4$ and $\lambda_{sty} = 10$. During training, the Adam optimizer is used, the learning rates of the generator and the discriminator are set to: $lr_G = 1e - 5$, $lr_D = 5e - 5$. Each training batch contains 8 content images and 8 style images, which are trained on two RTX 2080Ti.

4.2 Comparison with Other Methods

In this section, we evaluate our style transfer model from the following aspects and compare it with other advanced methods.

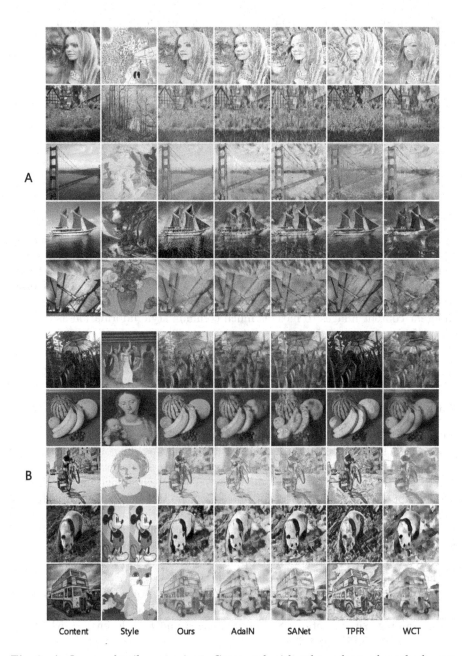

Content   Style   Ours   AdaIN   SANet   TPFR   WCT

Fig. 3. A: Images detail comparison. Compared with other advanced methods, our method generates more detailed artistic images. **B**: Comparison of style generalization ability. The style images come from 6 categories of artistic images randomly selected, which have not appeared in the training set. Our method performs better in these unlearned style categories.

Clearer Image Details. Compared with other methods, our algorithm maintains local construct invariance, and reconstructs the image details more clearly when the content image has a rich local detail structure.

Part A in Fig. 3 shows the comparison between our algorithm and other current methods. It can be seen from the results that other algorithms generate too many meaningless lines and color blocks in the blank areas of the image, and there is a sense of blur in the local details. In the comparison of the first row, our results clearly restore the texture of the hair and transform the style characteristics. In the last line of the picture, our result has the texture of an oil painting and maintains the structural information of the original content image.

Better Style Generalization Ability. Arbitrary style transfer requires the model to learn a general mapping in a limited style category, which can be generalized to arbitrary style category image outside the training set.

In the experiment, the random six categories of style images are not used in training. For these six unlearned styles, the comparison between our method and other current advanced methods is shown part B in Fig. 3.

From the results, it can be found that our method performs better in the category of style images that have not appeared before. In the comparison in the first row, our method generates the correct image color and artistic texture, while the TFPR algorithm [27] generates a large area of irrelevant colors, and other algorithms lose the green of the leaves. In the third row of comparison, the conversion results of other algorithms are blurred, and the image structure has different degrees of distortion.

Content and Style   Ours   AdaIN   SANet   Content and Style   Ours   AdaIN   SANet

Fig. 4. Results at high resolution. The content images in the left group and the right group are 1024 × 1024 pixels and 1536 × 1536 pixels. Our results are clearer in image details.

Results at High Resolution. When the content image has a higher resolution, the comparison of the conversion results is shown in the Fig. 4. Our method better restores the structure of the content image on the better resolution image, and maintains the stylized effect.

In Fig. 4, the resolution of the content pictures in the left group is 1024×1024, and the content pictures in the right group are 1536 × 1536. It is seen that the results in other methods are prone to a large number of fuzzy areas and overlapping lines, but our results are more clear in conversion details.

4.3 Ablation Experiments

In this section, we verify the effectiveness of the proposed AdaCNet module and each loss function through various experiments.

Figure 5 shows the results of the ablation experiment. It can be seen that the AdaCNet module can effectively improve the effect of style transfer, which not only maintains the structure of the image content, but also has obvious styliza-tion characteristics. The content reconstruction loss based on the local structure invariance effectively maintains the local structure of the content image, so that it will not be distorted during the image upsampling process, and avoids the appearance of meaningless fuzzy blocks in the image. Contrary to the loss of content reconstruction, the loss of style consistency makes the generated image not fully retain the characteristics of the content image, but has the character-istics of the style image in terms of graphic texture and color. The additional auxiliary classification loss utilizes the classification information of the art image data set, so that the model has a better performance in the style categories in the training set. Of course, experiments have also proved that this does not weaken the style generalization ability of the model.

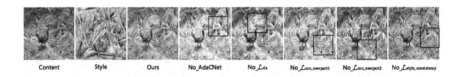

Content   Style   Ours   No_AdaCNet   No_$\mathcal{L}_{da}$ No_$\mathcal{L}_{con\_newpart1}$ No_$\mathcal{L}_{con\_newpart2}$ No_$\mathcal{L}_{style\_consistency}$

Fig. 5. Ablation experiments.

5 Conclusion

In this paper, we proposed an arbitrary style transfer algorithm based on adap-tive channel network, which combines WGAN-Div and InfoGAN structure. The AdaCNet module we proposed can decouple the style information and content information on the feature channel, so that the content structure is restored while still having rich style information (such as image texture, etc.). On this basis, we designed the new content reconstruction loss based on local structure invariance to restore more image content details, and the new style consistency loss to make the image have rich style information. Experimental results show that compared with the current advanced arbitrary style transfer algorithms, our algorithm weighs content structure and style information, eliminates some defects such as fuzzy blocks, and can effectively synthesize stylized images.

References

1. Azadi, S., Fisher, M., Kim, V., Wang, Z., Shechtman, E., Darrell, T.: Multi-content gan for few-shot font style transfer. In: Conference on Computer Vision and Pattern Recognition, pp. 7564–7573 (2018)
2. Bousmalis, K., Silberman, N., Dohan, D., Erhan, D., Krishnan, D.: Unsupervised pixel-level domain adaptation with generative adversarial networks. In: Conference on Computer Vision and Pattern Recognition (CVPR), pp. 95–104 (2017)
3. Chen, D., Yuan, L., Liao, J., Yu, N., Hua, G.: Stylebank: an explicit representation for neural image style transfer. In: Conference on Computer Vision and Pattern Recognition (CVPR), pp. 2770–2779 (2017)
4. Chen, T., Schmidt, M.: Fast patch-based style transfer of arbitrary style. In: NeurIPS (2016)
5. Chen, X., Duan, Y., Houthooft, R., Schulman, J., Sutskever, I., Abbeel, P.: Infogan: interpretable representation learning by information maximizing generative adversarial nets. In: NeurIPS (2016)
6. Deng, J., Dong, W., Socher, R., Li, L., Li, K., Fei-Fei, L.: Imagenet: a large-scale hierarchical image database. In: Conference on Computer Vision and Pattern Recognition, pp. 248–255 (2009)
7. Dumoulin, V., Shlens, J., Kudlur, M.: A learned representation for artistic style. ICLR (2017)
8. Gatys, L.A., Ecker, A.S., Bethge, M.: Image style transfer using convolutional neural networks. In: Conference on Computer Vision and Pattern Recognition (CVPR), pp. 2414–2423 (2016)
9. Goodfellow, I.J., et al.: Generative adversarial nets. In: NeurIPS (2014)
10. Huang, X., Belongie, S.: Arbitrary style transfer in real-time with adaptive instance normalization. In: International Conference on Computer Vision (ICCV), pp. 1510–1519 (2017)
11. Isola, P., Zhu, J., Zhou, T., Efros, A.A.: Image-to-image translation with conditional adversarial networks. In: Conference on Computer Vision and Pattern Recognition (CVPR), pp. 5967–5976 (2017)
12. Jimenez-Arredondo, V.H., Cepeda-Negrete, J., Sanchez-Yanez, R.E.: Multilevel color transfer on images for providing an artistic sight of the world. In: IEEE Access 5, pp. 15390–15399 (2017)
13. Johnson, J., Alahi, A., Fei-Fei, L.: Perceptual losses for real-time style transfer and super-resolution. In: Leibe, B., Matas, J., Sebe, N., Welling, M. (eds.) ECCV 2016. LNCS, vol. 9906, pp. 694–711. Springer, Cham (2016). https://doi.org/10.1007/978-3-319-46475-6_43
14. Kotovenko, D., Sanakoyeu, A., Lang, S., Ommer, B.: Content and style disentanglement for artistic style transfer. In: International Conference on Computer Vision (ICCV), pp. 4421–4430 (2019)
15. Kunfeng, W., Yue, L., Yutong, W., Fei-Yue, W.: Parallel imaging: a unified theoretical framework for image generation. In: 2017 Chinese Automation Congress (CAC), pp. 7687–7692 (2017)
16. Li, N., Zheng, Z., Zhang, S., Yu, Z., Zheng, H., Zheng, B.: The synthesis of unpaired underwater images using a multistyle generative adversarial network. IEEE Access 6, 54241–54257 (2018)
17. Li, Y., Fang, C., Yang, J., Wang, Z., Lu, X., Yang, M.: Diversified texture synthesis with feed-forward networks. In: Conference on Computer Vision and Pattern Recognition (CVPR), pp. 266–274 (2017)

18. Li, Y., Fang, C., Yang, J., Wang, Z., Lu, X., Yang, M.: Universal style transfer via feature transforms. In: Neural Information Processing Systems, vol. 30, pp. 386–396. Curran Associates, Inc. (2017)
19. Li, Y., Wang, N., Liu, J. and Hou, X.: Demystifying neural style transfer. In: Proceedings of the Twenty-Sixth International Joint Conference on Artificial Intelligence, IJCAI-17, pp. 2230–2236 (2017)
20. Liu, M., et al.: Few-shot unsupervised image-to-image translation. In: International Conference on Computer Vision (ICCV), pp. 10550–10559 (2019)
21. Park, D.Y., Lee, K.H.: Arbitrary style transfer with style-attentional networks. In: Conference on Computer Vision and Pattern Recognition (CVPR), pp. 5873–5881 (2019)
22. Phillips, F., Mackintosh, B.: Wiki Art Gallery Inc: a case for critical thinking. Issues Account. Educ. **26**(3), 593–608 (2011)
23. Sheng, L., Lin, Z., Shao, J., Wang, X.: Avatar-net: multi-scale zero-shot style transfer by feature decoration. In: Conference on Computer Vision and Pattern Recognition, pp. 8242–8250 (2018)
24. Shiri, F., Porikli, F., Hartley, R., Koniusz, P.: Identity-preserving face recovery from portraits. In: Winter Conference on Applications of Computer Vision (WACV), pp. 102–111 (2018)
25. Simonyan, K., Zisserman, A.: Very deep convolutional networks for large-scale image recognition. CoRR abs/1409.1556 (2015)
26. Song, C., Wu, Z., Zhou, Y., Gong, M., Huang, H.: Etnet: error transition network for arbitrary style transfer. In: NeurIPS (2019)
27. Svoboda, J., Anoosheh, A., Osendorfer, C., Masci, J.: Two-stage peer-regularized feature recombination for arbitrary image style transfer. In: Conference on Computer Vision and Pattern Recognition (CVPR), pp. 13813–13822 (2020)
28. Vo, D.M., Le, T., Sugimoto, A.: Balancing content and style with two-stream fcns for style transfer. In: Winter Conference on Applications of Computer Vision (WACV), pp. 1350–1358 (2018)
29. Wang, W., Shen, W., Guo, S., Zhu, R., Chen, B., Sun, Y.: Image artistic style migration based on convolutional neural network. In: 2018 5th International Conference on Systems and Informatics (ICSAI), pp. 967–972 (2018)
30. Wu, J., Huang, Z., Thoma, J., Acharya, D., Van Gool, L.: Wasserstein divergence for GANs. In: Ferrari, V., Hebert, M., Sminchisescu, C., Weiss, Y. (eds.) ECCV 2018. LNCS, vol. 11209, pp. 673–688. Springer, Cham (2018). https://doi.org/10.1007/978-3-030-01228-1_40
31. Sheng, L., Lin, Z., Shao, J., Wang, X.: Separating style and content for generalized style transfer. In: Conference on Computer Vision and Pattern Recognition, pp. 8447–8455 (2018)

Fast Single Image Dehazing Using Morphological Reconstruction and Saturation Compensation

Shuang Zheng[1] and Liang Wang[1,2](✉)

[1] Faculty of Information Technology, Beijing University of Technology, Beijing, China
[2] Engineering Research Center of Digital Community, Ministry of Education, Beijing, China
wangliang@bjut.edu.cn

Abstract. Despite having effective dehzing performance, single image dehazing methods based on the dark channel prior (DCP) still suffer from slightly dark dehazing results and oversaturated sky regions. An improved single image dehazing method, which combines image enhancement techniques with DCP model, is proposed to overcome this deficiency. Firstly, it is analyzed that the cause of darker results mainly lies in the air-light overestimation caused by bright ambient light and white objects. Then, the air-light estimation is modified by combining morphological reconstruction with DCP. Next, it is derived that appropriately increasing the saturation component can compensate for transmission underestimate, which can further alleviate the oversaturation. Finally, the image dehazed with modified air-light and transmission is further refined by linear intensity transformation to improve contrast. Extensive experiments validate the proposed method, which is on par with and even outperforms the state-of-the-art methods in subjective and objective evaluation.

Keywords: Single image dehazing · Dark channel prior · Morphological reconstruction · Saturation compensation

1 Introduction

The quality of hazy images captured in bad weather conditions, such as fog and haze, dramatically degrades due to the light scattering caused by suspended particles in the air. The resulting poor visibility, low contrast, and edge blur seriously hinder image-based applications. Therefore, image dehazing, which aims to diminish haze effects in hazy images, has attracted more and more attention.

Early image dehazing methods generally require additional information that is hard to obtain in practice, such as multiple images of the same scene [1] under different weather conditions. A more realistic solution is to diminish haze

---

This work was partially supported by the NSFC under Grant No. 61772050.

B. Þór Jónsson et al. (Eds.): MMM 2022, LNCS 13141, pp. 493–504, 2022.
https://doi.org/10.1007/978-3-030-98358-1_39

using a single image. There are mainly two categories of single image dehazing methods: image enhancement-based and physical model-based. The first category need not consider the reasons for the hazy image degradation. Some of them directly adjust contrast and improve visual effect using image enhancement [2] techniques. However, they often lead to image distortion. The others apply deep convolutional neural networks (CNN) to dehazing [3,4]. Despite obtaining good dehazing results, they demand a large amount of hard-acquired training data.

The second category analyzes the causes of the hazy degradation and establishes the corresponding model to diminish haze. Various priors and hypotheses are applied to modelling the degradation. The dark channel prior (DCP) [5] is the widely used model. To improve computational efficiency, soft matting in [5] is substituted by guided filtering [6] and median filtering [7,8]. However, there is the halo effect [6] and edge information loss [7,8]. Then, the bilateral filtering [9] and multi-scale information [10] are used to optimize the results, while the computational cost increased. Some other methods exploited depth information [11] or image segmentation [12] to dehaze images. However, recovering scene depth from a single image and image segmentation themselves are challenging. Recently, the DCP is re-formulated by the saturation component of the hazy image, then is used to improve dehazing results by iterativley increasing the saturation to prevent transmission under-estimation [13]. Besides, some other priors, such as the color attenuation prior [14], patch recurrence prior [15], color-line [16] and haze-line [17–19], are proposed. In most cases, these methods have an apparent dehazing effect. Unfortunately, when bright ambient light and white objects occur, these methods would overestimate the air-light, which leads to darker dehazing results and oversaturated sky regions.

Few works have noticed this deficiency. To remedy the air-light overestimation caused by directly taking the maximum intensity of hazy image pixels corresponding to the dark channel map's upmost 0.1% brightest pixels as the air-light, soft matting is applied in the DCP method [5]. However, its computational cost significantly increases. Then, Salazar-Colores et al. [20] apply morphological reconstruction to optimize the transmission, which can overcome the deficiency to some extent. However, morphological reconstruction with the fixed size structuring element still couldn't handle large highlight regions, such as the sky. So, an improved single image dehazing method is proposed in this paper. Different from [5,13] and [20], it first detects and removes the dark channel map's highlight regions corresponding to bright ambient light and white objects using image enhancement. Then, the mean intensity of hazy image's pixels corresponding to the upmost 0.1% brightest pixels in the modified dark channel map is taken as the air-light. Besides, the transmission is appropriately increased to compensate for underestimation and optimized with fast guided filtering. The proposed method can effectively improve the air-light overestimation, sky region oversaturation, and computational cost. Extensive experiments validate the proposed method, which is on par with and even outperforms the state-of-the-art methods.

The main contributions of this paper are as follows. 1. An improved image dehazing method combining image enhancement techniques with the physical model is proposed. 2. The morphological reconstruction with an adaptive structuring element is proposed to improve the air-light estimation by removing the dark channel map's regions corresponding to bright ambient light and white objects. 3. The dehazed image's oversaturation, especially in sky regions, is effectively reduced by appropriately increasing and optimizing the transmission.

The rest of this paper is organized as follows. Section 2 introduces the preliminaries. Section 3 presents the proposed method in detail. Section 4 reports the experimental results. Finally, conclusions are given in Sect. 5.

2   Preliminaries

2.1   Hazy Image Formation Model

The widely used hazy image formation model is proposed by Koschmieder [21]

$$\mathbf{I(x)} = t(\mathbf{x}){\cdot}\mathbf{J(x)} + [1 - t(\mathbf{x})]{\cdot}\mathbf{A}. \tag{1}$$

where $\mathbf{x}$ is the pixel coordinates, $\mathbf{I(x)}$, $\mathbf{J(x)}$ and $t(\mathbf{x})$ is the observed intensity, true radiance and transmission of the scene point imaged at $\mathbf{x}$ respectively, and $\mathbf{A}$ is the air-light. The aim of image dehazing is recovering $\mathbf{J}$ from given $\mathbf{I}$.

2.2   Dark Channel Prior

The DCP [5] is a statistical observation of outdoor haze-free images. It shows that most of patches in non-sky regions of outdoor haze-free images have at least one pixel with a very low intensity in one of its color channel (r, g or b), i.e.,

$$\min_{\mathbf{y}\in\Omega(\mathbf{x})}\min_{c\in\{r,g,b\}} \mathbf{J}^c(\mathbf{y}){\rightarrow}0, \tag{2}$$

where $\mathbf{y}$ is a pixel contained in the patch centred in pixel $\mathbf{x}$ in a haze-free image $\mathbf{J}$, $\Omega(\mathbf{x})$. Then, the dark channel map $\mathbf{I}^{dk}$ of a hazy image $\mathbf{I}$ can be defined as

$$\mathbf{I}^{dk}(\mathbf{x}) = \min_{\mathbf{y}\in\Omega(\mathbf{x})}\min_{c\in\{r,g,b\}} \mathbf{I}^c(\mathbf{y}). \tag{3}$$

2.3   Morphological Reconstruction

The closing and opening by reconstruction are used to remove bright ambient light and white objects in the dark channel map to improve the air-light estimation. The closing by reconstruction of size n of an image $\mathbf{I}$ is defined as

$$C_R^{(n)}(\mathbf{I}) = R_{\mathbf{I}}^E(\mathbf{I}\oplus n\mathbf{B}) \tag{4}$$

where $\mathbf{I}\oplus n\mathbf{B}$ denotes n successive grayscale dilations by $\mathbf{B}$, starting with $\mathbf{I}$, and $R_{\mathbf{I}}^E(\mathbf{F})$ denotes the morphological reconstruction by erosion of $\mathbf{I}$ by $\mathbf{F}$

$$\mathbf{R}_{\mathbf{I}}^E(\mathbf{F}) = \mathbf{E}_{\mathbf{I}}^{(k)}(\mathbf{F}) \tag{5}$$

with k such that $\mathbf{E}_\mathbf{I}^{(k)}(\mathbf{F}) = \mathbf{E}_\mathbf{I}^{(k+1)}(\mathbf{F})$. $\mathbf{E}_\mathbf{I}^{(n)}(\mathbf{F})$ is the geodesic erosion of size n,

$$\mathbf{E}_\mathbf{I}^{(n)}(\mathbf{F}) = \mathbf{E}_\mathbf{I}^{(1)}(\mathbf{E}_\mathbf{I}^{(n-1)}(\mathbf{F})) \tag{6}$$

with $\mathbf{E}_\mathbf{I}^{(0)}(\mathbf{F}) = \mathbf{F}$ and $\mathbf{E}_\mathbf{I}^{(1)}(\mathbf{F}) = (\mathbf{F}\ominus\mathbf{B})\vee\mathbf{I}$. Here $\ominus$ denotes the gray erosion and $\vee$ denotes the point-wise maximum operator.

Similarly, the opening by reconstruction of size n of an image $\mathbf{I}$ is defined as

$$O_R^{(n)}(\mathbf{I}) = R_\mathbf{I}^D(\mathbf{I}\ominus n\mathbf{B}) \tag{7}$$

where $\mathbf{I}\ominus n\mathbf{B}$ denotes n successive grayscale erosion by $\mathbf{B}$, starting with $\mathbf{I}$, and $R_\mathbf{I}^D(\mathbf{F})$ denotes the morphological reconstruction by dilation of $\mathbf{I}$ by $\mathbf{F}$

$$R_\mathbf{I}^D(\mathbf{F}) = \mathbf{D}_\mathbf{I}^{(k)}(\mathbf{F}) \tag{8}$$

with k such that $\mathbf{D}_\mathbf{I}^{(k)}(\mathbf{F}) = \mathbf{D}_\mathbf{I}^{(k+1)}(\mathbf{F})$. $\mathbf{D}_\mathbf{I}^{(n)}(\mathbf{F})$ is the geodesic dilation of size n

$$\mathbf{D}_\mathbf{I}^{(n)}(\mathbf{F}) = \mathbf{D}_\mathbf{I}^{(1)}(\mathbf{D}_\mathbf{I}^{(n-1)}(\mathbf{F})) \tag{9}$$

with $\mathbf{D}_\mathbf{I}^{(0)}(\mathbf{F}) = \mathbf{F}$ and $\mathbf{D}_\mathbf{I}^{(1)}(\mathbf{F}) = (\mathbf{F}\oplus\mathbf{B})\wedge\mathbf{I}$. Here $\oplus$ denotes the gray dilation and $\wedge$ denotes the point-wise minimum operator.

3   The Proposed Method

As shown in Fig. 1, our method first estimates the air-light by combining morphological processing with DCP, then refines the transmission using saturation compensation and fast guided filtering, and finally recovers the haze-free image.

3.1   Air-Light Estimation

DCP generally selects the utmost intensity of each color channel of hazy image's pixels corresponding to the upmost 0.1% of brightest pixels in the dark channel as the air-light's component. A majority of existing methods apply this strategy, whereas it often undesirably chooses the intensity of bright ambient light and white objects in the scene as the air-light. To avoid this mistake, we combine the morphological reconstruction with the DCP to correctly estimate the air-light.

Firstly, the dark channel map of the input hazy image, $\mathbf{I}^{dk}$, can be computed by Eq.(2). Next, the closing by morphological reconstruction is applied to the minimal channel map $\mathbf{I}^{min}(\mathbf{y}) = \min\limits_{c\in\{r,g,b\}} \mathbf{I}^c(\mathbf{y})$ to remove small dark objects.

$$\mathbf{I}^{cr}(\mathbf{x}) = C_\mathbf{R}^{(n)}(\mathbf{I}^{min}(\mathbf{x})), \tag{10}$$

where the dilation structuring element $\mathbf{B}$ is a square of size 15×15.

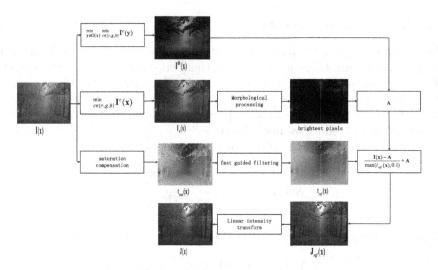

Fig. 1. Flowchart of the proposed method.

Next, the opening by reconstruction with an adaptive structuring element is applied to $\mathbf{I}^{cr}(\mathbf{x})$ to remove small bright objects.

$$\mathbf{I}^{or}(\mathbf{x}) = O_R^{(n)}(\mathbf{I}^{cr}(\mathbf{x})). \tag{11}$$

Here, an adaptive structuring element is applied, which is a square with the side length adaptively varying with the hazy image size, $\max\{40, \mathrm{ceil}(0.1\max(w, h))\}$, where w and h is the width and height of the hazy image.

Then, the pixels corresponding to bright ambient light and white objects in the scene, which leads to the air-light estimation mistakes, can be expressed as

$$\mathbf{I}^{hl}(\mathbf{x}) = \mathbf{I}^{cr}(\mathbf{x}) - \mathbf{I}^{or}(\mathbf{x}). \tag{12}$$

Generally, Eq.(13) only detects large highlight regions corresponding to bright ambient light and white objects. To obtain small highlight regions, dilation is applied to $\mathbf{I}^{hl}(\mathbf{x})$. Denote the obtained image of highlight regions as $\mathbf{I}^{rm}(\mathbf{x})$, we have

$$\mathbf{I}^{rm}(\mathbf{x}) = \mathbf{I}^{hl}(\mathbf{x}) \oplus \mathbf{B}. \tag{13}$$

After that, the dark channel map, $\mathbf{I}^{dk}$, is refined by removing highlight regions $\mathbf{I}^{rm}(\mathbf{x})$,

$$\mathbf{I}^{dk}(\mathbf{x}) = \mathbf{I}^{dk}(\mathbf{x}) - \mathbf{I}^{rm}(\mathbf{x}). \tag{14}$$

Finally, the mean intensity of hazy image's pixels corresponding to the upmost 0.1% of brightest pixels in the refined dark channel map is taken as the air-light $\mathbf{A}$.

3.2   Transmission Estimation

The bright ambient light and white objects in the scene often lead to the air-light overestimation and transmission underestimation, which further results in the dehazed image oversaturation. The transmission is analyzed using the saturation component by converting the hazy image into HSV color space to overcome this deficiency. It is found that an appropriate increase of saturation can increase transmission and reduce oversaturation.

In HSV color space, the saturation component is

$$S(\mathbf{I}(\mathbf{x})) = 1 - \frac{\min\limits_{c\in\{r,g,b\}}(\mathbf{I}^c(\mathbf{x}))}{\max\limits_{c\in\{r,g,b\}}(\mathbf{I}^c(\mathbf{x}))}. \tag{15}$$

Take the saturation component on both sides of Eq.(1) and simplify it. We have

$$t(\mathbf{x}) = \frac{\mathbf{A} - (1 - S(\mathbf{x})(\mathbf{I}^c(\mathbf{x}))) * \max\limits_{c\in\{r,g,b\}}(\mathbf{I}^c(\mathbf{x}))}{\mathbf{A} - \min\limits_{c\in\{r,g,b\}}(\mathbf{J}^c(\mathbf{x}))}. \tag{16}$$

The transmission is generally constant in a small neighbourhood. The actual transmission can be computed by taking the minimal in a small neighbourhood on both sides of Eq.(16),

$$\tilde{t}_{act}(\mathbf{x}) = \frac{\mathbf{A} - \max\limits_{c\in\{r,g,b\}}(\mathbf{I}^c(\mathbf{x})) * \min\limits_{y\in\Omega(\mathbf{x})}(1 - S(\mathbf{y}))}{\mathbf{A} - \min\limits_{y\in\Omega(\mathbf{x})}(\min\limits_{c\in\{r,g,b\}}(\mathbf{J}^c(\mathbf{y})))}. \tag{17}$$

From Eq.(2), the estimated transmission follows

$$\tilde{t}_{est}(\mathbf{x}) = \frac{\mathbf{A} - \max\limits_{c\in\{r,g,b\}}(\mathbf{I}^c(\mathbf{x})) * \min\limits_{y\in\Omega(\mathbf{x})}(1 - S(\mathbf{y}))}{\mathbf{A}}. \tag{18}$$

Since $\min\limits_{y\in\Omega(\mathbf{x})}(\min\limits_{c\in\{r,g,b\}}(\mathbf{J}^c(\mathbf{y})))\geq 0$ holds, $\tilde{t}_{est}\leq\tilde{t}_{act}$, i.e., the estimated transmission will be lower than the actual one. It results in a darker dehazed image with blurred details. If the saturation component of the hazy image, $S(\mathbf{I}^c)$, increases, the corresponding transmission will also increase. Therefore, the transmission can be appropriately compensated by increasing the hazy image's saturation to increase the overall brightness of dehazed image.

By taking into account both the increasing of saturation and the computational efficiency, we take the following rectified linear function to increase the saturation,

$$S_1(\mathbf{x}) = \min(S(\mathbf{I}^c(\mathbf{x})) * \alpha + \beta, 1), \tag{19}$$

where S_1 is the increased saturation of the hazy image, α and β are positive parameters. α can slightly refine the range of S_1. β can adjust the overall intensity of S_1. If β is too large, S_1 will be excessively increased, which leads to the dehazed image oversaturation rather than effective haze removing. On the contrary, the increase of S_1 will be too slight to effectively remove the halo and oversaturation. In this paper, two positive parameters are empirically set as

$$
\alpha = \begin{cases} 0.7 & mean\_S \geq 0.2 \\ 2.3 & 0.2 > mean\_S \geq 0.1 \, , \\ 0.3 & others \end{cases} \tag{20}
$$

and $\beta = 0.3$ respectivelly, where $mean\_S$ is the mean of $S(\mathbf{I}^c)$. Then, the improved transmission is

$$
t_{coa}(\mathbf{x}) = \frac{\mathbf{A} - \max_{c \in \{r,g,b\}} (\mathbf{I}^c(\mathbf{x})) * (1 - S_1(\mathbf{x}))}{\mathbf{A}}. \tag{21}
$$

Finally, the fast guided filtering (FGF) [22] is used to further optimize the transmission to remove noise and maintain edges in the field with discontinuous depth.

$$
t_{ref} = FGF(t_{coa}). \tag{22}
$$

3.3 Image Dehazing

Once the air-light and transmission are obtained, the image can be dehazed according to the atmosphere scattering model,

$$
\mathbf{J}(\mathbf{x}) = \frac{\mathbf{I}(\mathbf{x}) - \mathbf{A}}{max(t_{ref}(\mathbf{x}), 0.1)} + \mathbf{A}. \tag{23}
$$

In order to further increase the dynamic range and the contrast between the foreground and the background, and make the distribution of the intensity more uniform, it is necessary to perform linear intensity transformation to stretch the intensity range. First, pixels with the 0.1% lowest and highest intensity are pruned, then the intensity of remaining pixels are normalized to [0,1]. Denote the pruned image is $\mathbf{J}_{crop}(\mathbf{x})$, then the normalized formula is

$$
\mathbf{J}(\mathbf{x}) = \frac{\mathbf{J}_{crop}(\mathbf{x}) - min(\mathbf{J}_{crop}(\mathbf{x}))}{max(\mathbf{J}_{crop}(\mathbf{x})) - min(\mathbf{J}_{crop}(\mathbf{x}))}. \tag{24}
$$

The proposed method can be summarized as the following Algorithm 1.

4 Experiments

A series of experiments are performed on open datasets with different lighting conditions and haze concentration ranges, such as RESIDE (REalistic Single-Image DEhazing) [23], and Weizmann dataset [15], to verify our method. Except for subjective evaluation on dehazing results, some objective evaluation indices are also used, such as SSIM, PSNR, and NIQE. To make comparisons, He [6], Zhu [14], Salazar [20], Zhao [10], Berman [19], Cai [4] and Lu [13] are also performed.

Algorithm 1

Input: hazy image $\mathbf{I}(\mathbf{x})$

1. Calculate the dark channel image $\mathbf{I}^{dk}(\mathbf{x})$ via Eq.(3);
2. Refine the dark channel image $\mathbf{I}^{dk}(\mathbf{x})$ via Eq.(14) by removing highlight regions;
3. Calculate the air-light $\mathbf{A}$ with the refined $\mathbf{I}^{dk}(\mathbf{x})$;
4. Refine the saturation $S(\mathbf{I}(\mathbf{x}))$ cacluated by Eq.(15) to obtain $S_1(\mathbf{x})$ via Eq.(19);
5. Improve the coarse transmission $t_{coa}(\mathbf{x})$ caculated by Eq.(21) with the fast guided filtering;
6. Restore the coarse scene radiance $\mathbf{J}(\mathbf{x})$ via Eq.(23);
7. Refine $\mathbf{J}(\mathbf{x})$ via Eq.(24);

Output: dehazed image $\mathbf{J}(\mathbf{x})$

Fig. 2. Dehazing results of 2 images randomly selected from RESIDE. For each row, the image corresponds to the ground truth, hazy image, result of He [6], Zhu [14], Salazar [20], Zhao [10], Berman [19], Cai [4], Lu [13] and our method from left to right.

4.1 Experiments with Synthetic Data

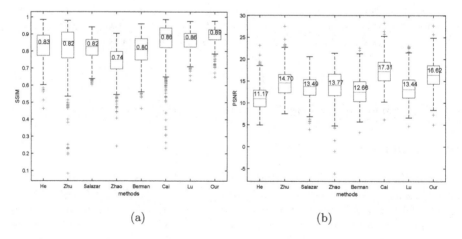

(a)   (b)

Fig. 3. Objective results on RESIDE. (a) The SSIM. (b) The PSNR.

Table 1. Runtimes of different methods (seconds).

Methods	Image size (pixels)			
	460×620	550×410	1024×768	4288×2848
He [6]	2.36	1.83	5.8	97.61
Zhu [14]	4.42	3.42	12.62	519.93
Salazar [20]	0.44	0.38	0.56	7.31
Zhao [10]	2.34	1.97	7.02	173.13
Berman [19]	6.22	4.32	10.14	512.05
Cai [4]	2.56	2.1	6.87	251.10
Lu [13]	0.04	0.03	0.11	1.66
Our method	0.45	0.44	0.71	7.44

To assess the proposed method, we randomly select 500 synthetic outdoor images from the RESIDE dataset [23]. Figure 2 shows the dehazing results of 2 randomly selected images among them. It can be seen that the proposed method has better subjective visual effect of dehazing. It can effectively reduce the halo effect in oversaturated sky regions and discontinuous depth fields while retains true color and more details. For further objective assessment, the structural similarity (SSIM) and peak signal-to-noise ratio (PSNR) of each method on all 500 dehazed images are computed and shown in Fig. 3 (a) and (b), respectively. A higher SSIM value indicates a better result and a higher PSNR also indicates a better result. From the median value of SSIM and PSNR shown as the red midline within each box and the mean of SSIM and PSNR indicated by the number within each box, it can be seen that the proposed method has the best SSIM and the second-best PSNR, where only the deep learning-based method, Cai [4], has slightly better PSNR. From the quartile range, i.e., the blue rectangle, it can be seen that the proposed method has the most compact quartile range. So it is the most robust. In addition, it can be seen from the numbers of outliers, i.e., red cross outside of the blue rectangle, that the proposed method has more generalization ability.

Besides, the mean runtimes of these methods for different size images on our computer with a 3.00 GHz CPU and 8 GB memory are reported in Table 1. As shown in Table 1, although our method is inferior to the method of Lu [13] and Salazar [20] on operation time, it is superior to other methods and on par with the fast dehazing method, the method of Salazar [20]. Considering that our method has a better subjective and objective dehazing effect than the method of Lu [13] and Salazar [20], it has the better overall performance than the state-of-the-arts.

4.2 Experiments with Natural Images

The Weizmann dataset [15] consists of 40 images of various natural scenes, which also provides the ground truth of the air-light. As shown in Fig. 4(a), the

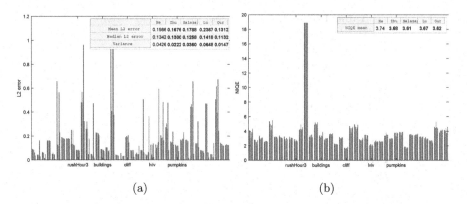

(a)   (b)

Fig. 4. Results on Weizmann dataset. (a) The L_2 errors of the air-light estimation. (b) The NIQE of dehazing images.

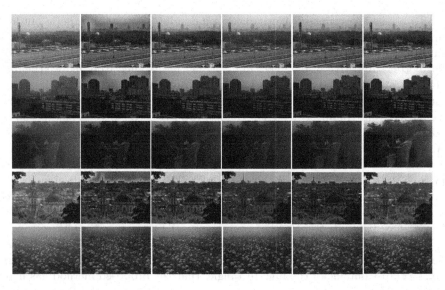

Fig. 5. Some dahazing results on Weizmann dataset. For each row, the image corresponds to the hazy image, result of He [6], Zhu [14], Salazar [20], Lu [13] and our method from left to right.

estimated air-light is quantitively evaluated by the L_2 errors relative to the ground truth, where a lower L_2 error indicates that the result is closer to the ground truth. Here, only results of the methods of He [6], Zhu [14], Salazar [20] and Lu [13], which show the better overall performance in the above experiments with synthetic data, are used to make a comparison. It can be seen that our method has the least L_2 errors in terms of all the mean, median and variance of L_2 errors.

All images are further dehazed. Some of them are shown in Fig. 5. We can see that the proposed method has the best subjective visual effect. Since there is no ground truth, the natural image quality evaluator (NIQE) is used to objectively evaluate dehazing results, where a smaller NIQE value indicates better dehazing result. As Fig. 4(b) shown, the method of Salazar [20] has the smallest NIQE and the proposed method is on a par with the method of Salazar [20] on NIQE. So the proposed method has a good dehazing effect. Considering both the quality of the air-light estimation and that of the dehazing results, the proposed method has the best overall performance, which is entirely consistent with the conclusion of experiments with synthetic data.

5 Conclusion

Although existing single image dehazing methods have obtained apparent dehazing results, the problem is that dehazing images are darker, and sky regions are oversaturated due to the inaccurate air-light and transmission estimation. An improved single image dehazing method based on image enhancement techniques and DCP prior is proposed to alleviate this problem. Extensive experiments on synthetic and real image data validate the proposed method. It can effectively reduce the halo effect in oversaturated sky regions and discontinuous depth fields while retains true color and more details. It is on par with and even better than most of the state-of-the-arts on the overall performance.

References

1. Shwartz, S., Namer, E., Schechner, Y.: Blind haze separation. In: Proceedings IEEE Conference on Computer Vision and Pattern Recognition, pp. 1984–1991. New York, NY, USA (2006)
2. Kim, T., Paik, J., Kang, B.: Contrast enhancement system using spatially adaptive histogram equalization with temporal filtering. IEEE Trans. Consum. Electron. 44(1), 82–87 (1998)
3. Ren, W., Pan, J., et al.: Single image dehazing via multi-scale convolutional neural networks with holistic edges. Int. J. Comput. Vis. 128, 240–259 (2020)
4. Cai, B., Xu, X., et al.: DehazeNet: an end-to-end system for single image haze removal. IEEE Trans. Image Process. 25(11), 5187–5198 (2016)
5. He, K., Tang, X.: Single image haze removal using dark channel prior. IEEE Trans. Pattern Anal. Mach. Intell. 33(12), 2341–2353 (2011)
6. He, K., Tang, X.: Guided image filtering. IEEE Trans. Pattern Anal. Mach. Intell. 35(6), 1397–1409 (2013)
7. Tarel, J., Hautiere, N.: Fast visibility restoration from a single color or gray level image. In: Proceedings International Conference on Computer Vision, pp. 2201–2208. Kyoto, Japan (2009)
8. Tarel, J., Hautiere, N., et al.: Vision enhancement in homogeneous and heterogeneous fog. IEEE Intell. Transp. Syst. Mag. 4(2), 6–20 (2012)
9. Tomasi, C., Manduchi, R.: Bilateral filtering for gray and color images. In: Proceedings of International Conference on Computer Vision, pp. 839–846. Bombay, India (1998)

10. Zhao, D., Xu, L., et al.: Multi-scale optimal fusion model for single image dehazing. Sig. Process. Image Commun. **74**, 253–265 (2019)
11. Liu, Q., Gao, X., He, L., Lu, W.: Single image dehazing with depth-aware nonlocal total variation regularization. IEEE Trans. Image Process. **27**(10), 5178–5191 (2018)
12. Salazar-Colores, S., Moya-Sanchez, E., et al.: Fast single image defogging with robust sky detection. IEEE Access **8**, 149176–149189 (2020)
13. Lu, Z., Long, B., Yang, S.: Saturation based iterative approach for single image Dehzing. IEEE Sig. Process. Lett. **27**, 665–669 (2020)
14. Zhu, Q., Mai, J., Shao, L.: A fast single image haze removal algorithm using color attenuation prior. IEEE Trans. Image Process. **24**(11), 3522–3533 (2015)
15. Bahat, Y., Irani, M.: Blind dehazing using internal patch recurrence. In: Proceedings of IEEE International Conference on Computational Photography, pp. 1–9. Evanston, IL, USA (2016)
16. Fattal, R.: Dehazing using color-lines. ACM Trans. Graph. **34**(1), 13 (2014)
17. Berman, D., Treibitz, T., Avidan, S.: Non-local image dehazing. In: Proceedings of IEEE Conference on Computer Vision and Pattern Recognition, pp. 1674–1682. Las Vegas, NV, USA (2016)
18. Berman, D., Treibitz, T., Avidan, S.: Air-light estimation using haze-lines. In: Proceedings of IEEE International Conference on Computational Photography, pp. 1–9. Stanford, CA, USA (2017)
19. Berman, D., Treibitz, T., Avidan, S.: Single image dehazing using haze-lines. IEEE Trans. Pattern Anal. Mach. Intell. **42**(3), 720–734 (2020)
20. Salazar-Colores, S., Cabal, E., et. al.: A fast image dehazing algorithm using morphological reconstruction. IEEE Trans. Image Process. **28**(5), 2357–2366 (2019)
21. Koschmieder, H.: Theorie der horizontalen sichtweite. Beitrage zur Physik der freien Atmosphare, pp. 33–53 (1924)
22. He, K., Sun, J.: Fast guided filter. arXiv **1505**, 00996 (2015)
23. Li, B., Ren, W., et al.: Benchmarking single image dehazing and beyond. IEEE Trans. Image Process. **28**(1), 492–505 (2019)

One-Stage Image Inpainting with Hybrid Attention

Lulu Zhao[1], Ling Shen[2(✉)], and Richang Hong[1]

[1] School of Computer Science and Information Engineering, Hefei University of
Technology, Hefei 230601, China
luluzhao@mail.hfut.edu.cn
[2] School of Internet, Anhui University, Hefei 230039, China

Abstract. Recently, attention-related image inpainting methods have
achieved remarkable performance. They reconstruct damaged regions
based on contextual information. However, due to the time-consuming
two-stage coarse-to-fine architecture and the single-layer attention manner, they often have limitations in generating reasonable and fine-detailed
results for irregularly damaged images. In this paper, we propose a
novel one-stage image inpainting method with a Hybrid Attention Module (HAM). Specifically, the proposed HAM contains two submodules,
namely, the Pixel-Wise Spatial Attention Module (PWSAM) and the
Multi-Scale Channel Attention Module (MSCAM). Benefit from these,
the reconstructed image features in spatial dimension can be further
optimized in channel dimension to make inpainting results more visually realistic. Qualitative and quantitative experiments on three public
datasets show that our proposed method outperforms state-of-the-art
methods.

Keywords: Image inpainting · Contextual information · Hybrid
attention

1 Introduction

Image inpainting is an important research hotspot in computer vision and graphics communities. It refers to synthesizing the missing or damaged parts of an
image with a plausible hypothesis. This task can be utilized in many practical
applications such as photo editing, object removal, and so on [1,4,15]. Despite
decades of studies, synthesizing not only visually realistic but semantically plausible pixels for the missing regions still remains challenging.

Existing methods for image inpainting roughly fall into two categories,
namely, traditional and learning-based methods. Traditional image inpainting
methods [1–4] mostly attempt to borrow contents or textures from surroundings
to fill the missing regions. In particular, the PatchMatch [1], iteratively searches
for best-matching image patches from non-hole regions. However, traditional
methods often have difficulty in producing semantically reasonable predictions
due to the insufficient ability to obtain high-level semantics.

© Springer Nature Switzerland AG 2022
B. Þór Jónsson et al. (Eds.): MMM 2022, LNCS 13141, pp. 505–517, 2022.
https://doi.org/10.1007/978-3-030-98358-1_40

In recent years, with the development of convolutional neural networks (CNNs), learning-based methods have achieved remarkable success in computer vision tasks, especially in image inpainting. Pathak et al. [15] propose a Context Encoder (CE) algorithm, which utilizes a simple encoder-decoder pipeline connected by a channel-wise fully-connected layer. It can generate semantically meaningful contents for rectangular holes located around the center of the image, but it cannot handle irregularly damaged images properly. To solve this problem, Liu et al. [11] and Yu et al. [23] replace the standard convolutions in the encoder-decoder network with partial convolutions and gated convolutions, respectively. Although these learning-based methods can generate semantically plausible results, they fail to effectively utilize contextual information. Thus, they often generate boundary artifacts, distorted structures, or blurry textures inconsistent with surrounding areas.

Inspired by the traditional PatchMatch methods, some recent researchers introduce spatial attention mechanisms to image inpainting and propose a series of attention-related methods [12,20,22]. For example, Yu et al. [22] propose a contextual attention layer to model long-term correlations between distant contextual information and the hole regions. However, these attention-related methods only use spatial attention in feature space. In fact, the importance of the spatial-reconstructed feature maps is variant for different channels. In addition, most of them use a time-consuming two-stage coarse-to-fine network with a fixed-scale attention layer. They have insufficient ability to perceive and reconstruct both structure and texture information.

To overcome the above limitations, we propose a novel end-to-end image inpainting method with a Hybrid Attention Module (HAM) (see Fig. 1). In which, we adopt the P-UNet as the backbone. It is a U-Net [16] structure with partial convolution layers [11]. Partial convolutions can capture the local information around the damaged irregular holes accurately and fill them appropriately. Meanwhile, a new Hybrid Attention Module (HAM) is proposed to generate fine-detailed textures and structures for missing regions following a Reconstruction-to-Optimization strategy. Similar to the Convolutional Block Attention Module (CBAM) [19], the HAM combines a spatial attention module named Pixel-Wise Spatial Attention Module (PWSAM) and a channel attention module named Multi-Scale Channel Attention Module (MSCAM) (see Fig. 2). The former contains a pixel-wise Contextual Attention layer [22]. The latter consists of four groups of dilated convolutions [21] and a Coordinate Attention [6] operation embedded the positional information. Specifically, the PWSAM perceives contextual information and performs multi-scale missing contents reconstruction in feature space. The MSCAM concatenate them with the original features in channel dimension for further optimization in an adaptive manner. Besides, the PatchGAN [9] discriminator and the pre-trained VGG-16 feature extractor [18] are combined to obtain more realistic details.

Qualitative and quantitative experiments are conducted on standard datasets Paris StreetView [5], CelebA-HQ [10], and Places2 [26]. The experiments results demonstrate that our method can generate more visually realistic and structurally coherent results. The main contributions of this paper are summarized as follows:

- A learnable attention-based inpainting method with a Reconstruction-to-Optimization strategy is presented. It is more effective to perceive and reconstruct image content in an adaptive manner.
- We propose a novel hybrid attention module containing a pixel-wise spatial attention submodule and a multi-scale channel attention submodule. It can produce image content with exquisite details by exploiting multi-scale contextual information in both spatial and channel space.
- A joint loss function is used to obtain more detailed inpainting results. The experiments on three public benchmark datasets demonstrate the superiority of our method.

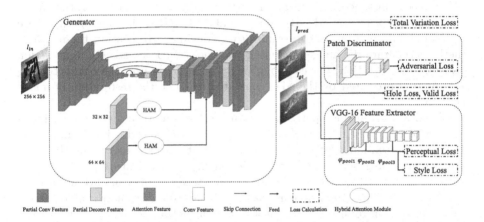

Fig. 1. Overall architecture of our proposed model.

2 Related Works

2.1 Image Inpainting

In the literature, existing image inpainting methods can generally be divided into two categories: traditional methods and learning-based methods.

Traditional Methods. Traditional image inpainting methods are mainly based on the correlation between pixels and the similarity of contents for prediction, which can be broadly classified into diffusion-based and patch-based methods. The former [2,3] generate locally smooth results by propagating known information to the holes based on the boundary information. The latter [1,4] assume that the missing regions of damaged images can be represented by known patches. They fill the missing region by globally searching for the image patches with the highest similarity to the missing regions. However, due to the difficulty in capturing high-level semantics, the performance of traditional methods is still limited when dealing with damaged images in large proportion.

Learning-Based Methods. Learning-based image inpainting methods generate pixels for the holes by using deep learning strategies. Context Encoders [15] is the first to adopt an encoder-decoder network and the adversarial training strategy for image inpainting. Later, Iizuka et al. [8] add global and local discriminators to the encoder-decoder network to ensure the global and local consistency of the generated images. Shen et al. [17] involve a densely skip connection in a battery of symmetric encoder-decoder groups to extract more semantics. However, these methods are limited to generating reasonable predictions for rectangular missing regions and produce poor results when processing irregularly masked images. To address this limitation, PConv [11] and GatedConv [23] replace the standard convolutions with partial convolutions and gated convolutions, respectively, and improve the performance of inpainting models effectively. Moreover, to address the mean and variance shifts in existing inpainting networks, RN [24] replaces instance normalization with two region-wise normalization modules, namely, basic RN (RN-B) and learnable RN (RN-L). Some methods use structural information as constraints to guide image inpainting tasks. These methods separate the image inpainting task into two parts: structure prediction and image completion. For example, EdgeConnect [14] uses the complete edge information predicted by the edge generator to guide the restoration of image contents.

Besides, introducing spatial attention mechanisms to use contextual information of the damaged images effectively is also a powerful inpainting strategy. These attention-related methods are dedicated to reconstructing the missing regions (foreground) by searching for highly similar feature patches in the surroundings (background). Yu et al. [22] propose a contextual attention layer (CA) to explicitly borrow similar feature patches from distant spatial locations. Liu et al. [12] introduce a coherent semantic attention layer (CSA), which not only considers the correlation between distant contextual information and the hole regions but also considers the coherency inside the hole regions. Yi et al. [20] adopt the idea of CA [22] and propose a contextual residual aggregation mechanism, which borrows not only features but also residuals from contexts. These methods utilize a two-stage architecture and restore damaged images in a coarse-to-fine manner. Although they improve the quality of texture details, they consume more time compared to one-stage approaches.

2.2   Channel Attention Mechanism

The channel attention mechanism has been widely used in object detection, scene segmentation, and classification tasks due to its remarkable effectiveness in enhancing the representation power of CNNs [6,7,19]. It allows the model to focus more on the most informative channel features and suppress those that are not important. Representative channel attention modules mainly include SE-Net [7], CBAM [19], and Coordinate Attention [6]. SE-Net simply squeezes each 2D feature map to build interdependencies between the channels efficiently. CBAM further advances this idea by sequentially applying channel and spatial attention modules. Later, Coordinate Attention embeds positional information into channel attention to efficiently capture positional information and channel-wise relationships.

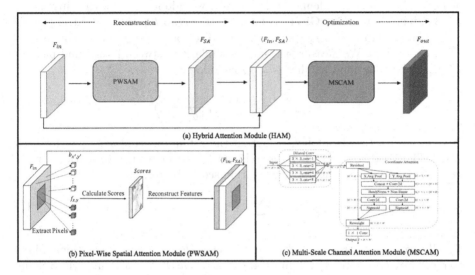

Fig. 2. The architecture of Hybrid Attention Module (HAM) and its two submodules.

3 Approach

3.1 Overall Architecture

The overall architecture of our proposed one-stage end-to-end inpainting model is shown in Fig. 1. We adopt the P-UNet with symmetrical encoder-decoder structure as the backbone of the generator, which has been shown effective in processing irregularly damaged images. Considering the computing resources and quality of inpainted results, the proposed Hybrid Attention Module (HAM) is added to the third-to-last and fourth-to-last layers in the decoding network to make use of multi-layer contextual information effectively. A pre-trained VGG-16 feature extractor [18] and a Patch-GAN discriminator with spectral normalization [13] are used to ensure more realistic detail generation.

3.2 Hybrid Attention Module

The HAM is proposed to make full use of multi-scale contextual information. It is composed of a pixel-wise spatial attention module (PWSAM) and a multi-scale channel attention module (MSCAM) (see Fig. 2(a)). The details of them are as follows.

Pixel-Wise Spatial Attention Module. As shown in Fig. 2(b), the PWSAM reconstructs missing image content based on the spatial attention mechanism. In order to avoid using misleading or even incorrect attention information and achieve the similarity calculation effectively, we adopt 1×1 patches instead of 3×3 patches in CA [22]. Given an input feature map F_{in}, we first extract pixels (1×1 patches) in the background (unmasked regions) and reshape them as convolutional filters. We measure the cosine similarity between foreground patches $\{f_{x,y}\}$ and background patches $\{b_{x',y'}\}$ as follows:

$$s_{x,y,x',y'} = \left\langle \frac{f_{x,y}}{\|f_{x,y}\|}, \frac{b_{x',y'}}{\|b_{x',y'}\|} \right\rangle \tag{1}$$

A softmax function is applied to obtain the attention score $s^*_{x,y,x',y'}$ for each pixel. Then, we adopt a left-right followed by a top-down propagation with a kernel size of k to propagate the attention scores better:

$$s'_{x,y,x',y'} = \sum_{i,j\in\{-k,...,k\}} s^*_{x+i,y+j,x'+i,y'+j} \tag{2}$$

Finally, we reuse extracted background patches $\{b_{x',y'}\}$ as deconvolutional filters to reconstruct the foreground (masked regions). We then concatenate the original feature maps F_{in} and the reconstructed feature maps F_{SA} as $\langle F_{in}, F_{SA} \rangle$.

Multi-Scale Channel Attention Module. The structure of the MSCAM is shown in Fig. 2(c). It combines four groups of dilated convolutions [21] with different rates and a Coordinate Attention operation [6] to optimize the concatenated feature maps $\langle F_{in}, F_{SA} \rangle$. Specifically, we feed $\langle F_{in}, F_{SA} \rangle$ into the dilated convolutions block with different rates (rate = 1, 2, 4, 8) to extract multi-scale contextual information and increase receptive fields. The aggregated multi-scale feature maps are expressed by $f_{dilated}(\langle F_{in}, F_{SA} \rangle)$. Considering the different influence of image features in channel dimension for image inpainting, we borrow the idea of Coordinate Attention [6], which embeds positional information into channel attention. It can merge the feature maps in an adaptive manner while preserving positional information, which is essential for capturing spatial structures of images. The process of the Coordinate Attention block can be divided into three steps, namely, 1) coordinate information embedding, 2) coordinate attention generation, and 3) channel reweighting. We use $f_{coor}()$ to represent the Coordinate Attention operation. Moreover, the pixel-wise convolution operation is used to match the channel number to the original channel number in the end of the MSCAM. The final output of our MSCAM can be expressed as $F_{out} = f_{conv}(f_{coor}(f_{dilated}(\langle F_{in}, F_{SA} \rangle)))$.

3.3   Loss Functions

Perceptual Loss and Style Loss. Perceptual loss and style loss are used to maintain high-level structure and style consistency. We calculate perceptual loss

$L_{perceptual}$ and style loss L_{style} by comparing feature maps $\phi_{pool_i}^{gt}$ from ground truth I_{gt} with feature maps $\phi_{pool_i}^{pred}$ from generated images I_{pred}. ϕ_{pool_i} is the feature map from the ith pooling layer of the pre-trained VGG-16 network.

$$L_{perceptual} = \mathbb{E}\left[\sum_{i=1}^{N}\left\|\phi_{pool_i}^{gt} - \phi_{pool_i}^{pred}\right\|_1\right] \tag{3}$$

$$L_{style} = \mathbb{E}\left[\sum_{i=1}^{N}\left\|G\left(\phi_{pool_i}^{gt}\right) - G\left(\phi_{pool_i}^{pred}\right)\right\|_1\right] \tag{4}$$

where G means the Gram matrix on the feature maps, $G(\phi) = \phi^T\phi$.

Adversarial Loss. Considering the task of irregularly masked image inpainting where there may be multiple holes with any shape at any location, we use a Patch-GAN discriminator [9] to evaluate whether each image patch belongs to the real or fake distribution. Spectral normalization is used in the discriminator to stabilize the training [13]. The adversarial loss L_{adv} can enhance the detailed expression of images and make the generated images visually more realistic.

Total Variation Loss. Total variation loss is introduced to eliminate the checkboard artifacts and enhance the spatial smoothness of the generated images. We calculate the total variation loss as follows:

$$L_{tv} = \mathbb{E}\left[\sum_{x,y}\left(\|m_{x,y} - m_{x+1,y}\|_1 + \|m_{x,y} - m_{x,y+1}\|_1\right)\right] \tag{5}$$

where $m_{x,y}$ refers to the pixel value at location (x,y) of damaged regions.

Hole Loss and Valid Loss. Hole loss L_{hole} and valid loss L_{valid} which calculate L1 differences in the damaged regions and undamaged regions respectively are also used in our model.

$$L_{hole} = \mathbb{E}\left[\sum_{i,j,k}\left\|p_{i,j,k}^{gt\_hole} - p_{i,j,k}^{pred\_hole}\right\|_1\right] \tag{6}$$

$$L_{valid} = \mathbb{E}\left[\sum_{i,j,k}\left\|p_{i,j,k}^{gt\_valid} - p_{i,j,k}^{pred\_valid}\right\|_1\right] \tag{7}$$

where i,j,k represent the height, width, and channel of the generated image and ground truth, respectively.

Overall Loss. In summary, our overall loss functions are expressed as follows:

$$L_{overall} = \lambda_{perceptual}L_{perceptual} + \lambda_{style}L_{style} + \lambda_{adv}L_{adv} + \lambda_{tv}L_{tv}$$
$$+\lambda_{hole}L_{hole} + \lambda_{valid}L_{valid} \qquad (8)$$

4   Experiments

We evaluate our model and the comparison methods on Paris Sreetview [5], CelebA-HQ [10], and Places2 [26] datasets. For masks, we use irregular mask dataset from the work of PConv [11] and augment these irregular masks by introducing four rotations ($0°$, $90°$, $180°$, $270°$). All the masks and images for training and testing are with the size of 256×256. We first use 2×10^{-4} as our initial learning rate to train our model with a batch size of 6 and then we finetune our model with a learning rate of 5×10^{-5}. The Adam Optimizer [25] is used to optimize our generator and discriminator. For the hyper-parameters, we choose 0.05, 120, 0.1, 0.1, 6, 1 for $\lambda_{perceptual}$, λ_{style}, λ_{adv}, λ_{tv}, λ_{hole}, λ_{valid} respectively. All models are trained with PyTorch framework on two GTX 1080 Ti GPUs. We compare our approach with four state-of-the-art methods including Contextual Attention (CA) [22], Partial Convolutions (PConv) [11], EdgeConnect (EC) [14], and Region Normalization (RN) [24].

5   Results

5.1   Qualitative Comparisons

Figure 3 presents the qualitative comparison results on Paris StreetView, CelebA-HQ, and Places2 datasets. As shown in Fig. 3, the CA can roughly restore the contents of the masked regions, but distorted structures, blurry textures, and artifacts are obvious. The results of the PConv are generally good, but the boundaries of masked regions are not recovered well, and visible distortions around the mask boundaries are very severe. As for EC, it can produce results extremely similar to the ground truth on Paris StreetView dataset. However, some broken or blurred edges are observed on CelebA-HQ dataset. RN can generate reasonable structures and style, while it cannot generate detailed textures, such as the walls, hair, and patterns. Our method can significantly reduce the checkerboard artifacts and distorted structures and provide more detailed textures compared with these state-of-the-art methods. Especially on CelebA-HQ dataset, our method generates better details and more visually realistic face images.

5.2   Quantitative Comparisons

We also compare our model with comparison methods quantitatively. Here, we adopt the commonly used metrics, namely, L1 loss, peak signal-to-noise ratio (PSNR), and structural similarity index (SSIM) for quantitative comparisons.

Meanwhile, the inference time metrics is used to evaluate time consumption. Table 1 lists the quantitative comparison results on Places2 and CelebA-HQ datasets. Our method ranks second on L1 and PSNR metrics and performs best on SSIM metrics on Places2 dataset. For CelebA-HQ dataset, our method has almost the best performance. Although the RN method performs the best on L1 and PSNR metrics on Places2 dataset, its inpainting results are very blurred and far inferior to our method in terms of texture details (see Fig. 3). Besides, compared with CA, an attention-related inpainting model that uses a two-stage coarse-fine architecture, the inference time for our one-stage model is significantly shorter.

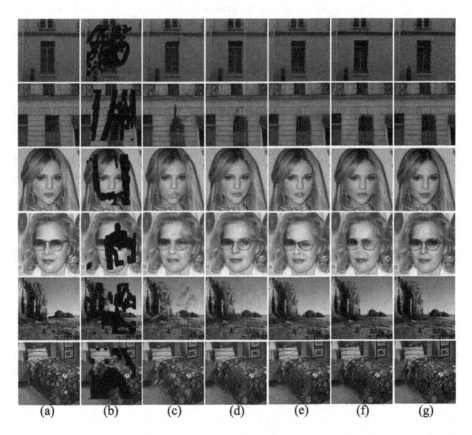

(a)   (b)   (c)   (d)   (e)   (f)   (g)

Fig. 3. Qualitative comparison results. From Left to right are: (a) Ground truth, (b) Masked image, (c) CA, (d) PConv, (e) EC, (f) RN, (g) Ours. First and second rows are results of Paris StreetView, third and fourth are results of CelebA-HQ, fifth and sixth are results of Places2.

Table 1. Quantitative results on Places2 and CelebA-HQ datasets. -Lower is better. +Higher is better.

Metrics	Mask ratio	Places2					CelebA-HQ				
		CA	PConv	EC	RN	Ours	CA	PConv	EC	RN	Ours
L1(%)-	20–30%	4.04	2.82	2.85	**2.08**	2.79	3.98	**1.49**	1.55	1.70	1.70
	30–40%	7.22	4.15	4.09	**3.13**	4.08	5.64	2.76	2.61	2.63	**2.55**
	40–50%	9.32	5.61	5.64	**4.68**	5.56	7.35	3.69	3.84	3.62	**3.59**
PSNR+	20–30%	21.03	23.59	23.71	**24.98**	24.34	22.01	27.90	27.69	28.33	**28.42**
	30–40%	19.15	21.88	21.94	**22.73**	22.66	19.96	26.59	26.76	26.98	**27.10**
	40–50%	17.79	20.46	20.48	**20.62**	20.60	18.38	24.51	24.84	25.01	**25.22**
SSIM+	20–30%	0.779	0.803	0.858	0.867	**0.889**	0.819	0.936	0.928	0.930	**0.945**
	30–40%	0.698	0.735	0.800	0.804	**0.826**	0.751	0.890	0.897	0.900	**0.910**
	40–50%	0.592	0.665	0.732	0.738	**0.753**	0.676	0.839	0.846	0.857	**0.865**
Time-(ms)	/	22.39	/	/	/	**7.96**	/	/	/	/	/
User study+	30–40%	2.03	3.73	4.16	3.96	**4.25**	/	/	/	/	/

5.3   User Study

In order to compare each method at the human visual level, we conduct human evaluation via user study. In which, 20 participants are asked to vote for 20 inpainted images with the mask ratio of 30–40% from Places2 dataset. The evaluation criteria are poor, fair, satisfactory, good,or excellent assigned with the score range from 1 to 5. Table 1 shows that our method outperforms the others based on human evaluation.

5.4   Ablation Studies

We conduct some experiments to analyze the effectiveness of the proposed HAM and its two submodules, the PWSAM and MSCAM. We remove the entire HAM, the MSCAM, and the PWSAM in our model, respectively. Figure 4 shows the inpainting results of each experiment on Paris StreetView dataset. From Fig. 4, we can see: (1) the texture details in masked regions can be repaired well by using the PWSAM; (2) the structural distortion phenomenon can be significantly improved by using the MSCAM; (3) our model with the proposed HAM can generate reasonable and fine-detailed results. Table 2 lists the quantitative results of each model with the mask ratio of 30–40%.

(a) Masked image   (b) w/o HAM   (c) w/o MSCAM   (d) w/o PWSAM   (e) Ours

Fig. 4. Qualitative results of ablation experiments on Paris StreetView dataset.

Table 2. Quantitative results of ablation experiments on Paris StreetView dataset.

Model	w/o HAM	w/o MSCAM	w/o PWSAM	Ours
PSNR/SSIM	24.77/0.811	25.01/0.820	25.46/0.836	**25.97/0.848**

6 Conclusion

In this paper, we propose a novel one-stage architecture with multi-scale hybrid attention layers for irregularly masked image inpainting. The hybrid attention layer combines two attention mechanisms to exploit multi-scale image contextual information and optimize feature representation in spatial dimension and channel dimension effectively. Extensive quantitative and qualitative comparisons demonstrate the superiority of the proposed method in both performance and efficiency.

Acknowledgement. This work was supported in part by the National Natural Science Foundation of China (Grant 61932009).

References

1. Barnes, C., Shechtman, E., Finkelstein, A., Goldman, D.B.: Patchmatch: a randomized correspondence algorithm for structural image editing. ACM Trans. Graph. **28**(3), 24 (2009)
2. Bertalmio, M., Sapiro, G., Caselles, V., Ballester, C.: Image inpainting. In: Proceedings of the 27th Annual Conference on Computer Graphics and Interactive Techniques, pp. 417–424 (2000)
3. Bertalmio, M., Vese, L., Sapiro, G., Osher, S.: Simultaneous structure and texture image inpainting. IEEE Trans. Image Process. **12**(8), 882–889 (2003)
4. Criminisi, A., Pérez, P., Toyama, K.: Region filling and object removal by exemplar-based image inpainting. IEEE Trans. Image Process. **13**(9), 1200–1212 (2004)

5. Doersch, C., Singh, S., Gupta, A., Sivic, J., Efros, A.: What makes paris look like paris? ACM Trans. Graph. **31**(4), 103–110 (2012)

6. Hou, Q., Zhou, D., Feng, J.: Coordinate attention for efficient mobile network design. In: Proceedings of the IEEE/CVF Conference on Computer Vision and Pattern Recognition, pp. 13713–13722 (2021)

7. Hu, J., Shen, L., Sun, G.: Squeeze-and-excitation networks. In: Proceedings of the IEEE Conference on Computer Vision and Pattern Recognition, pp. 7132–7141 (2018)

8. Iizuka, S., Simo-Serra, E., Ishikawa, H.: Globally and locally consistent image completion. ACM Trans. Graph. (ToG) **36**(4), 1–14 (2017)

9. Isola, P., Zhu, J.Y., Zhou, T., Efros, A.A.: Image-to-image translation with conditional adversarial networks. In: Proceedings of the IEEE Conference on Computer Vision and Pattern Recognition, pp. 1125–1134 (2017)

10. Karras, T., Aila, T., Laine, S., Lehtinen, J.: Progressive growing of gans for improved quality, stability, and variation. arXiv preprint arXiv:1710.10196 (2017)

11. Liu, G., Reda, F.A., Shih, K.J., Wang, T.C., Tao, A., Catanzaro, B.: Image inpainting for irregular holes using partial convolutions. In: Proceedings of the European Conference on Computer Vision (ECCV), pp. 85–100 (2018)

12. Liu, H., Jiang, B., Xiao, Y., Yang, C.: Coherent semantic attention for image inpainting. In: Proceedings of the IEEE/CVF International Conference on Computer Vision, pp. 4170–4179 (2019)

13. Miyato, T., Kataoka, T., Koyama, M., Yoshida, Y.: Spectral normalization for generative adversarial networks. arXiv preprint arXiv:1802.05957 (2018)

14. Nazeri, K., Ng, E., Joseph, T., Qureshi, F.Z., Ebrahimi, M.: Edgeconnect: Generative image inpainting with adversarial edge learning. arXiv preprint arXiv:1901.00212 (2019)

15. Pathak, D., Krahenbuhl, P., Donahue, J., Darrell, T., Efros, A.A.: Context encoders: feature learning by inpainting. In: Proceedings of the IEEE Conference on Computer Vision and Pattern Recognition, pp. 2536–2544 (2016)

16. Ronneberger, O., Fischer, P., Brox, T.: U-Net: convolutional networks for biomedical image segmentation. In: Navab, N., Hornegger, J., Wells, W.M., Frangi, A.F. (eds.) MICCAI 2015. LNCS, vol. 9351, pp. 234–241. Springer, Cham (2015). https://doi.org/10.1007/978-3-319-24574-4_28

17. Shen, L., Hong, R., Zhang, H., Zhang, H., Wang, M.: Single-shot semantic image inpainting with densely connected generative networks. In: Proceedings of the 27th ACM International Conference on Multimedia, pp. 1861–1869 (2019)

18. Simonyan, K., Zisserman, A.: Very deep convolutional networks for large-scale image recognition. arXiv preprint arXiv:1409.1556 (2014)

19. Woo, S., Park, J., Lee, J.Y., Kweon, I.S.: Cbam: convolutional block attention module. In: Proceedings of the European Conference on Computer Vision (ECCV), pp. 3–19 (2018)

20. Yi, Z., Tang, Q., Azizi, S., Jang, D., Xu, Z.: Contextual residual aggregation for ultra high-resolution image inpainting. In: Proceedings of the IEEE/CVF Conference on Computer Vision and Pattern Recognition, pp. 7508–7517 (2020)

21. Yu, F., Koltun, V.: Multi-scale context aggregation by dilated convolutions. arXiv preprint arXiv:1511.07122 (2015)

22. Yu, J., Lin, Z., Yang, J., Shen, X., Lu, X., Huang, T.S.: Generative image inpainting with contextual attention. In: Proceedings of the IEEE Conference on Computer Vision and Pattern Recognition, pp. 5505–5514 (2018)

23. Yu, J., Lin, Z., Yang, J., Shen, X., Lu, X., Huang, T.S.: Free-form image inpainting with gated convolution. In: Proceedings of the IEEE/CVF International Conference on Computer Vision, pp. 4471–4480 (2019)
24. Yu, T., et al.: Region normalization for image inpainting. In: Proceedings of the AAAI Conference on Artificial Intelligence, vol. 34, pp. 12733–12740 (2020)
25. Zhang, Z.: Improved adam optimizer for deep neural networks. In: 2018 IEEE/ACM 26th International Symposium on Quality of Service (IWQoS), pp. 1–2. IEEE (2018)
26. Zhou, B., Lapedriza, A., Khosla, A., Oliva, A., Torralba, A.: Places: A 10 million image database for scene recognition. IEEE Trans. Pattern Anal. Mach. Intell. **40**(6), 1452–1464 (2017)

Real-Time FPGA Design for OMP Targeting 8K Image Reconstruction

Jiayao Xu, Chen Fu, Zhiqiang Zhang, and Jinjia Zhou[✉]

Graduate School of Science and Engineering, Hosei University, Tokyo, Japan
zhou@hosei.ac.jp

Abstract. During the past decade, implementing reconstruction algorithms on hardware has been at the center of much attention in the field of real-time reconstruction in Compressed Sensing (CS). Orthogonal Matching Pursuit (OMP) is the most widely used reconstruction algorithm on hardware implementation because OMP obtains good quality reconstruction results under a proper time cost. OMP includes Dot Product (DP) and Least Square Problem (LSP). These two parts have numerous division calculations and considerable vector-based multiplications, which limit the implementation of real-time reconstruction on hardware. In the theory of CS, besides the reconstruction algorithm, the choice of sensing matrix affects the quality of reconstruction. It also influences the reconstruction efficiency by affecting the hardware architecture. Thus, designing a real-time hardware architecture of OMP needs to take three factors into consideration. The choice of sensing matrix, the implementation of DP and LSP. In this paper, a sensing matrix, which is sparsity and contains zero vectors mainly, is adopted to optimize the OMP reconstruction to break the bottleneck of reconstruction efficiency. Based on the features of the chosen matrix, the DP and LSP are implemented by simple shift, add and comparing procedures. This work is implemented on the Xilinx Virtex UltraScale+ FPGA device. To reconstruct a digital signal with 1024 length under 0.25 sampling rate, the proposal method costs 0.818 μs while the state-of-the-art costs 238 μs. Thus, this work speedups the state-of-the-art method 290 times. This work costs 0.026s to reconstruct an 8K gray image, which achieves 30FPS real-time reconstruction.

Keywords: Compressed Sensing · Reconstruction Algorithm · Orthogonal matching pursuit (OMP) · Field Programmable Gate Array (FPGA) · Real-Time Reconstruction

1 Introduction

Nowadays, digital signals, such as images, connect with people's life closely. The traditional method to obtain the digital signals is based on the Nyquist-Shannon sampling theory. This theory indicates that to sample the digital signals, the

The original version of this chapter has been revised. The measurement matrix has been updated as "Walsh matrix". A correction to this chapter can be found https://doi.org/10.1007/978-3-030-98358-1_50

© Springer Nature Switzerland AG 2022, corrected publication 2024
B. Þór Jónsson et al. (Eds.): MMM 2022, LNCS 13141, pp. 518–529, 2022.
https://doi.org/10.1007/978-3-030-98358-1_41

digital sampling frequency must be at least twice the highest frequency of the original analog signal. This leads to numerous redundancy in the digital signals and requires considerable storage. Thus, compression is an essential procedure after sampling. With the development of the technology, this method of compression after sampling can not meet the requirements of the explosive growth of digital signals.

To sample the digital signal, in the same time, compress it, the D Donoho, E Candes, T Tao and other scientists proposed a theory named Compressed Sensing (CS) [3] in 2006. Compressed Sensing guarantees that signals can be reconstructed effectively with few samples far less than Nyquist-Shannon theory requires. Different from the traditional method, the compression procedure of Compressed Sensing is just a simple linear projection while the reconstruct procedure is much complicated. Hence, the choice of the reconstruction algorithm is crucial to the reconstruction efficiency and quality.

Orthogonal Matching Pursuit (OMP) [12] is one of the classic reconstruction algorithms in Compressed Sensing, which can achieve good quality results in a shorter time. Recently, implementing OMP on Field Programmable Gate Array (FPGA) to achieve real-time reconstruction has gained attention from researchers. The reconstruction procedure of OMP includes Dot Product (DP) and Least Square Problem (LSP). DP is applied by the vector-based multiplications mainly. LSP has division calculations and numerous vector-based multiplications. Because of the limitation of the hardware, division calculations demand a big overhead and need to be avoided. Thus, implementing LSP is the key difficulty for implementing OMP on hardware.

Many methods are proposed to substitute the LSP. In the relevant literature, there are two main approaches, the Cholesky decomposition method [2,8] and the QR decomposition [1,10,11]. The first OMP on FPGA framework was designed by Septimus and Steinberg [9] in 2010. They used the Cholesky decomposition to prevent division calculations. But, the Cholesky decomposition has high computation complexity, the QR decomposition was proposed to overcome this problem. Because QR decomposition contains square root calculation, Ge et al. [5] presented a Square-Root-Free QR Decomposition method to decline the reconstruction time.

Besides the works illustrated above, to decrease the reconstruction time, other methods are adopted by the existing works. Li et al. [6] presented an approach using Gram-Schmidt Orthogonalization to substitute the LSP calculations in the iterations of reconstruction. In this method, the LSP is only be used once in the reconstruction procedure. Fardad et al. [4] proposed a deterministic matrix to replace the random matrix to decrease the reconstruction difficulty and save the hardware cost.

Because of the complexity of the image signals, most of existing works are sparsity signal based, only several works [1,10,11] verified their works on natural images. However, none of them achieves real-time image reconstruction when the image size is bigger than 1080p.

Not only the reconstruction algorithm but also the sensing matrix is a key point that affects the reconstruction quality. The sensing matrix also influences the reconstruction efficiency by affecting the design of hardware architecture.

Thus, choosing a proper sensing matrix is also a key point for hardware implementation.

To fulfill the goal of real-time image reconstruction, the main contributions of this paper include the following aspects.

1. In the proposed architecture, a sensing matrix obtained by multiplying the Walsh matrix with the Fast Walsh-Hadamard transform matrix is adopted. This chosen sensing matrix is sparse and includes zero vectors mainly. And the reconstruction results by this sensing matrix has good quality.
2. Based on the features of the chosen sensing matrix, the DP and LSP are applied by simple add, shift and comparing calculations to replace the complicated vector-based multiplications and division calculations.
3. Because the image signals are complicated, to guarantee the quality of the reconstructed results, the sparsity level of this architecture is not set as a certain value but in a range.
4. This proposed architecture achieves the real-time reconstruction of 8k 30FPS under 0.25 sampling rate.

2   Background

2.1   Compressed Sensing (CS)

Assuming the length of original image signal X is $N * 1$. Using a transform matrix marked as ψ with the size of $N * N$, transforming the original signal to the transform domain to gain the sparse signal called θ with the size of $N * 1$. Sparse means, in the signal, there are only a few elements are non-zero elements. The sparsity level is marked as k. Projecting the original signal on the measurement matrix ϕ, then the compressed signal Y called measurements is obtained. The size of measurement matrix is $M * N$, the size of signal Y is $M * 1$. The relationship between k, M, N is $K << M < N$. The M/N represents the sampling rate. Multiplying the measurement matrix with the transform matrix is the sensing matrix A. The theory of CS is as Eq. 1 shows.

$$Y = \phi_{M*N} X_{N*1} = \phi_{M*N} \psi_{N*N} \theta_{N*1} = A_{M*N} \theta_{N*1} \tag{1}$$

Compressed Sensing has two main principles. One is the sparsity of the original signals. This means the signal is compressible. The other one is incoherence. The measurement matrix with the transform matrix should have incoherence. The incoherence ensures the possibility of reconstructing the original. In other words, the sensing matrix, which is gained by multiplying the measurement matrix with the transform matrix, determines the quality of the reconstruction results. Thus, choosing proper sensing matrix is important.

2.2   Orthogonal Matching Pursuit (OMP)

Orthogonal Matching Pursuit (OMP) is a reconstruction algorithm that belongs to the greedy algorithm. To reconstruct the original image signal, OMP first uses

Dot Product to find the index of the column vector of the sensing matrix with the highest contribution, then puts this index into the index set. After that, the column vectors in the index set are used to approximate the original signal and update the residual. Both the procedure of approximating the original signal and the procedure of updating the residual include the Least Square Problem. The procedure of OMP reconstruction is as follows:

a. Initialize the residual $r_0 = Y$, the iteration counter $t = 1$, the index set $S_0 = \emptyset$.
b. Find the index of the highest contribution column vector of the sensing matrix. $Index_t = argmax|A^T * r_{t-1}|$.
c. Update the index set $S_t = S_{t-1} \cup Index_t$.
d. Use Least Square Problem to approximate the original signal. $\hat{\theta} = (A_S^T * A_S)^{-1}A_S^T * Y$
e. Judge if satisfy the quit condition or not. If yes, go to g. If not, go to f.
f. Update residual. $r_t = Y - A_S * \hat{\theta}$, then go back to b.
g. Inverse the approximate signal to obtain the reconstructed image signal. $\hat{X} = \psi_{N*N} * \hat{\theta}$.

OMP is an iteration-based reconstruction algorithm. If the reconstruction procedure satisfies the quit condition, the approximation signal will multiply with the transform matrix to obtain the reconstructed image signal. The iteration time is usually regarded as the sparsity level of the signal in the transform domain. But the sparsity is unknown for practical image reconstruction. If the iteration time is too long, the reconstruction time will be considerable. If the iteration time is too less, the quality of the result will be worse. Thus, the strategy of the quit condition is crucial in the design.

3 Proposals

3.1 Chosen Matrices and Features of Sensing Matrix

In this work, the Walsh matrix is adopted as the measurement matrix, the Fast Walsh-Hadamard transform matrix is chosen as the transform matrix. The sensing matrix A, which is used in the reconstruction procedure, is as the Eq. 2 and Fig. 1 shows.

$$A(i,j) = \begin{cases} 2*V, i=j=1 \\ V, i=j \cup i=1 \cap j \neq 1 \\ 0, others \end{cases} \tag{2}$$

In the Eq. 2, the value of V changes with the different choices of M and N. Especially, the range of i is $0 < i \leq M$, the range of j is $0 < j \leq N$. It is easy to find that when $j > M$, $A(i,j)$ is zero. That is, if the vector index is bigger than M, the column vectors are all zero vectors. Besides, the non-zero column vectors of the chosen sensing matrix are sparse vectors, which contain zero elements mainly. Based on these features, the Dot Product and Least Square Problem are optimized further to reduce the time cost to achieve the aim of real-time reconstruction.

16	0	0	0	0	0	0	0	0	0	0	0	0	0	0	0
8	8	0	0	0	0	0	0	0	0	0	0	0	0	0	0
8	0	8	0	0	0	0	0	0	0	0	0	0	0	0	0
8	0	0	8	0	0	0	0	0	0	0	0	0	0	0	0

Fig. 1. An example of sensing matrix ($M = 4$, $N = 16$, Sampling rate is 0.25)

3.2 Optimized Dot Product

This subsection introduces the optimized Dot Product implementation. The Dot Product is used to find the index of the highest contribution column vector of the sensing matrix. The original calculation is illustrated in Eq. 3.

$$Index = argmax|A^T * r| \qquad (3)$$

Because the column vectors with index bigger than M are all zero vectors, the vector-based multiplication results of these vectors are zero. Hence, the Dot Product in Eq. 3 is optimized as Eq. 4 shows.

$$result_{DP} = A^T_{j,j=1..M} * r \qquad (4)$$

In addition, the column vectors from 1 to M are sparse vectors, the calculation in Eq. 3 can be revised further. Deleting the calculations of zero elements, the Dot Product calculation is as Eq. 5 shows.

$$result_{DP}(j) = V * \begin{cases} 2 * y_1 + y_2 + ... + y_M, j = 1 \\ y_j, 1 < j \leq M \end{cases} \qquad (5)$$

After obtaining the result of the Dot Product, this result will be sort to find the index of the highest contribution column vector of the sensing matrix. This sort procedure is implemented by 2-to-1 comparison calculation. As Eq. 5 presents, there is a common divisor in the result of Dot Product. The multiplication with this common divisor, which is represented as V in Eq. 5, can be deleted to save both time and hardware cost.

$$Index = argmax|result_{DP}(j)| \qquad (6)$$

$$result_{DP}(j) = \begin{cases} 0, j = 1 \\ y_j, 1 < j \leq M \end{cases} \qquad (7)$$

Because in the first iteration, the residual is equals to the measurements, and the values of measurements are positive numbers, the $result_{DP}(1)$ must be the biggest value. That is, the $Index$ of the first iteration must be 1. In OMP, all of the column vectors only can be chosen once. Based on these conditions, in the first iteration, the procedure in Eq. 3 is omitted, the result of *Index* in the first iteration is set as 1 and the $result_{DP}(1)$ in other iterations is set as 0. The implemented procedure of finding the index of the highest contribution column vector is as Eq. 6, Eq. 7 present.

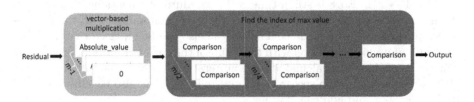

Fig. 2. Finding the index of the highest contribution column vector

Figure 2 shows the diagram of the implemented procedure when the iteration index is bigger than 1. First, the first element of the residual is set as 0, other elements are set as its absolute value. Then using the 2 to 1 comparison to find the biggest value. Last, outputting the index of the biggest value.

3.3   Optimized Least Square Problem

This subsection introduces the optimized Least Square Problem (LSP). The LSP is the key point at both residual update in the iteration and the original signal approximation after quitting the iteration. The calculation of LSP is as Eq. 8 shows.

$$\hat{\theta} = (A_S^T * A_S)^{-1} A_S^T * Y \qquad (8)$$

As mentioned in Sect. 3.1, the A_S contains sparse column vectors. Hence, in the vector-based multiplication of $A_S^T * A_S$, only several situations, which are illustrated in Eq. 9, get non-zero results.

$$Result_{Non-zero} = \begin{cases} A_S^T(1) * A_S(j), \\ A_S^T(j) * A_S(j), & 1 < j \le M \\ A_S^T(j) * A_S(1), \end{cases} \qquad (9)$$

Marking the $A_S^T * A_S$ as $Result_{matrix}$, the Eq. 10 shows the equation of $Result_{matrix}$.

$$Result_{matrix}(i,j) = \begin{cases} P, i = j = 1 \\ Q, i = 1 \cap j \ne 1 \\ Q, j = 1 \cap i \ne 1 \\ Q, i = j \cap i = j \ne 1 \end{cases} \qquad (10)$$

The range of i is $1 \le i \le index_{iteration}$, the range of j is $1 \le j \le index_{iteration}$. The $index_{iteration}$ represents the iteration index. The value of P and Q depends on the iteration index.

Because the value of matrix $Result_{matrix}$ is certain in each iteration, the value of $Result_{matrix}^{-1}$ is certain too. Hence, the complicated inverse calculation is substituted as using a Look Up Table (LUT) to find the value of $Result_{matrix}^{-1}$ of each iteration. But the inverse value leads to fractional numbers which is hard to implement in hardware, shifting the input is indispensable.

The $A_S^T * Y$ in Eq. 8 is still a time cost procedure. As mentioned in Sect. 2.2, the index set S unions the max index of the current iteration with the indexes stored in the previous iterations. The $A_S^T * Y$ also can be replaced by combining the result of previous iteration with the result of the current iteration. So only the new result of $A_S^T * Y$ is calculated in each iteration. Besides, the column vectors of A_S^T are sparsity, so the vector-based multiplication can also be substituted by the simple shift and add calculations.

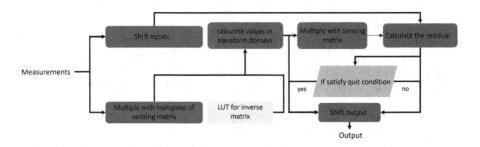

Fig. 3. The implementation of the Least Square Problem

The implementation details of the Least Square Problem is as Fig. 3 shows. First, multiply measurements with the transpose of sensing matrix. Then multiply it with the inverse matrix, which is stored as LUTs, to obtain the approximate signals in transform domain. Next, multiply the approximate signals in transform domain with the sensing matrix. After that, use the shift measurements to update the residual. Judge if meets the quit condition or not. If yes, output the shift value of the approximate signals in transform domain. If not, output the shift values of updated residual.

3.4   Overall Framework

Figure 4 shows the overall architecture of this work. As illustrated in Sect. 3.2, the first iteration of the reconstruction omits the Dot Product procedure. The result of the Dot Product in the first iteration is defaulted as 1. So the reconstruction procedure of this work starts from LSP to update the residual. In the LSP, if the quit condition is satisfied, LSP will output a flag named *reconstruction_finish* and the shift of the approximate signals in transform domain. If the *reconstruction_finish* is not equals to 1, the output residual of LSP will put into the Dot Product to find the index of the highest contribution

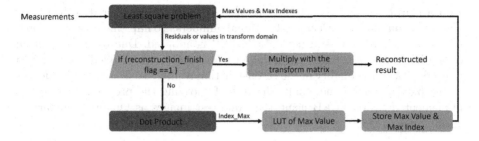

Fig. 4. The overall architecture

column vector of the sensing matrix. As mentioned in Sect. 3.3, there are calculations duplicate in every iteration. Thus, the max value of residual and max index of column vector are stored in every iteration. These parameters are inputs of LSP. This loop will be quit until the *reconstruction_finish* is 1. Then multiplying the output of the LSP with the transform matrix to obtain the reconstructed result.

4   Experiments

4.1   Design Details

Quality Comparison with Gaussian. Most of the existing works adopt the Gaussian matrix as the measurement matrix to verify their proposals. The Gaussian matrix is the classic random matrix of Compressed Sensing. But it consists of floating values, which is difficult to implement on the hardware. To compare with the matrix chosen by the existing work, 200 images with the size of 320 * 480 are chosen from the database BSD 500 [7] to do the experimental test. The transform matrix to test the Gaussian matrix is Discrete Cosine Transform (DCT). The MATLAB is used to do this comparison test. As Table 1 shows, the result quality of matrices chosen by this work outperforms that of the Gaussian matrix.

Table 1. Result quality comparison

Matrix name	Sampling rate	PSNR	SSIM
Gaussian with DCT	0.25	19.86	0.312
Matrices of this work	0.25	**26.30**	**0.640**
Gaussian with DCT	0.5	23.85	0.550
Matrices of this work	0.5	**29.48**	**0.818**
Gaussian with DCT	0.75	27.02	0.726
Matrices of this work	0.75	**32.37**	**0.908**

Fixed Point. In Sect. 3.3, the inverse of the $Result_{matrix}$ is stored in the LUTs. The inversion procedure leads to fractional numbers. To implement the fractional numbers on hardware, shifting data in LSP is adopted. Due to the limitation of the hardware, the fractional numbers only can be set as fixed point. Fixed point decreases the quality of the reconstruction results. To decline the influences of the fixed point on the result, the test of choosing the proper fixed point is implemented in MATLAB using the same test images as Quality Comparison with Gaussian uses.

Table 2. Test result of fixed point (Sampling rate is 0.25)

Fixed point	PSNR	PSNR increase
8	25.23	–
9	26.06	0.836
10	26.19	0.124
11	26.26	0.076
12	26.28	0.013

The Table 2 shows the test result of the fixed point under the sampling rate of 0.25. The PSNR increase is calculated by using PSNR of the current line to diminish the PSNR of the upper line. Because the PSNR increase of fixed point 12 is lower than 0.05, the fixed point of this work is set as 11.

Quit Condition and Sparsity. As mentioned in Sect. 2.2, the sparsity of the natural images is unknown. If the sparsity is too large, the iteration time will be high then the reconstruction time will be numerous. If the sparsity is too small, the quality of the results will be worse. To balance this trade-off, in the proposed architecture, the sparsity is set as 8, which is half of the M. If the iteration index equals 8, the iteration will be quit. Besides, if the residual in the iteration equals 0, the iteration will be quit too.

Design Parameters. To lay the foundation on the future works, the experimental images are separated into 8 * 8 blocks to do the compression. The reconstruction architecture is implemented by $N = 64$, $M = 16$, $k = 8$.

4.2   Design Performance

Design Verification Environment. Verilog is adopted to describe the proposed architecture. The proposed architecture is synthesised and implemented by the Xilinx Vivado 2020.2 on Virtex UltraScale+ FPGA.

Hardware Cost and Reconstruction Time Comparison. In the existing works, the signal length is set as 1024. To compare the hardware cost and reconstruction time with the existing works, this paper initializes 16 reconstruction blocks with the length of 64. The comparison details are as Table 3 presents.

Table 3. Comparison this work with existing works

	This work	[1]	[4]	[5]
FPGA	Virtex UltraScale+	Virtex-6	Virtex-6	Kintex-7
Signal size	1024	1024	1024	1024
Number of measurement	256	256	248	256
Sparsity	(up to) 128	36	36	36
Sparsity fixed	No	Yes	Yes	Yes
Frequency (MHz)	133.33	100	123	210
Reconstruction time (μs)	0.818	622	333	238
Occupied Slices	47624	32010	853	28443
LUT	266542	–	–	59414
FF	64713	–	–	–
DSP	80	261	7	523
BRAM	0	258	4	386

Comparing with the existing 3 works, only this work is sparsity unfixed, which makes the proposed design more flexible. Because the sensing matrix is embedded in the reconstruction procedure, this work costs 0 BRAM. The most notable point is that the reconstruction time of this work surpasses the existing works obviously. Reconstructing a signal with length of 1024 only needs 0.818 us.

Table 4. Reconstruction time under different image sizes (Sampling rate is 0.25)

Resolution	Reconstruction time (s)
1080p (1920 × 1080)	0.0017
4K (38402160)	0.0066
8K (76804320)	0.0265

Table 4 shows the reconstruction time under different image sizes. The proposed architecture can afford 1080p (1920 × 1080)×120 FPS, 4K (38402160)×120 FPS and 8K (76804320)× 30 FPS real-time reconstruction.

Figure 5 illustrates an example of reconstructed image result under sampling rate of 0.25. It is well known that if an image contains more backgrounds, it has more low-frequency information at the transform domain. On the other hand, if an image contains more details, it has more high-frequency information at the transform domain. Figure 2 shows that if the index to the column vector of the sensing matrix is bigger than M, the column vectors are all zero vectors. In other words, this sensing matrix keeps more low-frequency information at the transform domain. To compare the reconstruction quality between high-frequency image and low-frequency image, there are two block images of the reconstructed image are selected. In Fig. 5, the left block image contains more backgrounds while the right block image contains more details. The reconstruction quality of the left image outperforms than right image. Thus, the proposed hardware is more friendly to images with low-frequency information mainly.

Fig. 5. An example of reconstructed image result (Sampling rate is 0.25). The PSNR of this reconstructed image is 32.3647, the SSIM of this reconstructed image is 0.7334. Two block images of the reconstructed image with the size of 100 * 100 are selected. Block image at left contains backgrounds mainly, block image at right contains details mainly.

5   Conclusion

This paper introduces a hardware implementation of OMP named Real-time FPGA Design for OMP Targeting 8K Image Reconstruction. In the implementation of OMP on hardware, there are three factors that infect the efficiency and quality of the results. The choice of sensing matrix, the design of Dot Product (DP), and the design of Least Square Problem (LSP). In this work, a sparse sensing matrix, which contains zero vectors mainly, is obtained by multiplying the Walsh matrix with the Fast Walsh-Hadamard transform matrix. The features of this sensing matrix make that optimizing the DP and LSP is possible.

The complicated divisions and vector-based multiplications of DP and LSP are replaced by the simple shift, add, and comparing calculations. These optimizations make achieving the goal of 8K real-time reconstruction possible. The result shows that to reconstruct an 8K gray image, the proposed architecture costs only 0.026s with reasonable quality. Comparing with the State-of-the-art method, the proposed architecture speedups the reconstruction efficiency with 290 times. And the proposed architecture meets the requirement of reconstructing 8K × 30 FPS real-time.

References

1. Bai, L., Maechler, P., Muehlberghuber, M., Kaeslin, H.: High-speed compressed sensing reconstruction on FPGA using OMP and AMP. In: 2012 19th IEEE International Conference on Electronics, Circuits, and Systems (ICECS 2012), pp. 53–56. IEEE (2012)
2. Blache, P., Rabah, H., Amira, A.: High level prototyping and FPGA implementation of the orthogonal matching pursuit algorithm. In: 2012 11th International Conference on Information Science, Signal Processing and their Applications (ISSPA), pp. 1336–1340. IEEE (2012)
3. Donoho, D.L.: Compressed sensing. IEEE Trans. Inf. Theory **52**(4), 1289–1306 (2006)
4. Fardad, M., Sayedi, S.M., Yazdian, E.: A low-complexity hardware for deterministic compressive sensing reconstruction. IEEE Trans. Circ. Syst. I Regul. Pap. **65**(10), 3349–3361 (2018)
5. Ge, X., Yang, F., Zhu, H., Zeng, X., Zhou, D.: An efficient FPGA implementation of orthogonal matching pursuit with square-root-free qr decomposition. IEEE Trans. Very Large Scale Integr. (VLSI) Syst. **27**(3), 611–623 (2018)
6. Li, J., Chow, P., Peng, Y., Jiang, T.: FPGA implementation of an improved OMP for compressive sensing reconstruction. IEEE Trans. Very Large Scale Integr. (VLSI) Syst. **29**(2), 259–272 (2020)
7. Martin, D., Fowlkes, C., Tal, D., Malik, J.: A database of human segmented natural images and its application to evaluating segmentation algorithms and measuring ecological statistics. In: Proceedings Eighth IEEE International Conference on Computer Vision. ICCV 2001, vol. 2, pp. 416–423. IEEE (2001)
8. Rabah, H., Amira, A., Mohanty, B.K., Almaadeed, S., Meher, P.K.: FPGA implementation of orthogonal matching pursuit for compressive sensing reconstruction. IEEE Trans. Very Large Scale Integr. (VLSI) Syst. **23**(10), 2209–2220 (2014)
9. Septimus, A., Steinberg, R.: Compressive sampling hardware reconstruction. In: Proceedings of 2010 IEEE International Symposium on Circuits and Systems, pp. 3316–3319. IEEE (2010)
10. Stanislaus, J.L., Mohsenin, T.: High performance compressive sensing reconstruction hardware with QRD process. In: 2012 IEEE International Symposium on Circuits and Systems (ISCAS), pp. 29–32. IEEE (2012)
11. Stanislaus, J.L., Mohsenin, T.: Low-complexity FPGA implementation of compressive sensing reconstruction. In: 2013 International Conference on Computing, Networking and Communications (ICNC), pp. 671–675. IEEE (2013)
12. Tropp, J.A., Gilbert, A.C.: Signal recovery from random measurements via orthogonal matching pursuit. IEEE Trans. Inf. Theory **53**(12), 4655–4666 (2007)

Speech and Music

Time-Frequency Attention for Speech Emotion Recognition with Squeeze-and-Excitation Blocks

Ke Liu⬩, Chen Wang⬩, Jiayue Chen⬩, and Jun Feng(✉)⬩

The School of Information Science and Technology, Northwest University, Xi'an 710127, Shaanxi, China
likwix@stumail.nwu.edu.cn, fengjun@nwu.edu.cn

Abstract. In the field of Human-Computer Interaction (HCI), Speech Emotion Recognition (SER) is not only a fundamental step towards intelligent interaction but also plays an important role in smart environments e.g., elderly home monitoring. Most deep learning based SER systems invariably focus on handling high-level emotion-relevant features, which means the low-level feature difference between time and frequency dimensions is rarely analyzed. And it leads to an unsatisfactory accuracy in speech emotion recognition. In this paper, we propose the Time-Frequency Attention (TFA) to mine the significant low-level emotion feature from the time domain and the frequency domain. To make full use of the global information after feature fusion conducted by the TFA, we utilize Squeeze-and-Excitation (SE) blocks to compare emotion features from different channels. Experiments are conducted on a benchmark database - Interactive Emotional Dyadic Motion Capture (IEMOCAP). The results indicate that proposed model outperforms the sate-of-the-art methods with the absolute increase of 1.7% and 3.2% on average class accuracy among four emotion classes and weighted accuracy respectively.

Keywords: Speech Emotion Recognition · Convolutional Neural Network · Time-Frequency Attention · Low-Level Emotion Feature

1 Introduction

Human-Computer Interaction (HCI) is becoming more and more ubiquitous with the rapidly increasing demand on smart devices. Speech Emotion Recognition (SER) is a vital part in the intelligent HCI, since the speech carries various information in human communication. One of the most crucial parts for the success of a SER system is feature extraction [9]. Increasing deep learning methods have been adopted to find effective emotion representations in the feature extraction stage, which can significantly enhance the performance of SER.

Recently, deep learning methods combined with the attention mechanism have been extensively used in SER. Convolutional Neural Networks (CNNs) are always adopted

---

This work was supported by the National Key Research and Development Program of China under grant 2020YFC1523302.

© Springer Nature Switzerland AG 2022
B. Þór Jónsson et al. (Eds.): MMM 2022, LNCS 13141, pp. 533–543, 2022.
https://doi.org/10.1007/978-3-030-98358-1_42

to get time-frequency representations from raw inputs because of the translation invariance of the processing on the time and frequency axes [5]. [11] investigated convolution filters with different scales to capture the features from the time and frequency dimensions, and the result demonstrated the significance of learning both frequency and temporal information. Most attention based SER systems added the attention mechanism at the end of the deep learning network architecture to learn high-level emotion representations. However, the low-level emotion features, e.g., energy, pitch, are not fully used, which limits the performance of a SER task.

Therefore, in this paper, we propose a novelty way to explore the importance of low-level emotion features in the SER task. We introduce the Time-Frequency Attention to a deep convolutional neural network to extract robust low-level emotion features from time-specific and frequency-specific domains. Furthermore, Squeeze-and-Excitation (SE) [7] blocks are used to perform the feature recalibration to selectively emphasise features which are more relevant to the emotion classification from the channel level. With the TFA and SE blocks, the proposed model significantly improves the state-of-the-art speech emotion recognition accuracy, which indicates that specialized learning of the emotion information contained in low-level features is beneficial for SER performance.

2   Related Work

In the early year of SER [12, 15, 18], hand-crafted features occupied the leading status. Gaussian Mixture Models (GMM) were proposed by Slaney et al. to handle SER tasks [19]. Luengo et al. [14] used Support Vector Machine (SVM) to train emotion classifiers with the prosodic parameters. However, traditional methods may not achieve the satisfactory performance in the emotion recognition using speech.

With the rapid development of deep learning methods [3, 6, 25, 26], a growing number of feature extracting algorithms have been introduced to this field. Lee et al. [10] proposed a bi-directional Long Short-Term Memory (LSTM) network for emotion classification. Xixin Wu et al. [23] adopted a system based on capsule networks for the speech emotion recognition. A CNN based multi-time-scale convolution layer was applied to SER and it made classification results better [5].

The performance of the attention mechanism has been greatly improved after Google proposed the transformer which entirely based on self-attention [20]. [27] proposed an attention based fully convolutional network for SER to make the model be aware of the emotion-relevant time-frequency region. Mingke Xu et al. [24] used a multiscale area attention to attend emotional features with varied granularities. Most attention based deep learning methods [1, 20, 24] extracted emotion representations with fixed size filters, which may ignore differences between time and frequency characteristics in SER [11] proposed two specially designed filters to extract temporal and frequency information from the input spectrogram. However, there is no further exploration on the time-frequency feature obtained by the elaborate filters, which means low-level features (features that are paramount for SER [8]) in speech are not well utilized. The optimization of the channel feature after feature fusion of representations at different scales has not been paid much attention to yet.

In this paper, we propose a Time-Frequency Attention (TFA) based feature learning method to excavate low-level emotion features and use two auxiliary Squeeze-and-Excitation (SE) blocks to learn global information. The structure of our network is shown in Fig. 1. We design two parallel convolution filters with different shapes to learn cross-time and cross-frequency feature representations. Then we fed the learned representations into a TFA module to dig the effective low-level emotional characteristics. In order to obtain robust global information, two differently designed SE blocks follow the second and the third convolution layer respectively. Finally, the classification of emotion classes is completed by the following neural network layers. The effectiveness of the proposed model has been quantitatively evaluated using the benchmark IEMO-CAP dataset [2]. The results manifest that the model can achieve an overall accuracy of 79.6% and an average class accuracy of 75.0%. To the best of our knowledge, the results of these two metrics are the state of the art on IEMOCAP corpus.

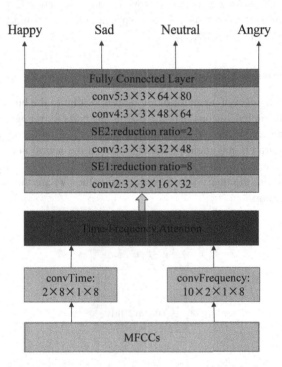

Fig. 1. The CNN architecture combined with TFA and SE blocks. Convolution filters are denoted by height × width × input channels × output channels.

3   Proposed Method

In this section, we first introduce the method of data preprocessing. Then we propose a novel and effective time-frequency attention mechanism to take better advantage of emotion-relevant features obtained by the initial temporal domain and frequency domain convolution layers. TFA can greatly improve the accuracy of the SER task by extracting the low-level feature more effectively than the previous works. Finally, SE blocks are adopted to emphasize characteristics of the channel dimension with more useful details, which contain global information.

3.1 Data Preprocessing

The length of raw utterances in IEMOCAP database is in the range of a second to 20 s. In order to get more data, we divide each utterance into 2-s segments with 1 s overlap in training data and 1.6 s overlap in testing data. Any audio file less than 2 s is dropped and the sampling rate of the audio files is 16 KHz. First, a hamming window with a hop length of 512 is used to perform a short term Fourier transform on the processed utterance. Then the log Mel-spectrogram is obtained by a set of Mel filters. Finally, the initial input tensor of our network is Mel-scale Frequency Cepstral Coefficients (MFCCs), a feature which is wildly used in speech emotion recognition, calculated by the discrete cosine transform (DCT).

3.2 Time-Frequency Attention

The working mechanism of an attention method is similar to the human primary visual cortex [4], which emphasises on the relative arresting parts for recognizing objects. This mechanism makes the subtle and meaningful differences of similar objects be identified easily. Similarly, traditional attention mechanisms in the neural network always focus on the most relevant region of the input sequence. Self attention is a variant form of the attention [17], where the query (Q), key (K) and value (V) are the same vectors from the input feature map.

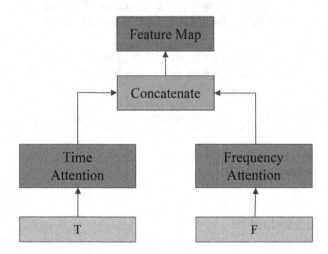

Fig. 2. The structure of TFA. T and F are the outputs of convTime and convFrequency respectively.

In the SER field, normal self attention based models take the high-level emotion features as the research target, which means the low-level but crucial prosodic features are not well utilized. TFA is an effective method which focuses on learning robust low-level emotion features from time and frequency dimensions. The importance of the low-level feature extraction and the validity of TFA have been proved in Sect. 4. Figure 2 shows the structure of the TFA module. Time Attention and Frequency Attention are used to learn more effective emotion related features. The outputs of them are concatenated for further feature learning. As a case study, Fig. 3 shows the detailed Time Attention structure (the Frequency Attention has the same realization mechanism). Different from normal self attention mechanism and the Convolutional Block Attention Module (CBAM) [22], we use the output of the time convolution layer as the input of Time Attention i.e. the feature map extracted by convTime is the initial Q, K and V of the Time Attention mechanism. The dot product in Fig. 3 acts on the spatial dimension which contains specific time and frequency features i.e. spatial features from the time domain and the frequency domain have different stresses. In this way, the self attention operation can be performed on multiple channels at the same time and the distribution of the original channel feature can be preserved completely for the subsequent channel optimization conducted by SE blocks. And we use the Dropout function in the proposed attention mechanism to overcome the over-fitting on account of the limited size of IEMOCAP database. The final output of the Time Attention $X' \in \mathbb{R}^{C \times H \times W}$ is obtained by:

$$X' = F_{att}(Q, K, V) = Dropout\left(Softmax\left(\frac{QK^{T}}{\sqrt{D_K}}\right)\right)V \qquad (1)$$

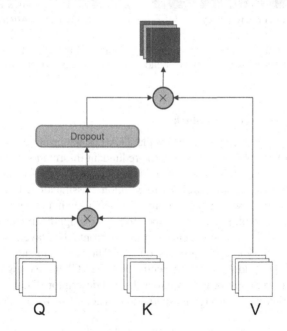

Fig. 3. The structure of time attention.

In Eq. (1), Q, K and V denote the same input matrix, the scaling factor D_K refers to the dimension of K.

In order to better explain why TFA is effective, we visualize the feature maps before and after the TFA module in Fig. 4. (a) and (b) illustrate that Time Attention can enhance the expressiveness of time-domain features and uncover neglected sentiment features. (c) and (d) show that features extracted by the frequency-specific convolution layer ignore a large number of emotion-related features, which can be attended on by the Frequency Attention. Furthermore, It can be seen from Fig. 4 that the features of time and frequency domains have different emphases in the SER task.

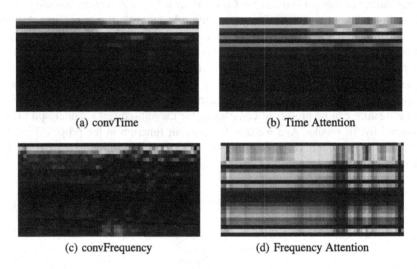

(a) convTime   (b) Time Attention

(c) convFrequency   (d) Frequency Attention

Fig. 4. The visualisation of feature maps. (a), (b), (c) and (d) are the outputs of the convTime layer, Time Attention, convFrequency layer and Frequency Attention respectively.

3.3 Squeeze-and-Excitation Block

Although the feature map generated by the TFA has better emotion representations, the complexity of the global feature and the redundant information have also increased after the feature fusion. SE block can weight each channel of the feature map and effectively ignore features that are unrelated to emotion classification. It is a computationally lightweight module which means it imposes only a slight increase in computational burden and model complexity [7]. SE block focuses on significant channels in the feature map $U \in \mathbb{R}^{C \times H \times W}$, which is generated by the front CNN layer. And it performs a squeeze and an excitation operation in sequence. The two main steps of SE algorithm are denoted as $F_{sq}(\cdot)$ and $F_{ex}(\cdot, W)$ respectively. It uses Global Average Pooling (GAP) to squeeze global spatial information into a channel descriptor. The $c - th$ element of z, generated by shrinking U through its spatial dimensions $H \times W$, is calculated by:

$$z_c = F_{sq}(u_c) = \frac{1}{H \times W} \sum_{i=1}^{H} \sum_{j=1}^{W} u_c(i, j) \qquad (2)$$

Where $u_c \in \mathbb{R}^{H \times W}$ refers to the $c - th$ channel of U. Following the squeeze operation, a simple gating mechanism with a Sigmoid activation is used to fully capture channel-wise dependencies, as shown in Eq. (3).

$$s = F_{ex}(z, W) = \sigma(g(z, W)) = \sigma(W_2 \delta(W_1 z)) \tag{3}$$

Where δ is the ReLu function, σ refers to a Sigmoid activation, $W_1 \in \mathbb{R}^{\frac{C}{r} \times C}$ and $W_2 \in \mathbb{R}^{C \times \frac{C}{r}}$. Symbol r is a reduction ratio which is used to limit model complexity. The final output $\widetilde{X} = \left[\widetilde{X}_1, \widetilde{X}_2, ..., \widetilde{X}_c \right]$ of a SE block is obtained by:

$$\widetilde{X}_c = F_{scale}(u_c, s_c) = s_c u_c \tag{4}$$

Where $\widetilde{X}_c$ ($F_{scale}(u_c, s_c)$) is the channel-wise multiplied by the feature map $u_c \in \mathbb{R}^{H \times W}$ and the scalar s_c.

4 Results and Discussion

4.1 Dataset

In this work, we choose Interactive Emotional Dyadic Motion Capture (IEMOCAP) database as the experimental database, which is established by the University of Southern California. It is a multimodal dataset and wildly used as the benchmark dataset in the speech emotion recognition filed. IEMOCAP contains 5 sessions, each session has one female and one male actor. The experienced actors perform scripted scenarios or improvisations, specially to represent various emotional expressions. IEMOCAP provides a total of 5531 utterances that are labeled with 9 types of emotion - Happiness, Anger, Sadness, Excitement, Fear, Frustration, Surprise, Neutral state and Other. For our experiments, we use the improvised raw audio samples, as actors can focus on the emotional expression itself and have no need to put the undesired contextual information from the script on agenda. In addition, the improvised dataset has been used by most SER studies.

Following the previous works, We choose four emotion types for our experiments - happiness, excitement, sadness, and neutral state. The distribution of the four classes in IEMOCAP is imbalanced, including 49% neutral emotion, around 12% angry, 12% happy and the rest of the 27% refers to Sad.

4.2 Experiment Setup

In accordance with prior works [13, 16, 17, 21], all results are reported on 5-fold cross validation and the gender and emotion classes are distributed evenly in both train and test datasets. We choose Weighted Accuracy (WA) and Unweighted Accuracy (UA) for the performance comparison. Weighted Accuracy refers to the overall accuracy, and Unweighted Accuracy is the average accuracy over selected emotion classes. The two metrics have been broadly employed in SER literature for evaluation because of the data imbalance. For segments from the same utterance, the prediction results of which are averaged to obtain the final score.

We make use of the PyTorch for the model training with a mini-batch size of 32. The Adam optimizer is used to optimize the model and the loss function is cross-entropy (CE). The proposed model is trained 60 epochs. The initial learning rate is 0.001 and it becomes one-tenth of the current value every ten epochs. We use Max pooling and Batch normalization after CNNs to reduce the chance of over-fitting. Based on the analysis of related works in Sect. 2, we selected the hyperparameters before conducting the five-fold cross validation experiment.

4.3   Comparison with Sate-of-the-art Methods

In Table 1, we compared our final accuracy with other published SER results in order to prove the performance of the proposed model. They use the same data division method and emotion types (happy, sad, angry, neutral state) as our experiment. And we all use IEMOCAP as the benchmark dataset. The result shows that proposed model has improved the weighted accuracy to 79.6%, which is 3.2% higher than the previous work. As for unweighted accuracy, it has also brought an increase of 1.7% to 75.0% in accuracy. This result demonstrates the importance of low-level emotion features in SER.

Table 1. Comparison with state-of-the-art methods

Methods	WA(%)	UA(%)
Lee [10] (Bi-LSTM)	62.8	63.9
Muppidi [16] (QCNN)	\	70.46
Liu [13] (TFCNN+DenseCap+ELM)	70.34	70.78
Wang [21] (LSTM+DS_LSTM)	72.7	73.3
Nediyanchath [17] (MHA + PE + MTL)	76.4	70.1
Ours (CNN + TFA + SE)	**79.6**	**75.0**

4.4   Ablation Study

In Table 2, we conducted ablation experiments to show the effectiveness of our methods. CNN is the baseline architecture. CNN with TFA is the model which uses the Time-Frequency Attention to learn the most useful emotion information in time and frequency feature maps. The third model (CNN with SE blocks) uses Squeeze-and-Excitation blocks to obtain the channel dependencies from the CNN layers without the TFA mechanism. CNN with TFA and SE is the final model in our experiment, it uses both TFA and SE blocks. From Table 2 we can see that either CNN with TFA or SE blocks can enable the model to achieve better accuracy than the baseline (CNN). The last model in Table 2, the best network architecture in our work, achieves the first-class performance. It has given a regarding 75.0% average class accuracy (UA) and the overall accuracy (WA) has been improved to 79.6%, to the state-of-the-art result.

Table 2. Ablation experiment

Methods	WA(%)	UA(%)
CNN	73.4	68.7
CNN + TFA	78.0	72.1
CNN + SE	77.9	73.3
CNN + TFA + SE	**79.6**	**75.0**

4.5 Average Class Accuracy

The IEMOCAP has a limited size and there is data imbalance among the four emotions. Therefore, the average class accuracy (unweighted accuracy) is the best metric to measure the effectiveness of the model. As shown in Fig. 5, the confusion matrices ((a), (b), and (c)) are presented to summarize the performance of the classification.

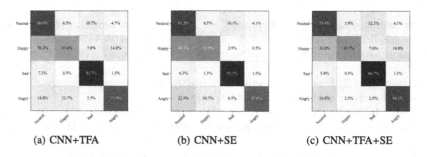

	(a) CNN+TFA	(b) CNN+SE	(c) CNN+TFA+SE

Fig. 5. Confusion matrices to show the average class accuracies

As discussed in Sect. 4.1, Happy and Angry are the classes which are underrepresented in the IEMOCAP dataset. Therefore, it can be seen from (a) and (b) that the classification accuracies of them are lower than Neutral and Sad classes. However, the proposed model (c) shows that the combination of the TFA module and the SE block can greatly improve the classification accuracy of the Angry class, which improves the accuracy of this emotion around by 10% compared to (a) and (b). It also indicates that the proposed method is able to learn more useful information in the Angry class than in the Happy class. Meanwhile, The classification performance of the Neutral class decreased slightly and the classification accuracy of the Happy class is between the results presented by the CNN+SE and the CNN+TFA, which can be attributed to the better generalization. As a result, there is a significant improvement in the unweighted accuracy beyond the state-of-the-art results.

5 Conclusion

In this paper, we propose a novel CNN architecture combined with the Time-Frequency Attention and SE blocks for speech emotion recognition. TFA can take into account differences of the low-level emotion feature between time and frequency domains. SE blocks manifest great performance in paying close attention to more valuable channel features. Experimental results conducted on IEMOCAP database demonstrate the importance of the low-level emotion features in the SER task. The proposed model outperforms other state of the art methods, which is able to achieve 75.0% average class accuracy and 79.6% weighted accuracy.

Due to the better emotion recognition capability of the proposed model, we believe it can greatly improve the performance of the SER system in smart environments. In the future, we will continue to explore more effective methods to learn low-level emotion features.

References

1. Bhosale, S., Chakraborty, R., Kopparapu, S.K.: Deep encoded linguistic and acoustic cues for attention based end to end speech emotion recognition. In: ICASSP 2020–2020 IEEE International Conference on Acoustics, Speech and Signal Processing (ICASSP), pp. 7189–7193 (2020)
2. Busso, C., et al.: Iemocap: interactive emotional dyadic motion capture database. In: Language Resources and Evaluation vol. 42, pp. 335–359 (2008)
3. Chen, M., He, X., Yang, J., Zhang, H.: 3-D convolutional recurrent neural networks with attention model for speech emotion recognition. IEEE Sig. Process. Lett. 25(10), 1440–1444 (2018)
4. Ebrahimpour, M.K., et al.: Ventral-dorsal neural networks: object detection via selective attention. In: 2019 IEEE Winter Conference on Applications of Computer Vision (WACV), pp. 986–994 (2019)
5. Guizzo, E., Weyde, T., Leveson, J.B.: Multi-time-scale convolution for emotion recognition from speech audio signals. In: ICASSP 2020–2020 IEEE International Conference on Acoustics, Speech and Signal Processing (ICASSP), pp. 6489–6493 (2020)
6. Han, K., Yu, D., Tashev, I.: Speech emotion recognition using deep neural network and extreme learning machine. In: INTERSPEECH, pp. 223–227 (2014)
7. Hu, J., Shen, L., Sun, G.: Squeeze-and-excitation networks. In: 2018 IEEE/CVF Conference on Computer Vision and Pattern Recognition, pp. 7132–7141 (2018)
8. Jagdale, S.M.: Speech emotion recognition with low level and prosodic features: a review. Digit. Sig. Process. 8(6), 154–158 (2016)
9. Kim, J., Saurous, R.A.: Emotion recognition from human speech using temporal information and deep learning. In: Interspeech 2018, pp. 937–940 (2018)
10. Lee, J., Tashev, I.: High-level feature representation using recurrent neural network for speech emotion recognition. In: INTERSPEECH, pp. 1537–1540 (2015)
11. Li, P., Song, Y., McLoughlin, I.V., Guo, W., Dai, L.: An attention pooling based representation learning method for speech emotion recognition. In: Interspeech 2018, pp. 3087–3091 (2018)
12. Li, Z.: A study on emotional feature analysis and recognition in speech signal. J. China Inst. Commun. (2000)

13. Liu, J., Liu, Z., Wang, L., Guo, L., Dang, J.: Speech emotion recognition with local-global aware deep representation learning. In: ICASSP 2020–2020 IEEE International Conference on Acoustics, Speech and Signal Processing (ICASSP), pp. 7174–7178 (2020)
14. Luengo, I., Navas, E., Hernaez, I.: Automatic emotion recognition using prosodic parameters. In: INTERSPEECH, pp. 493–496 (2005)
15. Montero, J., Gutiérrez-Arriola, J., Colás, J.: Analysis and modelling of emotional speech in Spanish (1999)
16. Muppidi, A., Radfar, M.: Speech emotion recognition using quaternion convolutional neural networks. In: ICASSP 2021–2021 IEEE International Conference on Acoustics, Speech and Signal Processing (ICASSP), pp. 6309–6313 (2021)
17. Nediyanchath, A., Paramasivam, P., Yenigalla, P.: Multi-head attention for speech emotion recognition with auxiliary learning of gender recognition. In: ICASSP 2020–2020 IEEE International Conference on Acoustics, Speech and Signal Processing (ICASSP), pp. 7179–7183 (2020)
18. Petrushin, V.A.: Emotion in speech: Recognition and application to call centers (1999)
19. Slaney, M., McRoberts, G.: Baby ears: a recognition system for affective vocalizations. Speech Commun. 39(3), 367–384 (2003)
20. Vaswani, A., et al.: Attention is all you need. In: Proceedings of the 31st International Conference on Neural Information Processing Systems vol. 30, pp. 5998–6008 (2017)
21. Wang, J., Xue, M., Culhane, R., Diao, E., Ding, J., Tarokh, V.: Speech emotion recognition with dual-sequence LSTM architecture. In: ICASSP 2020–2020 IEEE International Conference on Acoustics, Speech and Signal Processing (ICASSP), pp. 6474–6478 (2020)
22. Woo, S., Park, J., Lee, J.Y., Kweon, I.S.: Cbam: convolutional block attention module. In: Proceedings of the European Conference on Computer Vision (ECCV), pp. 3–19 (2018)
23. Wu, X., et al.: Speech emotion recognition using capsule networks. In: ICASSP 2019–2019 IEEE International Conference on Acoustics, Speech and Signal Processing (ICASSP), pp. 6695–6699 (2019)
24. Xu, M., Zhang, F., Cui, X., Zhang, W.: Speech emotion recognition with multiscale area attention and data augmentation. arXiv preprint arXiv:2102.01813 (2021)
25. Xu, Y., Xu, H., Zou, J.: HGFM : A hierarchical grained and feature model for acoustic emotion recognition. In: ICASSP 2020–2020 IEEE International Conference on Acoustics, Speech and Signal Processing (ICASSP), pp. 6499–6503 (2020)
26. Zhang, L., Shi, Z., Han, J., Shi, A., Ma, D.: FurcaNeXt: end-to-end monaural speech separation with dynamic gated dilated temporal convolutional networks. In: Ro, Y.M., et al. (eds.) MMM 2020. LNCS, vol. 11961, pp. 653–665. Springer, Cham (2020). https://doi.org/10.1007/978-3-030-37731-1_53
27. Zhang, Y., Du, J., Wang, Z., Zhang, J., Tu, Y.: Attention based fully convolutional network for speech emotion recognition. In: 2018 Asia-Pacific Signal and Information Processing Association Annual Summit and Conference (APSIPA ASC), pp. 1771–1775 (2018)

Speech Intelligibility Enhancement By Non-Parallel Speech Style Conversion Using CWT and iMetricGAN Based CycleGAN

Jing Xiao[1,2]([✉]), Jiaqi Liu[1,2], Dengshi Li[3], Lanxin Zhao[3], and Qianrui Wang[3]

[1] National Engineering Research Center for Multimedia Software,
School of Computer Science, Wuhan University, Wuhan 430072, China
jing@whu.edu.cn
[2] Hubei Key Laboratory of Multimedia and Network Communication Engineering,
Wuhan University, Wuhan 430072, China
[3] School of Artificial Intelligence, Jianghan University, Wuhan 430056, China

Abstract. Speech intelligibility enhancement is a perceptual enhancement technique for clean speech reproduced in noisy environments. Many studies enhance speech intelligibility by speaking style conversion (SSC), which relies solely on the Lombard effect does not work well in strong noise interference. They also model the conversion of fundamental frequency (F0) with a straightforward linear transform and map only a very few dimensions Mel-cepstral coefficients (MCEPs). As F0 and MCEPs are critical aspects of hierarchical intonation, we believe that adequate modeling of these features is essential. In this paper, we make a creative study of continuous wavelet transform (CWT) to decompose F0 into ten temporal scales that describe speech at different time resolutions for effective F0 conversion, and we also express MCEPs with 20 dimensions over baseline 10 dimensions for MCEPs conversion. We utilize an iMetricGAN network to optimize the speech intelligibility metrics in strong noise. Experimental results show that proposed Non-Parallel Speech Style Conversion using CWT and iMetricGAN based CycleGAN (NS-CiC) method outperforms the baselines that significantly increased speech intelligibility in robust noise environments in objective and subjective evaluations.

Keywords: Non-parallel SSC · Intelligibility enhancement · CWT · iMetricGAN · CycleGAN

1 Introduction

For decades, a speech intelligibility enhancement technique has been used in the auditory phase of multimedia communications as a perceptual enhancement of its reproduction of clean (non-noisy) speech in noisy environments, which has aroused great concern. About speech intelligibility enhancement, recent theoretical developments have

This work was supported by the National Key Research and Development Program of China (1502-211100026).

B. Þór Jónsson et al. (Eds.): MMM 2022, LNCS 13141, pp. 544–556, 2022.
https://doi.org/10.1007/978-3-030-98358-1_43

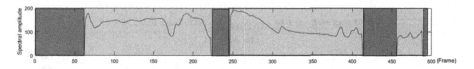

Fig. 1. Spectrogram of F0. F0 is a 1-dimensional discontinuous feature, and the blue area indicates unvoiced frames, the red area indicates voiced frames. (Color figure online)

revealed that based on acoustic masking principles and Digital Signal Processing (DSP) algorithms will cause a serious decline in the naturalness of speech.

A new data-driven approach named Speaking Style Conversion (SSC) [12] aimed at modifying the style of a given speech signal while keeping the speaker's acoustic characteristics is applied based on one particular vocal effort called Lombard effect [4] to enhance speech intelligibility. It uses normal style speech and Lombard style speech to train a normal-to-Lombard style conversion system. This approach utilizes the data to learn and model these changes named parameterization method can perform more comprehensive processing while keeping the converted voice quality good and natural. In this paper, we follow the same strategy and use the parameterized method based on the well-known WORLD vocoder [11].

The mainstream method of SSC nowadays is divided into parallel SSC and non-parallel SSC. Similar with the popular visual signal enhancement tasks [5,7–9], parallel SSC methods rely on the availability of parallel utterance pairs of the source (normal) and target (Lomdard) speech, and parallel data learning techniques are usually utilized, such as Gaussian Mixture Models (GMM) [6], Deep Neural Network (DNN) architectures [15] and more recently Recurrent Neural Network (RNN) architectures [10]. However, the speaker usually has a slower speech rate under the Lombard reflex. Parallel SSC needs time-alignment operations to preprocess training data conducted by lossy algorithms (e.g., dynamic time warping), resulting in some feature distortions. It encourages the use of non-parallel SSC to avoid time-alignment operations. Some recent studies have incorporated cycle-consistent generative adversarial networks (CycleGANs) to learn a generative distribution closed to the target without explicit approximation. With CycleGANs, they have got non-parallel SSC with better intelligibility and naturalness than parallel SSC.

However, there are still two main limitations:
Limitation 1: Fundamental frequency (F0), a 1-dimensional feature, is firstly affected by both short term dependencies and long term dependencies. Secondly, as shown in Fig. 1, F0 is discontinuous due to the presence of clear and turbid sounds. Another important feature named Mel-cepstral coefficients(MCEP) is a high-dimensional continuous properties, [16] co-map MCEPs with the one-dimensional F0 causes distribution blending. In addition, baseline extraction of 40-dimensional MCEPs with only 10-dimensional mapping does not represent the full Lombard style.

Limitation 2: It is considering the limitations of the strength of the Lombard effect in terms of its performance in different noise environments. SSC only with the Lombard effect still does not work well in strong noise interference with very low signal-to-noise ratios (SNRs), especially in SNR $\leq$ 0 dB.

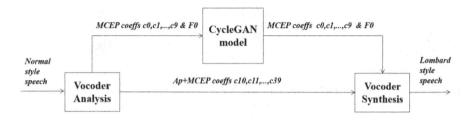

Fig. 2. Schematic diagram of non-parallel SSC.

To overcome the first limitation, in this paper, we consider a multi-resolution analysis framework to map temporal dependencies of F0 using continuous wavelet transform (CWT) and use 20-dimensional MCEPs features over baseline 10 dimensions to comprehensively represent the acoustic. Indeed, CWT has been suggested to describe speech parameters at several time scales in many fields such as [14].

To overcome the second limitation, we propose the use of iMetricGAN, which is a Generative Adversarial Network (GAN) system that consists of a generator to enhance the speech signal as the intelligibility enhancement module and a discriminator. Instead of discriminating fake from real, the discriminator aims to closely approximate the intelligibility metrics as a learned surrogate, and then the generator can be trained properly with the guidance of this surrogate.

The main contributions of this paper include: 1) We propose a higher resolution non-parallel SSC framework using CWT and iMetricGAN based CycleGAN named NS-CiC method; 2) Dealing the lack of time correlation in linear F0, we use CWT transform to process low-dimensional F0 into CWT coefficients at ten time scales and map higher-dimensional MCEPs features; 3) We utilize an iMetricGAN approach to optimize the speech intelligibility metrics with generative adversarial networks (GANs). We outperform the baseline [16] approaches and increased speech intelligibility through our high-quality SSC.

2   Baseline: Non-Parallel SSC Framework

2.1   Basic Framework

The non-parallel SSC framework of the latest baseline methods [16] is given as Fig. 2. The source speech (input) is speech utterances in the normal style, while the target speech (output) is the same utterances in the Lombard style. The system mainly consists of three parts: vocoder analysis, features mapping, and vocoder synthesis. Firstly, speech features are extracted from the input signal by the vocoder analysis. Then, the features, which are closely related to SSC, are converted by a mapping system. Finally, the mapped and unmodified features are fed to the vocoder, which synthesizes the target speech of the Lombard style.

2.2   CycleGAN

A CycleGAN is incorporated with three losses: adversarial loss, cycle-consistency loss, and identity-mapping loss, learning forward and inverse mapping between source and target. For the forward mapping, it is defined as:

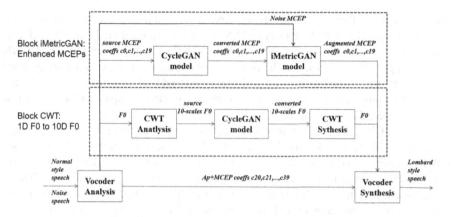

Fig. 3. Schematic diagram of the proposed NS-CiC method. Block iMetricGAN: iMetricGAN is used to enhance intelligibility in noisy environments. Block CWT: F0 is decomposing by CWT to 10-time scales.

$$L_{ADV}(G_{X \to Y}, D_Y, X, Y) = \mathbb{E}_{y \sim P(y)}[D_Y(y)]$$
$$+ \mathbb{E}_{x \sim P(x)}[\log(1 - D_Y(G_{X \to Y}(x)))] \tag{1}$$

The closer the distribution of converted data with that of target data, the smaller L_{ADV} becomes. In order to guarantee that the contextual information of x and $G_{X \to Y}$ will be consistent, the cycle-consistency loss is given as:

$$L_{CYC}(G_{X \to Y}, G_{Y \to X}) = \mathbb{E}_{x \sim P(x)}[\|G_{Y \to X}(G_{X \to Y}(x)) - x\|_1]$$
$$+ \mathbb{E}_{y \sim P(y)}[\|G_{X \to Y}(G_{Y \to X}(y)) - y\|_1] \tag{2}$$

This loss encourages $G_{X \to Y}$ and $G_{X \to Y}$ to find an optimal pseudo pair of (x, y) through circular conversion. To preserve the linguistic information without any external processes, an identity mapping loss is introduced as below:

$$L_{ID}(G_{X \to Y}, G_{Y \to X}) = \mathbb{E}_{x \sim P(x)}[\|G_{Y \to X}(x) - x\|] + \mathbb{E}_{y \sim P(y)}[\|G_{X \to Y}(y) - y\|] \tag{3}$$

3   Proposed Method: Non-Parallel SSC Using CWT and iMetricGAN Based CycleGAN

The baseline method only maps discontinuous 1-dimensional F0 and co-trains it with continuous 10-dimensional MCEPs. Furthermore, the state-of-the-art systems were also not good at dealing with strong noise interference. To overcome these limitations, we propose the NS-CiC method.

3.1   Framework

The whole phase of the proposed framework is given in Fig. 3. The widely used WORLD vocoder performs analysis and synthesis with a 5-ms frameshift. Based on the two essential features of speech, we have divided the entire framework into two parts as block CWT and block iMetricGAN. First, we extracted the F0 and MCEP features of the speech signal using the vocoder. Then the whole system uses CycleGAN as the mapping base model, and the two features extracted by the vocoder are mapped using the processes in block CWT and block iMetricGAN, respectively. Finally, the predicted features and the repair-altered features are used as inputs to the vocoder to synthesize the enhanced speech.

In block CWT, F0 is a 1-dimensional feature. It is noted that F0 features extracted from the WORLD vocoder are discontinuous due to the voiced/unvoiced parts. Since CWT is sensitive to the discontinuities in F0, we perform the following pre-processing steps for F0: 1) linear interpolation over unvoiced regions; 2) transformation of F0 from linear to a logarithmic scale; 3) normalization of the resulting F0 to zero mean and unit variance. We first apply CWT to decompose 1-dimensional F0 into 10-time scales and interpolate the discontinuous F0 as a continuous feature. Then we use CycleGAN network to map the source and target training data, which are from the same speaker but consist of different styles and energy. At last, we reconstruct the mapped F0 with CWT synthesis approximation method.

In block iMetricGAN, spectral envelope is represented as 40th-order MCEPs, and the first 20 MCEPs (C0 $\sim$C19) were taken as training data. In the first stage, Cycle-GAN was used to learn forward and inverse mappings simultaneously using adversarial and cycle-consistency losses. After CycleGAN predicting, the MCEPs of normal speech was converted into Lombard features. In the second stage of training, iMetricGAN is used as intelligibility enhancement in strong noise environments. We use the pre-extracted noise features and the converted MCEP as the input to the iMetricGAN model, enhanced MCEPs can be obtained.

3.2   Block: Continuous Wavelet Transform (CWT)

Wavelet transform provides an easily interpretable visual representation of signals. Using CWT, a signal can be decomposed into different temporal scales. We note that CWT has been successfully used in speech synthesis and voice conversion.

Given a bounded, continuous signal k_0, its CWT representation $W(k_0)(\tau, t)$ can be written as:

$$W\left(k_0\right)(\tau, t) = \tau^{-1/2} \int_{-\infty}^{+\infty} k_0(x)\psi\left(\frac{x-t}{\tau}\right) dx \tag{4}$$

where ψ is the Mexican hat mother wavelet. The original signal k_0 can be recovered from the wavelet representation $W(k_0)$ by inverse transform, given as:

$$k_0(t) = \int_{-\infty}^{+\infty} \int_0^{+\infty} W\left(k_0\right)(\tau, x)\tau^{-5/2}\psi\left(\frac{t-x}{\tau}\right) dx d\tau \tag{5}$$

However, if all information on $W(k_0)$ is not available, the reconstruction is incomplete. In this study, we fix the analysis at ten discrete scales, one octave apart. The decomposition is given as:

$$W_i\left(k_0\right)(t) = W_i\left(k_0\right)\left(2^{i+1}\tau_0, t\right)(i+2.5)^{-5/2} \tag{6}$$

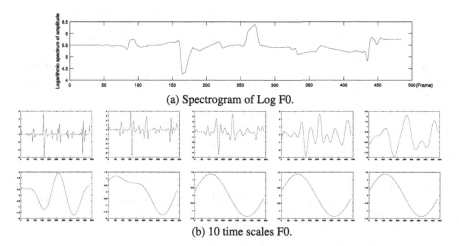

(a) Spectrogram of Log F0.

(b) 10 time scales F0.

Fig. 4. (a) denotes the continuous signal after interpolation and mean value of the 1-dimensional discontinuous F0. (b) denotes the transformation of a 1-dimensional F0 into a 10-scale F0 using CWT.

The reconstructed k_0 is approximated as:

$$k_0(t) = \sum_{i=1}^{10} W_i\,(k_0)\,(t)(i+2.5)^{-5/2} \tag{7}$$

where $i = 1, \ldots, 10$ and $\tau_0 = 5$ ms. These timing scales were originally proposed in [17]. We believe that the prosody of utterance is expressed differently at different time scales. Figure 4(b) gives 10-scales CWT components, while Fig. 4(a) can only represent a discontinuity in one dimension. With the multi-scale representations, lower scales capture the short-term variations, and higher scales capture the long-term variations. In this way, we are able to model and convert the F0 variants from the micro-prosody level to the whole utterance level for style pairs.

3.3 Block: iMetricGAN

The model framework is depicted in Fig. 5. It consists of a generator (G) network and a discriminator (D) network. G receives speech s and noise w and then generates the enhanced speech. The final processed speech is notated as $G(s, w)$. The cascading D is utilized to predict the intelligibility score of the enhanced speech $G(s, w)$, given s and w. The output of D is notated as $D(G(s, w), s, w)$ and is expected to be close to the true intelligibility score calculated by a specific measure. We introduce the function $Q(.)$ to represent the intelligibility measures to be modeled, i.e., speech intelligibility in bits with a Gaussian channel (SIIB Gauss) [19] and extended short-time objective intelligibility (ESTOI) [1] (which have achieved state-of-the-art performance). With the above notations, the training target of D, shown in Fig. 5 (a), can be represented to minimize the following loss function:

$$L_D = \mathbb{E}_{s,w}\left[(D(G(s, w), s, w) - Q(G(s, w), s, w))^2\right] \tag{8}$$

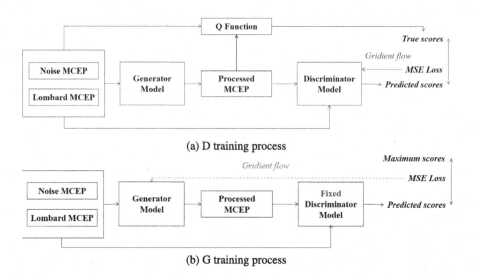

(a) D training process

(b) G training process

Fig. 5. The framework of iMetricGAN and its training process. D is updated via Q Function's scores; G is updated via updated D.

In the D training process, the loss function is extended to Eq. (9).

$$L_D = \mathbb{E}_{s,w}[D(G(s,w),s,w) - Q(G(s,w),s,w))^2 + (D(\hat{s},s,w) - Q(\hat{s},s,w))^2] \quad (9)$$

Equation (9) can be seen as the loss function with auxiliary knowledge, while Eq. (8) is the loss function with zero knowledge. Note that $\hat{S}$ should not be regarded as the ground truth or the training label. For the G training process shown in Fig. 5 (b), D's parameters are fixed and G is trained to reach intelligibility scores as high as possible. To achieve this, the target score t in Eq. (10) is assigned to the maximum value of the intelligibility measure.

$$L_G = \mathbb{E}_{s,w}\left[(D(G(s,w),s,w) - t)^2\right] \quad (10)$$

G and D are iteratively trained until convergence. G acts as an enhancement module and is trained to cheat D in order to achieve a higher intelligibility score. On the other hand, D tries to not be cheated and to accurately evaluate the score of the modified speech. This minimax game finally makes both G and D effective. Consequently, the input speech can be enhanced to a more intelligible level by G.

4   Experiments

4.1   Experimental Setup

Dataset: We chose the latest open-source Lombard corpus (without using video data) as the dataset, which is named Lombard Grid [2]. This corpus contained 30 female

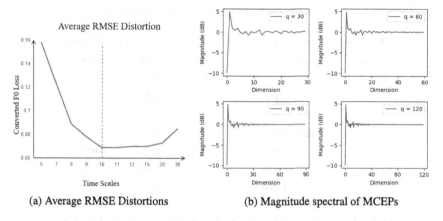

(a) Average RMSE Distortions   (b) Magnitude spectral of MCEPs

Fig. 6. (a) RMSE distortions of different time scales F0. (b) Magnitude spectral of MCEPs in different dimensions.

speakers and 24 male speakers that each speaker recorded 50 normal style utterances and 50 Lombard style utterances at a 16 kHz sampling rate. The 2/3 and 1/3 of the corpus were used for training and evaluation, respectively. We also chose a German corpus [18], which contains 40 phrases from 8 speakers, each utterance with three different Lombardnesses as 0, 55, 70, as a test set.

Environmental Noise: Three types of noise were involved in the experiments from NOISEX-92 database [20], referring to relevant studies. They were Factory1 (non-stationary), Factory2 (non-stationary), and Volvo (stationary). We set the Volvo noise SNR as -25 and -15 dB, while Factory1 and Factory2 noise are set to -5 and 0 dB.

Compared Methods: We set up three sets of comparison experiments. They are the baseline method named CycleGAN, our proposed 10-dimensional MCEP called NS-CiLC, and the 20-dimensional MCEP named NS-CiHC method. Normal speech was added to the experiments for validating speech intelligibility enhancement effects.

Proposed Method Implementation: In CycleGAN, we used the same parameter settings as the baseline. In iMetricGAN, as shown in Fig. 5, the input features for D are 3-channel spectrograms, i.e., (processed, unprocessed, noise). D consists of five layers of 2-D CNN with the following number of filters and kernel size: [8 (5, 5)], [16 (7, 7)], [32 (10, 10], [48 (15, 15)], and [64 (20, 20)], each with LeakyReLU activation. Global average pooling is followed by the last CNN layer to produce a fixed 64-dimensional feature. Two fully connected layers are successively added, each with 64 and 10 nodes with LeakyReLU. The last layer of D is also fully connected, and its output represents the scores of the intelligibility metrics. Therefore, the number of nodes in the last layer is equal to that of the intelligibility metrics. We normalize the ESTOI score ranges from 0 to 1. So, when training with ESTOI score, the sigmoid activation function is used in the last layer.

Table 1. Average RMSE distortion for F0 conversion.

Language	Gender	Voice clarity	CycleGAN	NS-CiLC	NS-CiHC
English	Female	Clear	0.085	**0.078**	**0.078**
		Unclear	0.097	**0.093**	**0.093**
	Male	Clear	0.089	**0.081**	**0.081**
		Unclear	0.099	**0.095**	**0.095**
German	Female	Clear	0.052	**0.048**	**0.048**
		Unclear	0.062	**0.057**	**0.057**
	Male	Clear	0.056	**0.050**	**0.050**
		Unclear	0.065	**0.059**	**0.059**

Table 2. iMetricGAN for enhanced Lombard speech on SIIB and ESTOI scores.

Language	Gender	SNRs	Normal	Lombard	NS-CiHC
English	SIIB Gauss	Mild	66.0	89.5	**91.1**
		Severe	34.7	39.7	**51.7**
	ESTOI	Mild	0.297	0.445	**0.447**
		Severe	0.183	0.301	**0.394**
German	SIIB Gauss	Mild	44.0	143.9	**144.2**
		Severe	18.6	47.2	**70.3**
	ESTOI	Mild	0.284	0.442	**0.444**
		Severe	0.157	0.307	**0.401**

Hyperparameter Setting: CWT Time-Scales Setting: We decomposed F0 into CWT coefficients of different time scales and compared the weights of CWT coefficients, the degree of influence on feature transformation, and the complexity of implementation, respectively. As shown in Fig. 6(a), the decomposition of F0 into CWT coefficients of 10-time scales is more suitable in terms of the quality and complexity of the feature transformation. MCEPs dimension Setting: Fig. 6(b) shows the MCEPs spectrum for the same sentence with different vocalisation styles ($q = 40$). Comparing MCEPs features in different dimensions, a clear difference in values can be seen at approximately $q \leq 20$, while after 20 dimensions, the MCEP values are all around zero, and no difference can be seen from the coarse-grained speech spectrograms. We experimented with the spectral features in 40 dimensions and selected the first 20 dimensions as the mapping features.

Objective Experimental Setting: We perform an objective evaluation to assess the performance of F0 mapping by Root Mean Squared Error (RMSE) [3], and SIIB Gauss scores and ESTOI scores are Measured to demonstrate improved intelligibility in strong noise environments by iMetricGAN model. Finally, we compared the overall performance for all methods.

We use RMSE to report the performance of F0 prediction. The RMSE between the converted F0 and the corresponding target F0 is defined as:

$$RMSE = \sqrt{\frac{1}{N} \sum_{i=1}^{N} (F0_i^c - F0_i^t)^2} \tag{11}$$

where $F0_i^c$ and $F0_i^t$ denote the predicted and target interpolated F0 features, respectively. N is the length of F0 sequence. We note that a lower RMSE value represents better F0 prediction performance.

Subjective Experimental Setting: The subjective listening evaluation was conducted by comparison mean opinion score (CMOS) standard [13]. The listeners were asked to give a relative score of two methods on the same utterance from -3 to 3 rating: -3) much worse; -2) worse; -1) slightly worse; 0) about the same; 1) slightly better; 2) better; 3) much better. The ratings were based on intelligibility, naturalness, and comfort. Twenty participants tested in an anechoic chamber with the Audio-Technica ATH-M50x headphones, where the speech had been processed and mixed with noise. They were aged 18 to 30 with fluent spoken English. Due to the limited selection of listeners, we did not conduct a subjective listening test of the German test set. We chose Factory1 and Factory2 at SNR = -5 and 0 dB and Volvo at SNR = -15 and -25 dB as severe and mild noise environments. Each listener tested 96 records: 3 methods per utterance $\times$ (2 females + 2 males) $\times$ 6 noise scenarios $\times$ 3 groups of comparisons.

4.2 Property Performance

F0 Conversion: As we can see from Table 1, F0 distortion is more severe in the female group than in the male group due to female has higher F0 value. The RMSE value is lower for the recorded clearer speech initially than for the initially less clear speech. In contrast to baseline's CycleGAN co-training method, NS-CiLC with F0 decomposed into 10-time scales of CWT coefficients has a more optimistic distortion profile and a significant improvement in the intelligibility of speech, as seen in the intelligibility metric of about 8% SIIB Gauss scores and 10% ESTOI scores.

Intelligibility Enhanced by iMetricGAN: Table 2 reports the SIIB Gauss scores and ESTOI scores for Normal, Lombard, and iMetricGAN post-speech with different SNRs. As we can see from the above table, relying solely on the Lombard effect gives a significant boost in the noisy environment of mild. Still, it does not achieve the enhancement in the noisy environment of Severe. The above table shows that the iMetricGAN approach can enhance intelligibility by about 23.2% for SIIB Gauss scores and 23.6% for ESTOI scores in a strong noise environment.

4.3 Overall Experiment

Objective Evaluation: SIIB Gauss and ESTOI are used to estimate the amount of information shared between the speaker and listener in bits/s. Figure 7 (a)–(c) give

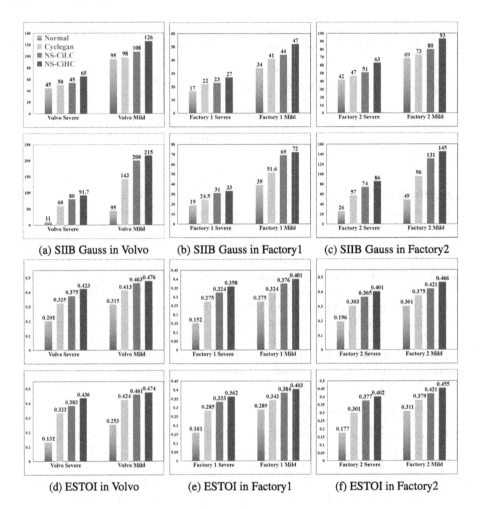

(a) SIIB Gauss in Volvo   (b) SIIB Gauss in Factory1   (c) SIIB Gauss in Factory2

(d) ESTOI in Volvo   (e) ESTOI in Factory1   (f) ESTOI in Factory2

Fig. 7. (a)–(c) denote the SIIB Gauss scores for different noise types at different SNRs. The top shows SIIB Gauss under English, and the bottom shows the values under German. (d)–(f) denote the ESTOI scores for different noise types at different SNRs.

objective evaluation scores, where confidence intervals are omitted because the scores among utterances are very close. Compared to normal, NS-CiHC improves SIIB Gauss 50% in severe noise while ESTOI scores are 115%. In a mild noise environment, due to the clarity of normal voice itself, the enhancement reaches about 35%, ESTOI scores increase 50%. Compared to CycleGAN, our method improves SIIB Gauss scores mainly 25%, and ESTOI scores are 30%. The increase in MCEPs dimension on intelligibility is also considerable, raising the SIIB Gauss and ESTOI scores by roughly 17% and 18.6%. Figure 7 (d)–(f) shows significant enhancements on the German set. Overall, NS-CiHC improves intelligibility more than several other methods.

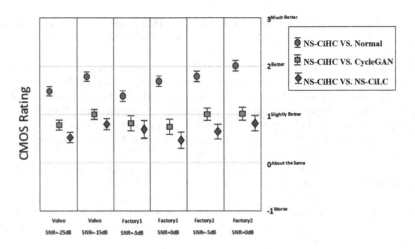

Fig. 8. MEAN CMOS ratings with 95% confidence intervals.

Subjective Evaluation: As shown in Fig. 8, there is no score below 0, which means the proposed method has steady improvements over reference methods. The CMOS scores indicate that the NS-CiC is significantly better in quality than the Normal utterances, gets about 1.8 scores. Compared to CycleGAN, it reaches about 0.9 scores. Compared to in a mildly noisy environment, our method has a higher 10% intelligibility lift in severe noise environments. Overall, the results of subjective experiments are consistent with the performance of objective experiments.

5 Conclusion

In this paper, we propose a high-quality parallel-data-free speech style conversion framework. We perform both spectrum and pitch conversion based on CycleGAN. We provide a non-linear method that studies the use of CWT to decompose F0 into ten temporal scales for effective F0 conversion. We also use 20-dimensional MCEPs features over baseline 10 dimensions to more comprehensively represent the acoustic features for MCEPs conversion. Considering that Lombard effect does not perform particularly well in strong noise environments, we further enhance it using iMetricGAN technology. Experimental results show that our proposed framework outperforms the baselines 25% SIIB Gauss and 30% ESTOI in objective evaluations; we get 0.9 CMOS score lifting in subjective evaluations. We effectively enhance speech intelligibility.

References

1. Alghamdi, A., Chan, W.Y.: Modified ESTOI for improving speech intelligibility prediction. In: 2020 IEEE Canadian Conference on Electrical and Computer Engineering (CCECE), pp. 1–5 (2020)
2. Alghamdi, N., Maddock, S., Marxer, R., Barker, J., Brown: a corpus of audio-visual lombard speech with frontal and profile views. J. Acoust. Soc. Am. **143**(6), EL523–EL529 (2018)

3. Chai, T., Draxler, R.R.: Root mean square error (RMSE) or mean absolute error (MAE)?-arguments against avoiding RMSE in the literature. Geosci Mod. Dev **7**(3), 1247–1250 (2014)
4. Garnier, M., Henrich, N.: Speaking in noise: How does the lombard effect improve acoustic contrasts between speech and ambient noise? Comput. Speech Lang. **28**(2), 580–597 (2014)
5. Hu, M., Xiao, J., Liao, L., Wang, Z., Lin, C.W., Wang, M., Satoh, S.: Capturing small, fast-moving objects: frame interpolation via recurrent motion enhancement. IEEE Trans. Circ. Syst. Video Technol. 1 (2021). https://doi.org/10.1109/TCSVT.2021.3110796
6. Kawanami, H., Iwami, Y., Toda, T., Saruwatari, H., Shikano, K.: GMM-based voice conversion applied to emotional speech synthesis (2003)
7. Liao, L., Xiao, J., Wang, Z., Lin, C.W., Satoh, S.: Image inpainting guided by coherence priors of semantics and textures. In: CVPR, pp. 6539–6548 (2021)
8. Liao, L., Xiao, J., Wang, Z., Lin, C.-W., Satoh, S.: Guidance and evaluation: semantic-aware image inpainting for mixed scenes. In: Vedaldi, A., Bischof, H., Brox, T., Frahm, J.-M. (eds.) ECCV 2020. LNCS, vol. 12372, pp. 683–700. Springer, Cham (2020). https://doi.org/10. 1007/978-3-030-58583-9_41
9. Liao, L., Xiao, J., Wang, Z., Lin, C.W., Satoh, S.: Uncertainty-aware semantic guidance and estimation for image inpainting. IEEE J. Sel. Top. Sig. Process. **15**(2), 310–323 (2021)
10. Ming, H., Huang, D.Y., Xie, L., Wu, J., Dong, M., Li, H.: Deep bidirectional LSTM modeling of timbre and prosody for emotional voice conversion. In: Interspeech, pp. 2453–2457 (2016)
11. Morise, M., Yokomori, F., Ozawa, K.: World: a vocoder-based high-quality speech synthesis system for real-time applications. IEICE Trans. Inf. Syst. **99**(7), 1877–1884 (2016)
12. Paul, D., Shifas, M.P., Pantazis, Y., Stylianou, Y.: Enhancing speech intelligibility in text-to-speech synthesis using speaking style conversion. arXiv preprint arXiv:2008.05809 (2020)
13. Rec, I.: P. 800: Methods for subjective determination of transmission quality. ITU (1996)
14. Ribeiro, M.S., Clark, R.A.: A multi-level representation of f0 using the continuous wavelet transform and the discrete cosine transform. In: ICASSP, pp. 4909–4913. IEEE (2015)
15. Seshadri, S., Juvela, L., Räsänen, O., Alku, P.: Vocal effort based speaking style conversion using vocoder features and parallel learning. IEEE Access **7**, 17230–17246 (2019)
16. Seshadri, S., Juvela, L., Yamagishi, J., Räsänen, O.: Cycle-consistent adversarial networks for non-parallel vocal effort based speaking style conversion. In: ICASSP. IEEE (2019)
17. Sisman, B., Li, H.: Wavelet analysis of speaker dependent and independent prosody for voice conversion. In: Interspeech, pp. 52–56 (2018)
18. Soloducha, M., Raake, A., Kettler, F., Voigt, P.: Lombard speech database for German language. In: Proceedings of of DAGA 42nd Annual Conference on Acoustics (2016)
19. Van Kuyk, S., Kleijn, W.B., Hendriks, R.C.: An evaluation of intrusive instrumental intelligibility metrics. IEEE ACM Trans. Audio Speech Lang. Process. **26**(11), 2153–2166 (2018)
20. Varga, A., Steeneken, H.J.: Ii. noisex-92: a database and an experiment to study the effect of additive noise on speech recognition systems. Speech Commun. **12**(3), 247–251 (1993)

A-Muze-Net: Music Generation by Composing the Harmony Based on the Generated Melody

Or Goren[1]([⊠]), Eliya Nachmani[1,2], and Lior Wolf[1]

[1] The Blavatnik School of Computer Science, Tel-Aviv University, Tel-Aviv, Israel
[2] Facebook AI Research, New York, USA

Abstract. We present a method for the generation of Midi files of piano music. The method models the right and left hands using two networks, where the left hand is conditioned on the right hand. This way, the melody is generated before the harmony. The Midi is represented in a way that is invariant to the musical scale, and the melody is represented, for the purpose of conditioning the harmony, by the content of each bar, viewed as a chord. Finally, notes are added randomly, based on this chord representation, in order to enrich the generated audio. Our experiments show a significant improvement over the state of the art for training on such datasets, and demonstrate the contribution of each of the novel components.

Keywords: Music generation · Midi processing · Recurrent neural networks

1 Introduction

We present a new method of symbolic music generation called A-Muze-Net. The method employs relatively low-capacity models, such as LSTM networks, and is trained on a relatively small dataset. In order to generalize well despite the lack of training data, it employs various techniques that are inspired by the common practices of human composers.

First, the harmony is composed after the melody is determined, and is conditioned on the melody. Second, the notes are represented in a way that is scale invariant, by considering the gap in pitch between the notes. Third, instead of separating notes to pitch and length, a single token captures both.

A crucial component of the method is that the melody is encoded by considering the notes at each generated bar and identifying the closest chord to this set of notes. Finally, a heuristic that employs the same chord-view adds random notes in order to make the generated audio more complete.

We demonstrate the advantage of our method over existing methods using a collection of 243 Midi files of Bach music. In addition, an ablation study demonstrates the value of each of the above mentioned contributions.

© Springer Nature Switzerland AG 2022
B. Þór Jónsson et al. (Eds.): MMM 2022, LNCS 13141, pp. 557–568, 2022.
https://doi.org/10.1007/978-3-030-98358-1_44

2   Related Work

Music generation methods can be divided into a few categories based on the generation domain. Many of the recent works, generate raw audio. **WaveNet** [14] is a convolutional neural network which inputs are raw audio files, and it generates new raw audio files. Since each raw audio timestamp is represented as a 16-bit integer, quantization is applied to reduce the output space [16]. A followup research by Manzelli et al. [12] employs the same quantization method but employs a biaxial LSTM model [10] which is built as two different LSTM models, one for the time-axis and one for the note-axis. The note-axis LSTM takes two inputs, the previous input as well as the final output from the time-axis LSTM model. **MP3net** [2] generates new mp3 files given mp3 files by using a CNN, their representation is based on the mp3 compression. The most evolved out of these methods is **Jukebox** [4], which compresses the raw audio data to discrete representation and apply high capacity transformer networks [18] to generate songs from many music genres, such as rock and jazz. It is trained on massive amounts of recorded data.

Many of the classical music composition approaches generate music scores [15,20,21], and this line of work has continued into the era of deep learning. **MidiNet** [21] employs a GAN in which both the generator and the discriminator are CNN models, **FlowComposer** [15] which uses Constrained Markov Models [17]. The Part-Invariant model [20] is a single RNN layer model that generates a composition based on an initial part.

Our model generates Midi notes given a prompt that it continues. Recent works that perform the same task include **MuseGan** [6] by Dong et al., which generates novel multi-track Midi files using a GAN model [7] trained on a large scale dataset. A multi-track Midi file contains a separate track for multiple instruments, such as guitar, piano, and drums. It is represented as a **Multi-Track Piano-Roll**. A single Piano-Roll is illustrated in Fig. 1, which is a binary-valued matrix where each row index represent a pitch value and each column index represent a time frame. Dong et al. have later on used a convolutional GAN to generate polyphonic music [5]. Binary neurons are used to generate the binary piano-roll representation, which was found to be more successful than using regular Hard Threshold (HT) or Bernoulli Sampling (BS) as was done in their earlier work.

Boulanger-Lewandowski et al. [1] also used the piano-roll representation but employed the Restricted Boltzmann Machine (RBM) on top of the RNN model in order to generate high-dimensional sequence. The dual-track generator of Lyu et al. [11] generates piano classical music. Similar to our method, it first generates the right-hand part and then the left-hand. In their model, the right-hand is generated by an LSTM, and the left-hand is subsequently generated using a Multi Layer Perceptron. Our left-hand generator is considerably more evolved as it's an LSTM that considers the chord embedding of the right-hand. In addition, while Lyu et al. represent the data as Piano-Rolls, we employ the normalized Midi representation, similar to **BachProp** [3].

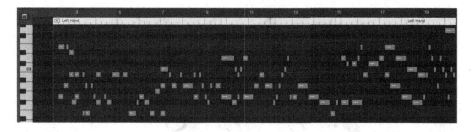

Fig. 1. Midi representation of prefug3 left-hand track, taken from Complete Bach Midi Index Dataset and opened with Logic Pro software

DeepJ [13] generates specific music styles: Baroque, Classical and Romantic. Similar to MuseGAN, a piano roll is employed as the underlying Midi representation. They employ a biaxial LSTM model [10], similar to the approach of [12]. Two LSTM models are used, one for the notes pitches and one for the duration of each such note. In order to pass the music genre information an embedding layer is used.

Music Transformer [9] is a transformer model with relative attention that generates symbolic music based on multi-track piano-roll representation of Bach's Chorales dataset. For the Piano-e-Competition dataset they have used the Midi events as their domain. **BachProp** is another LSTM model which is trained on given Midi files and composes new compositions. The normalized Midi representation it employs transforms the Midi into a sequence of notes, each with an associated length. The representation is defined as follows $note[n] = (T[n], P[n], dT[n])$, where $T[n]$ is the duration of the note, $P[n]$ is the pitch and $dT[n]$ is the time interval between the current note and the previous one. Their implementation employs three LSTM models, one per each input. **DeepBach** [8] is a deep learning model that uses the Bach's Chorales dataset, and generates new Chorales like Midi files. They are using only the Chorales, separating these to four different voices, where each voice has a single note at a time. Wu et al. [19] employed a Hierarchical-RNN (HRNN) to generate symbolic music. This was done using a slightly different Midi representation, in which the input domain is the Midi events note-on and note-off, and the time interval since the last event, like [9]. Their HRNN is built from three conditioned RNN models based on the bars, beat and notes.

Our representation is slightly different and employs notes and duration only. Furthermore, we employ a scale-invariant representation, see Sect. 3. In addition, we employ one LSTM for each hand, which are trained subsequently, and do not split the LSTM networks by the type of information of the note tuple.

3   Method

We describe the way the midi file is represented, the model we propose, and its training.

Fig. 2. All allowed notes lengths, First line from left to right: 1/32, 1/16, 1/8, 3/16 and 1/4. Second line from left to right: 3/8, 1/2, 3/4 and 1. The note images were obtained from https://www.freepik.com/.

3.1 Midi Representation

Given a Midi file, we apply a parser that outputs the note's pitch and length values for each note in the Midi file for each track. The obtained representation follows closely the music notes representation. The output is a string, in which the alphabet is a sequence of tokens. A sample token is '5-X-1/8', which means note 'X' at the fifth octave and length 1/8.

Each token is converted to an integer in the following way. First, we quantize the note's length into one of the following common values: 1/32, 1/16, 1/8, 3/16, 1/4, 3/8, 1/2, 3/4 and 1, as illustrated in Fig. 2. If, for example, the note's length is 11/16 which is rare, then we assign it to be 3/4.

The note integer representation which the networks employ is the product space of the nine length values and the 128 possible values of a note's midi-num[1].

The notes themselves are not taken as absolute notes, such as C (do), D (re), etc. Instead, we represent the Midi data in a way that is invariant to the musical scale used. A Midi file contains the scale information, and we compute each note's interval in the scale from the first note of the scale.

Two separate sequences are then generated. Specifically, for piano music one sequence is generated for the right-hand and one for the left. In some of the Midi files of the dataset, the separation is not provided. To overcome this, the average pitch for each track is calculated, and the track which has the lowest average pitch is chosen to be the left-hand track, and the maximal average pitch track is chosen to be the right-hand track. This stems from the position of the left hand on the keyboard relatively to the right hand, on the side of the lower notes.

Our representation assumes that there is no more than one note played simultaneously for each track. In case that the input contains multiple simultaneous notes, the right-hand selects the note with the highest pitch, and the left-hand the one with the lowest. Thus, heuristic relies on the observation that in the

---

[1] The Midi-num table assigns for each piano keyboard note a number, see https://computermusicresource.com/midikeys.html.

melody (right-hand) the highest note is more descriptive than the other ones, and vice versa for the harmony (left-hand).

3.2   Models

Our method relies on the common practice to compose the melody first and the harmony afterwards[2]. Therefore, the **Right Hand LSTM Model** is applied first. Subsequently, the **Left Hand LSTM Model** is applied conditioned on the output of the **Right Hand LSTM Model**.

The architecture of the **Right Hand LSTM Model** is depicted in Fig. 3. The embedding layer converts each of the possible 1161 integer values of the music representation into an embedding vector in $\mathbb{R}^{128}$. This is followed by two LSTM layers with a hidden size of the same dimensionality (128) and there are two layers. This is followed by a dropout layer with a factor of 0.5. Finally, a linear layer projects the LSTM output to a vector of length 1161 that produces the pseudo-probabilities (using softmax) of the next element in the sequence.

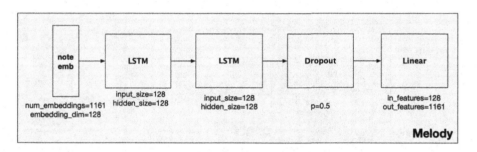

Fig. 3. Right Hand LSTM model architecture

In our method, the harmony generator network is conditioned on a new type of signal we propose, which is the chord analysis of the melody. The architecture of the **Left Hand LSTM Model** is depicted at Fig. 4. It is similar to the **Right Hand LSTM Model**. The main difference is that a second embedding layer is used. This added embedding, termed the **Chord Embedding Layer** captures the chord that is being played by the right-hand on the current bar. The number of items this embedding encodes is 253 and the embedding dimension is 128. Each of the 253 options encoded a specific combination of notes in the current bar played by the Right Hand Side. Formally, the input of the LSTM after the embedding is:

$$x_{emb} = E_{notes}(x) + E_{chords}(f(R)) \tag{1}$$

where x_{emb} is the LSTM input, x is the current left-hand note, E_{notes} is the **Notes Embedding Layer**, E_{chords} is the **Chords Embedding Layer**, R is

---

[2] See, for example, https://www.artofcomposing.com/how-to-compose-music-part-3-melody-or-harmony-first.

the current right-hand bar's notes and f is a function that maps a list of notes to their correspondent chord.

For this purpose, we employ a chords hash table that maps the chord's name to its right form, for example the chord **C** is mapped to notes "C", "E", "G". Also we gather groups of 7-chords, 6-chords, 13-chords, 9-chords, diminished chords and augmented chords, by adding/changing the original chord values. For example the chord **Cmaj7** is constructed by "C", "E", "G", "B", and **Ddim** is constructed by "D", "F", "$G^{\#}$". We apply this method to all possible chords and finally obtain the 253 chords mentioned above.

For recovering the chord associated with a specific bar, we gather all of the notes in that bar, and each chord is scored based on how many notes from a given bar belong to this chord. For example, if the notes are "C", "E" and "G" then chord **Cmaj7** will get a score of 3 and chord **Am** will get a score of 2, However chord **C** will get a score of 13 as these notes are the exact notes within the **C** chord, and it would be picked up. In case of a tie the more common chord would be chosen, i.e., **D** would be picked up rather than **D7**.

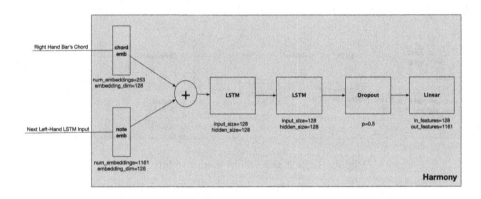

Fig. 4. Left Hand LSTM model architecture

3.3   A-Muze-Net Model Training

The model training process is depicted in Fig. 5. The given dataset is constructed from multiple Midi files, and we feed one Midi file at a time to the A-Muze-Net Model. The Midi file goes through the parsing methods, and is then divided into batches (the batches do not mix between multiple files).

Prediction - The prediction method inputs are:

1. A list of initial Melody notes (right-hand)
2. A list of initial Harmony notes (left-hand)
3. The number of notes to generate

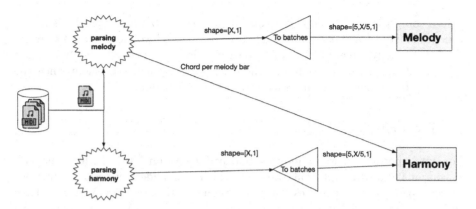

Fig. 5. A-Muze-Net model architecture

At start the hidden layers of the two LSTM models are initialized and are not being reset throughout the generation part, in order to keep the composition context. The initial melody sequence is fed to the already trained melody LSTM model while using teacher forcing to preserve the specified initial melody. This will set the hidden layer to preserve the initial melody context. Then, the last output from the initial feeding is essentially the first note prediction by the LSTM model. As the output is a probability for each note, only the top-k values are considered and a random value is chosen amongst them, after filtering the "break" notes. Then the chosen note is the next input of the melody LSTM model and again chooses the next predicted note from the next top-k ones. This process is finished when the given **number of notes to generate** is reached.

After this process is finished the chords for each melody bar are calculated and preserved as a sequence for chord per bar.

Then, the Harmony LSTM (Left-hand) is trained the same way as the other one, but the current right-hand bar's chord is passed through to the **Chord Embedding Layer** while the notes are passed through to the **Note Embedding Layer**. The initial sequence is also done in this method with teacher forcing, while the rest of the sequence up until the **number of notes to generate** is done without any teacher forcing.

After both the right-hand track and the left-hand track are generated, we apply a heuristic to add simultaneous notes. For each note in the harmony which is inside the current composition's scale, there is a 50% chance that it'll be accompanied with its perfect-fifth interval note and another 50% chance that it'll be also accompanied by its third interval note which is in the scale.

For example if the current scale is **C** and the current harmony note is **E** then in 50% chance the note **B** (fifth) would be added simultaneously, and another 50% that **G** (third - to form **Em** essentially) would be added.

For out of scale notes the method is different. Instead of adding their fifth or third interval, we add this note again but from a different octave. For example, if in a composition of scale C the current note is $4 - B^b$, for which B^b is at the fourth octave, then there is a 50% chance that $5 - B^b$ would be added as well.

For harmony, we apply a similar heuristic. However, instead of a 50% chance of generating simultaneous notes, there is a 10% to generate them since the harmony often generates simultaneous notes to form chords.

4   Experiments

For our experiments, we employ the **Complete Bach Midi Index** dataset[3]. It contains approximately 243 Midi files which are divided into several different genre topics, such as chorales, cantatas, fugues and more. The Midi files have different scales and different time-signatures. Most of these Midi files contain two tracks, one for the right-hand (melody) and one for the left-hand (harmony).

As baselines we employ two methods: **MuseGan** [6] and to Lyu et al. research [11]. Since our model is piano-based, we compare our results with the MuseGan piano track.

In addition to comparing with the baselines, we also compare with two ablation variants of our model.

Ablation 1 - No Conditioning of the Harmony on the Melody - In this experiment we trained the right-hand (melody) LSTM model and left-hand (harmony) LSTM model separately, meaning that we canceled the **Chords Embedding Layer** from the left-hand LSTM model. This way, both models are independent on one another. After the training was done we generated the Midi files.

Ablation 2 - Note Embedding Instead of Chord Embedding - In this ablation, we maintain the conditioning of the harmony on the melody, but instead of the **Chords Embedding Layer** we simply take the summation of all of the notes' embeddings of the right-hand bar and add them to the current left-hand note's embedding. In other words, we employ the following embedding

$$x_{emb} = E_{notes}(x) + \sum_{n \in R} E_{notes}(n) \tag{2}$$

Where x is the current left-track note, x_{emb} is the embedding output and the input to the LSTM layer, E_{notes} is the **Notes Embedding Layer**, R is the list of the corespondent right-hand bar notes.

Ablation 3 - Without the Notes Addition Method - In this ablation, we remove the part that adds random harmonic notes. In other words, the results are the output of the LSTM models without any further post-processing steps

The training perplexity of the full method is shown in Fig. 6(a). As can be seen, while the harmony and melody seemingly converged kind of the same way, still the melody converged faster than the harmony.

---

[3] http://www.bachcentral.com/midiindexcomplete.html.

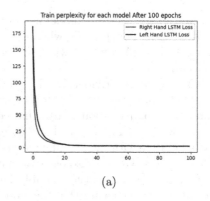 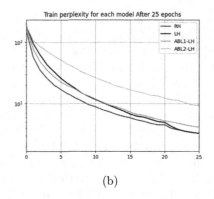

(a)   (b)

Fig. 6. (a) Train perplexity for the Right-Hand LSTM model and for the Left-Hand LSTM model. (b) Train perplexity with ablation studies.

The training perplexity of the full method compared to the ablation studies training perplexity is shown in Fig. 6(b). One can observe that **ABL1-LH**, which is the Left-Hand LSTM model of ablation study 1 is slightly above our Right-Hand LSTM model and below our Left-Hand LSTM model. This is expected since the **ABL1-LH** is not dependant on the Right-Hand LSTM model, and so its perplexity should be the same as the Right-Hand LSTM model. As for **ABL2-LH**, the obtained loss is considerably above our Left-Hand LSTM model and it takes it longer to converge. This emphasizes the importance of the **Chords Embedding Layer**.

4.1   Results

Following previous work, we consider the following quantitative metrics:

1. **QN (Qualified Note)** - The percentage of notes that were generated with a valid length. For example a note with length lower than $1/32$ is considered faulty.
2. **UPC (Unique Pitch Class)** - The average amount of different pitches per bar.
3. **TD (Tonal Distance)** - A number that specifies how much the two tracks are aligned chromatically, lower numbers are better.
4. **OOS (Out Of Scale)** - The percentage of generated notes that were out of scale.

Table 1 presents the results for our algorithm in comparison to the baselines. As can be seen, our model's **QN** achieves 100%, which means that all notes have a valid length size. This is because we maintain an allowed lengths list that each generated note has one of these lengths. This way, all of the generated notes are of qualified note lengths, and our method does not get fragments of notes, e.g. notes with length less than 1/32. Also we can see that our model achieves the closest **UPC** value to the True Music UPC value. For the **TD**, where lower values are better, we achieved a lower TD value than **MuseGan**, which means that our tracks are more coherent to each other.

Table 1 also depicts the results of the ablation study. Evidently, the UPC values for the ablation methods are lower, which indicates that the tracks are not aligned and do not complete one another. The second ablation study achieved the lowest score which might indicate that the addition of many right-hand notes together with the current left-hand one maybe interfere with the learning method of the model, causing it to generate much fewer notes. We can also observe that the TD values are much higher, and as expected the TD value of the first ablation study is higher than the TD value of the second one, which means that the model with no conditioning at all achieved a worse coherence score.

Our model has a higher OOS percentage in comparison to our ablation studies, which is consistent with the model's higher UPC value. In a music scale there are only seven notes which are inside the scale, and the five others are considered as out of scale. Since we have UPC value which is higher than seven, we have a high percentage of out of scale notes. Almost all music compositions uses notes from out of scale to generate unique sounds, as is evidenced from the high UPC value of True Music baseline. For example if a composition at scale C uses the **D** chord, it necessarily uses the $F^{\#}$ note which is out of scale. Interestingly, the second ablation study achieved 20% OOS although it uses less than seven notes, which reveals a mismatch with the notes being used at the harmony side, pointing to the significance of using the Chord Embedding Layer.

Table 1. Quantitative comparison to outher methods.

Experiment	QN	UPC	TD	OOS
True Music	98.70%	9.83	–	–
Lyu et al. Pianoroll CNN [11]	91.20%	2.35	–	–
Lyu et al. Embedding Atten-LSTM [11]	90%	7.79	–	–
MuseGan	64%	4.57	0.94	–
A-muse-Net - Ablation1	**100%**	7.30	0.95	18%
A-muse-Net - Ablation2	**100%**	6.80	0.90	20%
A-muse-Net - Ablation3	**100%**	7.70	0.90	18%
A-muse-Net	**100%**	**9.54**	**0.86**	29%

4.2   User Study

We asked 17 people to rate the A-Muze-Net generated songs with scores from 1–5 and to state their musical background level, as in **MuseGan** [6] and in Lyu et al. [11]. Each individual listened to ten different clips, which are of length of four-bars, as also was done in the MuseGan research. Table 2 presents their average satisfaction out of our generated songs on a scale from one to five.

As can be seen, our method outperforms the baseline methods. Interestingly, while MuseGAN is second by the user rating, it is far lower on the quantitative results.

Table 2. User study results.

Experiment	US
True music	3.80
Lyu et al. Pianoroll CNN [11]	2.40
Lyu et al. Embedding Atten-LSTM [11]	2.70
MuseGan	3.16
A-muse-Net	**3.28**

5 Conclusions

While high-capacity models have now been shown to be able to model music based on very large corpora [4], such models remain computationally inaccessible to most research labs and amassing such data if a copy free way is next to impossible. Furthermore, while such models teach us about AI and large-scale pattern extraction, there is little advancement with regard to the foundations of music making.

In this work, we employ a well established machine learning architecture and try to answer fundamental questions about music representation: (1) How to link the melody and the harmony effectively? (2) How to represent symbolic music in an accessible way? (3) How to capture the transient essence of the melody? (4) How to enrich the generated music?

Our answers to each of these questions have led to an improvement over the options that have been used in the previous work. Collectively, our method provides a sizable improvement in all metrics in comparison to the existing methods.

Acknowledgements. This project has received funding from the European Research Council (ERC) under the European Union's Horizon 2020 research and innovation programme (grant ERC CoG 725974).

References

1. Boulanger-Lewandowski, N., Bengio, Y., Vincent, P.: Modeling temporal dependencies in high-dimensional sequences: application to polyphonic music generation and transcription. arXiv preprint arXiv:1206.6392 (2012)

2. Broek, K.v.d.: Mp3net: coherent, minute-long music generation from raw audio with a simple convolutional GAN. arXiv preprint arXiv:2101.04785 (2021)
3. Colombo, F., Gerstner, W.: BachProp: learning to compose music in multiple styles. arXiv preprint arXiv:1802.05162 (2018)
4. Dhariwal, P., Jun, H., Payne, C., Kim, J.W., Radford, A., Sutskever, I.: Jukebox: a generative model for music. arXiv preprint arXiv:2005.00341 (2020)
5. Dong, H.W., Yang, Y.H.: Convolutional generative adversarial networks with binary neurons for polyphonic music generation. arXiv preprint 1804.09399 (2018)
6. Dong, H.W., et al.: MuseGAN: multi-track sequential generative adversarial networks for symbolic music generation and accompaniment. In: AAAI (2018)
7. Goodfellow, I., et al.: Generative adversarial nets. In: NIPS (2014)
8. Hadjeres, G., Pachet, F., Nielsen, F.: DeepBach: a steerable model for bach chorales generation. In: International Conference on Machine Learning (2017)
9. Huang, C.Z.A., et al.: Music transformer. arXiv preprint arXiv:1809.04281 (2018)
10. Johnson, D.D.: Generating polyphonic music using tied parallel networks. In: Correia, J., Ciesielski, V., Liapis, A. (eds.) EvoMUSART 2017. LNCS, vol. 10198, pp. 128–143. Springer, Cham (2017). https://doi.org/10.1007/978-3-319-55750-2_9
11. Lyu, S., Zhang, A., Song, R.: Dual-track music generation using deep learning. arXiv preprint arXiv:2005.04353 (2020)
12. Manzelli, R., Thakkar, V., Siahkamari, A., Kulis, B.: An end to end model for automatic music generation: combining deep raw and symbolic audio networks. In: Proceedings of the Musical Metacreation Workshop at 9th International Conference on Computational Creativity, Salamanca, Spain (2018)
13. Mao, H.H., Shin, T., Cottrell, G.: DeepJ: style-specific music generation. In: International Conference on Semantic Computing (ICSC) (2018)
14. van den Oord, A., et al.: WaveNet: a generative model for raw audio (2016)
15. Papadopoulos, A., Roy, P., Pachet, F.: Assisted lead sheet composition using Flow-Composer. In: International Conference on Principles and Practice of Constraint Programming (2016)
16. Recommendation, C.: Pulse code modulation of voice frequencies. In: ITU (1988)
17. Roweis, S.T.: Constrained hidden Markov models. In: NIPS (1999)
18. Vaswani, A., et al.: Attention is all you need. In: Advances in Neural Information Processing Systems, pp. 5998–6008 (2017)
19. Wu, J., Hu, C., Wang, Y., Hu, X., Zhu, J.: A hierarchical recurrent neural network for symbolic melody generation. IEEE Trans. Cybern. 50(6), 2749–2757 (2019)
20. Yan, Y., Lustig, E., VanderStel, J., Duan, Z.: Part-invariant model for music generation and harmonization. In: ISMIR, pp. 204–210 (2018)
21. Yang, L.C., Chou, S.Y., Yang, Y.H.: MidiNet: a convolutional generative adversarial network for symbolic-domain music generation. arXiv:1703.10847 (2017)

Melody Generation from Lyrics Using Three Branch Conditional LSTM-GAN

Abhishek Srivastava[2], Wei Duan[1], Rajiv Ratn Shah[2], Jianming Wu[3],
Suhua Tang[4], Wei Li[5], and Yi Yu[1(✉)]

[1] Digital Content and Media Sciences Research Division, National Institute
of Informatics, SOKENDAI, Tokyo, Japan
{weiduan,yiyu}@nii.ac.jp
[2] MDMA Lab, Indraprastha Institute of Information Technology, Delhi, India
{abhishek18124,rajivratn}@iiitd.ac.in
[3] KDDI Research, Inc, Tokyo, Japan
ji-wu@kddi-research.jp
[4] Graduate School of Informatics and Engineering, The University
of Electro-Communications, Tokyo, Japan
shtang@uec.ac.jp
[5] School of Computer Science and Technology, Fudan University, Shanghai, China
weili-fudan@fudan.edu.cn

Abstract. With the availability of paired lyrics-melody dataset and advancements of artificial intelligence techniques, research on melody generation conditioned on lyrics has become possible. In this work, for melody generation, we propose a novel architecture, Three Branch Conditional (TBC) LSTM-GAN conditioned on lyrics which is composed of a LSTM-based generator and discriminator respectively. The generative model is composed of three branches of identical and independent lyrics-conditioned LSTM-based sub-networks, each responsible for generating an attribute of a melody. For discrete-valued sequence generation, we leverage the Gumbel-Softmax technique to train GANs. Through extensive experiments, we show that our proposed model generates tuneful and plausible melodies from the given lyrics and outperforms the current state-of-the-art models quantitatively as well as qualitatively.

Keywords: Melody generation from lyrics · LSTM · GAN

1 Introduction

In the artificial intelligence field, automating the process of melody generation conditioned on lyrics has been a challenging research task. Songwriting is one of the creative human endeavors [16]. Typically, during songwriting, a musician either writes the lyrics for a song and then tries to compose a melody to match

---

A. Srivastava—was involved in this work during his internship at the National Institute of Informatics, Tokyo, Japan.
The second author has the same contribution as the first author for this work.

© Springer Nature Switzerland AG 2022
B. Þór Jónsson et al. (Eds.): MMM 2022, LNCS 13141, pp. 569–581, 2022.
https://doi.org/10.1007/978-3-030-98358-1_45

the lyrics or composes a melody for a song and then writes lyrics to fit the melody. In this work, we consider the task of melody generation from lyrics as a sequence-to-sequence task whereby for a given lyrics, *i.e.*, a sequence of syllables, we want to generate a melody, *i.e.*, a sequence of discrete-valued triplets of music attributes.

Our goal is to design and implement a generative model for melody generation from lyrics that can capture the correlations that exist between segments of lyrics and patterns in a melody. However, generating a melody based on music data and learning the association between multimodal music data [20] have been challenging research topics in the field of intelligent music. The task of melody generation from lyrics is intrinsically challenging since there is no unique mapping between a lyrics and melody [18]. This poses a problem especially during the evaluation phase due to a lack of metric that can evaluate a generated melody qualitatively and quantitatively. Moreover, training GANs on discrete data is not straightforward since the generator output is non-differentiable.

In this work, for melody generation, we design Three Branch Conditional (TBC)-LSTM-GAN conditioned on lyrics which is composed of three main components: i) an LSTM-based generator which models long term dependency in melody and contains three identical and independent lyrics-conditioned LSTM-based sub-networks, each responsible for generating an attribute of the melody; ii) a lyrics-conditioned LSTM-based discriminator which not only models long term dependency in melody but also provides informative feedback for generator updates; iii) the Gumbel-Softmax [6] to train GANs for generation based on discrete-valued sequence.

2   Related Works

Generally, in this work, melody generation from lyrics can be regarded as conditional sequence-to-sequence generation where a sequence of syllables is taken as the input to generate a sequence of discrete-valued triplets of music attributes. This is one of interesting music generation tasks.

2.1   Music Generation

Automating the process of music composition through computational techniques has been studied since the 1950s [5]. More recently an elaborate study [13] related to music composition through algorithmic methods has been conducted. Lately, various techniques of shallow and deep learning have shown promising results for lyrics-conditioned melody generation. ALYSIA [1], for instance, is a song-writing system based on Random Forest that generates a set of sample melodies when given a short lyrical phrase. Also, a sequence-to-sequence framework [2] was adopted to develop a melody composition model. To produce notes together with the corresponding alignment it uses a hierarchical decoder and a couple of encoders for the lyrics and melody. More recently, a LSTM based GAN architecture [19] was proposed that uses a quantization framework to discretize its continuous-valued output and generate melodies from the given lyrics.

2.2   Discrete Data Generation Using GANs

GANs were originally designed to generate continuous-valued data like images. Lately, however, GANs have been used for discrete sequence generation tasks. However, using GANs for discrete sequence generation is not straightforward since during discrete data generation, the output of the generator is non-different-iable due to which standard gradient-based algorithms cannot be used to train the model. Recently, two types of strategies have been explored to deal with the non-differentiability problem arising from discrete data generation using GANs. The first one is based on the reinforce algorithm and the second one is based on transform the problem from discrete data to the continuous space.

More recently, a wide variety of GANs for discrete data generation, especially for text generation, have relied on the reinforcement learning (RL) methods to train the model. SeqGAN [17] for instance, bypasses the generator differentiation problem through the use of policy gradient methods [15]. RankGAN [8] uses a rank-based discriminator instead of the binary classifier and is optimized through policy gradient techniques. LeakGAN [4] lets the discriminator leak high-level features it has learned to the generator and guides it. In this way, it allows the generator to incorporate intermediate information during each generation step. MaskGAN [3] resorts to a seq2seq model and propose an action-critic CGAN that fills the missing text by conditioning on the context surrounding it.

Lately, GANs, for discrete data generation, have relied on either working in a continuous space or approximating the discreteness. C-LSTM-GAN [19] for lyrics-conditioned melody generation, for instance, uses a quantization framework to discretize the continuous-valued output it generates. The quantization scheme they adopt constraints the generated continuous-valued music attributes to their closest discrete value. Approximating the argmax operation, TextGAN [21] exploits an annealed softmax relaxation at the output of the generator. ARAE [22] uses an auto-encoder module to reformulate the problem into a continuous latent space to avoid the issue of non-differentiability. RELGAN [11] applies the Gumbel-Softmax to train GANs based on discrete data.

3   Methodology

Our proposed model, TBC-LSTM-GAN, for lyrics-conditioned melody generation is shown in Fig. 1. We train the proposed model for the alignment relationship between the melody and lyrics. The proposed model is composed of three main components: 1) a lyrics-conditioned LSTM-based generator to learn long sequence dependencies in melody; 2) a lyrics-conditioned LSTM-based discriminator to provide meaningful updates to the generator; 3) the Gumbel-Softmax relaxation for training GANs on discrete data.

3.1   GANs

In GAN, the generator learns a mapping, $G(z; \theta_g)$ from a prior noise distribution $p_z(z)$ to the data space to capture the generator distribution p_g over the data

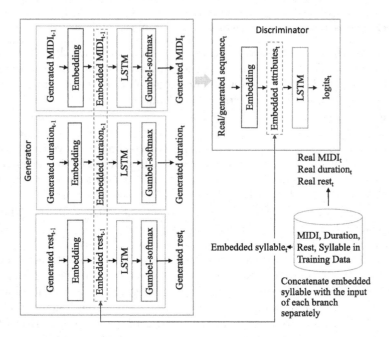

Fig. 1. Architecture of TBC-LSTM-GAN

x. The discriminator, $D(x; \theta_d)$, outputs a probability estimate that x is sampled from the training data instead of p_g. The generator and discriminator networks are trained simultaneously such that, we adjust the parameters of the generator to minimize $\log(1 - D(G(z)))$ while we adjust parameters of the discriminator to minimize $\log(D(x))$.

$$\min_G \max_D \mathbb{E}_{\mathbf{x} \sim p_{\text{data}}(\mathbf{x})}[\log D(\mathbf{x})] + \mathbb{E}_{\mathbf{z} \sim p_{\mathbf{z}}(\mathbf{z})}[\log(1 - D(G(\mathbf{z})))] \qquad (1)$$

We can easily extend a GAN to a conditioned model [10] by conditioning both the generator and discriminator with additional information y. We combine the prior input noise $p_z(z)$ and y in a joint hidden representation in the generator network. In the discriminator, we present x and y as inputs. The objective function of a two-payer minimax game is given as

$$\min_G \max_D \mathbb{E}_{\mathbf{x} \sim p_{\text{data}}(\mathbf{x})}[\log D(\mathbf{x}|\mathbf{y})] + \mathbb{E}_{\mathbf{z} \sim p_{\mathbf{z}}(\mathbf{z})}[\log(1 - D(G(\mathbf{z}|\mathbf{y})))] \qquad (2)$$

where $\mathbf{y}$ is the condition vector.

3.2   Problem Formulation

We can formulate our research problem as follows: we are given a lyrics, *i.e.*, a sequence of syllables represented by $X = [x_1, \ldots, x_T]$ such that $x_i \in \mathbb{R}^{20}$ and we want to generate a melody, *i.e.*, sequence of triplets of discrete-valued music attributes represented by $Y = [y_1, \ldots, y_T]$ where $y_i = \{y_i^{MIDI}, y_i^{dura}, y_i^{rest}\}$ such that $y_i^{MIDI} \in \mathbb{R}^{100}$, $y_i^{dura} \in \mathbb{R}^{12}$, and $y_i^{rest} \in \mathbb{R}^7$ respectively.

3.3 Gumbel-Softmax

When we train the GANs for generating discrete-valued data, there is a critical issue of non-differentiability. Due to this, the parameters of the generator, θ_G, cannot be updated and hence it cannot learn during the training phase. To mitigate the issue of non-differentiability we leverage the Gumbel-Softmax at the output of the generator. The Gumbel-Softmax relaxation technique, more recently, has been used to train GANs for text generation [11]. The task of discrete sequence generation involves generating a sequence of discrete-valued tokens such that each token belongs to the vocabulary V of the underlying data. When using an RNN based generator, we generate a single token at every time step. Let $|V|$ denote the size of the vocabulary and let $o_t \in \mathbb{R}^{|V|}$ denote the output logits, at time step t. Then, we can obtain the next one-hot token $y_{t+1} \in \mathbb{R}^{|V|}$ following Eq. 3.

$$y_{t+1} \sim softmax(o_t) \tag{3}$$

The sampling from a multinomial distribution depicted in Eq. 3 is a non-differentiable operation, this implies that there is a step function at the output of the generator. Because the derivative of a step function is zero almost everywhere, we have $\frac{\partial y_{t+1}}{\partial \theta_G} = 0$. Using the chain rule, we can see that the gradients of the generator loss l_G w.r.t. θ_G will be

$$\frac{\partial l_G}{\partial \theta_G} = \sum_{t=0}^{T-1} \frac{\partial y_{t+1}}{\partial \theta_G} \frac{\partial l_G}{\partial y_{t+1}} = 0 \tag{4}$$

Now, because $\frac{\partial l_G}{\partial \theta_G}$ is zero, the generator cannot get an update signal via the discriminator and hence the generator cannot be updated. For discrete data generation, there is the non-differentiability problem during training of GANs. By applying the Gumbel-Softmax relaxation at the output of the generator, for discrete data, we can solve the problem of non-differentiability. The Gumbel-Softmax approximates samples from a categorical distribution by defining a continuous distribution over a simplex [6,9]. The Gumbel-Softmax relaxation is composed of two parts which include the Gumbel-Max trick and relaxation of the discreteness. Using the Gumbel-Max trick we can reparameterize the non-differentiable sampling operation in Eq. 3 as

$$y_{t+1} = one\_hot(arg\ max_{1 \le i \le |V|}(o_t^{(i)} + g_t^{(i)})) \tag{5}$$

where $o_t^{(i)}$ denotes the ith entry of o_t and $g_t^{(i)}$ is from $i.i.d$ standard Gumbel distribution, $i.e.$, $g_t^{(i)} = -\log(-\log U_t^{(i)})$ with $U_t^{(i)} \sim Uniform(0,1)$. Reparameterization of the sampling operation in Eq. 3 is one part of the solution since the argmax operation in Eq. 5 is non-differentiable in nature. So, now we relax the discreteness by approximating the one-hot with argmax by softmax given as

$$\hat{y}_{t+1} = softmax(\beta(o_t + g_t)) \tag{6}$$

where β represents a tunable parameter which is always bigger than 0 and called *inverse temperature*. Since $\hat{y}_{t+1}$ in Eq. 6 is differentiable, so we can use it as the input into the discriminator instead of y_{t+1}.

3.4 Generator

In our work, the generator is used to generate a melody, $\hat{Y}$ conditioned on the lyrics, X. The generator is composed of three branches of identical and independent sub-networks which are used to generate a sequence of MIDI numbers, $\hat{Y}^{MIDI} = [\hat{y}_1^{MIDI}, \ldots, \hat{y}_T^{MIDI}]$, a sequence duration values, $\hat{Y}^{dura} = [\hat{y}_1^{dura}, \ldots, \hat{y}_T^{dura}]$, and a sequence of rest values, $\hat{Y}^{rest} = [\hat{y}_1^{rest}, \ldots, \hat{y}_T^{rest}]$ respectively. We sequentially align the sequences generated at the output of the three branches to assemble a melody for the given lyrics. Since the sub-network in each branch of the generator is identical, we will only explain how a branch of the generator generates a sequence of MIDI numbers by the forward pass.

At the tth time step, we input the embedded syllable x_t and the one-hot approximation of MIDI number generated in the last time step $\hat{y}_{t-1}^{MIDI}$ to the sub-network. To obtain an embedding of $\hat{y}_{t-1}^{MIDI}$ we pass it into a fully connected (FC) layer with a linear activation. We learn the embedding of MIDI number during the training. We then concatenate the embedded syllable x_t with the embedded MIDI representation and use a FC layer with ReLU activation to obtain the intermediate representation which is then passed through a couple of LSTM layers. The output of the LSTM layer is then inputted into a FC layer with linear activation to get the output logits, $o_t \in \mathbb{R}^{100}$. For the one-hot approximation of generated MIDI number, during the tth time step, $\hat{y}_t^{MIDI}$ we exploit the Gumbel-Softmax on o_t. We repeat the entire procedure for T time steps to generate $\hat{Y}^{MIDI}$. At the initial time step $t = 1$, $\hat{y}_{t-1}^{MIDI} \sim Uniform(0, 1)$.

3.5 Discriminator

The discriminator is responsible to determinate whether the input melody conditioned on the lyrics is true. The discriminator is a LSTM-based network to model long term dependencies in melody and provide informative signals for generator updates.

At the tth time step, we input the embedded syllable x_t, MIDI number y_t^{MIDI}, duration value y_t^{dura}, and rest value y_t^{rest} to the discriminator. We first embed the MIDI number, duration and rest values by passing them through a FC layer with linear activation. The embedded representation of MIDI number, duration, rest and syllable are then concatenated together to form a joint representation of syllable conditioned music attribute triplet. This joint representation is then inputted into a FC layer with ReLU activation to obtain an intermediate representation which is then passed through a couple LSTM layers. The output of the LSTM layer is then inputted into a FC layer with linear activation to get the output logits, $o_t \in \mathbb{R}$. We repeat the entire procedure for T time steps to obtain output logits $o = [o_1, \ldots, o_T]$. At last, we compute the average logit to calculate the loss. Specifically, o and $\hat{o}$ indicate the output logits which can be gained when a generated and a real melody conditioned on lyrics is inputted into the discriminator respectively. The loss function of discriminator is the relativistic standard GAN (RSGAN) [7] which can be given by

$$l_D = \log sigmoid(\frac{1}{T}\sum_{t=1}^{T} o_t - \frac{1}{T}\sum_{t=1}^{T} \hat{o}_t) \tag{7}$$

Intuitively, the loss function in Eq. 7 directly estimates that, compared with the generated melody, whether real melody is more realistic. In addition, the generator loss is $l_G = -l_D$.

4 Experiments and Evaluation

The data [19] for our task is composed of a collection of 13,9251 melody-lyrics pairs aligned at the note-syllable level. We randomly split the data in the ratio of 8:1:1 to create the training, validation and testing sets. In the data, a lyrics is represented as a sequence of syllables and a melody is represented as a sequence of triplets of music attributes. Each triplet is composed of the MIDI number of the musical note, the duration of the note, and the length of rest that follows the note. MIDI number is a discrete variable and its value ranges from 0 to 127. The temporal attributes, duration, and rest are also discrete in nature and assume values that represent the time they last with a single beat represented by a unity. In the data, there are 100 distinct MIDI numbers, 12 distinct duration values, and 7 distinct rest values. In this work, we work with sequences of length 20, *i.e.*, each lyrics contains 20 syllables and each melody contains 20 triplets of music attributes, one triplet of music attributes corresponding to each syllable in the lyrics. Before we commence the adversarial training, we pre-train the generator for several epochs using the standard maximum likelihood estimation (MLE) objective. We use the pre-trained generator of our proposed model as a baseline, we define it as the TBC-LSTM-MLE in our experiments. Besides TBC-LSTM-MLE, we use C-LSTM-GAN [19] as a strong baseline.

4.1 Experimental Setup

During the training phase, we use the Adam optimizer and set β_1 to 0.9 and β_2 to 0.99. Then, we apply gradient clipping to make the gradients not exceed 5. When we start training, firstly, we exploit the MLE objective as loss function of pre-train generator network for 40 epochs and set the learning rate to 0.01. Secondly, both the generator and discriminator are adversarial trained for 120 epochs and set the learning rate to 0.01. In addition, there are a single discriminator step and a single generator step in each step of adversarial training. During the adversarial training, we use a maximum temperature $\beta_{max} = 1000$ and set the batch size to 512.

4.2   Quality and Diversity Evaluation

Evaluation of GANs is an active area of research [14]. One of the challenges we face during the evaluation is the lack of a metric that can be used to simultaneously measure the quality and diversity of generated samples. Moreover, measuring the quality of the generated melody is subjective in nature. Nevertheless, the Self-BLEU score is used to measure the diversity of generated samples. Further, we conduct a subjective evaluation [19] as a means to measure the quality of the generated melody.

In Fig. 2, we show the sheet music corresponding to a sample lyrics at epoch 1, 40 and 160 respectively. From the figure, it is evident that as the training progresses the quality of melody improves.

(a) Model trained for 1 epoch

(b) Model trained for 40 epochs (end of pre-training)

(c) Model trained for 160 epochs (end of training)

Fig. 2. Sheet music for a sample lyrics at different stages of training.

Diversity Evaluation Using Self-BLEU. GANs are susceptible to mode collapse therefore it is important to evaluate the diversity of samples generated by GANs. We use the Self-BLEU score to measure the diversity of the generated samples. The value of the Self-BLEU score ranges from 0 to 1. The diversity of the generated samples is inversely proportional to the value of Self-BLEU with a lower value of Self-BLEU indicating there is a higher probability of sample diversity and lesser probability of mode collapse. The BLEU score [12] aims to assess the similarity between two sequences. By considering one generated sample as a hypothesis and the rest of the generated samples as the references, for each generated sample, we can calculate its BLEU score and consider the average BLEU score as the Self-BLEU score.

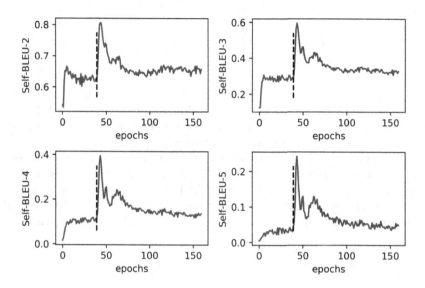

Fig. 3. Training curves of self-BLEU scores on testing dataset.

In the Fig. 3, we show the trend of Self-BLEU score on the testing data during the training. The pre-training and adversarial training stages are separated by the dotted line as shown in the figure. During the pre-training stage, the value of Self-BLEU does not change much and there is no observable trend. At the start of an adversarial train, the value for Self-BLEU score increases (upto epoch 50) indicates deteriorating sample diversity. However, as the adversarial training progresses, we observe a decreasing trend of Self-BLEU score indicating improved diversity of generated samples.

4.3   Music Quantitative Evaluation

To quantitatively evaluate the melody generated by the proposed model against the baselines, we can extract a sequence of individual music attributes and compute the following properties as described in [19]: MIDI number span, 3-MIDI number repetitions, 2-MIDI number repetitions, number of unique MIDI numbers, average rest value within a song, and song length.

Table 1. Metrics evaluation of in-songs attributes.

	Ground truth	TBC-LSTM-GAN	TBC-LSTM-MLE	C-LSTM-GAN
MIDI span	10.8	12.4	13.70	7.7
3-MIDI repetitions	3.8	2.7	2.1	2.2
2-MIDI repetitions	7.4	10.2	9.1	9.7
Unique MIDI	5.9	6.1	6.2	5.1
Notes without rest	15.6	15.6	12.7	16.7
Average rest value	0.8	0.7	1.1	0.6
Song length	43.3	41.7	51.0	39.2

We summarize the results in Table 1. From the table, we can observe that the proposed model, TBC-LSTM-GAN, is the closest to the ground-truth for every temporal song attribute as well as a couple of MIDI related song attributes such as MIDI number span and unique MIDI numbers.

We also visualize the transition between MIDI numbers which is an crucial music attribute. Figure 4 shows the MIDI number transition in the melodies generated by the proposed model, TBC-LSTM-GAN, the ground truth, and baseline models. As we can observe from the figure it is evident that the MIDI number transition of our proposed model is closest to the ground truth.

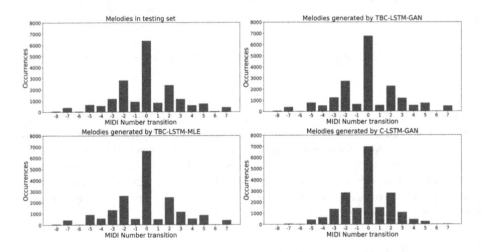

Fig. 4. Distribution of transitions.

4.4 Subjective Evaluation

To this end we randomly select three lyrics from the dataset and accordingly obtain melodies using the baseline models, the proposed model and the ground truth. We use Synthesizer V^1 to synthesize the generated melody and lyrics. We invite eight subjects to listen to the generated melodies and play the lyrics synthesized melody three times in a random order. For each melody played, we ask the subjects to answer three questions: i) how about the entire melody? ii) how about the rhythm? and iii) does the melody fit the lyrics well?

The subjects give a score between 1 and 5 for each question. Here, a score of 1 corresponds to very bad, 2 to bad, 3 to OK, 4 to good, and 5 to very good. The results of subjective evaluation are shown in Fig. 5. From the figure we can observe that the proposed model, TBC-LSTM-GAN outperforms other methods and generates melodies closest to human compositions. The generated melodies are available in the link[2].

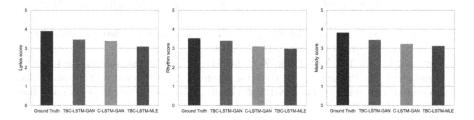

Fig. 5. Subjective evaluation results.

5   Conclusion

In this work, for melody generation, we proposed a novel architecture, TBC-LSTM-GAN conditioned on lyrics. Our proposed model is composed of an LSTM-based generator to learn the correlation between segments of lyrics and patterns in the melody. It uses an LSTM-based discriminator to model long term dependency in melody and provide informative feedback for generator updates. We exploited the Gumbel-Softmax technique to train GANs for generation based on discrete-valued sequence. In particular, through quantitative measurements including MIDI related and temporal song-attributes along with MIDI number transition, we have shown that the proposed model best approximates the ground-truth. Also, through subjective evaluation we have shown that the proposed model is the closest to the ground-truth with respect to the quality of generated melodies. Further, we showed how the quality and diversity of generated samples improves as the adversarial training progresses.

---

[1] https://synthesizerv.com/en/.
[2] https://drive.google.com/file/d/1Ov0YYZt84KxPpSuR8quEV05Gy9hY-f6n/view.

References

1. Ackerman, M., Loker, D.: Algorithmic songwriting with ALYSIA. CoRR abs/1612.01058 (2016). http://arxiv.org/abs/1612.01058
2. Bao, H., et al.: Neural melody composition from lyrics. CoRR abs/1809.04318 (2018). http://arxiv.org/abs/1809.04318
3. Fedus, W., Goodfellow, I.J., Dai, A.M.: Maskgan: better text generation via filling in the. ArXiv abs/1801.07736 (2018)
4. Guo, J., Lu, S., Cai, H., Zhang, W., Yu, Y., Wang, J.: Long text generation via adversarial training with leaked information. ArXiv abs/1709.08624 (2018)
5. Hiller, Jr., L.A., Isaacson, L.M.: Musical composition with a high-speed digital computer. J. Audio Eng. Soc. **6**(3), 154–160 (1958). http://www.aes.org/e-lib/browse.cfm?elib=231
6. Jang, E., Gu, S., Poole, B.: Categorical reparameterization with gumbel-softmax (2016)
7. Jolicoeur-Martineau, A.: The relativistic discriminator: a key element missing from standard gan. ArXiv abs/1807.00734 (2019)
8. Lin, K., Li, D., He, X., Zhang, Z., Sun, M.T.: Adversarial ranking for language generation. In: Proceedings of the 31st International Conference on Neural Information Processing Systems, NIPS 2017, pp. 3158–3168. Curran Associates Inc., Red Hook (2017)
9. Maddison, C.J., Mnih, A., Teh, Y.W.: The concrete distribution: a continuous relaxation of discrete random variables (2016)
10. Mirza, M., Osindero, S.: Conditional generative adversarial nets. CoRR abs/1411.1784 (2014). http://arxiv.org/abs/1411.1784
11. Nie, W., Narodytska, N., Patel, A.B.: Relgan: relational generative adversarial networks for text generation. In: ICLR (2019)
12. Papineni, K., Roukos, S., Ward, T., Zhu, W.J.: Bleu: a method for automatic evaluation of machine translation, October 2002. https://doi.org/10.3115/1073083.1073135
13. Rodriguez, J.D.F., Vico, F.J.: AI methods in algorithmic composition: a comprehensive survey. CoRR abs/1402.0585 (2014). http://arxiv.org/abs/1402.0585
14. Semeniuta, S., Severyn, A., Gelly, S.: On accurate evaluation of gans for language generation (2018)
15. Sutton, R., Mcallester, D., Singh, S., Mansour, Y.: Policy gradient methods for reinforcement learning with function approximation. Adv. Neural Inf. Process. Syst. **12**, February 2000
16. Wiggins, G.A.: A preliminary framework for description, analysis and comparison of creative systems. J. Knowl. Based Syst. **19**(7), 449–458 (2006)
17. Yu, L., Zhang, W., Wang, J., Yu, Y.: Seqgan: sequence generative adversarial nets with policy gradient. In: Proceedings of the Thirty-First AAAI Conference on Artificial Intelligence, AAAI 2017, pp. 2852–2858. AAAI Press (2017)
18. Yu, Yi., Harscoët, Florian, Canales, Simon, Reddy M, Gurunath, Tang, Suhua, Jiang, Junjun: Lyrics-conditioned neural melody generation. In: Ro, Yong Man, Cheng, Wen-Huang., Kim, Junmo, Chu, Wei-Ta., Cui, Peng, Choi, Jung-Woo., Hu, Min-Chun., De Neve, Wesley (eds.) MMM 2020. LNCS, vol. 11962, pp. 709–714. Springer, Cham (2020). https://doi.org/10.1007/978-3-030-37734-2_58
19. Yu, Y., Srivastava, A., Canales, S.: Conditional lstm-gan for melody generation from lyrics. ACM Trans. Multimedia Comput. Commun. Appl. (2020)

20. Yu, Y., Tang, S., Raposo, F., Chen, L.: Deep cross-modal correlation learning for audio and lyrics in music retrieval. ACM Trans. Multimedia Comput. Commun. Appl. **15**(1), February 2019. https://doi.org/10.1145/3281746
21. Zhang, Y., Gan, Z., Fan, K., Chen, Z., Henao, R., Shen, D., Carin, L.: Adversarial feature matching for text generation. In: Proceedings of the 34th International Conference on Machine Learning - Volume 70. pp. 4006–4015. ICML'17, JMLR.org (2017)
22. Zhao, J.J., Kim, Y., Zhang, K., Rush, A.M., LeCun, Y.: Adversarially regularized autoencoders. In: ICML (2018)

Multimodal Analytics

Bi-attention Modal Separation Network for Multimodal Video Fusion

Pengfei Du[1,2], Yali Gao[1,2], and Xiaoyong Li[1,2(✉)]

[1] Beijing University of Posts and Telecommunications, Beijing, China
[2] Key Laboratory of Trustworthy Distributed Computing and Service (BUPT),
Ministry of Education, Beijing, China
{dupf,gaoyali}@bupt.edu.cn

Abstract. With the increasing popularity of video sharing websites such as YouTube and Facebook, multimodal video understanding has received increasing attention from the scientific community. Video is usually composed of multimodal signals, such as video, text, image and audio, etc. The main method addressing this task is to develop powerful multimodal fusion techniques. Multimodal data fusion is to transform data from multiple single-mode representations to a compact multimodal representation. Effective multimodal fusion method should contain two key characteristics: the consistency and the difference. Previous studies mainly focused on applying different interaction methods to different modal fusion such as late fusion, early fusion, attention fusion, etc., but ignored the study of modal independence in the fusion process. In this paper, we introduce a fusion approach called bi-attention modal separation fusion network(BAMS) which can extract and integrate key information from various modalities and performs fusion and separation on modality representations. We conduct thorough ablation studies, and our experiments on datasets MOSI and MOSEI demonstrate significant gains over state-of-the-art models.

Keywords: Multimodal fusion · Video understanding · Deep learning · Transformer

1 Introduction

Video understanding is one of the major challenges in computer vision and has various applications such as sentiment analysis, violence detection and searching. Video is a typical multimodal data which usually consist of three channels: visual, acoustic and text data. Different patterns in the same data segment usually complement each other. For example, By simply analyzing the sentence "I like apple", we can't confirm the category of apple, but if a person is saying this sentence with a mobile phone in the video scene, we can easily distinguish an apple from a mobile phone through visual information. For another example, if a person says "you're so great", we will think that he is praising simply in the literal sense, but if the person's tone is sarcastic and his expression is contemptuous, the meaning of this sentence becomes sarcasm. Different modalities in the

ⓒ Springer Nature Switzerland AG 2022
B. Þór Jónsson et al. (Eds.): MMM 2022, LNCS 13141, pp. 585–598, 2022.
https://doi.org/10.1007/978-3-030-98358-1_46

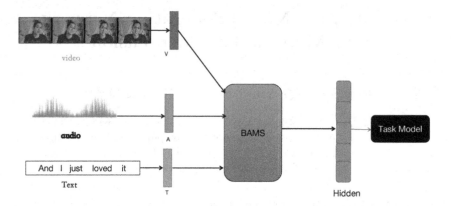

Fig. 1. Overall architecture for multimodal task. Output features embedding from different modalities and fused by our BAMS and then output to the final task.

video are sometimes consistent and sometimes independent of each other. Multimodal fusion is an extremely important research direction and core technology in multimodal data analysis. Research in multimodal fusion can provide three main benefits [3]: (1) more robust predictions, (2) capture complementary information, (3) operate when one of the modalities is missing. A crucial issue in multimodal language processing is how to integrate heterogeneous data efficiently, and a good fusion approach should extract and integrate meaningful information from multiple modalities while preserving their mutual independence. Figure 1 illustrates our proposed model for multimodal fusion task.

Baltrušaitis et al. classify fusion approach into two main categories: model-agnostic approaches that are not directly dependent on specific machine learning methods and model-based approaches that explicitly address fusion in their construction [3]. Atrey et al. split multimodal fusion approach into late (i.e., decision-based), early (i.e., feature-based) and hybrid fusion based on the stage in which fusion occurs during the associated procedures [2]. With the widespread use of unimodal pre-training models, the boundaries between stages have become less clear. So recent studies mainly focus on more flexible intermediate fusion, which allow fusion to occur on multiple layers of a deep model. Zhang et al. categories three main types [31]: simple operation-based, attention-based and tensor-based methods, which covers the main modal interactions' method between different modalities. Simple operation-based fusion is just a simple concatenation or weighted sums, and can't learn the deep interaction between different modalities. Attention-based and tensor-based methods correspond to the inner-product and outer-product operations of the matrix respectively. Tensor-based method is limited because of outer-product operations' large parameters and computation complexity. Attention-based mechanisms especially self-attention [23] method are widely used for fusion attributed to effective learning of interaction features between modalities and simple computation. Despite the advances, attention-based fusion techniques are often challenged by the modality gaps persisting between heterogeneous modalities. In addition, we want to fuse complementary information to minimize redundancy and integrate different information sets.

Our approach mainly focuses on attention-based method, motivated by attention in a bimodal transformer and advanced modality-specific representation learning, we propose bi-attention modal separation fusion network(BAMS), a novel multimodal fusion framework that provides better representations as input to fusion and assures mutual independence between modalities. Our fusion scheme consists of three bi-modal fusion operations with multi-head self-attention, Our model takes three modality pairs, TA(text-acoustic), AV(acoustic-video) and TV(text-video) as respective inputs for its two bimodal learning modules. To minimize information redundancy and keep independence between different modalities, we introduce in our BAMS an orthogonality constraint as a local regularizer that divides the feature space of different modalities. We evaluated our model on subtask of multimodal sentiment analysis using two datasets: CMU-MOSI, CMU-MOSEI. Experimental results outperform state-of-the-art models. Our main contributions can be summarized as follows:

- Uses BERT-based [7] transformers as the feature extractor for different modalities including video, audio and text.
- A bi-attention fusion scheme which can fusion as many modalities as possible.
- In order to reduce information redundancy and maintain the independence between modalities, we use an orthogonality regularizer to constraint learning during fusion processes.

2   Related Work

In this section, we briefly overview multimodal video fusion and bi-attention transformer.

2.1   Multimodal Video Fusion

Fusion is a key research topic in multimodal video analysis, which integrates the information extracted from different unimodal data sources into a compact multimodal representation. Early and late fusion based on the stage in which fusion occurs during are classic fusion method on video analysis especially in multimodal video sentiment analysis [8,17,18]. Another classic model is temporal based Fusion which accounts for view-specific and cross-view interactions and continuously models them over time [13,29]. Recent studies on learning multimodal fusion mainly focus on modalities' interaction to incorporate modalities. As mentioned in Sect. 1, tensor-based and attention-based are the two main approaches. Tensor Fusion Network calculates the out product of video, audio and text feature to represent comprehensive features [28]. In order to reduce computational complexity caused by outer-product, many approaches were proposed, while the low-rank method is a more efficient method [15]. There are also many researchers who apply the transformer's self-attention operation to provide a natural mechanism to connect multimodal signals. Multimodal Transformer (MulT) [22] proposed crossmodal attention mechanism to solve the long-range dependencies between elements across modalities. Sahay et al. [20] proposed a Fused Cross-modal Transformer and Low-Rank Fusion Transformer for encoding multimodal sequences for classification. Multimodal Attention (MMA) module reweight modalities through a Gram Matrix of self-attention [14]. To improve the performance of the fusion, some approach models the fine-grained structure for word-level fusion [19,24]. Another improvement is to constraints modal dependencies between different modalities [9,10]. There are two key points in the above approach, the fusion method between different modalities and the method to improves efficiency and preserving their mutual independence. Our approach mainly focuses on these two points.

2.2 Bi-attention Transformer

Inspired by BERT's success at language modelling, bi-attention transformer training tasks to learn joint representations of different modalities. ViLBERT extends BERT to include two encoder streams to process visual and textual inputs separately. These features can then interact through parallel co-attention layers [16]. LXMERT uses independent encoders to learn intermodality features for each modality and a cross-modality encoder on a higher level to learn cross-modality features using additional cross-attention layers [21].

3   Our Approach

In this section, we firstly define the problem and then describe our proposed bi-attention modal separation fusion network(BAMS). The goal of the BAMS is to acquire information-rich multimodal representations by joint learning the multimodal task and modal separation task.

Problem Defnition: In our research, the video mainly consists of three modalities: t (text), a (acoustic) and v (video), which are $2D$ tensors denoted by $M_t \in \mathbb{R}^{T_t \times d_t}$, $M_a \in \mathbb{R}^{T_a \times d_a}$ and $M_v \in \mathbb{R}^{T_v \times d_v}$, where T_m and d_m separately represent the sequences length and dimension of modality m. We regard the task of Multimodal Sentiment Analysis (MSA) as a regression task.

3.1   Network Architecture

Our core approach consists of three parts: the feature extraction module, modal fusion module, and modal separation module (see Fig. 2). The feature extraction module is used to extract the context-level information from three different modalities by three transformers separately. Modal fusion module is responsible for fusing three modalities(video, text and audio). In this module, the bimodal attention framework is employed, where an attention function is applied on the representations of pairwise modalities such as text-visual, acoustic-text and visual-acoustic to obtain bimodal representations. Since each unimodal has

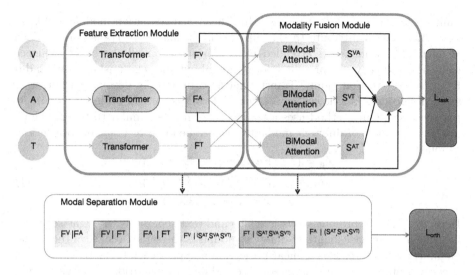

Fig. 2. Overall architecture for our BAMS, which compose of feature extraction module, modal fusion module and modal separation module.

different information, the purpose of multimodal fusion is to fully use the complementary information of multimodal data. We note that the bi-attention module also has the ability to capture the global and local connections. Therefore, a prominent part of our contribution in this paper is the introduction of the bidirectional attention module into multimodal fusion. For any utterance, each modality has unique characteristics, including stylistic information that is sensitive to the speaker. Such heterogeneous details are usually not related to other modalities and are considered as noise. Nevertheless, these details could be useful in predicting the affective state. In order to ensure the specific representation capture different aspects of the final input and provide a comprehensive multimodal representation of the utterance, a modal separation module is used. So our final learning task is a multitask with final task loss (regression loss or classification loss) and orthogonality constraints loss. We will describe each component in detail in the following subsections.

3.2   Feature Extraction Module

The feature extraction module is used to model the contextual relationship among neighbouring subword on text, visual and acoustic carried along each word. Also, all neighboring tokens are not equally important in the task. So, it is necessary to highlight which subword are more important to predict the target. Many studies in the past use Long Short-Term Memory(LSTM) [11] as the feature extractor [5,10,25,28]. Different from these approachs, our approach uses transformer as the feature extractor for all modalities' feature extract. Transformer is non-recurrent neural architecture designed for modeling sequential data, compared with Long Short-Term Memory(LSTM), it can break the limits of long-distance dependence. Multi-head Self-Attention module and position embedding contribute to the superior performance of Transformers. Each element of a sequence is attended by conditioning on all the other sequence elements, and they can provide information about the relationship between different subwords. Commonly, Transformer uses an encoder-decoder paradigm. A stack of encoders is followed by a stack of decoders to map an input to an output sequence. Our method uses a transformer encoder similar to the BERT [7] model. The input of different modalities are embedding to the same dimension, as follows:

$$\mathbf{Z_a} = (z_{\text{cls}}, \mathbf{E}a_1, \mathbf{E}a_2, \ldots, \mathbf{E}a_N) + \mathbf{p}$$
$$\mathbf{Z_t} = (z_{\text{cls}}, \mathbf{E}t_1, \mathbf{E}t_2, \ldots, \mathbf{E}t_N) + \mathbf{p} \tag{1}$$
$$\mathbf{Z_v} = (z_{\text{cls}}, \mathbf{E}v_1, \mathbf{E}v_2, \ldots, \mathbf{E}v_N) + \mathbf{p}$$

Here, a, v and t represent acoustic, video and text separately, N is the sequence length. The sequence length of different modals is the same because of the modal alignment operation. E is a linear projection mapping each token to $\mathbb{R}^d$, z_{cls} is a special token prepended to this sequence and its representation serves as a representation of the entire sequence. p is learned position embedding added to token embedding to retain position information. Then L layers transformer encoder is used to encoder the input embedding. Each transformer layer is same as the traditional transformer which consists of Multi-Head Self-Attention(MHA), Layer Normalisation(LN) and Multilayer Perceptron(MLP). The output layer of each modal represent as:

$$\mathbf{y}^l = \text{MHA}\left(\text{LN}\left(\mathbf{Z}^l\right)\right) + \mathbf{Z}^l$$
$$\mathbf{z}^{l+1} = \text{MLP}\left(\text{LN}\left(\mathbf{y}^l\right)\right) + \mathbf{y}^l. \tag{2}$$

The input of MHA is embedding of different modal $\mathbf{Z_a}$, $\mathbf{Z_t}$ and $\mathbf{Z_v}$, and each layers' output as the input of the next transformer layer.

3.3   Modal Fusion Module

The purpose of multimodal fusion is to make full use of the complementary information of different modals. Attention module can connect the information between different modalities and it has the ability to capture global and local connections. The essence of the attention function can be described as the mapping of a Q(query) to a series of K-V(key-value) pairs, the common setting of the traditional attention mechanism is that the key and value are the same. So, the formula of attention is: $\text{Attention}(Q, K, V) = \text{softmax}\left(\frac{QK^T}{\sqrt{d_k}}\right)V$, where d_k is the dimension of input. Usally, we use multi-headed attention block which can perform the attention function in parallel. A contribution of our solution is to propose the introduction of bi-attention into multimodal fusion. The mechanism of bi-attention fusion is used to exchange the information and align the entities between the two modalities in order to learn cross-modality representations. Given intermediate audio and text representations $\mathbf{Z_a}$ and $\mathbf{Z_t}$, the module computes query, key, and value matrices as in a standard transformer block. However, keys and values from each modality are passed as input to the other modality's multi-headed attention block. We define the Query as $Q_a = Z_a W_{Q_a}$, Keys as $K_t = Z_t W_{K_t}$, and Values as $V_t = Z_t W_{V_t}$, where $W_{Q_a} \in \mathbb{R}^{d_a \times d_k}$, $W_{K_t} \in \mathbb{R}^{d_t \times d_k}$ and $W_{V_t} \in \mathbb{R}^{d_t \times d_k}$ are weights. The latent adaptation from a to t is presented as: $C_{a \to t} := \text{Bi\_Attn}_{a \to t}(Z_a, Z_t)$:

$$
\begin{aligned}
C_{a \to t} &= \text{Bi\_Attn}_{a \to t}(Z_a, Z_t) \\
&= \text{softmax}\left(\frac{Q_a K_t^\top}{\sqrt{d_k}}\right) V_t \\
&= \text{softmax}\left(\frac{Z_a W_{Q_a} W_{K_t}^\top Z_t^\top}{\sqrt{d_k}}\right) Z_t W_{V_t}.
\end{aligned}
\tag{3}
$$

The bimodal multi-head self-attention can define as: $M_{a\_t} = concat(C_{a\_t}^0, C_{a\_t}^1 ... C_{a\_t}^h)$, where h is head number of the attention. Separately, we calculated three different modality pairs' bimodal multi-head self-attention and then concat them as:

$$
\begin{aligned}
M_{a\_t} &= concat(C_{a\_t}^0, C_{a\_t}^1 ... C_{a\_t}^h) \\
M_{v\_t} &= concat(C_{v\_t}^0, C_{v\_t}^1 ... C_{v\_t}^h) \\
M_{a\_v} &= concat(C_{a\_v}^0, C_{a\_v}^1 ... C_{a\_v}^h) \\
H_{a\_v\_t} &= concat(M_{a\_t}, M_{v\_t}, M_{a\_v})
\end{aligned}
\tag{4}
$$

In order to enrich the final results, we add three different modes to the final fusion results:

$$
H_{final} = concat(H_{a\_v\_t}, Z_a, Z_t, Z_v)
\tag{5}
$$

Tensor Fusion method [28] can also used for models the unimodal, bimodal and trimodal interactions without using an expensive 3-fold Cartesian product from modality-specific embeddings. The method leverages weights directly approximate the multitensor outer product operation. The low-rank matrix factorization operation is used where the interaction space is very large [15]. It can reduces the number of parameters as well as the computation complexity involved in tensorization from being exponential to linear and reduce redundant information in the fusion process. Different from the Tensor Fusion operation, the self-attention is dot-product operation so the number of parameters is not so large, but it also has the problem of information redundancy, especially our final approach has too many input. In the next subsection, we will introduce how to reduce redundant information and keep modal independence.

3.4   Modal Separation Module

The modal separation module is used to factorize the latent space into independent or private information of each modal. Therefore, we need to realize non-redundancy between different modalities. For this purpose, we can use some matrix dimensionality reduction method after the fusion process [1, 15], or train a classifier to discern which modality these representations come from [9]. Our approach enforcing a soft orthogonality constraint between different modalities representations [4,10]. Our orthogonality constraints are encoded as minimizing the Frobenius norm of the inner product between latent spaces, which results in minimizing the scalar products between each pair of modalities. After transforming input modalities' hidden vector Z_m to have zero mean and unit l_2 norm we got matrix $\hat{Z}_m$. The same operation on Ha_v_t, we got $\hat{H}a\_v\_t$. Then we can calculate the orthogonality constraint as:

$$\left\| \hat{\mathbf{Z}}_{\mathbf{m}}^{\top} \hat{\mathbf{H}}\mathbf{a\_v\_t} \right\|_F^2 \tag{6}$$

$\| \cdot \|_F^2$ here is the squared Frobenius norm. We also add orthogonality constraints between different modality vectors. Orthogonality loss is then computed as:

$$\mathcal{L}_{\text{orth}} = \sum_{m \in \{t,v,a\}} \left\| \hat{\mathbf{Z}}_{\mathbf{m}}^{\top} \hat{\mathbf{H}}\mathbf{a\_v\_t} \right\|_F^2 + \sum_{\substack{(m_1,m_2) \in \\ \{a,v,t\}}} \left\| \hat{\mathbf{Z}}_{\mathbf{m_1}}^{\top} \hat{\mathbf{Z}}_{\mathbf{m_2}} \right\|_F^2 \tag{7}$$

3.5 Learning

The final loss function of our model can be written as:

$$L = L_{\text{Task}} + \gamma L_{\text{Orth}} \tag{8}$$

where γ is hyper-parameter. For classification tasks, task loss use the standard cross-entropy loss whereas for regression tasks, we use mean squared error loss. For batch-size N, these are calculated as:

$$\mathcal{L}_{\text{task}} = \begin{cases} -\frac{1}{N} \sum_{i=0}^{N} \mathbf{y}_i \cdot \log \hat{\mathbf{y}}_i & \text{for classification} \\ \frac{1}{N} \sum_{i=0}^{N} \|\mathbf{y}_i - \hat{y}i\|_2^2 & \text{for regression} \end{cases} \tag{9}$$

4 Experiments

4.1 Datasets

CMU-MOSI Dataset. The CMU-MOSI(CMU Multimodal Opinion Sentiment Intensity) Dataset was developed in 2016 by Amir Zadeh et al. [27]. The dataset contains 2199 short monologue video clips taken from 93 opinion videos collected from YouTube video-blogs where many users can express their opinions about many different subjects. Human annotators label each sample with a sentiment score from −3 (strongly negative) to 3 (strongly positive).

CMU-MOSEI Dataset. The CMU-MOSEI dataset was developed in 2018 by Zadeh et al. [30]. CMU-MOSEI is a large scale dataset that consists of 23,453 annotated video segments (utterances), from 5,000 videos, 1,000 distinct speakers and 250 different topics. Each utterance in the dataset was labeled with one of eight sentiments: strongly positive (labeled as +3), positive (+2), weakly positive (+1), neutral (0), weakly negative (−1), negative (−2), strongly negative (−3).

Most researches use CMU-MOSI and CMU-MOSEI datasets to evaluate the performance of their models in multimodal sentiment analysis.

4.2 Features

Visual Feature Extraction. Both MOSI and MOSEI use Facet[1] to extract a set of visual features including facial landmarks, facial action units, head pose, gaze tracking and HOG features.

Acoustic Features Extraction. COVAREP [6] acoustic analysis framework is used for acoustic feature extraction. It includes 74 features of speech polarity, glottal closure instants, spectral envelope, pitch tracking.

Text Feature Extraction. Both MOSI and MOSEI videos are transcribed by the Youtube API and then corrected manually. Pre-trained BERT [7] is used to obtain word vectors from transcripts.

Modality Alignment. We used P2FA [26] to align acoustic and visual signals to text. The tool automatically divides a large number of frames into groups and matches each group with a marker by averaging their representation vectors into a new representation vector.

4.3 Baselines

To fully validate the performance of the BAMS, we make a fair comparison with the following baselines and state-of- the-art models.

TFN. TFN(Tensor Fusion Network) [28] calculates a multi-dimensional tensor based on outer-product to capture different modal interactions.

LMF. LMF(The Low-rank Multimodal Fusion) [15] is an improvement over TFN, where low-rank multimodal tensors fusion technique is used to improve efficiency.

MFN. MFN(The Memory Fusion Network) [29] has separate LSTMs to model each modality separately and a multi-view gated memory to synchronize among them.

MulT. MulT(The Multimodal Transformer) [22] use three sets of Transformers and combines their output in a late fusion manner to model a multimodal sequence.

RAVEN. RAVEN(Recurrent Attended Variation Embedding Network) [24] models the fine-grained structure of nonverbal subword sequences and dynamically shifts word representations based on nonverbal cues.

---

[1] https://imotions.com/platform/.

MAG-BERT. MAG-BET(The Multimodal Adaptation Gate for Bert) [19] apply multi-modal adaptive gate alignment data at different layers of the BERT backbone, it is an improvement over RAVEN.

MISA. MISA(Modality-Invariant and -Specific Representations) [10] also motivated by previous work in domain separation task, this work regards signals from different modalities as data in different domains and similarly constructs two kinds of feature spaces to finish the fusion process.

BBFN. BBFN(Bi-Bimodal Fusion Network) [9] consists of two bi-modal fusion modules, it is different from traditional ternary symmetric one. The model introduce a classification task to separate different modalities to tackle the problem of feature collapse.

4.4   Implementation Details

We train our models using the Adam [12] optimizer with weight a linear-decayed learning rate schedule [7] and a peak learning rate at 0.000001. We train our model for 60 epochs with a batch size of 48. The model's parameters are initialized with a BERT-base pretrained model. The position embedding parameters of acoustic and video modes are the same as those of text modes. The max sequence length set to 50 for each modal. For MOSI and MOSEI we take formulate it as a regression problem and report Mean-absolute Error (MAE) and the correlation of model predictions with true labels(Corr). And we convert the regression outputs into categorical values to obtain binary classification accuracy(Acc-2) and F1 score. For mae, lower values is better, while for other metrics, higher values is better. The whole training process on 3 GTX-1080Ti.

5   Results and Discussion

5.1   Summary of Results

We list the results with baselines on all datasets in Table 1. BAMS archives the best performance in both datasets and surpasses the baselines across metrics F1 and acc-2. Moreover, we reproduce three SOTA models, "MISA", "MAG-BERT", and "BBFN" under the same conditions. They are suitable fusion methods to ensure the consistency and difference between modes. We find that our model surpasses them on most metrics.

5.2   Ablation Study

To further explore the contributions of BAMS, we perform comprehensive ablation analysis.

Table 1. Results on MOSI and MOSEI. (B) means the language features are based on BERT; Models with * are reproduced under the same conditions. ** indicates results in the corresponding line are excerpted from previous papers. In Acc-2 and F1-Score, the left of the "/" is calculated as "negative/non-negative" and the right is calculated as "negative/positive". Best results are highlighted in bold.

Model	MOSI				MOSEI			
	MAE	Corr	Acc-2	F1-Score	MAE	Corr	Acc-2	F1-Score
TFN(B)**	0.901	0.698	-/80.8	-/80.7	0.593	0.700	-/82.5	-/82.1
LMF(B)**	0.917	0.695	-/82.5	-/82.4	0.623	0.677	-/82.0	-/82.1
MFN **	0.965	0.632	77.4/-	77.3/-	-	-	76.0/-	76.0/-
RAVEN**	0.915	0.691	78.0/-	76.6/-	0.614	0.662	79.1/-	79.5/-
MulT(B)**	0.861	0.711	81.5/84.1	80.6/83.9	0.58	0.703	-/82.5	-/82.3
MISA(B)*	0.783	0.761	81.8/83.4	81.7/83.6	0.555	0.756	83.6/85.5	83.8/85.3
MAG-BERT(B)*	**0.731**	0.789	82.54/84.3	82.59/84.3	**0.539**	0.753	83.79/85.23	83.74/85.08
BBFN(B)*	0.776	0.755	84.3/84.1	84.2/84.1	**0.529**	0.767	86.2/86.3	86.1/86.2
BAMS(B)*	**0.74**	**0.798**	**85.55/86.98**	**85.6/86.95**	0.58	**0.785**	**86.558/86.6**	**86.30/ 86.5**

Table 2. An ablation study of BAMS' different fusion combinations on the test set of CMU-MOSI.

Description	MAE	Corr	Acc-2	F1
TV only	0.86	0.71	80.1	80.6
VA only	1.4	0.3	55.1	54.8
TA only	0.83	0.73	81.8	81.0
TA+VA+AV	0.76	0.75	83.9	83.8
TA+VA+AV+T+V+A	0.78	0.78	83.1	83.0
TA+VA+AV+T+V+A(BAMS)	0.74	0.798	85.55	85.6

Results of Different Fusion Combinations. To further explore the influence of the different fusion combinations in BAMS, we conducted a series of ablation experiments. Specifically, we (1) use modality pairs VA, TA and TV; (2) concatenating the three different modality pairs; (3) concatenating three modality pairs and three different modalities. The results show in Table 2.

We observe that the performance sharply drops when using VA. Similar drops are not observed in AT and VT, showing that text modality has significant dominance over the visual and audio modalities. The reason could be the text's data quality is inherently better, and pre-trained BERT's model parameters are more fit for text feature representation than unfiltered audio and raw visual signals.

The model of type(2) outperformed those of type (1) on metrics, which indicates that fusion of different modality pairs is important. On the other hand, the performance of model type(3) degrades than model type(2), this is because with the introduction of more modal information, the model becomes redundant, and it cause harmful effects bringing in malicious noise. Therefore, the introduction of modal separation module effectively avoids this situation.

Table 3. Ablation study for orthogonality constraints. Here, (L) represents add orthogonality constraints.

Model	MOSI		MOSEI	
	MAE	F1-Score	MAE	F1-Score
TA+VA+AV	0.75	83.8	0.69	84.0
TA+VA+AV+T+V+A	0.78	83.0	0.70	83.8
(L)TA+VA+AV	**0.74**	**85.9**	**0.65**	**85.9**
(L)TA+VA+AV+T+V+A	**0.74**	**86.95**	**0.58**	**86.5**

Importance of Orthogonality Constraints. To quantitatively verify the importance of orthogonality constraints, we take the TA+VA+AV and TA+VA+AV +T+V+A fusion models in each dataset, we re-train them by ablating the orthogonality loss. To nullify the loss, we set γ to 0. Results are observed in Table 3. As seen, the best performance is achieved when we add orthogonality loss. In a closer look, we can see with orthogonality loss more input modalities can be fused.

Fine-Tuning Effect. We study whether or not the superior performance of the BAMS is related to the successful finetuning of the models. We suppose that any transformer with architecture like BERT would achieve superior performance regardless of being pretrained. By randomly initializing the weights of BERT within BAMS, we get 76.2 on Acc-2 for the CMU-MOSI, even on the larger CMU-MOSEI dataset, we only get Acc-2 of 78.1. This indicates that fact that fine-tuning is successful in our BAMS architecture.

6   Future Works

In the future, we will plan to explore more advanced fusion methods and architectures and introduce more modalities into our model and extend the BAMS to other tasks. And we will build an end-to-end multimodal learning network for exploring more effective fusion methods.

Acknowledgements. This work was supported in part by the NSFC-General Technology Fundamental Research Joint Fund under grant U1836215, National Nature Science Foundation of China under grant 62102040, and China Postdoctoral Science Foundation under grant 2020M680464.

References

1. Learning factorized multimodal representations. In: 7th International Conference on Learning Representations, ICLR 2019 (2019)
2. Atrey, P.K., Hossain, M.A., El Saddik, A., Kankanhalli, M.S.: Multimodal fusion for multimedia analysis: a survey. Multimedia Syst. **16**(6), 345–379 (2010)

3. Baltrušaitis, T., Ahuja, C., Morency, L.-P.: Multimodal machine learning: a survey and taxonomy. IEEE Trans. Pattern Anal. Mach. Intell. **41**(2), 423–443 (2018)
4. Bousmalis, K., Trigeorgis, G., Silberman, N., Krishnan, D., Erhan, D.: Domain separation networks. Adv. Neural Inf. Process. Sys. (Nips) **29**, 343–351 (2016). ISSN 10495258
5. Clark, K., Luong, M.T., Manning, C.D., Le, Q.V.: Semi-supervised sequence modeling with cross-view training. In: Proceedings of the 2018 Conference on Empirical Methods in Natural Language Processing, EMNLP 2018, pp. 1914–1925 (2020). https://doi.org/10.18653/v1/d18-1217
6. Degottex, G., Kane, J., Drugman, T., Raitio, T., Scherer, S.: Covarep-a collaborative voice analysis repository for speech technologies. In: 2014 IEEE International Conference on Acoustics, Speech and Signal Processing (ICASSP), pp. 960–964. IEEE (2014)
7. Devlin, J., Chang, M.-W., Lee, K., Toutanova, K.: Bert: Pre-training of deep bidirectional transformers for language understanding. arXiv preprint arXiv:1810.04805 (2018)
8. Gkoumas, D., Li, Q., Lioma, C., Yijun, Yu., Song, D.: What makes the difference? an empirical comparison of fusion strategies for multimodal language analysis. Inf. Fus. **66**, 184–197 (2021)
9. Han, W., Chen, H., Gelbukh, A., Zadeh, A., Morency, L.P., Poria, S.: Bi-Bimodal modality fusion for correlation-controlled multimodal sentiment analysis. In: Proceedings of the 2021 International Conference on Multimodal Interaction, vol. 1. Association for Computing Machinery (2021). http://arxiv.org/abs/2107.13669
10. Hazarika, D., Zimmermann, R., Poria, S.: MISA: modality-invariant and -specific representations for multimodal sentiment analysis. In: MM 2020 - Proceedings of the 28th ACM International Conference on Multimedia, pp. 1122–1131 (2020). https://doi.org/10.1145/3394171.3413678
11. Hochreiter, S., Schmidhuber, J.: Long short-term memory. Neural Comput. **9**(8), 1735–1780 (1997)
12. Kingma, D.P., Ba, J.: Adam: A method for stochastic optimization. arXiv preprint arXiv:1412.6980 (2014)
13. Liang, P.P., Liu, Z., Zadeh, A., Morency, L.-P.: Multimodal language analysis with recurrent multistage fusion. arXiv preprint arXiv:1808.03920 (2018)
14. Liu, Y., et al. iqiyi-vid: A large dataset for multi-modal person identification. arXiv preprint arXiv:1811.07548 (2018a)
15. Liu, Z., et al.: Efficient low-rank multimodal fusion with modality-specific factors. In: ACL 2018–56th Annual Meeting of the Association for Computational Linguistics, Proceedings of the Conference (Long Papers), vol. 1, pp. 2247–2256 (2018b). https://doi.org/10.18653/v1/p18-1209
16. Lu, J., Batra, D., Parikh, D., Lee, S.: Vilbert: Pretraining task-agnostic visiolinguistic representations for vision-and-language tasks. arXiv preprint arXiv:1908.02265 (2019)
17. Morency, L.P., Mihalcea, R., Doshi, P.: Towards multimodal sentiment analysis: harvesting opinions from the web. In Proceedings of the 13th International Conference on Multimodal Interfaces, pp. 169–176 (2011)
18. Nojavanasghari, B., Gopinath, D., Koushik, J., Baltrušaitis, T., Morency, L.-P.: Deep multimodal fusion for persuasiveness prediction. In Proceedings of the 18th ACM International Conference on Multimodal Interaction, pp. 284–288 (2016)
19. Rahman, W., et al.: Integrating Multimodal Information in Large Pretrained Transformers. pp. 2359–2369 (2020.) https://doi.org/10.18653/v1/2020.acl-main.214

20. Sahay, S., Okur, E., Kumar, S.H., Nachman, L.: Low Rank Fusion based Transformers for Multimodal Sequences, 29–34 (2020). https://doi.org/10.18653/v1/2020. challengehml-1.4
21. Tan, H., Bansal, M.: Lxmert: Learning cross-modality encoder representations from transformers. arXiv preprint arXiv:1908.07490 (2019)
22. Tsai, Y.H.H., et al.: Multimodal transformer for unaligned multimodal language sequences. In: ACL 2019–57th Annual Meeting of the Association for Computational Linguistics, Proceedings of the Conference, pp. 6558–6569 (2020). ISSN 0736–587X. https://doi.org/10.18653/v1/p19-1656
23. Vaswani, A., et al.: Attention is all you need. Adv. Neural Inf. Process. Syst. 2017-Decem (Nips), 5999–6009 (2017). ISSN 10495258
24. Wang, Y., Shen, Y., Liu, Z., Liang, P.P., Zadeh, A., Morency, L.P.: Words can shift: dynamically adjusting word representations using nonverbal behaviors. In: 33rd AAAI Conference on Artificial Intelligence, AAAI 2019, 31st Innovative Applications of Artificial Intelligence Conference, IAAI 2019 and the 9th AAAI Symposium on Educational Advances in Artificial Intelligence, EAAI 2019, pp. 7216–7223 (2019a). ISSN 2159–5399
25. Wang, Y., Shen, Y., Liu, Z., Liang, P.P., Zadeh, A., Morency, L.P.: Dynamically adjusting word representations using nonverbal behaviors: Words can shift. In: Proceedings of the AAAI Conference on Artificial Intelligence, vol. 33, pp. 7216–7223 (2019)
26. Yuan, J., Liberman, M., et al.: Speaker identification on the scotus corpus. J. Acoust. Soc. Am. **123**(5), 3878 (2008)
27. Zadeh, A., Zellers, R., Pincus, E., Morency, L.P.: Mosi: multimodal corpus of sentiment intensity and subjectivity analysis in online opinion videos. arXiv preprint arXiv:1606.06259 (2016)
28. Zadeh, A., Chen, M., Poria, S., Cambria, E., Morency, L.-P.: Tensor fusion network for multimodal sentiment analysis. arXiv preprint arXiv:1707.07250 (2017)
29. Zadeh, A., Poria, S., Liang, P.P., Cambria, E., Mazumder, N., Morency, L.P.: Memory fusion network for multi-view sequential learning. In: 32nd AAAI Conference on Artificial Intelligence, AAAI 2018, pp. 5634–5641 (2018a)
30. Zadeh, A.B., Liang, P.P., Poria, S., Cambria, E., Morency, L.P.: Multimodal language analysis in the wild: CMU-mosei dataset and interpretable dynamic fusion graph. In: Proceedings of the 56th Annual Meeting of the Association for Computational Linguistics (Volume 1: Long Papers), pp. 2236–2246 (2018b)
31. Zhang, C., Yang, Z., He, X., Deng, L.: Multimodal intelligence: representation learning, information fusion, and applications. IEEE J. Select. Top. Sig. Process. **14**(3), 478–493 (2020)

Combining Knowledge and Multi-modal Fusion for Meme Classification

Qi Zhong, Qian Wang$^{(\boxtimes)}$, and Ji Liu

College of Computer Science, Chongqing University, Chongqing 400044, China
{zhongqi,wangqian,liujiboy}@cqu.edu.cn

Abstract. Internet memes are widespread on social media platforms such as Twitter and Facebook. Recently, meme classification has been an active research topic, especially meme sentiment classification and meme offensive classification. Internet memes contain multi-modal information, and the meme text is embedded in the meme image. The existing methods classify memes by simply concatenating global visual and textual features to generate a multi-modal representation. However, these approaches ignored the noise introduced by global visual features and the potential common information of meme multi-modal representation. In this paper, we propose a model for meme classification named MeBERT. Our method enhances the semantic representation of the meme by introducing conceptual information through external Knowledge Bases (KBs). Then, to reduce noise, a concept-image attention module is designed to extract concept-sensitive visual representation. In addition, a deep convolution tensor fusion module is built to effectively integrate multi-modal information. To verify the effectiveness of the model in the tasks of meme sentiment classification and meme offensive classification, we designed experiments on the Memotion and MultiOFF datasets. The experimental results show that the MeBERT model achieves better performance than state-of-the-art techniques for meme classification.

Keywords: Meme classification · Multi-modal fusion · Self-attention mechanism

1 Introduction

Because of their novelty, internet memes are widely applied to share ideas and sentiment on social media. Meme sentiment classification is one of the tasks of Memotion analysis [18], which was first introduced at the International Workshop on Semantic Evaluation (SemEval) 2020. Another work [22] proposed the meme offensive classification task.

With the development of multi-modal machine learning [2], many multi-modal models have been proposed for meme classification [3,22]. However, the existing methods suffer from two limitations. First, as shown in Fig. 1, for each sample, the text is embedded in the image, so directly extracting the global features of the image introduces noise. In addition, the existing text-based methods

© Springer Nature Switzerland AG 2022
B. Þór Jónsson et al. (Eds.): MMM 2022, LNCS 13141, pp. 599–611, 2022.
https://doi.org/10.1007/978-3-030-98358-1_47

(a) Positive meme   (b) Negative meme   (c) Neutral meme

Fig. 1. Three examples from Memotion datasets. The text is embedded in the image.

are employed to capture both the syntactic and semantic information in meme text but ignore the important semantic relationships that exist in Knowledge Bases (KBs). Second, most existing multi-modal meme classification methods rely on simply concatenating feature vectors of different modalities. However, they ignore the potential common information between the modalities.

To address these two limitations, in this research, the MeBERT model is proposed based on the BERT [6] architecture. In addition, external knowledge is introduced into the MeBERT model to enhance meme semantic information. To address the first limitation, first, we retrieve the knowledge that is not explicitly contained within the meme from external knowledge sources, such as Probase [23]. For example, consider the following meme text: "when Chuck Norris left for college he told his father you are the man of the house now"; the existing methods may treat "Chuck Norris" as a new word and cannot capture "Chuck Norris" as a "person". Therefore, the *isA* semantic relation is used to retrieve the conceptual information of each meme text from the KB. Then, we treat conceptual information as an extra modality to bridge the meme text to the image. A concept attention mechanism is developed to align the concept with the image region to obtain a concept-sensitive visual representation. Therefore, the image region related to the concept receives more attention. To address the second limitation, the deep convolutional tensor network is used to build the fusion module, which extracts potential common information from the unimodal information and then integrates all unimodal information with the common information to generate a multi-modal representation for meme classification.

The distinct contributions of our work are as follows: (1) Conceptual information is introduced from an external knowledge base to enhance the semantic representation of the meme. (2) The concept-image attention module is proposed to obtain the concept-sensitive visual representation. (3) A convolution-tensor fusion module that effectively integrates multi-modal information is proposed. (4) The results of extensive experiments on two public datasets, the Memotion dataset [18] and MultiOFF dataset [22], show that our model exhibits competitive performance.

2   Related Work

2.1   Multi-modal Fusion

One of the key challenges in meme classification is to associate and fuse textual and visual modalities. Multi-modal fusion can be divided into model-agnostic and model-based approaches. Model-agnostic methods are not directly dependent on a specific machine learning method, such as early fusion, late fusion, and hybrid fusion. Early fusion integrates features into a single feature vector immediately after the features are extracted, after which the combined features are input into the classifier [16] for prediction. Late fusion integrates the decisions of the classifiers [26] trained on each modality. Hybrid fusion combines the outputs from early fusion and late fusion. A delta-memory attention network [28] is proposed to identify cross-view interactions. Model-based approaches use deep learning networks to solve the fusion problem in their construction. mBERT [25] and TomBERT [25] approaches generate multi-modal representation by using stacked additional transformer layers. MMBT [12] projects image embeddings to text token space to jointly fine-tune unimodal pre-trained ResNet-152 and BERT encoders. The VisualBERT [14] method was proposed to utilize the self-attention mechanism to find correspondences between elements of the input text and image regions. ViLBERT [15] introduced a novel co-attentional transformer layer to implement the information exchange between image regions and text segment modalities.

2.2   Meme Classification

Different solutions have been proposed for meme classification. The text-only approach is proposed for the meme sentiment classification task in [11]. [7] analyzed meme image content and proposed an image detection algorithm for detecting offensive content in the image. Moreover, other studies combined text and image information for meme classification. SESAM [3] evaluated alignment-based and fusion-based techniques on the task of meme sentiment classification. [10] utilized late fusion to ensemble the output of multiple classifiers. A parallel channel method [27] was designed for sentiment analysis of memes. A new multi-modal learning framework [9] was built to generate joint representations for meme sentiment analysis. Late fusion was adopted in [18] to solve the problem of missing modalities in meme prediction. In [19], transfer learning was introduced to analyze memes. The analysis-aware offensive meme detection (AOMD) [17] framework was developed to detect offensive analogy meme classification. DisMultiHate [4] disentangled the representations of target entities in memes for offensive classification. Although multi-modal technologies have been applied to meme classification, this work is not yet fully developed. In this paper, an innovative multi-modal method improves the performance of meme classification by reducing the noise of the meme image and integrating multi-modal information.

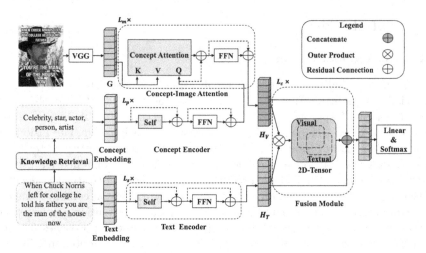

Fig. 2. The overall architecture of the MeBERT model. "Self" and "FFN" are abbreviations for self-attention sub-layers and feed-forward sub-layer.

3   Proposed Methodology

In this section, the proposed MeBERT method is introduced, as shown in Fig. 2. There are three steps. First, the concept set is retrieved, and text and concepts are encoded. Second, concept-sensitive visual representation is extracted. Finally, the multi-modal representation is generated for prediction. In addition, each input meme $x \in X$ consists of a foreground text T and image I.

3.1   Concept and Text Encoder

Knowledge Retrieval. We associate each meme text with its relevant concepts in the Probase [23] KB by using the *isA* relation. Specifically, given a sentence, entity linking [5] is applied to identify text entities and obtain a set of entities ε. Then the concept set C of each entity is retrieved from Probase. For example, consider the following meme text: "when Chuck Norris left for college he told his father you are the man of the house now"; we obtain the entity set $\varepsilon = \{ChuckNorris\}$ by entity linking. Then concept set $C = \{celebrity, star, actor, person, artist\}$ of entity $ChuckNorris$ is obtained from Probase by conceptualization.

Concept and Text Representation. For concept representation, a concept set is first split into words $\{c_1, c_2, ...c_M\}$ with length M by the same WordPiece tokenizer [24] in [6]. Then, the concept embedding is a sum of the token, segment, and position embeddings. Third, the input embedding is mapped to learned encodings through the concept encoder. The concept encoder is composed of L_p stacked BERT [6] layers. For each BERT layer, first, the output of the multi-head is obtained based on the self-attention mechanism. Then, a residual is added between the output and input of the self-attention mechanism, followed by a layer norm [1]. Next, a feed-forward layer and another residual connection are connected. Finally, the final hidden state of the first token is the conceptual representation $H_C \in \mathbb{R}^{d \times M}$, and d is represented as the dimensional size of the hidden state. Similar to the concept encoding process, a sentence T containing N words can be indicated as $H_T \in \mathbb{R}^{d \times N}$ after encoding.

3.2   Concept-Image Attention

First, image I is resized to 224×224 and divided into 7×7 regions. Each region $I_j (j = 1, 2, ..., 49)$ is then given to the pre-trained VGG19 [20] model to acquire the output $VGG(I) = \{r_j | r_j \in \mathbb{R}^{512}, j = 1, 2, ..., 49\}$ of the last convolutional layer. As a result, an image I is represented as $VGG(I) \in \mathbb{R}^{512 \times 49}$. Then, a linear transformation is applied to encode the image representation to project the visual features into the same space of textual features: $G = W_v VGG(I)$, where $W_v \in \mathbb{R}^{d \times 512}$ is a learnable parameter, and d is the dimension of the concept feature. The encoded image features can be denoted as $G \in \mathbb{R}^{d \times 49}$.

Concept Attention. The multi-head concept attention mechanism aligns the concept and the image so that the image region related to the concept receives more attention. For the input of this module, the concept features $H_C \in \mathbb{R}^{d \times M}$ is used as queries, and the image feature $G \in \mathbb{R}^{d \times 49}$ is adopted as keys and values. The i-th head concept attention layer is defined in the following form:

$$CATT_i(G, H_C) = softmax(\frac{[W_i^Q H_C]^T [W_i^K G]}{\sqrt{d_k}})[W_i^V G]^T \qquad (1)$$

where $d_k \in \mathbb{R}^{d/h}$, $CATT_i(G, H_C) \in \mathbb{R}^{M \times d_k}$, and $\{W_i^Q, W_i^K, W_i^V\} \in \mathbb{R}^{d \times d_k}$ are trainable parameters. Next, after concatenating the outputs of multi-heads, the following linear transformation is performed:

$$MATT(G, H_C) = [CATT_1(G, H_C), ..., CATT_h(G, H_C)]^T W^O \qquad (2)$$

where h represents the number of parallel attention heads, and $W^O \in \mathbb{R}^{d \times d}$ is a trainable parameter. Afterward, the concept feature and the output of the concept-attention layer are subjected to a residual connection, and then layer normalization (LN) [1] is applied as follows:

$$Z = LN(H_C + MATT(G, H_C)) \qquad (3)$$

Furthermore, a feed-forward network (a.k.a MLP) and another residual connection are applied to Z to acquire the output $CIA(Z) = LN(Z + MLP(Z))$ of the first BERT layer. $CIA(Z) \in \mathbb{R}^{M \times d}$ represents the output of the first concept attention layer. The final visual feature representation of the meme is produced by stacking such attention layers: $H_V = CIA_{L_m}(Z)$, where $H_V \in \mathbb{R}^{d \times M}$, and L_m is presented as the number of attention layers.

3.3 Fusion Module

To obtain the multi-modal representation, the idea of convolution kernels is applied to develop a tensor fusion module to extract common information from textual and visual representation. Therefore, the convolution kernels of an appropriate size are adopted as the feature extractor in this module. The joint representation $F_{TV} \in \mathbb{R}^{k_t \times k_v}$ of the tensor is obtained by calculating the outer product of the latent embeddings $f_{TV} = \sigma(H_T W_{tv} + b_{tv})$ and $f_{VT} = \sigma(H_V W_{vt} + b_{vt})$ of textual and visual features by the following formula:

$$F_{TV} = f_{TV} \otimes f_{VT} \tag{4}$$

where $f_{TV} \in \mathbb{R}^{1 \times k_t}$ and $f_{VT} \in \mathbb{R}^{1 \times k_v}$. $[W_{tv}, b_{tv}]$ and $[W_{vt}, b_{vt}]$ are hyperparameters. Next, $\mathcal{G}_{TV} = \sigma(Conv(F_{TV}))$ is obtained as the non-linear interactions in F_{TV} by using convolution filters. $\mathcal{G}_{TV}$ is represented as the output of the convolutional layer and a subsequent fully connected layer as follows:

$$H_{TV} = \sigma(\mathcal{G}_{TV} W_{TV} + b_{TV}) \tag{5}$$

The H_{TV}, H_T, and H_V feature vectors are concatenated and then fed into a feedforward layer. The softmax function is applied to obtain the final predicted $\hat{y}$. In our work, the cross-entropy loss function is applied to optimize all parameters of the MeBERT model as follows:

$$\mathcal{J} = -\frac{1}{|X|} \sum_{x=1}^{|X|} [y_x \log \hat{y}_x + (1 - y_x) \log(1 - \hat{y}_x)] \tag{6}$$

where $|X|$ is the number of training samples, and $\mathcal{J}$ is the loss function. $\hat{y}_x$ and y_x are the predicted value and true label of a sample x, respectively.

Table 1. Datasets statistics of Memotion [18] and MultiOFF [22]. Pos: positive, Neg: negative, Neu: Neutral, Off: offensive, and N-off: non-offensive. '–' means that no validation set data is in Memotion [18].

	Memotion dataset			MultiOFF dataset	
	Pos	Neg	Neu	Off	N-off
Train	4160	631	2201	187	258
Validation	–	–	–	59	90
Test	1111	173	594	59	90

4 Experiments and Analysis

4.1 Dataset Description

To validate our approach, we designed experiments based on the Memotion [18] and MultiOFF [22] datasets. The Memotion dataset contains approximately

8k annotated memes. In the meme sentiment classification task, each meme is labeled positive, negative, or neutral. MultiOFF contains 743 memes of two classes: offensive and non-offensive. The detailed statistics are summarized in Table 1.

4.2 Implementation Details

Our method is implemented within the PyTorch and performed on an NVIDIA Tesla P-100 GPU. For optimization, ADAM [13] is adopted, and the initial learning rates of the Memotion and MultiOFF datasets are set to 2e-5 and 6e-6, respectively. The batch size is set to 32. To avoid overfitting, a dropout [21] rate of 0.1 is applied. The maximum lengths of the sentence input and concept sequence are $N = 64$ and $M = 32$, respectively. The numbers of BERT layers for the text and concept encoders are both set to 12, i.e., $L_s = L_p = 12$. In addition, the parameters for both encoders are initialized from the pre-trained cased $BERT_{base}$ model with 768 hidden states and 12 attention heads. In this paper, the macro-F1 score is adopted as the evaluation metric for the Memotion dataset [18], and the F1 (F1), precision (P), and recall (R) are used as performance metrics for the MultiOFF dataset [4].

4.3 Competitors

We compare the performance of MeBERT with various existing models and typical visual-linguistic methods. Unimodal methods such as BiLSTM [8], BERT [6], VGG16 and VGG19 [20]. For the Memotion dataset, the baseline and top three methods 'Vkeswani IITK', 'Guoym', and 'Aihaihara' are reported in [18]. For the MultiOFF dataset, the StackedLSTM+VGG16, BiLSTM+VGG16, and CNN-Text+VGG16 baselines are described in [22]. DisMultiHate [4] improves performance by disentangling the representations of offensive-related target entities. The meme classification task is relatively new, so few studies have benchmarked it. Therefore, as additional baselines, we reproduced five advanced multi-modal methods on Memotion and MultiOFF datasets: mBERT [25], TomBERT [25], MMBT [12], VisualBERT [14], and ViLBERT [15].

4.4 Experimental Results and Analysis

Comparative Evaluation. The results of the methods on the Memotion and MultiOFF datasets are reported in Tables 2 and 3. For unimodal methods, BERT outperforms LSTM by 4.1% (Macro-F1) on the Memotion dataset and 26.4% (F1), 14.1% (P), 34.7% (R) on the MultiOFF dataset. In addition, VGG19 outperforms the VGG16 in both datasets. Therefore, BERT and VGG19 are chosen as textual and visual feature extractors. Compared with BERT and VGG19, MeBERT boosts the performance of the macro-F1 score by 4.3% and 16.5% on the Memotion dataset, respectively. It obtains F1-score performance improvements of 10.7% and 17.7% on the MultiOFF dataset, respectively.

For meme sentiment classification, as shown in Table 2, the baseline, 'Vkeswani IITK' [19], 'Gyoum' [10] and 'Aihaihara' systems obtain macro-F1 scores of 0.218, 0.355, 0.352, and 0.350, respectively. Compared with these methods, MeBERT obtains a macro-F1 score of 0.370 with improvements of 15.2% against the baseline and 1.5% against the 'Vkeswani IITK' system. In the visual-linguistic models, both TomBERT and VisualBERT obtain a macro-F1 score of 0.344. MeBERT achieves a 2.6% improvement over these two models. For meme offensive classification, as shown in Table 3, we observe that MeBERT outperforms DisMultiHate by 2.5% (F1), 2.5% (P), and 2% (R). Moreover, MeBERT achieves a 6.5% (F1), 5.5% (P), and 6.7% (R) improvement over MMBT models.

Text-based approaches perform better than visual-based approaches for meme classification because the information contained within meme text is richer than that contained within the meme image. Across the two meme classification tasks, we observe that MeBERT reports competitive results for both cases compared with previous methods, which verifies the effectiveness of MeBERT. In addition, for meme classification, the generalization and performance of MeBERT are better than those of the visual-linguistic models in Tables 2 and 3.

Table 2. Quantitative comparisons against various methods on the Memotion dataset. The best results are in bold. Method*: Values are taken from [18].

Methods	Macro-F1
VGG16	0.180
VGG19	0.205
BiLSTM	0.286
BERT	0.327
Baseline*	0.218
Aihaihara*	0.350
Guoym*	0.352
Vkeswani IITK*	0.355
TomBERT	0.344
mBERT	0.309
MMBT	0.248
VisualBERT	0.344
ViLBERT	0.327
MeBERT	**0.370**

Table 3. Quantitative comparisons against various methods on the MultiOFF dataset. The best results are in bold. F1: F1-score, P: Precision, R: Recall. Method*: Values are taken from [4].

Methods	F1	P	R
VGG16	0.240	0.410	0.160
VGG19	0.494	0.495	0.495
BiLSTM	0.300	0.420	0.230
BERT	0.564	0.561	0.577
StackedLSTM+VGG16*	0.463	0.373	0.661
BiLSTM+VGG16*	0.480	0.486	0.584
CNNText+VGG16*	0.463	0.373	0.661
DisMultiHate*	0.646	0.645	0.651
TomBERT	0.574	0.614	0.582
mBERT	0.498	0.501	0.501
MMBT	0.606	0.615	0.604
VisualBERT	0.562	0.579	0.580
ViLBERT	0.557	0.557	0.558
MeBERT	**0.671**	**0.670**	**0.671**

Ablation Study. To emphasize the contribution of submodules of MeBERT, ablation experiments were conducted. From Tables 4 and 5 we find the following. First, the MeBERT (w/o cpt-att) is obtained by removing the concept-image attention module. The performance decrease of this model indicates that it is effective to consider the consistency between the concept and the image. Second, the MeBERT (w/o fusion) is produced by removing the fusion module. This model causes dropped results, which means that it is worthwhile to extract common information from multi-modal representation. Third, the MeBERT(w/o concept) is obtained by replacing the concept with text modality as the input of the attention module. The performance degradation of this model means that the introduction of external knowledge is beneficial to meme classification. Finally, our MeBERT model outperforms the others in Tables 4 and 5. Therefore, the concept-image attention module, the fusion module, and external knowledge are indispensable in MeBERT.

Table 4. Ablation study on Memotion dataset. (w/o: without)

Methods	Macro-F1
Baseline	0.218
MeBERT (w/o cpt-att)	0.345
MeBERT (w/o fusion)	0.336
MeBERT (w/o concept)	0.359
MeBERT	**0.370**

Table 5. Ablation study on MultiOFF dataset. (w/o: without)

Methods	F1	P	R
BiLSTM+VGG	0.480	0.486	0.584
MeBERT (w/o cpt-att)	0.641	0.644	0.640
MeBERT (w/o fusion)	0.600	0.637	0.630
MeBERT (w/o concept)	0.652	0.649	0.652
MeBERT	**0.671**	**0.670**	**0.671**

Model Analysis. Since the concept-image and fusion modules in MeBERT may stack multiple layers, we analyze the impact of their layer numbers L_m and L_c. The results are shown in Fig. 3(a) and 3(b). First, as the number of layers L_c increases, the performance of the model is improved. However, adding layers is not very effective once the number of convolutional layers exceeds 3. Consequently, L_c is set as 3. Second, the MeBERT model performs best on the Memotion and MultiOFF datasets when L_m is 2 and 1, respectively. Upon further increasing L_c and L_m, the result worsens probably due to the increase in model parameters. In addition, we also tested the sizes of convolution filters 3 and 5. As shown in Fig. 3(c) and 3(d), compared to filter-size 5, filter-size 3 obtains slightly better results on the Memotion and MultiOFF datasets. The reason is that more overlapping regions between segments may cause convolution to be more effective on multi-modal representation.

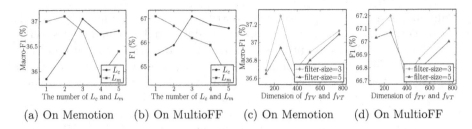

(a) On Memotion   (b) On MultioFF   (c) On Memotion   (d) On MultioFF

Fig. 3. The (a) and (b) figures compare the number of hidden layers of the concept-image attention (L_m) and the convolution fusion layer (L_c) in MeBERT. The (c) and (d) figures show the impact of convolution kernel size on MeBERT performance.

Case Study. Figure 4 presents concept-image attention visualization examples. The concept-image attention module is designed to obtain visual features related to the concept. Therefore, the image regions related to the concept are given higher attention weights. As shown in Fig. 4(a), we observe that the concept-image attention module plays an important role in extracting visual features. In the first example, the MeBERT model focuses on the regions related to the "Harry Hermione Ron", which corresponds to the concept information. Similar situations are observed in the remaining examples.

Error Analysis. We analyze the error cases induced by our proposed model. Most of these error cases can be summarized into three categories. First, some memes embed only text on the image, resulting in little visual information being provided. Second, long-tail entities only have a few useful conceptual information in KB due to the incompleteness of KB. Third, some texts are too short and lack contextual information. For example, a meme that only embeds the short text "Feel The BERN" is difficult to classify as offensive. It takes some form of reasoning to understand the emotions expressed by memes.

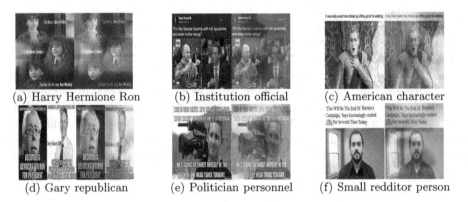

(a) Harry Hermione Ron   (b) Institution official   (c) American character

(d) Gary republican   (e) Politician personnel   (f) Small redditor person

Fig. 4. Concept-image attention visualization examples. Examples (a), (b), and (c) from Memotion dataset. Examples (d), (e), and (f) from MultiOFF dataset.

5   Conclusions

In this paper, we address two limitations of meme classification. First, external concept knowledge is introduced to enhance the semantic information of the meme. To reduce the meme image noise, a concept-image attention module is designed to extract concept-sensitive visual representations. Second, the fusion module is proposed to integrate multi-modal information. Finally, the effectiveness and generalization of the MeBERT model are verified for meme sentiment classification and offensive classification tasks.

In the future, we will focus on solving the problem of automatic extraction of meme concept information. We found that some meme variants are produced by changing meme images, and the same conceptual information has different effects on different meme images. Therefore, we will improve the concept information extraction method based on the MeBERT model, so as to encourage the model to not only make full use of the extracted active concept information but also decrease the weights of misleading information. Moreover, as very little work has been performed on meme classification, we will combine strategies from visual-linguistic fields to explore meme reasoning classification problems.

Acknowledgement. This work is supported by the Chongqing Research Program of Basic Research and Frontier Technology under Grant No. cstc2019jcyj-msxmX0033.

References

1. Ba, J.L., Kiros, J.R., Hinton, G.E.: Layer normalization. arXiv preprint arXiv:1607.06450 (2016)
2. Baltrušaitis, T., Ahuja, C., Morency, L.P.: Multimodal machine learning: a survey and taxonomy. IEEE Trans. Pattern Anal. Mach. Intell. **41**(2), 423–443 (2018). https://doi.org/10.1109/TPAMI.2018.2798607
3. Bonheme, L., Grzes, M.: SESAM at SemEval-2020 task 8: investigating the relationship between image and text in sentiment analysis of memes. In: Proceedings of the Fourteenth Workshop on Semantic Evaluation, pp. 804–816 (2020)
4. Cao, R., Fan, Z., Lee, R.K., Chong, W., Jiang, J.: Disentangling hate in online memes. arXiv preprint arXiv:2108.06207 (2021)
5. Chen, J., Hu, Y., Liu, J., Xiao, Y., Jiang, H.: Deep short text classification with knowledge powered attention. In: Proceedings of the AAAI Conference on Artificial Intelligence, vol. 33, pp. 6252–6259 (2019). https://doi.org/10.1609/aaai.v33i01.33016252
6. Devlin, J., Chang, M.W., Lee, K., et al.: BERT: pre-training of deep bidirectional transformers for language understanding. arXiv preprint arXiv:1810.04805 (2018)
7. Gandhi, S., Kokkula, S., Chaudhuri, A., et al.: Image matters: detecting offensive and non-compliant content/logo in product images. arXiv preprint arXiv:1905.02234 (2019)
8. Greff, K., Srivastava, R.K., Koutník, J., et al.: LSTM: a search space odyssey. IEEE Trans. Neural Netw. Learn. Syst. **28**(10), 2222–2232 (2016). https://doi.org/10.1109/TNNLS.2016.2582924

9. Guo, X., Ma, J., Zubiaga, A.: NUAA-QMUL at SemEval-2020 task 8: utilizing BERT and densenet for internet meme emotion analysis. arXiv preprint arXiv:2011.02788 (2020)

10. Guo, Y., Huang, J., Dong, Y., Xu, M.: Guoym at SemEval-2020 task 8: ensemble-based classification of visuo-lingual metaphor in memes. In: Proceedings of the Fourteenth Workshop on Semantic Evaluation, pp. 1120–1125 (2020)

11. Keswani, V., Singh, S., Agarwal, S., Modi, A.: IITK at SemEval-2020 task 8: unimodal and bimodal sentiment analysis of internet memes. In: Proceedings of the Fourteenth Workshop on Semantic Evaluation, pp. 1135–1140 (2020)

12. Kiela, D., Bhooshan, S., Firooz, H., et al.: Supervised multimodal bitransformers for classifying images and text. arXiv preprint arXiv:1909.02950 (2019)

13. Kingma, D.P., Ba, J.: Adam: a method for stochastic optimization. In: Proceedings of ICLR (2015)

14. Li, L.H., Yatskar, M., Yin, D., et al.: VisualBERT: a simple and performant baseline for vision and language. arXiv preprint arXiv:1908.03557 (2019)

15. Lu, J., Batra, D., Parikh, D., Lee, S.: ViLBERT: pretraining task-agnostic visiolinguistic representations for vision-and-language tasks. In: Advances in Neural Information Processing Systems (NeurIPS), pp. 13–23 (2019)

16. Majumder, N., Hazarika, D., Gelbukh, A., Cambria, E., Poria, S.: Multimodal sentiment analysis using hierarchical fusion with context modeling. Knowl.-Based Syst. **161**, 124–133 (2018). https://doi.org/10.1016/j.knosys.2018.07.041

17. Shang, L., Zhang, Y., Zha, Y., Chen, Y., Youn, C., Wang, D.: AOMD: an analogy-aware approach to offensive meme detection on social media. Inf. Process. Manag. **58**(5), 102664 (2021). https://doi.org/10.1016/j.ipm.2021.102664

18. Sharma, C., et al.: SemEval-2020 task 8: memotion analysis-the visuo-lingual metaphor! In: Proceedings of the Fourteenth Workshop on Semantic Evaluation, pp. 759–773 (2020)

19. Sharma, M., Kandasamy, I., Vasantha, W.: Memebusters at SemEval-2020 task 8: feature fusion model for sentiment analysis on memes using transfer learning. In: Proceedings of the Fourteenth Workshop on Semantic Evaluation, pp. 1163–1171 (2020)

20. Simonyan, K., Zisserman, A.: Very deep convolutional networks for large-scale image recognition. In: Proceedings of ICLR (2015)

21. Srivastava, N., Hinton, G., Krizhevsky, A., Sutskever, I., Salakhutdinov, R.: Dropout: a simple way to prevent neural networks from overfitting. J. Mach. Learn. Res. **15**(1), 1929–1958 (2014)

22. Suryawanshi, S., Chakravarthi, B.R., Arcan, M., Buitelaar, P.: Multimodal meme dataset (multioff) for identifying offensive content in image and text. In: Proceedings of the Second Workshop on Trolling, Aggression and Cyberbullying, pp. 32–41 (2020)

23. Wu, W., Li, H., Wang, H., Zhu, K.Q.: Probase: a probabilistic taxonomy for text understanding. In: SIGMOD, pp. 481–492 (2012). https://doi.org/10.1145/2213836.2213891

24. Wu, Y., Schuster, M., Chen, Z., et al.: Google's neural machine translation system: bridging the gap between human and machine translation. arXiv preprint arXiv:1609.08144 (2016)

25. Yu, J., Jiang, J.: Adapting BERT for target-oriented multimodal sentiment classification. In: IJCAI, pp. 5408–5414 (2019). https://doi.org/10.24963/ijcai.2019/751

26. Yu, W., Xu, H., Meng, F., et al.: CH-SIMS: a Chinese multimodal sentiment analysis dataset with fine-grained annotation of modality. In: Proceedings of the 58th Annual Meeting of the Association for Computational Linguistics, pp. 3718–3727 (2020). https://doi.org/10.18653/v1/2020.acl-main.343
27. Yuan, L., Wang, J., Zhang, X.: YNU-HPCC at SemEval-2020 task 8: using a parallel-channel model for memotion analysis. In: Proceedings of the Fourteenth Workshop on Semantic Evaluation, pp. 916–921 (2020)
28. Zadeh, A., Liang, P.P., Mazumder, N., Poria, S., Cambria, E., Morency, L.P.: Memory fusion network for multi-view sequential learning. In: Proceedings of the AAAI Conference on Artificial Intelligence, pp. 5634–5641. AAAI Press (2018)

Non-Uniform Attention Network
for Multi-modal Sentiment Analysis

Binqiang Wang[1,2,3($\boxtimes$)], Gang Dong[1,2,3], Yaqian Zhao[1,2,3], Rengang Li[1,2,3],
Qichun Cao[1,2,3], and Yinyin Chao[1,2,3]

[1] Inspur (Beijing) Electronic Information Industry Co., Ltd., Beijing, China
{wangbinqiang,donggang,zhaoyaqian,lrg,caoqichun,chaoyinyin}@inspur.com
[2] Inspur Electronic Information Industry Co., Ltd., Jinan, China
[3] Shandong Massive Information Technology Research Institute, Jinan, China

Abstract. Remarkable success has been achieved in the multi-modal sentiment analysis community thanks to the existence of annotated multi-modal data sets. However, coming from three different modalities, text, sound, and vision, establishes significant barriers for better feature fusion. In this paper, we introduce "NUAN", a non-uniform attention network for multi-modal feature fusion. NUAN is designed based on attention mechanism via considering three modalities simultaneously, but not uniformly: the text is seen as a determinate representation, with the hope that by leveraging the acoustic and visual representation, we are able to inject the effective information into a solid representation, named as tripartite interaction representation. A novel non-uniform attention module is inserted into adjacent time steps in LSTM (*Long Shot-Term Memory*) and processes information recurrently. The final outputs of LSTM and NUAM are concatenated to a vector, which is imported into a linear embedding layer to output the sentiment analysis result. The experimental analysis of two databases demonstrates the effectiveness of the proposed method.

Keywords: Multi-modal information fusion · Video sentiment analysis · Attention mechanism

1 Introduction

Multi-modal sentiment analysis, including text, sound, and vision, requires finding the complementary between different modalities and outputting sentiment analysis results [1,2]. For example, to identify the sentiment disposition is positive or negative for the man in Fig. 1, we must consider the three different modalities: *even the facial expression seems negative for the man, but the semantic of*

This work was supported in part by the Shandong Province Key R&D Program (Major Technological Innovation Project) Project under Grant 2019TSLH0201 and in part by the Shandong Provincial Natural Science Foundation, China, under Grant ZR2021QF145.

B. Þór Jónsson et al. (Eds.): MMM 2022, LNCS 13141, pp. 612–623, 2022.
https://doi.org/10.1007/978-3-030-98358-1_48

text can show that the sentiment disposition is positive. Thus, fusing information from different modalities is a focus research point in the sentiment analysis community.

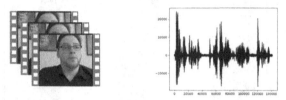

I bet if you put them next to the new film that the style would be similar enough that you wouldnt be able to really tell what the difference is 0.6

Fig. 1. The example transfers a relative positive (0.6) disposition with a neutral facial expression and positive text.

How should we build a model to perform information fusion in sentiment analysis tasks? Prior works [3–11] have explored various approaches from feature concatenation [12] to tensor factorization [3,4] or importing attention mechanism [13,14] in RNN (*Recurrent Neural Network*) or Transformer. Gkoumas *et al.* [12] adopt feature concatenation after paralleling feature extraction of LSTMs, in which three modalities are treated equally. By introducing an attention mechanism, Amir *et al.* do the same attention mechanism between each pair of two modes. Chen *et al.* [15] propose a fusion pipeline for speech and visuals considering correlations of features. Although these models are capable of performing information fusion, their fusion representations are constructed based on representations equally from different modalities that are not in line with common sense. Common sense is that *the information provided by different modalities is not equal for sentiment analysis.*

Common sense is illustrated by the phenomenon that the text plays a determinative role in emotion analysis. Specific experiments are designed that the sentiment analysis results are inducted from a single modality with the same model. Figure 2 shows the experimental fact of single modality on CMU-MOSI [16] (detail information about CMU-MOSI will be introduced in Sect. 4.1), lowest Mean Absolute Error (MAE) and highest binary accuracy prove the determinative role of text in sentiment analysis. To show more detailed information about samples in the test set, we counted the number of samples that are predicted correctly only by the model trained from one modality. Out of 686 testing samples, 164 samples can only be predicted correctly by the model trained on textual modality. For visual modality, the number is 25 and for acoustic modality, the number is 27. In a word, the textual representation performs best compared

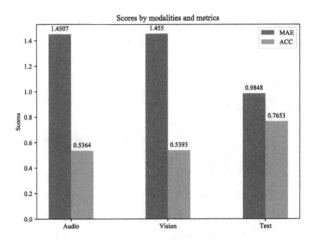

Fig. 2. Experimental facts: "MAE" represents the mean absolute error evaluated on singular modality regarding the sentiment analysis as a regression task. "ACC" represents the accuracy evaluated on different modalities respectively treating the sentiment analysis as a binary classification task. For "MAE", textual modality obtains the lowest score. For "ACC", the highest score corresponds to the text modal.

with the acoustic representation and visual representation. This common sense is consistent with the conclusions of previous research work [17,18].

In this paper, an alternative way is proposed to facilitate information fusion with a non-uniform attention module. Our proposed Non-Uniform Attention Network (NUAN) augments the deterministic representation for sentiment analysis in the video with a semantic interactive feature. The key idea of the proposed NUAN is to construct **tripartite interaction representation** mainly based on textual representation. A non-uniform attention mechanism is adopted to absorb the discriminative information contained in the acoustic representation and visual representation. Concretely, the original text from the data set is initialed with a pre-trained language model to obtain text representation. Acoustic and vision materials utilize the CMU-Multi-modal Data SDK[1] to extract acoustic representation and visual representation respectively. Then, three LSTM is used to encode three different modalities' data into feature vectors. Then, the outputted feature vectors are input into NUAM to construct the tripartite interaction representation. The tripartite interaction representation is also utilized to update the weights of LSTM. Finally, the tripartite interaction representation and hidden states of the final output of LSTM are concatenated to a full representation, that a linear embedding is followed to output the sentiment analysis result.

---

[1] https://github.com/A2Zadeh/CMU-MultimodalSDK.

The contribution of this paper can be summarized as follows: 1) A novel non-uniform attention module is designed based on the experimental phenomenon that text plays a determinative role in the process of multi-modal emotion analysis; 2) LSTM, in its' adjacent time steps NUAN is inserted, is applied to capture the temporal dynamic information from different modalities in the video; 3) Extensive experiments are conducted to validate the effectiveness of the proposed method.

2 Related Work

Initial research on sentiment analysis is focused on uni-modal approaches, either text [19] or image [20]. However, researchers have paid more attention to multi-modal emotion analysis with the emerging multi-modal data available on the internet [12,21]. The total pipeline of multi-modal sentiment analysis includes feature extraction, feature fusion, and decision making. Neural networks have become a powerful alternative to hand-crafted methods for feature extraction and are used in many communities [19,22], including sentiment analysis. Rather than providing a review of the whole pipeline, we focus here on the efforts recently proposed in the literature that address the problem of feature fusion. For exhaustive reviews of the literature in this field, readers are referred to [23].

There are two types of strategy according to the position in the pipeline to fuse the feature: early fusion and late fusion. These two strategies are implemented in [12] which are denoted as EF-LSTM and LF-LSTM. The features from three modalities are concatenated to a whole vector before or after LSTM. A multistage fusion network is proposed in [24], in which the feature fusion is completed through a multistage style. Tensor fusion network is proposed to model intra-modality and inter-modality dynamics [3] in multi-modal sentiment analysis. The attention mechanism is applied in the task and the multi-attention recurrent network [13] is constructed to capture the multi-view of different modalities. However, these methods do not treat different modal features differently and adopt a uniform method to treat different features equally. On the contrary, this paper proposes a non-uniform sentiment analysis method based on the different characteristics of different modalities.

3 Methods

3.1 Long Short-Term Memory

We choose Long Short-Term Memory (LSTM) as our backbone structure, which can be the main-stream architecture for the RNN-based video sentiment analysis methods. There are three modalities of data, we take text data as an example to illustrate the LSTM structure. Given text sequences $S = \{w_t\}_{t=1,2,...,N_w}$, where S represents a sentence with N_w words and each word is presented by w_t. LSTM is trained to produce the contextualized word representations $\mathbf{S} = \{\mathbf{w}_t\}_{t=1,2,...,N_w}$.

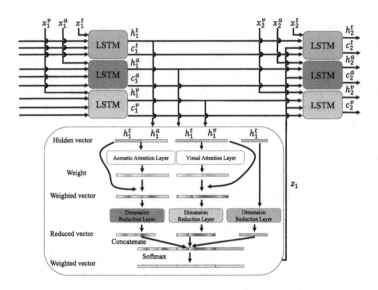

Fig. 3. Framework of the proposed method. Three LSTMs are the main component of the framework, which is used to extract features from different modalities. Between the adjacent steps in LSTM, a novel non-uniform attention module is inserted to output tripartite interaction representation z_*. Inputs of the non-uniform attention module include all the outputs of LSTMs.

As the recurrent structure of LSTM, the latter word representations contain the information memorized by the memory cell from previous time steps in LSTM. The memory cell with self connections is packed into a memory block devised with gate mechanisms to control the flow of information. Generally, a memory block contained an *input gate*, a *forget gate*, and an *output gate*. The amount of information that comes from the current time step's input data is controlled by the *input gate*. Part of the information contained in the memory cell is forgotten by the *forget gate*. The current memory cell, after being updated by the *input gate* and *forget gate*, is multiplied with the *output gate* to obtain hidden states. The hidden states are viewed as word representation directly or after embedding by a linear layer with an activation function.

To learn the precise timing of the outputs, a novel LSTM architecture is designed with *peephole connections* to control the gates with memory cells, which is ignored by the origin LSTM. Inspired by the *peephole connections* [25], a **tripartite interaction representation**, which contains the information from three different modalities, is conducted to decide the gates. Formally, the memory block used in this paper can be formulated as:

$$\mathbf{i}_t = \sigma \left(\mathbf{W}_{\mathbf{ix}}\mathbf{x}_t + \mathbf{W}_{\mathbf{ih}}\mathbf{h}_{t-1} + \mathbf{W}_{\mathbf{iz}}\mathbf{z}_{t-1} + \mathbf{b}_i \right), \tag{1}$$

$$\mathbf{f}_t = \sigma \left(\mathbf{W}_{\mathbf{fx}}\mathbf{x}_t + \mathbf{W}_{\mathbf{fh}}\mathbf{h}_{t-1} + \mathbf{W}_{\mathbf{fz}}\mathbf{z}_{t-1} + \mathbf{b}_f \right), \tag{2}$$

$$\mathbf{o}_t = \sigma \left(\mathbf{W}_{\mathbf{ox}}\mathbf{x}_t + \mathbf{W}_{\mathbf{oh}}\mathbf{h}_{t-1} + \mathbf{W}_{\mathbf{oz}}\mathbf{z}_{t-1} + \mathbf{b}_o \right), \tag{3}$$

$$c_t = f_t \circ c_{t-1} + i_t \circ \tanh\left(\mathbf{W_{cx}x_t} + \mathbf{W_{ch}h_{t-1}} + \mathbf{W_{cz}z_{t-1}} + b_c\right), \qquad (4)$$

$$h_t = o_t \circ \tanh\left(c_t\right), \qquad (5)$$

where i_t, f_t, and o_t are respectively *input gate*, *forget gate*, and *output gate*. $\mathbf{W_{**}}$ terms are learnable parameters, $\mathbf{b_*}$ terms denote bias vectors, σ is the logistic sigmoid function, tanh is the activation function in Eq. 4 and Eq. 5, $\circ$ is the element-wise product of the vectors, $\mathbf{x_t}$ is the input of t-th step, which is the word embedding vector corresponding to w_t, $\mathbf{h_t}$ denotes the hidden state of t-th step, which can also be seen as the $\mathbf{w_t}$ herein, $\mathbf{c_t}$ is the memory cell of t-th step, which pertains the information during steps, $\mathbf{z_t}$ is the **tripartite interaction representation**, which is the output of NUAM taking previously hidden status from three modalities as input.

This structure is just the same for acoustic data and visual data. However, the steps in LSTM of acoustic data and visual data are NOT defined by the origin audio signal or single frame picture in a video. The segment of audio corresponding to one word is compressed as one acoustic feature vector, which is denoted as $\mathbf{x_t^a}$. Following a similar process, several consecutive frames corresponding to one word are compressed as one visual feature vector, referred to as $\mathbf{x_t^v}$. To maintain the unity of form, the textual input of word w_t is denoted as $\mathbf{x_t^t}$. Note that the t in the upper right corner means the textual input while the t in the lower right corner means the t-th step in LSTM.

3.2 Attention Mechanism in Multi-modal Sentiment Analysis

To construct **tripartite interaction representation** during the information flow in LSTM, a non-uniform attention mechanism is introduced to extract information from different modalities. Given one modality input at t-th step, such as textual input $\mathbf{x_t^t}$, the attention mechanism is organized as follows: Firstly, the textual input is encoded into a semantic content vector, using a linear layer following a dropout layer. Then the attention score is obtained by a linear layer with a sigmoid function. To prevent over-fitting, a dropout layer is inserted before the sigmoid function. Specifically, the attention mechanism used in this paper can be formulated as:

$$\mathbf{x_t^{tc}} = Dropout\left(\mathbf{W_{tc}x_t^t} + \mathbf{b_{tc}}\right) \qquad (6)$$

$$\mathbf{s_t^{tc}} = softmax\left(\sigma\left(Dropout\left(\mathbf{W_{ts}x_t^t} + \mathbf{b_{ts}}\right)\right)\right) \qquad (7)$$

$$\mathbf{x_t^{attend}} = \mathbf{s_t^{tc}} \circ \mathbf{x_t^{tc}} \qquad (8)$$

where $\circ$ is element-wise multiplication, $\mathbf{W_{**}}$ and $\mathbf{b_{**}}$ are learnable parameters, the dropout layer is denoted as $Dropout$, $\mathbf{x_t^{tc}}$ is the semantic content vector, $\mathbf{s_t^{tc}}$ is the attention score, and $\mathbf{x_t^{attend}}$ is the output vector of the attention layer in this paper. The operations are packaged into an *attention* layer:

$$\mathbf{x_t^{attend}} = attention\left(\mathbf{x_t^t}\right) \qquad (9)$$

Note that the vector is changed from input space into semantic space and the dimension is adjusted by the shape of $\mathbf{W_{**}}$ and $\mathbf{b_{**}}$.

3.3   Non-uniform Attention Module

This section details the structures of Non-uniform Attention Module. The purpose of this module is to derive semantically meaningful tripartite interaction representation. Hidden states vectors from separate LSTMs are seen as ingredients to organize tripartite interaction representation. Experimental facts in Sect. 1 illustrate the textual determinate part in the process of sentiment analysis. Thus the hidden status vector of textual is utilized as partial conditional input. As shown in Fig. 3, 1-th step of LSTMs output textual hidden state vector $\mathbf{h}_1^t$ is concatenated with acoustic hidden state vector $\mathbf{h}_1^a$. Then the concatenated vector is passed through an acoustic attention layer whose structure is detailed in Sect. 3.2. This process can be formulated as:

$$\mathbf{h}_a^{attend} = attention\left(conca\left(\mathbf{h}_1^t, \mathbf{h}_1^a\right)\right) \tag{10}$$

where $\mathbf{h}_a^{attend}$ represents the output of acoustic attention layer, named as a weighted acoustic vector, $attention$ represents the attention layer and $conca$ represents the vector concatenation operation.

Similarly, the visual attention layer can be formulated as:

$$\mathbf{h}_v^{attend} = attention\left(conca\left(\mathbf{h}_1^t, \mathbf{h}_1^v\right)\right) \tag{11}$$

where $\mathbf{h}_v^{attend}$ represents the output of the visual attention layer, named as weighted visual vector. Note that weights of the visual attention layer and acoustic attention layer are not shared.

Following weighted vectors, dimension reduction layers are conducted to generate compact embedding vectors, called reduced vectors. Detail structures of the dimension reduction layer are composed of one linear embedding layer and one dropout layer. To maintain origin semantic information contained by weighted vectors, there is no activation function of the linear embedding layer. Except for weighted acoustic vector and weighted visual vector, hidden state vector of textual $\mathbf{h}_1^t$ is also imported into the dimension reduction layer to get compact representation. Outputs of three dimension reduction layers are concatenated together to form a combined representation containing information from three modalities. This representation is passed through a softmax function to output tripartite interaction representation $\mathbf{z}_1$.

The operation mentioned before can be seen as a part of cell computation process of LSTM. Tripartite interaction representation is updated as the step going of LSTM. Finally, N_w-th step's output contains the final tripartite interaction representation $\mathbf{z}_{N_w}$, final hidden state vectors from three modalities: $\mathbf{h}_{N_w}^t$, $\mathbf{h}_{N_w}^a$, $\mathbf{h}_{N_w}^v$, and final memory cell vectors from different modalities: $\mathbf{c}_{N_w}^t$, $\mathbf{c}_{N_w}^a$, $\mathbf{c}_{N_w}^v$. The final tripartite interaction representation $\mathbf{z}_{N_w}$ and final hidden state vectors from three modalities: $\mathbf{h}_{N_w}^t$, $\mathbf{h}_{N_w}^a$, $\mathbf{h}_{N_w}^v$, are concatenated as the final representation which is input into a classifier to complete the sentiment analysis.

3.4   Multi Attention Mechanism

Inspired by the multi attention structure in [13], K times of attention is conducted in each attention layer. Instead of repeating K times directly, the embedding dimension in Eq. 7 is expanded K times. Then softmax is conducted after splitting the embedding output to K parts. Outputs of K times attention are concatenated to a vector that can represent K different semantic views.

4 Experiments

4.1 Databases and Competitors

Databases. Carnegie Mellon University Multimodal Opinion Sentiment Intensity (CMU-MOSI) [16] is a popular database used in the sentiment analysis community [26]. CMU Multimodal Opinion Sentiment and Emotion Intensity (CMU-MOSEI) [27] is a larger database compared with CMU-MOSI.

The splits and preprocessing schedule follow the paper [12]. Databases used in this paper can be downloaded here[2].

Competitors. As for competitors, we follow previous literature [12,21] and choose Early Fusion LSTM (EF-LSTM) and Late Fusion LSTM (LF-LSTM) as baseline models, as well as Recurrent Multistage Fusion Network (RMFN) [24], Tensor Fusion Network (TFN) [3], Multi-Attention Recurrent Network (MARN) [13], Recurrent Attended Variation Embedding Network (RAVEN) [14], and Memory Fusion Network (MFN) [28].

4.2 Experimental Setup

The grid search strategy is adopted to determine these hyper parameters, Specifically, the textual embedding is initialized with GloVe [29], these weights and other trainable parameters in models are fine-tuned by conducting a fifty-times random grid search on predefined hyper parameters spaces. Following the schedule of [12], Adam optimizer is used with L1 loss for CMU-MOSI and CMU-MOSEI.

To measure the performance of methods, Mean Absolute Error (MAE), F1 score, Pearson product-moment correlation coefficients (Corr), and accuracy are used as metrics for CMU-MOSI and CMU-MOSEI. Specifically, Acc_2 represents the sentiment analysis is treated as a binary classification task using 0 as the boundary, and Acc_7 represents the output between –3 to 3 is embedded into seven classes by rounding operation.

4.3 Experimental Results

We first evaluate NUAN on CMU-MOSI. It can be seen in Table 1 that the proposed NUAN outperforms the competitors except for RAVEN according to Acc_2, F1, and Corr. These results prove the effectiveness of the proposed method.

---

[2] https://www.dropbox.com/s/7z56hf9szw4f8m8/cmumosi_cmumosei_iemocap.zip? dl=0.

Table 1. Evaluation on the CMU-MOSI

Method	Acc_7	Acc_2	F1	MAE	Corr
EF-LSTM [12]	32.7	75.8	75.6	1.000	0.630
LF-LSTM [12]	32.7	76.2	76.2	0.987	0.624
RMFN [24]	32.3	76.8	76.4	0.980	0.626
TFN [3]	34.9	75.6	75.5	1.009	0.605
MARN [13]	31.8	76.4	76.2	0.984	0.625
RAVEN [14]	34.6	78.6	78.6	0.948	0.674
MFN [28]	31.9	76.2	75.8	0.988	0.622
Ours	**26.8**	**78.3**	**77.9**	**1.034**	**0.654**

Observing the Acc_7 and Acc_2 metric of methods, an interesting phenomenon is that with the increase of metric Acc_2, Acc_7 is decreased. We argue that the main reason is that the L1 loss function is not dedicated to classification. The main goal of this article is to explore the results of sentiment analysis, not simply to improve the classification results. Another reason may be the uneven distribution of the seven-category data. As shown in Fig. 4, the relative imbalance of samples in CMU-MOSI causes the result predicted by models trained with L1 loss to be unsuitable for multi-classification. For the binary classification task, the samples of positive and negative are almost the same.

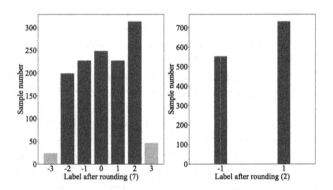

Fig. 4. The sample distribution of the training set from CMU-MOSI.

Next, to further validate the effectiveness of the proposed method, experimental are conducted on CMU-MOSEI. Due to the huge difference in the amount of data and the more complicated patterns included, a hidden layer is added here between the attention layer and the dimension reduction layer. As reported in Table 2, NUAN outperforms the most competitors on all metrics. For RAVEN [14], The NUAN is almost the same in terms of Corr and is better for other metrics.

Table 2. Evaluation on the CMU-MOSEI

Method	Acc_7	Acc_2	F1	MAE	Corr
EF-LSTM [12]	45.7	78.2	77.1	0.687	0.573
LF-LSTM [12]	47.1	79.2	78.5	0.655	0.614
TFN [3]	47.3	79.3	78.2	0.657	0.618
MARN [13]	47.7	79.3	77.8	0.646	0.629
RAVEN [14]	47.8	80.2	79.8	0.636	0.654
MFN [28]	47.4	79.9	79.1	0.646	0.626
Ours	**48.6**	**81.2**	**80.6**	**0.624**	**0.653**

4.4 Ablation Studies

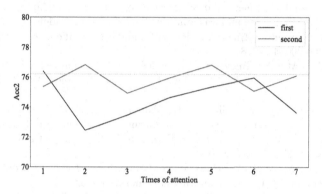

Fig. 5. The curve of accuracy according to attention times setting on CMU-MOSI. (Color figure online)

To study the influence of the attention times in attention layers, we conduct ablation studies by changing the attention times on CMU-MOSI. Experiments are conducted twice for setting attention times from 1 to 7, and results are shown in Fig. 5. If the attention mechanism is not used, the model degenerates to LF-LSTM, and the red dashed line in the figure represents the accuracy of LSTM. The blue line in Fig. 5 represents the result of the first experiment, and the green line represents the result of the second experiment. The only difference between the two experiments is the random seed. It can be concluded that times of attention influence the model's performance, but there is no unified setup guidance for the attention times. This should be set according to the purpose performance on the specific database in practice.

5   Conclusions

Based on the determinate role of text during experiments, a non-uniform atten-tion module is designed to complete the sentiment analysis. It can effectively extract discriminate features from three different modalities. To construct tripartite interaction representation between adjacent steps in LSTMs, textual features play the dominant part while acoustic and visual features play a complementary role. Experimentally, we show that the proposed method exhibits the best performance when compared to prior competitors.

References

1. Hu, M., Chu, Q., Wang, X., He, L., Ren, F.: A two-stage spatiotemporal attention convolution network for continuous dimensional emotion recognition from facial video. IEEE Signal Process. Lett. **28**, 698–702 (2021)
2. He, J., Mai, S., Hu, H.: A unimodal reinforced transformer with time squeeze fusion for multimodal sentiment analysis. IEEE Signal Process. Lett. **28**, 992–996 (2021)
3. Zadeh, A., Chen, M., Poria, S., Cambria, E., Morency, L.P.: Tensor fusion network for multimodal sentiment analysis. arXiv preprint arXiv:1707.07250 (2017)
4. Liu, Z., Shen, Y., Lakshminarasimhan, V.B., Liang, P.P., Zadeh, A., Morency, L.P.: Efficient low-rank multimodal fusion with modality-specific factors. arXiv preprint arXiv:1806.00064 (2018)
5. Abdullah, S.M.S.A., Ameen, S.Y.A., Sadeeq, M.A., Zeebaree, S.: Multimodal emotion recognition using deep learning. J. Appl. Sci. Technol. Trends **2**(02), 52–58 (2021)
6. Hazarika, D., Poria, S., Mihalcea, R., Cambria, E., Zimmermann, R.: Icon: interactive conversational memory network for multimodal emotion detection. In: Proceedings of the 2018 Conference on Empirical Methods in Natural Language Processing, pp. 2594–2604 (2018)
7. Nguyen, D., Nguyen, K., Sridharan, S., Ghasemi, A., Dean, D., Fookes, C.: Deep spatio-temporal features for multimodal emotion recognition. In: 2017 IEEE Winter Conference on Applications of Computer Vision (WACV), pp. 1215–1223. IEEE (2017)
8. Tzirakis, P., Trigeorgis, G., Nicolaou, M.A., Schuller, B.W., Zafeiriou, S.: End-to-end multimodal emotion recognition using deep neural networks. IEEE J. Sel. Topics Signal Process. **11**(8), 1301–1309 (2017)
9. Xu, H., Zhang, H., Han, K., Wang, Y., Peng, Y., Li, X.: Learning alignment for multimodal emotion recognition from speech. arXiv preprint arXiv:1909.05645 (2019)
10. Mittal, T., Bhattacharya, U., Chandra, R., Bera, A., Manocha, D.: M3er: multiplicative multimodal emotion recognition using facial, textual, and speech cues. In: Proceedings of the AAAI Conference on Artificial Intelligence, vol. 34, pp. 1359–1367 (2020)
11. Mittal, T., Guhan, P., Bhattacharya, U., Chandra, R., Bera, A., Manocha, D.: Emoticon: Context-aware multimodal emotion recognition using frege's principle. In: Proceedings of the IEEE/CVF Conference on Computer Vision and Pattern Recognition, pp. 14234–14243 (2020)
12. Gkoumas, D., Li, Q., Lioma, C., Yu, Y., Song, D.: What makes the difference? an empirical comparison of fusion strategies for multimodal language analysis. Inf. Fusion **66**, 184–197 (2021)
13. Zadeh, A., Liang, P.P., Poria, S., Vij, P., Cambria, E., Morency, L.P.: Multi-attention recurrent network for human communication comprehension. In: Proceedings of the AAAI Conference on Artificial Intelligence, vol. 32 (2018)

14. Wang, Y., Shen, Y., Liu, Z., Liang, P.P., Zadeh, A., Morency, L.P.: Words can shift: dynamically adjusting word representations using nonverbal behaviors. In: Proceedings of the AAAI Conference on Artificial Intelligence, vol. 33, pp. 7216–7223 (2019)
15. Guanghui, C., Xiaoping, Z.: Multi-modal emotion recognition by fusing correlation features of speech-visual. IEEE Signal Process. Lett. **28**, 533–537 (2021)
16. Zadeh, A., Zellers, R., Pincus, E., Morency, L.P.: Mosi: multimodal corpus of sentiment intensity and subjectivity analysis in online opinion videos. arXiv preprint arXiv:1606.06259 (2016)
17. Rosas, V.P., Mihalcea, R., Morency, L.P.: Multimodal sentiment analysis of Spanish online videos. IEEE Intell. Syst. **28**(3), 38–45 (2013)
18. Poria, S., Cambria, E., Gelbukh, A.: Deep convolutional neural network textual features and multiple kernel learning for utterance-level multimodal sentiment analysis. In: Proceedings of the 2015 Conference on Empirical Methods in Natural Language Processing, pp. 2539–2544 (2015)
19. Fu, Y., Guo, L., Wang, L., Liu, Z., Liu, J., Dang, J.: A sentiment similarity-oriented attention model with multi-task learning for text-based emotion recognition. In: Lokoč, J., Skopal, T., Schoeffmann, K., Mezaris, V., Li, X., Vrochidis, S., Patras, I. (eds.) MMM 2021. LNCS, vol. 12572, pp. 278–289. Springer, Cham (2021). https://doi.org/10.1007/978-3-030-67832-6_23
20. You, Q., Jin, H., Luo, J.: Visual sentiment analysis by attending on local image regions. In: Thirty-First AAAI Conference on Artificial Intelligence (2017)
21. Tsai, Y., Bai, S., Liang, P.P., Kolter, J.Z., Salakhutdinov, R.: Multimodal transformer for unaligned multimodal language sequences. In: Proceedings of the 57th Annual Meeting of the Association for Computational Linguistics (2019)
22. Zhang, Y., Yuan, Y., Feng, Y., Lu, X.: Hierarchical and robust convolutional neural network for very high-resolution remote sensing object detection. IEEE Trans. Geosci. Remote Sens. **57**(8), 5535–5548 (2019)
23. Chen, M., He, X., Yang, J., Zhang, H.: 3-d convolutional recurrent neural networks with attention model for speech emotion recognition. IEEE Signal Process. Lett. **25**(10), 1440–1444 (2018)
24. Ghosal, D., Akhtar, M.S., Chauhan, D., Poria, S., Bhattacharyya, P.: Contextual inter-modal attention for multi-modal sentiment analysis. In: Proceedings of the 2018 Conference on Empirical Methods in Natural Language Processing (2018)
25. Gers, F.A., Schraudolph, N.N., Schmidhuber, J.: Learning precise timing with LSTM recurrent networks. J. Mach. Learn. Res. **3**(Aug), 115–143 (2002)
26. Rahman, W., et al.: Integrating multimodal information in large pretrained transformers. In: Proceedings of the Conference. Association for Computational Linguistics. Meeting, vol. 2020, p. 2359. NIH Public Access (2020)
27. Zadeh, A.B., Liang, P.P., Poria, S., Cambria, E., Morency, L.P.: Multimodal language analysis in the wild: cmu-mosei dataset and interpretable dynamic fusion graph. In: Proceedings of the 56th Annual Meeting of the Association for Computational Linguistics, vol. 1: Long Papers, pp. 2236–2246 (2018)
28. Zadeh, A., Liang, P.P., Mazumder, N., Poria, S., Cambria, E., Morency, L.P.: Memory fusion network for multi-view sequential learning. In: Proceedings of the AAAI Conference on Artificial Intelligence, vol. 32 (2018)
29. Pennington, J., Socher, R., Manning, C.: Glove: global vectors for word representation. In: Proceedings of Empirical Methods Natural Language Processing, pp. 1532–1543 (2014)

Multimodal Unsupervised Image-to-Image Translation Without Independent Style Encoder

Yanbei Sun, Yao Lu$^{(\boxtimes)}$, Haowei Lu, Qingjie Zhao, and Shunzhou Wang

School of Computer Science and Technology, Beijing Institute of Technology,
Beijing, China
vis_yl@bit.edu.cn

Abstract. The multi-modal image-to-image translation frameworks often have the problems of complex model structure and low training efficiency. In addition, we find that although these methods can maintain the structural information of the source image well, they cannot transfer the style of the reference image well. To solve these problems, we propose a novel framework called Multimodal-No-Independent-Style-Encoder Generative Adversarial Network (MNISE-GAN) that simplifies the overall network structure by reusing the front part of the discriminator as the style encoder so it can achieve multi-modal image translation more effectively. At the same time, the discriminator directly uses the style code to classify real and synthetic samples, so it can enhance the classification ability and improve training efficiency. To enhance the style transfer ability, we propose a multi-scale style module embedded in the generator, and propose an Adaptive Layer-Instance-Group Normalization (AdaLIGN) to further strengthen the generator's ability to control texture. Extensive experiments on four popular image translation benchmarks quantitative and qualitative results demonstrate that our method is superior to state-of-the-art methods

Keywords: Generative Adversarial Networks · Image-to-image translation · Adaptive normalization

1 Introduction

Image-to-image (I2I) translation aims to solve the mapping problem between different visual fields, and is widely used in image inpainting [5,6], image colorization [26], super-resolution [2], etc. Given extensive efforts to collect paired images between domains, current research [3,18,21] focuses more on unsupervised scenes that do not require pairing information features.

Recently, No-Independent-Component-for-Encoding GAN (NICE-GAN) [21] is proposed to use the discriminator as the encoder to derive a more compact

This work is supported by the National Natural Science Foundation of China (No.61273273), by the National Key Research and Development Plan (No.2017YFC 0112001), and by China Central Television (JG2018-0247).

B. Þór Jónsson et al. (Eds.): MMM 2022, LNCS 13141, pp. 624–636, 2022.
https://doi.org/10.1007/978-3-030-98358-1_49

(a) dog → cat   (b) summer → winter   (c) photo → vangogh

Fig. 1. Example results of our MNISE-GAN. The first column and the first row represent source and reference image, and the remaining images are the result of translation.

and efficient I2I translation framework. However, they can only get one result for one input, ignoring the diversity of translation. To achieve a variety of image translations, some researchers focus on solving multi-modal I2I translation [15, 17,20]. They decouple and map the image to the shared content space and the style space of a specific domain. However, these methods generally have problems such as complex model structure and low training efficiency. In addition, current effective I2I translation frameworks [15,16,18,21], only inject style information at the deepest bottleneck layer of the network. However, this structure cannot handle multi-modal image translation tasks well in the experiment. Specifically, the structure information of the source image is retained well, but the style changes made according to the reference image are relatively poor.

To address the above problems, we propose a novel GAN-based model called Multimodal-No-Independent-Style-Encoder GAN (MNISE-GAN), which reuses the front part of the discriminator as the style encoder. Thanks to the removal of the independent style encoder, the overall network structure has become more compact. At the same time, compared with directly using images for authenticity classification, the discriminator of MNISE-GAN uses the image style code to classify real samples and synthetic samples, which can enhance the classification ability of discriminator and make the model more effective for training. In addition, we explore the location of injecting style information into the generator. We note that the upsample layer of the generator can extract multi-level semantic information from high-level structure information to low-level texture information. So we design a multi-scale style injection module in the upsample layer, which can adaptively synthesize textures and transform local shapes by fusing style information on different scales feature maps. Furthermore, we propose an adaptive normalization function for the generator, which divides channels with similar characteristics into a group through Group Normalization (GN) [24] to further improve local shape transformation and texture style transfer. Figure 1 shows the multi-modal results of our method on multiple datasets. To summarize, the contributions of our method are three-fold: **1)** We propose a new multimodal I2I translation framework, called MNISE-GAN. By reusing the discriminator as style encoder can simplify the network structure and achieve image translation more effectively. **2)** We design a multi-scale style injection module in the upsampling layer for learning to interpret and translate style feature, so that the generator can better complete the image style translation. **3)** Our new adaptive normalization function can more effectively control the translation of image texture styles while transforming local shapes, and improve the visual performance of the resulting texture details.

2   Related Work

2.1   Image-to-image Translation

Image-to-image translation method first appeared in conditional GAN [9]. Based on this framework, Pix2Pix [4] learned the mapping function from the source domain to the target domain. BicycleGAN [10] added a variational autoencoder to cGAN. Although these methods have produced impressive results, they need paired images in the training process. Unfortunately, it is difficult and expensive to collect such paired training data in many image translation scenarios.

To realize image translation with unpaired images, CycleGAN [3], Disco-GAN [13] and DualGAN [14] adopt cycle consistency loss to preserve the critical content information between the input and output. UNIT [7] assumed that two domains mapped to potential share space and learns a unimodal mapping. To deal with multimodal translation problems, MUNIT [15], DRIT [16], and DRIT++ [17] introduced the idea of decoupling on the basis of UNIT, which separated the features of a specific domain. Recently studies showed that enhanced the expression ability of the model can improve the quality of image transformation. U-GAT-IT [18] combined a new attention module to enhance the effect of network feature extraction. DSMAP [20] enhanced the mapping ability between two domains by using two additional domain-specific mappings. NICE-GAN [21] showed that reused the discriminator as an encoder can simplify the network structure, making the model more compact and more effective during training. Compared with NICE-GAN, our method can realize multi-modal image translation by reusing the discriminator as style encoder and improve the style injection ability of the network, so it can generate more flexible and high-quality translation results.

2.2   Normalization

The normalization function has been successfully applied to many computer vision tasks [27–29]. For image-to-image translation task, the normalization function significantly impacts the quality of the translation results for various datasets with different amounts of change in shape and texture. Ulyanov et al. [23] first found that replaced the traditional Batch Normalization [19] with Instance Normalization (IN) [23] can make it easier to transfer the image style. In addition, Karras proposed the Adaptive Instance Normalization (AdaIN) [25], which used the mean and standard deviation of the style image as an affine parameter so that they can achieve any style translation of the image. Recently, U-GAT-IT [18] proposed Adaptive Layer-Instance Normalization (AdaLIN),

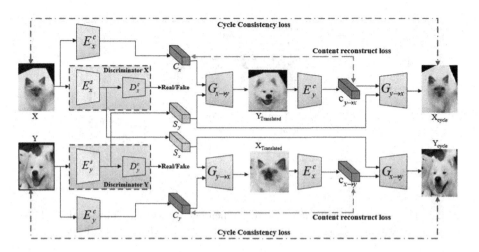

Fig. 2. The overall framework of MNISE-GAN. Green and blue represent domain X(cat) and domain Y(dog). The discriminator extracts style code of the reference image, and the content encoder extracts content code of the source image. (Color figure online)

which combined AdaIN and Layer Normalization [22] to transform the image style better. In comparison, our new adaptive normalization functions can divide channels with similar characteristics into a group for processing, thereby improving the texture details of the result.

3   Method

3.1   General Formulation

Assuming that $x \in X$ and $y \in Y$ are the images of the source domain and the target domain, respectively. The goal of the unsupervised I2I translation is to learn the mapping $f_{x \to y}$ to convert x to domain Y and $f_{y \to x}$ to convert y to domain X through unpaired images. In most of existing frameworks, the translation $f_{x \to y}$ is composed of an encoder E_x (resp. E_y) and a generator $G_{x \to y}$ (resp. $G_{y \to x}$). By combining them all together, it gives

$$
\begin{aligned}
y_{translated} &= f_{x \to y}(x) = G_{x \to y}(E_x(x)) \\
x_{translated} &= f_{y \to x}(y) = G_{y \to x}(E_y(y)),
\end{aligned}
\tag{1}
$$

The GAN training fashion is usually adopted to enable the translated output to fit the distribution of the target domain. Namely, we use a discriminator D_y (resp. D_x) to classify between the true image x and the translated image $x_{translated}$ (resp. y and $y_{translated}$).

As mentioned in introduction, we decompose the discriminator D_y of domain Y into the style encoding part E_y^s and classification part D_y^c. The front part E_y^s is responsible for extracting the style code s_y of the reference image y, and the

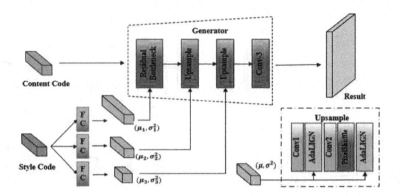

Fig. 3. The architecture of the generator, which can incorporate multi-scale style features. The bottom right corner is the specific details of each upsample layer.

remain part D_y^c is used to complete the classification task of the discriminator in domain Y. At the same time, a content encoder E_x^c of domain X is introduced to extract the content code c_x of the source image x. In this way, we can get $c_x = E_x^c(x)$, $s_y = E_y^s(y)$. Then input them into the generator $G_{x \to y}$ to get

$$
\begin{aligned}
y_{translated} &= G_{x \to y}(E_x^c(x), E_y^s(y)) \\
x_{translated} &= G_{y \to x}(E_y^c(y), E_x^s(x)),
\end{aligned}
\tag{2}
$$

where $y_{translated}$ represents the translation result of x to domain Y according to the style of y and $x_{translated}$ represents the translation result of y to domain X according to the style of x. Multimodal translation results can be realized by combining content code with different style codes. At the same time, like some previous work, we have introduced the idea of cycle consistency in the model. Specifically, the result x_{cycle} obtained after the translation result $y_{translated}$ through the generator $G_{y \to x}$ should be as close to the original image x as possible. The specific description is as follows

$$
\begin{aligned}
x_{cycle} &= G_{y \to x}(E_y^c(y_{translated}), E_x^s(x)) \\
y_{cycle} &= G_{x \to y}(E_x^c(x_{translated}), E_y^s(y)),
\end{aligned}
\tag{3}
$$

where $E_x^s(x)$ and $E_y^s(y)$ represents the style code of original images in their respective domains. Figure 2 illustrates our overall framework.

3.2   Network Architecture

Discriminator. As mentioned above, to achieve a compact and efficient multimodal image translation, we remove the independent style encoder in the usual multi-modal framework and replace it with the discriminator. Through such improvement, the style encoder is directly guided by the discriminator adversarial loss during training so that the model can be trained more effectively.

Generally, the style information plays a vital role in judging which domain it belongs to. In our method, the discriminator directly uses the style code to classify the real sample and the synthetic sample, so compared to NICE-GAN using the overall code of the image, it can enhance the classification ability of the discriminator and improve the training efficiency.

Generator. We analyse that current successful image translation methods like U-GAT-IT [18] and NICE-GAN [21], their generator only inject the style information at the deepest bottleneck layer, which leads to the weak style information transfer ability. To address this problem, we also use adaptive normalization layer to inject style information in the upsample part of the generator, as shown in Fig. 3. Specifically, the style code obtained by E^s in the discriminator is sent to multiple fully connected layers to generate scaling and translation parameters of different scales. Then input them to the adaptive normalization layer in the bottleneck and upsample layers to complete the injection of multi-scale style information. As shown in the lower right corner of Fig. 3, each upsample module contains two adaptive normalization layers. Such improvements can enhance the generator's style translation capabilities and improve the quality of the translation results.

3.3 Adaptive Layer-Instance-Group Normalization

The previously proposed AdaLIN [18] is not enough to transfer the texture style information of the local area from the reference image to the generated image in the task of multimodal I2I translation. For example, the shape and texture of cat' s eyes may be distributed in partial channels of the feature map, while both LN using all-channels and IN using single-channel information cannot control the degree of texture and shape changes well. Dividing channels with similar features into a group through Group Normalization (GN) can better adjust the scale and deviation of the input feature statistics. For this reason, we propose an Adaptive Layer-Instance-Group Normalization (AdaLIGN) method, the specific formula is as follows

$$AdaLIGN(x) = \gamma_s \cdot (\rho_1 \cdot a_I + \rho_2 \cdot a_L + \rho_3 \cdot a_G) + \beta_s, \qquad (4)$$

where γ_s and β_s are obtained from the style code through fully connected layers of different scales. The details of each part are as follows

$$a_I = \frac{x - \mu_I(x)}{\sqrt{\sigma_I^2(x) + \epsilon}}, a_L = \frac{x - \mu_L(x)}{\sqrt{\sigma_L^2(x) + \epsilon}}, a_G = \frac{x - \mu_G(x)}{\sqrt{\sigma_G^2(x) + \epsilon}}, \qquad (5)$$

where x represents the feature map to be normalized, μ_I, μ_L, μ_G and σ_I, σ_L, σ_G represent the mean and variance of channel-wise, layer-wise, and group-wise, respectively. ρ represent the weight of each part which satisfies

$$\rho_{1,2,3} \leftarrow clip_{[0,1]}(\rho_{1,2,3} - \tau \Delta \rho_{1,2,3}), \qquad (6)$$

τ is the learning rate. $\Delta \rho_{1,2,3}$ indicates the parameter update vector determined by the optimizer. The values of ρ_1, ρ_2, ρ_3 are constrained to the range of [0,

1] simply by imposing bounds at the parameter update step, simultaneously satisfying $\rho_1 + \rho_2 + \rho_3 = 1$ constraints. The larger the ρ is, the corresponding normalization layer plays a more critical role.

3.4   Loss Function

For the source image x and reference style image y, we use four kinds of loss to optimize the training goals, the details of each loss will be introduced below. For brevity, only the part converted from domain x to domain y is given.

Adversarial Loss. To enhance the stability of training, we use LS-GAN [8] to minimize the discrepancy between the distributions of the real images and the generated images. The min-max game is conducted by

$$\min_{G} \max_{D} L_{gan}^{x \to y} = \frac{1}{2}\mathbb{E}_{y \sim \mathbf{y}}\left[D_y(y)^2\right] + \frac{1}{2}\mathbb{E}_{x \sim \mathbf{x}, y \sim \mathbf{y}}\left[(D_y(G_{x \to y}(c_x, s_y)) - 1)^2\right],$$

(7)

where $c_x = E_x^c(x)$ represents the content code of the source image, $s_y = E_y^s(y)$ represents the style code of the target image.

Cycle-consistency Loss. The cycle-consistency loss proposed by CycleGAN proved to be valuable and effective, which forces the generator to be able to restore the source image after converting it into another domain.

$$\min_{G} L_{cycle}^{x \to y} = \mathbb{E}_{x \sim \mathbf{x}, y \sim \mathbf{y}}\left[\left|x - G_{y \to x}(E_y^c(G_{x \to y}(c_x, s_y)), s_x))\right|_1\right].$$

(8)

Style Reconstruction Loss. To ensure that the style encoder in the discriminator can encode more meaningful style features, the style information contained in the result should be close enough to the reference image, which can help to encourage diverse outputs given different style codes. The loss is defined as

$$\min_{G} L_{style}^{x \to y} = \mathbb{E}_{x \sim \mathbf{x}, y \sim \mathbf{y}}\left[\left|s_y - E_y^s(G_{x \to y}(c_x, s_y))\right|_1\right],$$

(9)

where E_y^s is the style encoder in the discriminator D_y.

Content Reconstruction Loss. Similar to the style loss, for the consistency of the structural content information in the images before and after translation, the content information in the translation result and the source image should be close enough. Out of this consideration, the loss is defined as follows.

$$\min_{G} L_{content}^{x \to y} = \mathbb{E}_{x \sim \mathbf{x}, y \sim \mathbf{y}}\left[\left|c_x - E_y^c(G_{x \to y}(c_x, s_y))\right|_1\right].$$

(10)

Full Objective. In summary, we combine each pair of dual terms together and the total loss is as follows.

$$\min_{G} \lambda_{gan}L_{gan} + \lambda_{cyc}L_{cycle} + \lambda_{s}L_{style} + \lambda_{c}L_{content},$$

$$\max_{D} \lambda_{gan}L_{gan}.$$

(11)

Here $\lambda_{gan}, \lambda_{cyc}, \lambda_s, \lambda_c$ are hyper-parameters to balance the relationship between each loss. We fix them as $\lambda_{gan} = 1, \lambda_{cyc} = 10, \lambda_s = 10, \lambda_c = 10$ in experiment.

4   Experiments

4.1   Experimental Settings

Baselines. We compared MNISE-GAN with state-of-the-art unsupervised I2I translation, including CycleGAN [3], U-GAT-IT [18], and NICE-GAN [21], as well as multi-modal methods MUNIT [15], DRIT++ [16], and DSMAP [20]. For the sake of fairness, all methods are implemented using open source code and the same hyper-parameters, such as iteration number and batch size, etc.

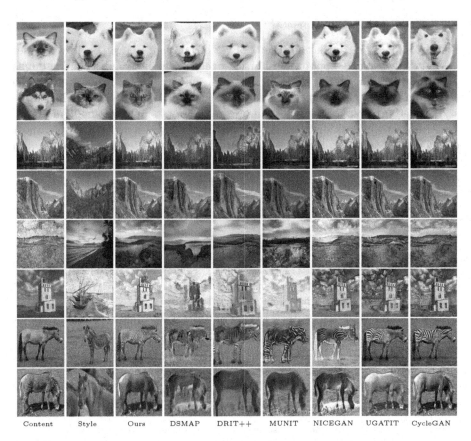

Content   Style   Ours   DSMAP   DRIT++   MUNIT   NICEGAN   UGATIT   CycleGAN

Fig. 4. Examples of generated outputs by various methods. The first and second columns are the source image and the reference style image, respectively. The third to sixth columns are the multi-modal methods and the rest of the few columns are the results of single-mode methods.

Dataset. We conduct experiments on four popular benchmarks of unpaired I2I translation task: **cat** ↔ **dog**, **summer** ↔ **winter**, **vangogh** ↔ **photo**, and **horse** ↔ **zebra**. The specific train-test splits for each dataset are respectively: 771/100 (cat), 1,264/100 (dog); 1,231/309 (summer), 962/238 (winter); 400/400 (vangogh), 6,287/751 (photo); 1,067/120 (horse), 1,334/140 (zebra). All images of all datasets are cropped and resized to 256 256 for training and testing.

Implementation Details. We use spectral normalization in the discriminator to improve model stability. The batch size of all experiments is set to 1, and we use the Adam optimizer to train all models with 10k iterations. Both learning rate and weight decay rate are set to 0.0001. Empirically, we set the GN group in AdaLIGN to 8 will achieve better results.

4.2   Qualitative Comparison

Figure 4 shows the translation results of various methods in cat ↔ dog, summer ↔ winter, vangogh ↔ photo and horse ↔ zebra. The first and second columns are the source image and the reference style image, respectively. The third to sixth columns are the multi-modal methods which is translated according to the style image. The rest of the few columns are the results of single-mode methods.

Although the data distribution of the cat ↔ dog is relatively simple, most of the current methods have the problem of fuzzy detail texture information in

Table 1. The FID and KID results of different methods on multiple datasets, where KID is multiplied by 100. All methods are trained for 10k iterations.

Method	Dataset							
	dog → cat		winter → summer		photo → vangogh		zebra → horse	
	FID↓	KID↓	FID↓	KID↓	FID↓	KID↓	FID↓	KID↓
MNISE-GAN	**43.24**	**0.93**	**75.33**	**0.93**	**121.70**	3.53	**131.10**	2.45
DSMAP [20]	60.81	6.35	92.28	4.46	161.94	8.76	136.17	4.44
DRIT++ [17]	69.22	4.04	79.17	1.03	155.94	7.20	177.34	7.41
MUNIT [15]	66.44	2.05	98.71	4.75	148.57	6.06	209.20	8.60
NICE-GAN [21]	48.79	1.88	77.01	1.32	141.20	4.36	145.05	3.41
U-GAT-IT [18]	56.95	1.87	79.58	1.54	130.71	4.27	150.55	3.26
Cycle-GAN [3]	58.01	1.11	88.17	3.12	126.36	3.76	136.38	3.21
Method	Dataset							
	cat → dog		summer → winter		vangogh → photo		horse → zebra	
	FID↓	KID↓	FID↓	KID↓	FID↓	KID↓	FID↓	KID↓
MNISE-GAN	33.95	**0.58**	**77.11**	**0.73**	**110.40**	2.84	**45.05**	**0.74**
DSMAP [20]	**30.99**	0.59	113.15	5.74	129.35	7.36	48.48	2.07
DRIT++ [17]	66.60	3.64	80.51	1.20	123.95	3.08	73.35	2.66
MUNIT [15]	71.37	2.19	109.90	4.93	153.59	6.80	116.10	5.48
NICE-GAN [21]	44.67	1.20	79.63	1.06	121.02	3.51	65.46	1.66
U-GAT-IT [18]	59.68	1.74	87.02	1.18	126.10	3.96	92.76	3.32
Cycle-GAN [3]	135.60	7.87	78.70	0.82	134.88	5.51	72.50	1.82

the translation results. Since our method adds a multi-scale style injection module and proposes an adaptive normalization layer that combines partial channel information, the model can learn the style features better from the reference image. For example, the results of cat ↔ dog have clearer species characteristics and more realistic hair textures. In addition, in winter → summer, our method can properly migrate the color and texture of the grass in the summer mountains and obtain closer real and better quality results. Other methods such as MUNIT, DSMAP, and DRIT++ only inject style information at the deepest bottleneck layer, so they cannot integrate the style of the reference image well, which ultimately leads to more artifacts in the result. The remaining single-modal methods cannot refer to the style image for translation, so the result is not like a real summer scene.

In other words, MNISE-GAN can better learn from the style of the reference image to generate more meaningful translation results with fewer artifacts.

4.3   Quantitative Comparison

FID and KID. Heusel proposes Frechet Inception Distance (FID) [11], which calculates the frechet distance with mean and covariance between the real and the fake image distributions. Similar to FID, Kernel Inception Distance (KID) [12] is an improved measure of GAN convergence and quality. It is the squared Maximum Mean Discrepancy between inception representations. Lower FID and KID indicates more visual similarity between real and generated image.

Table 2. Ablation of MNISE-GAN on cat ↔ dog dataset, where NISE represents No Independent Style Encoder and MSG represents Multi-Scale G.

Method	Dataset			
	dog → cat		cat → dog	
	FID↓	KID↓	FID↓	KID↓
w/o NISE	44.65	0.98	44.78	1.23
w/o MSG	45.89	1.03	35.6	0.63
w/o AdaLIGN	46.57	1.19	53.30	1.82
MNISE(Ours)	**43.24**	**0.93**	**33.95**	**0.58**

As shown in Table 1, our method achieves the lowest FID and KID scores in multiple datasets except for cat → dog. DSMAP uses an additional inter-domain mapping network to enhance the expressive ability of the network, which leads to better results on the cat → dog. However, in view of multiple task scenarios, our method can achieve better quality results than DSMAP. Compared with NICE-GAN, our method separates the content and style information of the image and improves the style injection ability of the network by improving the generator and adaptive normalization function, so we can get better metric results on multiple datasets. Note that the metrics in vangogh ↔ photo and zebra → horse tasks are relatively poor, because it is more challenging to generate real scene images from artistic paintings, and the background information in the zebra dataset is more complicated. However, MNISE-GAN still achieves better metrics than other methods, which shows the advancement of our method.

4.4   Ablation Study

We conduct ablation experiments with FID and KID metrics on the cat ↔ dog dataset to verify the effectiveness of each module of our method, the result is shown in Table 2. The case of **w/o NISE** means that two independent encoders are used to extract content and style codes respectively. By reusing the discriminator through NISE, the style encoder can be trained more effectively and improve the quality of the results. For example, the FID/KID value dropped from 48.66/1.30 to 43.24/0.93 in cat → dog, and 46.80/1.36 to 33.95/0.58 in dog → cat. **w/o MSG** means that the style information of the reference image is only injected into the deepest bottleneck layer of the network. The results show that the value of FID and KID can be reduced by adding a multi-scale style injection module in generator, which proves MSG can play a positive role in image translation. The group of **w/o AdaLIGN** represents the use of previous AdaLIN [18] for style information injection. The transfer of style information can be enhanced, reflected in the decline of FID and KID metrics which verifies the effectiveness of improving the adaptive normalization. Overall, by combing all components, MNISE-GAN remarkably outperforms all other variants.

Content   Style   MNISE-GAN   w/o NISE   w/o MSG   w/o AdaLIGN

Fig. 5. Visual comparison of the contributions of MNISE-GAN.

The visual comparison of the contribution of each component is shown in Fig. 5. It can be seen from the figure that without using the NISE, the style encoder can only be trained indirectly by the generator's adversarial loss, which weakens the style extraction ability, so the generated results cannot better match the style of the reference image. In addition, the removal of the MSG and AdaLIGN will weaken the generator's style injection ability, thereby reducing the quality of the translation result. For example, in the result of **w/o AdaLIGN**, the dog's mouth becomes unreal, and the texture of the cat's eyes becomes more blurred. In the result of **w/o MSG** from dog ↔ cat, the style between the translation result and the reference image cannot satisfy good consistency. In summary, the full version of MNISE-GAN can get better texture details similar to the reference image and more realistic results.

5 Conclusion

In this paper, we propose a new multi-modal unsupervised image-to-image translation network, called MNISE-GAN. By reusing the front part of the discriminator as a style encoder, the network structure can be simplified, and the model can be trained more effectively. To enhance the ability of style transfer, a multiscale style injection upsample layer and an adaptive normalization function are proposed for learning to interpret and translate style information. Finally, experiments on multiple datasets show that our method has higher performance than existing methods.

References

1. Goodfellow, I., et al.: Generative adversarial nets. In: NIPS, Montreal, pp. 2672–2680 (2014)
2. Wu, X., Li, X., He, J., Wu, X., Mumtaz, I.: Generative adversarial networks with enhanced symmetric residual units for single image super-resolution. In: MMM, Thessaloniki, pp. 483–494 (2019)
3. Zhu, J.Y., Park, T., Isola, P., et al.: Unpaired image-to-image translation using cycle-consistent adversarial networks. In: CVPR, Honolulu, pp. 2223–2232 (2017)
4. Isola, P., Zhu, J. Y., Zhou, T., Efros, A.A.: Image-to-image translation with conditional adversarial networks. In: CVPR, Honolulu, pp. 1125–1134 (2017)
5. Xiao, Z., Li, D.: Generative image inpainting by hybrid contextual attention network. In: MMM, Online, pp. 162–173 (2021)
6. Huang, Z., Qin, C., Li, L., Liu, R., Zhu, Y.: Confidence-based global attention guided network for image inpainting. In: MMM, Online, pp. 200–212 (2021)
7. Liu, M.Y., Breuel, T., Kautz, J.: Unsupervised image-to-image translation networks. In: NIPS, Long Beach, pp. 700–708 (2017)
8. Mao, X., Li, Q., Xie, H., Lau, R.Y., Wang, Z., Paul Smolley, S.: Least squares generative adversarial networks. In: CVPR, Honolulu, pp. 2794–2802 (2017)
9. Mirza, M., Osindero, S.: Conditional generative adversarial nets. arXiv preprint arXiv:1411.1784 (2014)
10. Zhu, J.Y., Zhang, R., Pathak, D., Darrell, T., et al.: Toward multimodal image-to-image translation. In: NIPS, Long Beach, pp. 465–476 (2017)

11. Heusel, M., Ramsauer, H., Unterthiner, T., et al.: Gans trained by a two time-scale update rule converge to a local nash equilibrium. In: NIPS, Long Beach, vol. 30 (2017)

12. Bińkowski, M., Sutherland, D.J., Arbel, M., Gretton, A.: Demystifying mmd gans. arXiv preprint arXiv:1801.01401 (2018)

13. Kim, T., Cha, M., Kim, H., et al.: Learning to discover cross-domain relations with generative adversarial networks. In: ICML, Sydney, pp. 1857–1865 (2017)

14. Yi, Z., Zhang, H., Tan, P., Gong, M.: Dualgan: unsupervised dual learning for image-to-image translation. In: CVPR, Honolulu, pp. 2849–2857 (2017)

15. Huang, X., Liu, M. Y., Belongie, S., Kautz, J.: Multimodal unsupervised image-to-image translation. In: ECCV, Munich, pp. 172–189 (2018)

16. Lee, H.Y., Tseng, H.Y., Huang, J.B., et al.: Diverse image-to-image translation via disentangled representations. In: ECCV, Munich, pp. 35–51 (2018)

17. Lee, H.Y., Tseng, H.Y., Mao, Q., et al.: Drit++: diverse image-to-image translation via disentangled representations. In: IJCV, pp. 2402–2417 (2020)

18. Kim, J., Kim, M., Kang, H., Lee, K.: U-gat-it: unsupervised generative attentional networks with adaptive layer-instance normalization for image-to-image translation. arXiv preprint arXiv:1907.10830 (2019)

19. Ioffe, S., Szegedy, C.: Batch normalization: accelerating deep network training by reducing internal covariate shift. In: ICML, Lille, pp. 448–456 (2015)

20. Chang, H.Y., Wang, Z., Chuang, Y.Y.: Domain-specific mappings for generative adversarial style transfer. In: ECCV, Online, pp. 573–589 (2020)

21. Chen, R., Huang, W., et al.: Reusing discriminators for encoding: towards unsupervised image-to-image translation. In: CVPR, Seattle, pp. 8168–8177 (2020)

22. Ba, J.L., et al.: Layer normalization. arXiv preprint arXiv:1607.06450 (2016)

23. Ulyanov, D., Vedaldi, A., Lempitsky, V.: Improved texture networks: maximizing quality and diversity in feed-forward stylization and texture synthesis. In: CVPR, Honolulu, pp. 6924–6932 (2017)

24. Wu, Y., He, K.: Group normalization. In: ECCV, Munich, pp. 3–19 (2018)

25. Karras, T., Laine, S., Aila, T.: A style-based generator architecture for generative adversarial networks. In: CVPR, Long Beach, pp. 4401–4410 (2019)

26. Lee, J., et al.: Reference-based sketch image colorization using augmented-self reference and dense semantic correspondence. In: CVPR, Seattle, pp. 649–666 (2020)

27. Zhou, T., Li, J., Wang, S., Tao, R., Shen, J.: Matnet: motion-attentive transition network for zero-shot video object segmentation. IEEE TIP **29**, 8326–8338 (2020)

28. Zhou, T., Wang, S., Zhou, Y., Yao, Y., Li, J., Shao, L.: Motion-attentive transition for zero-shot video object segmentation. In: AAAI, New York, pp. 13066–13073 (2020)

29. Zhou, T., Wang, W., Qi, S., Ling, H., Shen, J.: Cascaded human-object interaction recognition. In: CVPR, Seattle, pp. 4263–4272 (2020)

Correction to: Real-Time FPGA Design for OMP Targeting 8K Image Reconstruction

Jiayao Xu, Chen Fu, Zhiqiang Zhang, and Jinjia Zhou

Correction to:
Chapter 41 in: B. Þór Jónsson et al. (Eds.):
MultiMedia Modeling, **LNCS 13141,**
https://doi.org/10.1007/978-3-030-98358-1_41

In the originally published chapter 41, measurement matrix was mistakenly referred to as the "Hadamard matrix". The measurement matrix has been updated as "Walsh matrix".

The updated version of this chapter can be found at
https://doi.org/10.1007/978-3-030-98358-1_41

Author Index

Printed in the United States
by Baker & Taylor Publisher Services